EQUAL JUSTICE UNDER LAW
Constitutional Development
1835–1875

The

New American Nation Series

EDITED BY

HENRY STEELE COMMAGER

AND

RICHARD B. MORRIS

EQUAL JUSTICE UNDER LAW

Constitutional Development

1835 ★ 1875

By HAROLD M. HYMAN
and WILLIAM M. WIECEK

ILLUSTRATED

1817

HARPER & ROW, PUBLISHERS, New York
Cambridge, Philadelphia, San Francisco, London
Mexico City, São Paulo, Sydney

FIRST EDITION

Library of Congress Cataloging in Publication Data

Hyman, Harold Melvin, 1924–
  Equal justice under law.
  (The New American Nation series)
  Bibliography: p.
  Includes index.
  1. United States—Constitutional history. 2. Law—United States—History and criticism. I. Wiecek, William M., 1938–   II. Title.   III. Series.
KF4541.H89   42.73′029   81-47658
ISBN 0-06-014937-X   47.30229   AACR2

82 83 84 85 86 10 9 8 7 6 5 4 3 2 1

FOR FERNE, AND FOR M.

Acknowledgments

M ANY librarians and archivists have given us invaluable assistance. Reference librarians, especially Ferne B. Hyman at Rice
University and Anne Edwards of the University of Missouri-
Columbia, were unfailingly helpful and gracious in locating information and in exploiting interlibrary loan facilities, and they
deserve special mention. Librarians and archivists elsewhere who
made the resources of their institutions available to us, often at
inconvenient times, include Dr. Mark E. Neely, Jr., Director of the
Louis A. Warren-Lincoln Library and Museum, Fort Wayne, Indiana, Dr. Richard Baker, Historian of the United States Senate and
his staff, and Mr. Ross Cameron of the National Archives. Our
colleagues Thomas B. Alexander and Noble E. Cunningham helped
resolve some problems. Several doctoral students at Rice University, including Barbara Guidry and Thomas Mackey, dug on our
behalf; to them warmest thanks, as to Corona Machemer and her
assistant, Liza Pulitzer, the Harper & Row editors who helped us in
several ways to bring this book to its present form.

We and our book benefited immeasurably from the critical observations of Richard B. Morris and Henry Steele Commager, the
general editors of this series. We took full advantage of this chance
to exploit the knowledge, insights, and judgments of these two
extraordinary individuals, and we take pleasure in acknowledging
our great debt to them.

The Research Council of the University of Missouri-Columbia generously provided funds to support typing a part of this manuscript.

HAROLD M. HYMAN
WILLIAM M. WIECEK

Contents

x CONTENTS

Illustrations

MAPS

Editors' Introduction

Equal Justice Under Law addresses itself to the third major era of American constitutional history. The first—the formative era of State and Federal Constitution making—laid the permanent foundations of written constitutions, the federal system, separation of powers, independence of the judiciary, and the protection of the fundamental liberties of men. The second embraced the era of nationalism dominated by powerful jurists like Jay, Marshall, and Story, who presided over an experiment unique in the history of nationalism, for only in the United States can it be said that nationalism was in large measure a product of Law, Courts, and Judges. The third, which Professor Wiecek and Professor Hyman here recount, though not the most affluent was clearly the most critical, for it would determine, as its greatest spokesman made clear, whether a nation "so conceived and so dedicated could long endure." The story here is that of a half-century of challenge, testing, conflict, and, in the end, resolution, out of which emerged, almost imperceptibly, our modern Constitution. For it was Lincoln and Johnson who inaugurated and presided over the greatest constitutional revolution in our history—the shift in the center of gravity of both liberty and of authority, from states to nation.

It was not, in the realm of politics, an inventive generation, but so compelling were the new economic and social forces making for change—railroads, corporations, the growth of cities, the impact of large scale immigration, the re-alignment of parties, the emergence of Blacks (if not to freedom, at least to a position where they could contemplate and struggle for freedom)—that the Courts, and through them the Constitution, responded, even if reluctantly, to the new challenges.

On the whole, the Court failed to realize the potentialities of the greatest constitutional decision in American history—that made by Grant's success at Appomattox. These potentialities were to enlarge the Constitution to its full possibilities, a task that had to be resumed by the Hughes, Stone, and Warren Courts of the twentieth century. To this extent the Courts of the period were not so much conservative as unenterprising.

Could a constitution based originally on the principle of limited government be adapted to the exigent demands of the new economy, the new power structure, the emergence of four million blacks to freedom and to a new but as yet untested political and social status?

This is the fundamental problem whose vicissitudes Professors Wiecek and Hyman so luminously interpret. They recount here in rich detail how Slavery, threatened by the new nationalism of Marshall and Story, constructed for itself new constitutional defenses of States Rights; how this States Rights philosophy challenged traditional nationalism, and how that same philosophy undermined the Confederacy itself, and, in the end, led to the defeat not only of the seceding States, but to the defeat of the principle of State Sovereignty by the forces and the power of Unionism. They analyze, too, the complex, but compelling, constitutional problems created by war—a war which by posing unique legal and constitutional problems all but defied constitutional management or interpretation.

Professor Hyman, with new speculations and new insights, takes up the familiar—but ever-puzzling—story of Reconstruction. This chapter of our constitutional history saw a decisive shift in the center of gravity from the judicial to the executive and, more decisively, to the legislative branch. It was the Congress which fixed the terms of the new constitutionalism by its reconstruction policies, its intimidation of the Executive, and above all, its enactment of the Fourteenth Amendment. This extraordinary Amendment—unquestionably the most significant in our history—was, as it turned out, a revolution *in posse*, rather than *in esse*. Its esoteric words and phrases, such as "citizens," "person," "privileges and immunities," "life, liberty and property," "equal protection of the laws," like the great phrases of the Declaration of Independence and of the First Amendment, were pregnant with meaning for each individual and new generation, and contained within themselves the dynamic of revolution—as well as the guarantee of limitless litigation!

But if the Judiciary did not exercise political power, it did greatly expand its economic and administrative authority. Confronted with the nationalization of the economy this was unavoidable. Upon it then fell responsibility for accomodation of law and administration to the problems raised by the new corporate economy, the demands of organized labor, taxation, banking, and finance. The Court, not otherwise distinguished for its philosophical vision, proved competent and effective in these more mundane areas. Yet at the same time it avoided, or evaded, the urgent problems of accommodating the interests of blacks, women, and labor to the clear dictates of the new Constitutional amendments. As it turned out, it took almost a century for the Court to shoulder its responsibilities here.

This volume is one of six volumes of a series on constitutional history in the New American Nation Series, a comprehensive, cooperative history of the area now embraced in the United States from the days of discovery to the present. Other volumes in the series by Professor Loren P. Beth and Professor Paul L. Murphy have covered the period from 1876 to 1969. Still to come are volumes on the foundations of American constitutionalism, on the era of Jay and Marshall, and a final volume on the constitutional developments of the post-Warren era.

HENRY STEELE COMMAGER
RICHARD B. MORRIS

EQUAL JUSTICE UNDER LAW

Constitutional Development
1835–1875

CHAPTER 1

The Democratic Constitution: Sovereignty, Union, Slavery

IN 1836, the United States government was approaching its semi-centennial under the Constitution. Like all valedictory occasions, this half-century anniversary marked ends and beginnings. As if to mark the occasion, to take leave of the Republic he had done so much to establish, James Madison, the last surviving Framer, died that year. John Marshall, the first great Chief Justice of the United States, had died a year earlier, closing the first creative era of the United States Supreme Court. The administration of Andrew Jackson was nearing its end, but the elections of 1836 resulted in the continuation of Jacksonian Democratic dominance in national politics.

Valedictories are times for reaffirming principles. Had a contemporary compiled an agenda of constitutional issues that would dominate Americans' concerns in the nation's second half-century, the list would have been headed by these matters: (1) the scope of popular sovereignty; (2) democratization of political mechanisms; (3) maintenance of the American union; and (4) protection for Afro-American slavery.

The French observer Alexis de Tocqueville extolled "the principle of the sovereignty of the people," which he saw was "recognized by the customs and proclaimed by the laws" in America. "The people reign in the American political world," he enthused; "they are the cause and the aim of all things; everything comes from them, and everything is absorbed in them."[1] The next two decades demonstrated that Tocqueville's breathless claim was not exaggerated.

From the settled coastal cities to the frontier, Americans made popular sovereignty a working principle of their governments. When Arkansas came into the Union in 1836, its Constitution proclaimed that

all power is inherent in the people; and all free government is founded on their authority, and instituted for their peace, safety, and happiness. For the advancement of these ends, they have, at all times, an unqualified right to alter, reform or abolish their government, in such manner as they may think proper.[2]

In the West, the Republic of Texas declared its independence in 1836, justifying its acts by "the inherent and unalienable right of the people to appeal to first principles and take their political affairs into their own hands."[3]

This reliance on the people's sovereignty was the constitutional mainspring of American politics up to the Civil War. Though embedded in the Revolutionary-era Constitutions, its origins reached far back into the colonial period. A strain of radical democracy has marked the appearance of popular sovereignty in American constitutional thought, beginning with the founding of Rhode Island in 1643, described by contemporaries as a "democracie, or popular government; that is to say, it is in the power of the body of the freemen orderly assembled, or the major part of them," to legislate.[4] Roger Williams insisted at the time that "the soveraigne, originall, and foundation of civill power lies in the people," and he was echoed by John Wise, writing in Massachusetts two generations later.[5] The radical strain flourished during the Revolution, finding its most thorough exposition in the radical tract *The People the Best Governors* (1776) and in the 1776 Pennsylvania Constitution. Seem-

[1]Alexis de Tocqueville, *Democracy in America*, trans. Henry Reeve (1835; 2 vols., reprint New York, 1945), I, 57–60.

[2]Arkansas Constitution (1836), Art. II, sec. 2, in Francis Newton Thorpe (comp.), *The Federal and State Constitutions* (7 vols., Washington, 1909), I, 269; see also Michigan Constitution (1835) for nearly verbatim formulation of this popular-sovereignty clause, *ibid.*, IV, 1930.

[3]The Texas Declaration of Independence, Mar. 2, 1836, *ibid.*, VI, 3528.

[4]Quoted in "Rhode Island—Interference of the Executive in the Affairs of," House Reports, 28 Cong., 1 sess., ser. 447, doc. 546, June 7, 1844.

[5]Roger Williams, *The Bloudy Tenent, of Persecution, for cause of Conscience, discussed* . . . (1644), in *The Complete Writings of Roger Williams* (New York, 1963), III, 249. John Wise, *A Vindication of the Government of the New England Churches* . . . (1717; reprint Gainesville, Fla., 1958), p. 44.

ingly validated by the Declaration of Independence and by the Virginia Declaration of Rights (1776),[6] which was the parent of most later popular-sovereignty clauses (including Arkansas's), the idea that government derived its legitimacy and authority from the people persisted through the Jacksonian era and justified the only revolutionary republican movement that occurred after the Revolution: the Dorr Rebellion of 1842 in Rhode Island. The Rebellion became a dramatic focus for the development of popular sovereignty in America, pitting as it did the hallowed though vague Revolutionary republican impulse against a state's need to suppress an actual rebellion.

Industrialization hit Rhode Island earliest and hardest among the American states. Its cities and mill villages filled with native workingmen and immigrants. Yet the Rhode Island Charter of 1663, still the state's Constitution in 1842, imposed on this teeming social order an archaic, inflexible constitutional system that enshrined the twin evils of malapportionment and disfranchisement. Estimates of disfranchisement suggest that as many as 90 percent of adult white males in Providence may have been voteless, principally because of the "freehold" requirement: a constitutional and statutory provision denying the vote to anyone owning less than $134 worth of real property.

In 1834, Thomas W. Dorr, who was to give his name to the radical reform movement, insisted that "it is one of the essential parts of the definition of a Republican Government, or Representative Democracy, that it is a government resulting from the will of the majority ascertained by just and equal representation."[7] When, in 1842, suffrage reformers despaired of relief from the hands of the conservative-dominated General Assembly, they applied their theory literally, calling an extralegal "People's Convention" to revise the Charter, electing delegates to it by universal (i.e., adult male) suffrage, drafting a new constitution, seeing to its ratification by

[6]Declaration of Independence: ". . . to secure these rights, Governments are instituted among Men, deriving their just powers from the consent of the governed, That whenever any Form of Government becomes destructive of these ends, it is the right of the People to alter or to abolish it, and to institute new Government. . . ." Virginia Declaration of Rights: ". . . all power is vested in, and consequently derived from, the people; that magistrates are their trustees and servants, and at all times amenable to them. [Art. II] . . . when any government shall be found inadequate or contrary to these purposes, a majority of the community hath an indubitable, unalienable and indefeasible right to reform, alter or abolish it. . . ." [Art. III]; Thorpe, *Federal and State Constitutions*, VII, 3813.

[7]Thomas W. Dorr et al., *An Address to the People of Rhode Island* (Providence, 1834), p. 22.

universal suffrage, and electing a government to take office under it, headed by Dorr as People's Governor. A crisis arose when the existing government refused to relinquish its authority, promoted its own constitution (which was rejected in a restricted referendum vote), and grimly clung to power, using state militia to suppress the Dorrites.

This incipient civil war provoked an outburst of ideological controversy over the nature of popular sovereignty. Supporters of the People's Government rested their arguments on Revolutionary texts—the 1776 Virginia Declaration of Rights, the Declaration of Independence, George Washington's Farewell Address—to justify the actual, direct assumption of sovereign power by the people.[8] Sympathetic Democrats in the United States House of Representatives summed up these ideas as "the inherent sovereign right of the people to change and reform their existing government at pleasure."[9] Even Dorr's opponents were forced to accept the principle publicly (though rejecting it in private communications among themselves), modifying it with the reservation that "the people" consist only of those who exercise legitimate power under extant law.[10]

The Dorr Rebellion was settled by a combination of constitutional reform and military repression, though the issues were to rekindle in the United States Supreme Court seven years later.[11]

[8]See, e.g., the "Nine Lawyers' Opinion on the Right of the People of Rhode Island to Form a Constitution," in Sidney S. Rider (comp.), *Bibliographical Memoirs of Three Rhode Island Authors* (Providence, 1880), pp. 68–92; [Benjamin Cowell], *A Letter to Hon. Samuel W. King . . .* (n.p., [1842]); memorial of Democratic members of Rhode Island General Assembly, 1843, reprinted in "Rhode Island—Interference of the Executive in the Affairs of"; *A Democratic Catechism: Containing the Self-Evident and Fundamental Principles of Democracy. The People are Sovereign* (Providence, 1846); Orestes A. Brownson to Thomas W. Dorr, May 14, 1842, in Dorr Mss., John Hay Library, Brown University, Providence, R.I.

[9]Conclusions of the majority of the House Select Committee on Rhode Island, 1844, printed in "Rhode Island—Interference of the Executive in the Affairs of," p. 83.

[10]William Giles Goddard, *An Address to the People of Rhode-Island . . .* (Providence, 1843), pp. 40–41; John Quincy Adams, *The Social Compact Exemplified in the Constitution of the Commonwealth of Massachusetts . . .* (Providence, 1842), p. 16. For private reservations, see Edwin Noyes to James M. B. Potter, June 23, 1842, and Elisha R. Potter to D. J. Pearce, Dec. 20, 1841, in Elisha R. Potter Mss., Rhode Island Historical Society, Providence, R.I.

[11]See the discussion of Luther *v.* Borden (1849) in ch. 3 below.

The literal Dorrite interpretation of popular sovereignty did not succeed in Rhode Island, but as a constitutional dynamic the doctrine remained paradoxically more potent than ever. In the Helderberg Mountains of New York, it became the basis of an extremely democratic ideology in the Anti-Rent Wars of 1839–46, in which upstate farmers holding their lands on long-term leases from the pre-Revolutionary patroonships demanded an end to the annual payment of land rents. The Anti-Renters insisted that "all men are equal, sovereign and independent. . . . We believe that all power reposes in and emanates from the people, not the few, but all." This creed became the foundation of a sweeping reformist program that called for the inalienability of homesteads, free land to settlers, opposition to monopolies, universal public education, and religious liberty.[12]

Popular sovereignty also justified resort to people's tribunals created outside the established legal order, and sometimes even in defiance of it. In 1837, James Buchanan, United States Senator from Pennsylvania, grandly declared that when the rights of the majority in a state (he was speaking of Maryland) had long been violated, he would "invoke the peaceable aid of the people, in their sovereign capacity to remedy these evils. They are the source of all power; they are the rightful authors of all Constitutions. . . . Whoever denies this position condemns the principles of the Declaration of Independence and of the American Revolution."[13] Throughout the antebellum period, like-minded Americans justified vigilante justice in the name of the people's sovereignty. The clearest instance of this was provided by the San Francisco Vigilantes of 1856, who boldly declared:

Embodied in the principles of republican governments are the truths that the majority should rule, and that when corrupt officials, who have fraudulently seized the reigns [sic] of authority, designedly thwart the execution of the laws and avert punishment from the notoriously guilty, the power they usurp reverts back to the people from whom it was wrested . . . all law emanates from the people, so that, when the laws thus enacted are not

[12]An anonymous 1847 Anti-Rent manifesto, quoted in Henry Christman, *Tin Horns and Calico: A Decisive Episode in the Emergence of Democracy* (New York, 1945), p. 290.
[13]*Congressional Globe,* 24 Cong. 2 sess., app. p. 75 (Jan. 2, 1837). As President twenty years later, Buchanan was to ignore popular majorities in forcing the Lecompton Constitution on reluctant Kansans; see below, Ch. 6.

executed, the power returns to the people, and is theirs whenever they may choose to exercise it.[14]

The Vigilantes' claims that they represented the people were self-serving; but no one in America openly repudiated the principles they invoked.

The legal and extralegal realization of the ideal that the people are sovereign in America brought with it an essential consequence: the structures and mechanics of American politics changed to reflect the increasing role of the people in public affairs. This "democratization" of political life in Jacksonian America did not mean increased access to political power for everyone. To the contrary: women remained excluded from political participation, and blacks actually lost ground. But more and more white males gained entrée to the exuberant political life captured in the genre paintings of George Caleb Bingham. This expansion of political participation was achieved despite an ambivalence that reflected not just the fears of Whig ideologues but also deeper tensions in American society that transcended mere party differences.

Democratization found constitutional expression in several ways, often in the drafting of constitutions for the new states and in constitutional revisions in the older. High on the agendas for these conventions were problems of malapportionment and disfranchisement that plagued Rhode Island. Population movements created an endemic imbalance of political power within each state, with the older settled regions enjoying relatively greater legislative power than the new areas. To redress this, the decade of the 1830s began with an extraordinary constitutional convention in Virginia (1829–30), ennobled by the presence of Madison, James Monroe, John Randolph, and John Marshall as delegates, acting in a solemn constitutional capacity for the last time.

The Virginia Convention was a symbol of the constitutional tensions of the epoch. Its dominant issue, at the outset, was the reallocation of legislative representation so as to equalize the voting strength of the supposedly more democratic Piedmont as against the "aristocratic" Tidewater. But democratization challenged un-

---

[14]*Constitution and Address of the Committee of Vigilance of San Francisco* (1856), excerpted in Charles M. Haar (ed.), *The Golden Age of American Law* (New York, 1965), pp. 483–486.

spoken assumptions and fears of the entire white population. What began as a straightforward drive for reapportionment and broadened franchise quickly expanded into a sweeping review of the nature of the American constitutional order. What remains striking about this review is the defeat of democratic forces.

Few of the Virginia delegates joined John Randolph's unrestrained condemnation of all reform as "the newest, theoretical, pure, defecated Jacobinism," as "this besetting sin of Republican Governments, this *rerum novarum libido*."[15] But an impressive group of younger conservatives—John Tyler, Benjamin Watkins Leigh, Abel Parker Upshur, Philip Pendleton Barbour—challenged the democratic assumptions of the Piedmont delegates, pointing out that manhood suffrage and one-man-one-vote reapportionment would challenge the constitutional status of all property, but particularly the property in human beings. Suavely and adeptly the Tidewater conservatives divided the reform interest so that what emerged from the convention was a vestigial freeholder/taxpayer suffrage[16] and only a mild remedy for malapportionment and disfranchisement. This was accomplished by complex constitutional formulas that left the slaveholding Tidewater almost as securely in power as before. The convention did extend the great 1776 Declaration of Rights by incorporating into it Jefferson's Statute for Religious Freedom and explicit guarantees for freedom of speech and press, the privilege of the writ of habeas corpus, and prohibitions of ex post facto laws, laws impairing the obligation of contracts, and the taking of private property without just compensation. These changes produced a mixture of constitutional restraints on legislative power dear to both libertarians and conservatives.[17]

The results of constitutional change were similar in Georgia, Maryland, and North Carolina, which avoided complete democratization while conceding mild reforms. In general, the southern con-

[15]Quoted from excerpt of convention speech in Merrill D. Peterson (ed.), *Democracy, Liberty, and Property: The State Constitutional Conventions of the 1820s* (Indianapolis, 1966), pp. 432–434. The Latin phrase means "lust for new things."

[16]Manhood suffrage would extend the vote to all adult white male citizens. Freeholder suffrage would extend the vote to those with a specified minimum ownership of real property. Taxpayer suffrage would enfranchise persons who paid a minimum tax. Militia suffrage would permit all men enrolled in the militia to vote.

[17]The new constitutional provisions are in Thorpe, *Federal and State Constitutions*, VII, 3824–3826.

stitutional conventions of the thirties extended the suffrage by reducing or eliminating property-holding and religious qualifications for voting and officeholding. They made the governor elected directly by the people, rather than by the legislature, and curtailed the powers of the legislature slightly, by prohibiting special legislative divorce, by making legislative sessions biennial, by providing for popular election rather than appointment of lesser public officials and some judges, and by providing for periodic reapportionment.[18]

If democratization was as irresistible in the Jacksonian period as Tocqueville and others thought, why did it produce such ambivalent half-measures in state constitutional amendment? Tocqueville suggested one explanation when he pointed to American lawyers as "the most powerful existing security against the excesses of democracy." In words that remain applicable today, the French observer —no stranger to aristocracy himself—identified the elitist traits of the American bar: "a certain contempt for the judgment of the multitude"; a "secret contempt of the government of the people"; an "eminently conservative and antidemocratic" outlook; "inclinations natural to privileged classes."[19] (Tocqueville did not regret or condemn these traits; he considered them an essential counterpoise to the power of the people.) Lawyers' attitudes, training, and opportunities gave them an unusual opportunity to make public policy, largely by being able to cast policy issues in legal terms. The intellectual leaders of the antebellum American bar, the men who dictated the terms of constitutional discourse, were conservative judges and lawyers: Joseph Story, James Kent, Lemuel Shaw, Daniel Webster. Though one can point to reform-minded lawyers and judges here and there, such men were always counterbalanced by an equally eminent conservative colleague: Marcus Morton in Massachusetts offset by Rufus Choate, David Dudley Field in New York offset by Charles O'Conor, Judge William Gaston of North Carolina offset by Judge Thomas Ruffin. Moreover, reformist lawyers of the 1830s sometimes tended with time to degenerate into a wooden conservatism, a condition often attributed to the malign influence of Jacksonian Democracy: witness Benjamin Hallett of Massachusetts, Levi Woodbury of New Hampshire.

The Democratic party itself was an incubus on democracy and

[18]Fletcher M. Green, *Constitutional Development in the South Atlantic States, 1776–1860* (1930; reprint New York, 1966), 251–253.
[19]De Tocqueville, *Democracy in America,* I, 283–290, *passim.*

constitutional reform. The trauma of the Missouri crises of 1819–21 had molded the party's attitudes in the 1820s, giving it a social orientation not only static but reactionary. Democrats of all regions agreed that the internal security of slavery in the South was an absolute value, to be protected at any cost. The party's method of protecting slavery was control of the national government by controlling the White House and the Senate. This would give control of the United States Supreme Court. By the 1830s, demographic trends made it certain that the House of Representatives was irrevocably lost to the South. Democrats controlled the White House by nominating for the presidency either a southerner posing as a man of the West (Andrew Jackson) or a "northern man with southern principles": Martin Van Buren and his successors Franklin Pierce and James Buchanan. Control of the Senate was achieved by the de facto pairing of new states, so as to preserve a parity between slave and free states. Assuming the southern Senators voted as a bloc on slavery-related issues, some northern Democratic colleagues could always be found to vote with them because of party ties, logrolling, or other political pulls.[20] The system worked well until 1846, and might have gone on indefinitely had it not been for the Mexican War. But in the 1830s, given its commitment to the security and welfare of slavery, the Democracy, as it then called itself, was an antidemocratic force in American life.

But the ideology of the Democratic party and the policies of Andrew Jackson did have lasting constitutional significance. In his Farewell Address (1837), Jackson condemned what he called "the moneyed interest" and "monopoly and exclusive privileges."[21] This Jacksonian hostility to "privilege" created a fund of ideas and attitudes freely drawn on later by those who opposed the excesses of wealth and monopoly capitalism. Jacksonians' tirades against the abusive power of privileged concentrations of wealth had a curious staying power, a lingering echo that never faded out of American political rhetoric.

For good or ill, Jackson also passed on the legacy of a strong presidency. His vigorous personal involvement in the conduct of foreign affairs, a belligerent readiness to use force coupled with a

[20]Richard H. Brown, "The Missouri Crisis, Slavery, and the Politics of Jacksonianism," *South Atlantic Quarterly*, LXV (1966), 55–72.
[21]James D. Richardson (comp.), *A Compilation of the Messages and Papers of the Presidents* (22 vols., New York, 1897–1917), IV, 1525.

sincere desire to avoid doing so, and a simplistic world view based on a Manichaean vision of forces of light (American democracy) contending against the forces of darkness (European corruption and intrigue), all have their modern counterparts. Jackson also transformed his domestic constitutional role by use of the veto. What had been previously considered a "monarchical" trait in the American Constitution became, in Jackson's eyes, a vindication of the will of the people. The Bank Veto Message (1832) asserted a heightened presidential legislative role that is one of the preconditions of the power of the modern presidency. Jackson's contempt for federal judicial power still serves to inhibit unrestrained judicial review, though his claim to an independent constitutional authority equal in dignity to the Supreme Court's and not answerable to it was untenable even when conceived. Few Presidents have made so much of the office: Jefferson, Lincoln, the Roosevelts, Wilson certainly; perhaps Washington, Polk, Truman, and the second Johnson.

Jackson contributed even more profoundly to the third constitutional challenge of his era, preservation of the Union and a functional federal system. By its semicentennial in 1836, the Union seemed secure, though not free of problems. Under the Constitution, federalism had evolved into a remarkably flexible machinery for reconciling the competing impulses of nationalism and particularism. The Union had weathered its two most serious challenges, the disunionist sentiment among New England Federalists before and during the War of 1812, and the nullification crisis in South Carolina of 1832. The resolution of the nullification controversy was a triumph for the Union, in the short run. Andrew Jackson seemed to have the last word in his unbending "Proclamation to the People of South Carolina" (December 10, 1832). Denouncing nullification and secession as revolutionary, not constitutional, Jackson thumpingly insisted that "the Constitution of the United States, then, forms a *government,* not a league . . . in which all the people are represented, which operates directly on the people individually." "Be not deceived by names," he warned; "disunion by armed force is treason."[22] Jackson's Proclamation joined the list of classic unionist texts: Washington's Farewell Address, Marshall's opinion in *McCulloch* v. *Maryland,* Webster's reply to Hayne.

[22]*Ibid.,* III, 1203–1219 at 1211, 1217 (italics in original).

The nullification dispute called forth a unionist voice from the grave of James Madison eighteen years later. In 1834, Madison had drafted "Advice to My Country," in a spidery hand enfeebled by advanced age. Anticipating posthumous publication, he called it a message that "may be considered as issuing from the tomb where truth alone can be respected." Musing on his extraordinary career, Madison invoked "the experience of one who has served his country in various stations through a period of forty years, who espoused in his youth and adhered through his life to the cause of its liberty and who has borne a part in most of the great transactions which will constitute epochs of its destiny." From that vantage, Madison offered "the advice nearest to my heart":

Let the Union of the States be cherished & perpetuated. Let the open enemy to it be regarded as a Pandora with her box opened; and the disguised one, as the serpent creeping with his deadly wiles into Paradise.[23]

This ghostly voice of the Father of the Constitution was not actually heard until 1850; Virginia Unionists published it then to refute southern invocation of Madison as authority for another nullification effort. But it was Madison's valedictory, and a fitting theme for the mid-thirties.

At the same time that he penned "Advice to My Country," Madison enlarged on an idea that Washington and Jefferson had already addressed magisterially, Washington in his Farewell Address and Jefferson, with prophetic pessimism, in 1821 during the aftermath of the Missouri crisis. Madison gravely viewed the danger of sectionalism, as his predecessors had, but he also surveyed countervailing tendencies:

A return of danger from abroad . . . may aid in binding the States in one political system, or . . . the geographical and commercial ligatures, may have that effect; or . . . the present discord of interests between the North & the South, may give way to a less diversity in the applications of labour, or to the mutual advantage of a safe & constant interchange of the different products of labour in different sections.[24]

[23]From facsimile of draft in Madison's hand, reproduced adjacent to p. 530 of Irving Brant, *James Madison: Commander in Chief, 1812–1836* (Indianapolis, 1961).
[24]Madison to Edward Coles, Aug. 29, 1834, in Gaillard Hunt (ed.), *The Writings of James Madison* (11 vols., New York, 1910), IX, 536–542 at 541–542.

Madison did not live to see his hopes fulfilled, but each of the ties of the Union he itemized, except what he delicately referred to as "less diversity in the applications of labour," was to be effectuated.

The "danger from abroad" that Madison apprehended soon took shape. Anglo-American tensions along the northern frontier of the United States erupted into bloodshed in 1838 when Canadian militiamen burned an American steamboat, the *Caroline,* killing one American. Throughout the ensuing winter, Maine and New Brunswick lumberjacks and militia skirmished bloodlessly in territory disputed between the United States and Great Britain because of the imperfect cartography of 1783. But these frictions were soothed by the Webster-Ashburton Treaty of 1842, which adjusted the northern frontier lines in a way that not only settled existing controversies but also ultimately gave the United States an invaluable economic bonus: the Mesabi iron range of northern Minnesota.

Madison also expected that "commercial ligatures" would bind the Union together. As he wrote, they were already in place. The Erie Canal had been opened in 1825; its success in the next decade stimulated an outburst of canal-building in the western states. Though few of the western canals enjoyed the profits of the Erie, cumulatively they created a network of water-borne commerce that dominated American transportation until after the Civil War. Their importance was amplified by steamboats on the western rivers and lakes, creating what Chief Justice Roger B. Taney would characterize in 1851 as "a great and growing commerce . . . upon them between different States and a foreign nation, which is subject to all the incidents and hazards that attend commerce on the ocean."[25]

The canal's future rival, the railroad, had already appeared. Before 1830, little specialized short-lines were laid in Massachusetts, Pennsylvania, New Jersey, Maryland, and South Carolina. By 1836, larger multistate lines had extensive trackage: the Boston and Worcester, the Boston and Albany, the Louisville, Cincinnati and Charleston, and the predecessor of the Atlantic Coast Line. By 1840, the United States had nearly twice as much railroad track as all Europe combined.[26]

[25]Propellor Genesee Chief *v.* Fitzhugh, 12 How. (53 U.S.) 443 (1851) at 453. On this case, see below, ch. 3.

[26]United States: 3,328 miles; Europe: 1,818 miles. Richard B. Morris, *Encyclopedia of American History* (New York, 1976), p. 606.

Together the railroads and canals encouraged a boom in state and local financing of internal improvements, where states, counties, and municipalities eagerly subscribed to bond issues, took second mortgages, or provided other subventions to finance what historians term the Transportation Revolution. Seldom did the governments own and operate the railroads (Pennsylvania's Main Line is the conspicuous exception, and even that was sold off in the 1850s). Instead, governments provided financial support to private enterprise, usually relinquishing control of the enterprise. In this way, the United States established the precedent of public-sector support for private profitmaking activity, in contrast to Europe's policy of public ownership. This policy was compounded by the tradition of feeble governmental supervision of the railroads' behavior, which created in the nineteenth century what Wallace Farnham has called "the weakened spring of government": a condition of subsidy without regulation or supervision that failed to ensure either justice or order.[27]

The last great challenge of the Democratic Constitution, slavery, proved to be a constitutional cancer. It had never been in true remission since Independence. But there had been periods—1807 to 1819, 1822 to 1833—when the controversy had seemed to abate, in the sense that it did not occupy much time on the floor of Congress. Even in these periods disputes over slavery surfaced, but the controversies were confined largely to one section of the country. The second of these quiescent periods came to an end rudely in 1833 after northern abolitionists and blacks had begun to condemn slavery in effective propaganda media and to demand its immediate abolition. As if in resonance with this rejuvenated abolition sentiment, in 1831 a slave preacher in southern Virginia, Nat Turner, led a black uprising that left some sixty whites, mostly women and children, dead, before it was bloodily suppressed.

The Turner Rebellion, followed by the founding of the American Anti-Slavery Society in Philadelphia (1833), proved to be the prelude to an outburst of controversy over slavery that dominated the 1830s. In 1835, a mob in Charleston, South Carolina, rifled mail

[27]Wallace D. Farnham, "The Weakened Spring of Government: A Study in Nineteenth-Century American History," *American Historical Review*, LXVIII (1963), 662–680.

sacks of the United States Post Office in order to seize and burn abolitionist propaganda. Postmaster General Amos Kendall, a member of Jackson's cabinet, gave his tacit approval and recommended executive and legislative action that would exclude antislavery material from the mails.[28] For his part, Jackson first thought that informal rather than formal suppression of abolitionists' First Amendment rights was preferable; he recommended that postmasters publish the names of recipients of mail from abolitionists to "put them in Coventry." But he soon decided that action against the source rather than the target of propaganda would work better and recommended legislation excluding abolitionist propaganda from the mails.[29]

From 1834 through 1836, antiabolition and antiblack mobs troubled northern communities as well as southern: New York (July, 1834); Philadelphia (August, 1834); numerous small towns in Ohio (1835); Utica, New York (October, 1835); Boston (October, 1835); Cincinnati (July, 1836); Palmyra, Missouri, and St. Louis (May, 1836). This violence culminated in the mob murder of abolitionist editor Elijah Lovejoy in Alton, Illinois, on October 26, 1836.

Jackson responded to this violence by berating its victims. In his Farewell Address (March 4, 1837), which was drafted by Roger B. Taney, Jackson sternly condemned abolitionists and encouraged antiabolitionist mobs: "the citizens of every State should . . . frown upon any proceedings within their borders likely to disturb the tranquillity of their political brethren in other portions of the union." He went on to repeat a fundamental assumption of the American constitutional order: ". . . each State has the unquestionable right to regulate its own internal concerns according to its own pleasure." This seeming truism was a euphemistic way of saying that the control of slavery was exclusively a concern of the states, and that the federal government, other states, or individuals and groups in other states could not legitimately interfere in the formation of policy toward slavery in any particular state. Jackson warned

[28]"Report of the Postmaster General," House Executive Documents, 24 Cong., 1 sess., ser. 286, doc. 2 (1835), 396–398.

[29]Andrew Jackson to Amos Kendall, Aug. 9, 1835, in John Spencer Bassett (ed.), *Correspondence of Andrew Jackson* (Washington, 1926–35), V, 360–361; Andrew Jackson, seventh annual message, Dec. 7, 1835, in Richardson, *Messages and Papers of the Presidents*, IV, 1395.

that all efforts on the part of people of other States to cast odium upon their institutions, and all measures calculated to disturb their rights of property or to put in jeopardy their peace and internal tranquillity, are in direct opposition to the spirit in which the Union was formed, and must endanger its safety.[30]

Congress, meanwhile, tried to achieve more decorously what the people-out-of-doors were doing in the streets: both Houses attempted to exclude the discussion of slavery in a series of "gag" resolutions adopted in the spring of 1836. The gags, automatically tabling all petitions coming into either House on the subject of slavery, had two immediate effects. First, they stimulated abolitionists to redouble efforts in their petition campaigns. Antislavery agents got half a million signatures to petitions on various constitutional topics, such as slavery and the slave trade in the District of Columbia; the admission of Arkansas and other slave states; slavery in the territories; the annexation of Texas; the interstate slave trade; the privileges and immunities of whites and blacks traveling in the South; and the rights of free blacks. Second, though there was little love throughout the North for abolitionists, and even less for blacks, northerners began to see that the slavery of blacks required the repression of some whites, and that it might require further sacrifices from whites, and not just abolitionists.

Jackson, like the party he led, cherished slavery as the only conceivable answer to the otherwise insoluble problem of finding a workable constitutional niche for blacks in the multiracial society of the United States. He and the Democracy were determined to protect the internal security of slavery where it was; to encourage its expansion to areas where it had not yet penetrated or where it had been abolished; and to commit the nation's diplomatic and military forces to promoting these ends.[31] Jackson spent his last days in office attempting unsuccessfully to persuade the Senate to ratify the annexation of the Republic of Texas. His failure left the issue of Texas to fester in American national politics for a decade.

These controversies stimulated John C. Calhoun, representing South Carolina in the Senate, to rethink the nature of the federal

[30] *Ibid.*, IV, 1511–1527 at 1513–1514, 1516.
[31] Edward Pessen, *Jacksonian America: Society, Personality, and Politics*, rev. ed. (Homewood, Ill., 1978), pp. 301–303.

Union, the locus of sovereignty, and the place of slavery in the American constitutional order. Calhoun's resulting reinterpretation of the Constitution was premised on an idea first publicly articulated in 1835 by South Carolina Governor George McDuffie in a message to the legislature. McDuffie declared that slavery was "manifestly consistent with the will of God" and "therefore, instead of being a political evil, is the cornerstone of our republican edifice."[32] Calhoun popularized the idea, though it shocked the free states on first hearing, by restating it as his "positive-good" thesis: slavery is a positive blessing, not an evil, to white and black alike and, in any event, is inseparable from the social and constitutional order of the southern states.

Calhoun presented the constitutional expression of this insight in a set of resolutions he offered to the Senate on December 27, 1837, declaring that:

1. In ratifying the Constitution, "the States adopting the same acted, severally, as free, independent, and sovereign States."

2. "The States retained, severally, the exclusive and sole right over their own domestic institutions"; therefore any "intermeddling" by other states or organizations, like the antislavery societies, in the internal affairs of other states is "subversive of the objects for which the Constitution was formed."

3. The federal government is nothing more than "a common agent" of the sovereign states, with its powers merely "delegated" by them; it must therefore use those powers to give "increased stability and security to the domestic institutions of the States."

4. Slavery "composes an important part of [the] domestic institutions" of the southern states and "an essential element in the distribution of its powers among the states" (Calhoun here referred to northern objections to the "three-fifths clause" of Article I, section 2, which permitted 60 percent of the slaves to be counted as part of a state's population for purposes of apportioning seats in the House of Representatives.)

5. Any northern effort to abolish slavery in the District of Columbia or the territories "under the pretext that it is immoral or sinful" would be a "direct and dangerous attack on the institutions of all the slaveholding States."

6. "The union of these States rests on an equality of rights and advantages among its members." Therefore any refusal to admit new slave states

[32]Printed in *Journal of the General Assembly of . . . South Carolina . . . 1835* (n.p., n.d.), pp. 5–9.

or annex new slave territories would deprive the slave states of the equality
due them under the Constitution.[33]

The Senate, apparently regarding the first four as unobjectiona-
ble, adopted them, but somehow saw the latter two as innovative or
controversial in ways that the first four were not, and refused to
endorse them. The Calhoun resolutions embodied a new theory of
the Union, radically different from the assumptions that underlay
the drafting of the Constitution fifty years earlier. Their power
derived not from their grounding in precedent nor from a universal
consensus on their validity but simply because no one had a better
alternative to offer that spoke to the emerging tensions between
North and South.

No one, that is, but the despised abolitionists. Calhoun had begun
a process of taking three separate sources of constitutional dyna-
mism—popular sovereignty, union, slavery—and fusing them, so
that it became increasingly difficult to filter out one of them to deal
with it isolated from the others. The abolitionist alternative, of
course, would not have appeased anxious slavocrats jittery over the
bogey of slave insurrections and the precipitous decline in slave
prices in the decade 1836–45. But abolitionists did offer a coherent,
equally plausible, variant interpretation of the Constitution. For the
period 1833–37, a time of relatively short-lived harmony and mutual tolerance among organized abolitionists, the precepts of abolitionist constitutional thought included these basic ideas:

1. Slavery was contrary to natural law, the proclamation of equality in the
Declaration of Independence, and the principles of republican government.
2. It must therefore be abolished immediately.
3. Black people should "share an equality with the whites, of civil and
religious privileges."
4. Congress had no power to abolish slavery; each state has the "exclusive
right to legislate in regard to its abolition in said State."
5. But Congress could and should constitutionally act to:
a. abolish slavery in the District of Columbia and all federal territories
    and possessions;
b. abolish the interstate slave trade;
c. refuse to admit new slave states;

[33]*Congressional Globe*, 25 Cong., 2 sess., 55 (Dec. 27, 1837).

d. refuse to assist in suppressing slave insurrections;

e. refuse to enforce the fugitive slave clause;

f. abrogate the three-fifths clause (presumably by amendment).[34]

Calhoun and the abolitionists had done something more than just make explicit two "extremist" positions, one pro-slavery and the other anti-. Rather, both pointed out that the constitutional assumptions of 1836 were proving inadequate as a matrix within which the controversy over slavery, Union, and sovereignty could be resolved. The old constitutional order was not dying, but it was not sufficient to the needs of the nation as it entered upon its second half-century. Calhoun and the abolitionists each worked out, from their differing historical assumptions, a vision of future constitutional development. In 1836, the constitution was entering a new and dangerous period of growth, and Americans were faced with the disagreeable necessity of thinking about sovereignty, slavery, and Union in unprecedented ways.

But despite this ominous note, the constitutional priorities of the 1830s—popular sovereignty, democracy, Union, slavery—seemed reasonably secure. The national government had established its preeminence in the federal system by 1836 to an extent that realized the hopes of the nationalists who had created it fifty years earlier. Despite Madison's twilight pessimism, national supremacy was a fact, not an aspiration, in 1836. The sweeping imperatives of Marshall's great decisions—*McCulloch* v. *Maryland* (1819) foremost— and Joseph Story's assertion of federal judicial supremacy in *Martin* v. *Hunter's Lessee* (1816) survived the carpings of Jefferson, John Taylor, and Spencer Roane. The South Carolinians' railing at what Thomas Cooper called "consolidation"—that is, national supremacy—merely confirmed this national preeminence.

Joseph Story captured best this triumph of national power that he himself had helped achieve. The American people, he wrote benignly in his *Commentaries on the Constitution* (1833), saw the federal government as

---

[34]Distilled from the Constitution and the Declaration of Sentiments (1833) of the American Anti-Slavery Society, reprinted with constitutional exegesis in *The Declaration of Sentiments and Constitution of the American Anti-Slavery Society; Together with Those Parts of the Constitution of the United States, Which are Supposed to have any Relation to Slavery* (New York, 1835); see William M. Wiecek, *The Sources of Antislavery Constitutionalism in America, 1760–1848* (Ithaca, 1978).

the parental guardian of our public and private rights, and the natural ally of all the state governments, in the administration of justice, and the promotion of general prosperity. It is beloved, not for its beneficence; not because it commands, but because it sustains the common interests, and the common liberties, and the common rights of the people.[35]

The rights of the people, the preservation of the Union, the protection of liberty: these were some of the constitutional ideals of the Jacksonian era. Would the second half-century under the Constitution see them as well served as the first had? Story's nationalism notwithstanding, that was a question that would be answered primarily in the states, not at Washington.

[35]Joseph Story, *Commentaries on the Constitution of the United States* (Boston, 1833), sec. 515.

CHAPTER 2

The Public Law

THE American Union before the Civil War was a federation of states. It was further along the road to nationhood than the old Confederation of 1776–89 had been, but the states still retained internal sovereignty[1] and remained important sources of constitutional development. Hence a constitutional history of the antebellum years necessarily reviews the public law of the states. For it was in the mundane areas of railroad finance, women's rights, tort law, and the like that antebellum Americans worked out constitutional issues later subsumed by the federal government: the relationship of the individual to the state, the meaning of republican government, the limitations on state power.

At the beginning of the second half-century of the American Republic, the judges of the state courts were creatively applying doctrines of "higher law" that imposed limits on the power of state legislatures, designed to protect property rights as an element of republican liberty. Judges displayed a special tenderness for corporations, those new artificial legal beings so necessary to a dynamic, modern capitalist economy. At the same time, the state legislatures

---

[1]Sovereignty = "the supreme, absolute, and uncontrollable power by which any independent state is governed; supreme political authority; paramount control of the constitution and frame of government and its administration; the self-sufficient source of political power, from which all specific political powers are derived." *Black's Law Dictionary,* 5th ed., "Sovereignty."

were responding to Jacksonian demands, partly entrepreneurial, partly democratic, for general incorporation laws. In the exuberance of their creativity, judges of the state courts created two new bodies of law: torts and contracts. Conservative lawyers fought off efforts to make the law comprehensible and accessible to the common people, successfully resisting a movement to codify the law until the twentieth century, when codification was accomplished on lawyers' terms. Finally, the public law of the states responded to the reform movements of the Jacksonian era, absorbing some reforms, repelling others. As never before or since, the public law of the states distributed privilege and power, burdens and discriminations, among various groups of American society. Legal historians justly call this the "Formative Era" and the "Golden Age" of American law.[2]

The antebellum period proved to be a time of judicial activism. State judges confidently seized the chance to mold public policy and did not hesitate to challenge legislatures. Whig judges in particular, concerned that the democratic impulse might lead legislative majorities to experiment with legislation that threatened the security or the opportunities of private property, eagerly sought explicit limitations on legislative power in the state Constitutions. Often, however, they could not find them because the early Constitutions were comparatively spare, terse documents. They conformed to Chief Justice Marshall's description: if a Constitution were "to contain an accurate detail of all the subdivisions of which its great powers will admit, [it] would partake of the prolixity of a legal code, and could scarcely be embraced by the human mind. . . . Its nature, therefore, requires, that only its great outlines should be marked. . . ."[3] So when judges could not find a suitable text, they fell back on higher-law doctrines. The higher-law tradition holds that human lawmaking authority can enact laws only in conformity to principles derived from some higher source of law, usually divine. William Blackstone, in his *Commentaries on the Laws of England* (1765), boldly declared that "the law of nature . . . dictated by God himself, is of course superior in obligation to any other. It is binding over all the

---

[2]Roscoe Pound, *The Formative Era of American Law* (Boston, 1938); Charles M. Haar (ed.), *The Golden Age of American Law* (New York, 1965).
[3]McCulloch v. Maryland, 4 Wheat. (17 U.S.) 316 (1819) at 407.

globe, in all countries, and at all times: no human laws are of any validity if contrary to this."[4] Classical American constitutional jurisprudence absorbed Blackstone's higher-law principles: Judge William Paterson's Circuit Court opinion in *Van Horne's Lessee* v. *Dorrance* (1795); Marshall's majority opinion and Justice William Johnson's concurrence in *Fletcher* v. *Peck* (1810), in which Johnson impiously maintained that higher-law ideas bind even God; Chancellor Kent's *Commentaries;* and Joseph Story's *Commentaries on the Constitution.* [5]

The leading exposition of this view was United States Supreme Court Justice Samuel Chase's opinion in *Calder* v. *Bull* (1798), in which he asserted, in dictum, that "there are acts which the federal or state legislature cannot do, without exceeding their authority. There are certain vital principles in our free republican governments, which will determine and overrule an apparent and flagrant abuse of legislative power. . . . The genius, the nature, and the spirit of our state governments, amount to a prohibition of such acts of legislation; and the general principles of law and reason forbid them."[6]

But after the *Dartmouth College* case (1819),[7] higher-law principles in their vague, generalized *Calder* v. *Bull* formulations disappeared from the language of the United States Supreme Court, save for an occasional opinion by Justice Story.[8] Following Marshall's lead, the federal courts voided state legislation only because of conflict with a specific clause of the United States Constitution. The contracts clause of Article I, section 10, was usually the prime candidate for this sort of employment, and it displaced higher law in the federal courts.

In the state courts, however, higher law flourished. It evolved

[4]William Blackstone, *Commentaries on the Laws of England* (first edition: Oxford, 1765), I, *41.

[5]2 Dall. 304 (C.C.D. Pa. 1795); 6 Cranch (10 U.S.) 87 (1810); James Kent, *Commentaries on American Law* (New York, 1826–30), II, 339–340; Joseph Story, *Commentaries on the Constitution of the United States* (Boston, 1833), sec. 1399.

[6]3 Dall. (3 U.S.) 386 (1798) (Chase, J. seriatim). "Dictum" is a statement appearing in a judicial opinion that is unnecessary to the holding of the case. It is an expression of the judge's opinion, and is not binding on later judges.

[7]On the significance of this case, see p. 27.

[8]Terrett v. Taylor, 9 Cranch (13 U.S.) 43 (1815); U.S. *v.* La Jeune Eugenie, 26 Fed. Cas. 832 (No. 15551) (C.C.D. Mass. 1822); Wilkinson *v.* Leland, 2 Pet. (27 U.S.) 627 (1829).

from a demand that statutes affecting property be general, not special, to an insistence that such laws not be punitive or retroactive in application. Courts in Connecticut, Tennessee, Maryland, and Delaware paraphrased the vague *Calder* v. *Bull* phrases to void state statutes violating "eternal principles of justice," "obvious dictates of reason," "the nature and spirit of the social compact," and "the nature and spirit of our republican form of government."[9] Higher-law ideas became associated with specific constitutional texts, chiefly the law-of-the-land or due process clauses of the state constitutions.[10] Chief Judge Thomas Ruffin of the North Carolina Supreme Court and Judge Greene C. Bronson of the New York Supreme Court pioneered this effort.[11]

In the 1840s, two types of social-reform legislation attracted the attention of judges employing higher law in defense of property: Married Women's Property Acts and temperance legislation. In order to strike down laws vesting title in women to property they owned at the time of marriage, or statutes prohibiting the retail sale of liquor, judges relied indiscriminately on federal constitutional provisions like the contracts clause and state law-of-the-land provisions to bludgeon women's emancipation and prohibition.[12] But they were soon stymied by a formidable new doctrine: the police power. Chief Justice Lemuel Shaw of the Massachusetts Supreme Judicial Court, a peer of Marshall, Story, and Taney, originated the doctrine in *Commonwealth* v. *Alger* (1851), where he defined the police power as "the power vested in the legislature to make . . . all manner of wholesome and reasonable laws . . . not repugnant to the constitution, as they shall judge to be for the good and welfare of the commonwealth." Shaw explained that in a

well ordered civil society, . . . every holder of property, however absolute and unqualified may be his title, holds it under the implied liability that his

[9]*Goshen* v. *Stonington*, 4 Conn. 209 (1822) (dictum); *Bank of the State* v. *Cooper*, 2 Yerg. 599 (Tenn. 1831); *Regents of the University of Maryland* v. *Williams*, 9 Gill & J. 365 (Md. 1838); *Rice* v. *Foster*, 4 Harr. 479 (Del. 1847).

[10]The common ancestor of these provisions was Art. 8 of the Virginia Declaration of Rights (1776): ". . . no man be deprived of his liberty, except by the law of the land or the judgment of his peers." Thorpe, *Federal and State Constitutions*, VII, 3813.

[11]*Hoke* v. *Henderson*, 4 Dev. Law 1 (N.C. 1833); *Taylor* v. *Porter*, 4 Hill 140 (N.Y. 1843).

[12]*White* v. *White*, 5 Barb. S.C. 474 (N.Y. Supreme Court, 1849); *Rice* v. *Foster*, 4 Harr. 479 (Del. 1847).

use of it may be so regulated, that it shall not be injurious to the equal enjoyment of others having an equal right to the enjoyment of their property, nor injurious to the rights of the community. . . . Rights of property, like all other social and conventional rights, are subject to such reasonable limitations in their enjoyment, as shall prevent them from being injurious, and to such reasonable restraints and regulations established by law, as the legislature [may impose].[13]

Thus expressed, police power was a potentially serious threat to property rights of all kinds and to the higher-law doctrines protecting them. Because Chief Justice Roger B. Taney of the United States Supreme Court was a devotee of the police power doctrine for his own purposes, viewing it as a means of protecting the states' exclusive control of slavery, the state courts had to work out their own responses to the threat posed by the new doctrine. This task was made all the more difficult because the United States Supreme Court, though badly divided over commerce-clause issues, sustained the constitutionality of some forms of liquor prohibition in the *License Cases* (1847).[14] Moreover, the Marshall Court had already held that the United States Constitution's Fifth Amendment requirements of public purpose and just compensation for the taking of property were not applicable as restraints on the states' exercise of police power.[15] But the New York Court of Appeals met this challenge successfully in *Wynehamer* v. *People* (1856)[16] when it struck down a state prohibition statute. Judge George F. Comstock asserted that "theories of public good or public necessity may be so plausible or even so truthful as to command public majorities. But whether truthful or plausible merely, and by whatever numbers they are assented to, there are some absolute private rights beyond their reach, and among these the constitution places the right of property."

Married Women's Property Acts and prohibition statutes were not the only sources of concern for conservative jurists. Proponents of higher-law doctrines also feared that legislative majorities might regulate corporations in ways that would discourage the entrepreneurial risk-taking so important in a capital-scarce, industrializ-

[13]7 Cush. (61 Mass.) 53 (1851) at 84–85.
[14]5 How. (46 U.S.) 504 (1847); on this case, see below, Ch. 3.
[15]Barron v. Baltimore, 7 Pet. (32 U.S.) 243 (1833).
[16]13 N.Y. 378 (1856) at 387.

ing economy. And with good reason: reform-minded Democrats and others did seek to limit the scope of corporate power, while investors' spokesmen sought boundless opportunities for corporate activity. The struggle between these groups was so contentious partly because the private, profitmaking corporation was a new creature of the law, radically different from its legal ancestor, the public corporation.

A series of technological innovations after Independence left America poised on the threshold of the Industrial Revolution: the factory (Samuel Slater built the first water-powered cloth mill in Pawtucket, Rhode Island, 1790); the factory system of production (Eli Whitney devised a system of assembling precision-made interchangeable parts in the manufacture of muskets, 1800); a new source of power (Oliver Evans perfected a high-pressure steam engine in 1787); an expanded market for the products of the industrial system (John Fitch and Robert Fulton devised steam-powered vessels, 1787–1807, and Peter Cooper built the first railroad in America in South Carolina, 1830). Samuel F. B. Morse's invention of the telegraph—the first message was sent in 1844—revolutionized business communications. But entrepreneurs' ability to exploit these technological innovations was hampered by the lack of a suitable financial mechanism for amassing the large amounts of capital needed for long-term investment.

The traditional partnership was unsuitable because it terminated with the death or withdrawal of a partner, and because each partner was liable for the debts of the entire enterprise. So investors before 1820 experimented with a variety of economic and legal forms for accumulating capital: limited partnerships (in which only some partners were fully liable for the partnership's debts); the business trust (with management in the hands of "trustees," and profits accruing for the benefit of "beneficiaries," the investors); and chartered "companies" or "associations" in a seemingly infinite variety of forms.[17] Out of this trial-and-error, there emerged a new form that provided investors with the vehicle they sought: the private business corporation, a modification of the old public corporation, "an artificial person, existing in contemplation of law, and endowed with certain powers and franchises which . . . are . . . considered as

[17]Lawrence M. Friedman, *A History of American Law* (New York, 1973), pp. 176–177.

subsisting in the corporation itself, as distinctly as if it were a real personage."[18] The private business corporation proved to be an improvement on all earlier forms because it survived the death of any of its shareholders or officers; because, after a period of experimentation, its shareholders were not liable for more than the value of the shares they held or subscribed; and because it gave greater flexibility in amassing investment capital from numerous investors. But before this was achieved, the new corporation became the center of a controversy between investors, who sought to maximize its power and minimize its responsibility, and some political leaders, who sought the reverse. The legal history of the private business corporation before the Civil War is the story of how these opposing demands were compromised by legislative and judicial action.

At their most extravagant, investors insisted that corporations were virtually free from any form of state regulation—enclaves of uncontrolled economic power in the republic. Less grandiosely, investors sought three specific advantages over the partnership form: corporate immortality, limited liability, and transferability of shares. That is, they wanted a legal entity that would survive the death of an investor or officer; that would be exclusively responsible for its debts, rather than the investors or officers being liable; and that provided an easy means for an investor to come in or withdraw.

These demands, together with some fast-and-loose financial practices in the early banking corporations, created a climate of hostility among many political leaders. Virginians were among the most prominent enemies of the corporation. Judge Spencer Roane of the Virginia Supreme Court of Appeals thought that corporations were inherently suspect under Article IV of the Virginia Declaration of Rights, which stated that "no . . . set of men, are entitled to exclusive or separate emoluments or privileges from the community, but in consideration of publick services." From this, he drew the conclusion that "if [the investors'] object is merely private or selfish; if it is detrimental to, or not promotive of, the public good, they have no adequate claim on the legislature for the privilege [of a charter]."[19] Old Jeffersonians like United States Supreme Court Justice Peter V. Daniel carried this attitude with them to the grave. Daniel

[18]Story, J., concurring in Dartmouth College *v.* Woodward, 4 Wheat. (17 U.S.) 418 (1819) at 667.
[19]Currie's Administrators *v.* The Mutual Assurance Society, 4 Hen. & Munf. 315 (Va. 1809).

provided in his will that his executor could convert his real property into stocks and bonds, "excluding the stocks or bonds of banks, railroads, or corporations or joint stock companies of any kind."[20]

While Virginia Republicans voiced extreme views, others were more influential in shaping public policy around two principal points. First, the people, through their representatives in the legislature, must be able to exercise some control over corporations. Second, creditors must have some claim against money invested or pledged by shareholders. Between these demands for public accountability on one hand and opportunity for investors on the other, public policy took form in the courts and statehouses. In 1819, two major decisions, both conventionally seen as triumphs for the private business corporation, harmonized these demands. John Marshall's majority opinion in *Dartmouth College* v. *Woodward* (1819)[21] is usually hailed as the great shield of the corporation, protecting it from arbitrary state interference. But the case was paradoxical, potentially restraining corporations as much as it did the state legislatures. Justice Story in his *Dartmouth College* concurrence conceded a point earlier established by the Massachusetts Supreme Judicial Court in *Wales* v. *Stetson* (1806):

a corporation cannot be controlled or destroyed by any subsequent statute, unless a power for that purpose be reserved to the legislature in the act of incorporation. . . . If the legislature mean to claim such an authority, it must be reserved in the grant [i.e., in the corporate charter].[22]

State legislatures did just that: both in special charters and in general incorporation acts they reserved power to amend or abrogate the charter, or imposed limitations on its powers. Moreover, corporations did not have innate powers; they could exercise only those powers specifically granted in the charter or necessary for the powers expressly granted.[23] Thus some public control was legitimated and preserved.

Similarly with the other great corporation case of 1819, *Spear* v. *Grant,* in which the Massachusetts Supreme Judicial Court established the principle of limited liability by holding that the debts of

---

[20]John P. Frank, *Justice Daniel Dissenting: A Biography of Peter V. Daniel, 1784–1860* (Cambridge, Mass., 1964), p. 289.

[21]4 Wheat. (17 U.S.) 518 (1819).

[22]2 Tyng (2 Mass.) 143 (1806) at 146.

[23]Kent, *Commentaries,* II, *298.

the corporation were not the debts of the individual investors.[24] Chief Justice Isaac Parker held that it was up to the legislature to establish the extent of a shareholder's liability for the debts of the corporation he invested in, and even suggested that a remedy might be available against a shareholder who had pledged to buy, but not yet paid for, stock of a defunct corporation.

The Massachusetts legislature then went to the extreme of imposing unlimited liability on all shareholders of manufacturing corporations. These drastic measures, unique to the Bay State, effectively converted such corporations to partnerships for liability purposes.[25] New York's Chancellor James Kent sarcastically commented that "whether [this policy] be well or ill founded, it is admirably well calculated to cure all undue avidity for charters of incorporation."[26] Bowing to reality, Massachusetts began abandoning the rule in 1837.

States preserved control and accountability of corporations in other ways, too. They provided for the automatic expiration of a corporate charter after a specified term; prohibited fraud on creditors; and legislated detailed regulations governing corporate activities, either in charters or in general corporation statutes. When legislatures made extravagant concessions of immunity from taxation, indignant judges rebuked them.[27]

Jacksonian Democrats enthusiastically promoted general incorporation statutes in the 1830s. Before the nineteenth century all corporations were created by a special act, the granting of a charter, by the king or the state legislature. The practice invited abuses, the most common being that friendly (or bribed) legislators would rush through corporate charters, sometimes in the closing days of legislative sessions, loaded with special concessions that escaped the attention of their colleagues. Often, in another practice Chief Justice Taney complained of in 1854, incorporators themselves drafted the corporate charter.[28] Hence Jacksonians demanded general incorporation statutes: laws providing a model, pattern, or outline of

[24]16 Tyng (16 Mass.) 9 (1819).
[25]Joseph K. Angell and Samuel Ames, *A Treatise on the Law of Private Corporations Aggregate,* 2nd ed. (Boston, 1843), p. 483. The first edition of this book (1832) was the earliest Anglo-American treatise on the law of modern private corporations.
[26]Kent, *Commentaries,* II, *272.
[27]Mott v. Pennsylvania Railroad, 30 Penn. St. 9 (1858).
[28]Ohio Life Insurance and Trust Co. v. Debolt, 16 How. (57 U.S.) 415 (1854) at 435.

a corporate charter, and including some regulation of powers, stock ownership, rights of creditors, voting powers, and other routine aspects of corporate activity. Jacksonians hostile to monopolies and special privileges demanded open access to corporate charters for all who had money to invest. The experience of Wisconsin in drafting its first state constitution between 1846 and 1848 provides some examples. The Democratic Racine *Advocate* insisted that

if corporate powers are necessary, let them be made as limited as possible in extent, and as available as possible to all. Let general incorporation laws alone be passed, even for villages and cities, so that . . . all may avail themselves of them.

A Racine County mass meeting adopted resolutions demanding

that all exclusive privileges and monopolies, whereby the few may be enabled to amass wealth at the expense of the many, are contrary to the spirit of a government of true equality. . . . [Corporations] should be regulated by general laws for the privileges of which none can be excluded who comply with their provisions.[29]

Responding to such demands, the Wisconsin Constitution of 1848 forbade the charter of any banking corporations unless approved twice by popular referenda, and required that all other corporations be created only by "general laws" unless the legislature determined that the objects of a particular corporation could not be achieved under the general incorporation act. The same article also contained a clause common to constitutions and statutes of the period, providing that corporate charters, whether general or special, could be altered or repealed by the legislature at any time.[30]

Special charters did not vanish after the Jacksonian period, but the democratization of investment opportunity at least freed legislatures from the task of considering every new corporate charter. Similar trends of the period abolished special legislative divorces, and, in Congress, special legislative hearings on every claim against the federal government.

One technological innovation, the railroad, quickly availed itself of the legal and financial opportunities opened up by the new pri-

[29]Quoted in George J. Kuehnl, *The Wisconsin Business Corporation* (Madison, Wis., 1959), p. 72.
[30]Wisconsin Constitution, Art. XI, in Thorpe, *Federal and State Constitutions*, VII, 4093.

vate corporation. Railroads played a role second only to banks in the development of corporate law. They became so important to the nation's economy that by midcentury railroad law constituted a legal realm unto itself, indicated first by the appearance of *Angell on Carriers* (1849) and then in 1858 by *Redfield on Railways.* [31] Paraphrasing a eulogy to Chief Justice Lemuel Shaw, Leonard Levy has written that "the first puff of the [railroad] engine on the iron road announced a capitalist revolution in the common law."[32] The impact of the railroad on public law in America can be illustrated in three areas: the doctrine of eminent domain; legislative and administrative control of railroads; and the use of law to encourage investment. In all three areas, Shaw and the Supreme Judicial Court of Massachusetts "practically established the railroad law for the country."[33]

Eminent domain is a surprisingly modern legal concept. The phrase itself and the ideas it connotes did not appear before the nineteenth century. The power of government to take private property for public purposes had long been recognized by the common law, though, the classic illustrative case being the power to raze a building as a firestop during a conflagration. The milldam acts of the colonies, and of the territories and states after Independence, were a distinctly American application of this doctrine. These statutes reversed the common-law rule that flooding the land of another was an actionable injury and the dam itself an abatable nuisance,[34] by enabling gristmill proprietors to dam a stream to provide a head of water to power their mill. The milldam acts gave the owner of flooded lands a right to statutory damages, but by the early nineteenth century, this right was becoming one of diminishing value. Any loss beyond statutory damages was *damnum absque iniuria,* that convenient common-law concept meaning loss without actionable injury. But the theory sustaining the constitutionality of

---

[31]Joseph K. Angell, *A Treatise on the Law of Carriers* . . . (Boston, 1849); Isaac Redfield, *The Law of Railways* . . . (Boston, 1858). Lawyers customarily refer to such classic legal treatises as, e.g., *Redfield on Railways.*

[32]Leonard W. Levy, *The Law of the Commonwealth and Chief Justice Shaw* (Cambridge, Mass., 1957), p. 165.

[33]Charles Warren, *A History of the American Bar* (Boston, 1911), p. 485.

[34]An actionable injury is a wrong for which the injured party may seek redress in a legal proceeding. An abatable nuisance is an activity or physical condition that an injured party may seek to have suppressed by a suit in equity.

the milldam acts was compatible with common law. Gristmills were in the category of quasi-public businesses that operated under a mixture of privilege and control because they performed a vital public service and they monopolized some unique natural resource.[35]

The milldam acts helped introduce the idea of eminent domain into the public law of the states. Thus, when the new legal concept appeared in an 1831 railroad case decided by Chancellor Reuben Walworth of New York, it did not seem as alien, novel, or radical as it would appear to Daniel Webster and other worried conservatives in a few years.[36] In *Beekman* v. *Saratoga and Schenectady Railroad Co.*, Walworth upheld the practice of granting eminent domain power to railroads.[37] The legislature, he stated, had a right to exercise the power of eminent domain, or permit corporations to do so, "whenever the public interest requires it." Though there must be a "benefit to the public," Walworth defined this loosely as "even the expediency of the state." Two requirements had to be satisfied. The state had to pay just compensation, and the taking had to be according to procedures specified by law. As the price of this boon, the railroads had to recognize that the power given them was a "franchise" that the legislature could regulate in such things as fares and charges, routes, schedules, and so on. Or, an Ohio judge stated in 1849, the railroad "must be made a public work for all purposes, not solely for that of appropriating the citizen's land."[38]

Chief Justice Shaw adapted Walworth's ideas to Massachusetts jurisprudence and extended it to manufacturing corporations, on the theory that economic development of any sort created public benefits great enough to transform the taking of private property into a "public use" as required by the Massachusetts Constitution of 1780. Flooding to create a head of water to power a factory was a public use because it was "an object of great public interest, especially since manufacturing has come to be one of the great

---

[35]In 1877, Chief Justice Morrison Waite cited milling as illustrative of traditional regulation of the common callings: Munn v. Illinois, 94 U.S. 113 at 125.

[36]See Webster's arguments in West River Bridge v. Dix (1848), quoted below, ch. 3, at p. 65.

[37]3 Paige 44 (New York Chancery, 1831) at 73.

[38]Matter of Cincinnati, Hamilton, and Dayton Railroad (Ohio Court of Common Pleas, 1849), quoted in Harry N. Scheiber, *Ohio Canal Era: A Case Study of Government and the Economy, 1820–1861* (Athens, Ohio, 1969), p. 279.

public industrial pursuits of the commonwealth."[39]

In reality, land or other property involuntarily contributed to railroads and factories constituted a forced subsidy to private enterprise. To the extent that the real damage to the owner exceeded the amount of compensation, the private use of eminent domain was a crude and discriminatory form of taxation, falling only on those who happened to own property in the area of expansion. The contribution was especially galling in the case of railroads because of superadded damages inflicted on the landowner after the road was built, such as flooding by stagnant pools, wandering cattle being run down by trains, and fires set by sparks from engines.

The eminent domain power contained a potential for jurists to extend some measure of public regulatory authority over corporations. Judges could interpret the requirement of public purpose to classify a corporation enjoying eminent domain powers as a

public work, established by public authority, intended for the public use and benefit, the use of which is secured to the whole community. . . . All property of the railroad is in trust for the public. The company have not the general power of disposal, incident to the absolute right of property; they are obliged to use it in a particular manner, and for the accomplishment of a well defined public object.[40]

Yet even in this 1842 case, Chief Justice Shaw used eminent domain doctrine to extend a tax immunity, not restrict it. Though Leonard Levy sees the origin of modern public utilities law in the linkage between eminent domain and regulatory power,[41] the regulatory hand of the state lay lightly on railroad corporations before the Civil War. The experience of Ohio and New York suggests that the real beginnings of regulatory law derive rather from the administrative bodies that administered canals. The canal boards of both states had extensive regulatory powers, including the power to set rates, and both exercised these powers vigorously. In contrast, in Ohio the regulation of railroad rates was nominal, while in New York it was effectively nonexistent.[42]

Meanwhile, having served its purpose as a justification for grant-

---

[39]Hazen v. Essex Co., 12 Cush. (66 Mass.) 475 (1853) at 478.

[40]Inhabitants of Worcester v. Western Railroad Corp., 4 Metc. (45 Mass.) 564 (1842) at 566.

[41]Levy, *Law of the Commonwealth and Chief Justice Shaw*, pp. 259, 307–308.

[42]Scheiber, *Ohio Canal Era*, ch. 10, "State Rate-Making and Market Allocation, 1827–1851" (canals), p. 280 (railroads).

ing legislative powers to private, profitmaking enterprises, eminent domain and its American source, the milldam acts, were falling into disfavor—or, as Morton Horwitz suggests, undergoing a transformation that dissipated their potential for redistributing wealth in America in ways harmful to the newly triumphant corporate-capitalist elite.[43]

Although the United States Supreme Court in 1848 upheld the constitutionality of the state's eminent domain power when used to condemn the charter of a bridge,[44] state courts began to voice reservations about the milldam acts and eminent domain. Judge Augustus C. Hand of the New York Supreme Court, in an 1848 opinion inconsistent with Chancellor Walworth's *Beekman* decision, flatly rejected the use of eminent domain for milldams of any sort.[45] The Wisconsin Supreme Court sustained the state's milldam act only on the basis of *stare decisis,* and stated that were it a case of first impression, the court would hold the statute unconstitutional.[46] Finally, after the Civil War, Chief Judge Thomas M. Cooley of the Michigan Supreme Court struck down a statute authorizing a milldam for factories, largely on the grounds that falling water used as a power source had become technologically obsolete with the introduction of the stationary steam engine. He was careful, however, to except railroads from his holding, thus saving the fruit of the doctrine of eminent domain while throwing away its obsolete husk, the milldam acts.[47]

The controversy over railroads' eminent domain powers was symptomatic of broader public dissatisfaction with railroads and their performance. Railroads, like other corporations before the 1840s, were chartered by special act. But the pressures that led to general incorporation laws were more intense for railroad corporations. Dissatisfied consumers, on one hand, complained of high fares, poor service, bribery and corruption, rate discrimination, and monopoly—the same catalog of grievances that later stirred the

[43]Morton J. Horwitz, *The Transformation of American Law, 1780–1860* (Cambridge, Mass., 1977), pp. 47–53, 63–66, 259–261.

[44]West River Bridge *v.* Dix, 6 How. (47 U.S.) 507 (1848).

[45]Hay *v.* Cohoes Co., 3 Barb. S.C. 42 (N.Y. Supreme Court, 1848).

[46]Fisher *v.* Horicon Iron and Mfg. Co., 10 Wis. 293 (1860). *Stare decisis* is the legal principle requiring a court to adhere to a legal doctrine it has adopted in later cases involving substantially the same facts. A case of first impression is one raising a legal issue for the first time before a particular court.

[47]Ryerson *v.* Brown, 35 Mich. 332 (1877).

Grangers and Populists. At the same time, corporate promoters, fearing that the odor of monopoly and special privilege threatened corporations generally and might lead to "an ill-directed zeal for the disallowment of any corporate grants," supported the Jacksonian demand for general incorporation laws.[48]

These pressures produced a new article on "Corporations" in the New York Constitution of 1846 that prohibited special corporate charters unless the objects of the corporation could not be attained under a general incorporation statute.[49] Four years later, the New York legislature enacted the first "Free Railroad Law," a general incorporation act for railroads. Though the act reserved to the legislature some power to control rates and other details of railroad operation, it created a climate of laissez-faire for railroads. Any twenty-five persons, merely by filing articles of incorporation, could automatically become incorporated, get the power of eminent domain, and run lines anywhere they wished.[50]

Railroad laissez-faire was later partially offset by administrative regulation of railroads, which began in New England and was confined to that region until after the Civil War. The first of the new railroad commissions, the Rhode Island Board of Railroad Commissioners, was founded in 1839 to ensure access of all citizens to railroad services and to stop collusion between railroads and steamship lines.[51] New Hampshire's came into being as a rubber stamp that enabled railroads to condemn lands, a privilege denied them under eminent domain law in the Granite State. Connecticut's was established to enforce railroad safety measures.[52] The earliest commissions did not have full-time salaried staffs and lacked effective coercive authority. Though Massachusetts did not establish a permanent railroad commission, from time to time it set up special commissions, usually for rate-setting purposes and with investiga-

[48]Lee Benson, *Merchants, Farmers, & Railroads: Railroad Regulation and New York Politics, 1850–1887* (Cambridge, Mass., 1955), pp. 1–9; quote, p. 3.

[49]New York Constitution of 1846, Art. VIII, sec. 1, in Thorpe, *Federal and State Constitutions,* V, 2669.

[50]Benson, *Merchants, Farmers, & Railroads,* p. 5; New York Laws 1850, ch. 140.

[51]Rhode Island Laws 1839, pp. 23–24; Edward C. Kirkland, *Men, Cities and Transportation: A Study in New England History, 1820–1900* (Cambridge, Mass., 1948), II, 230–241.

[52]New Hampshire Laws 1844, ch. 128. Connecticut Public Acts 1850, ch. 60. "Condemn" in this context refers to a legal taking of lands.

tory powers. The Supreme Judicial Court upheld their powers to set rates, impose schedules, and perform other wide-ranging administrative tasks on the grounds that they exercised a discretion, based on expertise, that courts would not question as long as they performed within the area of their statutory authority.[53] Railroad commissions did not exist elsewhere, except for a short-lived experiment in New York.[54]

Another casualty of the era was the "mixed-enterprise" system, by which states, municipalities, and counties provided financial aid to encourage the construction of canals and railroads. Stimulated by the success of the Erie Canal in the 1820s, the seaboard states that had passable routes to the trans-Appalachian West eagerly went in for building canals and railroads. But the Depression of 1837, and another exactly twenty years later, cooled the ardor of the states for mixed enterprise. In its 1846 Constitution, New York forbade state aid to private corporations and prohibited the state from borrowing more than one million dollars without referendum approval. The western states of Illinois (1848), Wisconsin (1849), Michigan (1850), and Ohio (1851), soured by canal investments that did not approach the Erie Canal's success, prohibited state aid to private companies and prohibited borrowing for public improvements projects. Maryland followed suit in 1851 after the state-assisted Chesapeake and Ohio Canal was eclipsed by the Baltimore-supported Baltimore and Ohio Railroad. In Pennsylvania, opponents of local aid to railroad companies challenged the constitutionality of the entire mixed enterprise system. In *Sharpless* v. *Mayor* (1853),[55] Chief Judge Jeremiah S. Black repulsed this challenge, but opponents of public investment had the last word by sponsoring a constitutional amendment in 1857 that flatly forbade both state and local investment, which a popular referendum ratified by a 9–1 margin. The state thereupon sold its engineering hybrid, the Main Line, a system of railroads and canals linking Philadelphia and Pittsburgh, to the Pennsylvania Railroad.

---

[53]Vermont and Massachusetts Railroad Co. *v.* Fitchburg Railroad Co., 9 Cush. (63 Mass.) 369 (1852); Boston and Worcester Railroad Corp. *v.* Western Railroad Corp., 14 Gray (80 Mass.) 253 (1859); Lexington and West Cambridge Railroad Co. *v.* Fitchburg Railroad Co., 14 Gray (80 Mass.) 266 (1859).
[54]Benson, *Merchants, Farmers & Railroads*, p. 8.
[55]21 Pa. St. 147 (1853).

Judge-made law tipped the economic scales in favor of railroad investors in their conflicts with workers and customers. By the Civil War, railroads and other industries used law to pass off their operating and construction costs onto workers and consumers.

In preindustrial economies in the West, excepting areas of traditionally unfree labor organization (the mines, the military, plantation agriculture, and merchant shipping), the relationship between employer and employee was characterized by something close to a one-to-one ratio, by a somewhat flexible work regime and schedule, by guild and apprenticeship systems having some paternalistic features, by the worker's ownership of his tools, by low technology, and by energy derived from wood and human or animal labor. Industrialization changed each of those features, invariably to the disadvantage of labor. Every industrializing economy, whether feudal, capitalist, or socialist, has accumulated savings at the expense of labor, through paying low wages and by dumping social costs on the working force, their communities, or the larger society. The American experience in the nineteenth century was no exception. The work forces in factories found themselves massed in uncomfortable and dangerous workplaces, regimented and disciplined in unpleasant ways, underpaid, and forced to live in squalor.

Judges who wanted to promote the accumulation of capital devised ways to help entrepreneurs pass the social costs of their businesses onto others, thereby saving funds that could then be available for investment. The classic legal examples of passing on costs in this way were the fellow-servant rule, and the doctrine of assumption of risk, invented by Lemuel Shaw in 1842. Both exempted an employer from liability to one of his workers injured by the negligence of a co-worker. They permitted investors to fob off the costs of industrial accidents onto workers or their widows and orphans. In *Farwell v. Boston and Worcester Railroad* (1842),[56] Shaw held on two grounds that a railroad was not liable for injury to an engineer caused by the negligence of a switchman. First, a person "takes upon himself the natural and ordinary risks and perils" of a job when he hires on. Second, an employee has two options when he observes that a fellow employee is negligent: he can warn the employer, or he can quit.

[56] 4 Metcalf (45 Mass.) 49 (1842); see Levy, *Law of the Commonwealth and Chief Justice Shaw*, ch. 10, "The Fellow-Servant Rule."

Shaw's *Farwell* opinion was an early example of legal "formalism": a state of mind in which a judge worked out rules of law abstracted from social reality, deduced by logical categories that hid from the judge himself the real policy considerations implicit in his opinion. Shaw envisioned a world of one-to-one employment relationships characteristic of a seventeenth-century master and journeyman but archaic in the Industrial Revolution when the individual employees of large corporations were poor and powerless. *Farwell,* an immediate triumph in America and in England, delayed the enactment of workmen's compensation acts until the eve of World War I by casting over them the vague aura of unconstitutionality.

So much for workers. Consumers could also be made to bear the costs of the Industrial Revolution, but in subtler, more technical, less drastic ways. At common law, a common carrier, like a railroad, had a high degree of liability for goods entrusted to it for shipment. It was virtually an insuror (that is, responsible for loss even if that loss occurred without fault on its part); only war or an act of God were good defenses. Naturally, railroads sought to evade this responsibility either by general notice, such as signs on walls that limited their liability for baggage, or by special notice, such as a disclaimer printed on a ticket or a bill of lading. Judges were at first hostile to such efforts and held the railroads to absolute liability. But as the railroads grew in power, this attitude faded.[57] Joseph Story, in his *Commentaries on the Law of Bailments,* stated that carriers could contract out of liability for goods, except for that based on "gross negligence and fraud."[58] By 1847, his Supreme Court colleague Justice Samuel Nelson confirmed this trend when he reformulated the rule to hold that any carrier could contract out of common-carrier liability by "express stipulation," written or oral, and could thus avoid responsibility for negligence on its part that was less than gross.[59] In this way, railroads were able to pass on some costs of doing business to their customers.

American public law in its golden age favored entrepreneurial risk-taking in indirect ways as well. Here, too, railroads were a prime beneficiary of judges' concern to protect capital investments. Concurrent with the Industrial Revolution in America, Anglo-American

[57]*Redfield on Railways,* 2nd ed. (Boston, 1858), pp. 266–270.
[58]*Story on Bailments* (4th ed., 1846), sec. 549.
[59]New Jersey Steam Navigation Co. *v.* Merchants Bank, 6 How. (47 U.S.) 344 (1847).

judges created an entire new body of law: torts, the law of civil wrongs. They shaped its doctrines to accommodate the needs of corporate capitalism and a market economy. The law of torts encouraged firms to pass on costs to others and promoted the rationalization of economic behavior.

Primitive and early modern law concerned with distributing the burden of civil wrongs tended toward absolute liability: the plaintiff had only to show that his injury was caused by the act of the defendant. Questions of fault were secondary, if relevant at all. Such premises were inappropriate to a capital-scarce economy during a period of intensive industrialization. As the New York Court of Appeals indignantly suggested, absolute liability would have forced railroads to compensate everyone they injured. In *Ryan* v. *New York Central Railroad* (1866), a case involving negligent destruction of plaintiff's building 130 feet distant from defendant railroad, the court proposed an alternative policy. In denying recovery, the court held that "no private fortune would be adequate" to bear the costs of the railroad's negligent conduct in the case of a spreading fire caused by an engine's sparks. The burden of loss, in the name of sustaining a "civilized society," the court held, had to be shifted to the sufferers: "In a commercial country, each man, to some extent, runs the hazard of his neighbor's conduct, and each, by insurance against such hazards, is enabled to obtain a reasonable security against loss."[60] The court did not consider whether individuals could better bear catastrophic loss than corporations, nor did it question its assumptions that the costs of industrialization should more appropriately fall on the victim rather than the large and wealthy cause of the injury. The *Farwell* case was the product of the same assumptions.

Chief Justice Shaw was virtually the creator of this new body of tort law, and its early development reflected his policy assumptions. The first significant tort case in America, *Brown* v. *Kendall* (1850), had immeasurable consequences. In a suit for an unintended injury (defendant had accidentally struck plaintiff while trying to break up a dogfight), Shaw held that plaintiff must "show either that the [defendant's] intention was unlawful, or that the defendant was in fault; for if the injury was unavoidable, and the conduct of the defendant was free from blame, he will not be liable." Shaw held the

[60]35 N.Y. 210 (1866) at 217.

defendant to the standard of "ordinary care," which "means that kind and degree of care, which prudent and cautious men would use, such as is required by the exigency of the case, and such as is necessary to guard against probable danger."[61] Under these seemingly reasonable and obvious propositions, however, there lay a movement of enormous significance in public law.

Liability was to be based only on fault; in cases where the injury was nonintentional, fault could be imputed only by showing negligence. Negligence depended on a standard of ordinary care, determined by judges. The paragon for that standard of care was the "reasonable man," that wraithlike figure so beloved of modern judges. Thus a whole new field of law was born. Tort law ever since has been dominated by concepts of negligence and fault. Seemingly so reasonable, so unarguable a moral judgment, Shaw's no-fault–no-liability equation nevertheless rationalized economic decision-making indispensable to capitalism.

In *Brown* v. *Kendall,* Shaw innovated another doctrine, contributory negligence, a doctrine that would prove almost as important as the ordinary-care standard in denying recovery to victims of industrialization. Though defendant was negligent, "if the plaintiff was also chargeable with negligence," there could be no recovery unless plaintiff could show that "his own negligence did not contribute as an efficient cause to produce" the injury. Or, to put it the way railroad attorneys immediately construed the rule, if defendant can show some degree of plaintiff's contributory negligence, defendant is not liable, no matter how culpable or how great the share of its own negligence in the ratio.

Shaw's reliance on causality suggested another element that favored corporate defendants: proximate cause. Plaintiff had to show that defendant's act was the proximate, or immediate, cause of the injury. If the act of someone else intervened to deflect injury, as it were, toward plaintiff, defendant might escape liability. Yet another useful doctrine for defendants antedated the new tort law: the principle of the nonsurvival of actions for death by wrongful act. At common law, a cause of action for acts causing the death of a potential plaintiff died with him; his survivors (in the case of indus-

---

[61]6 Cush. (60 Mass.) 292 (1850) at 296–297; for a critique of the view that judicial decisions in tort and railroad law subsidized industrialization, see Richard A. Posner, "A Theory of Negligence," *Journal of Legal Studies,* I (1972), 29–96.

trial workers, usually widows and orphans) could not recover for his death.[62]

The pro-defendant bias of early American tort law reflects a determination to protect risky investments in new technologies, as well as two legal developments then undergoing rapid change: the extent of jury discretion and the growth of insurance. One of the consequences of proving plaintiff's contributory negligence is that the case does not go to the jury; the judge dismisses it. Defending this result, Judge Seward Barcolo of the New York Supreme Court explained in 1852 that

> in certain controversies between the weak and the strong—between a humble individual and a gigantic corporation, the sympathies of the human mind naturally, honestly and generously run to the assistance and support of the feeble and apparently oppressed; and that compassion will sometimes exercise over the deliberations of the jury, an influence which, however honorable to them as philanthropists, is wholly inconsistent with the principles of law and the ends of justice.[63]

A judge could assume that "the principles of law and the ends of justice" were incompatible with "compassion" for the victims of the Industrial Revolution, because judges and legal commentators stress that the morality of law is "conventional." Nathan Dane, America's Blackstone and the patron of Joseph Story at the Harvard Law School, explained that "the law of the land and morality are the same" only in "some special cases," but separate "when policy, or arbitrary rules must also be regarded." "Virtue alone is the subject of morality, but law has, often, for its object, the peace of society, and what is practicable."[64]

Insurance was a different problem. At common law before the nineteenth century, an individual could not insure against his own negligence. This rule tended to support the absolute liability of carriers by suggesting that a carrier could not contract out of responsibility for its own negligence. When marine insurance split off from the larger, emergent subject of general insurance around 1830, and nonmarine insurance expanded to cover some risks of

[62]See Richard B. Morris, *Studies in the History of American Law* (New York, 1930), pp. 247–258.

[63]Haring *v.* New-York and Erie Railroad Co., 13 Barb. S.C. 2 at 15–16 (New York Supreme Court, 1852).

[64]Nathan Dane, *A General Abridgement and Digest of American Law* (1823), quoted in Horwitz, *Transformation of American Law*, p. 183.

industrialization in a national market economy, judges accepted the idea that corporations could insure against damage caused by the negligence of their employees. Until then, risk could not be financially spread or actuarially anticipated. But, as the *Ryan* case suggests, even when the concept of insurability became familiar to judges, the plight of plaintiffs was not necessarily eased.

Legislatures moderated the severity of common-law tort rules almost as quickly as judges created them. States, following the lead of Lord Campbell's Act in England, enacted Wrongful Death Acts that either reversed the common-law rule of nonsurvival of wrongful death actions or created some statutory right in survivors— usually, however, with a ceiling on liability.[65] Statutory liability, sometimes approaching the stringency of primitive-law absolute liability, derived from statutes that imposed certain specific safety requirements on railroads and made them liable for all damages resulting from accidents where plaintiff could show noncompliance with the statutory requirement.

The second great body of law created by antebellum judges, contract, also reflected their developmental, entrepreneurial bias. Contract law was not wholly new in 1830; it had been evolving slowly over the previous four centuries, chiefly in judge-made modifications of some half-dozen forms of action at common law. But as an independent, substantive body of law, contract scarcely existed before the nineteenth century. Such law as there was consisted of one venerable piece of legislation, the Statute of Frauds (1677), adopted in all American jurisdictions, which requires certain kinds of contracts to be in writing, together with a few scattered cases from the colonial and early national courts. These cases tended to emphasize equitable considerations in the adjudication of disputes. They looked to the fairness of the transaction, left much discretion to jury verdicts to achieve fair results as measured by community standards, and emphasized the remedies of restitution and specific performance.[66] Contract in the preindustrial era was also closely tied to concepts of property; it generally involved the

[65]Lord Campbell's Act, 9 and 10 Vict. 93, was the model for a line of state statutes, beginning with New York in 1847. Morris, *Studies in the History of American Law*, p. 258.

[66]Restitution is an equitable remedy that, in general, seeks to restore both parties to their original condition after a contract is rescinded. Specific performance is another equitable remedy that compels a party to perform his obligation as he promised. Both are alternatives to the legal remedy of damages.

transfer of title to tangible, extant property.[67]

All these characteristics were eclipsed by the emergence of modern contract law serving an industrialized society oriented to a national market. In a constitutional sense, the nineteenth century was "the golden age of the law of contract," as Lawrence Friedman has called it.[68] The age began with *Fletcher* v. *Peck* (1810), when the United States Supreme Court held that state legislative acts were contracts for purposes of the contracts clause of the United States Constitution, and extended to 1897, when the same Court articulated the doctrine of "liberty of contract" as yet another limitation on state legislative power in the case of *Allgeyer* v. *Louisiana*. [69] In between, in all the states, the common law of contract flourished, as judges ambitiously grasped policymaking power in the regulation of the economy.

The formation of a national and an international market created a large network of impersonal economic relationships, in which objectivity, predictability, and reliability became prime virtues. Speculative trading in commodities futures began around 1800, and no traditional categories of the law of personal property could regulate that new economic activity. Contract law in the mid-nineteenth century therefore was transformed from the inchoate muddle of Blackstone's few pages on the subject to an overarching jurisprudential theory influential enough to establish itself by the end of the century as one of the basic fields of law[70] and to remake American public and constitutional law in the image of its jurisprudential assumptions.

The new contract law was based on a set of assumptions called the "will theory." The essence of a contract was a mutually agreed-upon assent to an economic relationship. The law had no business inquiring into the fairness of an exchange; its function was to determine whether there had been "a meeting of the minds." "Every contract," wrote William Wetmore Story, son of Justice Joseph Story and author of the first comprehensive treatise on contracts

[67]Horwitz, *Transformation of American Law*, ch. 6, "The Triumph of Contract."

[68]Friedman, *History of American Law*, p. 244.

[69]6 Cranch (10 U.S.) 87 (1810); 165 U.S. 578 (1897).

[70]The first casebook ever published, which was the foundation of modern legal education, was Christopher C. Langdell's *A Selection of Cases on the Law of Contracts* (Boston, 1881).

that reflected the new jurisprudential assumptions of an impersonal market economy, "is founded upon the mutual agreement of the parties." Even an implied contract, where the law creates a contractual relationship, is based on a presumed assent of the parties.[71] The will theory necessarily presumed that both parties to the transaction stood upon a footing of equality vis-à-vis each other, and that the market price was a measure of each one's estimate of the worth of the relationship to himself, which the law would not second-guess. Under such assumptions, no contract could be exploitative; if it were, by definition, the exploited party would not have entered into it. "Modern contract law was thus born staunchly proclaiming that all men are equal because all measures of inequality are illusory."[72] Chancellor Kent displayed a dogmatic hostility to the ideal of equality:

The legislature has no right to limit the extent of the acquisition of property. . . . A state of equality as to property is impossible to be maintained, for it is against the laws of our own nature; and if it could be reduced to practice, it would place the human race in a state of tasteless enjoyment and stupid inactivity. . . . Liberty depends essentially upon the structure of government, the administration of justice, and the intelligence of the people and it has very little concern with equality of property and frugality of living.[73]

With the triumph of the will theory, the elements of modern contract law fell into place: offer and acceptance (which were the formal and external manifestations of the parties' wills); "consideration," that mysterious *quid pro quo,* but now increasingly an evidentiary requirement used to prove the meeting of the minds, rather than to assure fair, nonopprobrious dealings. Judges began to squint suspiciously at old equitable elements of contract. The old doctrine of "a sound price warrants a sound commodity" gave way to the new and pitiless doctrine of *caveat emptor:* let the buyer beware. The result of the divergence between the law of contracts and considerations of equity and the community sense of fairness was, in Morton Horwitz's terms, "a great intellectual divide between a system of

[71]William W. Story, *A Treatise on the Law of Contracts,* 5th ed. (Boston, 1874), I, 4 (first ed.: 1844).
[72]Horwitz, *Transformation of American Law,* p. 161.
[73]Kent, *Commentaries on American Law,* II, *328, *330.

formal rules—which judges and treatise writers managed to identify exclusively with the 'rule of law'—and those ancient precepts of morality and equity, which they were able to render suspect as subversive of 'the rule of law' itself."[74]

But as judges were creating these new domains of common law, legal reformers were subjecting the entire legal system to criticism, and demanding its reform. Hostility to the common law was not altogether new in American society. Earlier disputes over the reception of the English common law had carried over into the Jacksonian period. But in the 1830s, various reform movements attacked the conservative bar and the common-law legal system it administered, or sought to use law to achieve social reforms that the bar mistrusted. These efforts coalesced in the movement to codify the common law.

By the Jacksonian period, the common law had been "received" in every American jurisdiction. Through constitutional provision, statute, and judicial decision, the customary law of England expounded in the decisions of the royal courts before American Independence was adopted as law in America unless it was inconsistent with American circumstances or was specifically declared inapplicable by statute. But the reception of the common law did not quiet controversy over adopting judge-made law. On the contrary; republican ideological emphasis on the role of the legislature, Jeffersonian hostility to the decisions of the Marshall Court, and democratic insistence on popular sovereignty all combined to make the role of judges suspect, especially when they thwarted popular or legislative will by holding a statute unconstitutional. Hence attacks on the common law were fueled not only by Anglophobia but also by suspicions about the role of courts in a democracy.

The talented Irish-American lawyer William Sampson demanded that the "stubborn forms [of common law] be taught to bend to the convenience and exigencies of the people for whose use it subsists." He heaped ridicule on the common law: it was

A mysterious essence like the Dalai Lama, not to be seen or visited in open day; of most indefinite antiquity; sometimes in the decrepitude of age, and sometimes in the bloom of infancy, yet still the same that was, and was to be, and evermore to sit cross-legged and motionless upon its antique altar,

[74]Horwitz, *Transformation of American Law,* p. 188.

for no use or purpose, but to be praised and worshipped by ignorant and superstitious votaries. Its attributes were all negative, its properties all enigmatical, and its name a metaphor. Taken in many senses, it had truly none. It was oral tradition opposed to written law; it was written law, but presuming the writing lost; it was that of whose origin there was no record or memory, but of which the evidence was both in books and records. It was opposed to statute law, to civil law, to ecclesiastical law, to military law, to maritime and mercantile law, to the law of nations; but most frequently contrasted with equity itself. It was common sense, but of an artificial kind, such as is not the sense of any common man.[75]

Reflecting the philosophical attitudes of Jeremy Bentham as much as the antijudicial bias of Jacksonian Democrats, the prominent Massachusetts Jacksonian attorney and political leader Robert Rantoul, in his widely noted "Oration at Scituate" (1836), summed up the attack on the common law. "Statutes, enacted by the legislature, speak the public voice"; but judge-made law "usurps legislative power." Therefore, Rantoul concluded, "the whole body of the law must be codified."[76]

The demand for codification sprang from several sources. Many of the men who administered the law in America, especially justices of the peace and law-enforcement officials, were not lawyers—none of the judges of the Rhode Island Supreme Court was a lawyer, for example. These laymen needed a clear and concise guide to what the law was. Law reports had begun to proliferate, and many judges and lawyers, including Joseph Story, looked uneasily over their shoulder at the increasingly indigestible mass of law being accumulated in America. Some areas of law, such as the law of commercial paper, were inherently suited to being codified, while others —civil procedure—were moss-covered with old and meaningless intricacy. Moreover, codes were not a novelty in America. The earliest laws of New England and New York were codes; all the colonies codified some parts of their laws in the eighteenth century; and Louisiana, because of its Franco-Spanish civil-law heritage, blended code and common law in a unique legal environment.

Though he was appalled at the anti-common-law, antilawyer, an-

[75]William Sampson, *An Anniversary Discourse . . . 1823 . . . Showing the Origin, Progress, Antiquities, Curiosities, and the Nature of the Common Law,* excerpted in Perry Miller (ed.), *The Legal Mind in America* (1962; reprint Ithaca, N.Y., 1969), pp. 122–124.
[76]Rantoul, "Oration at Scituate," *ibid.,* pp. 223–225.

tijudicial sentiments of Sampson and Rantoul, Story recognized the value of a limited and controlled codification for some areas of law, and promoted moderate codification in the twenties and thirties. Seeing law as a science, Story believed that it could be reduced to basic principles in some fields of law and that these principles could be collected in printed form and enacted as a code.[77] In 1837, as the head of a commission appointed to advise the General Court on the feasibility of codifying Massachusetts law, Story cautiously recommended three codes: the "general principles" of property, contracts, and personal rights; the entire criminal law; and the entire law of evidence.[78]

Story's limited proposal was overtaken by a crusade for more thoroughgoing codification led by the New York lawyer David Dudley Field. The brother of Stephen J. Field, a future justice of the United States Supreme Court, Field was a prominent constitutional lawyer, later participating as counsel in much of the post–Civil War constitutional litigation. But his enduring fame rests on the codes he drafted and promoted, largely without success, for New York: a criminal code, a procedural code, and a comprehensive civil code. Basing his approach on a judicial commonplace of the time—the function of judges is to declare the law, not to make it—Field hoped that the legislature, by adopting his codes, would "render the existing law as accessible and as intelligible as we can, . . . to cast aside known rules which are obsolete, to correct those which are burdensome, or unsuitable to present circumstances, to reject anomalous or ill-considered cases, to bring the different branches into a more perfect order and agreement."[79]

Field and other enthusiasts for codification believed that because law was a science, its elements could be categorized and classified according to its central principles, which were supposedly compatible with the legal profession's interests deriving from technology and growth. Both principles and technical details could then be

[77]Joseph Story, "The Progress of Jurisprudence" (1821), in William W. Story (ed.), *The Miscellaneous Writings of Joseph Story* (Boston, 1852), pp. 198–241.
[78]Story, "A Report of the Commissioners . . . 1837," *ibid.*, pp. 699–734 at pp. 715–716.
[79]David Dudley Field, "Introduction to the Completed Civil Code," in A. P. Sprague (ed.), *Speeches, Arguments, and Miscellaneous Papers of David Dudley Field* (New York, 1884–90), I, 327.

taught more systematically to law students, and be available in convenient form to practicing lawyers and to judges. Ill-educated practitioners would have the benefit of rationalized, standard sources. Instead of the increasing hodgepodge of case reports, recorded according to no agreed style, more uniform reporting would give trial lawyers a precision that clients and judges would appreciate.

But despite these advantages to the bar, codification made little progress in the nineteenth century. Field's procedural code was adopted in New York and elsewhere, and "code pleading," as it came to be called, replaced the perverse, antiquated mystery of common-law pleading. But Field's own state, New York, rejected his substantive law codes. Only a few states, mostly in the West, adopted them after the Civil War. Resistance to the codes was led by conservative leaders of the bar, who confused Field and his codes with more radical attacks on the law itself. The conservative elite of American lawyers identified the "rule of law" with their own clients' interests and ambitions, indiscriminately condemning as anarchic all demands for reform, attacks on lawyers, and criticisms of capitalism.

Rufus Choate lyricized about "the sacred sentiments of obedience and reverence and justice, of the supremacy of the calm and grand reason of the law over the fitful will of the individual and the crowd." He denied that law was the product of human will— a convenient fiction useful to the hegemony of the elite—least of all was it, or could it be, the product of the will of a majority. He hoped to "raise the law itself, in the professional and in the general idea, almost up to the nature of an independent, superior reason, in one sense out of the people, in one sense above them."[80] James C. Carter, a New York lawyer and American Bar Association president, dismissed the codes as nothing more than Field's effort to gratify his own ambition or vanity, and condemned codification per se as something borrowed from the jurisprudence of "despotic nations."[81]

[80]Rufus Choate, "The Position and Functions of the American Bar, as an Element of Conservatism in the State" (1845), in Miller (ed.), *Legal Mind in America,* pp. 261, 270.
[81]James C. Carter, *The Proposed Codification of Our Common Law* (1884), excerpted in Spencer L. Kimball, *Historical Introduction to the Legal System* (St. Paul, 1966), pp. 377–382.

Yet in one of history's ironies, at the time of Field's death in 1894 codification stood on the threshold of its great twentieth-century triumphs, thanks in some measure to the conservative elite who opposed the sweeping codes that Field proposed. Beginning with the creation of the National Conference of Commissioners on Uniform State Laws (1892), spurred by approval of the Uniform Negotiable Instruments Act (1896), cresting to early success with the Uniform Sales Act (1906), and then sweeping the entire field of commercial law with the Uniform Commercial Code (adopted in all American jurisdictions between 1953 and 1970), the codification movement eventually triumphed, though in a way different from what Field had envisioned.

Other reform movements impinged on the public law less directly. Nevertheless, the common law and the legal profession were affected at numerous points by the gaudy swirl of meliorist and radical movements of the 1830s. Three are illustrative: labor organization, penal reform, and women's rights.

Workers were not entirely passive in the face of entrepreneurs' efforts to accumulate investment capital at the expense of labor. Early in the nineteenth century, journeymen artisans began to experiment with primitive forms of labor organization. At first, reflecting their lingering semientrepreneurial status, workers' associations resembled businessmen's price-fixing combinations. But as workers sank in status from journeymen to wage earners, their labor organizations took on noticeably modern characteristics, most particularly in pitting worker against employer. Employers and judges reacted predictably, beginning with the famous Philadelphia and New York *Cordwainers' Cases* (1806–10), declaring unions to be criminal conspiracies. Their attitudes were best reflected in an opinion of New York's Chief Justice John Savage in *People* v. *Fisher* (1835).[82] Holding that workers' organizations violated New York's conspiracies statute, Savage claimed that workers' "extravagant demands for wages" would interfere with the beneficent, natural operation of the free market. "It is important to the best interests of society that the price of labor be left to regulate itself, or rather, be limited by the demand for it."

In such a climate of opinion, the decision of Chief Justice Shaw

[82]14 Wend. 6 (New York Court for the Correction of Errors, 1835).

in *Commonwealth* v. *Hunt* (1842)[83] appears almost revolutionary. Overturning a conviction for the common-law crime of conspiracy, Shaw applied the traditional means-ends test for conspiracies and held that labor organization for purposes of establishing what is now called a closed shop was not in itself illegal, nor were the means (collective refusal to work). While *Commonwealth* v. *Hunt* did not relieve embryonic unions from all legal harassment, it did lift the stigma fixed on them since 1806 that suggested that workers' concerted efforts were criminal.

The boundaries of the criminal law contracted slightly in the Jacksonian period. Many states revised the substantive law of crimes, mostly by modifying the severe penalties left over from the eighteenth century. The scope of common-law crimes shrank, as the criminal law was reduced to written form. By the Civil War, all states had abolished imprisonment for debt. None of these reforms was especially controversial.

The reform of postconviction penal systems was another matter. Two reform efforts provoked controversy: the abolition of capital punishment and the improvement of prisons. Edward Livingston, a transplanted New Yorker who drew up Louisiana's Civil Code of 1825, was the first prominent nineteenth-century leader of the movement to do away with the death penalty. Like opponents ever since, he stressed that the death penalty was no deterrent to crime. Rather, he urged legislators, "study the passions which first suggested the offence, and apply your punishment to mortify and counteract them."[84] This theme was echoed by some Jacksonian Democratic reformers, chief among them Robert Rantoul of Massachusetts and John L. O'Sullivan of New York.

They enjoyed limited success: Michigan abolished the death penalty in 1847, Rhode Island in 1852, and Wisconsin in 1853. But the movement provoked a vigorous and popular countermovement to retain capital punishment, led chiefly by conservative clergymen

[83]4 Metcalf (45 Mass.) 45 (1842); see Levy, *Law of the Commonwealth and Chief Justice Shaw*, ch. 11, "Labor Law." For the use of criminal conspiracy in these years to thwart collective action by labor, see Richard B. Morris, Introduction to J. R. Commons, et al. (eds.), *A Documentary History of American Industrial Society* (rev. ed., New York, 1958), III, i–xii.

[84]Edward Livingston, "Report on the Project of a New Penal Code" (1824), excerpted in Haar, *Golden Age of American Law*, pp. 300–308; quote pp. 302–303.

who considered the death penalty sanctioned by God. An 1844 referendum in New Hampshire resulted in a vote of two to one in favor of retaining the death penalty, and a spectacular murder trial and subsequent execution of Harvard Professor John Webster in Massachusetts provided opponents with an easily understood dramatic event that could be turned to good propaganda use. After the Wisconsin success, the movement was eclipsed during the war, and languished afterward.

Prison reform was equally unpopular. New York pioneered the "Auburn system," named after the state prison in the town, in which inmates were permitted to work during the day and confined to separate cells at night. New York also introduced the idea of a separate system for housing and treating juvenile offenders, the House of Refuge, in 1825. In the following decade, prison reform was an issue taken up by reformers in both Europe and America— it was the original reason for Alexis de Tocqueville's mission to America in 1832. But prison reform butted up against two hard realities: one was costs; the other was the widely popular notion that convicts are sent to prison to be punished, not coddled. Effective systems of penal reform were expensive because they required new buildings, or at least extensive remodeling, and expanded staff, including professionals. As a result, the Auburn idea lost its dynamic, and most prisons remained places of horror. Local lockups were even worse.

If the lot of convicts in American society remained unchanged, the place of women was beginning to undergo rapid transition. The influences of this social movement and law were reciprocal. Women benefited from a jurisprudential transformation, first identified by Sir Henry Maine, that was redirecting Western law in the nineteenth century. In his classic *Ancient Law* (1861), he suggested that as a legal system matures, "the movement of the progressive societies has hitherto been a movement from Status to Contract."[85] From being determined by birth, class, sex, race, or pedigree, a person's place in society was coming to be based on relationships based on will and therefore to some extent on ability and initiative. J. Willard Hurst has emphasized that the first half of the nineteenth century sought to promote the release of individuals' creative energy by

[85]Sir Henry Maine, *Ancient Law* (1861; reprint New York, 1917), p. 100.

protecting their decisionmaking capacity and expanding the scope of decisions they could make.[86] Artificial impediments on human endeavor ran against the current of the nineteenth century. Women benefited from this shift of status to contract. At the beginning of the nineteenth century, their legal status, when married, was comparable in the eyes of the law to that of slaves, convicts, children, and lunatics. Women had little legal capacity. As Chancellor Kent put it: "the husband and wife are regarded [by the law] as one person, and her legal existence and authority in a degree lost or suspended, during the continuance of the matrimonial union." With unconscious irony, he went on to observe that the wife's legal "dependence" on her husband "furnishes powerful motives to the promotion of harmony and peaceful cohabitation in married life."[87] But this debased legal status was culturally and economically anomalous. Women ran plantations and businesses, organized reformist groups, and constituted a significant market for ideas and products, as indicated by the commercial success of women's magazines like *Godey's Lady's Book*. A southern frontier jurisdiction, Mississippi, enacted the first statute recognizing women's legal capacity in 1839. The forms of law simply followed economic and social reality in a state where many farms and plantations were run by women. By 1850, about half the states had enacted Married Women's Property Acts, giving married women some measure of control over their own property. To the extent that this divested husbands of extant rights in their wives' property, judges caught up in higher-law enthusiasm balked. Judge Barcolo of the New York Supreme Court lamented that "the ancient muniments, hitherto deemed 'essential to the inviolability of the nuptial contract and to the maintenance of the institution of marriage' are crumbling and falling before the batteries of modern reformers. The old landmarks are being removed. The principles of former times are fast receding from view."[88] But such attitudes did not deflect the irresistible triumph of contract as the determinant of human relations.

Divorce was another issue affecting the status of women. In the

[86]J. Willard Hurst, *Law and the Conditions of Freedom in the Nineteenth-Century United States* (Madison, 1956), ch. 1, "The Release of Energy."
[87]Kent, *Commentaries*, II, *129.
[88]Holmes v. Holmes, 4 Barb. S.C. 295 (New York Supreme Court, 1848). A muniment is a documentary evidence of title.

colonial period, divorce was rare and, when granted, came only by legislative act. After Independence a few of the states began to experiment with judicial divorce. Yet legislative divorce did not disappear. Either from a sense of power or to provide an element of flexibility that general divorce did not, lawmakers sought to retain some divorce-granting power despite the work involved for them. But Chancellor Kent voiced the suspicion that a legislative divorce might not be valid in any state except the one where granted, the full-faith-and-credit clause of the federal Constitution's Article IV, section 1, notwithstanding, and legislative divorce became increasingly unpopular and suspect.[89]

General divorce laws raised the question of what grounds should be adequate for divorce. The "strict" states, led by New York, prohibited divorce for any reason but adultery. The "liberal" states experimented with other grounds: desertion, pregnancy at marriage by another, drunkenness, cruelty. The legal remedy of annulment, based on the theory that the marriage was invalid from the beginning, persisted, but divorce *a mensa et thoro* ("from table and bed"), a legal separation prohibiting either partner from remarrying, slowly fell into disuse.

The movement to liberalize divorce provoked a debate between those who feared that freer divorce would encourage orgies of lewdness and those critical of the harshness or hypocrisy of strict laws. Chancellor Kent proposed a solution that found little official support. He suggested that it might be desirable to legalize the double standard, so that only the husband could get a divorce on grounds of his wife's adultery. He explained that "the violation of the marriage vow, on the part of the wife, is the most mischievous, and the prosecution ought to be confined to the offence on her part."[90] In the variety of grounds, the states differed among themselves, from South Carolina, which into the Jacksonian period prided itself on never having granted either a legislative or a judicial divorce, to Indiana, which in the same period was something of a quickie divorce haven having liberal laws and a relatively brief residence requirement. But supporters of strict grounds slowly had to give

[89]Kent, *Commentaries*, II, *117–118.
[90]*Ibid.*, *106.

way as the conviction spread that, in Lawrence Friedman's words, "a divorceless state is not a state without adultery, prostitution, fornication. It is, more likely than not, a place sharply divided between official law and unofficial behavior. A country with rare or expensive divorce is a country with two sets of divorce laws, one for the rich, and one for the poor."[91]

Despite some progress in the matters of property rights and divorce, women were still subjected to many forms of discrimination before the war. They could not vote, legislators often rejected their legislative petitions with vulgarity and contempt, they were excluded from the professions of law, medicine, and clergy, and inequalities in legal capacity lingered. The dissatisfaction of less compromising women's rights advocates like Elizabeth Cady Stanton produced the famous Seneca Falls Declaration (1848) which, using the Declaration of Independence as a form, cataloged the wrongs to women as Jefferson had once cataloged the wrongs to America:

[man] has never permitted her to exercise her inalienable right to the elective franchise. He has made her, if married, in the eye of the law, civilly dead. He has taken from her all right in property, even to the wages she earns.

"Resolved," they concluded, "That woman is man's equal."[92] But equality before the law for American women still lay a long way off.

The public law of Jacksonian America played a central role in assigning rights and duties, privileges and handicaps, among the varying groups of American society. One dominant trend appeared as midcentury approached: law, especially judge-made law, promoted the interests of investors in order to encourage the accumulation of investment capital. It developed the new device of the corporation and adapted its forms to the needs of railroad, manufacturing, and insurance interests. But all this took place in a heterogeneous Union, and the public law of the states sometimes reflected that heterogeneity in an undesirable diversity, clogging the national market and the federal system that the law sought to protect. As the

[91]Friedman, *History of American Law*, p. 183.
[92]Henry S. Commager (ed.), *Documents of American History*, 9th ed. (Englewood Cliffs, N.J., 1973), I, 315–317.

Union matured, the need for a central authority to reconcile American public law became ever more apparent. The United States Supreme Court under John Marshall had begun to do that. Many observers of the Court wondered whether it could expand that role under the direction of its new chief, the Jacksonian Democrat Roger B. Taney.

CHAPTER 3

The Taney Court

THE *Charles River Bridge* case of 1837 stands as one of three major decisions of the new Chief Justice's first term that pointed to the directions the Taney Court might travel. The case raised as many important issues of the day as could plausibly be crammed into a single legal-constitutional controversy. These included: the role of law in fostering technological innovation; the regulatory power of the state; the future of corporations; the scope of the vested-rights doctrine; the role of the states in protecting investment. All these questions, Taney noted with understatement, "are pregnant with important consequences."[1]

In 1785, the Massachusetts General Court[2] created a corporation, the proprietors of the Charles River Bridge, authorizing it to span the Charles between Boston and Charlestown and to charge tolls. The charter contained no provisions that protected the bridge from competition or that gave it monopolistic or exclusive rights to control the Boston-Charlestown traffic. As Boston and its northern hinterland grew, the Charles River Bridge became both more profit-

---

[1] 11 Pet. (36 U.S.) 420 (1837) at 536; McLean, J. would dismiss for lack of jurisdiction; Story, J. dissented. See Stanley I. Kutler, *Privilege and Creative Destruction: The Charles River Bridge Case* (Philadelphia, 1971).

[2] In Massachusetts, Maine, and New Hampshire, "the General Court" was, and remains today, the name of the legislature. The highest court in Massachusetts and its daughter state, Maine, is known as the Supreme Judicial Court.

able and more inadequate for the volume of traffic. In 1828, after the old bridge's shares had increased 625 percent in value, the General Court decided to charter a second bridge, the Warren Bridge, with a Boston terminus only 825 feet from the old bridge. The new bridge would become toll-free after its construction costs had been recouped. Because this would make the stock of the old bridge worthless, its proprietors sought an injunction that would halt the construction of the new bridge. The Massachusetts Supreme Judicial Court, evenly divided (2–2) over the substantive issues of the case, denied the injunction and dismissed the petition, thus opening the way for an appeal to the United States Supreme Court. The case was first argued before Chief Justice Marshall, but illness and disagreements among the justices prevented the Court from disposing of the case promptly, and it lay over to become the most significant case awaiting the attention of the new Chief Justice.

In arguments before Taney, Daniel Webster, counsel for the old bridge, made a point Chancellor Kent had helpfully suggested in his *Commentaries:* the charter of the old bridge had to be read to contain an implicit assurance that the old bridge would not have to compete with a nearby rival. Otherwise investors would be reluctant to advance risk capital for new ventures, since the state might nullify the value of their investment at any time. Webster suggested that this would be a taking of property without compensation in violation of Article X of the Massachusetts Constitution.[3]

Taney rejected this bold gambit. He shrewdly drew on a Marshall opinion in *Providence Bank* v. *Billings* (1830)[4] to support his contention that a "State ought never to be presumed to surrender this power [to encourage transportation improvements] because, like the taxing power, the whole community have an interest in preserving it undiminished."[5] Strictly construing the charter of the old bridge, Taney laid down a general rubric of construction that clarified the relationship between states and corporations: "in charters . . . , no

[3]Kent, *Commentaries*, 3rd ed. (New York, 1836), III, 457–458. Kent seems to have added this point to his section "Of Franchises" in his first edition (1828) in anticipation of a controversy involving the Charles River Bridge. Webster's argument survives in fragmentary form in the notes of the Court's Reporter, Richard Peters, reprinted from Peters's original reports in 9 L.Ed. 811–819.

[4]4 Pet. (29 U.S.) 514 (1830).

[5]This and following quotations are at 11 Pet. at 547, 549, 552.

rights are taken from the public, or given to the corporation, beyond those which the words of the charter, by their natural and proper construction, purport to convey." With no implied provision guaranteeing the old bridge a monopoly, Massachusetts' creation of the new bridge did not violate the obligation-of-contracts clause.

In these passages, Taney created a flexible doctrine that served as a paradigm for cases where the state's power to regulate corporations and the economy clashed with the claims of investors who sought to protect the security of their venture capital. Taney managed to preserve adequate scope for the states' regulatory role while at the same time making it possible for investors to, in effect, bargain with the state at the time of incorporation to secure explicit assurances of profitmaking opportunity. In the *Charles River Bridge* paradigm, both capitalism and the states' power of governance were well served. The doctrine was adaptable and in harmony with the emergent legal emphasis on the role of private autonomy in the American economy.

Taney's peroration suggests how sensitive the justices were to the implications of their constitutional views for the future of technology in America:

If this court should establish the principles now contended for, what is to become of the numerous railroads established on the same line of travel with turnpike companies; and which have rendered the franchises of the turnpike corporations of no value? Let it once be understood that such charters carry with them these implied contracts, and give this unknown and undefined property in a line of travelling, and you will soon find the old turnpike corporations awakening from their sleep, and calling upon this court to put down the improvements which have taken their place. The millions of property which have been invested in railroads and canals, upon lines of travel which had been before occupied by turnpike corporations, will be put in jeopardy. We shall be thrown back to the improvements of the last century, and obliged to stand still, until the claims of the old turnpike corporations shall be satisfied, and they shall consent to permit these States to avail themselves of the lights of modern science, and to partake of the benefit of those improvements which are now adding to the wealth and prosperity, and the convenience and comfort of every other part of the civilized world.

Conservatives wrongly interpreted Taney's opinion as an attack on vested rights. Story, who had heard arguments in the case under two Chief Justices, grew elegiac in his dissent, which was a *tour de force* of elegant learning:

I stand upon the old law; upon law established more than three centuries ago . . . in resisting any such encroachments upon the rights and liberties of the citizens, secured by public grants.[6]

In private correspondence, he composed his judicial epitaph: "I am the last of the old race of Judges. I stand their solitary representative, with a pained heart, and a subdued confidence."[7] In an anonymous law review article, a dismayed Chancellor Kent bemoaned Taney's decision: "What a deep injury has this decision inflicted on the Constitution, jurisprudence, and character of the United States."[8] In this critique, Kent began a tradition of interpretation that lasted a century, in which critics contrasted the Taney Court invidiously with its predecessor. Kent, however, exaggerated the discontinuities and ignored the fact that Taney and Marshall labored in two differing political environments.

The conservative laments were misplaced. Taney was no enemy of vested rights, corporations, or capital, any more than Marshall was hostile to all state regulatory power. Both men sought to maintain a dynamic equilibrium in the American Constitution, protecting entrepreneurial capitalism that operated under republican forms of state government in a political culture that aspired to democracy. The *Charles River Bridge* decision exemplified what Willard Hurst has identified as the nineteenth century's preference for "dynamic" as opposed to "static" capital. By stimulating the release of energy necessary to the realization of men's creative capabilities, judges encouraged the types of investment that would promote the exploitation of resources. Legal policymakers frowned on mere coupon-clipping that provided nothing more than income to bondholders without the multiplier benefits accruing to the whole community from capital-in-motion. Rather than clinging stand-pat to vested rights, Hurst argues, "the nineteenth-century United States valued change more than stability. . . . We were concerned with protecting

---

[6]11 Pet. at 598.

[7]Story to Harriet Martineau, Apr. 7, 1837, in William W. Story (ed.), *The Life and Letters of Joseph Story* (Boston, 1851), II, 277.

[8]Quoted in Carl B. Swisher, *The Taney Period: 1836–64* (vol. 5 of the Holmes Devise *History of the Supreme Court of the United States*) (New York, 1974), p. 95.

private property chiefly for what it could do. . . . What we did in the name of vested rights had less to do with protecting holdings than it had to do with protecting ventures."[9]

But in one sense, Story's lament, "I am the last of the old race of Judges," was correct. The Taney Court was a body of new men. Only one of its members, Story, had participated in most of the important Marshall cases. Congress expanded the size of the Court from seven to nine in 1837,[10] but even aside from these new seats, a majority of the Court were not associated with the great cases of Marshall's epoch.

The new Chief Justice (1777–1864) was the scion of Maryland's old Catholic families. Born into the comfortable circumstances of a large slaveholding plantation family, Taney graduated from Dickinson College and was admitted to the Maryland bar in 1799. He began a lucrative practice in the town of Frederick, forty miles northwest of both Washington and Baltimore. After serving a term in the Maryland House as a Federalist, Taney broke with the party at the time of the War of 1812. After the war, he served in the state senate for five years. Thereafter, he removed his practice to Baltimore. A supporter of Andrew Jackson in 1824, Taney was appointed Maryland attorney general, and then from 1831 to 1833, Attorney General of the United States, and, briefly, acting Secretary of War.

Taney made his reputation as a partisan Jacksonian during the "Bank War." His own experiences and strongly held convictions led him to oppose rechartering the Bank, and he drafted that part of Jackson's veto message (1832) that denied that the President was bound to accept the Supreme Court's interpretation of the Constitution. "The Congress, the Executive, and the Court must each for itself be guided by its own opinion of the Constitution," Taney wrote as Jackson's amanuensis. "The opinion of the judges has no more authority over Congress than the opinion of Congress has over the judges, and on that point the President is independent of both. The authority of the Supreme Court must not, therefore, be permitted to control the Congress or the Executive when acting in

[9]Willard Hurst, *Law and the Conditions of Freedom in the Nineteenth-Century United States* (Madison, 1956), p. 24.
[10]Act of Mar. 3, 1837, ch. 34, 5 Stat. 176.

their legislative capacities, but to have only such influence as the force of their reasoning may deserve."[11] The authorship of the veto message was no secret, so it is understandable that conservatives reacted with distress to the news that the author of this passage was to become the Chief Justice of the United States.

Taney also supported removal of federal deposits from the Bank of the United States. Though the Senate refused to confirm his appointment as Secretary of the Treasury, Taney was able to effect removal while holding that office as a recess appointee. His role in removal confirmed the conservatives' view of him as a radical and a partisan, and also established the entirely unfounded opinion that Taney was a mere cat's-paw of Jackson. After Taney resigned from the cabinet, Jackson nominated him as an associate justice of the Supreme Court, but he again failed of confirmation in the Senate. However, he was confirmed as Chief Justice in 1836 and served until his death in 1864.

Taney manumitted nearly all his own slaves, save for several superannuated slaves whom he kept in order to provide support in their old age. In his personal relationships, he was a loving parent, a kindly, paternalistic master, and a warm friend in his narrow circle of intimates. But in his public capacity, he was supremely self-assured, capable of pugnaciously promoting his views, intolerant of disagreement, and dogmatic to a fault. Deeply conscious of his Maryland roots, Taney was to the core a southerner, fiercely defensive of his region against the "aggressions" of the northern states. These attitudes served him poorly as Chief Justice.

Joseph Story (1779–1845), the senior associate Justice in point of service, had begun his career as an attorney in Salem, Massachusetts, after graduation from Harvard College and a stint reading law in law offices. Though he was a Jeffersonian in a staunchly Federalist community, Story served two terms in the state legislature and one in Congress, where he opposed his President's Embargo policies. Returning to the Massachusetts General Court, he served briefly as Speaker of the House until his appointment to the United States Supreme Court in 1811. His erudite opinions, written in a graceful though formal style, displayed a breadth of learning that did not in

[11]Richardson, *Messages and Papers of the Presidents*, III, 1145 (message of July 10, 1832).

any way detract from the vigor of his positions. Story was the Court's expert on admiralty, equity, and federal jurisdiction, among other topics, and was a more vigorous proponent of higher-law doctrines than even Chief Justice Marshall and Justice William Johnson. He shared with them and with Justice Bushrod Washington a militant nationalism, disdaining the attacks on him and the Court coming from Virginia jurists who objected to the extension of federal jurisdiction. While serving on the Supreme Court, Story also found time to write his classical treatises on agency, bailments, the Constitution, equity, equity pleading, conflicts, partnership, bills of exchange, and promissory notes. In addition, he served as the first Dane Professor at the Harvard Law School and virtually created that institution single-handedly.

Smith Thompson (1768–1843), the next senior justice, had sat on the New York Supreme Court, where he was chief justice from 1814 to 1819. From 1819 until his appointment to the United States Supreme Court in 1823, Thompson served as Secretary of the Navy in the Monroe administration. During the Marshall years, Thompson distanced himself from the Chief Justice by dissents in *Brown* v. *Maryland* (1827) and *Craig* v. *Missouri* (1830), and by siding with the majority over Marshall's dissent in *Ogden* v. *Saunders* (1827), thus establishing himself as less a nationalist than Marshall and Story.[12]

John McLean (1785–1861), who began his career as a Jeffersonian Republican, served in Congress during the War of 1812, and then on the Ohio Supreme Court from 1816 to 1822. He became commissioner of the United States Land Office and, shortly thereafter, Postmaster General. During his long tenure on the U.S. Supreme Court (1829–1861), McLean never shook himself free from political involvements, and in his later years semiopenly courted the Republican nomination for the presidency. Though McLean was hostile to slavery's expansion and political power, he firmly supported enforcement of the Fugitive Slave Act.

Henry Baldwin (1780–1844) was the most erratic member of the Taney Court. He was the half-brother of Abraham Baldwin, the distinguished Georgia delegate to the Constitutional Convention of 1787. Baldwin read law in the office of Alexander Dallas and estab-

---

[12]Respectively: 12 Wheat. (25 U.S.) 419 (1827); 4 Pet. (29 U.S.) 410 (1830); 12 Wheat. (25 U.S.) 213 (1827).

lished a practice in the Pittsburgh area. In 1830 Andrew Jackson appointed him to the Supreme Court, where he sat until his death in 1844. Despite his northern background, Baldwin adopted an extremist proslavery position but was otherwise not known for any significant opinion.

A majority of the Court, five justices, were appointed between 1835 and 1837 by President Jackson; as of 1837, all but two justices were Jackson appointees—a calamity from a Whig point of view. James M. Wayne (1790–1867) of Georgia represented his state in Congress during Jackson's presidency and chaired the House Foreign Relations Committee. Appointed to the United States Supreme Court in 1835, he served there until his death in 1867 and distinguished himself as the standard-bearer of the Marshall-Story nationalist tradition. During the Civil War, despite strong ties to his home state, he remained a Unionist.

The "Virginia seat" on the Court, if it may be called that, was occupied briefly by Philip Pendleton Barbour (1783–1841), who came from a family prominent in Virginia Jeffersonian politics. He had served in Congress and presided with distinction over the Virginia constitutional convention of 1829–30. He had also represented the Virginia viewpoint, hostile to the position of Story and Marshall, as counsel for the commonwealth in *Cohens* v. *Virginia* (1816). His brief service on the Court (1836–41), cut short by early death, give him little opportunity to make a name for himself there. He was succeeded by Peter V. Daniel (1784–1860), who served from 1841 to 1860. Daniel was ideologically an Old Republican, unbending in his state-rights views and even more fanatically dedicated to the protection of slavery than the Chief Justice. He was the Court's preeminent dissenter, speaking for the Court in a significant constitutional case only once in his twenty years there, and finding himself always in dissent when the Court adopted a nationalist position or when he considered the majority position as being hostile to state powers.

The two new seats were filled without much distinction by John McKinley and John Catron. McKinley (1780–1852), an Alabama legislator and United States Senator, was a Jacksonian Democrat. He sat on the Court from 1837 until his death in 1852. Catron (1786–1865) had been chief judge of the Tennessee Supreme Court of Errors and Appeals for a decade. Jackson appointed him to the United States Supreme Court in 1837, where he sat unspectacularly until death terminated his tenure in 1865. Like Wayne, Catron remained attached to the cause of the Union during the war.

The Taney Court displayed a continuity of personnel. Thompson was succeeded by his fellow New York judge, Samuel Nelson, and Baldwin by another Pennsylvanian, Robert Grier. Levi Woodbury, Benjamin R. Curtis, and Nathan Clifford succeeded Story in the "New England chair." Woodbury and Clifford, both Democrats, were *epigone*, but Curtis was a jurist of distinction whose learning did no discredit to the seat once occupied by Story. John A. Campbell followed his fellow Alabamian McKinley. Despite these changes, the intellectual complexion of the Court changed little during Taney's term as Chief Justice. Hence it is not misleading to speak of a "Taney Court," a body cohesive in membership, if not in opinions.

Charles River Bridge had involved the relationship between a state and its own creature, a corporation that it had chartered. But what were the mutual powers of a state and a "foreign" corporation, that is, one chartered by a sister state? The Court shortly turned to this question in *Bank of Augusta* v. *Earle* (1839),[13] where Taney once again adopted a developmentally open posture toward the conflicts between states and foreign corporations, leaving it to a dissent and a concurrence to expound extreme positions on one side and the other. After Justice John McKinley on circuit held that a foreign corporation lacked power to contract outside the state that chartered it, an ideological and partisan explosion burst on the heads of the justices. The Democratic press, including the Van Buren administration's organ, the Washington *Globe,* extolled the circuit decision as a blow against "these money-mongering monsters," the banks and other corporations. Whigs were aghast at the implications of McKinley's ruling, seeing it as striking "at the root of all commercial intercourse between the states" and being another stride forward in "the march of agrarianism" (that is, socialism).[14] Political rhetoric aside, the circuit court holding would have dis-

[13]13 Pet. (38 U.S.) 519 (1839).
[14]Quotations at Charles Warren, *The Supreme Court in United States History* (Boston, 1923), II, 329, 333.

rupted interstate business seriously if not ruinously, so the Taney Court found itself with a case of major economic importance on its hands.

Taney resolved the issue judiciously, using the *Charles River Bridge* paradigm to preserve a field for the exercise of state regulatory power yet not defeat investors' expectations and the national market. He held that a corporation was "a mere artificial being, invisible and intangible, yet it is a person, for certain purposes, in contemplation of law."[15] As such, it could make contracts, and thus could do business outside the state where it was chartered, much as an individual could carry on business outside the state of his residence. States could regulate the activities of foreign corporations, or even exclude them altogether, but they had to do so explicitly. In the absence of explicit state policy, comity required that states be presumed to acquiesce in foreign corporations doing business within their borders.[16] Here, as in *Charles River Bridge,* Taney left the door open for state legislatures to regulate as broadly as they wished, but held them to specific regulations and refused to permit judge-made presumptions or policy to interfere with business activity.

Justices McKinley dissenting and Baldwin concurring espoused the polar extremes. McKinley, the former Alabama state legislator and Congressman, stood by his ruling below and urged an implied policy of exclusion by insisting that rules of comity were inapplicable in the American federal union. Baldwin, by contrast, insisted that the privileges-and-immunities clause of the federal Constitution voided even explicit exclusions by states.[17] McKinley's position would have produced commercial disaster, balkanizing the nation-wide market in bills of exchange, a disruption the country scarcely needed in its slow recuperation from the Depression of 1837. Bald-

---

[15]13 Pet. at 588.

[16]Taney drew on analogies and doctrines from international law to shed light on the relations between states and their legal creatures in the American federal system. Comity has been defined as the principle by which "the courts of one state or jurisdiction will give effect to the laws and judicial decisions of another state or jurisdiction, not as a matter of obligation, but out of deference and mutual respect." *Black's Law Dictionary,* 5th ed., "Comity."

[17]Baldwin's failure to deliver his opinion to the Court's Reporter, Richard Peters, has required that historians rely on newspaper accounts for the content of the orally delivered version. Swisher, *Taney Period,* p. 120, citing an account in the New York *Courier and Enquirer,* Mar. 12, 1839.

win's view would have negated the police power of the states in commercial and financial matters.

In *Bank of Augusta,* Taney did not need to explore the concept of police power. But the 1848 case of *West River Bridge* v. *Dix,* which called forth a fervid attack by Daniel Webster on eminent domain, required the Supreme Court to review the scope of the police power. The Vermont legislature had chartered a corporation to operate a toll bridge. Later, using its power of eminent domain and paying compensation for the taking, the legislature destroyed the franchise by making the bridge part of a toll-free highway. Webster, counsel for the bridge corporation, warned of the dangers that eminent domain posed to American institutions. He noted that eminent domain was a relatively new legal concept, based on the proposition "that all the powers heretofore regarded as the incidents of sovereignty must be existing in some department of State authority," a proposition that he denied. But he recognized that police power and eminent domain were here to stay, despite the danger that "the existing will of the existing majority" might pose to corporate property. If legislatures were to be the judges of the extent of eminent domain power, Webster warned somewhat hysterically, "the most levelling ultraisms of Anti-rentism or agrarianism or Abolitionism may be successfully advanced."[18]

Webster's base plea to the proslavery passions of the Court's majority proved unavailing. Unimpressed by his rhetoric, Justice Peter V. Daniel, a dogged opponent of corporations, wrote for the majority upholding Vermont's action. He confused eminent domain with police power, defining the former in terms appropriate only to the latter, and holding it "paramount to all private rights vested under the government," which are "held in subordination to this power, and must yield in every instance to its proper exercise."[19] *West River Bridge* established the point that the power of taking could extend not only to material things (land, buildings) but to what

[18]Webster's argument may be found in the report of the case at 12 L.Ed. 540. His mention of "Anti-rentism" referred to the contemporary Anti-Rent Wars of New York State. "Agrarianism" was a pejorative term for socialist doctrines expounded by pre-Marxian writers including Gracchus Babeuf, Charles Fourier, Robert Owen, and Pierre Joseph Proudhon.

[19]6 How. (47 U.S.) 507 (1848) at 532; McLean and Woodbury, JJ. concurred in separate opinions; Wayne, J. dissented.

lawyers call "incorporeal" property: rights, powers, expectations that nevertheless represent valuable financial opportunities. Though *West River Bridge* was a potentially serious inroad into the *Charles River Bridge* doctrine, judges later softened its impact by hedging about the eminent domain power with restrictions based on federal and state constitutional provisions that prohibited the taking of private property except for public use and with payment of just compensation. A writer in the Boston *Post* noted how well the *West River Bridge* decision fit into the *Charles River Bridge* formula: "under this decision, any State has the power to check the assumption of these corporations, while, at the same time, all the necessary privileges of corporations are as well secured as ever, and their real value and utility enhanced by thus harmonizing them with popular sentiment."[20]

The Court continued to respect both sides of the dynamic balance established by *Charles River Bridge,* supporting the power of the state when explicitly exercised and refusing to read implied monopoly grants or other benefits into charters. In *Planters Bank* v. *Sharp* (1848),[21] decided in the same term as *West River Bridge,* the Court upheld the binding effect of an expressly granted corporate power. The Court held that the contracts clause of Article I, section 10, prohibited a state from voiding express charter provisions that empowered banks to assign bills and notes. (Mississippi had tried to do that in retaliation for a banking practice its legislators considered morally repugnant: banks refused to accept their own depreciated notes in payment of debts due them.) And the Court affirmed the other side of the *Charles River Bridge* formula in *Richmond, Fredericksburg, and Potomac Railroad* v. *Louisa Railroad* (1852)[22] by refusing to imply into a railroad's charter any guarantee against competition in freight hauling by subsequently chartered lines.

But usually two or more justices dissented in all these cases. Together with the concurrences, this multiplicity of voices suggested that the *Charles River Bridge* formula would be sorely tested if the Court was presented with cases clearly setting vested rights and entrepreneurial opportunity against popular sovereignty and

[20]Boston *Post,* Feb. 4, 1848, quoted in Warren, *Supreme Court in United States History,* II, 439.
[21]6 How. (47 U.S.) 301 (1848).
[22]13 How. (54 U.S.) 71 (1852).

the police power, especially if such cases arose against a politically volatile backdrop. Three such cases came to the court in the mid-fifties as the result of a struggle between Ohio banks and the Democratic majorities of that state's legislature.

In the aftermath of the Panic of 1837, Ohio Democrats refused to renew expired charters of Ohio banks, thereby building up pro-banking pressure that was prevented from flowing into its normal financial outlet. When the Whigs came into power briefly in 1845, they opened the sluice gates by enacting a general banking act that contained what amounted to an exemption from taxation for Ohio banks by taxing only profits, not gross revenue. Back in power two years later, resentful Democrats first enacted a general bank tax, then, in an 1850 constitutional convention, amended the state constitution to subject all bank property to taxation "without deduction." Under the aegis of this provision, they then reenacted the bank tax.

The first case to come to the High Court out of this party struggle, *Piqua Bank* v. *Knoop* (1854),[23] produced a 6–3 split, with Ohioan John McLean for the majority holding that the state could not revoke the tax exemption for banks charted under the Whig general banking act of 1845 without violating the contracts clause. Joining Daniel and John A. Campbell in dissent, Justice John Catron insisted that states could not permanently surrender their taxing powers, and that therefore no corporate charter containing a perpetual tax exemption could tie the hands of a subsequent legislature, the contracts clause notwithstanding.

The *Piqua Bank* decision ignited anti-Court sentiment throughout Ohio. The Cincinnati *Enquirer* complimented the Court on being a "citadel of silk-gowned fogeydom, a goodly portion of it imbecile with age."[24] But at the same time, and still within the paradigmatic limits of *Charles River Bridge,* the Court determined in *Ohio Life Insurance Co.* v. *Debolt* (1854)[25] that banks chartered by special enact-

[23]16 How. (57 U.S.) 369 (1854); Taney concurred in the result but expressly disavowed the majority's reasoning.
[24]Quoted in Warren, *Supreme Court in United States History,* II, 526.
[25]16 How. (57 U.S.) 416 (1854). There was no majority opinion in Debolt. Taney delivered the judgment of the Court and an opinion for himself and Grier. Catron, Daniel, and Campbell each concurred separately; McLean, Wayne, Curtis, and Nelson dissented.

ment before the 1845 general banking incorporation act would not have an implied grant of a tax exemption read into their charters.

The third of the triad of Ohio bank cases, *Dodge* v. *Woolsey* (1856),[26] posed the severest challenge to doctrines of police power and popular sovereignty. A 6–3 majority held the second bank tax unconstitutional as applied to banks whose charters contained an explicit exemption, on the grounds that the people could no more void a contractual obligation by constitutional amendment than they could by ordinary legislation. But *Dodge* v. *Woolsey* was no ordinary bank-tax case. Here, for the first time in its history, the United States Supreme Court held a provision of a state Constitution—not just an ordinary statute—void because of a conflict with the federal Constitution. This rekindled the embers of Virginia's opposition to the review powers of federal courts, a fire that had been banked but not extinguished by Story's opinion in *Martin* v. *Hunter's Lessee* (1816) and Marshall's in *Cohens* v. *Virginia* (1821).

The combination of novelty, seriousness, and partisan controversy evoked unusually passionate opinions from Justice James M. Wayne for the majority, and Justice Campbell for the dissenters. After a Marshallesque dissertation on the supremacy of the federal Constitution and the importance of judicial review, Wayne sermonized: "moral obligations never die. If broken by states and nations, though the terms of reproach are not the same with which we are accustomed to designate the faithlessness of individuals, the violation of justice is not the less."[27] Campbell, joined by Catron and Daniel in dissent, responded in Jeffersonian terms, condemning banks as "a caste made up of combinations of men for the most part under the most favorable conditions in society, who will habitually look beyond the institutions and the authorities of the state to the

---

[26]18 How. (59 U.S.) 331 (1856). The suit on which the appeal in Dodge was based was patently collusive, an inconvenient fact that the majority brushed aside to the frustration of the three indignant dissenters. A collusive suit, between "friendly" parties who have no true adversary interest and who cooperate in bringing litigation just to create a test case, cannot be one of the "Cases" or "Controversies" requisite for federal court jurisdiction under Art. III of the United States Constitution. Lord v. Veazie, 8 How. (49 U.S.) 251 (1850). Nonetheless, some classics of American constitutional jurisprudence, most notoriously Pollock v. Farmers Loan and Trust (1895, 1896), the *Income Tax* cases, were collusive. The viability of a collusive suit requires a Court majority sympathetic to the colluders.

[27]18 How. at 360.

central government for the strength and support necessary to maintain them in the enjoyment of their special privileges and exemptions."[28]

But banks were too important in the national economy, and too profitable, to be withered by Old Republican tirades. The balance of *Charles River Bridge* survived the bank wars intact: investors were assured that states could not break explicit promises, while devotees of popular sovereignty knew that state legislatures might still specify what powers the people retained over banks and other corporations.

In police power cases that were not complicated by the need to protect investment opportunity, the Taney Court demonstrated its sensitivity to states' interests. Only in this respect was its orientation significantly different from the early Marshall Court's. But this different outlook surfaced immediately in Taney's first term, and was largely responsible for the mistaken belief that a Court of Democratic appointees reversed Marshallian values, moving from nationalism to states' rights.

But, to be fair to Taney's conservative critics, *Briscoe* v. *Bank of Kentucky* (1837)[29] did seem a break with the past. In contrast with *Charles River Bridge,* decided at the same term, where Taney supported his position by drawing on the authority of a Marshall precedent (*Providence Bank* v. *Billings,* 1830), in *Briscoe* the Court seemed to be reversing a policy set by Marshall only a few years earlier. In *Craig* v. *Missouri* (1830),[30] Marshall had antagonized the capital-scarce southern and western states by holding that the bills-of-credit clause of Article I, section 10, voided a state monetary scheme by which the state issued loan-office certificates that served, in effect, as a limited currency. Taney, a Marylander, was sensitive to the intense hostility *Craig* had provoked in the South and West, areas that were avid for investment capital and a circulating medium adequate to sustain economic growth. When *Briscoe* challenged a monetary mechanism resembling Missouri's, Taney designated Justice McLean, who had dissented in *Craig,* to write the opinion sustaining the Kentucky measure. Kentucky had modified the Missouri

[28] 18 How. at 373.
[29] 11 Pet. (36 U.S.) 257 (1837).
[30] 4 Pet. (29 U.S.) 410 (1830).

scheme by chartering a bank wholly owned and controlled by it. The bank then issued notes that were not backed by the credit of the state. The new Court held that these banknotes were not the "Bills of Credit" banned by the federal Constitution. Story alone dissented, noting in elegiac tones that had Marshall still lived he would have joined in dissent.

Story and others who feared that the Court was heading off in dangerous new directions might have taken comfort from the decision in the contracts-clause case of *Bronson* v. *Kinzie* six years later.[31] *Bronson* arose out of the vexed history of debtor relief in the United States. In response to the Panic of 1837 and ensuing mortgage foreclosures, the states enacted a variety of measures protecting mortgagors against exacting foreclosures. These relief statutes usually contained one or both of the following provisions: a "stay" or moratorium, giving the debtor an option to repurchase foreclosed property within a specified period; and the requirement of a minimal amount, specified as a fraction or percentage of market value, below which property could not be sold at foreclosure. Such statutes were naturally unpopular with creditors and their Whig supporters. Taney, to the gratification of the aged and ill Story, held an Illinois foreclosure statute unconstitutional as an impairment of contracts. But he extracted from an earlier Story opinion in *Green* v. *Biddle* (1823)[32] a concession to the states that bore fruit a century later. Taney emphasized that though states could not impair the substantive obligation of a contract, they could tinker with the remedies available to parties under it, a qualification that would have saved some forms of stay legislation. Such reasoning influenced Taney's remote successor, Chief Justice Charles Evans Hughes, in the Minnesota mortgage moratorium case that played so prominent a constitutional role in the early New Deal.[33]

The police power and contracts-clause cases demonstrated that the federal courts could not avoid the difficult and delicate role of mediating conflicts between the state, on one hand, and either the federal government or large economic interests on the other. But to support federal judges in this politically sensitive role, the Mar-

[31] 1 How. (42 U.S.) 311 (1843); McLean, J. dissenting.
[32] 8 Wheat. (21 U.S.) 1 (1823).
[33] Home Building and Loan Assn. v. Blaisdell, 290 U.S. 398 (1934).

shall-era classic dissertations on the nature and scope of judicial power were no longer sufficient. Their magisterial authority remained undiminished, but Court and nation had moved on into a new era wherein the thinking of Marshall, Story, and William Johnson would have to be brought up to date, and, in two instances, significantly modified. Thus the Taney Court decisions on the scope of judicial power constitute some of its most enduring monuments.

One of these judicial-power cases, *Swift* v. *Tyson* (1842),[34] remains little known outside scholarly and legal circles, despite its considerable influence on American constitutional development, an influence that lasted for good or ill almost a century until its doctrine was overturned in 1938. In one of the less-well-known sections of the celebrated Judiciary Act of 1789, Congress provided that "the laws of the several states . . . shall be regarded as rules of decision in trials at common law in the courts of the United States, in cases where they apply."[35] This doubly ambiguous provision left it unclear just what the "laws of the several states" were. Were they only statutes, or did they include common law, that is, the decisions of the state courts expounding the states' bodies of unwritten law? And where *did* they apply? This raised delicate but important questions of federalism.

The economic conditions of the late Jacksonian period provided a backdrop for the resolution of these questions. A severe depression had set in after 1837, with little relief before 1843. The national market was impeded by the variety of local laws in various commercial fields, and this same multifariousness hampered the orderly expansion of credit. There were thus strong pressures for judicial development of uniformity in commercial law topics, especially in those areas relating to negotiability of commercial paper. *Swift* v. *Tyson* resolved some of the ambiguities of the rules-of-decision section while at the same time promoting uniformity in commercial law.

The question presented in *Swift* was whether a Federal District Court sitting in New York had to follow the common law of that

[34] 16 Pet. (41 U.S.) 1 (1842), Catron, J. concurring in result.
[35] Act of Sept. 24, 1789, ch. 20, sec. 34, 1 Stat. 73. This is commonly referred to as the "rules of decision" section. A rule of decision is the law applicable to the facts of the case that determines the legal outcome. In a federal system, a court may have to choose between a state rule of decision and a federal one, if they differ.

state on a commercial law question, or whether it could seek its rule of decision in some other body of law. Story, writing for a unanimous Court, chose the latter option in a carefully drawn opinion that nevertheless had sweeping consequences. He partially resolved the ambiguity of section 34 by holding that its phrase "laws of the several states" meant "state laws strictly local, that is to say, . . . the positive statutes of the state, and the construction thereof adopted by the local tribunals, and . . . rights and titles of things having a permanent locality, such as the rights and titles to real estate." Section 34 therefore did not oblige federal courts to follow state judicial decisions on commercial law subjects. There, federal judges were to seek their rule of decision in "the general principles and doctrines of commercial jurisprudence."[36]

Story's primary object in promulgating the *Swift* doctrine was to establish national uniformity in commercial law, based on the international body of commercial law derived from mercantile custom— the "general principles of commercial jurisprudence" he mentioned. Story entertained an expansive vision of a unitary body of international commercial law and approvingly quoted Cicero, who had said there is not one law at Rome and another at Athens.

Story was not primarily concerned with aggrandizing federal judicial power, though that was certainly a result of his decision. In his *Swift* opinion, he carried with him even that unsleeping watchdog of states' rights, Justice Daniel, suggesting that the problems of federalism in this case were subordinated to considerations relating to credit, negotiability, and the national market. Story and his colleagues viewed heterogeneity and indeterminacy in commercial law questions as a nuisance, and sought to replace them with a unitary law.

Nor was Story determined to impose a federal common law on the states. The Marshall Court had rejected the possibility of a federal common law of crimes,[37] and the suggestion of a federal common law in civil areas would have touched off vociferous dissents by Daniel, Taney, and McKinley at least. But section 34 was ambiguous, and Story provided a welcome resolution of part of its ambiguities, by freeing federal judges from the multiplicity of state rules.

[36]16 Pet. at 18–19.
[37]United States *v.* Hudson and Goodwin, 7 Cranch (11 U.S.) 32 (1812).

The *Swift* decision caused little furor in its time, largely because of a prevailing consensus that the commercial law of the states required some unifying supervision. But it shortly underwent expansion, concurrent with the post–Civil War growth of federal court jurisdiction, and soon earned the enmity of powerful legal commentators and judges, including Justice Oliver Wendell Holmes, Jr., who sneeringly called the general body of commercial common law that Story adulated "a brooding omnipresence in the sky."[38] His associate, Justice Louis Brandeis, finally repudiated the rule in *Erie Railroad* v. *Tompkins* (1938), discarding it as unconstitutional.[39] But in its time, the *Swift* rule led lower federal judges to develop uniform national rules in the law of wills, torts, mineral conveyances, contracts, and damages—an impressive career for any single rule of law.

Other Taney Court decisions on the scope of judicial power proved to be even more enduring. Two of them, one concerning corporations and the other dealing with admiralty jurisdiction, each undid a Marshall Court's premature and unwise solution to a novel problem. In *Louisville, Cincinnati, and Charleston Railroad Co.* v. *Letson* (1844), Justice Wayne attacked the knotty problem of a corporation's citizenship.[40] Article III of the Constitution gives federal courts jurisdiction of "Cases . . . between Citizens of different States." Lawyers refer to this as "diversity jurisdiction"; the parties are said to be "diverse." But of what state could that new and intangible legal creature, the corporation, be said to be a citizen if its stockholders and officers resided in different states? The novelty of the problem baffled John Marshall and led him astray. In *Bank of the United States* v. *Deveaux* (1809)[41] Marshall held that in order for federal courts to entertain diversity suits in which a corporation is a party, all of its shareholders must have citizenship diverse from the parties on the other side. This became an impossibly constrictive rule as corporations matured in the national market. Had it not been

---

[38]Southern Pacific Railroad v. Jensen, 244 U.S. 205 (1917) at 222 (Holmes, J. dissenting). For Holmes's hostility to Swift, see Black and White Taxicab Co. v. Brown and Yellow Taxicab Co., 276 U.S. 518 (1928) at 533–535 (Holmes, J. dissenting).
[39]304 U.S. 64 (1938).
[40]2 How. (43 U.S.) 497 (1844).
[41]5 Cranch (9 U.S.) 84 (1809).

abandoned, the doors of federal courts would have been shut to all but the smallest and most local corporations. In *Letson,* Justice James M. Wayne overruled *Deveaux* to hold that for diversity purposes, a corporation was deemed a citizen of the state in which it was chartered. Jurisdiction would not be defeated if some of the shareholders were nondiverse with parties on the other side. Wayne eased the shock of overruling precedent by asserting that Marshall himself in private conversation later regretted *Deveaux.* The *Letson* rule, being eminently serviceable, has proved lasting, and has been reaffirmed by recent congressional legislation.[42]

Another increasingly unwelcome inheritance of the Marshall era was the so-called tidewater rule that restricted the jurisdiction of federal courts sitting in admiralty to causes of action that occurred in tidal waters or the high seas, and excluded cases arising on fresh waters, including the inland rivers and the Great Lakes. The tidewater rule, English in origin, was adopted by Joseph Story for American courts in *The Thomas Jefferson* (1825).[43] Why he should have done so remains a mystery. His early law practice was in the oceanport of Salem, Massachusetts, and this may have given him an oceangoing orientation. At the time of the decision, steam vessels had not yet been perfected, though they were already plying the inland waters. But Story's position, in spite of these rationales, remains uncharacteristically shortsighted for him, especially in view of the fact that he was at the same time the Court's most outspoken exponent of expanding the jurisdiction of the federal courts as well as its chief admiralty expert.[44]

As steamboats opened the commerce of the interior, technology again came knocking insistently at the law's door, as it did in *Charles River Bridge.* With federal courts barred from taking jurisdiction of fresh-water suits, inland maritime law was left to the states, which soon developed a lush diversity of rules that hindered development of the national market. Story's sensitivity in *Swift* v. *Tyson* to the nuisance of one law at Rome and another at Athens somehow did not extend to the anomaly of one law of seaman's wages at Cincinnati and another at St. Louis. Finally, after Story's death, Taney

[42]Act of July 25, 1958, now 28 U.S.C. sec. 1332(c).
[43]10 Wheat. (23 U.S.) 428 (1825).
[44]Anon., "From Judicial Grant to Legislative Power: The Admiralty Clause in the Nineteenth Century," *Harvard Law Review,* LXVII (1954), 1214–1237.

decided that the tidewater rule should be interred with its American foster-parent. In *The Genesee Chief* v. *Fitzhugh* (1851),[45] Taney overruled *The Thomas Jefferson* and extended federal admiralty jurisdiction to nontidal waters. *The Genesee Chief* ranks with *Charles River Bridge* as a triumphant marriage of technological development and legal advance, based on a realistic appraisal of the policy consequences of adopting one rule of law or another. As Taney said, the Great Lakes

are in truth inland seas. Different States border on them on one side, and a foreign nation on the other. A great and growing commerce is carried on upon them between different States and a foreign nation, which is subject to all the incidents and hazards that attend commerce on the ocean. Hostile fleets have encountered on them, and prizes been made; and every reason which existed for the grant of admiralty jurisdiction to the general government on the Atlantic seas, applies with equal force to the lakes. . . .[46]

In place of the discarded tidewater rule, Taney announced a new constitutional test: navigability. The reputation of the Taney Court has been blighted by what a later Chief Justice of the United States called its "self-inflicted wound," the *Dred Scott* case. But as *The Genesee Chief* demonstrates, Taney and his associates molded the constitutional law of the United States in ways that have proved as enduring and beneficent as the achievements of the Marshall Court.

Perhaps Taney's most influential legacy has been the political question doctrine. The doctrine is an attempt to rationalize a sense that some kinds of questions coming before a court are unsuitable for resolution by judges. Alternatively, and more consonant with the Supreme Court's development of the doctrine, the ultimate issue behind the doctrine is "whether particular constitutional provisions yield judicially enforceable rights."[47] Alexander Bickel suggested some of the more subtle, intuitive pressures that lead judges to reach for the doctrine as a convenient way out:

the doctrine is based on the court's sense of a lack of capacity, compounded in unequal parts of the strangeness of the issue and the suspicion that it will have to yield more often and more substantially to expediency than to principle; the sheer momentousness of it, which unbalances judgment and

[45]12 How. (53 U.S.) 443 (1851).
[46]12 How. at 453.
[47]Laurence Tribe, *American Constitutional Law* (Mineola, N.Y., 1978), p. 73.

prevents one from subsuming the normal calculations of probabilities; the anxiety not so much that the judicial judgment will be ignored, as that perhaps it should be, but won't; and finally . . . the inner vulnerability of an institution which is electorally irresponsible.[48]

Taney may not have been the first to grasp these points, but he was the first justice of the United States Supreme Court to elevate them to the status of constitutional doctrine. He began elaborating the idea in a dissent in *Rhode Island* v. *Massachusetts* (1838), a case involving an ancient boundary dispute between the two states.[49] This suit was one of those rare instances of the United States Supreme Court's exercise of its original jurisdiction given in Article III, section 2, whereby a case comes before it in the first instance, without being tried before any inferior court, state or federal. The majority accepted jurisdiction of the suit and, after hearings, dismissed the bill. Taney dissented, claiming that though the Court might have jurisdiction if property rights were involved in the boundary-line dispute, it lacked jurisdiction if questions of state sovereignty were involved, as he thought they were in this case. The political question doctrine remained embryonic for a few years afterward, though, until it was revived spectacularly in that peculiar judicial aftermath of the Dorr Rebellion, *Luther* v. *Borden* (1849).

After Dorr's followers and their Democratic sympathizers in Congress finally abandoned political efforts to vindicate their cause by 1845, a few diehard Rhode Island suffragists decided to seek redress before the United States Supreme Court, seeking to have the Court declare the Freeholder Government's imposition of martial law unconstitutional. In this way, they hoped, the People's Government under Dorr might be found to be the only legitimate government of Rhode Island in 1842. This was a strange expectation, if the Dorrites were seeking any real remedy, as opposed to a mere rhetorical endorsement of their theory. Even though almost the entire bench in 1846 had been appointed by Democratic Presidents, it was bizarre to think that the Court would overthrow the peaceful and reasonably updated government of Rhode Island to vindicate an

48Alexander Bickel, "Foreword: The Passive Virtues," *Harvard Law Review*, LXXV (1961), 40–79 at 75.
4912 Pet. (37 U.S.) 657 (1838).

abstract theory. Nonetheless, Dorrites fashioned a judicial action out of one of the numerous incidents of Freeholder harassment and went to the United States Supreme Court on a pro forma certificate of division.[50] Whether or not the case was collusive, the certificate of division certainly was, because both United States Circuit Court judges, Joseph Story of the Supreme Court and Judge John Pitman of the United States District Court, were hostile toward the Dorrite cause.[51] The case came up to the United States Supreme Court in 1846 and, after postponements due to absences caused by illness and death, was finally decided in 1849 with Taney writing for the Court on the political-question doctrine.[52]

Taney began by listing the insuperable practical difficulties that would ensue if the Court were to declare the Rhode Island government illegitimate for the previous seven years. With disarming simplicity, he then introduced the political question doctrine:

the courts uniformly held that the inquiry proposed to be made [i.e., whether the government under the 1663 Charter was republican] belonged to the political power and not to the judicial; that it rested with the political power to decide whether the charter government had been displaced or not; and when that decision was made, the judicial department would be bound to take notice of it as the paramount law of the State. . . .[53]

He went on to support this idea, newborn and therefore vulnerable, by asserting that responsibility for enforcement of the guarantee clause of Article IV, section 4 , on which the Dorrite challenge relied, lay with Congress rather than with the courts.

Taney concluded his landmark opinion by noting that "much of the argument on the part of the plaintiff turned upon political rights and political questions, upon which the court has been urged to

[50]The United States Circuit Courts of the period consisted of two judges: a justice of the United States Supreme Court on circuit, and the judge of the United States District Court of the state where the Circuit Court sat. When they disagreed between themselves, producing a 1–1 split, they certified their division to the United States Supreme Court to have the difference resolved by the High Court.

[51]Story to John Pitman, Feb. 10, 1842, in Story (ed.), *Life and Letters of Story*, II, 416; Pitman to Story, Jan. 26, 1842, May 4, 1842, Nov. 7, 1842, in Joseph Story Papers, William L. Clements Library, University of Michigan–Ann Arbor.

[52]7 How. (48 U.S.) 1 (1849). Woodbury, J. dissented on a martial law point, but endorsed and amplified Taney's views on the political question and guarantee clause issues.

[53]7 How. at 39.

express an opinion. We decline doing so." He then did so, though, with a hollow verbal concession to Dorrite theory:

> No one, we believe, has ever doubted the position that, according to the institutions of this country, the sovereignty in every State resides in the people of the State, and that they may alter and change their form of government at their own pleasure. But whether they have changed it or not by abolishing an old government, and establishing a new one in its place, is a question to be settled by the political power.[54]

The political question doctrine has remained influential into modern times, though weakened or perhaps detoured by *Baker* v. *Carr* (1962). Whether cited explicitly or not, it lay behind the federal courts' reluctance to inquire whether American involvement in Vietnam was unconstitutional. Its doctrinal base is fluid, if not muddled, but it is still available to judges disinclined to become entangled in issues they sense to be nonjusticiable.[55]

The Taney Court cases involving banks, corporations, technological change, and the power of federal courts did not raise issues related to slavery. But, given slavery's pervasive influence in the Taney era, it was probably inevitable that sooner or later cases challenging the police power of the states, even if they did not deal directly with the constitutional status of slaves, would raise slavery questions. This inevitability was realized when the states' police power was pitted against the power of the federal government to regulate interstate and foreign commerce. The dynamic balance that the Court achieved in other cases between police power and the restraints of the contracts clause became impossible to attain in the commerce-clause area, where the cases were doctrinally skewed by the influence of the peculiar institution.

The third major case of Taney's first term, *Mayor of New York* v. *Miln* (1837), raised a question that on its face seemed far removed from slavery: the constitutionality of a New York statute requiring masters of incoming vessels to furnish the mayor of New York City with a passenger manifest. Its purpose was to control the entry of diseased and impoverished immigrants. But the generic problem of a state's power to control the entry of undesirable persons recalled

---

[54]7 How. at 47.
[55]A justiciable controversy is one suitable for resolution by a court (as opposed to one resolvable only by political or other nonjudicial means).

to sensitized southern minds a fifteen-year-old controversy that northerners scarcely took notice of: the constitutional flare over the Negro Seamen's Acts.

In 1822, Charleston, South Carolina, experienced a slave insurrection panic, caused by a supposed plot of slaves and free blacks under the leadership of an ex-slave named Denmark Vesey to seize the city. In response, terrified white Carolinians tried to quarantine the spread of abolitionist ideas. They procured enactment of the Negro Seamen's Act, a statute that required free black seamen to remain on board their vessels while in Carolina harbors, on pain of being jailed and sold into slavery if not redeemed by the ship's master. In the remainder of the decade, the other coastal slave states enacted similar legislation, causing diplomatic embarrassment to the United States government and considerable inconvenience to northern shippers because of the great numbers of seamen affected.[56] These laws, particularly South Carolina's parent-statute, provoked a long-lived, intense conflict between national and state authority. In *Elkison* v. *Deliesseline* (1823), United States Supreme Court Justice William Johnson, on circuit, held the Negro Seamen's Act unconstitutional as an interference with treaty obligations and an intrusion on the federal commerce power.[57] Johnson expanded on the commerce-clause point in his concurrence in *Gibbons* v. *Ogden* (1824), insisting that all state legislation affecting interstate commerce in any way was void if Congress has regulated the same subject.[58] Massachusetts federal judge Peleg Sprague and United States Attorney General William Wirt also considered the Seamen's Acts unconstitutional.[59]

Southern judges believed that these opinions endangered the police powers of the southern states in the control of slaves, free

---

[56]According to one estimate, almost half the seamen in the American merchant marine of the 1850s were black: Richard N. Current et al., *The Essentials of American History*, 2nd ed. (New York, 1976), p. 116.

[57]8 Fed. Cas. 493 (No. 4366) (C.C.D.S.C. 1823).

[58]Gibbons v. Ogden, 9 Wheat. (22 U.S.) 1 (1824), Johnson, J. concurring at 27–33. See Maurice G. Baxter, *The Steamboat Monopoly: Gibbons v. Ogden, 1824* (New York, 1972), pp. 57–60.

[59]The Cynosure, 6 Fed. Cas. 1102 (No. 3529) (D.C.D. Mass. 1844) (dictum); Wirt's opinion is reprinted, along with other documents generated by the controversy, in "Free Colored Seamen—Majority and Minority Reports," House Reports, 27 Cong., 3 sess., ser. 426, doc. 80 (1843).

blacks, and incoming abolitionists. Meanwhile, continuing British
and northern-state protests led President Jackson to refer the question of the Negro Seamen's Acts to his successive Attorneys General, John M. Berrien and Roger B. Taney. Both—Berrien in an
official opinion and Taney in an unpublished draft—upheld the
laws, Taney claiming that state police power overrode any inconsistent exercise of the federal treaty power, the polar opposite of
Justice Johnson's *Elkison* opinion. Taney added, anticipating his
Dred Scott opinion of twenty years later, that free blacks could not
be citizens of the United States and hence could not claim the
protection of federal courts.[60]

This background of controversy permeated the *Miln* opinion.
Chief Justice Taney assigned the majority opinion to his Virginia
colleague, Philip Pendleton Barbour, who simply avoided the commerce-clause–police-power conflict by holding that the New York
statute was not a regulation of commerce at all, but merely an
exercise of the police power. Barbour, however, affirmed the extent
of state police power in the broadest terms and hinted that anything
falling in the police power category lay outside the scope of federal
regulatory power: "all those powers which relate to merely municipal legislation, or what may, perhaps, more properly be called internal police, are not thus surrendered or restrained; and that, consequently, in relation to these, the authority of a state is complete,
unqualified, and exclusive."[61] This was too much for Justices Story
and Smith Thompson of New York. Story dissented, holding the
state act unconstitutional as an interference with commerce, and
Thompson concurred on the grounds that state regulation was valid
but only because there was no conflicting federal regulation. This
division on the court suggested that any case challenging state
power to control the entry of obnoxious persons, substances, or
ideas would prove to be controversial and difficult.

This was borne out a decade later in the *License Cases,* a group of
companion cases from three New England states presenting questions of the states' power to control the sale of liquor. Prohibition
became a contentious social-reform issue in the 1840s when the

[60]*Official Opinions of the Attorneys-General,* II, 427–442 (1852); Taney's ms. draft
reprinted in Carl B. Swisher, "Mr. Chief Justice Taney," in Allison Dunham and
Philip B. Kurland (eds.), *Mr. Justice* (Chicago, 1964), pp. 43–45.
[61]11 Pet. (36 U.S.) 102 (1837) at 139.

temperance movement was challenged by "cold-water" prohibi-
tionists who sought to outlaw alcoholic beverages, not just persuade
people to drink less of them. Chief Justice Shaw of the Massachusetts Supreme Judicial Court upheld Massachusetts' prohibition
statute under the police power rationale.[62] The question would not
have touched off intense controversy in the United States Supreme
Court but for two complications. First, prohibition interfered with
rights in existing property and with the expectation of future profits
from a business hitherto legitimate. This posed higher-law questions irresistible to conservative jurists and attorneys, including
those New Englanders who represented liquor interests in these
cases, including Daniel Webster and Rufus Choate. Second, the
Negro Seamen's Act controversy intruded itself in these cases. Boston merchants demanded repeal of the Seamen's Acts. They
memorialized Congress, and when that produced no results, the
Massachusetts General Court commissioned two distinguished, elderly political figures, Samuel Hoar and Henry Hubbard, to go to
South Carolina and Louisiana to seek repeal of the obnoxious legislation. Hubbard was threatened with lynching on arrival, and Hoar
was condemned in Charleston as a mad incendiary. Daniel Webster,
in his *License Cases* arguments, pointed out the connection between
Louisiana's desire to control the ingress of dangerous ideas and
Massachusetts' desire to control liquor, and incautiously invited the
Court to speak to that issue as well.[63]

Webster's invitation was unnecessary. The justices were so eager
to take up the issue that six of the eight sitting (McKinley was off
on circuit) wrote opinions.[64] Out of this plethora of views, no doctrine at all emerged, and scarcely any result, though the New England laws had not been struck down. The *License Cases* lack doctrinal significance, and are merely evidence of a Court badly divided
on unaddressed questions looming in the background.

The Court's inability to coalesce on doctrine is usually a sign of
controversial issues and a fluctuating state of the law caused by
intense social or economic conflicts. This became obvious when,
two years later, the Court once again slogged through the *Miln* and

---

[62]Commonwealth *v.* Kimball, 24 Pick. (41 Mass.) 359 (1837).
[63]Charleston [S.C.] *Courier*, Feb. 5, 1845, as quoted in Swisher, *Taney Period*, p. 371.
[64]*License* cases, 5 How. (46 U.S.) 504 (1847).

License Cases issues, with even less coherence—if that was possible. New York and Massachusetts had respectively taxed incoming passengers to support a marine hospital and permitted inspection and exclusion of immigrants who were diseased or mentally incompetent. Eight opinions reflected a 5–4 split on the court in the *Passenger Cases*, [65] but this time the majority held the statutes unconstitutional. The number of opinions in a case and the doctrinal clarity of the result bear an inverse relationship to each other, so it was again not possible to assess the significance of the cases, except as an indication that the Court was not going to produce any usable commerce-clause interpretations unless it could filter out slavery complications from commerce and police power issues.

The justices managed to do this in 1851 when, for the last time, the Taney Court was once again able to balance the claims of technological innovation against the expectations of investors and to mediate among conflicting regional economic interests. The Court's final contribution of constructive lawmaking began with *Cooley* v. *Board of Wardens of the Port of Philadelphia* (1851), where the Court dealt sensibly with a genuine commerce-clause question: Did local harbor pilotage regulations, including fees exacted for pilotage services, interfere with Congress's paramount authority over interstate and foreign commerce? Speaking through Justice Benjamin R. Curtis, the Court held that it did not. [66] Curtis drew a statesmanlike and long-lived distinction between national and local subjects of concern, the former "imperatively demanding a single uniform rule, operating equally on the commerce of the United States in every port; and some . . . as imperatively demanding that diversity, which alone can meet the local necessities of navigation." Hence, when the subjects of regulation "are in their nature national, or admit only of one uniform system," Congress's power was exclusive; but when local, as with pilotage, the states could regulate. Justices Wayne and John McLean dissented, insisting congressional regulation was exclusive, while at the opposite pole, Justice Daniel concurred on the grounds that the states' power to regulate on this subject was unimpeded by any national regulatory power. *Cooley*, like *Bank of Augusta* v. *Earle*, struck a sensible balance between the

[65] 7 How. (48 U.S.) 283 (1849).
[66] 12 How. (53 U.S.) 299 (1851) at 319.

extremes expressed in the dissents and concurrence, and provided the basis for an ongoing adjustment of the federal balance.

The Court took up another case having overtones of *Charles River Bridge* a few years later, one that reflected regional commercial rivalry and the competition between two technologies. To link the Cumberland Road on either side of the Ohio River at Wheeling, the Virginia legislature authorized construction of the Wheeling Bridge. Western Pennsylvania economic interests contested this, because the Cumberland Road would tie the commerce of the western states to an eastern depot at Baltimore. But if the road could remain effectively truncated by the river, linked only by a ferry that was interrupted by flood and ice, the lucrative western trade would be diverted northward to Pittsburgh and thence, via a chain of railroads and canals, to Harrisburg and Philadelphia. The bridge symbolized another struggle as well: if Pennsylvania was successful in forcing the bridge to be dismantled, the result would give an impetus to waterborne transportation, like that going to Pittsburgh on the Ohio River; but if the bridge stood, it would enable trains to capture much of the market for canal and river commerce.

Pennsylvania's petition for an injunction was heard by the Supreme Court in its original jurisdiction because a state was a party. Justice McLean found that the bridge did obstruct navigation on the Ohio, and ordered its erectors to raise or remove it.[67] Taney and Daniel dissented sharply, Taney insisting that there was no national regulation available to provide the basis for the Court's action. Though it provided no long-lived doctrine, the *Wheeling Bridge* case was a controversial case in its time. Bridge and railroad interests persuaded Congress to enact legislation declaring that the bridge was a lawful structure at its prelitigation height, thus providing the congressional declaration of policy that Taney said was missing, and invalidating McLean's majority opinion. A year later a storm destroyed the bridge, and when the company rebuilt it, Pennsylvania again tried to abate it. But this time the court held that Congress had precluded further judicial action.[68]

[67]Pennsylvania *v.* Wheeling and Belmont Bridge Co., 13 How. (54 U.S.) 518 (1852).
[68]Pennsylvania *v.* Wheeling and Belmont Bridge Co., 18 How. (59 U.S.) 421 (1856).

In cases untouched by slavery, Roger Taney and his associates molded early American constitutional law to an extent comparable to the Marshall Court. Taney's modification of the trajectory of Marshall's doctrine in contracts-clause cases provided a necessary balance to constitutional growth in that area. Taney promoted a dynamic, viable relationship between state regulatory power, based ultimately on the principle of popular sovereignty, and the powers of corporations which rested on higher-law assumptions about the place of property and contracts in the American constitutional order.

Taney gave life to two new doctrinal concepts, police power and political questions. Though both had been foreshadowed in decisions of the Marshall Court, the Taney Court called them into being. Both were potentially healthy checks on the abuse of judicial power, the police-power idea stressing the regulatory power of the legislature and the political-question doctrine serving as a reminder to judges that power, law, and order derive ultimately from the people and depend for their legitimacy on the people's consent.

The Taney Court also coped successfully with the emergence of the corporation, especially corporations doing multistate business, and with the gush of technological innovation. In these areas, Taney proved to have had as much vision as his predecessor, but a more reliable sense of balance and limits. His most useful service consisted of inhibiting conservative pretensions to unchecked corporate power. Investors of the time, abetted by counsel like Daniel Webster, desired corporations virtually free of regulatory restraint, almost having attributes of sovereignty. In asserting the power of the states to regulate, provided they do so explicitly, Taney preserved both popular sovereignty and the rule of law.

The Taney decisions construing the commerce clause were far less successful because of the polluting influence of slavery. Taney there bent the healthy doctrine of police power to serve the slave states' demands for internal security against the dangers of freedom. But in so doing, Taney, Daniel, and others warped the development of commerce-clause doctrine. They thereby lost an opportunity to clarify and inhibit the potential excesses of Marshall's and Johnson's opinions in *Gibbons* v. *Ogden,* and left commerce-clause development awash, to be brought around only after the Civil War.

If Roger Taney was not the giant Marshall was, neither was he the pygmy portrayed by his critics during and after the war. To the extent that he appears so, it is only because the intensity of his devotion to the welfare of slavery forced lapses in his judgment, aberrations of an otherwise sure instinct for constitutional statesmanship. Roger Taney, not his abolitionist contemnors, was his own worst enemy.

CHAPTER 4

The Nemesis of the Constitution: Slavery in the Courts

THE peculiar institution that dogged the achievements of Chief Justice Taney was not a new feature on the American constitutional landscape. It had been recognized by law in several mainland English colonies by the late seventeenth century. The colonies did not create slavery by statute, but they, and later the states, regulated it both by statute and by common law.[1] The law of slavery and its constitutional impact spread throughout the new nation along with the black men and women who were its primary victims. But it is incorrect to think of the United States at its semicentennial as being neatly divided between slave states and free. The very terms themselves were misleading, a complaint southerners often made.

The demographic reality of American slavery in Taney's day, and consequently its politico-constitutional influence, is better conveyed by a chiaroscuro. Patterns of black population density relative to white correlate with constitutional attitudes toward slavery and provide one of the suggestive ways of explaining the dynamics of the American political system of the 1850s. The demographic model also strikingly depicts the pattern of success and failure of the secessionist impulse in 1861.

[1]William M. Wiecek, "The Statutory Law of Slavery and Race in the Thirteen Mainland Colonies of British America," *William and Mary Quarterly,* XXXIV (1977), 258–280; A. Leon Higginbotham, *In the Matter of Color: Race and the American Legal Process: The Colonial Period* (New York, 1978), chs. 1–7.

The darkest part of this black population pattern denotes not only the densest black population but also the corresponding zone of slavery's greatest economic importance, and whites' most pervasive dedication to slavery. It ran in a band from tidewater Virginia down into South Carolina and Georgia and then into the Black Belt of Alabama and Mississippi and on to Louisiana. A bit lighter were Florida, parts of Virginia, Tennessee, North Carolina, Arkansas, and Texas. A third zone, the middle of the spectrum, was represented by the border states of Delaware, Maryland, Kentucky, western Virginia, and Missouri, plus the mountainous regions of southern Appalachia, where slavery enjoyed a legal existence. But its actual strength in the border and mountain regions was diluted by the limited size of the enslaved black population, a relatively large free black population in some areas, proximity to free states, or large segments of a nonslaveholding white population hostile to slavery or to the political power of the Democratic Establishment in the state. The fourth region, lighter but with a still-discernibly dark element, included the regions adjacent to the border states. In these areas, slavery was abolished, but large segments of the white population remained sympathetic to the anxieties of the slave states. These areas included southern Indiana, Ohio, and Illinois, New Jersey, and New York City (the last included here for commercial, not geographic reasons). The last zone in the United States is the remainder of the northern states—Wisconsin, Michigan, upper Ohio, Illinois, Indiana, upstate and western New York, virtually all of Pennsylvania and all of New England (though with Connecticut visibly splotched)—where blacks were few and where antislavery made some headway. Finally, British Canada represented the only zone on the North American continent of absolute freedom; only there could black people go to sleep at night with their doors unlocked.

Slavery and freedom were relative everywhere in America. Though Henry David Thoreau and William Lloyd Garrison exaggerated when they called Massachusetts a slave state, their harsh name is a reminder that a black person could be a slave there or in any of the other "free" states because of the constitutional protection afforded by the federal and state constitutions for masters' rights in fugitive and sojourning slaves. Southerners and one sect of abolitionists insisted the North not close its eyes to that fact.

Spokesmen for slaveowners insisted that only by a reliable respect for the continuation of the slave relationship throughout the United States, including all the territories, could slaveowners actually enjoy true equality with the owners of all other kinds of property. Anything less would be discrimination. As slaveowners came to see themselves the victims of such discrimination in the 1840s and 1850s, they became ever more insistent on political and constitutional guarantees for the security of their peculiar institution at home, in the western territories, and in the free states.

At the time of Independence, slavery was part of the American legal order. But a recent decision by the highest common-law court in England left Americans with a judicial legacy that eventually unsettled slavery's legal status. In *Somerset* v. *Stewart* (1772), William Murray, Baron Mansfield, the Chief Justice of King's Bench, rendered an opinion about the law of slavery that molded American constitutional development for ninety years.[2] The case involved an American slave, brought by his master to England for a temporary sojourn, who ran away but was recaptured by his master and consigned for sale to Jamaica. English emancipationists got a writ of habeas corpus[3] on his behalf, hoping to have Mansfield declare slavery illegitimate in Britain. Instead, Mansfield freed Somerset on the basis of two narrower, though significant, points of law. First, where a court must choose between competing systems of law to apply in a slavery case before it, it will follow the law of its own jurisdiction rather than the foreign law of the slave's domicile. Second, and more broadly, slavery is "so odious, that nothing can be suffered to support it but positive law." *Somerset* promptly passed into the mainstream of American law, where it influenced the workings of the federal system and left slavery vulnerable to legal challenge.

Even before 1787, slavery's place in the American constitutional order was ordained by two correlative assumptions: except in a few

[2]Somerset v. Stewart, Lofft 1, 98 Eng. Rep. 499 (K.B. 1772). See William M. Wiecek, *"Somerset:* Lord Mansfield and the Legitimacy of Slavery in the Anglo-American World," *University of Chicago Law Review,* XLII (1974), 86–146.

[3]The writ of habeas corpus is the single most important procedural guaranty of personal liberty in the Anglo-American legal tradition, and is accordingly known as "the Great Writ." Technically known as the writ of habeas corpus ad subjiciendum, it is a command from a court to someone detaining another person to bring the detainee before the court to test the legality of his detention.

specified matters, the federal government had no authority over the "domestic institutions" of the states, including slavery. Consequently, only the states could exercise any form of control over slavery in their jurisdictions.[4] This understanding later proved insufficient for the task of resolving the constitutional complications presented by slavery. But before that failure became apparent, the federal government established important precedents that enhanced slavery's place in American life.

The Philadelphia Convention of 1787 was twice beset by confrontations over slavery. James Madison and Gouverneur Morris both noted that slavery formed the real basis of divisions at the convention, not the split between large and small or "landed" versus "landless" states. Twice the Convention reached impasses that threatened to destroy any possibility of sectional agreement on the new Constitution. They were resolved by an intricate package of "compromises" that produced not only the three well-known slavery clauses of the Constitution but seven others as well, all inserted to enhance the political power of slavery. These were:

1. Article I, section 2: representatives in the House were apportioned among the states on the basis of population, computed by counting all free persons and three-fifths of the slaves (the "federal number" or "three-fifths" clause);

2. Article I, section 2, and Article I, section 9: two clauses required, redundantly, that direct taxes (including capitations) be apportioned among the states on the foregoing basis, the purpose being to prevent Congress from laying a head tax on slaves to encourage their emancipation;

3. Article I, section 9: Congress was prohibited from abolishing the international slave trade to the United States before 1808;

4. Article IV, section 2: the states were prohibited from emancipating fugitive slaves, who were to be returned on demand of the master;

5. Article I, section 8: Congress was empowered to provide for calling up the states' militias to suppress insurrections, including slave uprisings;

6. Article IV, section 4: the federal government was obliged to protect the states against domestic violence, again including slave insurrections;

7. Article V: the provisions of Article I, section 9, clauses 1 and 4 (pertaining to the slave trade and direct taxes) were made unamendable;

8. Article I, section 9, and Article I, section 10: these two clauses prohibited the federal government and the states from taxing exports, one pur-

---

[4]Wiecek, *Sources of Antislavery Constitutionalism, passim.*

pose being to prevent them from taxing slavery indirectly by taxing the exported products of slave labor.[5]

The Confederation Congress meeting simultaneously in New York enacted the Northwest Ordinance of 1787. In its celebrated sixth article, the Ordinance prohibited slavery in the Northwest Territory—the modern states of Ohio, Indiana, Illinois, Michigan, Wisconsin, and a small segment of eastern Minnesota. The same provision, in a clause vaguely similar to the Constitution's, permitted reclamation of fugitive slaves.[6] Though the Ordinance forbade slavery north of the Ohio River, it was a tacit permission for slavery to expand into the western lands south of the river.[7]

In 1793 Congress enacted the first Fugitive Slave Act.[8] Implementing the fugitive-slave clause of the Constitution, the statute provided that an owner or agent could seize an alleged runaway slave and bring him before a federal judge or local magistrate. Upon affidavit or oral testimony, the claimant would then receive a certificate of rendition authorizing him to remove the black to the master's domicile. In 1801 Congress enacted a slave code for the District of Columbia.[9] While Congress thus secured slavery, the original states north of Maryland began gradually abolishing it by *post-nati* and apprenticeship statutes providing that children born to a slave mother after a certain date, usually the Fourth of July, would be free but had to serve as apprentices to their mother's master to a certain age.[10]

[5]*Ibid.*, pp. 62–63.

[6]Art. VI, Northwest Ordinance, in Thorpe, *Federal and State Constitutions*, II, 962: "There shall be neither slavery nor involuntary servitude in the said territory, otherwise than in punishment of crimes whereof the party shall have been duly convicted: Provided, always, That any person escaping into the same, from whom labor or service is lawfully claimed in any one of the original States, such fugitive may be lawfully reclaimed and conveyed to the person claiming his or her labor or service as aforesaid."

[7]Staughton Lynd, "The Compromise of 1787" (1966), reprinted in Lynd, *Class Conflict, Slavery, and the United States Constitution* (Indianapolis, 1967), pp. 185–213.

[8]Act of Feb. 12, 1793, ch. 7, 1 Stat. 302.

[9]Act of Feb. 27, 1801, ch. 15, 2 Stat. 103. Congress here acted in its capacity as the legislative body for the District. The District code was supplemented by a body of regulations drawn up by the Corporation of the City, which derived its legislative authority from Congress. For the entire corpus of D.C. slave law, see the unofficial but thorough compilation: *The Slavery Code of the District of Columbia* (Washington, 1862).

[10]Arthur Zilversmit, *The First Emancipation: The Abolition of Slavery in the North* (Chi-

After a generation of relative quiescence, the slavery controversy flared again in 1819 when Missourians demanded that their territory be admitted as a slave state. The first Missouri controversy (1819–20) concerned the power of Congress to exclude slavery from the territories and require its prohibition as a condition of admitting new states. The second (1820–21) involved the power of states to exclude free blacks and provoked an exhaustive congressional review of the constitutional status of slavery and black people. Congress finally admitted Missouri as a slave state and excluded slavery from the remainder of the Louisiana Purchase territory north of it. But both sections had been alerted to the constitutional implications of slavery's westward expansion.

As the furor over Missouri was dying down, white South Carolinians in 1822 found themselves propelled into a dynamic new defense of slavery by the real or imagined slave uprising led by Denmark Vesey. The momentum of events convinced first the Carolinians, then most other white southerners, that they faced a serious threat to the internal security of slavery. In debates over Missouri's admission, southerners heard a few northern representatives put forth constitutional and policy arguments for the first time that implicitly challenged the legitimacy of slavery itself, not just its expansion across the Mississippi River. After Vesey, Carolinians linked slave insurrections with northern attitudes toward slavery. An unwelcome northern interest in using federal funds to promote colonization of free blacks, Virginia debates in 1829 and 1831 on the gradual abolition of slavery in the Old Dominion, and the constitutional clashes that led to the nullification crisis of 1832, all contributed to southern unease. The publication of black abolitionist David Walker's *Appeal to the Colored Citizens of the World* (1829), which hinted at violent slave resistance, the formation of the New-England Anti-Slavery Society (1831) and the American Anti-Slavery Society (1833), the appearance of William Lloyd Garrison's *Liberator* (1831), and British West Indian emancipation (1833) confirmed Carolinians in their fears and made some converts among other southerners. Nat Turner's bloody 1831 slave insurrection in southern Virginia seemed to cap a sinister progress of ideas that challenged the security of American slave societies.

---

cago, 1967); *post-nati* = "born-after."

These southern fears were not all fantasies. In the 1830s the slave states found themselves confronting a revitalized, resourceful antislavery movement. As part of their many-faceted argument, abolitionists turned to the American Constitution and began exploring possibilities for a legal and constitutional challenge to slavery. By 1845, three groups of abolitionists had articulated widely differing approaches to the problem of slavery and the Constitution. For shorthand purposes, they will be referred to as radical, moderate, and Garrisonian abolitionists.[11]

The radicals' principal publicists included New York lawyer Alvan Stewart, Boston freethinker and lawyer Lysander Spooner, and the itinerant reform editor William Goodell. After 1840, they marshaled their ideas around the central thesis that slavery was everywhere illegitimate. They therefore demanded that the federal government abolish slavery in the states, discarding what had been until then the universal assumption that the federal government lacked such power. Stewart and the others maintained that slavery violated the Fifth Amendment's due process guarantee, the Article IV guarantee of republican government, and various other clauses of the federal and state Constitutions.[12] Since the Revolution, they reasoned, the American Constitution had somehow become perverted by acquiescence in proslavery custom. Its true antislavery character could be redeemed by federal action.

Such ideas never won the support of more than a small fragment of organized abolition. The political and constitutional mainstream of the antislavery movement, led by western abolitionists like Salmon P. Chase, a Cincinnati attorney, rejected the radicals' view that slavery was innately illegitimate. They clung to the assumption that the federal government lacked power over slavery, and improved on that idea by claiming that the correlative to a lack of

[11]The next few paragraphs summarize the argument of Wiecek, *Sources of Antislavery Constitutionalism,* chs. 9–11.

[12]Compendia of radical thought include: Luther R. Marsh (ed.), *Writings and Speeches of Alvan Stewart, on Slavery* (New York, 1860); Lysander Spooner, *The Unconstitutionality of Slavery,* 4th ed. (Boston, 1860); William Goodell, *Views of American Constitutional Law, in Its Bearing upon American Slavery* (Utica, 1844); James G. Birney, "Can Congress, Under the Constitution, Abolish Slavery in the States?" newspaper articles, May, 1847, reprinted in Jacobus ten Broek, *Equal Under Law* (New York, 1965), pp. 296–319; Joel Tiffany, *A Treatise on the Unconstitutionality of American Slavery. . . .* (Cleveland, 1849).

federal power to abolish it anywhere was a lack of federal power to establish it. The moderates' constitutional thought shaded off into a political program having as its principal plank something they referred to as "divorcement." They wanted to separate slavery from its support by the federal government, so that, deprived of federal shelter, it would wither in the states where it existed. Sensing the widespread appeal of the Free-Soil idea, as it was embodied in the Wilmot Proviso, after 1846 moderates promoted fusion with disgruntled Whigs and Democrats on a Free-Soil platform, and in time became one of the principal groups that formed the Republican party.

The third, and most widely misunderstood, of the abolitionist group was composed of William Lloyd Garrison and his associates. Their foremost legal thinker was Wendell Phillips.[13] Garrisonians developed their political and constitutional theories out of the religious doctrine of perfectionism and the ecclesiastical tactic of disunion, both of which persuaded them that any participation in organizations that condoned slaveholding was sinful. Since they could easily demonstrate that the United States Constitution directly supported slavery in at least three different ways, they concluded that it was, in the words of Isaiah, a "covenant with death."[14] They called upon individuals to disavow their allegiance to the United States government and demanded that northern states secede from the Union, which they saw as a bulwark of slavery. Their belief in the proslavery character of the Constitution was symbolized in the famous incident of 1854 when Garrison held aloft a copy of the document and set fire to it.

Throughout the 1830s and 1840s, abolitionists had ample opportunity to test their evolving theories in state and federal courts. After 1830, cases involving the status of free blacks, slaves, and their white benefactors were tried and appealed at all judicial levels in the United States, from justice of the peace courts in obscure northern

[13]Glimpses of Garrisonian thought at one particular date or another can be caught in [Wendell Phillips (ed.)], *The Constitution a Pro-Slavery Compact, or Selections from the Madison Papers* (New York, 1844); "Constitutionality of Slavery," *Massachusetts Quarterly Review*, IV (1848), 463–509; William I. Bowditch, *Slavery and the Constitution* (Boston, 1849). But the best sense of the development of Garrisonian ideas over time can be gained only from the files of *The Liberator*, 1831–65.
[14]Isaiah 28:18.

hamlets all the way to the United States Supreme Court. In these cases, abolitionists encountered three pervasive judicial attitudes affecting blacks: racism, expressing itself in unquestioned assumptions that blacks could be assigned an inferior civil status in northern society simply because of their race; positivism, manifest as a firm refusal by judges to modify law, whether statutory or judge-made, to conform to appeals of conscience; and a proslavery bias that held most justices of the United States Supreme Court, as well as some lower federal court judges, in an iron grasp. Frequently, however, abolitionists also found northern state judges determined not to permit slavery to extend its reach into the free states.

Abolitionists' earliest judicial encounter with the collision of race and law involved not slaves, but free native blacks in the northern states. The 1820–21 Missouri controversy over the rights, privileges, and immunities of free blacks had already served notice that the anomalous status of black people who were not slaves would raise constitutional issues. A decade later, these questions were aired extensively in the Connecticut prosecution of Prudence Crandall. In 1832, Crandall, who ran a school for girls in the eastern Connecticut village of Canterbury, began to accept black pupils into her classes. When white parents objected, she converted her school to one exclusively for blacks. Indignant neighbors harassed her in petty ways and got the General Assembly to enact the so-called Connecticut Black Law, which prohibited anyone from running a school for nonresident blacks without first obtaining consent of the local selectmen and town meeting. Crandall, a stubborn Quaker who was supported by Massachusetts, Rhode Island, Connecticut, and New York abolitionists, refused to close her school and was convicted of violation of the statute. Although her conviction was later reversed on a technicality by the Connecticut Supreme Court, mob violence eventually forced the closing of the school, but not before abolitionists and supporters of the statute clashed in the courts over the relevance of the privileges and immunities clause of Article IV, section 2, to free blacks.

Arguments in the *Crandall* case turned on the question whether free blacks were "Citizens" within the meaning of that clause. Citizenship at the time was a poorly defined relationship between the individual and the state, centering on a reciprocal set of obligations: the individual owed allegiance to the state and obedience to its laws;

the state owed protection to the individual. But who citizens were and how citizenship was obtained were vexed questions, unsettled in the United States until ratification of the Fourteenth Amendment after the Civil War.[15] The question was even more complicated in the American federal system, where the same person might (or might not be) a citizen of both the state and the nation. Did citizenship of the one confer citizenship of the other? What rights accompanied either, and did they pertain to both? If free blacks were not citizens, the Black Law did not run into constitutional difficulties under the privileges and immunities clause, the position taken by the prosecuting attorney and a judge of the Supreme Court of Errors.[16] Abolitionists, on the other hand, maintained alternative positions on black citizenship. Either citizenship in any state conferred a national citizenship, or it conferred citizenship in every other state. Either way, blacks qualified as "Citizens" and were presumably immune from discrimination against them in another state.[17]

The Crandall episode ended inconclusively; not so the struggles over denial of the vote to blacks in Pennsylvania five years later. In *Hobbs* v. *Fogg* (1837),[18] Chief Judge John Bannister Gibson, one of the most distinguished jurists of the nineteenth century, disfranchised Pennsylvania's blacks on the grounds that a black was not a "freeman" as that term was used in the 1790 Pennsylvania Constitution. In an unsupported opinion that did no credit to his reputation, Gibson confessed that the result was determined by his personal race prejudice, and cited no authority for his unprecedented holding except an unnamed, unreported opinion decided years earlier and surviving only in the recollection of a member of the bar. Despite these weaknesses, the result of Gibson's opinion was popular, and a state constitutional convention sitting contemporaneously ratified Gibson's decision by explicitly restricting the vote to whites. In Massachusetts, Lemuel Shaw was also swayed by racial precon-

[15]See generally James H. Kettner, *The Development of American Citizenship, 1608–1870* (Chapel Hill, 1978).
[16]Arguments are set forth in *Andrew T. Judson's Remarks, to the Jury, on the Trial of the Case, State v. P. Crandall . . .* (Hartford, [1833]) and in State *v.* Crandall, 10 Conn. 339 (1834).
[17][Chauncey F. Cleveland], *Report of the Arguments of Counsel in the Case of . . . Crandall . . . v. State . . .* (Boston, 1834).
[18]6 Watts 553 (Pa. 1834).

ceptions when faced with a black challenge to racial segregation in the public schools of Boston. For more than twenty years, Boston had supported a separate and increasingly unequal grade school for black children, originally with the approval of their parents. But black dissatisfaction with segregated status, the deteriorating condition of the colored school and its distance from the homes of some of its pupils, and the exuberance of organized abolition in Boston produced a challenge to the constitutionality of school segregation under the provisions of Articles I and VI of the Massachusetts Constitution of 1780, providing that "all men are born free and equal" and prohibiting the grant of "particular and exclusive privileges."[19] In arguments before the Supreme Judicial Court, Whig political figure and egalitarian lawyer Charles Sumner maintained that segregation of itself conflicted with the principle of equality before the law and argued that segregation was psychologically harmful for both races. He claimed that "any institution founded on inequality or caste" violated the Massachusetts Constitution.[20]

Unimpressed, Shaw held in *Roberts* v. *City of Boston* (1849) that the school board had power to segregate schoolchildren by race.[21] He offered an alternate conception of legal equality to that suggested by Sumner. Conceding that "all persons without distinction of age or sex, birth or color, origin or condition, are equal before the law," Shaw held that "when this great principle comes to be applied to the actual and various conditions of persons in society," it did not abolish distinctions between men and women or adults and children. Rather, in Shaw's meaningless formulation, it meant that "the rights of all, as they are settled and regulated by law, are equally entitled to the paternal consideration and protection of the law." The legislature could give or withhold rights, and could do so on the basis of arbitrary categories such as race. Shaw dismissed abolitionist egalitarianism:

What those rights are, to which individuals, in the infinite variety of circumstances by which they are surrounded in society, are entitled, must depend on laws adapted to their respective relations and conditions.

[19]Thorpe, *Federal and State Constitutions,* III, 1889–1890.
[20]*Argument of Charles Sumner, Esq. Against the Constitutionality of Separate Colored Schools, in the Case of . . . Roberts vs. the City of Boston . . .* (Boston, 1849), p. 26.
[21]5 Cush. (59 Mass.) 198 (1849) at 206.

In the short run, blacks and abolitionists had the last say, in the Bay State at least. In the fervor of feeling aroused by fugitive-slave recaptures in Boston and repeal of the Missouri Compromise, the General Court prohibited racial segregation by statute in 1855. But the ghost of Shaw's *Roberts* opinion stalked throughout the late nineteenth century, and on into the twentieth, being invoked to bolster the constitutionality of Jim Crow schools and the legal doctrine of separate-but-equal. It was not laid to rest until *Brown* v. *Board of Education* in 1954.[22]

Enslaved blacks posed just as much of a problem for free-state jurists—and just as much an opportunity for abolitionists—as did free blacks in the 1840s. Slavery lingered on in some of the free states. Those where it persisted had enacted gradual emancipation statutes after the Revolution. Because such statutes freed only children born after a specified date, extant slaves remained unaffected, and the freed children were held in apprenticeship until some time in their adult years. New Jersey typified these reluctant states: it began the gradual abolition of slavery in 1804 with a *post-nati* act, freeing the children born to slave mothers after July 4 of that year; the child so freed would be "apprenticed" to its mother's owner, men until age twenty-five, women until twenty-one. The state also prohibited the kidnapping of free blacks and, in 1837, enacted a personal liberty law guaranteeing jury trials to alleged fugitive slaves. Then, in 1844, New Jersey amended its Revolutionary-era Constitution and adopted a Bill of Rights with a first article patterned on the classic Virginia and Massachusetts provisions, stating that "all men are by nature free and independent."

Interpreting this literally, abolitionist Alvan Stewart brought two companion test cases, one on behalf of a person who was a slave before 1804 and the other on behalf of a slave's child still apprenticed, seeking a declaration that the new constitution had abolished slavery. This argument had some force in the Quock Walker cases sixty years earlier, where similar reasoning had contributed to the speedy dissipation of slavery in Massachusetts. In these cases (1781–83), Chief Justice William Cushing of the Massachusetts Supreme Judicial Court was supposed to have held that slavery was incompatible with the free-and-equal provision of the Massachu-

---

[22]Levy, *Law of the Commonwealth and Chief Justice Shaw*, ch. 7, "Segregation."

setts Constitution of 1780.[23] In 1806, Virginia's venerable Chancellor George Wythe, under whom Thomas Jefferson had studied law, similarly construed the Virginia Declaration of Rights' Article I, the ancestor of the Massachusetts and New Jersey provisions, asserting that "freedom is the birthright of every human being, which sentiment is strongly inculcated in the first article of our 'political catechism,' the bill of rights." However, the Virginia Supreme Court of Appeals, on review, repudiated Wythe's statement as it pertained to blacks.[24]

But New Jersey blacks and their abolitionist friends were disappointed by the New Jersey court, which held that adoption of the free-and-independent provision did not abolish property rights or derange the social order. A majority of the New Jersey court—its most distinguished member, Chief Judge Joseph C. Hornblower, dissented without opinion—shrugged off the pivotal words as "certain general phrases of abstract natural right," and chided Stewart for appealing "to the feelings [rather] than to the legal intelligence of the court." The judges asserted that the constitutional convention that adopted the free-and-independent language "never designed to apply this language to man in his private, individual or domestic capacity."[25] The judges' distinction between "feelings" and "legal intelligence" was basic to northern judges' response to abolitionist arguments that slavery or its incidents violated the law of God or was inconsistent with the spirit of the Declaration of Independence. Such arguments, judges reproved abolitionist attorneys, were appeals to conscience or emotion, not to the laws that the judges were sworn to uphold.[26]

Apart from the moribund forms of residual slavery like New Jersey's, slaves might be found in northern states in one of two legal capacities: as runaways, or as "sojourners," slaves accompanying

[23]See John D. Cushing, "The Cushing Court and the Abolition of Slavery in Massachusetts: More Notes on the Quock Walker Case," *American Journal of Legal History*, V (1961), 118–144.

[24]Hudgins v. Wrights, 1 Hen. & M. 134 (Va. 1806).

[25]State v. Post and State v. Van Buren, 20 N.J. Law 368 (1845); Stewart's position is set forth at length in "Argument, On the Question Whether the New Constitution of 1844 Abolished Slavery in New Jersey," in Marsh (ed.), *Writings and Speeches of Alvan Stewart, On Slavery*, pp. 272–367.

[26]See Robert Cover, *Justice Accused: Antislavery and the Judicial Process* (New Haven, 1975).

their masters who were either passing through a free state or were there for a temporary residence. In either status, they were residents of another state, and thus raised the conflicts-of-laws questions broached in *Somerset*.[27] Sojourning slaves were common in certain areas of the north: at summer vacation areas like Saratoga Springs, at centers of commerce and shipping like New York City, at border ports like Cincinnati, and along major migration routes from the upper South to Missouri. In Boston suburbs activist abolitionist women found a slave girl, Med, six years old, accompanying her vacationing mistress, and secured attorneys to procure a writ of habeas corpus on her behalf. The resulting litigation was widely reported; Justice Story even expected it would be appealed to the United States Supreme Court.[28]

It was not, however. Med's case, formally titled *Commonwealth v. Aves* (1836), received its final disposition before Chief Justice Shaw. Shaw responded to the abolitionist challenge as Mansfield had in *Somerset*. Both men were conservatives; both feared the radical implications of arguments made by the slave's attorneys; both regretted the notoriety the case attained outside the court. But both were determined to dispose of it strictly by positive law. The result in both was a victory for slavery's foes. In *Med*, Shaw, unlike the New Jersey Court that same year, read the free-and-equal provisions of the Massachusetts Constitution as "precisely adapted to the abolition of negro slavery." Slavery could have been established in Massachusetts only by positive law, and there was no sojourners' statute permitting a visiting slaveholder to keep someone enslaved. As to arguments that Massachusetts ought to protect property relationships created by the laws of a sister state as a matter of comity, Shaw held that comity in Massachusetts' court extended only to property in things, not in humans. *Med* was as close as an American court ever came to completely absorbing *Somerset,* a fact recognized by the little girl's benefactresses, who renamed her "Med Maria Sommersett."[29]

[27]Conflicts of laws is defined as "that branch of jurisprudence . . . which . . . decides which law or system is to govern in the particular case, or settles the degree of force to be accorded to the law of another jurisdiction . . . either where it varies from the domestic law, or where the domestic law is silent or not exclusively applicable to the case in point." *Black's Law Dictionary,* 5th ed., "Conflict of Laws."
[28]Levy, *Law of the Commonwealth and Chief Justice Shaw,* ch. 5, "The Law of Freedom."
[29]Commonwealth v. Aves, 18 Pick. (35 Mass.) 193 (1836); see to the same effect,

Conflicts of laws and comity provided two bundles of doctrines to states dealing with questions of the status of slaves who were domiciled in another state. But America was a federal Union, and the problem of extradomiciliary slaves was a national one, too. In fact, under the federal Constitution, only extradomiciliary slaves could properly be the concern of any of the three branches of the federal government. Hence, despite slavery's importance to the national economy, few slavery cases came before the United States Supreme Court, and few federal statutes dealt with slavery during the first half-century of the Republic. But the intensification of the slavery controversy in the 1830s meant that Court and Congress would be hearing a good deal more about slavery. While state courts still remained important forums where the status of slaves would continue to be litigated, the federal courts were drawn relentlessly into the controversy.

The earliest slavery cases before the United States Supreme Court involved the application of international law and potentially raised the choice-of-law issues touched on in the *Somerset* case. In a United States Circuit Court decision of 1822, Joseph Story condemned the international slave trade as inconsistent with "the general principles of justice and humanity."[30] But the United States Supreme Court repudiated that position. John Marshall held in *The Antelope* that the maritime powers had legitimized the international slave trade by positive law. Marshall did, however, adopt the *Somerset* principle that slavery could be established only by positive law, though he stated that this could include customary, as well as statutory, law.[31] Marshall's holding and dicta left unresolved the question of what laws would be applied to adjudicate the status of slaves and the powers of masters or their agents when an extradomiciliary slave found himself caught in the meshes of federal justice.

The first cases to come before the United States Supreme Court involving such slaves arose out of the interstate and international slave trade. The Court's divisions on non-slavery-related issues of interstate commerce, first disclosed in *Mayor of New York* v. *Miln* (1837), were caused by unspoken attitudes toward the movement of

Jackson *v.* Bulloch, 12 Conn. 38 (1837).

[30]United States *v.* La Jeune Eugenie, 26 Fed. Cas. 832 (No. 15,551) (C.C.D. Mass. 1822) at 846.

[31]The Antelope, 23 U.S. (10 Wheat.) 66 (1825).

slaves, free blacks, abolitionists, and abolitionist writings across state lines. These attitudes had already been reflected in the disputes over the Negro Seamen's Acts formalized in *Elkison* v. *Deliesseline* and Justice William Johnson's concurrence in *Gibbons* v. *Ogden*. But the disputes did not end in 1824. They persisted in executive and diplomatic channels.

Roger Taney, as United States Attorney General in the cabinet of President Jackson, contributed to the controversy by drafting an opinion that refuted Justice Johnson and upheld the constitutionality of the Negro Seamen's Act. The states reserved to themselves all power to exclude persons who posed a threat to their internal security, and this power was not overridden by the federal commerce or treaty power, Taney insisted. He also set forth his conception of blacks that was to underlie his *Dred Scott* opinion twenty-five years later: blacks were "a separate and degraded people to whom the sovereignty of each state might accord or withhold such privileges as they might deem proper."[32] This opinion apparently did not circulate widely enough to influence public debate. In any event, it would have been influential only among United States Attorneys and other officials in the executive branch. It had no formal binding force on the judiciary or Congress. It did, however, prefigure the posture of southern jurists in later controversies.

Taney returned to this controversy in the only case ever to come before the United States Supreme Court directly involving the interstate slave trade, *Groves* v. *Slaughter* (1841). In 1832, Mississippi amended its Constitution to prohibit bringing slaves into the state for sale. The state hoped to check an outflow of capital, discourage speculative practices in slave trading, exclude suspected black insurrectionists exported from the eastern states or the West Indies, keep down the size of the black population, and perhaps keep up the prices of slaves within the state. A purchaser defaulted on a note given for some slaves. In a suit on the note, he argued that the transaction was void because prohibited by the state Constitution. But he was held liable, and appealed to the United States Supreme Court.

[32]Taney's unpublished opinion is excerpted in Carl B. Swisher, "Mr. Chief Justice Taney," in Allison Dunham and Philip B. Kurland (eds.), *Mr. Justice* (Chicago, 1964), pp. 43–45.

The Court split five ways on the slave-trade and commerce-clause issues posed by *Groves*. [33] Justice Smith Thompson's opinion evaded the slavery-related issues by holding the purchaser's defense insufficient because the state constitutional provision was not self-executing. It needed supplemental legislation, which the Mississippi General Assembly never enacted, and hence was unenforceable. But Justice McLean, concurring, suggested several lines of argument that paralleled elements of abolitionist constitutional thought at the time. He argued that federal power over the slave trade was exclusive of state power, that slaves were considered persons rather than property under the federal Constitution, and that "the character of property is given them by the local law." This last point seemed to be an endorsement of the *Somerset* principle that slavery is a creature of municipal legislation. These implications of McLean's provoked another concurrence by Taney. He repeated his 1832 Attorney General's opinion by claiming that state power over the ingress of blacks, slave or free, was exclusive of federal power, whether derived from the commerce or slave-trade clauses. Justice Henry Baldwin's opinion was an undisciplined heap of dicta supporting an extreme proslavery interpretation: federal power over the slave trade was exclusive, but also "conservative" (Baldwin's term) in the sense that it could be used only to protect, not harm, the trade; states could not prohibit the trade because that would interfere with the rights slaveowners enjoyed under the privileges and immunities clause of Article IV, section 2; the Fifth Amendment's due process clause protected owners' rights in slaves; and slaves were, in a constitutional sense, property, not persons.

On the related subject of the international slave trade, an inchoate consensus had been forming since the 1820s. Congressional prohibition of the trade was left feebly enforced. The navy's African Squadron was undermanned, the State Department opposed British demands for powers to search American flag vessels, and American consular officials falsified ship's papers for a bribe. The result was a steady, though modest, level of slave smuggling into the United

---

[33] 15 Pet. (40 U.S.) 449 (1841). The division of the Court was as follows: Thompson delivered the judgment of the Court and an opinion for himself and Wayne; Taney, McLean, and Baldwin concurred, each by separate opinion; McKinley and Story dissented without opinion; Catron did not participate because of illness; the seat vacated by Barbour's recent death had not yet been filled.

States, estimated at about one thousand slaves a year until the Civil War blockade effectively cut it off.[34] Finally, Congress would do nothing to inhibit the interstate slave trade, even when it was carried on in international waters.

The international trade was not at the top of the list of abolitionists' priorities for legal attack, but in 1839 they suddenly found themselves with a dramatic opportunity to try out their increasingly sophisticated constitutional arguments in a series of cases arising out of the mutiny of slaves aboard the Spanish slaver *Amistad.* Africans illegally imported into Cuba in violation of Spanish laws abolishing the high-seas slave trade rose up, killed the captain and cook, and commanded their terrified purchasers to steer toward Africa. The Cubans did so during the day, but set a northerly course at night, hoping to land in a friendly port in the southern United States. Instead, they were captured by an American naval vessel in Long Island Sound.

Only one of the several legal proceedings that were begun after the seizure of the slaver became doctrinally significant. In an 1839 admiralty action in the United States District Court, a team of four abolitionist attorneys led by Theodore Sedgwick, Jr., and Ellis Gray Loring opposed awarding salvage on the Africans on the grounds that they were freemen illegally enslaved and hence could not be the subjects of an *in rem* admiralty proceeding.[35] To their surprise, the judge concurred; the Circuit Court affirmed and sent the case on up to the United States Supreme Court. There the lawyers for the slaves, assisted by former President and now Congressman John Quincy Adams, confronted United States Attorney General Henry Gilpin, who supported the claim of the Cuban owners.

Roger Sherman Baldwin, for the Africans, insisted that the federal government lacked power to enslave anyone, as it would do by remitting the originally free captives to their claimants.[36] Again to

[34]Philip D. Curtin, *The Atlantic Slave Trade: A Census* (Madison, Wis., 1969), pp. 74–75.

[35]Admiralty is that branch of law dealing with civil and criminal maritime controversies. Salvage is compensation in admiralty awarded to persons who helped save a ship or its cargo from peril or wreck. An *in rem* proceeding is a legal action against property, rather than against a human party.

[36]Roger S. Baldwin, *Argument Before the Supreme Court of the United States, in the Case of the United States, Appellants, vs. Cinque, and others, Africans of the Amistad* (New York, 1841).

the surprise of everyone, Justice Story, for the Court, went a short
distance toward that abolitionist position by holding that there was
no valid proof that the Africans were slaves.[37] The cases provided
abolitionists with an invaluable propaganda opportunity. They exploited it zestfully by educating the captives, converting some to
Christianity, publicizing their cause in books, pamphlets, newspapers, and sermons, raising defense funds, and eventually providing
the blacks' transportation back to Guinea—where, according to an
ironic tradition, the mutineers' leader, Joseph Cinque, ended his
career as a slave trader himself.

Two years later, another mutiny aboard an American slaver engaged in the interstate trade presented abolitionists with legislative
and diplomatic opportunities. American slaves aboard the *Creole*
mutinied, killed a passenger, and forced the ship to the Bahamas
(then a British possession), where most of them were set free. Duti-
fully carrying out the proslavery policies of John Tyler's administration, Secretary of State Daniel Webster demanded that the British
compensate the American owners for the liberated slaves. Webster's communication touched off heated debates in the abolitionist
and legal press over the legal status of the men who mutinied
aboard the *Creole*.[38] In the House of Representatives, Congressman
Joshua Giddings, an Ohio Whig who agreed with the moderate
abolitionists, offered the "*Creole* Resolutions," which fused the implications of the *Somerset* decision with Baldwin's *Amistad* argument
by insisting that the slave status of the mutineers terminated at the
borders of the state whose positive law kept them enslaved, so that
on the high seas they reverted to their natural condition, freedom.[39]

Though the *Creole* matter did not come before the courts, Justice
Story condemned Webster's official position in private correspondence. He insisted that whether the British should recognize the
slave status of the *Creole* mutineers was entirely a matter of comity
which the United States could not demand as a right protected
under international law.[40] This was in accord with the view of comity

[37]U.S. v. The Amistad, 40 U.S. (15 Pet.) 518 (1841).

[38]Webster's position is set forth in an untitled Senate document, 27 Cong., 2 sess.,
ser. 397, doc. 137 (Feb. 21, 1842). An abolitionist legal rejoinder was *The Creole Case,
and Mr. Webster's Despatch* (New York, 1842).

[39]*Congressional Globe*, 27 Cong., 2 sess. 342 (Mar. 21, 1842).

[40]Story to Webster, Mar. 26, 1842, in C. H. Van Tyne (ed.), *The Letters of Daniel
Webster* (New York, 1902), pp. 263–266.

Story pioneered in his *Commentaries on the Conflict of Laws* (1834),[41] discarding the universal applicability of the law of the domicile state in favor of discretion on the part of the forum state to adopt or reject it on the basis of comity. The impact of the *Creole* mutiny was not confined to paper argument. Slavery's supporters in the House officially censured Giddings for offering the *"Creole* Resolutions" as a violation of the gag. Giddings resigned, went back to his Ohio district and ran for reelection to challenge his censure, and won a landslide victory. The gag rule, now in disarray, was repealed in 1844.

After the *Creole* incident, the issue of the international slave trade lay quiescent until the 1850s, when some southerners demanded repeal of the 1807 slave-trade ban and the reopening of the African slave trade. In the meantime, abolitionists and others turned to other areas of constitutional confrontation over slavery. The most problematical, before the Mexican War, was the problem of fugitive slaves in the free states. Challenges to enforcement of fugitive slave recaptures presented abolitionists with irresistible legal and propaganda opportunities. The Framers of the fugitive-slave clause did not use the terms "slave" or "slavery," substituting euphemisms instead. They also drafted the clause in the passive voice—a distinct invitation to mischief in any legal document—thus leaving the source of responsibility for its enforcement, if any, indeterminate. Congress's implementation of the clause, by the Fugitive Slave Act of 1793, created a simple, alternative federal-state procedure for legal recaptures of fugitives. It permitted an owner or owner's agent to seize an alleged runaway and obtain a certificate from a federal judge or local magistrate entitling him to haul the black to the owner's state. The simplicity of this early act created two technical problems. First, no state had more than one (or, during sittings of the United States Circuit Court, two) federal judges within its borders, making slave catchers dependent, as a practical matter, on the cooperation of state or local judges. Second, the 1793 statute made no provisions, other than the requirement of affidavit or oral assertion, for determining the status of the black. Kidnapping of blacks was an endemic problem in border states, especially when the prices

[41]Joseph Story, *Commentaries on the Conflict of Laws,* 2nd ed. (Boston, 1841), secs. 95–96a; on the subject of comity, especially as it pertains to Prigg *v.* Pennsylvania and all other slavery-related topics, see Paul Finkelman's outstanding *An Imperfect Union: Slavery, Federalism, and Comity* (Chapel Hill, 1981).

of slaves rose, and the federal act did little to discriminate effectively between slaves and free persons being kidnapped.

But abolitionists were less concerned with these relatively technical issues and more outraged at the fundamental immorality of using the law to capture a human being running to freedom and send him or her back to slavery. Here, principles and law intersected with propaganda. The inherent drama of a black man or woman fleeing to freedom at risk of life caught the attention of abolitionists long before Harriet Beecher Stowe dramatized it so effectively in the episode of Eliza clutching her baby, jumping across the ice floes of the Ohio River, in *Uncle Tom's Cabin.* Beginning in the 1830s, abolitionist lawyers and laypeople mounted challenges, invariably unsuccessfully, to the 1793 Act and to fugitive recaptures generally.

At first it seemed that the 1793 act was immune to constitutional challenge. Eminent jurists defended its constitutionality. Chief Judge William Tilghman of the Pennsylvania Supreme Court in 1819, Chief Justice Isaac Parker of the Massachusetts Supreme Judicial Court in 1823, and Justice Joseph Story (implicitly) in his *Commentaries on the Constitution,* all supported the statute.[42] But in 1836, New York Chancellor Reuben Walworth suggested in dicta that the statute was unconstitutional.[43] Thus the first major abolitionist challenge to the fugitive recaptures, the *Matilda* case of 1837, was not utterly fanciful.

Were it not for the combative determination of the abolitionist movement in Ohio, the fate of Matilda Lawrence in a petty Ohio court in 1837 would have been no different from that of countless blacks dragged back to slavery by federal power, unheard, unnoticed, undefended. But she happened to be a servant in the household of one of abolition's most spectacular converts, James G. Birney, then at the peak of his fame and enjoying the cachet of a recent mobbing that destroyed his antislavery press. Though he was himself a lawyer, Birney sought the assistance of Salmon P. Chase, then a young Cincinnati attorney, and together they worked out the legal theory challenging the 1793 Act in the first of the cases that were

[42]Wright *v.* Deacon, 5 Serg. & R. 62 (Pa. 1819); Commonwealth v. Griffith, 2 Pick. (19 Mass.) 11 (1823); Joseph Story, *Commentaries on the Constitution of the United States* (Boston, 1833), secs. 1811–1812.
[43]Jack *v.* Martin, 14 Wend. 507 (New York Court for the Correction of Errors, 1836) (Walworth, Ch. concurring).

to earn Chase the nickname in Kentucky and Ohio of "attorney general for runaway negroes."

Chase and Birney argued that the act violated the unreasonable search and seizure provisions of the Fourth Amendment, the due process clause of the Fifth (in a procedural sense only), and the guarantee of jury trial and habeas corpus in the Northwest Ordinance.[44] They also maintained that the federal Constitution had created a relationship of compact among the states, and that the fugitive-slave clause, a part of that compact, did not authorize the federal government to create a mechanism for enforcing something it lacked power to enforce. Finally, they adapted *Somerset*'s holding to maintain that when Matilda Lawrence came into Ohio, she became free, and her freedom became legally enforceable, because she left the confines of the positive law of the jurisdiction where she was enslaved. Slavery, Chase concluded, violated a natural right to freedom.

The court rejected these arguments, and Matilda's slave-catcher-kidnappers hurried her off to the New Orleans slave mart, but Birney had the argument printed and distributed through the North as a compendium of arguments for others to use in challenging fugitive renditions. As an innovation of abolitionist constitutional theory, the Chase/Birney *Matilda* arguments proved to be the overture to more than two decades of conflict among the free states, the slave states, the federal government, and abolitionist groups.

Both free and slave states became dissatisfied with the legal mechanism of the 1793 Act. A few northern states enacted "Personal Liberty Laws" that variously provided jury trial, the writ of habeas corpus, or other procedural safeguards to blacks caught up in the recapture mechanism.[45] None of these acts was meant to prevent the rendition of actual fugitive slaves, but white southerners resented them nonetheless. In order to settle questions about the constitutionality of these laws, Pennsylvania and Maryland cooperated in what was virtually a collusive prosecution of a Maryland

[44]*Speech of Salmon P. Chase, in the Case of the Colored Woman, Matilda* (Cincinnati, 1837). Northwest Ordinance, Art. 2: "The inhabitants of the said territory shall always be entitled to the benefits of the writ of habeas corpus, and of the trial by jury. . . ." The Northwest Ordinance was the first organic act for the state of Ohio.

[45]See generally Thomas D. Morris, *Free Men All: The Personal Liberty Laws of the North, 1780–1861* (Baltimore, 1974).

slave catcher for violation of a Pennsylvania 1826 personal liberty act by taking an alleged slave and her children to Maryland without the legal authorization required by either the state or the federal statutes. From affirmance of the conviction by the Pennsylvania Supreme Court, the case went by writ of error to the High Court.[46]

Far from allaying controversies over fugitive recaptures, the Court's response in *Prigg* v. *Pennsylvania* (1842) only intensified them.[47] Like *Dred Scott* later, the case produced a proliferation of opinions—seven in all—that made it difficult to determine just what the Court had held, that invited misunderstanding about who spoke for the Court, and that confused the distinction between what was holding and what was dicta. Justice Story's opinion was and is conventionally assumed to have been for the Court, though one of the points most often asserted to be the "holding" of *Prigg* v. *Pennsylvania* was a dictum that he alone supported. In any event, a majority in *Prigg* held that: (1) the Fugitive Slave Act of 1793 was constitutional; (2) the Pennsylvania Personal Liberty Law of 1826 was unconstitutional because it interfered with the rights of the master under the federal Constitution and statute; and (3) the master had a right to recapture his runaway slave in a state other than his domicile, though it is unclear whether this was a right derived from the Constitution or the common law.

Other points raised in the sprawl of opinions included the following: Justices Story, McLean, and Wayne claimed that a state could not enact legislation that supplemented enforcement of the federal law. Justices Daniel and Thompson disagreed, saying that a state could, and Chief Justice Taney going so far as to claim that a state must, enact supportive legislation. Taney's opinion represented the proslavery extreme of *Prigg*.

The antislavery extreme, if it may be called that, appeared in a dictum supported only by Justice McLean, who argued that states could enact statutes designed to prevent their free black citizens from being kidnapped, as long as the statute did not inhibit the

[46]The writ of error, long known to the common law, was the principal procedural means by which cases were appealed to the United States Supreme Court in the nineteenth century. It was a writ issuing from the appellate court to the inferior court, commanding that the lower court transmit the record of the case for purposes of correcting errors of law. It is obsolete today in federal practice.
[47]16 Pet. (41 U.S.) 539 (1842).

recapture of fugitives. Finally, Story made a point in dictum that he erroneously claimed to be a "Triumph of Freedom": states could prohibit their officials (sheriffs, magistrates, constables, judges, etc.) from participating in the enforcement of the federal act. This was a position unique to Story, and was not supported by any other member of the Court, then or later.

Unique or not, though, abolitionists quickly realized the value of this dictum, as well as other consequences of the *Prigg* decision, in the Latimer case of 1842, the Fugitive Slave Act's first national *cause célèbre*. [48] A Boston constable seized George Latimer as a runaway slave and detained him in the city jail while his alleged master's attorney sought a certificate of rendition. Two abolitionist appeals to Chief Justice Shaw to secure Latimer's release proved fruitless, because Shaw held that, under the recent *Prigg* decision, local procedures to challenge the detention of alleged fugitives could not be allowed to interfere with execution of the federal Fugitive Slave Act. But Boston abolitionists impeded enforcement so successfully that legal costs to the master began to approach Latimer's value as a slave, and the Virginian was induced to sell him to agents of the Latimer Defense Committee, who promptly freed him. Though George Latimer promptly and prudently faded into anonymity, the consequences of his close escape persisted to the eve of the Civil War. John Greenleaf Whittier best captured the emotional tone of the whole incident, and its impact on the Boston community, in his poem "Massachusetts to Virginia," with its memorable peroration:

> No slave-hunt in our borders,—no pirate on our strand!
> No fetters in the Bay State,—no slave upon our land!

The case proved to be a crisis of conscience for both abolitionists and lawyers, confronting both groups with a conflict between law and moral duty. Abolitionists were forced to recognize that conscience might compel them to refuse obedience to an otherwise valid law. For the first time Garrisonian abolitionists challenged the legitimacy of the American Constitution and laws. This produced

[48]Exhaustive primary-source collections are *The Latimer Journal and North Star* (1842–43), an ephemeral newspaper whose only complete run is at the Massachusetts Historical Society, Boston; and Henry I. Bowditch, *Proceedings of the Citizens of the Borough of Norfolk, on the Boston Outrage, in the Case of the Runaway Slave George Latimer* (Norfolk, Mass., 1843).

comprehensive expositions of the Garrisonian view that the Constitution was a covenant with death. Lawyers, for their part, chose law over conscience. For the next five years in law journals, judicial opinions, and private correspondence, they elaborated a rationale for enforcing laws that violated moral imperatives.

The *Latimer* incident stimulated enactment of what may be called the "Prigg personal liberty laws." Taking advantage of the hint tendered by Story, in 1843 Bay State abolitionists prevailed on the General Court to prohibit state and local officials from participating in the enforcement of the Fugitive Slave Act, from arresting alleged fugitives, and from using public facilities as barracoons to house fugitives awaiting rendition.[49] As the controversy over slavery intensified, these personal liberty laws became more radical in scope and content, especially after enactment of the federal Fugitive Slave Act of 1850. This trend culminated in passage of the Massachusetts 1855 personal liberty act, which granted comprehensive procedural protection to alleged fugitives, including representation by appointed counsel, jury trial, habeas corpus, and the writ of personal replevin.[50]

Before the northern states were pushed to this stance of defiance, the United States Supreme Court took up the challenge of law versus conscience that the *Latimer* case first posed. *Jones* v. *Van Zandt* (1847) gave Salmon P. Chase another forum to attack the Fugitive Slave Act a decade after his *Matilda* arguments. Defending a white man convicted of violating the enforcement provisions of the 1793 Act by assisting some blacks to escape from Kentucky, Chase in his *Van Zandt* argument updated *Somerset*'s ideas and adapted them to the circumstances of the American federal system. He maintained that because slavery was contrary to "natural right," it could be maintained only by "local and municipal" positive law, the force of which terminated at the jurisdictional line. In arguments reminiscent of his friend Congressman Giddings's *"Creole* Resolutions," Chase maintained that once a slave left the jurisdiction under whose laws he was enslaved, he became free "because he continues to be

---

[49]"An Act to Protect Personal Liberty," ch. 69, *Acts and Resolves . . . of Massachusetts . . . 1843.* A barracoon was a slave pen.

[50]*Massachusetts Acts and Resolves . . . 1855,* ch. 489. The writ of personal replevin, technically known as the writ de homine replegiando, was an old procedural device used to regain custody of one person from another.

a man and leaves behind him the law of force." Hence the Fugitive Slave Act was unconstitutional because the federal government lacked power to enslave anyone, because it violated the due process, unreasonable searches and seizures, and civil jury trial provisions of the Fourth, Fifth, and Seventh Amendments, and because the Tenth Amendment withdrew the power to regulate fugitive recaptures from the federal government and reserved it to the states.[51]

Justice Levi Woodbury, Story's successor on the Supreme Court, brusquely dismissed Chase's arguments and reaffirmed *Prigg*'s holding that the Fugitive Slave Act was constitutional.[52] He also took up the challenge to the judicial conscience raised so pointedly in his native New England. Woodbury insisted that the legitimacy of laws imposing slavery was a "political question, settled by each state for itself." Reaffirming a point Story had made in *Prigg*, Woodbury claimed that the fugitive-slave clause was a compromise essential to the South's entering the Union and ratifying the Constitution, and, as such, "one of [the] sacred compromises" of the Constitution. "This court has no alternative, while they exist, but to stand by the constitution and the laws with fidelity to their duties and their oaths." Woodbury's rationale was commonplace and served to palliate the conscience of nearly all northern judges who found themselves performing some judicial duty concerning slavery that offended their conscience.

After the Mexican War (1846–48), the controversies over slavery moved away from the static question of its internal security in the states where it existed to the dynamic questions of its spread westward into the territories and its penetration into the free states. Slavery threatened the constitutionally free status of the northern states. Thus an 1851 case that otherwise might not have been of great constitutional significance became critical. It marked a moment in time when slavery's defenders, feeling themselves besieged, lurched forward to a new salient in the constitutional defense of slavery. In *Strader* v. *Graham* (1851), Chief Justice Taney began exploring the constitutional basis of slavery's presence in the northern states. From a northern point of view, this opened up a danger-

---

[51] S. P. Chase, *Reclamation of Fugitives from Service. An Argument for the Defendant Submitted to the Supreme Court of the United States . . . in the Case of Wharton Jones vs. John Vanzandt* (Cincinnati, 1847).
[52] 5 How. (46 U.S.) 215 (1847).

ous reexamination of two fundamental bases for slavery's place in the American constitutional order. These were relevance of *Somerset,* and the assumption that the states had complete control over slavery within their borders. In this reexamination, Taney began to provide a comprehensive proslavery judicial theory that complemented John C. Calhoun's earlier political initiatives.

Graham v. *Strader* (1844) raised *Somerset* issues in the Kentucky Court of Appeals.[53] A Kentucky master permitted several of his slaves to go to Ohio and Indiana to work temporarily for wages as musicians. They returned to Kentucky, then ran away to freedom, allegedly journeying part of the way on a vessel owned by Jacob Strader. The master sued Strader for damages under a Kentucky statute making an abettor of fugitives liable to the owner for their value. Strader defended on the grounds that, at the time of their escape, the blacks were free men because of their sojourn in free states with their master's consent, and had not resumed their status as slaves upon their return to Kentucky. The Kentucky courts affirmed Strader's liability.

When *Strader* was decided by the Supreme Court in 1851, Taney first disposed of the entire issue on noncontroversial and unexceptionable grounds. He held that the United States Supreme Court lacked jurisdiction of the issue presented because the question of the status of the blacks was a matter exclusively to be determined by state courts on the basis of state law; this determination was conclusive on federal courts.[54] But Taney could not leave well enough alone in slavery cases. Anticipating his *Dred Scott* opinion again, he went on to try to give a definitive resolution to related constitutional questions in an effort to stifle abolitionist constitutional heresy for all time. Where his opinion was based on settled law, as it was on the threshold jurisdictional issue that should have disposed of the case, Taney's voice was clear and authoritative. But when he went on an unnecessary foray beyond that, stalking abolitionists, his utterance took on a peculiar, ambiguous quality. They seemed to be dicta, yet they could be made relevant to the dispute before him as he framed it.

[53] 5 B. Monroe 173 (Ky. 1844). The Court of Appeals was the highest court of the commonwealth.
[54] 10 How. (51 U.S.) 83 (1851).

Once beyond the safe bounds of the jurisdictional issue, Taney repeated the truism that "every state has an undoubted right to determine the status, or domestic and social condition, of the persons domiciled within its territory." But he immediately added a troubling qualification: "except in so far as the powers of the states in this respect are restrained, or duties and obligations imposed on them, by the Constitution of the United States." In *Groves* v. *Slaughter* a decade earlier, Justice Baldwin, concurring, had argued that slaveowners could not be deprived of property rights in their slaves. Was Taney endorsing that extraordinary claim? Was he suggesting that the privileges and immunities clause protected the rights of slaveowners in their human property when that human property was in a free jurisdiction? Did the contracts clause protect the master's right in his slaves? Whatever Taney might have been hinting at, if anything, a nervous northerner might reasonably have concluded that the Constitution as construed by Taney, hitherto considered neutral on slavery except for the three specified points (federal number, fugitive slaves, international slave trade), might actually be an instrument that forced slavery into the northern states where it had been abolished.

Even then, Taney would not stop. Recklessly and provocatively, he insisted that the Northwest Ordinance was defunct, its "forever . . . unalterable compact" no longer competent to prohibit slavery in the five western states carved out of its territory. This, in turn, implied that Congress could not impose an enforceable condition on the admission of a new state, a dictum at variance with a statement in *Permoli* v. *New Orleans* (1845) that Congress could stipulate provisions a territory must present in its constitution as a condition for granting statehood.[55] This proslavery tendency to unsettle what northerners regarded as fundamental constitutional settlements was repeated when Congress discarded the Missouri Compromise in 1854 and and when Taney held it unconstitutional anyway in *Dred Scott* three years after that.

Read with hindsight, Taney's words betray a sense of unease, an urgent need to settle constitutional issues threatening the Union. But it was already too late for judges to resolve slavery questions with finality. By 1851, slavery had become irreversibly politicized

[55] 3 How. (44 U.S.) 589 (1845) at 609–610.

and nationalized. For better or worse, solutions to slavery's problems would be argued in legislatures, on the stump, in newspapers and pamphlets and sermons. These solutions would have to be national in scope. Contrary to the constitutional wisdom of another 1851 decision of the Taney Court, *Cooley* v. *Board of Wardens,* which recognized the utility of local diversity in some commerce questions, solutions to the problems of slavery required national uniformity. Taney glimpsed this, and began to move toward uniformity. His solutions might well have nationalized slavery, not only in the territories but in the free states as well.

CHAPTER 5

Free Soil: The Constitution and the "Empire for Liberty," 1845–1852

CHIEF Justice Taney's injudicious determination to crush abolitionist constitutional efforts was the legal counterpart to a political counteroffensive that slavery's spokesmen and their northern Democratic allies waged after 1835. At first, the abolitionist challenge of the 1830s was diffuse, attacking all constitutional aspects of slavery, not singling any out for special emphasis. But as administration pressures for the annexation of Texas intensified in the 1840s, abolitionists concentrated their efforts on the future of slavery in the territories and the new states to be carved out of them. Southern leaders met this attack head on, producing a constitutional confrontation that relentlessly ground away centrist compromise proposals.

Before 1840, Americans had twice resolved crises over the future of slavery in the West—the area Thomas Jefferson called an "empire for liberty"[1]—by compromise settlements that took on constitutional status. The Northwest Ordinance combined a geographic allocation of lands to slavery and freedom with a fugitive-slave clause. The first Missouri Compromise in 1820 extended the geographic division, relying not on a convenient natural boundary like

[1]Thomas Jefferson to James Madison, Apr. 27, 1809, in Andrew A. Lipscomb and Albert E. Bergh (eds.), *The Writings of Thomas Jefferson* (Washington, 1905), XII, 274–277 at 277. Jefferson added: "I am persuaded no constitution was ever before so well calculated as ours for extensive empire and self-government."

the Ohio River but on a surveyor's line: 36°30'.

But the Missouri Compromise shortly began to look like a bad bargain for the slave states. The only territory it ensured for slavery was Arkansas, which at that time included the seemingly worthless and uninhabitable area of modern Oklahoma, designated as a refuge for Indians being driven out of regions east of the Mississippi. Slavery was excluded from all the remainder of the Louisiana Purchase above Missouri, an area likely to produce at least five more states. This addition of new free states would in time upset the pattern of paired admissions of free and slave states, giving the northern states a preponderance in the Senate. Simultaneously, the growth of population in the free states was outstripping that of the slave states, assuring an inescapable free-state predominance in the House. These trends threatened to destroy the fundamental political strategy of the Democratic party, thus removing an assurance of the internal security of the southern slave societies.

In 1842, Representative Henry Wise, a troubled Virginian, voiced the South's fears:

If Iowa be added on the one side, Florida would be added on the other; but there the equation must stop. Let one more Northern State be admitted and the Equilibrium is gone—gone forever. The balance of interests was gone; the safeguard of American property, of the American Constitution, of the American Union, vanished into thin air. This must be the inevitable result, unless, by a treaty with Mexico, the South can add more weight to her end of the lever. Let the South stop at the Sabine, [the eastern boundary of Texas], while the North may spread unchecked beyond the Rocky Mountains, and the southern scale must kick the beam.[2]

Hence southern leaders demanded the annexation of the independent Republic of Texas, hoping that its immense territory might be subdivided into perhaps five slave states.[3]

The Texans established their independence in 1836, but President Andrew Jackson's attempt to annex the Lone Star Republic failed because of the caution of Congress. Meanwhile, abolitionists

[2]*Congressional Globe*, 27 Cong., 2 sess., 174 (Jan. 26, 1842).
[3]The Joint Resolution of Mar. 1, 1845, 5 Stat. 797, admitting Texas provided that "new States, of convenient size, not exceeding four in number, in addition to said State of Texas, . . . may hereafter, by the consent of said State, be formed out of the territory thereof." Nothing ever came of this, though the idea has been occasionally revived in recent times; see, e.g., *New York Times*, Mar. 1, 1975, p. 19.

sniffed the western airs and detected the scent of a slavocratic conspiracy to expand slavery and its political influence. The tireless Quaker publisher Benjamin Lundy walked to Texas to investigate conditions there, and then walked back east to report his findings in a little book whose title summed up the abolitionist view: *The War in Texas: A Review of Facts and Circumstances, Showing that This Contest Is the Result of a Long Premeditated Crusade against the Government [of Mexico] Set on Foot by Slaveholders, Land Speculators, &c., With the View of Re-Establishing, Expanding, and Perpetuating the System of Slavery and the Slave Trade in the Republic of Mexico. . . .*[4]

Presidents Martin Van Buren and William Henry Harrison did not promote annexation, nor did President John Tyler before 1842. But after Daniel Webster's resignation as Secretary of State, Tyler gathered around himself a coterie of slavery expansionists avid for Texas. These included his new Secretary of State, the Virginian Abel Parker Upshur; John C. Calhoun, who became Secretary of State after Upshur's accidental death; Thomas W. Gilmer, another Virginia Congressman who became Secretary of the Navy; and Duff Green, a Missouri land speculator and editor who served as an informal envoy to Great Britain. Together these men secretly pushed Texas annexation and thereby stumbled into a swamp of constitutional problems.

The first was an issue that had been nagging New Englanders since the beginning of the century: the three-fifths clause. Article I, section 2, of the Constitution provided that

Representatives and direct Taxes shall be apportioned among the several States which may be included within this Union, according to their respective Numbers, which shall be determined by adding to the whole Number of free Persons . . . three-fifths of all other Persons.

The "other Persons" were slaves. Though abolitionists chose to quibble over this euphemism, the correlative of "free Persons" was unfree persons: slaves. This reading was confirmed by the 1840 publication of James Madison's *Notes* taken at the Philadelphia convention of 1787, containing the fullest account that has ever emerged of what went on at Independence Hall.[5] Madison's *Notes*

---

[4][Benjamin Lundy], *The War in Texas* . . . (Philadelphia, 1836).
[5]The 1840 posthumous publication of Madison's *Notes of Debates in the Federal Convention of 1787* was a historic event in its own right. Prior to 1840, only three

made it unmistakably plain that though the Framers used circumlo-
cutions, they meant slaves. The effect of the clause was to give
added weight in Congress to slave states based on 60 percent of
persons in their jurisdictions who could never vote.

Massachusetts political leaders complained about the three-fifths
clause persistently before and during the War of 1812. Their view
found constitutional expression in the Hartford Resolves of 1814,
which demanded repeal of the clause. The successful end of the war,
capped by Andrew Jackson's stirring victory at New Orleans, spread
an aura of disgrace over the Federalist party, but New England
resentment at the three-fifths clause never really disappeared.
Texas annexation reawakened it, and the Massachusetts General
Court adopted a joint resolution in 1843 demanding once again that
the clause be repealed.[6] Ohio adopted a similar resolution two years
later, indicating that New England's discontent had spread to the
West.

Congress refused to consider Massachusetts' demand for rescis-
sion of the three-fifths clause. But the demand itself revitalized a
second constitutional problem related to Texas annexation: the
gags. In 1836, Congress had adopted rules automatically tabling all
petitions related to slavery, in a persistently unsuccessful attempt to
shut off all floor debate hostile to the peculiar institution. But the
gags only proved counterproductive, because they stimulated more
petitions to Congress. They also invited challenge by John Quincy
Adams and other antislavery Congressmen, who twitted the slavoc-
racy repeatedly. Adams's acidulous personality flourished under the
arbitrary regime of the gags. Outraged southern representatives
moved that Adams be censured on the grounds that he had
breached the privilege of the House by introducing a petition relating to slavery, had committed contempt of the House, and had
offered to commit perjury and treason.[7] This gave Adams another

delegates had published their notes, and these were brief, sketchy, and inaccurate.
Madison's *Notes* provided an astonishingly detailed and revealing view of what took
place behind the secrecy imposed in Philadelphia. They disclosed, among other
things, the intensity of sectional competition and the concessions to slavery. They
are available in a modern edition: Adrienne Koch (comp.), *Notes of Debates in the Federal
Convention of 1787 Reported by James Madison* (1966; reprint New York, 1969).

   [6]*Acts and Resolves . . . Massachusetts . . . 1843,* Resolves ch. 60.

   [7]See the discussion in Samuel F. Bemis, *John Quincy Adams and the Union* (New York,
1965), ch. 20, "Trial for Censure."

opportunity for the kind of biting sarcasm that led his admirers to bestow on him the nickname "Old Man Eloquent." For ten days he fended off his attackers, leaving one of them, as he noted in his diary, "sprawling in his own compost."[8] Finally, the southern members gave up, recognizing that Adams was once again making fools of them.

During 1843 and 1844, the principal vehicles for attacks on the gags were petitions opposing the annexation of Texas, slavery in federal territories, or the admission of new slave states. The gag rule was impotent to quash these petitions as Adams and other antislavery Whig Congressmen found ways to circumvent the gags or to use a successful gagging as an opportunity to raise First Amendment issues relating to freedom of speech, press, and the right of petition. But proslavery Congressmen tried once more to enforce the House gag by censuring Ohio Representative Joshua Giddings for introducing the *"Creole* resolutions." This time, they did succeed in censuring the obnoxious Congressman, only to have their maneuver backfire. Giddings resigned his seat, returned to his district, ran for it again in a special election that was, in effect, a referendum on his antislavery position, and won in a landslide.[9] Seeing that the gags were hopeless, southerners gave up. In 1844, both Houses repealed the gags—in time to remove the last obstacles to free-for-all floor fights on other issues surrounding Texas annexation.

Free-state constitutional authorities challenged annexation on the grounds that the United States lacked constitutional power to annex an independent nation. Though the United States had three times previously annexed territory outside its boundaries—the Louisiana Purchase in 1803, West Florida in 1810–12, East Florida in 1819—each of these areas was a colonial dependency of a foreign power. Texas, on the other hand, was an independent republic, and nothing in the Constitution explicitly empowered the United States to absorb another nation. As on other issues, so-called strict and loose constructionists switched positions. Southerners like Tyler, Gilmer, and Calhoun, who made political careers out of proclaiming their adhesion to strict-construction doctrines, now shrugged off

[8]Charles Francis Adams (ed.), *Memoirs of John Quincy Adams, Comprising Portions of His Diary from 1795 to 1848* (Philadelphia, 1874–77), XI, 86 (diary entry of Feb. 5, 1842).
[9]James B. Stewart, *Joshua R. Giddings and the Tactics of Radical Politics* (Cleveland, 1970), pp. 73–76.

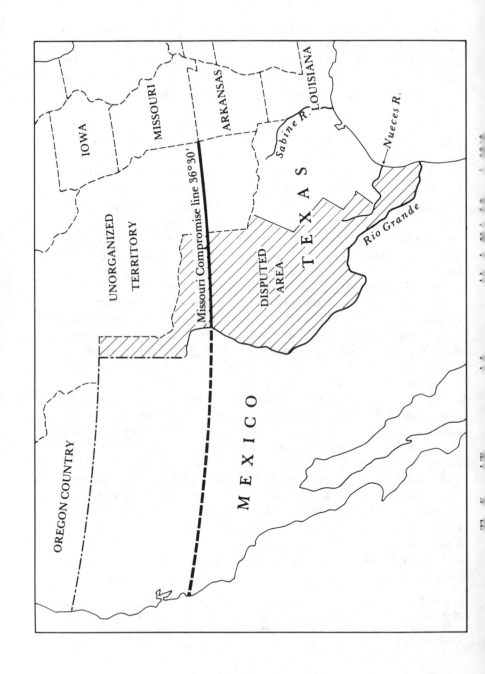

the constitutional objection as a quibble over a technicality—as in reality it was. Gilmer declared in a public letter that he was "a strict constructionist of the powers of our federal government; and I do not admit the force of mere precedent to establish authority under written constitutions. [However] the power conferred by the constitution over our foreign relations, and the repeated acquisitions of territory under it, seem to me to leave this question open, as one of expedience."[10]

On the other hand, advocates of a Hamiltonian, broad view of the Constitution—chiefly Daniel Webster, Joseph Story, and John Quincy Adams[11]—now scrutinized the territories clause with a Jeffersonian eye, claiming to see in it nothing that permitted conversion of an independent nation into a territory.

Precedent was on the side of those promoting annexation. If the Constitution does not explicitly authorize the acquisition of an independent nation, neither does it furnish any basis for a distinction between a nation and a dependency. Vermont was an independent republic like Texas at the time it was admitted under the Constitution in 1791. In *American Insurance Co.* v. *Canter* (1828), Chief Justice John Marshall sweepingly declared that the "Constitution confers absolutely on the government of the Union, the powers of making war, and of making treaties; consequently, that government possesses the power of acquiring territory, either by conquest or by treaty."[12] He suggested that this power to acquire territory derived not from any particular clause of the Constitution, but from the federal government's inherent sovereign powers. Marshall's doctrine has permitted the acquisition not only of Texas but also of the independent kingdom of Hawaii.

A weightier constitutional objection arose after the Senate voted down the treaty of annexation on June 8, 1844. President Tyler, perhaps reasoning that Texas, once acquired, would be promptly

[10]Gilmer to editor of Baltimore Republican, Jan. 10, 1843, reprinted in Frederick Merk, *Slavery and the Annexation of Texas* (New York, 1972), pp. 200–204 at 201.

[11]Adams (ed.), *Memoirs of John Quincy Adams*, XI, 330 (diary entry of Feb. 28, 1843). Daniel Webster to———Bigelow et al., Jan. 23, 1844, in Papers of Daniel Webster, microfilm edition, reel 19. Joseph Story to Joseph Tuckerman, July 25, 1837, in Fulmer Mood and Granville Hicks (eds.), "Letters to Dr. Channing on Slavery and the Annexation of Texas, 1837," *New England Quarterly*, V (1932), 587–601 at 593.

[12]American Insurance Co. *v.* Canter, 1 Pet. (26 U.S.) 511 at 542 (1828). See also Joseph Story's similar position in his *Commentaries on the Constitution*, sec. 1287.

admitted to the Union as a state, rather than being retained as a territory, hit on an expedient to get around the constitutional requirement of the two-thirds vote for ratification of a treaty in the Senate. He proposed, as an alternative, that Texas be annexed by joint resolution of both Houses, which would require only a majority vote in each. Annexation's opponents immediately objected, this time with greater effect. The transaction with Texas was a foreign-affairs issue of the gravest weight, both domestically and in foreign policy, and therefore was precisely what the Constitution contemplated as requiring the Senate's solemn assent. For in August, 1843, President Antonio Lopez de Santa Anna informed the United States that his government would "consider equivalent to a declaration of war against the Mexican Republic the passage of an act of the incorporation of Texas in the territory of the United States."[13]

If Texas were to be admitted by joint resolution or ordinary legislation, its constitutional basis would presumably be the New States clause. This attenuated support aroused conservative opposition. The venerable Albert Gallatin, a surviving Jeffersonian, joined with Rufus Choate, eminent Massachusetts attorney and spokesman for northern commercial Whiggery, in denouncing such use of the New States clause. But it was southern Whigs—chiefly William Cabell Rives, also an old Jeffersonian who, ironically, was John Tyler's replacement in the Senate after the latter's election to the Vice-Presidency; his Virginia colleague William S. Archer; and Georgian John M. Berrien—who furnished the most effective opposition to annexation by resolution. Rives warned his southern colleagues that the slave states should be "the very last to give up the conservative features of the constitution" lest some future majority in Congress use its power to harass or abolish slavery.[14]

Annexation's proponents recognized that their problem lay in the division of the Democratic party in both houses, and the opposition of the southern Whigs. Revising their resolutions to patch up the Democratic division and mollify the southern members, they picked up enough southern Whig support to enact joint resolutions of annexation. Texas came in immediately as a state, without a preliminary territorial period, and the Missouri Compromise line was ex-

[13]Quoted in Morris, *Encyclopedia of American History*, p. 225.
[14]Quoted in Merk, *Slavery and the Annexation of Texas*, p. 147.

tended through whatever part of the disputed northern area of Texas might be part of the United States. The Texas precedent later served to justify the admission of Hawaii by joint resolution as a means of circumventing anti-imperialist sentiment in the Senate in 1898.[15]

One other constitutional issue still remained: the modern one of the President's power to deploy American troops in a foreign war or to use them in ways that might commit the United States to an irreversible foreign policy without adequate congressional participation in policymaking. This question, first provoked by Tyler's orders to army and navy units to take up stations around Mexico in the event of Texan-Mexican hostilities before annexation, became absorbed in Whig opposition to the military policies of his successor, James K. Polk.

Compared with Polk, Tyler was circumspect about the exercise of his powers as Commander in Chief. Though he ordered naval units to patrol the Mexican coast in the Gulf, and stationed army units near Texas territory, he was scrupulously careful not to "invade" Texas soil, much less Mexican. When an American chargé d'affaires in Texas, William S. Murphy, gave written assurances of military assistance to the Texas government, Tyler promptly ordered him rebuked:

. . . you have suffered your zeal to . . . commit the President to measures for which he has no constitutional authority to stipulate. The employment of the army or navy against a foreign Power, with which the United States are at peace, is not within the competency of the President.[16]

Polk, on the other hand, deployed American forces with less restraint. When he took office, Texas annexation had already been accomplished. Mexico promptly broke off diplomatic relations, and its President, José Joaquín Herrera, recommended to his Congress that it declare war as soon as annexation was consummated or American troops moved into Mexico. Moreover, the United States had annexed a border dispute: historical Texas had extended to the Nueces River. Areas to the southwest of that river had always been part of Tamaulipas province. But both Polk and the Texans were

[15]Joint Resolution of July 7, 1898, 30 Stat. 750.
[16]John Nelson to William S. Murphy, Mar. 11, 1844, in Sen. Doc., 28 Cong., 1 sess., ser. 435, doc. 349 (June 1, 1844), 10–11 at 10.

determined to have Texas to the Rio Grande. Finally, Polk wanted to acquire California and other Mexican territory, in addition to Texas.

Polk unhesitatingly ordered naval squadrons to patrol both Mexican coasts and commanded General Zachary Taylor to occupy a site south of the Nueces. Naval units on the Pacific Coast were to maintain contact with potential California separatists. Polk sent John C. Frémont, an officer of the U.S. army's Topographical Corps, to California with at least a broad hint from the administration that he was to engage in some kind of military activity if war broke out. In his first annual message (December 2, 1845) Polk restated the Monroe Doctrine so vigorously that the policy he enunciated, warning the British and French to refrain from fishing in the troubled waters of Texas, Mexico, and California, is sometimes called the "Polk Doctrine." With an eye on Texas and perhaps California, Polk proclaimed that should any people on the North American continent "constituting an independent state, propose to unite themselves with our Confederacy, this will be a question for them and us to determine without any foreign interposition." He sternly warned against any application of "balance of power" principles.[17] With the failure of an American mission to Mexico seeking to buy Mexican territory, Polk decided on war. He found a pretext when Mexican troops attacked a small force of American dragoons in the disputed territory between the Nueces and the Rio Grande. In his war message, Polk declared that "Mexico has passed the boundary of the United States, has invaded our territory and shed American blood upon the American soil . . . war exists . . . by the act of Mexico herself."[18]

Polk now faced not only abolitionist opposition but also Whig partisan hostility, muffled antagonism from some New York Democrats (the result of an intraparty fight), and sectional opposition in the Northeast. Whigs controlled the House in the Thirtieth Congress and used their majority to harass the Democratic President. In December, 1847, Whig Representative Abraham Lincoln offered resolutions, immediately tabled, that requested the President to inform the House "whether the spot of soil on which the blood of

[17]Richardson, *Messages and Papers of the Presidents,* V, 2248.
[18]*Ibid.,* VI, 2292.

our citizens was shed" was within Mexican territory.[19] These "Spot Resolutions" prefigured the more successful resolution, adopted the next month, that declared the war to have been "unnecessarily and unconstitutionally begun by the President," implying that Polk had abused his powers as Commander in Chief.[20] Though obviously partisan, and scarcely a selfless assertion of principle, the antiwar resolution did convert a political issue into a perennial constitutional one.

In 1793, James Madison and Alexander Hamilton had set forth the opposing positions of the debate over the extent of the President's power to deploy American forces without congressional declaration of war. The resulting documents became as important for the constitutional guidelines of American foreign policy as the Jefferson-Hamilton debate in 1791 over the Bank was to become for domestic constitutional issues. Hamilton based his argument on the first clause of Article II: "The executive Power shall be vested in a President of the United States of America." Writing pseudonymously as "Pacificus," he argued that the President has an inherent executive power, not granted, but merely restrained, by the specific provisions of the Constitution. It was derived from "the general grant of [executive] power, interpreted in conformity with other parts of the Constitution, and with the principles of free government. The general doctrine of our Constitution then is, that the executive power of the nation is vested in the President; subject only to the exceptions and qualifications, which are expressed in the instrument."[21]

Madison rejected this expansive reading of the clause. Writing as "Helvidius," he maintained that the prerogative in foreign policy lay with Congress, rather than the President, by virtue of its power to declare war—that ultimate act of foreign policy—and that the President's powers were purely ministerial. He was to execute policy determined by Congress, not make it himself.[22]

Subsequent constitutional developments did not resolve this dis-

[19]*Congressional Globe*, 30 Cong., 1 sess., 64 (Dec. 22, 1847).
[20]*Congressional Globe*, 30 Cong., 1 sess., 95 (Jan. 3, 1848).
[21]The Pacificus letters are in Henry Cabot Lodge (ed.), *The Works of Alexander Hamilton* (New York, n.d.), IV, 432–489; quote at 439.
[22]The Helvidius letters are in Hunt (ed.), *Writings of James Madison*, VI, 138–188; see 146–149.

pute, so Polk maneuvered in a field cluttered with conflicting and ambiguous precedent. John Marshall began the ambiguity by declaring, as a Virginia Congressman before his appointment to the Supreme Court, that "the President is the sole organ of the nation in its external relations, and its sole representative with foreign nations."[23] On the other hand, just two years later, as Chief Justice of the United States, he declared that "the whole powers of war being, by the constitution of the United States, vested in congress, the acts of that body can alone be resorted to as our guides."[24] And three years after that, he managed to speak more precisely yet more ambiguously to the same issue:

It is by no means clear that the President of the United States, whose high duty it is to "take care that the laws be faithfully executed," and who is commander in chief of the armies and navies of the United States, might not, without any special authority for that purpose, in the then existing state of things [the undeclared naval war with France, 1798–99], have empowered the officers commanding the armed vessels of the United States, to seize [certain American vessels described in the Non-Intercourse Act of 1799].[25]

Congress did little to clarify the Delphic utterances from the High Court. Before hostilities broke out with France in 1798, Congress authorized the President to order the capture of French vessels. In 1802, it empowered President Jefferson to conduct naval warfare against Tripoli. The President was to "cause to be done all such other acts of precaution or hostility as the state of war will justify, and may, in his opinion, require."[26] Congress similarly authorized President Van Buren to "resist any attempt on the part of Great Britain to enforce, by arms" her claim to the disputed Maine–New Brunswick territory in the Aroostook War of 1839.[27] Only once did

[23][Thomas Hart Benton], *Abridgment of the Debates of Congress* (New York, 1857), II, 456 (Mar. 7, 1800).

[24]Talbot *v.* Seeman, 1 Cranch (5 U.S.) 1 (1801) at 28 (dictum).

[25]Little *v.* Barreme, 2 Cranch (6 U.S.) 170 (1804) at 177. Act of Feb. 9, 1799, ch. 2, 1 Stat. 613.

[26]Act of May 28, 1798, ch. 48, 1 Stat. 561; Act of Feb. 6, 1802, ch. 4, 2 Stat. 129. The latter statute was reenacted nearly verbatim to deal with a similar crypto-war against Algiers in 1815: Act of Mar. 3, 1815, ch. 90, 3 Stat. 230.

[27]Act of Mar. 3, 1839, ch. 89, 5 Stat. 355.

Congress engage in a full-dress review and debate of war policy before committing the United States to war: in 1812, in response to President Madison's request for a declaration of war against Great Britain. In each of these cases, however, a consensus existed between President and Congress on the necessity of some military response to an international conflict.

That consensus, if it existed at all in early 1846, was weak, and it dissolved with Whig congressional victories that autumn. Though Congress had acceded to Polk's request for a declaration of war, Whig, abolitionist, and sectional opposition raised an articulated constitutional opposition to his war policies. Congressman Abraham Lincoln, who supported the Whig resolution declaring the war unconstitutional, argued the point with his law partner William H. Herndon:

Allow the President to invade a neighboring nation whenever he shall deem it necessary to repel an invasion, . . . and you allow him to make war at his pleasure. Study to see if you can fix any limit to his power in this respect, after having given him so much power as you propose.[28]

Such opposition lapsed, however, with the conclusion of a successful peace by the Treaty of Guadaloupe Hidalgo (February 2, 1848). But by the time political opposition to the war had crystallized constitutionally, the issue of the President's war powers had been eclipsed by a constitutional controversy far more awesome—so much so that it may be considered the beginning of the terminal crisis of the Union.

On August 8, 1846, only three months into the Mexican War, Congressman David Wilmot, a Pennsylvania Democrat, offered an amendment to an appropriations bill providing that, "as an express and fundamental condition to the acquisition of any territory from the Republic of Mexico by the United States, . . . neither slavery nor involuntary servitude shall ever exist in any part of said territory, except for crime, whereof the party shall first be duly convicted."[29] The formula was hallowed: it was the language of the Northwest Ordinance, and so, in a sense, Wilmot was doing only what the

[28]Abraham Lincoln to William H. Herndon, Feb. 15, 1848, in Roy P. Basler (ed.), *The Collected Works of Abraham Lincoln* (7 vols., New Brunswick, N.J., 1953–55), I, 451.
[29]*Congressional Globe,* 29 Cong., 1 sess. 1217 (Aug. 8, 1846).

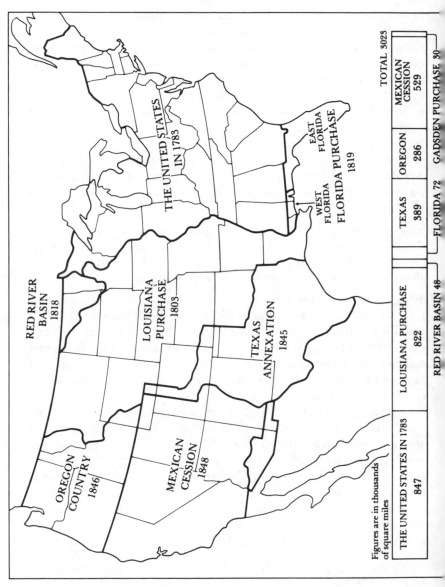

Territorial acquisitions of the United States from 1803 to 1853

RED RIVER BASIN 1818

THE UNITED STATES IN 1783

LOUISIANA PURCHASE 1803

TEXAS ANNEXATION 1845

OREGON COUNTRY 1846

MEXICAN CESSION 1848

EAST FLORIDA

WEST FLORIDA

FLORIDA PURCHASE 1819

Figures are in thousands of square miles

TOTAL 3023

THE UNITED STATES IN 1783	LOUISIANA PURCHASE		TEXAS	OREGON	MEXICAN CESSION
847	822		389	286	529

RED RIVER BASIN 48 — FLORIDA 72 — GADSDEN PURCHASE 30

Framers and their contemporaries had sanctioned. The Wilmot
Proviso, no matter how politically explosive, was not constitutionally innovative.

But it was explosive. Northern Democrats deserted the administration to support it. By 1848, every free-state legislature but one
instructed their Congressmen to support the Proviso. Politically,
Democratic congressional support for the Proviso signaled a rebellion by free-state representatives against southern dictation within
the party, a revolt made necessary by widespread popular support
for the Proviso back in their districts. The Proviso concentrated a
diffuse northern discontent with the political power of slavery and
provided a clear-cut, easily understood political response to a profound national transformation.

This transformation was in part geographic. The territory acquired between 1845 and 1853—by the annexation of Texas, the
Oregon settlement with Britain, the Mexican cession, and the Gadsden Purchase—increased the territory of the United States by 73
percent, adding roughly 1,234,000,000 square miles. The two settlements that had disposed of the slavery-expansion problem previously, the Northwest Ordinance and the Missouri Compromise,
were not operable to resolve the problem of slavery in this new
million and a quarter square miles of America.

Through 1845, even after the annexation of Texas, the Union was
not under intolerable stress. Both sections had accepted the Missouri Compromise line, despite their dissatisfactions, and were willing to let it partition America's land and resources between freedom
and slavery. The challenges posed by the abolitionists were, if not
irrelevant, at least insufficient to disrupt the Union. All the issues
they raised could be ignored, negotiated, or compromised as they
had been before 1846. But with the Mexican War, the United States
had become, in effect, a new nation once again, requiring a new
constitutional settlement.

Geography alone, no matter how immense the territory, does not
account for the appeal of the Wilmot Proviso in the North. It also
crystallized northern racial attitudes. Wilmot himself defended the
Proviso on the grounds that "the negro race already occupy enough
of this fair continent; let us keep what remains for ourselves, and our
children . . . for the free white laborer." A faction of New York
Democrats who supported the Proviso called it the "White Man's

Resolution." New York Senator John A. Dix insisted that Americans had a "sacred duty to consecrate these spaces to the multiplication of the white race."[30] Though the Proviso had some appeal to abolitionists—it *was*, after all, an antislavery measure, whatever the racial attitudes of its supporters might have been—its power in the North was not based on egalitarian ideals.

The Polk administration, some northern Democrats, and all southern political leaders fought the Proviso, and proposed four alternatives to it. In the four years following its introduction, the Proviso and these alternatives provided a range of alternative ways to deal with the problem slavery posed in the Empire for Liberty. The earliest in time was first embodied in the resolution annexing Texas (1845): an extension of the Missouri Compromise line through Texas. No one could identify precisely what Texas territory to which it might have applied in 1845, given the indefinite and disputed location of the Republic's boundaries. But the line might potentially be extended farther west through other territory to be acquired. An Indiana Congressman, William Wick, moved it as an alternative the same night Wilmot offered his Proviso, but it was promptly voted down. It soon attracted more substantial support, however: James Buchanan, Secretary of State in the Polk administration and seemingly front-runner for the Democratic presidential nomination in 1848, endorsed it in his widely reprinted "Old Berks" letter of 1847.[31] After some vacillation, Polk and the rest of his cabinet supported it too.

Extension of the Missouri line had an unusual appeal to southerners—unusual, given the growing belief among southern leaders that any restriction of slavery in the territories was unconstitutional. In 1847, Representative Armistead Burt of South Carolina, known to be speaking for Calhoun, offered it as an amendment to an Oregon admission bill. Its prompt rejection by northern Congressmen provoked Calhoun and the rest of the southern leadership to abandon compromise and move to developing the southern position.[32]

[30]All quotations from Richard H. Sewell, *Ballots for Freedom: Antislavery Politics in the United States, 1837–1860* (New York, 1976), pp. 172–173.

[31]James Buchanan to Charles Kessler, Aug. 25, 1847, in John B. Moore (ed.), *The Works of James Buchanan* (Philadelphia, 1908–11), VII, 386.

[32]*Congressional Globe*, 29 Cong., 2 sess., app. 116 (Jan. 14, 1847) (Burt), 454 (Feb. 19, 1847) (Calhoun).

United States Supreme Court Justice John Catron of Tennessee endorsed it,[33] and Delaware Senator John M. Clayton promoted it in 1848, unsuccessfully, as a compromise measure to resolve the increasingly tense sectional confrontation. In 1850, the Nashville Convention, a gathering of southern delegates called to consider the Compromise of 1850, indicated the Missouri line would be acceptable if the free states found the South's preferred position unacceptable.[34] The Missouri Compromise itself was repealed by the Kansas-Nebraska Act in 1854 and declared unconstitutional by Chief Justice Taney in the *Dred Scott* case (1857), but during secession winter (1860–61) Kentucky Senator John J. Crittenden resurrected it and proposed to run the line to the Pacific by a constitutional amendment as part of the "Crittenden Compromise" package.

The second alternative to the Wilmot Proviso was, operationally, the most successful: it was enacted, and it accomplished its real object. Historians call it the "Clayton Compromise," after the man who first proposed it, Senator Clayton. Moderate Congressmen found it attractive because it might get the entire question of slavery in the territories out of Congress, where it seemed to be both insoluble and incendiary. In 1848, during debates over the organization of California and New Mexico territories, Clayton moved that their organic acts contain no provisions concerning slavery, and that all questions involving slavery there be resolved by the territorial supreme court, whose decisions in such cases would be directly appealable to the United States Supreme Court.[35] Two years later, Congress adopted Clayton's proposal in the New Mexico and Utah territorial acts, part of the 1850 Compromise package. Congress thereby invited the United States Supreme Court to take up the slavery issue and resolve it as a constitutional question. The indirect result was Dred Scott's case. No matter how ill-advised the court's involvement there, it was by invitation.

[33]John Catron to Daniel Graham, July 12, 1848, James K. Polk Presidential Papers, Library of Congress (microfilm, ser. 2).

[34]Resolutions of the Nashville Convention, June 10, 1850, reprinted in Henry S. Commager (ed.), *Documents of American History,* 9th ed. (Englewood Cliffs, N.J., 1973), I, 324–325.

[35]Clayton's bill is in *Congressional Globe,* 30 Cong., 1 sess. 1002–1005 (July 26, 1848).

"Territorial sovereignty" (usually referred to as popular sovereignty) as a third alternative to the Wilmot Proviso was first suggested by Vice-President George M. Dallas, a Pennsylvania Democrat, and formally offered as a resolution introduced in Congress by Democratic Senator Daniel S. Dickinson of New York. Dallas proposed that the question of slavery in the territories be left "to the people of the territory . . . the business of settling the matter for themselves." Dickinson's resolution declared that "the true spirit and meaning of the Constitution [will] be observed . . . by leaving all questions concerning domestic policies [in the territories] to the legislatures chosen by the people thereof."[36] The weightiest support for the idea came from Michigan Senator Lewis Cass, a Democratic presidential hopeful for 1848, who declared in his "Nicholson letter" that the power of Congress to enact substantive legislation for a territory was "a doubtful and invidious authority." Cass did not then flatly say that congressional prohibition of slavery would be unconstitutional. Rather, he argued that the federal government was a government of limited and delegated authority, with all power over municipal legislation and domestic institutions left to the states and territories. He urged that slavery be left "to the people inhabiting [the territories] to regulate their internal concerns their own way." Cass insisted that the people of the territories had "the right to regulate [slavery] themselves, under the general principles of the constitution."[37] Neither Cass nor any other supporter of territorial sovereignty ever bothered to explain just what those "general principles of the constitution" were and how they would affect the status of slavery in the territories. So usefully ambiguous an idea could be made to appeal plausibly to both North and South, and thus territorial sovereignty retained its vitality long enough to become, in modified form, the centerpiece of the Kansas-Nebraska Act in 1854.

Territorial sovereignty's ambiguity proliferated constitutional

---

[36]Dallas and Dickinson are quoted in Chaplain W. Morrison, *Democratic Politics and Sectionalism: The Wilmot Proviso Controversy* (Chapel Hill, 1967), pp. 87–88. The phrase "territorial sovereignty," as a preferable alternative to "popular sovereignty" (already used above in an altogether different connotation) or "squatter sovereignty" (a disparaging term in its day), is taken from Arthur E. Bestor, Jr., "The American Civil War as a Constitutional Crisis," *American Historical Review*, LXIX (1964), 327–352.

[37]Cass's "Nicholson Letter" was printed in *Niles National Register*, Jan. 8, 1848.

doctrine, interpretation, and innovation. Cass, though insisting that he never deviated from his original conception of it, subtly modified the doctrine over the years until it was absorbed into the use Stephen Douglas made of it in 1854. Cass's refinements served as one of the principal vehicles for the development of an idea adopted by Taney in 1857: the notion that any congressional prohibition of slavery in the territories was unconstitutional. Cass first returned to the idea in 1850, with an argument only a lawyer would appreciate: the Wilmot Proviso was unconstitutional; but if it was not unconstitutional, it was inexpedient. Only the people of the territories had the power of substantive legislation.[38] This was a radical innovation. Never before 1847 were the people of a territory considered to be invested with the attributes of sovereignty. Then in the crucible of the Kansas-Nebraska debates, Cass flatly and for the first time unequivocally denied congressional power to exclude slavery. He insisted that the Territories clause empowered Congress only to dispose of the lands of the territory and to organize a territorial government, leaving municipal legislation to the territorial legislature. Cass was not a stalking horse for the southern clique; he rejected the southern doctrine of nonintervention. But the potential of his ideas could be bent as easily in a proslavery direction as in the opposite direction, and that is the use Taney made of them three years later.

Territorial sovereignty was based on a simplistic, readily comprehensible notion of democracy: let the people themselves control slavery in "their" territory. This had the added advantage of comporting with one of the most basic constitutional assumptions about slavery: that only the states, not the federal government, could control slavery in their jurisdictions. It also had the political advantage of not confronting the essential question lying just beyond the simple formulation of let-the-people-decide. That question was: When? Free-state leaders assumed that a decision to exclude slavery could be made at any point in the territorial stage by the territorial legislative body. Southerners, on the other hand, assumed that the decision could not be made before the territory was petitioning for admission as a state and had drawn up its state constitution. Pre-

---

[38]*Congressional Globe,* 31 Cong., 1 sess., 398 (Feb. 20, 1850).

sumably, if no bar existed to the admission of slaves before that point, slavery would have gained a foothold and would not be barred under the state constitution.

The ambiguity of territorial sovereignty was heightened by divergent sectional expectations for the future of slavery in the West. All northern proponents of the concept, including Cass and Douglas and even including some slave-state Whigs like Henry Clay, thought that the climate of the western territories was inhospitable to plantation agriculture. Therefore slavery and its black victims could not be transplanted there. James G. Blaine recalled an unnamed southern Congressman exclaiming in exasperation: "The whole controversy over the Territories . . . related to an imaginary negro in an impossible place."[39] Cass insisted that the Proviso was an unnecessary affront to southern pride, because it attempted to legislate what would occur in any event.

Proslavery and Free-Soil spokesmen, on the other hand, saw no natural bar to slavery in cold or arid regions. Slaves were used in mining and in industry; by the 1850s, southern corporations had begun to own slaves; and, if for no other purpose, slaves could be taken anywhere as personal servants.[40] Political leaders with long memories might have recalled that at the time of the Missouri crises, 1819–21, slaves profitably worked the lead mines of Galena, Illinois, diggings located in the cold northwest tip of the state. The existence of slavery at Galena was expressly secured, in modified form, in the Illinois Constitution of 1819. For centuries, slaves had been digging the mines of Spanish America and other seemingly inhospitable areas. Some southerners therefore found territorial sovereignty acceptable, but only if there was no direct impediment to slavery's penetration during the territorial stage.

Territorial sovereignty gained added flexibility, as well as antislavery overtones, by being tied to a constitutional consequence of the *Somerset* doctrine. In 1848, a New York judge, Greene Bronson, pointed out that under *Somerset,* Congress and a territorial legislature could exclude slavery from a territory simply by not enacting a slave code for it. Slavery not being established by positive law, any

---

[39]James G. Blaine, *Twenty Years of Congress* . . . (Norwich, Conn., 1884), I, 272.

[40]Robert S. Starobin, *Industrial Slavery in the Old South* (New York, 1970); Charles B. Dew, *Ironmaker to the Confederacy: Joseph R. Anderson and the Tredegar Iron Works* (New Haven, 1966); Sewall, *Ballots for Freedom,* pp. 192–197.

slave coming into the jurisdiction would be free, and under *Somerset,* the master would lack authority to hold the slave or compel the slave to return to some slave jurisdiction.[41] United States Supreme Court Justice John McLean, an opponent of slavery expansion, and future Justice John Archibald Campbell, a proslavery Alabamian, both conceded the validity of Bronson's argument.[42] Though current only in 1848, Stephen A. Douglas revived this idea as his "Freeport Doctrine" in 1858.

The ambiguity of territorial sovereignty made it useful to southern leaders, for a season. It was not inconsistent with the emerging proslavery doctrine of "nonintervention." By 1850, this became a name for a cluster of theories holding that: Congress could not exclude slavery from the territories; a territorial legislature was a creature of Congress, having no powers that Congress did not possess; a territorial legislature therefore could no more exclude slavery than could Congress; Congress could not permit a territorial legislature to exclude slavery, and any attempted exclusion, whether federal or territorial, was void; slaveowners had the same rights to migrate to the territories with their property, including slaves, as any other Americans had to migrate with theirs. Reinterpreted in the light of nonintervention, territorial sovereignty became a way of declaring that Congress *would* not take any action to inhibit the spread of slavery in the territories, with the vital but unspoken corollary that a territorial legislature *could* not.

Though territorial sovereignty retained its appeal for some southerners into the fifties, some concerned slave-state leaders concluded that it and the extension of the Missouri Compromise line were fatally defective because they conceded a vital constitutional point: the power of Congress to exclude slavery from the territories. After 1847, Calhoun and other southern leaders worked out a proslavery counterpart to the Wilmot Proviso to ensure that all territories were open to slavery. In 1847, Calhoun offered a set of resolutions in the

---

[41]Bronson is quoted in Joseph G. Rayback, *Free Soil: The Election of 1848* (Lexington, Ky., 1970), p. 253.

[42]McLean quoted in "Territorial Government," *United States Magazine and Democratic Review,* n.s., 23 (1848), 191–192; John A. Campbell to John C. Calhoun, Mar. 1, 1848, in Chauncey S. Boucher et al. (eds.), "Correspondence Addressed to John C. Calhoun, 1837–1849," American Historical Association *Annual Report . . . 1929* (Washington, 1930), p. 431.

Senate that extended the doctrinal content of his 1837 Resolutions. He maintained that: the territories were the common property of all the states; Congress could not discriminate between the states or between the citizens of the states by prohibiting slave-state citizens from taking their slave property into the territories; and Congress could not refuse to admit a new state because it permitted slavery.[43] Calhoun rejected the constitutionality of the Wilmot Proviso's central assumption that Congress had authority to exclude slavery from a territory. This was implicitly an attack on the constitutionality of the Missouri Compromise.

Next, the Nashville Convention of 1850 insisted that the property right Calhoun had specified is "entitled to the protection of the federal government" in the territories.[44] This implied that the federal government had to enact laws that protected a slaveowner's rights in human chattels. Richard Yeadon, a Charleston editor, perfected that idea by 1857 in claiming that the United States Constitution positively secured slavery "by federal protection and agency." The federal government had a duty of "guarantee, protection, and defense" of slavery in the territories.[45] This idea gathered force from a contemporary southern constitutional theory that slavery exists of its own force everywhere it is not affirmatively abolished. Missouri Senator James Green insisted that "the prohibition of slavery in the United States is local . . . the right to hold slave property wherever there is no prohibition is national."[46] To deal with the Bronson argument that slavery might be practically excluded from a territory by the absence of a federal and territorial slave code, Senator Jefferson Davis of Mississippi insisted in 1860 that it was the federal government's "duty" to provide a slave code for a territory failing to enact one; "and if experience should at any time prove that the judiciary does not possess power to insure adequate protection, it will then become the duty of Congress to

[43]*Congressional Globe,* 29 Cong., 2 sess. 455 (Feb. 19, 1847).

[44]Resolutions of the Nashville convention, reprinted in Commager, *Documents of American History,* I, 324–325.

[45]Richard Yeadon, *An Address Delivered before the . . . Literary Societies of Erskine College . . . 1857,* quoted in Theodore Parker, *The Present Aspect of Slavery in America . . .* (Boston, 1858), pp. 17–19.

[46]*Congressional Globe,* 36 Cong., 1 sess., app. 78 (Jan. 11, 1860).

supply such deficiency."[47] The southern wing of the Democratic party incorporated this idea into its 1860 platform as the final pre-secession statement of the South's position.

The southern view had the advantage of being supported by Calhoun's reconsideration of popular sovereignty, federalism, and slavery. In 1843, Calhoun began to write a systematic exposition of his constitutional views. The controversy ignited by the Wilmot Proviso, the accelerating pace of sectional polarization, and apprehension of his impending death spurred Calhoun on, and he completed two treatises, *A Disquisition on Government* and *A Discourse on the Constitution and Government of the United States* before his death in 1850. They were published posthumously. These two essays provided a philosophical underpinning to the southern position, and a program of constitutional alteration that would protect the security of slavery.

Calhoun's thought on the nature of humanity and the basis of government echoed Madison in the *Federalist*, Numbers 10, 37, 48, 51, and 63. All men were self-seeking, and would combine together in interest groups. These groups, in turn, would form coalitions in order to constitute a majority, which would seize the power of government to promote its own interests at the expense of a minority. This tendency of majoritarian oppression would take place not only within states, but also among states in a federation.

Here Calhoun parted company with Madison, who found security against this oppressive majoritarian coalition in the nature of representative republican government and in the size of the American federation. Instead, Calhoun argued that it was necessary to take

the sense of each interest or portion of the community, which may be unequally and injuriously affected by the action of the government . . . and to require the consent of each interest . . . to keep the government in action.

This required a structural modification of government to create

such an organism of the government . . . as will by dividing and distributing the powers of government, give to each division or interest, through its appropriate organ, either a concurrent voice in making and executing the laws or a veto on their execution.

[47]*Ibid.*, 1 sess. 658 (Feb. 2, 1860).

Calhoun called this the "concurrent majority." Translated into structural terms for the federal government, it meant a dual presidency, with each President representing one of the sections, and having a veto on all national legislation.[48]

Calhoun thought the idea that all men are born free and equal not only preposterous but dangerous. Blacks in particular were not, and never could be, the political or social equals of whites. Allowing them any form of freedom, equality, or political power would derange the only social organization by which blacks and whites could coexist in the same community: slavery. Slavery was thus a vital institution throughout the South. In the "Pakenham letter," which Calhoun composed as Secretary of State during the agitation over Texas annexation, he identified slavery as "in reality a political institution, essential to the peace, safety, and prosperity of those States of the Union in which it exists."[49] In that character, it enjoyed a special constitutional protection, being, uniquely, the only form of property particularly specified (though not by name) in the Constitution. Therefore any political action hostile to slavery, particularly its exclusion from the territories, was unconstitutional.

Slavery in the territories was important not only in its own right, but as an additional security for slavery in the older states. In trying to explain this idea, defenders of slavery frequently used the metaphor of a besieged citadel and its outposts. South Carolina Governor James Hamilton explained that the controversy over tariffs during the nullification crises was in reality "a battle at the outposts, by which, if we succeed in repulsing the enemy, the citadel would be safe."[50] Referring to the territorial issue, one of Calhoun's correspondents warned that "the necessary consequences of allowing all the outposts of Slavery to be carried, involves a certain destruction of the Citadel itself."[51] Seeing that his colleagues from the free

[48]Both the *Disquisition* and the *Discourse* are printed in Richard K. Cralle (ed.), *The Works of John C. Calhoun* (Charleston and New York, 1851–56), vol. I. Quotation at p. 25 *(Disquisition);* see p. 392 *(Discourse).*

[49]The Pakenham letter is in Sen. Doc., 28 Cong., 1 sess., ser. 435, doc. 341 (n.d.), 50–53 at 53.

[50]Hamilton to John Taylor, Sept. 14, 1830, in William W. Freehling (ed.), *The Nullification Era: A Documentary Record* (New York, 1967), pp. 100–101.

[51]Hilliard M. Judge to Calhoun, Apr. 29, 1849, reprinted in John Franklin Jameson (ed.), *Correspondence of John C. Calhoun,* in American Historical Association *Annual Report . . . 1899* (Washington, 1900), II, 1195–1197 at 1196.

states were being obtuse on this point, Senator Jefferson Davis tried
to lay it out for them in the simplest possible terms. "Why should
we care whether [slaves] go into other Territories or not?" he asked.
"Simply because of the war that is made against our institutions;
simply because of the want of security which results from the action
of our opponents in the northern States."[52]

But Calhoun could read the handwriting on the wall. He saw that
the North's numerical preponderance would lead—indeed, already
had led—to what he considered to be unconstitutional legislation
inimical to slavery (the Missouri Compromise, the tariff). What,
then, could the slave states do? Calhoun recurred to the nature of
the federal government, which was

a government emanating from a compact between sovereigns, and partak-
ing, in its nature and object, of the character of a joint commission, appointed to superintend and administer the interests in which all are jointly
concerned; but having beyond its proper sphere, no more power than if it
did not exist.[53]

Or, in other legal metaphors, the federal government was a trustee
or agent, with the states the principals. The terms of the trust were
set forth in the federal Constitution. If the federal government
abused its trust, as by enacting legislation hostile to the interests of
a state, the state could respond by declaring that the federal government had breached the terms of the trust—had, in other words,
acted unconstitutionally. The state would thus "nullify" the unauthorized act.

But that did not neutralize the North's population majority. Calhoun glumly foresaw that by repeated nibbling at slavery—abolishing it in the District of Columbia now, refusing to admit New Mexico
as a slave state later, then interfering with the interstate slave trade
—the free states might parlay their numbers in the House and
eventually in the Senate into a majority large enough to amend the
federal Constitution and override a single state's objection. What
then? The states could secede. Because the federal government was
a compact among sovereigns, or an agency set up by principals,
those who created it could withdraw from the compact when they

[52]*Congressional Globe*, 35 Cong., 1 sess. 619 (Feb. 8, 1858).
[53]"Address on the Relation which the States and General Government Bear to
Each Other" (1837) in Cralle, *Works of Calhoun*, VI, 73.

found that their creature was abusing their interests.[54]

Ten years after Calhoun's death, on Christmas Eve, 1860, the Convention of the people of South Carolina declared that in 1787

thus was established by compact between the States, a Government with defined objects and powers, limited to the express words of the grant . . . [but] the ends for which this Government was instituted have been defeated, and the [federal] Government itself has been destructive of them by the action of the nonslaveholding states.

The people of South Carolina therefore "have solemnly declared that the Union heretofore existing between this State and the other States of North America is dissolved."[55] The fatal logic of the Cast-Iron Man triumphed.

Even as Calhoun was dictating the *Disquisitions* and *Discourse* to his private secretary, people in the North were coalescing to form the cluster of interest groups that he foretold. Texas annexation had cut loose three disaffected political elements from their party moorings. Thus adrift, these three groups moved toward fusion among themselves. The result was the Free-Soil party.

The abolitionist movement, like the Protestant churches from which it drew its theology, discipline, and structure, was inherently prone to fission. Even after the movement split into Garrisonian and anti-Garrisonian wings in 1839, the latter could cohere only briefly. They espoused political action, and formed the Liberty party, which ran James G. Birney as its presidential candidate in 1840 and 1844. But this experiment proved divisive. Radicals split off because of disagreements over constitutional theory, while the mainstream of the Liberty party came under the leadership of its western wing. The westerners, led by Salmon P. Chase, energetically promoted the idea of a party organized around an antislavery platform, but that would attract significant numbers of Whigs and Democrats. Chase scoffed at splinter groups of ideological purists. He sought a real party that could challenge the Democrats and Whigs, gain votes, and elect candidates. He was quite willing to pay a price for political power by watering down the egalitarian element of abolition to appeal to the racial self-interest of whites in the western states who

[54]"Discourse on the Constitution," *ibid.*, I, 300.
[55]"The Declaration of the Causes of Secession," in Commager, *Documents of American History*, I, 373.

were electrified by the Wilmot Proviso. But Chase also believed that the core of the 1840 and 1844 Liberty platforms, the divorce of the federal government from the support of slavery, could be made compatible with the basis of an 1848 fusion party organized on the principle of "Free Soil."

As early as 1842, Chase spoke of the interests of "Free Labor" in the territories,[56] an irresistible issue to the people of the western states. The exclusion of slavery from the territories could be the first step toward a more comprehensive antislavery platform. This view derived from Liberty party constitutional beliefs. Since the federal government could not interfere with slavery in the states, it had to confine its acts to areas within its constitutional competence: fugitives, American slaves outside the United States, slavery in the territories, the District of Columbia, the interstate slave trade. Assuming the moral equivalence of these issues, why not seize on that one —slavery in the territories—that had the most widespread political appeal outside the abolitionist movement, and make it the central plank of a fusion platform?

The second element of a potential fusion group consisted of Whigs restless under their party's proslavery national leadership. These Whigs were most prominent in Massachusetts, where they came to be known as "Conscience Whigs" after 1846. In 1846, the year of the Wilmot Proviso, Conscience Whigs beckoned to abolitionists with a program that called not only for slavery's exclusion from the territories but its abolition in the District of Columbia, the abolition of the interstate slave trade, and opposition to the admission of new slave states. Charles Sumner went so far as to speak of "emancipation" as the true end of Conscience Whig policy.[57] Illinois Whig Congressman Owen Lovejoy thought that "the immediate object [of Free Soil] is one which we cordially approve, and the ultimate object is identical—the extinction of slavery."[58]

This, as it turned out, was based on a naïve misreading of the attitudes of the third group in the fusion coalition of 1848: disaffected Democrats. Some of them, especially those outside New York, were not opportunists: e.g., John Parker Hale of New Hamp-

[56]"Address of the Liberty Convention to the People of Ohio," *Emancipator and Free American*, Jan. 27, 1842.
[57]*The Works of Charles Sumner* (Boston, 1875–83), I, 313.
[58]Quoted in Sewell, *Ballots for Freedom*, p. 160.

shire, Marcus Morton of Massachusetts. But the core of the Democratic fusion group were New York Barnburners: men who had espoused the Wilmot Proviso in 1846 partly because of constituency pressure but mostly because of resentment at what they considered their betrayal in the 1844 Democratic convention and Polk's subsequent patronage policies. The Libertymen and egalitarian Whigs like Sumner had to shut their eyes to the avid racism of the Barnburners.

But New York Democrats' racism was momentarily overshadowed by their lust for revenge in 1848, and the Conscience Whigs and Libertymen, in turn, could interpret the ambiguity of Free Soil to their liking. A marriage of expedience was in order and was consummated at the fusion convention in Buffalo, August, 1848, where the Free Soil party was born. Evenhandedly, the new party drew its presidential candidate from the Barnburners (Martin Van Buren), its vice-presidential candidate from the Conscience faction (Charles Francis Adams, son of John Quincy Adams), and two of its planks, Free Soil and divorce, from the Libertymen. It marched into the 1848 elections under the honestly equivocal slogan, "Van Buren and Free Soil, Adams and Liberty."

The Free-Soil platform hinted at, but did not really adopt, the idea that congressional permission for slavery to enter the territories was unconstitutional. Drawing on some of the murkiest areas of abolitionist constitutional rhetoric, two of the planks declared that the Constitution "expressly denied to the Federal Government . . . all constitutional power to deprive any person of life, liberty, or property, without due legal process," leaving the unstated inference that slavery was such a denial, and that "Congress has no more power to make a Slave than to make a King; no more power to institute or establish Slavery, than to institute or establish a Monarchy. No such power can be found among those specifically conferred by the Constitution, or derived by just implication from them."[59] This really did not come to terms with the issue of constitutionality, except as a denial of the emerging southern position. Perhaps greater precision is too much to expect of a campaign platform.

[59]Donald B. Johnson and Kirk H. Porter (comps.), *National Party Platforms, 1840–1972* (Urbana, 1973), p. 13.

The results of the 1848 election were no less equivocal than the campaign. The regular Democrats nominated Lewis Cass of Michigan, at the time the leading exponent of territorial sovereignty. The Whigs cannily chose the apolitical war hero General Zachary Taylor, a Louisiana slaveholder, and refused to commit themselves to a platform or to any of the five alternative solutions to the problem of slavery in the territories. Thus the Whig victory on a nonplatform that ignored the most exigent issue of the time merely postponed the day of constitutional reckoning. The 1848 election did nothing to resolve the territorial question. The discovery of gold in California the next year only served to make that issue more urgent, because the territory was filling with settlers so fast that it would soon have the minimal population requisite for statehood. California's people were Free Soil in their sentiments.

Moreover, the crisis had broadened. Southern leaders no longer saw the issue as being confined to slavery in the territories. The whole furor over the Wilmot Proviso was but symptomatic of a larger problem having to do with the security of slavery in the states. They came to agree with the position that Calhoun had sketched in his 1847 resolutions: the South was in danger of being discriminated against by the free states, of being denied the right to expand into the West, and, ultimately, of being plunged into a civil war of slaves against masters because the slaves were being encouraged to become discontented with their lot by northern fanatics. Seeing the issue in these larger terms, southerners realized that the security of the slave system required more than a resolution of the territorial question alone. The issues raised by the Wilmot Proviso had escalated from being an abstract, though urgently felt "point of honor," as Georgia Congressman Robert Toombs called it,[60] to a grim choice between adequate security for slavery and disunion. This, and not just the unresolved choice among the Wilmot Proviso and its alternatives, produced the Crisis of 1850.

Henry Clay and Stephen A. Douglas worked out solutions to the constitutional components of the Crisis of 1850 in a series of bills they marshaled through Congress. The Compromise of 1850 consisted of the following elements:

[60]Robert Toombs to John J. Crittenden, Jan. 22, 1849, in Mrs. Chapman Coleman, *The Life of John J. Crittenden* (Philadelphia, 1873), I, 335–336.

1. California was admitted as a state; its Constitution excluded slavery.[61]

2. Congress dealt adroitly with two politically significant but constitutionally irrelevant problems by setting the Texas–New Mexico border at roughly its present location, and compensating Texas for the loss of the claimed territory by a $10 million grant, half of which was to go to holders of Texas securities, a straightforward buying-out of powerful speculators in Texas bonds.

3. Congress abolished the slave trade in the District of Columbia.[62] This had a double constitutional significance, neither of which was reassuring to southerners. First, it was a clear assertion of congressional power over the District of Columbia, even though slavery there remained intact and under the protection of federal law. This seemed a dangerous precedent to southerners; Calhoun had warned against it in his 1837 Resolutions. Second, it asserted federal power over the interstate slave trade, because it pertained explicitly to the importation and exportation of slaves into and out of the District. Southerners had long denied that Congress had power to ban the interstate trade.

4. Congress enacted the Fugitive Slave Act of 1850.

5. Congress organized the New Mexico and Utah regions as territories. Their enabling acts provided that when they attained the requisite population, they would be admitted as states "with or without slavery, as their constitution may prescribe" at the time of admission. The enabling acts also contained a suggestively ambiguous statement that "the legislative power of the territory shall extend to all rightful subjects of legislation, consistent with the Constitution." This presumably would invalidate provisions of the Mexican Constitution in Utah and New Mexico, under which slavery had been abolished.[63]

Whether the United States Constitution would of its own force have established slavery in the territories remained an open question. If the southern view was accepted—that slavery existed everywhere it was not affirmatively abolished—the extension of the fed-

[61]Act of Sept. 9, 1850, ch. 51, 9 Stat. 453; California Constitution of 1849, Art. I, sec. 18, in Thorpe, *Federal and State Constitutions,* I, 392.

[62]Act of Sept. 20, 1850, ch. 63, 9 Stat 467.

[63]Act of Sept. 9, 1850, ch. 49, secs. 2, 7, 10, 9 Stat. 446 (New Mexico); Act of Sept. 9, 1850, ch. 51, secs. 1, 6, 9, 9 Stat. 453 (Utah).

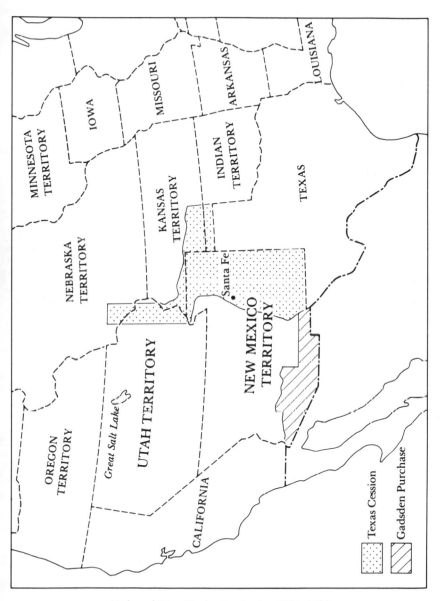

Utah and New Mexico territories, 1854–1858

eral Constitution over the territories would have established it there. Because slavery was not affirmatively excluded from these Territories, they were open to slave settlement, and a few slaves were in fact taken to New Mexico. In 1859, New Mexico adopted a territorial slave code.[64]

Ohio's Free-Soil Senator Salmon P. Chase declared that "the question of slavery in the territories has been avoided. It has not been settled."[65] He was referring to a threefold evasion in the Compromise. First, because California was admitted directly as a state, skipping entirely the territorial stage, Congress was able to avoid the territorial problem there. Second, though Congress did reject the Wilmot Proviso and the Missouri Compromise line for Utah and New Mexico, it did nothing to resolve the long-standing ambiguity of territorial sovereignty: could the territorial legislature exclude slavery at any point during the territorial phase? Third, Congress enacted the Clayton Compromise of 1848 by providing that any question decided by the territorial supreme court of Utah or New Mexico relating to the personal freedom of a black or to title to slaves could go on appeal directly to the United States Supreme Court by writ of error or appeal. Congress thereby confessed its impotence as a policymaking body to resolve the most pressing political issue of the day, and extended a dangerous, open-ended invitation to another body to do it.

But the Compromise did get the troublesome issue out of Congress, and both parties adopted platforms in 1852 pledging themselves to the "finality" of the Compromise measures as a total resolution of all issues relating to slavery. At last, party leaders insisted, the slavery issue had been disposed of once and for all.

Dissident groups on the extremes of the controversy sulked. In the South, secessionist radicals were doubly disappointed, first in the moderate, compromising, and Unionist tone of the platform adopted by the Nashville Convention in 1850. Convened by radicals hoping to denounce the Compromise, the Convention was dominated by moderates who endorsed a mild version of Calhoun's property theories but who concluded, almost amicably, that "this

[64]"An Act to provide for the protection of property in Slaves in this Territory," ch. 26, *Laws of the Territory of New Mexico . . . 1858–9*.
[65]*Congressional Globe*, 31 Cong., 1 sess. 1859 (Sept. 18, 1850).

controversy should be ended, either by a recognition of the constitutional rights of the Southern people, or by an equitable partition of the territories," an inconsistent posture from a purist viewpoint.[66] The "Georgia Platform," adopted in December, 1850, was also disappointing to southern radicals despite its hectoring tone. A Georgia convention called to consider the Compromise and secession resolved that it would accept the Compromise as "a permanent adjustment" of the sectional controversy, but warned that the state would secede if Congress took any action inimical to slavery in the District of Columbia, federal territories, and other sites of federal jurisdiction, such as forts; if Congress refused to admit a new state because it recognized slavery; if Congress tried to suppress the slave trade between slave states; if Congress prohibited the introduction of slaves into New Mexico and Utah territories; or if Congress enacted any law "materially modifying" the Fugitive Slave Acts of 1793 and 1850. For good measure, the Georgians warned the free states that the South expected a "faithful execution" of the Fugitive Slave Act.[67] For the moment, "finality" reigned as the dominant mood in the South.

It reigned as well in the North. New York Barnburners returned to the fold, leaving the Free-Soil coalition bereft of its most politically astute component. The Free-Soilers therefore made a disappointing showing in the 1852 election, and the divided antislavery movement seemed to dissolve into little sectarian groups that could do nothing more effective than squabble with each other. But as David Potter judiciously observed, a profound realignment of ideas was taking place. "Without embracing secession, the South had committed itself to the principle of secessionism; without embracing abolition, the North had committed itself to the principle of abolitionism."[68]

The Compromise of 1850 was an opportunistic maneuver to get an insoluble controversy out of the political arena, rather than to settle it. Alexander Stephens—not an extremist, but a Georgia Unionist—evaluated the consequences of this with unusual foresight before the compromise measures were enacted:

[66]The Resolutions of the Nashville Convention are excerpted in Commager, *Documents of American History,* I, 324–325.
[67]The Georgia Platform is reprinted *ibid.,* pp. 323–324.
[68]David M. Potter, *The Impending Crisis 1848–1860* (New York, 1976), pp. 143–144.

The present crisis may pass, the present adjustment may be made, but the great question of the permanence of slavery in the Southern states will be far from being settled thereby. And in my opinion the crisis of that question is not far ahead.[69]

As Stephens saw, the controversies of 1850 had gone far beyond slavery in the western territories; they involved the very existence of slavery itself. And *that,* all hopeful talk of "finality" notwithstanding, was further than ever from solution.

The most inflammatory element of the Compromise was the Fugitive Slave Act of 1850. It was a supplement to, not a replacement for, the original Act of 1793.[70] The first Fugitive Slave Act enabled slaveowners or their agents to seize a runaway, haul him before a federal judge or a local magistrate, prove title to the slave by affidavit or oral testimony, and get a certificate of rendition entitling them to remove the slave. Though enforcement of the statute between 1793 and 1842 provoked little controversy, abolitionists kept up a petition campaign to have the act abolished or modified in ways helpful to captured blacks.

After the furor in 1842 over the *Prigg* decision, the *Latimer* case in Boston, and the subsequent personal-liberty laws, southerners began to complain about what they considered a lackadaisical attitude toward the statute in the free states. In particular, the federal mechanisms under the 1793 Act seemed inadequate to them. In the federal court system of the time, only one federal judge sat in each state or district, except when a U.S. Supreme Court justice was circuit-riding there. Hence, for practical purposes, slave catchers depended chiefly on local magistrates for certificates of rendition. Some states explicitly forbade these magistrates from participating in fugitive slave hearings. Even where not disabled in that way, magistrates were likely to mirror the opinion of their communities, and that opinion, after 1842, became increasingly hostile to slave catching. The consequence was overstated by the Virginia General Assembly, but their views accurately reflect the way the South regarded enforcement of the Act after 1842. The master or slave catcher,

---

[69]Quoted *ibid.,* p. 124.
[70]Act of Sept. 18, 1850, ch. 60, 9 Stat. 462; Act of Feb. 12, 1793, ch. 7, 1 Stat. 302.

a stranger, must go into a free state, seize his slave without form or process of law, and unaccompanied by a single civil officer, must carry that slave, in the face of a fanatical and infuriated population, perhaps from the centre of extremists of the state, a distance of two or three hundred miles to the place where the judge may happen to reside . . .

and even then the slave catcher lacked effective process to secure the slave while leaving the state.[71]

Given extensive northern emotional revulsion at the intrusion of the Slave Power and at the recapture of fugitive slaves, often under pitiable or dramatic circumstances, the South's demand for more stringent fugitive-recapture mechanisms assured a sectional dogfight. The Act of 1850 was gratuitously offensive to northern whites—to say nothing of northern blacks. It contained the following innovations on the 1793 statute:

1. Owners and slave catchers were authorized to seize a black person either with a federal warrant or without legal process. The latter option made it easy for unscrupulous kidnappers to seize free blacks in the border states and secure their "rendition" through fraudulent affidavits.

2. Both warrants and certificates of rendition could be granted by federal judges, as under the 1793 act, but also by a class of pseudo-judicial officers, "commissioners," nominated by federal circuit courts and territorial superior courts.

3. The alleged slave was explicitly forbidden from testifying on his own behalf, a right he may arguably have been accorded under the 1793 Act.

4. For their services, commissioners earned a fee of $5 if their determination was in favor of the slave (i.e., that the individual before them was not the slave claimed) and $10 if their decision was in favor of the owner.

5. Obstruction or rescue was punishable by a fine of $1,000 and imprisonment for six months. These two points, taken together, prompted abolitionist Anson Burlingame's remark that the Fugitive Slave Act set the price of a Carolina Negro at $1,000 and a Yankee soul at $5.[72]

[71]Resolution of Feb. 7, 1849, in *Acts of the General Assembly of Virginia* [1849–50], 240–254 at 252.
[72]Quoted in Allan Nevins, *Ordeal of the Union* (New York, 1947), I, 381.

6. Commissioners and federal marshals could form a posse out of bystanders to assist in capture and rendition. Every adult male, by this provision, was made a potential slave catcher.

7. All legal process, such as habeas corpus, that might interfere with the rendition of the alleged slave was forbidden.

8. All expenses incurred to prevent rescues, as well as routine judicial administrative costs, were to be paid out of the federal treasury.

9. Federal marshals having fugitives in their custody were liable for the slave's full value if the slave escaped.

New York Senator William H. Seward's famous "higher law" speech (which was actually aimed at the territorial components of the 1850 Compromise, not the fugitive slave bill) announced northern resistance to the Act. His easily quotable comment—"But there is higher law than the Constitution . . ."—taken out of his restricted, quasi-religious context, suggested that even if the Fugitive Slave Act was constitutional, a point by no means conceded in the North, it was overridden by the law of conscience.[73] Abolitionist ministers amplified Seward's remark, publishing sermon after sermon swelling the corpus of abolitionist literature and affirming the duty of disobedience to immoral law.[74] The theological and propagandistic elements of these higher-law sermons had a constitutional impact, encouraging the elaboration of arguments Chase and Birney had begun in the *Matilda* case of 1837.

Substantive objections to the constitutionality of the Act fell under three heads:[75]

1. States' rights: building on a theme elaborated by Chase in his *Van Zandt* arguments of 1847, the fugitive-slave clause of Article IV,

[73]William Henry Seward, Senate speech of March 11, 1850, reprinted in George E. Baker (ed.), *The Works of William H. Seward* (Boston, 1884), I, 74.

[74]A compendium of the theological content of these sermons is William Hosmer, *The Higher Law, in the Relations to Civil Government: With Particular Reference to Slavery, and the Fugitive Slave Law* (Auburn, N.Y., 1852).

[75]This summary of the antislavery constitutional argument concerning the 1850 Act is derived from the following primary sources: Robert Rantoul, *The Fugitive Slave Law . . .* (n.p., n.d. [1851]), reprinted in pertinent part in William H. Pease and Jane H. Pease (eds.), *The Antislavery Argument* (Indianapolis, 1965), pp. 370–384; [William Jay,] "A Letter to the Hon. Samuel A. Eliot . . . in Reply to His Apology for Voting for the Fugitive Slave Bill" (1851), in William Jay, *Miscellaneous Writings on Slavery* (Boston, 1853) at pp. 572–592; Lysander Spooner, *A Defence for Fugitive Slaves* (Boston, 1850).

section 2, was more in the nature of a compact between the states than it was a clause granting power to the federal government. Hence the federal government derived no enforcement powers from it, nor did it authorize the federal government to impose duties on the states. This argument carried considerable weight because the fugitive-slave clause was located in Article IV, a collection of compactlike clauses dealing with interstate relations, rather than Article 1, section 8, dealing with the powers of the federal government, and because it was drafted in the passive voice, yet directed at states, not the federal government.

2. Judicial power: the commissioners were not judges and therefore not invested with the "judicial Power of the United States" specified in Article III, and hence incapable of making conclusive determinations on personal status or property rights. This argument, too, was persuasive, because the commissioners' determination was final everywhere and as to everyone except the master in the state of alleged escape. This argument received support from an unlikely source: United States Attorney General John J. Crittenden, a supporter of the Act, who in an 1851 official opinion determined that the commissioner under the Act "constituted a tribunal with exclusive jurisdiction" whose judgment was "conclusive upon every other tribunal."[76] But if conclusive on other courts, the commissioner's determination was at least arguably judicial, especially if Crittenden was right in designating him a "tribunal."

One possible way out of the conceptual difficulty Crittenden's opinion created would have been to argue that the fugitive-slave commissioners were a court, but not an Article III court (that is, one organized under Article III of the Constitution). The commissioners might have been found to be so-called Article I courts created under that clause of Article I, section 8, that empowers Congress to "constitute Tribunals inferior to the supreme Court." Such courts need not have the judicial attributes of Article III courts, yet may perform conclusive, judicial acts.

3. Civil liberties: the Act violated the jury trial, confrontation, cross examination, and habeas corpus provisions of the Sixth and

[76]Opinion of Sept. 18, 1850, in *Official Opinions of the Attorneys General of the United States*, V, 254–259 at p. 258. Crittenden insisted, however, that the Act, or at least its habeas corpus provision, was constitutional.

Seventh Amendments and Article I, section 9.

The United States Supreme Court did not speak to these issues until the 1859 case of *Ableman* v. *Booth*, in which Chief Justice Taney, in dictum, declared the Act constitutional, without going into detail, without offering any reasoning to support his position, and without citing any precedent.[77] Meanwhile, however, abolitionists resorted to lobbying state legislatures, persuading them to enact more advanced personal liberty laws; they justified popular disobedience of the Act; and they provided defense arguments in prosecutions for violation of the Act.

In revulsion at the Kansas-Nebraska Act of 1854, northern state legislatures struck at the action of Congress indirectly, by the only means available to them: enactment of personal liberty laws that went beyond the *Prigg*-era statutes of 1842–50. Generally, the earlier statutes merely took advantage of the loophole of Story's dictum and prohibited the use of the state's physical facilities (jails) or its officers (sheriffs, judges) for fugitive recaptures.[78] The more radical states of the 1850s openly defied both the spirit and the letter of the 1850 Compromise. Vermont in 1850 made the writ of habeas corpus available to detained fugitives, reaffirmed their right to jury trial, and required the state's attorneys in each county to assist fugitives in recovering their freedom.[79] In 1854–55, Vermont, Maine, Massachusetts, Connecticut, Rhode Island, and Michigan extended their personal liberty laws to prohibit state officials from participating in the enforcement of the federal fugitive laws, Massachusetts going furthest in vacating the office of any state official granting a certificate of removal, making such an individual incapable of holding state office, and disbarring attorneys representing claimants. They reenacted earlier provisions prohibiting the use of jails to house fugitives, an increasingly effective blow at fugitive recaptures, leaving the claimant and slave catchers to try to rent private rooms. These states prohibited kidnapping of free blacks under the pretense that they were fugitive slaves, a power that Justice John McLean in a *Prigg* dictum claimed belonged to the states. Vermont, Massachusetts, and Michigan extended the be-

[77]21 How. (62 U.S.) 506 (1859) at 526; on this case, see below, ch. 6.

[78]On these acts, see Thomas D. Morris, *Free Men All: The Personal Liberty Laws of the North, 1780–1861* (Baltimore, 1974).

[79]*Acts and Resolves . . . of Vermont . . . 1850*, No. 16.

nefits of the writ of habeas corpus and of jury trial to detained fugitives, and provided for the assistance of state's attorneys to fugitives.[80] Arguably, the habeas corpus, jury trial, and state's attorney provisions, as well as the Massachusetts removal provisions, conflicted with the federal statute and were hence invalid.[81]

Captures and rescues under the Fugitive Slave Act provided intense, real-life drama that supplemented the book and stage versions of *Uncle Tom's Cabin* and that drove the reality of slavery home to many northern people in their own communities. Five of these captures and/or rescues had constitutional significance: the "Christiana massacre," Pennsylvania, 1851; Jerry, Syracuse, New York, 1851; Thomas Sims, Boston, 1851; Anthony Burns, Boston, 1854; George McQuerry, Ohio, 1853. The Sims and Burns cases confronted the Boston bar and bench with a challenge to the constitutionality of the Fugitive Slave Act. The McQuerry case produced a similar confrontation for Justice John McLean, the only member of the United States Supreme Court who at the time might be suspected of entertaining antislavery sympathies. The "Christiana massacre" and the Jerry rescue tested the federal government's willingness to use prosecutions for treason to enforce the Fugitive Slave Act.

In 1851, after Chief Justice Shaw refused a writ of habeas corpus, a black mob rescued a detained fugitive, Shadrach.[82] The rescue alarmed President Millard Fillmore, who called a special cabinet meeting to discuss it, and went so far as to place federal soldiers at the disposal of the federal marshal to prevent further rescues. Shaw was primed for abolitionist efforts to have him declare the Fugitive Slave Act of 1850 unconstitutional. When another fugitive, Thomas Sims, was captured that year, the courthouse where Shaw sat was girded in chains and ropes, so that persons trying to enter, including the Chief Justice himself, had to stoop under the chains. This provided a propaganda coup for abolitionists, and Theodore Parker

[80]On these statutes, see generally Morris, *Free Men All,* pp. 159–185, and Stanley W. Campbell, *The Slave Catchers: Enforcement of the Fugitive Slave Law 1850–1860* (Chapel Hill, 1970), ch. 8, "The Personal Liberty Laws and Enforcement of the Fugitive Slave Law."

[81]These are the opinions of Campbell, *Slave Catchers,* pp. 181–182, and Levy, *Law of the Commonwealth and Chief Justice Shaw,* p. 106.

[82]On the Shadrach, Sims, and Burns affairs, see Levy, *Law of the Commonwealth and Chief Justice Shaw,* ch. 6, "The Fugitive Slave Law."

made the most of it: "the Supreme Court seemed to love the chains
round the Court House; for one by one the judges bowed and
stooped and bent and cringed and curled and crouched down, and
crawled under the chain. . . . It was a very appropriate spectacle,—
the southern chain on the neck of the Massachusetts court."[83]

Antislavery lawyers Samuel E. Sewall, Richard Henry Dana, and
Robert Rantoul sought a writ of habeas corpus on Sims's behalf
from the Supreme Judicial Court. Shaw denied the writ and upheld
the constitutionality of the Fugitive Slave Act in what was the preeminent judicial determination on that issue from any court, federal or
state. Like Story before him in the *Prigg* opinion, Shaw adopted a
version of the "historical-necessity" thesis, arguing that the fugitive-slave clause was essential to the ratification of the Constitution.
He found congressional power to enact the statute in the combination of that clause and the necessary-and-proper clause of Article I,
section 8. Relying on *Prigg*, which had upheld the constitutionality
of the 1793 Act, Shaw found the 1850 Act constitutional on the
same grounds, both as to the challenge that Congress lacked power
to enact either and as to the challenge that both failed to provide
for jury trial.[84] Shaw's reasoning was labored, yet it was in its time
"the highest authority,—to the degree that, in opinion of judges
. . . in later cases . . . it has been taken to preclude all further juristical
discussion."[85]

The rendition of Anthony Burns in 1854 was more significant as
drama than as constitutional discourse, but it did offer several
refinements to the state of the law as it was left in the *Sims* case.[86]
Burns was seized as a fugitive, held despite a large hostile crowd and

[83]Theodore Parker, *The Boston Kidnapping: A Discourse to Commemorate the Rendition
of Thomas Sims* . . . (Boston, 1852), p. 38. Parker paid the Boston bar this compliment:
"There are kennels of the courts wherein there settled down all that the law breeds
most foul, loathesome, and hideous and abhorrent to the light of day; slowly, stealth-
ily, continually agglomerating its fetid massy spontaneous cohesion, and sinking by
the irresistible gravity of rottenness into that abhorred deep, the lowest ghastliest pit
in all subterranean vaults of human sin. . . . the government has skimmed the top
and dredged the bottom of these kennels of the courts" to find commissioners. *Ibid.*

[84]In re Sims, 7 Cush. (61 Mass.) 285 (1851). See Leonard W. Levy, "Sims' Case:
The Fugitive Slave Law in Boston in 1851," *Journal of Negro History,* XXXV (1950),
39–74.

[85]John Codman Hurd, *The Law of Freedom and Bondage in the United States* (Boston,
1862), II, 653.

[86]A judicious compilation of documents pertaining to the case may be found in
Jane H. Pease and William H. Pease, *The Fugitive Slave Law and Anthony Burns: A
Problem in Law Enforcement* (Philadelphia, 1975).

a rescue attempt that resulted in the death of a deputy guarding him, and was marched back to Virginia slavery under massive federal, state, and local escort. Army artillery ringed the courthouse square. Marines marched Burns to the waiting ship with fixed bayonets; drunken militiamen, according to eyewitness abolitionist accounts, taunted the hostile crowds by singing "Carry me back to old Virginny." The Burns rendition produced an opinion by United States Commissioner Edward G. Loring upholding the constitutionality of the 1850 Act on the grounds that the duties of the commissioner were ministerial, not judicial, thereby affirming the legitimacy of the office and rendering it unnecessary to provide for jury trial since the fugitive-rendition proceedings were entirely nonjudicial.[87] In response to this federal show of force, and the enactment of the Kansas-Nebraska Act which occurred simultaneously with the Burns recapture, the Massachusetts General Court enacted the 1855 Personal Liberty Law, defiantly captioned "An Act to protect the Rights and Liberties of the People of the Commonwealth of Massachusetts," with its provision for ouster of officials granting certificates of rendition. Loring, who was a judge of probate, was promptly removed from office.

The Burns rendition provoked an outpouring of angry sermons, speeches, pamphlets, editorials, and books. The most stinging critique of all was Henry David Thoreau's condemnation of judges and the law in his essay "Slavery in Massachusetts" (1854). Thoreau extolled resistance to law. "The law will never make men free; it is men who have got to make the law free. They are the lovers of law and order who observe the law when the government breaks it." Thinking of Loring's and Shaw's reasoning, he wrote that "in important moral and vital questions, like this, it is just as impertinent to ask whether a law is constitutional or not, as to ask whether it is profitable or not." He stigmatized constitutional reasoning in a sharp metaphor:

The judge still sits grinding at his organ, but it yields no music, and we hear only the sound of the handle. He believes that all the music resides in the handle, and the crowd tosses him their coppers the same as before.[88]

[87]The relevant portion of Loring's opinion is reprinted in Pease, *Fugitive Slave Law and Anthony Burns,* pp. 72–73.
[88]Henry David Thoreau, "Slavery in Massachusetts," in *Miscellanies* (vol. 10 of *The Writings of Henry David Thoreau*) (Boston, 1893), pp. 181, 191.

United States Supreme Court Justice John McLean was sensitized to this challenge to the judicial conscience by Circuit Court hearings in the *VanZandt* case in 1843. McLean rejected the urging of his personal friend Salmon P. Chase that he consult conscience rather than law:

The law is our only guide. If convictions, . . . of what is right or wrong, are to be substituted as a rule of action in disregard of the law, we shall soon be without law and without protection . . . in this way, society may be resolved into its original elements, and then the governing principle must be force. Every approximation to this state is at war with the social compact.[89]

When the issue returned to plague him under the much harsher Act of 1850, in the *McQuerry* hearings a decade later, McLean accepted the *Prigg* decision on the constitutionality of the 1793 Act as equally conclusive of constitutional challenges to the 1850 Act, and then turned to one of the most forceful substantive objections raised to the 1850 Act during congressional debates. If a jury trial were not provided in the rendition state, to determine at least the alleged fugitive's identity, then the right to jury trial would prove illusory back in the "home" state for most recaptured blacks because, as a practical matter, a master who succeeded in bringing back a fugitive would not keep him, but would probably sell him off at the first opportunity, and would be likely to do so before the black had a chance to avail himself of whatever judicial mechanisms might be available to him in the slave state to determine his claim to freedom. McLean responded forthrightly to this challenge when made in argument, combining the Story disclaimer of responsibility with the argument to be made by Loring the next year on the provisional nature of fugitive hearings:

the inquiry [under the 1850 Act] is preliminary, and not final. It is true, it may be said, that the power of the master may be so exercised as to defeat a trial for the freedom of the fugitive. This must be admitted, but the hardship and injustice supposed arises out of the institution of slavery, over which we have no control. Under such circumstances, we cannot be held answerable.[90]

[89]Jones v. VanZandt, 13 Fed. Cas. 1047 (No. 7502) (C.C.D. Ohio, 1843), at 1048.
[90]Miller v. McQuerry, 17 Fed. Cas. 335 (No. 9583) (C.C.D. Ohio, 1853) at 340.

McLean's *McQuerry* opinion was influential in persuading southerners that free-state judges would stand by their duty in rendering
fugitives, and it acted as a deterrent to securing the acceptance of
abolitionist constitutional doctrines among northern judges.

Two rescues—Jerry in Syracuse, New York, 1851, and the "Christiana massacre" in southeastern Pennsylvania, 1851—tested the determination of the President and his legal advisers as well as the
federal judiciary to use the ultimate legal sanction, prosecutions for
treason, to enforce the Fugitive Slave Acts. Even before there were
any significant fugitive rescues, prominent Democratic and Whig
conservatives insisted that disobedience to the Fugitive Act would
be treason. The Massachusetts Jacksonian Benjamin Hallett, in a
bloodthirsty speech of 1850, exclaimed that resistance to it "is treason, rebellion, mobism, and anarchy, and he who risks it must risk
hanging for it."[91] Daniel Webster charged that legislative resolutions from Ohio, New York, and Massachusetts denouncing the new
statute were "distinctly treasonable." A fugitive rescue, he declared
would be "an act of clear treason," a "levying war against the
Union."[92]

The "Christiana massacre" was a foiled recapture incident in
which the white owner-claimant and three blacks were killed in a
September, 1851, shootout in southeastern Pennsylvania. Two local
Quakers who refused to participate in recapturing the runaways,
plus some forty others, were charged with treason. United States
District Court Judge John Kane, a Jacksonian Democrat, instructed
the grand jury that they should return an indictment for treason if
they found that the defendants had incited resistance to execution
of a federal law if accompanied or followed by force.[93] Kane's
charge was partially supported by precedent: in the aftermath of the
Whiskey Rebellion of western Pennsylvania in 1794, Judge William
Paterson charged a United States Circuit Court jury that if the
object of an uprising "was to suppress the excise offices, and to

[91]Speech, Nov. 26, 1850, recorded in *Proceedings of the Constitutional Meeting at Faneuil Hall . . .* (Boston, 1850), p. 21.
[92]"Speech to the Young Men of Albany" (1851) in *The Works of Daniel Webster* (Boston, 1851), II, 577–578.
[93]Charge to Grand Jury, Treason, 30 Fed. Cas. 1047 (No. 18276) (C.C.E.D. Pa. 1851); on the entire incident and its judicial aftermath, see Jonathan Katz, *Resistance at Christiana: . . . A Documentary Account* (New York, 1974).

prevent the execution of an act of Congress, by force and intimidation, the offence, in legal estimation, is high treason. . . ."⁹⁴ But the
Whiskey Rebellion involved an extensive, armed insurrection directly challenging one of the most sensitive exercises of federal
authority: the collection of taxes. Blacks exercising their right of
self-defense scarcely rose to the level of waging war against the
United States. Lawrence Friedman has noted that a totalitarian state
has trouble distinguishing between treason and ordinary crime.⁹⁵
The historical tradition of the United States, by contrast, has drawn
a rigid distinction between the two, with high substantive and evidentiary thresholds necessary for treason convictions. The resort to
treason in the fugitive slave cases is thus a measure of how far
toward totalitarianism the United States had been forced by the
pressures of slavery. But the results of the treason prosecutions
were, from the government's point of view, all failures. The first of
the Christiana defendants to be tried, Castner Hanway, was acquit-
ted after United States Supreme Court Justice Robert Grier, sitting
as a circuit judge, instructed the jury that the evidence did not
sustain the charge of treason because the blacks' resistance was not
"public," that is, not insurrectionary.⁹⁶ Federal attorneys then
dropped the prosecution of the remaining defendants.

A greater disappointment met federal prosecutors in Syracuse,
New York, that same month.⁹⁷ Rather than obscure Quakers and
runaway blacks, the Jerry rescue defendants included two of the
nation's leading white abolitionists, Samuel J. May and Gerrit
Smith, and a black abolitionist leader of national prominence, the
Reverend Jermain Loguen. The United States Attorney first hoped
to indict a large group of black and white abolitionists on charges
of "constructive treason," but later decided to go for the lesser
offence of violation of the 1850 Act's obstruction provisions. Even
on these lesser charges, he was able to secure only one conviction.
As a sidelight, Smith and other abolitionists turned the weapon of
the law against their persecutors by having a federal marshal arrested and charged with violation of New York's 1840 jury-trial law,

⁹⁴United States v. Mitchell, 26 Fed. Cas. 1277 (No. 15788) (U.S.C.C.D. Pa. 1795)
at 1281.
⁹⁵Friedman, History of American Law, p. 256.
⁹⁶U.S. v. Hanway, 26 Fed. Cas. 105 (No. 15299) (C.C.E.D. Pa. 1851).
⁹⁷On the Syracuse rescue, see Campbell, Slave Catchers, pp. 156–157.

a statute enacted under abolitionist pressure to provide jury trials for alleged fugitives. Smith, who had recently been admitted to the bar, developed an extensive argument on the unconstitutionality of the federal statute, but to no avail. The presiding justice of the New York Supreme Court held the federal statute constitutional and instructed the jury to return a verdict of not guilty, which they did. Both the 1851 treason prosecutions ended ingloriously for the government, and amounted to a victory for the abolitionists, whose practical harassment had obstructed enforcement of the Act and challenged the government to a stand-off.

Despite these clashes, the nation had achieved a seeming end to the conflict over slavery by 1852. Both major parties in the presidential election of that year pledged themselves to vigorous enforcement of the Compromise of 1850 and condemned further agitation of any slavery issues. Abolitionists and southern disunionists both seemed crushed. The Free-Soil party that year polled fewer votes than it had four years earlier, while the disunionists found themselves isolated ever since adoption of the Georgia Platform in 1850. The dangerous destabilization begun by Texas annexation and the Mexican War appeared to be contained. Congress buried the Wilmot Proviso, that flag of discord, and worked out a tolerable resolution of the major divisive issues of the time, slavery in the territories and fugitive slaves. But the illusion of peace was not to last long.

CHAPTER 6

The Crisis of the Union, 1853–1859

A MERICANS' yearning in 1852 for peace and finality on the slavery issue was pathetically misdirected. The compromises that achieved "finality" were evasive. They preserved the institutional structure of the federal government, but at the cost of failing to ease the stresses tearing at that structure. Franklin Pierce's America was no place to seek harmony on any issue. The vitality and violence of this society would have shredded a much sturdier political fabric than the Compromise of 1850.

Rescues and recaptures of fugitive slaves threw some northern communities into turmoils that were quieted only by force. Life imitated art. Real-life slavehunts mirrored the publishing and stage blockbuster of the nineteenth century, *Uncle Tom's Cabin,* whose scenes of runaway Eliza clutching her baby and jumping across the ice floes of the Ohio River to freedom electrified readers and audiences in the free states.

The peculiar, energetic movement that called itself Young America sought territorial expansion around the Golden Circle of the Caribbean in the name of republican liberty and for the cause of southern slavery. In New Orleans, crowds cheered southern volunteers and mercenaries called Filibusters, enlisted under a soldier of fortune, Narciso Lopez, as they went off to "liberate" Cuba from Spanish rule and to protect slavery there. When Spanish authorities hanged the Americans, Louisiana crowds went on a rampage and destroyed the Spanish consulate. In northwestern Mexico, the work of American topographical engineers bore fruit in a treaty negotiated by the South Carolinian James Gadsden that enlarged American territory by a strip of what is now southern Arizona and New Mexico in the Mesilla River valley. Southerners promoted the acquisition of this otherwise valueless area to facilitate construction of a transcontinental railroad terminating in New Orleans, raising the specter of a new avenue for slavery's westward expansion.

The fragmented political structure of America was recombining in new forms. Throughout the United States, the Whig party inexorably broke apart. In the South, sectional pressures drove Whigs into fellowship with Unionist Democrats. The Whig organization in New York, even with the advantage of having one of its own, Millard Fillmore, in the White House, split into antislavery and pro-Compromise factions. In Massachusetts, the prestige and numbers of the Cotton Whigs shriveled as the party lost its brightest young members like Charles Sumner and Horace Mann to local party reorganizations that appear in retrospect to be transitional between the dying Free-Soil coalition and the Republican party struggling to be born. Know-Nothings, a secret society opposed to the political power of Catholics and immigrants, eroded the base of Whig rank-and-file support throughout the country.

In Chicago, St. Louis, Memphis, and New Orleans, ambitious men dreamed of great commercial empires linking the Golden State of California and the trade of Asia with the Mississippi River and the settled parts of America. These four cities vied among themselves for the lucrative prize of being the eastern terminus of the railroad that was to bring the riches of the Orient to the eastern half of the United States. But before railroads could be built, territories had to be organized and Indian titles dissolved. Efforts in Washington to organize territories or provide aid to railroad construction died stillborn in the Thirty-second Congress (1851–53), but the young junior Senator from Illinois, Stephen A. Douglas, promptly resumed them in the first session of the Thirty-third. Douglas, chairman of the Senate Committee on Territories, reported out a bill to organize all the remaining territory of the United States north of the 36°30′ Missouri line, and thereby smashed the delicate Compromise of 1850.

The final form of the Kansas-Nebraska Act was quite different from the bill originally reported out by Douglas. The legislative history of the bill reveals the push-and-shove of great sectional forces contending for power and dominion, pursuing their goals through the forms of constitutional doctrine. The bill Douglas originally reported out contained three provisions concerning slavery in Nebraska Territory.[1] The first was a verbatim borrowing from the New Mexico and Utah enabling acts: "The legislative power of the territory shall extend to all rightful subjects of legislation consistent with the constitution of the United States. . . ." This provision contained two bits of calculated ambiguity, preserving the convenient lack of resolution that had made the Compromise of 1850 viable. Was slavery a "rightful subject of legislation" for a territorial legislature? If so, when and under what restrictions or qualifications? Because contradictory answers to these questions were plausible, both Free-Soilers and Calhounites could accept the phrasing as a reflection of their views. Was territorial legislation concerning slavery "consistent with the Constitution of the United States"? This was not only ambiguous, but seemingly truistic: obviously no legislature, state, national, or territorial, could enact laws that were not consistent with the federal Constitution. This conveniently equivocal provision remained intact in the final Act.

The Douglas bill contained two other provisions concerning slavery. The first seemed to be another constitutional truism of 1850, and nothing more than verbiage meant to soothe southern sensibilities: "when admitted as a State or States, the said territory, or any portion of the same, shall be received into the Union, with or without slavery, as their constitution may prescribe at the time of their admission." But it conceded a point vital to the southern position: it guaranteed that an incipient state that permitted slavery could not be excluded on that account, and thereby rejected the central demand of abolitionists and Free-Soilers. Finally, the bill reincorporated the Clayton Compromise, providing that suits involving title to slaves and issues of personal freedom were appealable to the United States Supreme Court. Both these provisions remained intact in the Act.

More important than the bill itself was the brief committee report

[1]Nebraska Territory then comprised all of the remaining Louisiana Purchase territory northwest of Missouri up to the Canadian line.

that accompanied the bill. Douglas forthrightly stated that the issue of the constitutionality of the Missouri Compromise was mooted, that the Territories Committee of the Senate would refuse to resolve or even consider it, and that Congress should neither repeal nor reenact the Missouri Compromise, nor even attempt declaratory legislation. Rather, the slavery provisions of the bill he reported out were grounded on the "great principle" that "all questions pertaining to slavery in the territories, and in the new states to be formed therefrom, are to be left to the decision of the people residing therein."[2] Douglas thus casually dismissed a constitutional settlement that had lasted half the entire time of the Republic's existence. Worse, he reopened issues that most Americans considered settled in 1820 and 1850. Seldom in American legislative experience has a political figure played so recklessly with explosive materials.

A small coterie of southern Senators, comprising what was called the "senatorial junto," pressured Douglas to repeal the Missouri Compromise explicitly.[3] Perhaps as a partial concession to these southern demands, Douglas added this section to the bill he had reported out:

In order to avoid all misconstruction, it is hereby declared to be the true intent and meaning of this act, so far as the question of slavery is concerned, to carry into practical operation the following propositions and principles, established by the compromise measures [1850] . . .: First, that all questions pertaining to slavery in the Territories, and in the new States to be formed therefrom, are to be left to the decision of the people residing therein, through their appropriate representatives.[4]

This obfuscating clarification enacted the principle of territorial sovereignty. It would have repealed the Missouri Compromise to the extent that it would be theoretically possible under the provi-

[2]Untitled Senate Report, 33 Cong., 1 sess., ser. 706, doc. 15, (Jan. 4, 1854).

[3]The junto consisted of four powerful Calhounite Democrats: David R. Atchison of Missouri, Robert M. T. Hunter and James M. Mason of Virginia, and Andrew P. Butler of South Carolina.

[4]*Congressional Globe*, 33 Cong., 1 sess., 222 (Jan. 23, 1854). This "true intent" provision seems to have been added to the bill a week after the amended bill was reported out. Douglas attributed its omission to clerical error. Potter, *Impending Crisis*, p. 159, interprets this implausible claim as a sign of southern pressure on Douglas and his willingness to make responsive concessions.

sion for a territorial legislature to enact a slave code. But an Alabama Representative, Philip Phillips, pointed out that the provision would have left the Missouri Compromise restriction intact until a territorial legislature enacted a slave code. Moreover, repeal of the Missouri restriction was in its own right a goal of most southerners, who agreed with Cass that it was a gratuitous slur on their states.

Southern dissatisfaction with Douglas's proffered ambiguity quickly surfaced. Kentucky Whig Archibald Dixon announced his intention to offer an amendment to the bill that would not only have repealed the compromise—"as if the [Missouri] act . . . had never been passed," in the odd language of the bill—but would have provided that all citizens "shall be at liberty to take and hold their slaves within any of the Territories of the United States, or of the States to be formed therefrom. . . ."[5] Dixon's amendment went further than any southern proposal, no matter how extremist, ever had. It absorbed the Calhounite position as worked out from 1848 to 1854, in that it opened all territories to slavery by positive congressional guarantee of entry. This applied not only to Nebraska, but also to Utah and New Mexico, already open to slaveholders, and to the territories that were free and were certain to remain so: Oregon, Washington, and Minnesota.[6] But in the phrase "or of the States to be formed therefrom," Dixon managed to go beyond the wildest suggestions of extreme proslavery, in forcing *states,* after admission, to permit slavery. Never had any southerner broached such an extraordinary demand, for the good reason that it was unconstitutional, according to orthodox southern constitutional thought.

Douglas was surprised by this maneuver, and he moved quickly and cleverly to roll back the southern offensive. Both congressional committees having jurisdiction of the territorial bills, as well as the senatorial junto, worked out revisions to the bill Douglas had originally offered. Douglas soon reported out from the Senate Territories Committee a substitute for the first bill, containing two major revisions of his first, both making significant concessions to southern demands but nothing as wholesale as the Dixon amend-

[5]*Congressional Globe,* 33 Cong., 1 sess., 175 (Jan. 16, 1854).
[6]These territories comprised not only the modern states of those names, but also all modern Idaho and sizable portions of Montana and the Dakotas.

ment. First, the territory was divided into two portions: Kansas, lying entirely west of Missouri and therefore convenient for settlement by slaveholding Missourians; and Nebraska, the immense remainder, lying west of the free state of Iowa and the free territory of Minnesota. Second, the substitute bill declared that the Missouri exclusion "was superseded by the principles of the legislation of 1850, commonly called the compromise measures, and is declared inoperative."[7] The word "void" was shortly added to "inoperative" as a further verbal concession to southern constitutional principles.

But these overtures still did not meet the demands of the southerners, who amended the latter statement to read that the Missouri Compromise was "inconsistent with the principle of nonintervention by Congress with slavery in the States and Territories, as recognized by the legislation of [1850], commonly called the compromise measures, [and] is hereby declared inoperative and void." This was considerably more than mere verbiage. The critical word "nonintervention," already a southern code word for their particular constitutional understanding, at last got official statutory recognition and, what is more, was made retroactive to 1850 if not to 1820. Second, the southerners added on an interpretive clause declaring that it was

the true intent and meaning of this act not to legislate slavery into any Territory or State, nor to exclude it therefrom; but to leave the people thereof perfectly free to form and regulate their domestic institutions in their own way, subject only to the Constitution of the United States.[8]

This was something more than territorial sovereignty; just how much more was not clear. Since 1847, southerners had been toying with the idea that the United States Constitution contained more guarantees for slavery than were traditionally assumed; that, for example, some clause of the Constitution might void the liberation of a slave in a free state. Since all the operative amendments to the original Nebraska bill were worked out in committee, caucus, and private gathering, we cannot know what specifically—if anything—was meant by this suggestive phrasing. But it was one further ambiguity heaped on the pile of opaque slavery-related provisions of the

[7] Congressional Globe, 33 Cong., 1 sess., 222 (Jan. 23, 1854).
[8] Congressional Globe, 33 Cong., 1 sess., 353 (Feb. 7, 1854).

Kansas-Nebraska Act, which became law after five months of acrimonious debate.[9]

The Kansas-Nebraska Act opened the Great Plains to slavery and surrounded the free states and Minnesota Territory with a cordon of potentially slave territories. The free state of California and the free territories of Washington and Oregon became isolated. But this immediate impact of the act was overshadowed by the indirect consequences of the Kansas-Nebraska struggle. The "finality" of 1850 was dissipated forever, and in its place there appeared an accelerating disequilibrium, where constitutional dysfunction became compounded. Each new outbreak of disorder, instead of being resolved or compromised or even temporized, immediately diminished the already enfeebled ability of the constitutional or political process to settle disagreement.

The struggles of 1854 also narrowed constitutional options drastically. Of the five constitutional alternatives open to the nation in 1848—Wilmot Proviso (Free Soil), territorial sovereignty, extension of the Missouri Compromise line, Calhounite slavery-ubiquity, and the Clayton Compromise—two lay dead or dying in 1854. The Missouri Compromise was politically defunct, and the view that it had always been unconstitutional was gaining support. Territorial sovereignty was perverted in northern eyes, stripped of its pseudodemocratic implications and revealed for what it was: a proslavery disguise, concealing the flanking movements of slavery in the western empire. This left only the Free-Soil and Calhounite polar opposites as constitutionally viable, together with the unpredictable Clayton possibility of abandoning the constitutional issue to federal judges. In this sense, Abraham Lincoln's "House Divided" speech of 1858 expressed an important constitutional truth. The constitutional house had become divided; the scope available for evasion and ambiguity had constricted; the time left for temporizing was running out.

If anyone doubted this, events in Kansas would soon disabuse him. Proslavery Missourians flocked over the border, while free-state emigrants came from Massachusetts and elsewhere to challenge them for control of the territory. The first territorial elections created a proslavery legislature by means of thousands of fraudulent

[9]Act of May 30, 1854, ch. 59, 10 Stat. 277.

Missouri votes. Missouri Senator David R. Atchison, personally leading Missouri Border Ruffians, announced that he intended "to kill every God-damned abolitionist in the district," which, in his terms of reference, meant every free-state settler.[10] With attitudes like that prevalent, violence shortly followed in "Bleeding Kansas." Free-state settlers responded by drafting and ratifying their own constitution and electing a shadow legislature, thus laying the groundwork for civil war: two governments in the same jurisdiction contesting for its control. Bushwhacking broke out in the winter of 1855–56, Missourians reinvaded, this time to use bullets rather than ballots, proslavery posses sacked the free-state town of Lawrence, and a murderous antislavery visionary, John Brown, retaliated by shooting five men near Pottawatomie Creek. Complementing the violence in Kansas, South Carolina Representative Preston Brooks beat Massachusetts Senator Charles Sumner senseless with a cane on the floor of the Senate, an act that to many northerners symbolized the aggressions of the Slave Power. Violence began to replace legal and political processes.

Back in Kansas, territorial governors came and went, phantom guerrilla armies marched in the night but did more posturing than shooting, and a proslavery constitutional convention met in 1857 at Lecompton. It produced a Constitution protecting the rights to slaves already in Kansas and authorized a referendum vote only on the Constitution "with slavery" or "without slavery" but not to accept or reject the entire Constitution. President James Buchanan supported this mode of referring the Constitution to the voters of the territory, thereby alienating Douglas, who saw in the restricted referendum a travesty of territorial sovereignty. Two elections were held. In the first, because free-state settlers abstained, proslavery Kansans and fraudulent Missouri voters supported the Lecompton Constitution with slavery (6,226 to 569). In the second election, antislavery voters went to the polls while the Missourians abstained, resulting in rejection of the Constitution entirely (10,226 against the Constitution, 24 for the Constitution without slavery, 138 for the Constitution with slavery). With these conflicting returns in hand, Buchanan proceeded to transform confusion into catastrophe by throwing all his political weight behind the Lecompton Constitu-

[10]Quoted in Potter, *Impending Crisis*, p. 203.

tion with slavery. An administration-backed measure passed that would resubmit the Constitution on the terms that rejection of the Constitution would delay admission as a state until the territorial population reached 90,000. Kansas voters promptly rejected the Constitution 11,300 to 788. So Kansas remained a territory, and the Democratic party split, its ability to play a nationalizing role mediating between the sections gone.

As the Kansas confusion broke out, a political revolt erupted spontaneously in the free states. Its clarion was the "Appeal of the Independent Democrats," a manifesto drafted by Senator Chase and Representative Giddings, with some help from Senator Sumner and Representative Gerrit Smith. (Giddings and Sumner were Whigs, Chase a Democrat, and Smith a political independent and abolitionist.) A masterpiece of political propaganda appearing on the eve of debates on Douglas's first Nebraska bill, the "Appeal" extolled the Missouri Compromise as a "solemn compact . . . universally regarded and acted upon as inviolable American law." It exposed Douglas's dishonest contention that the Compromise of 1850 implicitly superseded the Missouri Compromise, and called upon voters and ministers of the free states to resist turning the northern plains "into a dreary region of despotism, inhabited by master and slaves."[11]

The "Appeal" was extensively reprinted and quoted in editorials, sermons, and speeches. It hastened the formation of the Republican party throughout the northern states in the spring and summer of 1854. With the formation of the party, and the sectionalization of the Democracy, Jefferson's dire prediction of 1821 was realized:

a geographical line, coinciding with a marked principle, moral and political, once conceived and held up to the angry passions of men, will never be obliterated.[12]

By an irony, it was the very obliteration of the line (the Missouri Compromise) that Jefferson referred to that had the effect of holding marked moral and political principles up to the angry passions of men. Fragments of a new northern party organized around Free-

[11]The "Appeal" is substantially reprinted in Commager, *Documents of American History*, I, 329–331.
[12]Jefferson to John Holmes, Apr. 22, 1820, in Lipscomb and Bergh, *Writings of Jefferson*, XV, 248–250.

Soil principles had been around the American political scene since 1847. But it was the sectional crisis recklessly provoked by the Democrats in 1854 that united them. Suddenly, leadership, organization, ideology, and rank-and-file support appeared and constituted the Republican party.

With the demise of the Whigs and the cooptation of the Know-Nothings, a process completed by 1856, the Republicans now constituted a party vehicle for the elaboration of Free Soil, quasi-abolitionist views, giving those ideas a respectability and an entrée into political dialogue that they lacked as long as they were the theories of a reformist sect or a third party. In their platform of 1856, written with an eye to the contemporaneous Kansas struggle, the Republicans flatly declared that neither Congress nor territorial legislature could constitutionally establish slavery in any territory, and ambiguously grounded that constitutional conclusion on the Fifth Amendment premise that no person shall be deprived of life, liberty, or property without due process.[13]

Republican ideology was grounded on two fundamental constitutional principles. Out of these sprang all subsequent Republican political programs relating to slavery. First, Republicans cherished the *Somerset* axiom that slavery existed only where established by positive law. The obvious corollary was that where no positive law established slavery, it did not exist.[14] This became the basis of the Republican approach to the territorial question. Beyond that, the echoes of *Somerset* in Republican thought gave them a flexibility of response to constitutional issues. Lincoln expressed the *Somerset* idea aphoristically as the principle that "no law is free law"; that is, where no law exists securing slavery, a slave is free if he chooses to claim his freedom.[15] Hence the basis of the claim made by some

[13]Johnson and Porter, *National Party Platforms*, p. 27. On the formation of the Republican party, see generally Sewell, *Ballots for Freedom*, and Eric Foner, *Free Soil, Free Labor, Free Men: The Ideology of the Republican Party before the Civil War* (New York, 1970).

[14]Senator Daniel Clark of New Hampshire, *Congressional Globe*, 35 Cong., 1 sess., app. 87–89 (Mar. 15, 1858); Senator Jacob Collamer of Vermont, *Congressional Globe*, 34 Cong., 1 sess., app. 378 (April 4, 1856); editorial by Henry J. Raymond, *New York Times*, July 11, 1860.

[15]Lincoln's Peoria speech, Oct. 1854, quoted in Harry V. Jaffa, *Crisis of the House Divided: An Interpretation of the Issues of the Lincoln-Douglas Debates* (1959; reprint Seattle, 1973), p. 121; but it must be pointed out that in context Lincoln disparaged the principle as ineffectual compared to a statute enacted by Congress.

early Republicans that Congress can establish a free territory simply by not legislating a slave code for it.

The second pillar of Republican constitutional thought was the idea that only states, not the federal government, have any substantive power over slavery—any power to abolish, establish, or regulate it. Republicans conceded the legitimacy of slavery in the states where it existed, but they firmly denied any federal power to establish or promote slavery.

From these constitutional principles emerged two prolific slogans: "divorce" and "Freedom national." Divorce, the old Liberty idea, demanded "the absolute and unqualified divorce of the General Government from Slavery":[16] that it not establish slavery in the District of Columbia, that it not protect it on the high seas or in the interstate slave trade, that it not lend its force to the recapture of runaways. "Freedom national" was a derivative of *Somerset:* "Freedom is national; slavery only is local and sectional,"[17] Chase declared during Senate debates on the 1850 Compromise, and the idea passed on into all Republican thought of the ensuing decade.

These views made the Republican party a distinctly sectional but potentially majority party. No one realistically hoped that the South could be won over to such a constitutional program. But that of itself was only half the explanation for the disruption of a national party system. The other half was the Democrats' seemingly irreversible slide into the pit of proslavery constitutional belief. Steadily, until Douglas revolted against the Buchanan administration over Kansas in 1858, the Democrats adopted more and more of the southern canon. The loss of anti-Nebraska Democrats in 1854, and the spineless personal characteristics of Pierce and Buchanan, only hastened the slide.

Though of little direct constitutional significance, another event of 1854, coming only four months after enactment of the Kansas-Nebraska Act, compounded the forces of dissolution. Three American diplomats, Pierre Soulé (minister to Spain), John Y. Mason (France), and James Buchanan (Great Britain) met in Belgium and issued a confidential memorandum over their signatures that came to be known as the Ostend Manifesto. Soulé and Mason had by this time established reputations for themselves as proslavery extrem-

---

[16]Liberty platform of 1844, in Johnson and Porter, *National Party Platforms,* p. 4.
[17]*Congressional Globe,* 31 Cong., 1 sess., app. 474 (Mar. 26, 1850).

ists, and Buchanan was the archetype of the "northern man with southern principles" that was the Democratic ideal for the presidency. The three ministers asserted in the Manifesto that the United States should imperatively demand the cession of Cuba from Spain to prevent the "Africanization" of the island, that is, the abolition of slavery there. If Spain declined to sell it, the ministers recommended that the United States seize it by force, piously adding that such an act would be justified "by every law human and divine."[18] The Pierce administration promptly repudiated the Manifesto, but enraged northerners saw it as further confirmation of the Slave Power conspiracy alleged in the "Appeal of the Independent Democrats," seeking to promote the expansion of slavery at every cost, including military aggression against foreign nations.

Northern fears were confirmed by filibustering expeditions in 1855 led by a bizarre Tennessee adventurer, William Walker, successively physician, lawyer, journalist, author, and mercenary soldier, who attempted to seize Baja California, Nicaragua, and Honduras between 1855 and 1860, when the Hondurans finally tried and shot him. In reality, Walker was more a mercenary for isthmian canal interests than he was for slavery expansionists, but that did not much affect the North's perception of his activities. Another Filibuster, the Mississippian John Quitman, engaged in explicitly proslavery intervention in Cuba with the tacit support of Pierce's cabinet and enthusiastic public support in New Orleans. An articulated, centrally directed slavery-expansion conspiracy did not exist, but the pattern of events made northern suspicions reasonable.

The failures of Kansas policy were merely symptomatic of the inability of all branches of the federal government to resolve the most exigent political question of the late 1850s. Whether seen as an issue in its own right, or as a surrogate for the security of slavery in the extant states, or as a symbol for sectional confrontation, the problem of slavery in the territories daily became less amenable to political solutions while at the same time growing more urgent. Congress had managed to keep the national political processes operable only by deliberate ambiguity or procrastination. The policies of the Democrats in the White House, based on a proslavery

[18]The Ostend Manifesto is substantially excerpted in Commager, *Documents of American History*, I, 333–335.

"tilt," only inflamed the issues they touched. Under these circumstances, men yearned for a solution to the slavery/territories problem that was both decisive and apolitical.

For nearly a decade, Congress, seeking such a solution, had been inviting the United States Supreme Court to try its hand. A close reading of *Jones* v. *VanZandt* (1847) and *Strader* v. *Graham* (1851) would have suggested to Court observers that the justices were not disinclined, and that—making allowances for the particular details of the case—the result would not be displeasing to southerners.

Unknown to any of the great national figures who were contemplating the United States Supreme Court's confrontation with slavery, the vehicle for this involvement had been taking shape in Missouri. Just a month before the outbreak of hostilities with Mexico in 1846, two slaves, Dred Scott and his wife Harriet, began litigation in state courts to secure their freedom and that of their two daughters, Eliza and Lizzie, from their owner, Irene Emerson. Their claim to freedom was based on these events: in 1833, Dred Scott was owned by an army physician, John Emerson, who was stationed at Jefferson Barracks near St. Louis, Missouri. When Dr. Emerson was transferred to Fort Armstrong, Illinois (near modern Moline), he took his slave with him, despite the fact that Illinois was a free state under its Constitution and had been a free territory under its organic act, the Northwest Ordinance. In 1836, the army transferred Emerson to Fort Snelling, just west of modern St. Paul, Minnesota. It was located in the northern part of the Louisiana Purchase, and hence was free territory under the Missouri Compromise. There, Scott met and married Harriet, with the consent of their masters. He returned briefly to St. Louis with his bride, and thence went back to Fort Snelling. On the way, their first daughter was born somewhere on the Mississippi River north of Missouri—that is, in a free state or territory. In 1840, the three slaves returned once again to St. Louis. Three years later, Emerson died, leaving his wife a life estate in his property, including the slaves.

Scott's claim to freedom[19] was based on his two-year residence in the free state of Illinois and his four-year residence in federal terri-

[19]The separate suits of Harriet were consolidated with her husband's at all trial and appellate stages, and treated as standing on an identical footing, and will be so treated here, despite the fact that her claim to freedom did not include residence in Illinois.

tory free under the Missouri Compromise. Because his master took him to these free jurisdictions for long-term or indefinite residence, he claimed that he became free there, and that his slavery did not reattach upon his return to the slave state of Missouri. The legal basis for Scott's claim, grounded ultimately in the American extrapolations of *Somerset,* was supported by Missouri precedent. The Missouri Supreme Court, along with some other southern state courts, had repeatedly held that a master voluntarily taking a slave for permanent residence in a free jurisdiction thereby liberated him, and that the slave could bring suit to regain his freedom after a return to the slave state.[20] In a case nearly identical with Dred Scott's, *Rachael* v. *Walker* (1836), the Missouri Supreme Court held in 1836 that an army officer taking a slave for extended residence in Wisconsin Territory and Fort Snelling liberated her.[21]

In 1850, the Missouri Circuit Court entered a judgment affirming a jury verdict that Scott was free. Attorneys for his putative owner, the widow Emerson, appealed this result to the Missouri Supreme Court.

At this point, what had been a routine and unimportant freedom suit became politicized in the volatile social climate of Missouri in the 1850s. Along with other slave states, Missouri had grown increasingly resentful toward what it regarded as attacks on slavery after the introduction of the Wilmot Proviso. This attitude was reflected in a clash within the state Democratic party between a proslavery faction, led by Senator David Atchison, and the followers of Thomas Hart Benton. The militants supported all southern proslavery initiatives and succeeded in denying Benton the Senate seat he had held for thirty years. This conflict infected the Missouri Supreme Court, which was never above politics anyway, but particularly not after it became an elective bench in 1851. A majority of the Missouri bench, both before and after the transition to an elective judiciary, supported the proslavery wing of the state's Democracy and let that political-ideological attitude influence the substantive content of their opinions.

The outcome of Dred Scott's case in the Missouri Supreme Court

[20]See, e.g., Winny *v.* Whitesides, 1 Mo. 472 (1824); LaGrange *v.* Chouteau, 2 Mo. 20 (1828).
[21]4 Mo. 350 (1836).

was also influenced by two legal trends. First, the United States Supreme Court had recently handed down its decision in *Strader* v. *Graham* (1851), wherein Taney affirmed the right of the forum state to apply its own policy to slaves domiciled outside its jurisdiction and then returned to it.[22] He emphasized that the law of the state of residence was not controlling in the forum state. Second, Taney's *Strader* opinion reflected a turnabout in conflict-of-laws doctrine that had been under way for nearly a generation. Justice Joseph Story had been the leading proponent of a new view in the conflicts area, holding that the policy of the forum state, rather than respect for the policy of the foreign jurisdiction, should be controlling in choice-of-law cases. At first, this new view, stressing the interests of the forum jurisdiction, had an antislavery flavor.[23] But like all legal doctrine, it was capable of serving opposite ends too, as southern courts began to discover when they came to reconsider conflicts issues in the 1850s.

The consequence of these political and juridical currents left Dred Scott a slave. In *Scott* v. *Emerson* (1852),[24] a majority of the Missouri Supreme Court chose the new conflicts approach, stating that law in Missouri must reflect Missouri policy, not that of free jurisdictions. They concluded with a proslavery diatribe that must have been emotionally gratifying to the Democracy of the state but that did little credit to the reputation of its judges. In overruling *Rachael* v. *Walker*, the court explained:

Times are not now as they were when the former decisions on this subject were made. Since then not only individuals but States have been possessed with a dark and fell spirit in relation to slavery, whose gratification is sought in the pursuit of measures, whose inevitable consequences must be the overthrow and destruction of our government. Under such circumstances it does not behoove the State of Missouri to show the least countenance to

[22]In conflicts-of-law cases, the forum state is the state of the court rendering the decision.

[23]Anon., "American Slavery and the Conflict of Laws," *Columbia Law Review*, LXXI (1971), 74–99; Harold W. Horowitz, "Choice-of-Law Decisions Involving Slavery: 'Interest Analysis' in the Early Nineteenth Century," *U.C.L.A. Law Review*, XVII (1970), 587–601. For an important antislavery application of the new orientation, see *Polydore* v. *Prince*, 19 Fed. Cas. 950 (No. 11257) (D.C.D. Me. 1837). Story first articulated the new view in his *Commentaries on the Conflict of Laws*, 1st ed. (Boston, 1834).

[24]15 Mo. 576 (1852).

any measure which might gratify this spirit. . . . Although we may, for our own sakes, regret that the avarice and hard-heartedness of the progenitors of those who are now so sensitive on the subject, ever introduced the institution among us, yet we will not go to them to learn law, morality or religion on the subject.

Scott and his supporters did not give up after the Missouri decision. Rather, before the suit in the state court system was technically disposed of, Scott's attorneys initiated an entirely new suit in the United States Circuit Court for the District of Missouri. The form of the suit was still the plea of a fictitious assault and battery and false imprisonment, the traditional mode of bringing freedom suits in slave jurisdictions. But because Scott was now in a federal court he had to prove either one of two things: (1) under the diversity-of-citizenship clause of Article III, Scott could sue in a federal court if he could show that he was a citizen of the state where the suit was brought, the defendant was a citizen of some other state, and the amount in controversy between them was at least $500;[25] (2) or Scott could avoid the diverse-citizenship and amount-in-controversy requirements altogether by appealing from the state court result under section 25 of the Judiciary Act of 1789. By choosing this route, Scott would have to claim that the decision of the state court was adverse to a federal right.

At this time, Scott acquired both a new owner and new counsel. His new owner, John F. A. Sanford,[26] the brother of the widow Emerson who was the defendant in the original action, was a resident of New York, so the first alternative became available. One reading of *Strader* v. *Graham,* later endorsed by Chief Justice Taney, would have suggested that Scott would lose any appeal to the United States Circuit Court—technically, his appeal would be dismissed for want of jurisdiction—because the Missouri Supreme Court's decision on his status was controlling for all federal courts. So Scott's new counsel chose to relitigate the entire issue, going the diversity route, taking on himself the new burden of averring that Scott was a citizen of Missouri.

The new federal action was heard by only half the federal Circuit

[25]The amount-in-controversy requirement derived from the 1789 Judiciary Act: Act of Sept. 24, 1789, ch. 20, sec. 11, 1 Stat. 73.
[26]Sanford's name was misspelled in the reports of the case in the United States Supreme Court thus: Sandford.

Court, District Judge Robert W. Wells.[27] (His associate on the circuit bench, Justice James M. Wayne of the United States Supreme Court, was not able to attend circuit at that time because of an unusually long term of the Supreme Court.) Sanford's counsel responded to Scott's writ with a plea in abatement,[28] raising one of the fatal issues to come before the United States Supreme Court: he alleged that Scott was not a citizen of Missouri because he was black. Scott demurred and his demurrer was sustained on the grounds that, whatever the complexities of the total question of citizenship of blacks, Scott was enough of a citizen for purposes of initiating suit in federal courts. Sanford's counsel then pled to the merits, alleging Scott was still a slave.

Judge Wells's procedural ruling sustaining the plaintiff's demurrer had one astonishing implication. If Wells had been sustained in this ruling on appeal, ordinary freedom suits would have stopped enforcement of the 1850 Fugitive Slave Act. For if a black, any black, was citizen enough of a state to get into federal courts on the basis of diversity jurisdiction, then seized fugitives might claim access to jury trial in federal courts that could override the 1850 statute's procedures because the basis of their status as litigants was *constitutional:* that is, it was derived from Article III of the United States Constitution. Scott's counsel were aware of this possibility.[29] Perhaps this was one reason why Taney was so determined to annihilate

[27]For documents pertaining to Scott *v.* Sanford in the Circuit Court (defendant's name was spelled correctly at that level), see John D. Lawson (ed.), *American State Trials* (St. Louis, 1914–36), XIII, 243–252; and Dred Scott *v.* Sandford, 15 L. Ed. 692–694.

[28]This procedural technicality was important to the substantive outcome of the case. In common-law pleading, a plea in abatement was not a response to the merits of the plaintiff's claim; instead, it was a challenge to his ability to continue the suit, because of some defect either in his status or in his pleading. Technically, a plea in abatement was usually not a challenge to the jurisdiction of the court as such, but the U.S. Supreme Court chose to treat Sanford's plea as a jurisdictional challenge. Favorable action on the plea in abatement would have the effect of throwing plaintiff out of court, not of deciding against him on the merits. See *Chitty on Pleading,* 10th American ed. (1847), pp. 447–454, and Edward S. Corwin, "The Dred Scott Decision in the Light of Contemporary Legal Doctrines," *American Historical Review,* XVII (1911), 52–69.

[29]Roswell M. Field to Montgomery Blair, Jan. 7, 1855, typescript copy in Dred Scott Collection, Missouri Historical Society, St. Louis. A claim based on a constitutional right would take precedence over conflicting claims based on statutes because the Constitution is of superior authority.

any possibility that blacks could claim citizenship for diversity purposes, and the *Dred Scott* case may have been, among other things, Taney's effort to protect the 1850 Fugitive Slave Act from further abolitionist challenge. As the slavery issues of the 1850s intensified, they tended to fuse, as well, so that raising one issue seemed often to bring others trailing along with it.

Having reached the merits, Judge Wells instructed the jury that Scott was still a slave, relying principally on the decision of the Missouri Supreme Court in *Scott* v. *Emerson* and following the Supreme Court's directions in *Strader* v. *Graham.* The jury accordingly found for Sanford, and Wells entered judgment for the defendant.

New counsel for both sides entered the picture when the case went up to the United States Supreme Court by writ of error. Representing Scott in Washington was Montgomery Blair, son of the old Jacksonian Francis Preston Blair and Lincoln's future Postmaster General. Sanford and proslavery interests generally were now represented by Missouri's United States Senator Henry Geyer, who had taken Benton's seat, and the distinguished constitutional attorney Reverdy Johnson, a prominent conservative Maryland Unionist throughout the Civil War and Reconstruction. Blair, Geyer, and Johnson argued the cause first in February, 1856. Repeated conferences produced a divided Court, split over a jurisdictional issue not covered in the first argument: whether the United States Supreme Court on appeal could pass on the validity of the Circuit Court's ruling on the plea in abatement. The Court accordingly ordered reargument on that question and the logically consequent one: whether the Circuit Court *had* been correct in its ruling on the plea in abatement.

The Court heard rearguments in December, 1856, but these arguments were not confined to the jurisdictional question. They canvassed all the substantive issues the case had brought up to the Court. As the Court retired to reach a decision and write opinions, it had four questions before it:

1. Was the jurisdictional issue raised by the plea in abatement properly before the Court? The Court remained divided on this one.

2. If the Court took up the jurisdictional issue, how would it be resolved on its merits? That is, could a black in a freedom suit be considered a citizen for purposes of federal diversity jurisdiction?

Though important to the status of free blacks, this issue was not as momentous as the next two.

3. Was Scott free because he had been taken by his master to reside in a free *state* (Illinois)? This raised two subquestions, both already answered affirmatively in *Strader* v. *Graham:*

    a. Can a slave state determine that a black, whatever his status while residing in a free jurisdiction, resumes the status of slavery upon return to a slave state?

    b. Are federal courts bound by such a determination made by a state court?

4. Was Scott free because he had been taken by his master to reside in a free *territory?* This was the big question, involving as it did the constitutionality of the Missouri Compromise.

Between rearguments in December, 1856, and early March, 1857, the *Dred Scott* case became further politicized by an exchange of communications among members of the court and the President-elect, James Buchanan. Though not relevant to the larger significance of the case, these letters demonstrate the interaction between proslavery politics and the inner workings of the United States Supreme Court. The Court at first decided to sidestep the controversial issues of the case in an exercise of judicial self-restraint by merely affirming the decision of the Circuit Court and relying on *Strader* v. *Graham* as dispositive. That approach had the virtue of avoiding the territorial issue, though it did not eliminate the constitutional implications of allowing blacks to claim status as citizens for diversity purposes. But Buchanan wrote Justice John Catron, asking whether the case would be decided soon enough for him to allude to it in some way in his inaugural address. Catron replied, indicating the Court would not reach the territorial issue, relying instead on *Strader.* Justice Nelson set about writing such an opinion.

But in mid-February, the Court abruptly changed its course and Taney undertook to write the majority opinion, which would reach the territorial issue by holding the Missouri Compromise unconstitutional. At first Taney carried only his four fellow southerners with him on this question.[30] Catron accordingly wrote Buchanan again,

---

[30]The Court's sectional makeup was:

Roger B. Taney, C.J.   Maryland   manumitted nearly all his slaves thirty years earlier; supported secession.

asking him to exert pressure on his fellow Pennsylvanian, Justice Robert Grier, to side with the southerners, thus enhancing the majority and diminishing its starkly sectional appearance.[31] Buchanan did so, but he was misinformed about, or misunderstood, what the Court would do. His use of Catron's inside information in his inaugural address provides a revealing aside about the course of constitutional development in the preceding decade. Buchanan stated that:

A difference of opinion has arisen in regard to the point of time when the people of a Territory shall decide this question for themselves. This is, happily a matter of but little practical importance. Besides, it is a judicial question, which legitimately belongs to the Supreme Court of the United States, before whom it is now pending, and will, it is understood, be speedily and finally settled. To their decision, in common with all good citizens, I shall cheerfully submit, whatever this may be.[32]

Buchanan spoke as a Democrat with an eye on the divisions within his party, but he utterly missed the real constitutional point.

Since the Clayton Compromise was first suggested a decade earlier, congressional Democrats had moved from a vague, open-ended invitation to the Supreme Court to take up the territorial issue to a more focused approach. The original Clayton Compromise and its embodiments in the acts of 1850 and 1854 were broad enough to encompass the question of the power of Congress to exclude slavery there. But after Congress decisively rejected the Wilmot Proviso in 1850, and as the conviction spread between 1850 and 1856 that the Missouri Compromise was unconstitutional, the focus shifted to the constitutional question that was separating

John McLean	Ohio	aspirant for Republican presidential nomination 1856, 1860.
James M. Wayne	Georgia	Unionist during the war.
John Catron	Tennessee	Unionist during the war.
Peter V. Daniel	Virginia	
Samuel Nelson	New York	
Robert Grier	Pennsylvania	
Benjamin R. Curtis	Massachusetts	supported Fugitive Slave Act's enforcement in Bay State.
John A. Campbell	Alabama	Confederate subcabinet official during the war.

[31]Catron's letters were published in Philip Auchampaugh, "James Buchanan, the Court and the Dred Scott Case," *Tennessee Historical Magazine,* IX (1926), 231–240.
[32]Richardson, *Messages and Papers of the Presidents,* VII, 2962.

northern from southern Democrats: could the *territorial legislature* exclude slavery at any point before it drafted a constitution and applied for statehood? Territorial sovereignty in a northern interpretation answered "yes"; in the southern interpretation, "no." It was this issue that Buchanan thought the Court would resolve. But Taney and some of his associates were intent on going after the original, broader question: congressional power.

The Court delivered its judgment and opinions on March 6 and 7, 1857. Taney insisted that his opinion was for the Court. The Clerk of the Court, Benjamin Howard, his creature, so listed it in the official reports; and it was immediately accepted by all as being the majority opinion. But all nine justices wrote opinions, leading to the same plethora of judicial utterances that confused *Prigg* v. *Pennsylvania*, the *License Cases*, and the *Passenger Cases*. Hence contemporaries, lawyers, and scholars ever since have been trying to puzzle out just what the Court *did* decide. Unfortunately, multiplicity of voices was not the only source of confusion. The issues themselves presented an inherent conceptual circularity and dilemma. Any effort to resolve the threshold jurisdictional question—can a black be a citizen for diversity purposes?—inescapably required that the Court resolve the substantive issues before settling the procedural issue. Yet if those substantive issues were resolved in such a way as to conclude that the black was not a citizen, then the court conceptually never had jurisdiction of the party or the cause to begin with, and should have thrown it out on the jurisdictional issue without reaching the substantive merits.

Don Fehrenbacher has concluded, after close analysis of the case, that "none of the major rulings in Taney's opinion can be pushed aside as unauthoritative. . . . As a matter of historical reality, the Court decided what Taney declared that it decided . . . the Taney opinion *is,* for all practical purposes, *the* Dred Scott decision."[33] Taney's opinion is thus the most important determinant of the *Dred Scott* case and its impact on American constitutional development.

Taney began with an important technicality, holding that the plea in abatement was properly before the Court, thus presenting the question whether a black in a freedom suit could be a citizen for

[33]Don E. Fehrenbacher, *The Dred Scott Case: Its Significance in American Law and Politics* (New York, 1978), pp. 333–334, 337 (ital. in orig.).

diversity-jurisdiction purposes. In declaring that he could not, Taney expended nearly half his opinion excluding free blacks from the status and protection afforded by the United States Constitution. Without extenuating the abuses of his opinion in any way, it must be said for him that Taney here tried to resolve what was, in *his* time, one of the most confused and unprecedented areas of American constitutional development: the problem of citizenship. The Fourteenth Amendment resolved the relationship between federal and state citizenship, but it took nothing less than a Civil War and a constitutional amendment, addressing the question implicit in this part of Taney's opinion, to provide a definitive resolution of this problem. His solution of the relationship between federal and state citizenship was not only logically possible, but as valid as any other, given the uncertainties of the whole issue.[34]

Taney rejected Judge Wells's idea that there could be a differential citizenship, by which a black might be a citizen for some purposes and not for others. He then fused the questions of state and federal citizenship in such a way as to deny blacks the benefits of either as far as it was in his power to do so. Taney held that blacks were not state citizens, within the meaning of the diversity clause, because they were not citizens within the meaning of the privileges and immunities clause, and because they were not citizens of the United States. These two logical bases must strike a modern reader as perversely wrong-headed: the question before the Court was not whether Scott, as a putative citizen of Missouri, could sue in a federal court in some other state, but whether he could do so in Missouri; and that, in turn, depended not on whether he was a citizen of the United States, but rather on whether he was, in the words of Article III, one of the class "Citizens of different States." Hence nearly all this part of Taney's opinion is logically beside the point.

Taney, in fact, conceded the vital question supporting Scott's effort: that a free black could be, for *state* purposes, a citizen of a state. But he also tried to show that, as such, (1) blacks were objects of discrimination based on racial antipathy; (2) a black could not use his status of a citizen of state X to claim any rights, privileges, status, or immunities in state Y; (3) being a citizen of state X did not make

[34]Kettner, *Development of American Citizenship,* pp. 300–333.

a black a citizen of the United States; (4) he could not be one of the "Citizens of different States" for diversity purposes because he was not one of the "Citizens of each State" for privileges and immunities clause purposes. All four of these conclusions were irrelevent to the issue and logical non sequiturs; the last three may have been wrong as a matter of law in Taney's own time, though the confusion of the question makes it difficult to make that assertion with confidence.

The trek into irrelevance led Taney to make the most egregious mis-statements of his long opinion: blacks, he wrote,

were at that time [1787] considered as a subordinate and inferior class of beings, who had been subjugated by the dominant race, and, whether emancipated or not, yet remained subject to their authority, and had no rights or privileges but such as those who held the power and the Government might choose to grant them. . . . [In 1776] they had for more than a century before been regarded as beings of an inferior order, and altogether unfit to associate with the white race, either in social or political relations; and so far inferior, that they had no rights which the white man was bound to respect. . . .[35]

Then, to tie his historical digression to the state of law of his time, Taney set forth this canon of interpretation:

No one, we presume, supposes that any change in public opinion or feeling, in relation to this unfortunate race, . . . should induce the court to give to the words of the constitution a more liberal construction in their favor than they were intended to bear when the instrument was framed and adopted. . . . If any of its provisions are deemed unjust, there is a mode prescribed in the instrument itself by which it may be amended; but while it remains unaltered, it must be construed now as it was understood at the time of its adoption. It is not only the same in words, but the same in meaning. . . . Any other rule of construction would abrogate the judicial character of this court, and make it the mere reflex of the popular opinion or passion of the day.[36]

If this rule of interpretation had not been promptly discarded, the Constitution would have soon become a fossil, an inflexible and brittle historical document having a rapidly diminishing relevance to modern times. Taney, for his own purposes, was trying to create a static Constitution, changeless as a mummy.

---

[35]Dred Scott *v.* Sandford, 19 How. (60 U.S.) 393 (1857) at 405, 407.
[36]19 How. at 426.

Finally, in this segment of the opinion, Taney went on to construct the proslavery constitutional theory that made *Dred Scott* so vicious a judicial error. He declared that

The government of the United States had no right to interfere [with the states in their control of the black people] for any other purpose but that of protecting the rights of the owner, leaving it altogether with the several States to deal with this race, whether emancipated or not, as each State may think justice, safety, and the interests and safety of society, require.[37]

The federal government could not be neutral as to slavery; it had to protect it. Here as elsewhere, Taney took a constitutional half-truth and surrounded it with a judicial gloss reflecting attitudes developed two generations after the Framers drafted the Constitution. That this process contradicted his own canon of interpretation quoted above did not occur to him.[38]

If Taney had a majority with him on this point—that Dred Scott could not sue in federal courts because he was *black*—then he might well have ended his opinion there. But only two of his colleagues, Wayne and Daniel, explicitly agreed with this point. In addition, two other justices, the dissenters Curtis and McLean, thought the Court held blacks could not be citizens. (They disagreed, of course.) But this was obviously a shaky majority, if it can be called a majority at all. To make a more solid majority Taney went on to a conceptually different question: Could Scott sue in federal courts if he was a *slave?* That got Taney to the Missouri Compromise and free-state-residence issues. It was here that Republicans had to deny that Taney's opinion was valid, on the grounds that it was dicta. Their argument ran thus: Having shown the Court had no jurisdiction on one ground, the Court ought to have thrown the suit out at that point. Once having proved no jurisdictional competence, anything subsequently said to the merits was obiter.

This argument has misled those trying to make sense out of the case for over a century. If Taney indeed had only two of his brethren with him solidly on the black citizenship point, then he would have to go on to deal with the slave citizenship issue to put together a

[37]19 How. at 426.
[38]For a different critique of this segment of the Taney *Dred Scott* opinion, with which we agree but do not wish to paraphrase here, see Fehrenbacher, *Dred Scott Case*, ch. 15, "The Opinion of the Court: Negroes and Citizenship."

majority. That question is still moot, and it is certain that Taney felt
no reluctance to take up the Missouri Compromise issue—indeed,
the relish obvious in his words suggests that he welcomed the opportunity. Further, as Edward Corwin suggested over half a century
ago, it was considered proper for a court in that era to canvass all
issues that might support its holding, and not dismiss abruptly at the
first point in which it demonstrated a jurisdictional deficiency.
Hence, in a purely procedural sense, it was not improper for Taney
to take up the Missouri Compromise issue.[39]

In undertaking to hold the Missouri Compromise unconstitutional, Taney was confronted at the threshold with several formidable barriers, and it was his efforts to circumvent these that give the
latter half of his opinion its peculiar, tortuous, and oddly tentative
quality. First, Taney had to cling to his nationalist outlook, even
while denying a power to the national government, because national
power might prove useful to promote slavery in the territories.
Then, all precedents that existed were overwhelmingly on the side
of the constitutionality of the Missouri Compromise. Taney was
about to undo a constitutional consensus that had existed for at
least forty years, and in the process had to prove that he understood
the Framers' intentions better than they did themselves. Finally, in
the name of strict construction Taney had to construe out of existence an explicit clause, and then derive congressional power by
implication from another clause, and then strictly construe the implied power. Given these obstacles, the wonder is not that Taney's
opinion was as unpersuasive as it was, but rather that it was not
more obviously absurd.

Taney began by taking the most obvious textual basis for congressional power over the territories, the territories clause, of Article IV,
section 3, and declaring it irrelevant on the ground that it applied
only to territory held by the federal government in 1787 and not to
territory subsequently acquired, such as the Louisiana Purchase.
There was no historical evidence to support this position. Taney
had to evade the precedent of *American Insurance Company* v. *Canter*
(1828), in which Marshall had said that Florida Territory, not acquired until 1819, was "a territory of the United States, governed

[39]See the exceptionally clear discussion of this reciprocating procedural-substan-
tive dilemma *ibid.*, p. 332.

by virtue of that clause in the constitution which empowers Congress 'to make all needful rules and regulations respecting the territory or other property belonging to the United States.' "[40] Taney probably could not have carried a majority with him for overruling *Canter,* and in any event he had no desire to do so, because it might prove useful for various nationalist purposes such as the acquisition and governance of new slave territory like Cuba.

Though Taney had cast doubt on the constitutionality of the Northwest Ordinance in *Strader,* he seemed to realize that another such head-on challenge might not carry his brethren with him, because it was historically indefensible. For, to maintain his *Strader* position, he would have had to maintain that the Confederation Congress that adopted the Northwest Ordinance, plus Thomas Jefferson (who had proposed an earlier variant version of its slavery restriction in 1784), plus the Framers sitting in the First Congress that reenacted the Northwest Ordinance, all misunderstood the meaning of the Constitution. Taney was not above saying that he understood James Madison's mind better than Madison, but he decided, apparently for tactical purposes, to back off from the *Strader* salient and concede the relevance of the Northwest Ordinance, but only to the original territory of the United States, not its post-1800 acquisitions.

The other reason dictating that Taney avoid the territories clause is an idea forgotten today: all states are equal, and must be treated equally upon their admission. The corollary of this idea is that Congress can impose no restrictions or conditions on the admission of new states. Justice Catron, in a concurrence otherwise mostly at odds with the Taney opinion, referred to this doctrine as "that great fundamental condition of the Union—the equality of the states."[41] An early casualty of the Civil War, this idea was appealing to defenders of slavery before the war because it would invalidate any congressional refusal to admit a new slave state.

The state-equality idea led Taney to a more satisfactory textual source of congressional power, the new-states clause of Article IV, section 3. Such powers as Congress had to govern the territories

---

[40] 1 Pet. (26 U.S.) 511 (1828) at 542.
[41] 19 How. at 527. See generally William A. Dunning, "Are the States Equal under the Constitution," *Political Science Quarterly,* III (1888), 425–453. Taney had already used the idea in Strader v. Graham for proslavery purposes.

derived by implication from its power to admit new states. But because Congress could not impose conditions relegating new states to inferiority (as, for example, by denying them the opportunity to enter the Union as slave states, since nine states had already enjoyed that opportunity), it could not restrict them in the territorial stage. To maintain this position, Taney had to shut his eyes to historical experience under the Northwest Ordinance.

Then Taney turned to his second confirmation of Calhounian constitutional ideas, by insisting that whatever territory the federal government acquires, "it acquires for the benefit of the people of the several states who created it. It is their trustee acting for them and charged with the duty of promoting the interests of the whole people of the Union. . . ."[42] As trustee for the whole people, the federal government could not treat one class of citizens invidiously. It could not, in other words, exclude owners of slaves from a territory as long as it let owners of horses go there. (It ought to be needless to point out that Congress made no attempt to exclude slaveowners from the territories, or, for that matter, even slaves. In the Missouri Compromise, it merely forbade the legal establishment of slavery in the territories above Missouri. Taney glossed over this conceptual embarrassment.) Taney here shifted the argument from the macro level of powers of government to the micro level of the rights of individuals, and thereby came out at this remarkable assertion:

Thus the rights of property are united with the rights of person, and placed on the same ground by the fifth amendment to the constitution, which provides that no person shall be deprived of life, liberty, and property, without due process of law. And an act of Congress which deprives a citizen of the United States of his liberty or property, merely because he came himself or brought his property into a particular Territory of the United States, and who had committed no offense against the laws, could hardly be dignified with the name of due process of law.[43]

Historians have conventionally stated that Taney here enunciated the modern doctrine of "substantive due process," assuming that he had in mind the *Wynehamer* v. *New York* (1856) precedent, then only a year old. Thus regarded, Taney's Fifth Amendment point assumes

[42]19 How. at 448.
[43]19 How. at 450.

an importance coordinate with the issues of Negro citizenship and the Missouri Compromise. But a close reading[44] reveals that his statement is almost a throwaway line, a weak and passing allusion to one idea potentially great but here underdeveloped and unexploited. At most, this notion of substantive due process was one idea among many in Taney's 55 pages. He did not explicitly state that the Missouri Compromise was unconstitutional because it contravened the Fifth Amendment's due process clause. If this statement were to serve as the origin of substantive due process as an operative doctrine in the United States Supreme Court, it was a feeble beginning indeed. When, sixteen years later, Justice Samuel F. Miller stated with perplexity in the *Slaughterhouse* cases (1873) that "under no construction of [the due process clause] that we have ever seen, or any that we deem admissible, can [the Louisiana statute involved in that case] be held to be a deprivation of property within the meaning of that provision,"[45] he was accurately reflecting the slight weight to be attributed to Taney's passing invocation of the Fifth Amendment.

In the search for antebellum origins of substantive due process, a more likely candidate for the case marking the debut of the doctrine in the United States Supreme Court would be Justice Curtis's opinion in *Murray v. Hoboken,* decided a year before *Dred Scott.*[46] There, the Court unanimously sustained a federal statute authorizing an executive official, not a judge, to issue a distraint warrant against the property of a federal revenue officer. But Curtis noted with some sympathy the claim that this violated the due process clause of the Fifth Amendment, and he suggested that

it was not left to the legislative power to enact any process which might be devised. The Article [Fifth Amendment] is a restraint on the legislative as well as the executive and judicial powers of the government, and cannot be so construed as to leave the Congress free to make any process "due process of law," by its mere will.

Though conceptually still within the realm of procedural due process, Curtis's dictum was pregnant with possibilities realized later in

---

[44]Fehrenbacher, *Dred Scott Case,* pp. 378–384.
[45]16 Wall. (83 U.S.) 36 (1873) at 81.
[46]Murray v. Hoboken Land and Improvement Co., 18 How. (59 U.S.) 272 (1856); quotation at 276.

the century. *Murray* v. *Hoboken,* and not *Dred Scott,* was the true inception of substantive due process in the United States Supreme Court.

Having destroyed the raison d'être of the Republican party, Taney turned, in one of the few statements in his opinion that was truly dictum, to annihilate the position of northern Douglas Democrats. He asserted that if Congress lacked powers to prohibit slavery in the territories, "it could not authorize a territorial government to exercise them."[47] This swept away the structure of territorial sovereignty that Cass and Douglas had developed and left standing only the proslavery extreme position advocated by the followers of Calhoun. As if this were not plain enough, Taney drove the point home with his third assertion of Calhounian constitutional thought: "The only power conferred [on Congress] is the power coupled with the duty of guarding and protecting the [slave] owner in his rights."[48]

Then, almost anticlimactically, Taney at last got around to *Strader* v. *Graham,* enhanced it beyond its restricted 1851 scope, and held that it was controlling on the question of Scott's residence in Illinois. He relegated this pivotal issue to the tag end of his opinion for several reasons. For one thing, it would have no bearing on the case of Harriet Scott, consolidated with her husband's, since they were married after Dred's Illinois residence, nor would it affect their daughter Lizzie, whose exact birthplace was uncertain, or their daughter Eliza, born in Missouri. For another, one reading of *Strader* and its dicta might have aborted the whole proceeding on the jurisdictional question before Taney had a chance to get in his shots at the Republicans and at the Cass-Douglas wing of the Democracy.[49] That is, Taney might have treated *Strader* as dispositive at the outset, holding that the Missouri Supreme Court's determination of Scott's status in *Scott* v. *Emerson* was binding on all federal courts. This solution would have been somewhat clumsy and arbitrary, and not relevant to the status of Scott's wife and daughters, but it would have avoided what Chief Justice Charles Evans Hughes later characterized as the Court's great "self-inflicted wound."

[47]19 How. at 451.
[48]19 How. at 452.
[49]Again, for an alternative critique of the latter half of Taney's opinion, which we endorse but prefer not to repeat here, see Fehrenbacher, *Dred Scott Case,* ch. 16, "The Opinion of the Court: Slavery in the Territories."

And thus, finally, Taney got to the judgment of the Court, which no one contested as being the majority's disposition of the case. He reversed the judgment below and ordered that the case be dismissed for lack of jurisdiction. Around him lay, to his grim satisfaction, the fragments of antislavery, Free-Soil, Republican, and territorial-sovereignty constitutional thought.

Little needs to be said of the six concurrences, except that they gave ineffectual support to Taney's principal positions. Wayne and Grier indicated their entire support of Taney, and said little else, in brief opinions. Nelson submitted what was presumably the aboriginal *Dred Scott* opinion, holding that the Missouri court's determination of Scott's status was dispositive for federal courts. He did, however, inconclusively but suggestively allude to several points wholly outside the *Dred Scott* case, hinting that they would be resolved in a proslavery direction, as, for example, in his assumption that a military officer could not be prohibited from bringing his slave to reside with him when posted to duty in a free state.

Daniel, a Virginian, wrote an opinion that surpassed Taney's in the extremity of its substantive doctrine and in the intemperateness of its language. He insisted that slavery was a form of superproperty under the federal Constitution, enjoying explicit protection not conferred on other sorts of chattels; he was the only justice to hold the Northwest Ordinance unconstitutional; and he adopted an almost pure Calhounism in describing the relationship of the federal government to the states and the territories. Daniel was intellectually the most rigid and retrogressive of the members of the Court, and his *Dred Scott* opinion was his final word on the subjects of slavery and federalism.[50]

Justice Campbell reversed his earlier beliefs, expressed in private correspondence before his elevation to the bench, and held the Missouri Compromise unconstitutional, but in a temperate and reasoned opinion. Catron disagreed substantially with Taney, supporting Taney's conclusion that the Missouri Compromise was unconstitutional chiefly on the grounds that it violated the treaty of cession with France (1803), a point Taney did not raise.

Justices Curtis and McLean dissented, rebutting Taney's two

[50]John P. Frank, *Justice Daniel Dissenting* (Cambridge, Mass., 1964), esp. pp. 254–257.

principal points by holding that blacks could be citizens for diversity purposes and upholding the constitutionality of the Missouri Compromise. Curtis's effort was the longer, more tightly reasoned, and more persuasive of the two, and Republicans treated it as the correct disposition of the issues in the case. Curtis effectively used historical data and precedent to show that blacks were citizens at the time the Constitution was framed and that the territories clause was an ample source of congressional authority to legislate substantively for the territories. His amply documented opinion was conclusive to those who thought Taney wrong and who viewed his conclusions as dicta to be repudiated as soon as possible.

Dred Scott was a major historical event in its own right, and as such a shoal in the river of history around which events swirled for a time. The decision did not seriously diminish the prestige or power of the United States Supreme Court as an institution.[51] On the contrary, the Court continued to play a vital role as a coordinate branch of government throughout the war and Reconstruction. But the Court's majority did politicize itself. Taney's error-ridden dogmatism and Daniel's vituperation invited responses in kind, and they were not long in coming.

As might be expected, most southerners were delighted with the result, as were their northern racist fellows. The Augusta (Georgia) *Constitutionalist* crowed that "Southern opinion upon the subject of southern slavery . . . is now the supreme law of the land . . . and opposition to southern opinion upon this subject is now opposition to the Constitution, and morally treason against the Government." James Gordon Bennett's anti-Republican New York *Herald* agreed: "disobedience [to the decision] is rebellion, treason, and revolution." America's leading pseudoscientific racist of the time, New York physician John H. Van Evrie, later hailed Taney's words as implying "a universal recognition of 'slavery' as the natural relation of the races [as] the basis of the common law."[52]

Partisan and sectional attacks surprised no one. But soon several lengthy, reasoned criticisms of the Taney decision appeared in print

---

[51]Stanley I. Kutler, *Judicial Power and Reconstruction Politics* (Chicago, 1968), ch. 2, "The Healing Wound: The Supreme Court and National Politics, 1857–1866" and *passim*.

[52]*Constitutionalist* and *Herald* quoted in Fehrenbacher, *Dred Scott Case*, p. 418; Van Evrie, *The Dred Scott Decision: Opinion of Chief Justice Taney, with an Introduction by Dr. J. H. Van Evrie* (New York, 1863), p. iv.

and lent intellectual respectability to Republican condemnation of the decision. The first was a law review article, "The Case of Dred Scott," published by the erudite, scholarly young lawyer Horace Gray, later to occupy Benjamin Curtis's seat on the United States Supreme Court, and John Lowell, later a distinguished United States District and Circuit Court judge. Gray and Lowell supported Curtis, and, in a display of even temper rare for Bostonians that year, expressed regret rather than anger at Taney's legal and logical lapses, calling his opinion "unworthy of the reputation of that great magistrate."[53]

The Gray-Lowell effort was followed by others equally remarkable. Thomas Hart Benton, though dying of cancer, produced a book-length attack on the Missouri Compromise portion of Taney's opinion, supporting full congressional power in the territories.[54] John Codman Hurd, a learned Bostonian who wrote a monumental treatise defending the legitimacy of slavery, nonetheless subjected the same part of Taney's opinion to devastating scrutiny.[55] Other conservative legal commentators joined the criticism: the Philadelphia patrician Sidney George Fisher, the Harvard Law School professor Joel Parker, and Boston attorney George Ticknor Curtis, counsel for Scott in reargument in the Supreme Court and brother of Justice Curtis.[56]

The actions of northern courts and legislatures had a greater immediate impact than these scholarly rebuttals. In an advisory opinion requested by the Maine legislature, six of the seven members of the Maine Supreme Judicial Court asserted that blacks could vote in state and federal elections in Maine, rejecting Taney's opinion and relying instead on Curtis's dissent.[57] The Ohio Supreme Court defied Taney on a different legal issue, holding that any slave

[53][Horace Gray and John Lowell], "The Case of Dred Scott," *Monthly Law Reporter* (June, 1857), pp. 61–118; quote at p. 67.
[54]Thomas Hart Benton, *Historical and Legal Examination of that Part of . . . the Dred Scott Case, Which Declares the Unconstitutionality of the Missouri Compromise Act . . .* (New York, 1857).
[55]John Codman Hurd, *The Law of Freedom and Bondage in the United States* (Boston, 1858), I, sec. 502–536.
[56]Sidney George Fisher, *The Law of the Territories* (Philadelphia, 1859); Joel Parker, *Personal Liberty Laws and Slavery in the Territories* (Boston, 1861). On both these men, see Phillip S. Paludan, *A Covenant with Death: The Constitution, Law, and Equality in the Civil War Era* (Urbana, Ill., 1975), pp. 109–218. George Ticknor Curtis, *The Just Supremacy of Congress over the Territories . . .* (Boston, 1859).
[57]Opinion of the Justices, 44 Me. 505 (1857).

coming into the state with the consent of his master was freed, even if the slave was there only temporarily as a sojourner. For good measure, the Ohio court held that slave status did not reattach when the slave returned to a slave state.[58]

The New York Court of Appeals reached the same result in *Lemmon* v. *People* (1860), a case that was itself part of a larger problem inflamed by Dred Scott. To appreciate the significance and potential of the *Lemmon* case, it is necessary to realize that by the late 1850s, some northerners had come to believe that in one way or another, slavery was about to be forced into the free states themselves. A hundred and twenty-five years later, this fear seems fantastic, if not paranoid, and it was not enhanced in its day by being coupled with conspiracy fantasies. Yet events of the 1850s made the fear appear well grounded. For half a century, both sections had entertained the double apprehension of being both encircled and penetrated by the system—slavery or abolition—of the other. After Kansas-Nebraska and *Dred Scott,* it was plain to the free states that they were to be encircled by slavery, with even the free territories of Minnesota, Oregon, and Washington being threatened. The Fugitive Slave Act of 1850 and the dramatic legal confrontations under it provided one form of penetration; *Dred Scott* suggested there were more to come.

In *Strader* v. *Graham,* Taney, in a bit of seemingly deliberate judicial sloppiness characteristic of his slavery opinions, asserted the truism that every state had control over the status of persons within its jurisdiction, "except in so far as the powers of the states in this respect are restrained, or duties and obligations imposed on them, by the Constitution of the United States."[59] It was not clear what Taney was hinting at. If his remark was limited to the fugitive slave clause, it was truistic; but then it would have been easy enough to be more specific. Perhaps Taney was stalking bigger game, possibly broaching the idea that the sojourners laws enacted by a few northern states, limiting the time in which sojourning slaveholders could retain slaves within their jurisdictions, were unconstitutional. Or, conceivably, Taney might have been beginning a process of declaring the gradual abolition statutes and constitutional clauses of the northern states unconstitutional.

[58]Anderson *v.* Poindexter, 6 Ohio St. 623 (1857).
[59]10 How. at 93.

Georgia Senator Robert Toombs did not soothe northern fears by a remark he allegedly made, that he would one day call the roll of his slaves at the foot of Boston's Bunker Hill.[60] Nor did his Mississippi colleague in the United States Senate, Albert Gallatin Brown, who tactlessly proclaimed in 1858: "I would spread the blessings of slavery . . . to the uttermost ends of the earth, and rebellious and wicked as the Yankees have been, I would even extend it to them."[61] In the *Dred Scott* case Justice Nelson repeated Taney's *Strader* qualification almost verbatim ("subject only to such limitations as may be found in the Federal Constitution"). Justice Campbell, though no one outside the Court knew of it, amended the final printed draft of his *Dred Scott* opinion to bobtail this sentence: "Wherever the master is entitled to go, the slave may accompany him, unless prohibited by restrictive state or municipal legislation," by docking the final clause, thereby withdrawing the inference that restrictive laws were constitutional, and stating that the master may take his slave anywhere in the United States.[62]

Nor was it implausible that the United States Supreme Court might directly declare some or all northern abolition statutes unconstitutional. President Buchanan, in his last annual message, fervently denounced the personal liberty laws of the northern states as unconstitutional.[63] Taney's passing allusion to the due process clause of the Fifth Amendment, though not applicable to the states under the holding of *Barron* v. *Baltimore* (1833),[64] could nevertheless be translated into state constitutional doctrine via the law of the land or due process clauses that were everywhere parts of the state Constitutions. Gradual abolition statutes might just as easily have violated state constitutional guarantees of life, liberty, and property as the Missouri Compromise violated the Fifth Amendment. And, in fact, the organ of the Buchanan administration, the Washington

[60]Some time after the remark was supposedly made, Toombs denied having said it, claiming that he was being smeared by an abolitionist canard; see Pleasant A. Stovall, *Robert Toombs: Statesman, Speaker, Soldier, Sage* (New York, 1892), p. 119.
[61]M. W. Cluskey (ed.), *Speeches, Messages, and Other Writings of the Hon. Albert G. Brown* . . . (Philadelphia, 1859), pp. 588–599.
[62]This draft, corrected in Campbell's hand, is in U.S. National Archives, record group 267, appellate case file 3230.
[63]Buchanan, Fourth Annual Message, Dec. 3, 1860, in Richardson, *Messages and Papers of the Presidents*, VII, 3160.
[64]7 Pet. (32 U.S.) 243 (1833).

Union, asserted in November, 1857, that state abolition statutes were an unconstitutional attack on property rights.[65] This editorial was probably only an ill-advised trial balloon, and southern spokesmen in Congress immediately repudiated it. But a direct assault on northern abolition was not the only constitutional route to establish slavery in the North.

Some southern jurists argued that slavery was theoretically based on a contractual relationship between master and slave. If that were so, the contracts clause of Article I, section 10, might prohibit any impairment of that "contract."[66] Or the full-faith-and-credit clause of Article IV might protect the rights of out-of-state slaveholders bringing their slaves into the free states, conceivably even for sale. Or the privileges and immunities clause might similarly protect visiting slaveowners. A Vermont legislative committee maintained that that clause, interpreted in the light furnished by *Dred Scott,* "would convert every State into a slaveholding State, precisely as it now makes every Territory a slaveholding Territory."[67] Justice Henry Baldwin, in his *Groves* v. *Slaughter* concurrence (1841), had already stated that the clause did protect the rights of transient slaveowners, though he referred to an out-of-state slaveowner selling slaves in a slave state, not a free one.[68]

In 1854, as part of the response to the Kansas-Nebraska Act, northern political leaders and newspapers warned of "a continuous movement of slaveholders to advance slavery over the entire North." *Dred Scott* revived and compounded these fears.[69] Wisconsin Republican James R. Doolittle paraphrased the logic of Taney's opinion to hold that "the Constitution of the United States is the paramount law of every State, and if that recognizes slaves as property . . . no State constitution or State law can abolish it, or prohibit its introduction."[70]

[65]Washington *Union,* Nov. 17, 1857, excerpted at length in *Congressional Globe,* 35 Cong., 1 sess., app. 199–200 (Mar. 22, 1858).
[66]This possibility is considered in Samuel A. Foot, *An Examination of the Case of Dred Scott . . .* (New York, 1859), pp. 13–15.
[67]Vermont House of Representatives, *Report of the Select Committee on Slavery, the Dred Scott Decision, and the Action of the Federal Government Thereon* (Montpelier, 1858), p. 7.
[68]15 Pet. at 515–516.
[69]See the discussion in Sewell, *Ballots for Freedom,* 258–259, 299–300; quotation at p. 258; and Finkelman, *An Imperfect Union,* pp. 285–338.
[70]*Congressional Globe,* 35 Cong., 1 sess., 665 (Feb. 11, 1858); see also, to same effect, Senator James Harlan (R.—Iowa), *ibid.,* 1 sess., 385 (Jan. 25, 1858); Senator George Pugh (D.—Ohio), *ibid.,* 35 Cong. 2 sess., 1249–1251 (Feb. 23, 1859).

In the midst of these northern expressions of concern, the *Lemmon* case was working its way up through the New York courts. The prominent New York Jacksonian Charles O'Conor, counsel for the slaveowners in the case, insisted that the privileges and immunities clause of the federal Constitution protected the title of his clients to their slaves while passing through New York.[71] Alarmed antislavery observers warned that even if the New York courts rejected such arguments (which they did), the case would still serve as a vehicle to permit the United States Supreme Court to nationalize slavery.[72]

Abraham Lincoln voiced the same fears in his 1858 debates with Douglas. At Springfield, he noted that the Supreme Court had omitted "to declare whether or not the same Constitution permits a State, or the people of a State, to exclude [slavery]. . . . Put this and that together, and we have another nice little niche, which we may, ere long, see filled with another Supreme Court decision, declaring that the Constitution of the United States does not permit a state to exclude slavery from its limits."[73] Unlike others, Lincoln saw the supremacy clause of Article VI as the lever the Court would use to pry slavery into the free states. At Galesburg, he put the anticipated holding syllogistically:

> Nothing in the Constitution or laws of any State can destroy a right distinctly and expressly affirmed in the Constitution of the United States.
> The right of property in a slave is distinctly and expressly affirmed in the Constitution of the United States.
> Therefore, nothing in the Constitution or laws of any State can destroy the right of property in a slave.[74]

Taney never had the opportunity so to rule, but Lincoln's fears were not groundless or demagogic.

The northern judicial reaction to *Dred Scott* was complemented by legislative action in New York, Massachusetts, Ohio, Vermont, Maine, and Pennsylvania that expressed a mood of resistance to judicial proslavery. The most significant of New York's actions was

[71]20 N.Y. 562 (1860); O'Conor's argument summarized at 580.
[72]Samuel A. Foot, *Reasons for Joining the Republican Party . . .* (New York, 1855), p. 4; Theodore Parker, *The Present Aspect of Slavery in America and the Immediate Duty of the North . . .* (Boston, 1858), p. 20. See Paul Finkelman, "The Nationalization of Slavery: A Counterfactual Approach to the 1860s," *Louisiana Studies*, XIV (1975), 213–240.
[73]Robert Johannsen (ed.), *The Lincoln-Douglas Debates of 1858* (New York, 1965), p. 19.
[74]*Ibid.*, pp. 230–231.

a resolution that declared "this state will not allow slavery within her borders, in any form, or under any pretence, or for any time however short."[75] This was the doctrine vindicated by the Court of Appeals in *Lemmon*. Maine's legislature adopted resolutions directly critical of the Court and the decision, and enacted a statute freeing any slave brought into the state by his master. Ohio resolutions condemned the decision and forbade both sojourning and black kidnapping.[76] Vermont provided the most comprehensive response, not only to *Dred Scott* but to the larger tendency toward nationalization of slavery, by adoption of the Freedom Act of 1858,[77] which provided that: any slave coming into Vermont, with or without his master, was free; it was a misdemeanor to hold any such person as a slave; no person in Vermont could be vendible, held as a slave, or deprived of liberty or property without due process of law; jury trials were available in all fugitive-slave proceedings; slavery would not be grounds for denial of state citizenship.

Even before the Lincoln-Douglas debates, in June, 1857, Douglas had suggested that the right to take a slave into a territory, supposedly secured by the decision, required "appropriate police regulations and local legislation" to give it effect. These in turn, required popular support in the territory, and a territorial legislature reflecting the will of the people. "Hence," Douglas wrongheadedly concluded, "the great principle of popular sovereignty and self-government is sustained and firmly established by the authority of this decision."[78] At the time, this remark did not antagonize southern Democrats. But during the next twelve months, as the controversy over the Lecompton Constitution raged and Douglas broke with the Buchanan administration, he became anathema to the South.

Lincoln began the 1858 senatorial debates with Douglas with his famous "House Divided" speech,[79] where he linked the Kansas-Nebraska Act, Douglas's moral indifference to slavery, and *Dred Scott* in a conspiracy in which "Stephen [Douglas] and Franklin [Pierce]

[75]Resolution of Apr. 18, 1857, in *Laws of the State of New York . . . 1857*, p. 797.
[76]These legislative reactions are summarized in Fehrenbacher, *Dred Scott Case*, pp. 432–435.
[77]"An Act to Secure Freedom to All Persons within this State," no. 37, *Acts and Resolves of . . . Vermont . . . 1858*.
[78]*New York Times*, June 23, 1857. The "decision" was *Dred Scott*.
[79]Reproduced in relevant part in Commager, *Documents of American History*, I, 345–347.

and Roger [Taney] and James [Buchanan] all understood one another from the beginning, and all worked upon a common plan or draft drawn up before the first blow was struck." The result, he warned, would be that the Supreme Court would make Illinois a slave state. At Freeport, Lincoln propounded four interrogatories, two of which reiterated the dilemma that *Dred Scott* presented to northern Democrats:

Q. 2: Can the People of a United States Territory, in any lawful way . . . exclude slavery from its limits prior to the formation of a state constitution? Q. 3: If the Supreme Court of the United States shall decide that States cannot exclude slavery from their limits, are you in favor of . . . following such a decision as a rule of political action?

Douglas responded to the second question with what has come to be called the "Freeport Doctrine":

It matters not what way the Supreme Court may hereafter decide as to the abstract question whether slavery may or may not go into a Territory under the Constitution, the people have the lawful means to introduce it or exclude it as they please, for the reason that slavery cannot exist a day or an hour anywhere, unless it is supported by local police regulations.

He added, in a phrase that became a byword to his enemies in the Democratic party, that a territorial legislature could adopt "unfriendly legislation" to discourage slaveowners from migrating to the territory. But Douglas recognized that the third question—slavery in the free states—had trapped him, and he evaded it, insisting that the Supreme Court would never produce such a decision, though he did admit that it would be "moral treason" if such an unthinkable decision were ever handed down.[80] The most effective answer to this evasion came from a heckler in the Quincy debates, who shouted: "The same thing was said about the Dred Scott decision before it passed."[81]

Taney's final official[82] involvement came two years to the day

---

[80]Johannsen, *Lincoln-Douglas Debates,* pp. 79, 88, 91.
[81]Quoted in Jaffa, *Crisis of the House Divided,* p. 350.
[82]After 1859, the Chief Justice composed several draft "opinions" or memoranda on slavery and war-related issues as follows:

1. Supplement to Dred Scott opinion, reasserting that blacks could not be citizens and extending this to all blacks, not just descendants of slaves; published in Samuel Tyler, *Memoir of Roger Brooke Taney, LL.D.* (Baltimore, 1872), pp. 578–605.

after the last of the *Dred Scott* opinions had been read, in *Ableman v. Booth* (1859). This action arose out of northern judicial resistance to the encroachments of slavery, and its emotional intensity drew strength from northern anger at the Kansas-Nebraska Act and the subsequent events in Kansas.

In March, 1854, a United States marshal, accompanied by the claimant, Benammi Garland, seized an alleged fugitive slave, Joshua Glover, in Racine, Wisconsin, and lodged him in jail, preparatory to securing a certificate of rendition. The next day, a mob organized in part by Milwaukee abolitionist Sherman M. Booth rescued Glover and sent him on to Canada. This rescue prompted a welter of legal actions that pitted the Wisconsin courts against the United States Supreme Court. First, abolitionists had Garland arrested, charging him with assault on the slave. A United States District Court judge promptly released him on a petition for habeas corpus, holding that he claimed a right secured by the federal Constitution and laws and could not be molested by a state prosecution in exercising that right.[83] Then Booth was arrested on a federal warrant and charged with violation of the Fugitive Slave Act. He, in his turn, was promptly released by a writ of habeas corpus issued by a judge of the Wisconsin Supreme Court.[84] He was rearrested, tried in a federal District Court, found guilty, and sentenced to fine and imprisonment. Once again, he successfully sought release by habeas corpus, the Wisconsin Supreme Court again holding that the Fugitive Slave Act was unconstitutional. These cases were the first instance in which a State Supreme Court so held.[85] Then, back in the Federal District Court, Garland brought suit against Booth under the provisions of the Act allowing claimants to recover the value of a slave from those who aided in his escape, and won a verdict. At the same time, United States Attorney General Jeremiah S. Black sought a

---

2. Unpublished draft memorandum reasserting obligation of northern states to respect slavery and return fugitive slaves (1860–61?), in "Oddments" file, Roger B. Taney Papers, Mss. Div., Library of Congress.

3. Draft opinions holding Emancipation Proclamation, conscription, and legal tender acts unconstitutional; discussed in Carl Brent Swisher, *Roger B. Taney* (New York, 1936), pp. 564–572.

[83]U.S. ex rel. Garland *v.* Morris, 26 Fed. Cas. 1318 (No. 15811) (D.C.D. Wis. 1854).

[84]In re Booth, 3 Wis. 13 (1854).

[85]In re Booth and Rycraft, 3 Wis. 144 (1855).

writ of error directed to the Wisconsin Supreme Court from the United States Supreme Court. When the United States Attorney sought to serve the writ, he was advised by the clerk of the Wisconsin Supreme Court that the chief judge had instructed him to make no return to the writ and to make no entry on the records of the court concerning the writ. The Supreme Court of Wisconsin thus again defied the authority of the Supreme Court of the United States.

Chief Justice Taney eagerly took jurisdiction of the appeal, and, for a unanimous Court, condemned the action of the Wisconsin court.[86] *Ableman* v. *Booth* (1859) stands in striking contrast to *Dred Scott*. In the earlier case, two of Taney's fundamental values—the power of judicial review versus national power—were posed in conflict, and his resolution was strained, artificial, and marred by poor judicial craftmanship. In *Ableman,* by contrast, his opinion displayed an inner coherence because the values he asserted—judicial power and nationalism—were harmonious. *Dred Scott* has been almost universally discredited in modern times as a monument of error and arrogance; *Ableman* has been repeatedly reaffirmed and hailed as a benchmark in a line of cases from *Martin* v. *Hunter's Lessee* (1816) through the civil rights cases of the 1960s that vindicated federal judicial supremacy.

Taney began his opinion with a tactic he had successfully used in *Luther* v. *Borden,* by reciting a list of dreadful consequences that would follow a result opposite the one he intended to reach, with states everywhere obstructing the execution of federal laws. Then he returned to grand themes that had dominated American constitutional jurisprudence up to his time: a Marshallesque insistence that the federal government had to have the authority to enforce its own laws through its own courts, unobstructed by state resistance, if it was to preserve the Union; a reliance on federal supremacy and the correspondent limitations on state sovereignty ("although the State of Wisconsin is sovereign within its territorial limits to a certain extent, yet that sovereignty is limited and restricted by the Constitution of the United States"); and the creation of a new doc-

---

[86] 21 How. (62 U.S.) 506 (1859). The 1859 Court was identical to the *Dred Scott* Court, except that Justice Curtis, who had resigned in 1857, was replaced by the Maine Democrat Nathan Clifford.

trine that would be exploited half a century after his death for purposes he scarcely imagined: the doctrine of dual sovereignty. Taney wrote:

the powers of the general government, and of the State, although both exist and are exercised within the same territorial limits, are yet separate and distinct sovereignties, acting separately and independently of each other, within their respective spheres.

From these premises, he recurred to the spirit of Story's dissertation on federal judicial supremacy in *Martin* v. *Hunter's Lessee* (1816) and Marshall's in *Cohens* v. *Virginia* (1821), stating that "it was essential, therefore, to its very existence as a government, that it should have the power of establishing courts of justice, altogether independent of State power, to carry into effect its own laws. . . ."[87]

A reconstituted Wisconsin Supreme Court, though no less hostile to the proslavery implications of Taney's action, subsequently conceded that Taney's understanding of federal judicial power was correct and necessary. Moreover, when Booth once again applied for a writ of habeas corpus to release him from federal confinement, the new chief judge of the Wisconsin Court denied the writ and apologized to the United States Supreme Court, holding the Court's earlier action constituted "a breach of that comity, or good behavior, which should be maintained between the courts of the two governments toward each other."[88]

As a vindication of national judicial supremacy, and of the primacy of the federal government, Taney's *Ableman* effort has enjoyed an enduring relevance. Yet it bore the millstone of slavery around its neck and was temporarily obscured because many read it only in terms of its immediate end, which was the preservation of slavery's expansionist power. Taney, as always, was responsible for that, because he insisted in dictum "in the judgement of this court, the act of Congress commonly called the fugitive slave law is, in all of its provisions, fully authorized by the Constitution of the United States."

Ableman was a confrontation between "classical" doctrines of interposition and nullification, as expounded in the Virginia and Kentucky Resolutions of 1798–99, on the one hand, and state sovereign-

[87]Quotations from 21 How. at 516, 518, 526.
[88]Ableman v. Booth, 11 Wis. 517 (1860); Booth v. Ableman, 18 Wis. 519 (1864).

ty/state power doctrines on the other. The Jefferson/Madison exposition of interposition saw the state as interposing its sovereign power between an unconstitutional statute of Congress and the rights of one of its citizens. That was precisely what the Wisconsin courts were attempting to do here. Taney's nationalist opinion, rejecting this doctrine, instead, promoted federal judicial supremacy (vis-à-vis both states and Congress), the extraterritorial reach of state law, and, of course, the welfare of slavery. As was so often true of Taney opinions, things were not what they seemed at first:

federal judicial supremacy [according to Arthur Bestor] did not mean the supremacy of national policy over local or sectional policy. It meant precisely the reverse. It meant the denial to the federal government of any discretionary, policy-making function whatever in the matter of slavery.[89]

Ableman v. *Booth* will always speak with two voices. In one respect, it is a constitutional museum piece, a relic of judicial proslavery, extending the power of federal courts as the guardians of slavery and its aggressive outreach. Yet purged of its slavery contamination, the *Ableman* opinion vindicated the tradition of Marshall and Story over localist obstruction. In this latter respect, it remains one of Taney's monuments.

As Taney was delivering the *Ableman* opinion, the Union stood on the threshold of its gravest crisis. The previous year, in his "House Divided" speech, Lincoln explained this crisis:

this government cannot endure, permanently half slave and half free. I do not expect the Union to be dissolved . . . but I do expect it will cease to be divided. . . . Either the opponents of slavery will arrest the further spread of it, and place it where the public mind shall rest in the belief that it is in the course of ultimate extinction; or its advocates will push it forward, till it shall become alike lawful in all the States, old as well as new, North, as well as South.[90]

By 1859, Lincoln's prediction seemed well on the way to fulfillment, but in a proslavery direction. The free states of the Northeast were surrounded by a sweep of territory theoretically liable to become slave states. The executive branch committed its prestige and

[89]Arthur Bestor, "State Sovereignty and Slavery: A Reinterpretation of Proslavery Constitutional Doctrine, 1846–1860," *Journal of the Illinois State Historical Society,* LIV (1961), 117–180, at 141.
[90]Basler, *Collected Works of Lincoln,* II, 461–469 at 461–462.

federal power to secure slavery's penetration of the free states through the enforcement of the Fugitive Slave Act. Well might northern voters fear the reality of a Slave Power trampling the liberties of whites to perpetuate the enslavement of blacks. Lincoln was correct: the tensions of the 1850s would have to be resolved somehow, and the house cease to be divided.

CHAPTER 7

Secession: The Union Destroyed

TOCQUEVILLE wrote with profound insight in 1835 that "scarcely any question arises in the United States which does not become, sooner or later, a subject of judicial debate."[1] But after *Dred Scott*, the constitutional issues surrounding slavery became politicized again, because all save some forlorn administration Democrats recognized that the judiciary had tried its hand and failed. After being tossed back into the political arena, constitutional questions throughout 1860 and the ensuing "secession winter" were couched in political terms and articulated by politicians responding to political realities. These realities were principally two:

1. the United States in 1860 consisted of five distinct political regions, and constitutional questions would be resolved by coalitions among these regions; and

2. superimposed on this geographic division was a fissioning party process. The presidential election of 1860 was not unitary, but rather consisted of two independent contests, one North and one South, among, in effect, four parties, two of them being purely sectional.

The political regions of the United States in 1860 reflected shadings of attitudes toward slavery, rather than any other political,

[1]Tocqueville, *Democracy in America*, I, 284.

ideological, or constitutional issue.[2] The upper North, consisting of the New England states, western upstate New York, and those parts of the Old Northwest above the National Road[3] comprised the area most hostile to the territorial expansion of slavery and to enforcement of the Fugitive Slave Act. The lower North, consisting of the remainder of the free states south of the 41st parallel, contained some of the country's most important cities, including New York, Philadelphia, and Cincinnati. It had a larger black population—free, of course—than the region above it, and also closer commercial ties to the South. The new Pacific states, California (1850) and Oregon (1859), shared the attitudes, though not the geography or demography, of the lower North. The border region—Delaware, Maryland, the ultramontane region of old Virginia, Kentucky, and Missouri—consisted of slave states with relatively small black populations, relatively large numbers of free blacks, and indigenous pockets of white hostility to slavery. The upper South comprised the remainder of Virginia, North Carolina, and Tennessee. It and the Border States shared one dominant characteristic: slavery there was moribund economically and demographically. Finally, the deep or lower South, consisting of South Carolina, Florida, Alabama, Mississippi, Arkansas, Louisiana, and Texas, was the region where slavery was most vital, and where black population achieved its greatest density relative to the white.

The Democracy could no longer represent the views and aspirations of all these regions in one platform; the Republican party never even bothered to try. Instead the platforms and candidates of the parties sought to build coalitions based on some combination of two or more regions. The Republicans had carried almost every county in the upper North in the 1856 presidential contest. Their basic strategy for 1860 was to retain their strength there and do well enough in the lower North to enable them to carry the crucial states of New Jersey, Pennsylvania, Indiana, and Illinois. In other words, the Republicans sought a free-state coalition. The Democrats, on the other hand, were crippled by the unnatural split in their north-

[2]The political regions of 1860 were derived from demographic and ideological regional characteristics noted above, ch. 4, p. 86–87.

[3]The National Road was the predecessor of old U.S. 40, which is now Interstate 70. It ran from Cumberland, in the Maryland panhandle, to Vandalia, in south-central Illinois, roughly following the 41st parallel.

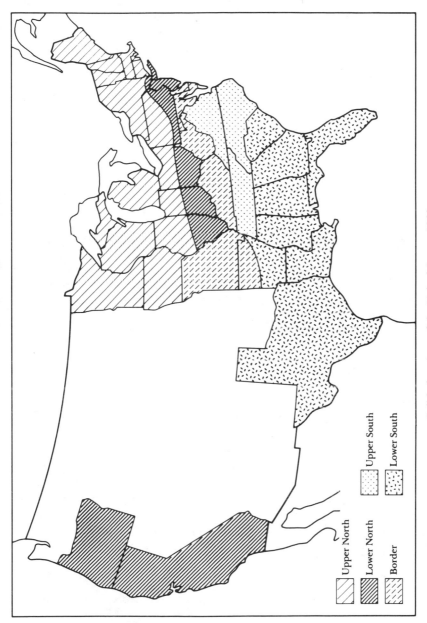

Political regions of the United States, 1860

ern wing. The President, a northern Democrat, dedicated himself to a pro-southern, proslavery policy at odds with the wishes of Democrats throughout the upper and lower North, who turned to Stephen Douglas as their spokesman. Moreover, the southern wing was determined to force its own views of orthodoxy on the slavery/territorial question on all the party, making their demands a shibboleth to test the commitment of their northern colleagues. Hence the obvious Democratic strategy of trying to appeal to a coalition of the lower North, the Border, and the upper South was doomed, and with it, party unity.

The last official position of the united Democracy had been the "Cincinnati Platform" of 1856, which articulated the long-prevalent constitutional consensus concerning slavery, and also the deliberate Democratic ambiguity concerning its spread into the territories:

Congress has no power under the Constitution to interfere with or control the domestic institutions of the several states, and that all such States are the sole and proper judge of everything pertaining to their own affairs not prohibited by the Constitution. . . . the American Democracy recognize and adopt the principles contained in the organic laws establishing the Territories of Nebraska and Kansas as embodying the only sound and safe solution of the slavery question: non-interference of Congress with slavery in the territories. . . .

The Democracy in the North could only be harmed by any substantial movement away from the basic position of the Cincinnati Platform.[4] After *Dred Scott,* Douglas disingenuously sought to find some way to salvage something of territorial sovereignty for Kansas and the other territories.

But Buchanan, determined to force slavery into Kansas, resolutely opposed Douglas and territorial sovereignty, defiantly proclaiming in February, 1858, that Kansas was then "as much a slave State as Georgia or South Carolina."[5] In his 1859 annual message, after Kansas voters rejected the Lecompton Constitution, Buchanan insisted that the *Dred Scott* decision had established the right of every slaveowner to take slaves into all American territories (includ-

[4]The 1856 Cincinnati Platform is in Johnson and Porter, *National Party Platforms,* pp. 23–27.

[5]Message of Feb. 2, 1858, in Richardson, *Messages and Papers of the Presidents,* VII, 3010.

ing those committed to freedom, such as Minnesota, Kansas, and Oregon, which was on the eve of statehood), and to have such slave property "protected there under the Federal Constitution."[6] That, in turn, led to Senator Jefferson Davis's demand that a federal slave code be imposed on all the territories.[7] That position became canonical for the southern Democratic leadership by 1860.

The emergence of this final southern position guaranteed that the Democratic National Convention meeting in Charleston in April would be tumultuous. Southern Democrats demanded that the 1856 "non-interference" plank be scrapped and, with it, territorial sovereignty, in favor of a "positive-protection" program. Accordingly, when Douglas forces defeated their demand for a platform proclaiming that it was the "duty of the Federal government, in all its departments to protect, when necessary the rights of persons and property . . . in the territories," nine southern delegations walked out.[8] When the party met again six weeks later in Baltimore, it split again, but this time the Douglas forces insisted on pushing through the nomination of their candidate. Southern delegates again walked out, met elsewhere in the city, adopted the territorial plank rejected at Charleston, and nominated John C. Breckinridge of Kentucky and Joseph Lane, a native North Carolinian transplanted to Oregon, as their presidential and vice-presidential nominees. The Democracy was now formally split, but this merely reflected a division that had existed in reality since 1846, when Democrats began casting about for alternatives to the Wilmot Proviso. Ambiguity and procrastination would no longer serve to hold the party together.

Douglas began the presidential campaign in the summer of 1860 as the exponent of territorial sovereignty, or whatever remnant of it he could salvage despite *Dred Scott* and the party's leadership. But he soon saw that his cause was hopeless, and that the Republican candidate would be elected. In an act of courageous statesmanship that transfigured his political career, he then switched his emphasis and threw himself utterly into the effort to avoid secession. He alone among the candidates campaigned, whistlestopping through the North, where Cassandra-like he tried to warn northern voters of the

[6]*Ibid.*, p. 3085.
[7]*Congressional Globe*, 36 Cong., 1 sess., 658 (Feb. 2, 1860).
[8]The Douglas and southern Democratic platforms are reprinted in Johnson and Porter, *National Party Platforms*, pp. 30–31.

reality of southern determination to secede if Lincoln were elected, and in the South, where he condemned disunion and secession. His efforts were in vain. Horace Greeley scoffed that "the South could no more unite upon a scheme of secession than a company of lunatics could conspire to break out of bedlam." Lincoln shrugged off secession threats from patronage-hungry southerners: "They won't give up the offices. Were it believed that vacant places could be had at the North Pole, the road there would be lined with dead Virginians."[9]

The Breckinridge Democrats, realistic candidates only in the slave states, stood by the Charleston platform of forcing slavery into all the territories. Breckinridge and Lane did not campaign, and neither ran as an overt secessionist.

The Republicans, keenly aware of the need to carry Illinois, Indiana, New Jersey, and Pennsylvania, bypassed the front-runner, New York Senator William H. Seward, in favor of Abraham Lincoln. Their platform reflected both a softening of their 1856 Free-Soil resolve and an outreach to interests not concerned about the slavery question. The party condemned the Buchanan/Taney/Davis doctrine that the Constitution of its own force implanted slavery in every territory, and denied the power of both Congress and territorial legislatures to establish slavery in a territory, vaguely linking this position to the due process clause of the Fifth Amendment. But it conspicuously did not condemn slavery or slaveholders; it was mute on the burning issues of the Fugitive Slave Act and the personal liberty laws; and it called for the "maintenance inviolate of . . . the right of each State to order and control its own domestic institutions according to its own judgement exclusively."

Instead of alienating moderates and conservatives on these issues, the Republicans opportunistically appealed to northern sectional interests by endorsing a protective tariff (a vital interest of Pennsylvania, the most important of the lower North states because it had almost as many electoral votes as Illinois, Indiana, and New Jersey combined); by endorsing the Homestead Bill and calling for recognition of the rights of squatters; by supporting rivers-and-harbors appropriations; by demanding "immediate and efficient" federal aid for a transcontinental railroad; and finally, by dumping

[9]Quoted in Potter, *Impending Crisis*, p. 432.

nativism and calling for the maintenance of the status quo of nationalization laws.[10]

The fourth party on the national scene, a collection of elderly
lower North and Border State Whigs, called itself the Constitutional
Union party. It took no position at all on the slavery issue, avowing
"no political principle other than the Constitution of the country,
the Union of the States and the enforcement of the Laws."[11] Its
presidential candidate was the Tennessee Unionist John Bell.

The Republican strategy of building a coalition of upper North
and lower North worked (as a bonus, they even carried California
and Oregon). The Breckinridge Democrats swept the deep South,
with the upper South and Border States splitting among Douglas,
Bell, and Breckinridge. Lincoln, though getting only a plurality of
the popular vote, was validly elected; he would have enjoyed the
same electoral college majority had all other candidates' votes, both
popular and electoral, been united for one person. But while Lincoln's victory was substantively legitimate, he was as politically alien
as the Emperor Napoleon III to nearly all the slave states. (He was
on the ballot only in Delaware, Missouri, Virginia, Maryland, and
Kentucky.) Thus his election was not legitimate in the eyes of southern editorialists and men-in-the-street. For this and many other
reasons, the only alternative facing would-be secessionists was, indeed, submission or independence.

After the election, a curious series of occurrences took place
within the next three months. The issues of the 1860 campaign had
clearly focused on the territorial question, and thus reflected the
ostensible contest between slave and free states. With the Republican victory, one might therefore have expected to find at least
rear-guard skirmishing over territorial issues. Yet by a supreme
irony, the parties in Congress proceeded to dispose of actual territorial issues promptly and without noisy controversy. Congress
created three new territories, Colorado, Nevada, and Dakota,[12]
making no provision of any sort concerning slavery in them. It dealt
dispassionately, almost indifferently, with New Mexico Territory,

[10]Johnson and Porter, *National Party Platforms,* pp. 31–33.
[11]*Ibid.*, p. 30.
[12]Dakota Territory comprised modern North and South Dakota, nearly all of
Montana, and about half of Wyoming. Nevada Territory was a shrunken version of
its present self.

declining to admit it immediately as a slave state yet making no move to exclude slavery from it or force it there. Finally, in January, 1861, it admitted Kansas, with little fanfare, as a free state. The territorial slavery issue, recently so real and so momentous, seemed to have been tossed aside like an orange peel, a strange denouement explained only by the fact that Lincoln's election was the culmination of the crisis of the Union, not just an abrupt settlement of the territorial question. Since the Wilmot Proviso controversy fourteen years earlier, southern political leaders had come to see the territorial issue as an adjunct to the real question, which was the security of slavery in the extant states. Whether or not they were correct in seeing slavery's freedom to expand into the territories as vital to its internal security in the old states, they did correctly apprehend Lincoln's election as at least a portent of a long-term assault on slavery, a struggle that they were certain to lose. Thus, like a kaleidoscope, the territorial question was transformed into the question of slavery's security where it was, rather than its prospects in the territories, and that, in turn, became transformed into the question of southern independence.

Seeing the issue as independence versus the impending demise of slavery, white southerners turned to the question of secession. They split into three groups: immediate secessionists who sought to secede promptly, permanently, and by separate state action if necessary; "cooperationists," a divergent group ranging from secessionists at one end to unionists at the other, who hoped to delay immediate secession for a variety of motives; and unconditional unionists like Senator Andrew Johnson of Tennessee who flatly opposed secession. This division of opinion was related to the regional differences that had played so prominent a role in the politics of the late fifties. The deep South housed the greatest number of immediate secessionists, and consisted of the first states to secede.[13] The upper South and the Border States contained a greater proportion of cooperationists and unionists. The upper South seceded only after it became outraged by federal coercion; the Border States remained in the Union, not altogether enthusiastically.

In promoting secession, the leaders of the southern indepen-

---

[13] On secessionist-cooperationist divisions in the deep South, see William L. Barney, *The Secessionist Impulse: Alabama and Mississippi in 1860* (Princeton, 1974).

dence movement could draw on a rich and venerable treasury of constitutional theory. Secession was rooted in three different yet related ideas: state sovereignty, interposition/nullification, and disunion. Disunion was not so much an idea as an impulse, sectionally based and accompanied by economic or religious rationalizations. New Englanders, particularly conservative Massachusetts Federalists, considered disunion in the period between the Louisiana Purchase in 1803 and the Treaty of Ghent (1815) as they sensed the hemorrhaging of political power from their section. Resenting the new western territories, the political power of the slave states based on the three-fifths clause, and the Virginia Dynasty, they contemplated an independent northeastern federation. Later, Garrisonian abolitionists, together with a few non-Garrisonians, relied on many of the same grievances to demand the separation of the free states from the South. Unlike the earlier disunionists, they were hostile to slavery as such. Their disunionism derived not from economic self-interest but from theological concepts sanctioned by the command in the Book of Revelation (18:4): "Come out of her, my people, that ye be not partakers of her sins, and that ye receive not of her plagues."

But the most consistent disunionists of the antebellum years were southern defenders of slavery, who with increasing frequency since the 1790s had been threatening to leave the Union if attacks on the peculiar institution did not cease. They played on the disunion theme so heavily that, like the boy crying "Wolf!" in the fable, they lost credibility by the time they were prepared to act on their demand. Whether northern or southern, disunionism of itself lacked constitutional justification.

Not so state sovereignty.[14] As an indispensable element of federalism, theories concerning the nature of the states' retained sovereignty were numerous in the Revolutionary period and had been amply replenished and updated ever since. The Tenth Amendment, ratified in 1791, referred explicitly to retained states' powers. James Madison and Thomas Jefferson, in the Virginia and Kentucky Resolutions (1798–99) developed the theory of a federal government of

[14]The fullest exposition of state sovereignty theories and their constitutional consequences, particularly the right of secession, is Alexander H. Stephens, *A Constitutional View of the Late War Between the States . . .* (Philadelphia, 1868), esp. vol. I.

specified and delegated powers,"reserving each State to itself, the residuary mass of right to their own self-government."[15] Virginians continued as special custodians, almost a temple priesthood, of the doctrine. St. George Tucker, the first American editor of Blackstone, affirmed state sovereignty in an early constitutional commentary. The feud between nationalists like John Marshall and Joseph Story, on one hand, and Jefferson, Spencer Roane, and John Taylor of Carolina on the other, drew forth from the Virginians lengthy dissertations, printed in the columns of Thomas Richie's Richmond *Inquirer,* on state sovereignty and the derivative character of the federal government.

If these men were a priesthood, their ally, John Randolph of Roanoke, was a cult figure. Stepson of St. George Tucker, Randolph spent his long congressional career opposing initiatives of federal power. Leaders of a political coterie of the 1820s known as the Quids, Randolph left an impressive intellectual legacy to Virginia opponents of federal power known more in reverence than in scorn as "Old Republicans." These men produced a succession of states' rights theorists and conservative political thinkers: Abel Parker Upshur, Benjamin Watkins Leigh, Thomas R. Dew, the seemingly innumerable Tuckers, including Nathaniel Beverly Tucker and Henry St. George Tucker, and United States Supreme Court Justices Philip Pendleton Barbour and Peter V. Daniel.

But despite this impressive intellectual tradition of the Old Dominion, South Carolinians assumed the role of leadership in developing state-sovereignty thought after 1820. Alarmed by the supposed slave revolt of Denmark Vesey in 1822, a line of Carolina publicists and political leaders elaborated on ideas sketched by Thomas Cooper in his diatribe *Consolidation* (1824), in which he denied that a national government had been created by the Constitution.[16] Cooper became one of the first Americans to develop a theory of secession. Other prominent Carolina states' rights theorists included Robert Turnbull, Robert Y. Hayne, George McDuffie, and James Henry Hammond. The leading theorist of state sovereignty, though a late recruit to the cause, was John C. Calhoun. Building on Turnbull's argument that the true sovereigns in Amer-

---

[15]From the Kentucky Resolution of 1798, substantially excerpted in Commager, *Documents of American History,* I, 178–182 at 178.

[16][Thomas Cooper], *Consolidation. An Account of Parties in the United States, from the Convention of 1787, to the Present Period* (Columbia, S.C., 1824).

ica were the people of the separate states, not the people of the entire country *en masse,* Calhoun spent the last twenty years of his life elaborating a theory of state sovereignty, with its related features of the agency character of the federal government and the various mechanisms by which the states might protect their sovereignty. Calhoun's thought was carried to its logical conclusion by three other Carolinians, William Lowndes Yancey, Edmund Ruffin, and Robert Barnwell Rhett, who had become secessionists by the early 1850s and who were leaders of the so-called fire-eaters demanding southern independence.[17]

The third of this triad of ideas, interposition/nullification, also derived from the Virginia and Kentucky Resolutions. The Virginia Resolution of 1798 spoke of the duty of the states to "interpose" their authority, and the Kentucky Resolution of 1799 extended Jefferson's thought of the year before by stating that "a nullification [by the states] of all unauthorized [federal] acts . . . is the rightful remedy."[18] Disappointed that his constitutional notions embodied in the 1837 Resolutions met with only partial success, Calhoun devised theories of nullification and secession.

After Calhoun's death in 1850, the idea of secession became associated with a hallowed American constitutional innovation, the popular convention. Originated in the Revolutionary era as a formal convocation of the people's representatives to perform some solemn act, like drafting or ratifying a constitution, the convention had become a vehicle that translated the theory of popular sovereignty into an actual mechanism of government.

Immediately upon Lincoln's election, Carolina secessionists secured elections for a convention to meet on December 17, 1860. On December 20, 1860, the convention adopted an Ordinance of Secession, and on Christmas Eve sent to the world at large a "Declaration of the Immediate Causes [of] Secession," a formal summary of wrongs the Carolinians endured and of the constitutional theory that underlay secession.[19] Unlike Edward Pollard's and Jefferson Davis's postwar constitutional defenses of secession, the 1860 Dec-

---

[17]Though usually associated with his adopted state, Alabama, Yancey was a native South Carolinian.

[18]Excerpted in Commager, *Documents of American History,* I, 182, 184.

[19]"Declaration of the Immediate Causes Which Induce and Justify the Secession of South Carolina from the Federal Union" (1860), in John A. May and Joan R. Faunt (comps.), *South Carolina Secedes* (Columbia, S.C., 1960).

laration placed slavery squarely at the heart of the controversy.[20]
The Carolinians accused the northern states, as parties to the national compact that constituted the Constitution, of reneging on
their obligations by tolerating antislavery activity, sheltering runaway slaves, attempting to exclude slaveholders from the territories,
enacting personal liberty laws, permitting blacks to vote, and condemning slavery as sinful. Therefore, the sovereign people of Carolina, acting through their convention, reassumed their status as "a
separate and independent state, with full power to levy war, conclude peace, contract alliances, establish commerce, and to do all
other acts and things which independent States may of right do."
By February 1, 1861, six other states—Georgia, Florida, Alabama,
Mississippi, Louisiana, and Texas—had followed South Carolina
into secession. The entire lower South had become what some
called, hopefully or derisively, the "Gulf Coast Confederacy."

Back in December, 1860, the Carolinians had had the foresight to
call for a meeting of commissioners at Montgomery, Alabama, on
February 4, 1861 to consider formation of a separate nation. With
remarkable speed, the commissioners met, adopted a Provisional
Constitution for the new confederacy, which was to be called the
Confederate States of America, and elected Jefferson Davis president of the new federated republic. The Montgomery Convention
played the historically unique role of serving as constitutional convention, electoral college, and proto-Congress.[21]

But then the momentum of secession stalled because of the
demographic and economic characteristics that differentiated the
three regions of the slave states. Although Virginia had been the
matrix of state-sovereignty thought earlier in the century, her declining slave population, shifting agricultural base, incipient industrialization, and historic ties to the Union muffled calls for secession.
She and the remaining seven slave states adopted a wait-and-see
attitude, conditioned chiefly on Lincoln's response to the crisis and
on compromise efforts. With the failure of compromise and the
firing on Fort Sumter, the upper South opted for the Confederacy,

Virginia in April, North Carolina, Tennessee, and Arkansas in May, 1861.

In the autumn of that year, a rump segment of the legislature of Missouri and a convention called by Kentucky Confederate soldiers declared their states seceded, thus making a total of thirteen stars in the Stars and Bars. But for all practical purposes, both those states remained in the old Union, so much so that Missouri boasted that it furnished more men to the Union armies than Massachusetts. Delaware made no move to secede, in great measure because of its historic ties to Pennsylvania (it was originally the "Lower Counties" of Penn's proprietary) and because by 1860 half its black population was free anyway. Maryland did not secede either, despite intense and extensive secessionist sentiment. (The modern state anthem, "Maryland, My Maryland," is actually an anti-Lincoln diatribe inviting the state to join her sister Virginia in secession.) But Lincoln's prompt and vigorous use of federal force preserved Baltimore and its environs for the Union, and with it the rest of the state.

At the time that the Old Dominion was taking itself out of the Union, delegates from its western counties began their own secessionist movement from the state, laying the foundations for the Unionist state of West Virginia, which Congress admitted in 1863. Finally, to round out the picture, occasional and atypical voices were heard in Iowa, Oregon, and throughout the lower North calling for secession of those states. In New York City, Mayor Fernando Wood, a southern sympathizer, formally proposed to the city council the bizarre scheme of having the city secede from New York State and declare itself a "Free City."[22] This never came to anything, but the Empire City remained a thorn in the side of the Union, sheltering southern sympathizers and being the scene of the bloodiest anti-draft riots in the nation in 1863.

The northern response to the disruption of the Union during secession winter was cautious to the point of immobility. President Buchanan temporized, partly, as he later claimed, to buy time for attempts at compromise efforts, partly to avoid forcing the remaining slave states into secession, and, above all, to do whatever he

[22]William C. Wright, *The Secession Movement in the Middle Atlantic States* (Rutherford, N.J., 1973); Wood's message, dated Jan. 6, 1861, is excerpted in Commager, *Documents of American History*, I, 374–376.

could to save the Union.[23] But because of his innate weakness, conflicting pressures on him from within his cabinet paralyzed him. Henry Adams described it thus:

It was a battle after the Homeric style. Mr. Cass [Lewis Cass of Michigan, Secretary of State] dragged him by the foot; Mr. Cobb [Howell Cobb of Georgia, Secretary of Treasury] by the head, and between impeachment and assassination, the feeble object of the furious contest could only weep with his ancient friends, and call upon the people to fast and pray.[24]

Where Lincoln was to find opportunities in constitutional and statutory provisions, Buchanan could see only constraints. Federal statutes shed little light on ways the President might respond to the unprecedented crisis of secession. The previous spring, Congress had refused to enact a seditious conspiracies statute.[25] Buchanan's temperamental inclination to procrastinate and evade was encouraged by his Attorney General, the proslavery Pennsylvanian Jeremiah S. Black. In an official opinion,[26] Black cautioned the President that his duty to see to the faithful execution of the laws was limited, not enlarged, by extant statutory authority, derived largely from revenue statutes and the title of the United States to federal property. Presidential ability to call up militia under the 1795 Enforcement Act[27] was limited to "defensive" responses to obstructions of the laws, and could not be activated where loyal courts were not functioning. Black went on to declare, gratuitously—no states had yet seceded—that if a state withdrew from the Union, the President could make no response, that being a function of Congress or the states in convention. But lest this encourage congressional action,

[23][James M. Buchanan], *Mr. Buchanan's Administration on the Eve of the Rebellion* (New York, 1866), p. 111.

[24]Henry Adams, "The Great Secession Winter," in George Hochfield (ed.), *The Great Secession Winter of 1860–61 and Other Essays* [by Henry Adams] (New York, 1958), p. 6.

[25]Catherine M. Tarrant, "To 'insure domestic Tranquility': Congress and the Law of Seditious Conspiracy, 1859–1861," *American Journal of Legal History,* XV (1971), 107–123.

[26]Opinion of Nov. 20, 1860 in *Opinions of the Attorney-General,* IX, 516–526.

[27]Militia Act of 1792, ch. 28, 1 Stat. 264; extended by Enforcement Act of 1795, ch. 36, 1 Stat. 424. By Act of Mar. 3, 1807, ch. 39, 2 Stat. 443, the President was authorized to use regular troops as well as militia to enforce federal laws and put down resistance to federal authority.

Black concluded by asserting that any attempt by Congress to coerce a seceding state militarily would "absolve" the state's constitutional obligations. "The Union must utterly perish" if Congress
should attempt to save it by force, he perversely declared.

Although Buchanan adopted Black's position in his last annual
message, his posture reflected a subtle difference in emphasis, sending a slightly stiffer pro-Union message to secessionists. He began
with Democratic orthodoxy, blaming the northern states for the
current crisis because of their personal liberty laws and their tolerance of antislavery agitation. He called for a constitutional convention, suggesting that its agenda include more stringent protections
for recapture of fugitive slaves and protection of slavery in the
territories. In the segment of his message that drew most northern
fire, the President declared that secession had no constitutional
basis, but then went on to state that neither was there authority for
presidential coercion of the seceding states. But he did conclude
with the constitutional formula later adopted by Lincoln as the
resolution of the dilemma posed by the fact that the Constitution
did not contemplate secession: he would continue to enforce federal laws in the seceded states. Buchanan found textual authority for
this in the provision of Article II, section 3, that requires that the
President "take Care that the Laws be faithfully executed. . . ."[28]
Buchanan backed his sentiments with action. Although secessionist
forces were seizing federal forts and arsenals throughout the South,
Buchanan refused to surrender Fort Sumter, South Carolina, and
Fort Pickens, Florida. Both were coastal installations and thus rein-
forceable by sea.

Despite this modest assertion of authority, northerners found
Buchanan's constitutional views insufficient. Senator William Seward sarcastically paraphrased the President: "it is the duty of the
President to execute the laws—unless somebody opposes him—and
that no state has the right to go out of the Union—unless it wants
to."[29] So other northern political leaders did what they could to
supply the deficiencies of the leadership in Washington. In an out-

[28]Annual Message of Dec. 3, 1860, in Richardson, *Messages and Papers of the Presidents,* VII, 3157–3169.
[29]William H. Seward to Frances A. Seward, Dec. 5, 1860, in Frederick W. Seward,
Seward at Washington, as Senator and Secretary of State, (New York, 1891), II, 480.

burst of spread-eagle patriotism, individual northerners spontaneously formed volunteer military companies or enlisted in militia
units, and governors and legislatures backed their antisecession
oratory with appropriations and militia call-ups. The decrepit commanding general of the army, Winfield Scott, supervised the fortifi-
cation of Washington and expressed his determination to prevent
any revolutionary interference with the certification of the 1860
election returns:

any man who attempted [to] interfere with the lawful count of the electoral
vote should be lashed to the muzzle of a twelve-pounder and fired out of
a window of the Capitol. I would manure the hills of Arlington with his
body.[30]

But it was to President-elect Lincoln that Americans necessarily
looked for policy guidance, and he deliberately refused to venture
beyond his previously stated positions. At various times between his
election (November 6, 1860) and his inauguration (March 4, 1861)
he reiterated the two fundamental points on which he and his party
had campaigned:

1. Slavery must not be permitted, either by congressional or by territorial
action, to expand into the territories; this was an essential first step in
placing slavery, as Lincoln had stated in his 1858 "House Divided" speech,
"in the course of ultimate extinction."
2. But the Republicans would protect slavery where it existed, and would
generously accommodate all southern demands for preservation of their
internal security for as long as slavery existed.

In pursuit of these aims, Lincoln proposed new legislation for
effective enforcement of the Fugitive Slave Act but, unlike the 1793
and 1850 statutes, that would not oblige private persons to participate in enforcement and that permitted "the usual safeguards to
liberty" for black "freemen." He also urged repeal of the personal
liberty laws.[31] Writing privately to Seward shortly before his inauguration, Lincoln insisted that the party not recede on its territorial
position, but "as to fugitive slaves, [slavery in the] District of Columbia, slave trade among the slave states, and whatever springs of

---

[30]Quoted in Allan Nevins, *The Emergence of Lincoln* (New York, 1950), II, 437.
[31]*Ibid.*, p. 396.

necessity from the fact that the institution is amongst us, I care but little, so that what is done be comely, and not altogether outrageous."[32] And in his inaugural address he expressed support for a constitutional amendment prohibiting federal interference with slavery in the states, stating that this was "now . . . implied constitutional law."[33]

Beyond that, however, Lincoln did not orchestrate a forceful northern response to secession before his inauguration. While this had the arguably desirable effect of giving compromise movements whatever chance they may have had to prevent bloodshed, it also furnished secessionists with an invaluable opportunity to organize armies and civilian governments. The old exponent of secession, Edmund Ruffin, mused in his diary that:

the imbecility of the executive department, added to the want of funds and means by the federal government, have prevented anything being done to coerce the seceded states. . . . This has given four months of unforeseen and almost undisturbed time for action. . . . Thus there has been avoided what I certainly counted upon, the interregnum of lawful power, or transition state of disorder, or illegal rule and perhaps revolutionary anarchy.[34]

Secession winter was thus an incubation period for the new Confederate state and federal governments.

Northerners, both prominent and obscure, shared Ruffin's concern about disorder, illegal rule, and anarchy. They, however, translated their concerns into a demand that secession be crushed in order to preserve the values of ordered liberty and local self-government. "A surrender to Secession is the suicide of government," trumpeted a Cincinnati newspaper, and throughout the North men enlisted or otherwise supported the Union's war efforts in order to stave off anarchy and to preserve their opportunity to govern themselves in their local communities.[35]

Given the intense and widespread determination in the North that

[32]Lincoln to Seward, Feb. 1, 1861, in Roy P. Basler (ed.), *The Collected Works of Abraham Lincoln* (New Brunswick, N.J., 1953–55), IV, 183.
[33]*Ibid.*, p. 270.
[34]Ruffin diary entry of Jan. 31, 1861, quoted in Nevins, *Emergence of Lincoln*, II, 341–342.
[35]Phillip S. Paludan, "The American Civil War Considered as a Crisis in Law and Order," *American Historical Review*, LXXVII (1972), 1013–1034; quotation at 1018.

secession must be put down, and the equally intense support in the South for southern independence, the compromise efforts of secession winter, viewed with hindsight, have a tragically hopeless quality about them. Because Lincoln was, in the word he chose to describe his position, "inflexible" on the territorial issue,[36] "compromise" on the Republican side could have no meaning but "surrender." Similarly with the secessionists: even before South Carolina began the chain of secessions, thirty anticooperationist southern senators and representatives published a manifesto declaring:

All hope of relief in the Union, through the agency of committees, Congressional legislation, or constitutional amendments, is extinguished. . . . We are satisfied the honor, safety, and independence of the Southern people are to be found in a Southern Confederacy. . . .[37]

The notion of compromise would therefore be meaningful only to "moderates"—in the North, persons indifferent to slavery and its expansion, in the South, Unionists concentrated in the Border States and the upper South. These men exercised great leverage in secession winter, but they were not in control. Their efforts were foredoomed because there was nothing the Republican party could offer, while preserving its raison d'être as a party, to the slave states that the slave states considered both credible and adequate. Compromise on either side required capitulation, and neither side was prepared to capitulate. Lincoln put it more eloquently in his second inaugural:

Both parties deprecated war, but one of them would *make* war rather than let the nation survive, and the other would *accept* war rather than let it perish,

"and the war came," he concluded.[38]

     But three efforts at compromise, all of them involving constitutional means and constitutional objectives, held the North's attention through secession winter. The first, which was actually a collection of alternative proposals, emerged out of the work of a special

[36]Lincoln to John A. Gilmer, Dec. 15, 1860, in Basler, *Collected Works of Lincoln*, IV, 152; see also Lincoln to Lyman Trumbull, Dec. 10, 1860, and Lincoln to William Kellogg, Dec. 11, 1860, *ibid.*, pp. 149, 150.
[37]The manifesto of Dec. 13, 1860, is printed in Edward McPherson, *The Political History of . . . the Great Rebellion . . .* (New York, 1864), p. 37.
[38]Richardson, *Messages and Papers of the Presidents*, VIII, 3477 (ital. in orig.).

committee of the Senate, known popularly as the "Committee of Thirteen." This body disgorged four proposals.[39] Two, offered by Mississippi Senator Jefferson Davis and Georgia Senator Robert Toombs, represented the South's demands—though with no likelihood that the deep South would abandon secession if they were met. Under the Davis/Toombs proposals, slavery would be protected everywhere like any other form of property, free from impairment by federal, state, and territorial legislatures. Habeas corpus and jury trial would be denied to fugitive slaves. A majority of slave state Congressmen had to assent to any federal statute affecting slavery. The slave states had to consent unanimously to any constitutional amendments affecting slavery. And northern states' sojourner laws would be voided. Northern Congressmen disdained these proposals.

A third set, offered by Senator Douglas, was no more satisfactory. Trading once again on racism, Douglas would have: prohibited blacks from voting or holding office anywhere; promoted colonization (that is, forced expatriation of free blacks); prohibited congressional abolition in the District of Columbia; forbidden interference with the domestic slave trade; stopped all further territorial expansion; required compensation from the federal treasury for unrecovered fugitive slaves; and frozen the status of all territories until their population reached 50,000, at which point they would promptly be admitted as states.

It was the fourth set of compromise proposals, that of the old Kentucky Whig John J. Crittenden, that commanded attention. In a package of six constitutional amendments and four precatory resolutions, Crittenden's amendments would: admit all new states with or without slavery as they might provide; prohibit abolition of slavery within the states and the District of Columbia; protect the interstate slave trade; provide federal compensation for unreclaimed runaways; make all constitutional amendments concerning slavery unamendable; soften the Fugitive Slave Act; call for repeal of the personal liberty laws; prohibit reopening of the African slave

[39]All these proposals may be found in "Report [of] the Committee of Thirteen," Sen. Rep. 36 Cong., 2 sess., ser. 1090, doc. 288 (Dec. 31, 1860); cf. the critique in Harold M. Hyman, "The Narrow Escape from a 'Compromise of 1860': Secession and the Constitution," in Hyman and Leonard W. Levy, *Freedom and Reform: Essays in Honor of Henry Steele Commager* (New York, 1967), pp. 149–166.

trade; and, in its centerpiece, extend the Missouri Compromise line of 36° 30' to the Pacific, excluding slavery to the north and establishing it south, and requiring its protection by territorial governments. Moreover, the Missouri Compromise line amendment would apply not only to extant territory but also to that "hereafter acquired," thus permitting if not inviting expansion, filibustering, and aggression of the Ostend Manifesto sort.

Crittenden submitted this package with the novel and audacious proposal that it be submitted to a national referendum. But his proposals were futile from the outset. Perceived in both sections as pro-southern—the secessionist New Orleans *Bee* commended them as "fully inspired by a sense of justice" to the South[40]—the proposals were unacceptable to the Republicans, who could not support the keystone Missouri line provision without committing party suicide. But their greatest weakness was simply that they did not resolve the core slavery problem, the long-term security of slavery in the existing states.

Two other compromise efforts were probably little more than tactical maneuvers, according to Henry Adams, designed to split the Border States and upper South from the deep South, and to dissipate secessionist sentiment in the upper South and the Border.[41] The first emerged from the House counterpart to the Committee of Thirteen, the Committee of Thirty-three. It consisted of two prongs. The first was the Fabian policy of the Maryland ex-Whig Henry Winter Davis. It would have immediately admitted New Mexico, with the tacit understanding that it would come in as a slave state, since it was already a slave territory.[42] This would have been a substantial accession of territory open to slavery, most of it north of the Missouri Compromise line. Republicans offered this "concession" cynically, believing that slavery could never establish itself there. Nevertheless, the proposal had its tactical effect, luring Border State representatives from secession and buying some time. The other prong was to be an unamendable amendment to the Constitution that would prohibit Congress from interfering with slavery in

[40]Quoted in Dwight L. Dumond (ed.), *Southern Editorials on Secession* (New York, 1931), p. 414.
[41]Adams, "The Great Secession Winter."
[42]"Fabian policy" is the evaluation of David M. Potter, *Lincoln and His Party in the Secession Crisis* (1942; rpt. New Haven, 1962), p. 303.

the extant states. Though misguided, this seems to have been a bona fide effort to reassure slaveholders of the Republicans' fundamental constitutional and social conservatism. The Winter Davis proposal failed, but both Houses of Congress approved the amendment and sent it out for ratification as the original "Thirteenth Amendment." Three states actually ratified it before it was overtaken by events.

On the same day that delegates were meeting in Montgomery to organize the Confederacy (February 4, 1861), the third center of compromise effort took up its work. It enjoyed the advantage of being independent of the federal government, though it met in Washington, having been called by ex-President John Tyler and sponsored by the Virginia legislature. But it suffered from the disadvantage implied in its popular name: the "Old Gentlemen's Convention." (Semiofficially it was more hopefully designated the "Washington Peace Conference.") It was not an official constitutional convention of the sort provided for in Aticle V, because it was not called by Congress on the application of two-thirds of the state legislatures. But its recommendations would come freighted with the prestige of the elder statesmen who constituted many of its delegates. The conference proposed a package similar in many respects to the Crittenden proposals, but with one vital difference: its amendment extending the Missouri Compromise line would not force slavery into the territories south of the line, but would rather leave its constitutional status there to be decided by federal courts —courts soon to be staffed by Republican appointees who could be assumed to espouse Republican constitutional views.[43] Despite wide support in the upper South, the Peace Conference proposals died ingloriously at the end of the short session of the Thirty-sixth Congress, being rejected in the Senate and not even submitted to a vote in the House, largely because of the perceived futility of yet another eleventh-hour overture to secessionists.

While the compromise efforts were dwindling, the reality of secession and southern independence appeared more pronounced. The Confederacy, under its provisional constitution, became a real-

[43]The Conference proposals may be found in the notes of one of the delegates: L. E. Chittenden, *A Report of the Debates . . . of the Conference Convention . . .* (New York, 1864), pp. 440–445.

ity, and a part of America seemed launched on a new republican experiment. The Texas secession convention declared that "the constitution of the Confederate States of America is copied almost entire from the constitution of the United States. The few changes made are admitted by all to be improvements . . . we still cling to the old constitution made by our fathers."[44] Whatever its contemporary rhetorical purpose, that assertion does not withstand an analysis of the Confederate Constitution. Despite a superficial similarity between the two documents, the Confederate Constitution was based on significantly different constitutional theories, and contained numerous modifications, not all of which improved the performance of the Confederate government. The Confederate Constitution's departures from the Constitution of 1787 occurred in four areas: state sovereignty, slavery, "Democratic" provisions, and tinkering with the mechanisms of government.[45]

The constitutionmakers of the Confederacy were obsessed with the reciprocal issues of "consolidation" and state sovereignty.[46] As Jabez Curry, an Alabama delegate to the Montgomery convention, explained, "the permanent [Confederate] Constitution was framed on the state rights theory to take from a majority in Congress unlimited control."[47] It represented a compromise between the conflicting pressures of localism and nationalism. The preamble of the Constitution declared that the Constitution was formed by the people of the "Confederate States, each State acting in its sovereign and independent character." All federal power was explicitly "delegated" (I/1);[48] certain federal officers could be impeached by state legislatures (I/2); the 1787 Constitution's general-welfare clause from the preamble and the tax/spend clause of Article I were omitted deliberately, Confederate theorists seeing them as dangerous

---

[44]"Address to the People of Texas" (1861), in Ernest W. Winkler (ed.), *Journal of the Secession Convention of Texas 1861* (Austin, 1912), p. 259.

[45]On the Confederate Constitution generally, see Charles R. Lee, *The Confederate Constitutions* (Chapel Hill, 1963), esp. its app. C, a parallel-column comparison of the U.S.A. and C.S.A. Constitutions. Cp. Carpenter, *South as a Conscious Minority*, ch. 7, "Applications in the Confederate Constitution."

[46]See, for example, the exposition of constitutional theory in "The Address of the People of South Carolina . . . to the People of the Slaveholding States" (1860), in May and Faunt, *South Carolina Secedes*, pp. 82–92.

[47]Jabez L. M. Curry, *Civil History of the Government of the Confederate States*, (Richmond, 1900), p. 69.

[48]All parenthetical citations to the C.S.A. Constitution in text will be to article, in Roman caps, and section, in Arabic.

sources of national authority (I/8) (yet, curiously, they retained the necessary-and-proper clause and the supremacy clause of the old Constitution); Confederate national courts were denied diversity jurisdiction (III/2); and the amendment process of Article V was revised to permit any three states to propose amendments and call a constitutional convention, while omitting any federal agency in proposing amendments (V).

Confederate constitutional authorities prized this state-sovereignty orientation of their Constitution and attempted to maintain it despite the pressures of war. Thomas Hill Watts, an Alabamian who served as attorney general of the Confederacy in 1862, wrote in an official opinion that

the Confederate Government is one of limited and specific powers; that no powers can be exercised by [the Confederate] Congress except such as are granted to that body by the Constitution. . . . a strict construction of the Constitution is essential to preserve the rights of the States, the Sovereign parties to the Constitutional compact. . . .

Later, Watts went so far as to state that the Confederate "Constitution itself is a little less than a power of attorney creating a Government and giving a few and well defined powers to its Departments."[49]

As might have been expected, the Montgomery Convention believed that the provisions of the mother-Constitution could be improved on the topic of slavery. They strictly prohibited the foreign slave trade, except from the slave states of the United States, and explicitly required Congress to "pass such laws as shall effectually prevent the same" (I/9); prohibited passage of federal laws "denying or impairing the right of property in negro slaves" (I/9); protected "the right of transit and sojourn" of slaves in each of the states (IV/2); protected the slave status of slaves "lawfully carried" into another state, and modified the language of the fugitive-slave clause to use the word *slave* instead of the old euphemisms (IV/3); and gave the full panoply of protection to slavery in the territories that Jefferson Davis had demanded from the United States government in 1860 (IV/3).

The founding fathers of the Confederacy reflected their predomi-

[49]Opinions of May 16, 1862, and Aug. 2, 1862, in Rembert W. Patrick (comp.), *The Opinions of the Confederate Attorneys General, 1861–1865* (Buffalo, 1950), pp. 94, 130.

nantly Democratic party antecedents in a number of provisions. (Three-fifths of the delegates had been Democrats.) When they excised the general-welfare clause, they also specified that taxes were to be raised only "for revenue necessary . . ." (I/8); they prohibited bounties and protective tariffs (I/8); banned all internal-improvement appropriations except navigational and rivers and harbors projects, which were required to pay for themselves (I/8); required the Post Office to pay its own way (I/8); and required a two-thirds majority to pass export taxes (I/9).

Finally, they adopted structural modifications of the machinery of government. They permitted cabinet officers a seat and voice in Congress (I/6); gave the president a line-item veto (I/7) and limited him to one six-year term (II/1); carefully circumscribed the appropriations process in technical ways (I/9); permitted executive removal of cabinet and diplomatic officials and prohibited the removal of all others except for cause (II/2).

Many of these innovations tended to impede effective government. The Confederacy's creators hampered political party operations leading to the effective administration of policy alternatives. Lacking the two-party politics that lubricated free-state governments, numerous direct national interventions within states occurred, as well as dangerous confrontations between Confederate and state authorities and private citizens.

The Confederacy aimed to create the fewest opportunities possible for changes to occur in what they had seceded to preserve: perpetual property in slaves. The revisions in the Confederacy's Constitution limited the Confederate national government in ways that blocked power in order to prevent change. The likelihood thereby declined of majorities weakening slavery through misdirected political action. In turn, this goal was advanced in the Confederate Constitution's limits on the sources of public funds. In the free states, such financial resources were the two parties' "money machines" that sustained party discipline and influence. In northern states the capacity of government to act and of adversary political parties to define alternative courses of government action were inseparable.[50]

The Confederate Constitution specified that each Confederate

---

[50]Clifton K. Yearley, *The Money Machines: The Breakdown and Reform of Governmental and Party Finance in the North, 1860–1920* (Albany, 1970), ch. 1.

state was sovereign. Participation in the federal union of Confederate States was therefore an exercise of state sovereignty, not a diminution or relinquishment of it. Yet the Confederate Constitution did not recognize state nullification, interposition, or secession. Southern whites saw secession as a single-shot weapon, a revolutionary remedy. In the old Union it was necessary because the free states always threatened slavery. But in a Union of all slave states, secession was irrelevant and impermissible.

Slavery was the basic state right. It received the Confederate Constitution's special protection. By its terms, the Confederate Congress could not impair private property rights in slaves. But, state sovereignty notwithstanding, neither could states impair their citizens' slave property. The Confederate Congress was required to protect slave property in Confederate territories. Experience suggested that a territory with slave property assured ensuing slave states, which is what the crises of 1820, 1850, 1854, and 1860–61 had been about.

These scattered provisions, though not concealing Confederates' slave concerns, were not the reckless defense of slavery that many contemporaries expected. That argument was already won, the Confederacy's Constitution-crafters assumed. Confederate Vice-President Alexander Stephens stated the proposition in 1861:

The new [Confederate] Constitution has put at rest forever all the agitating questions relating to our peculiar institutions—African slavery as it exists among us—the proper status of the negro in our form of civilization. This was the immediate cause of our late rupture and present revolution. . . . Our new Government is founded . . . upon the great truth that the negro is not the equal of the white man. That slavery—subordination to the superior race, is his natural and normal condition. . . . It is upon this [assumption that] . . . our actual fabric is firmly planted. . . . The progress of disintegration in the old Union may be expected to go on with almost absolute certainty. We are now the nucleus of a growing power, which . . . will become the controlling power on this continent.[51]

The real cost of this mummification of slave property was the virtual nondevelopment in the South of multiform connections, formal and informal, between governments, political parties, pri-

[51]Edward McPherson, *Political History of the United States during the Great Rebellion, 1860–1865,* eds. Harold M. Hyman and Hans Trefousse (1865; reprint New York, 1972), pp. 103–104.

vate associations, and individuals, common in free states. Long a region without viable political alternatives on basic matters such as race relations, the South, institutionalizing its Confederacy, saw only dangers in the slippages and discordances of two-party operations. The Confederate experience, like that of the prewar southern states in the Union, did not reward compromise politicians or inspire adaptive legal-constitutional doctrines. Their absence was destined to impede both the Confederate war effort and the Union's Reconstruction ends and means.[52]

The Confederate states shared with their northern counterparts the doctrine of plenary state police powers. In addition, the South's states were sovereign polities, according to dominant regional opinion. State legislatures met more frequently than in prewar years. Some states created special councils and commissions to control prices of scarce commodities and to suppress reconstructionists and other disloyal persons. Debt moratoria, anti-usury, and contract stay laws proved to be popular state measures. Suspensions of specie payments for both public and private debts, and bonuses for producers of goods in short supply, were also common state expedients. It appears that state governments devised more original responses to the war's impact, and attracted more talented and energetic men to public offices, than was true of the Confederate national government. This was the reverse of the Union's experience.

Despite states' sovereignty ideas, Confederate national authorities found it necessary to intrude rudely into states by means of laws and executive orders directly affecting individuals.[53] As in the North, the Confederate Congress enacted laws confiscating disloyalists' property. Confiscation proceedings were both by judicial process and by extraordinary commissions. Confederate conscription legislation never achieved the symmetry the North managed by 1863. No Confederate equivalent to the Provost Marshal General

[52]Eric McKitrick, "Party Politics and the Union and Confederate War Efforts," in William N. Chambers and W. D. Burnham (eds.), *American Party Systems* (Boston, 1961), p. 120; David Potter, "Jefferson Davis and the Political Factors in the Confederate Defeat," in David Donald (ed.), *Why the North Won the Civil War* (Baton Rouge, 1961), p. 113.

[53]Curtis A. Amlund, *Federalism in the Southern Confederacy* (Washington, 1966), esp. ch. 8, "Confederate-State Relations."

Bureau was to grace the southern War Department. Similarly, President Jefferson Davis, like Lincoln, proclaimed martial law, suspended habeas corpus protections, and authorized soldiers to arrest civilians suspected of disloyal tendencies.

Such policies are abrasive by nature. Southerners who became irritated or distressed by enforcements of these national policies learned to pit their state governors, legislatures, and judges against Davis and executive officers. The Confederate president usually failed to avoid the resulting nation-state confrontations. He lacked traditional resources Lincoln enjoyed with which to compromise issues with governors. Davis never called a governor's conference, as Lincoln did. The southerner was far less able than Lincoln to use patronage pressures on recalcitrant governors. Confederate Constitution provisions requiring only one item in an appropriation bill lessened possibilities for compromises by means of logrolling and other trades.[54]

Confederate federalism allowed no democratic alternatives on basic policies such as reconstructionism (i.e., acceptance of defeat, and reunion) and race. The white South could get on, as it had, without alternative politics, had it not resorted to war and lost it. The southern consensus on race was so pervasive and constraining as to be, in Daniel Boorstin's phrase, "an indwelling law."[55] A society so dependent upon agreed assumptions about its race-based superiority, though losing the war, could not risk change in existing arrangements.

Southerners remained hag-ridden by nightmare fears of government effectiveness that might one day diminish white controls over blacks. Instead, Confederates created, out of distorted Jeffersonian constitutionalism, what a historian of Georgia's secession described as "a litany disguised as historical analysis, an incantation which promised to create a South that never would be out of a South that never was."[56]

Confederate internal security policies, including arrests of civil-

[54]Paul D. Escott, *After Secession: Jefferson Davis and the Failure of Confederate Nationalism* (Baton Rouge, 1978).

[55]Daniel Boorstin, "The Perils of Indwelling Law," in Robert P. Wolff (ed.), *The Rule of Law* (New York, 1971), p. 85.

[56]Michael B. Johnson, *Toward a Patriarchal Republic: The Secession of Georgia* (Baton Rouge, 1977), p. 28.

ians by soldiers, habeas corpus suspensions, travel controls, censorship, and confiscations, never escalated onto more sophisticated policy-purpose levels. Antidisloyalty arrests could not, in the contracting South, become part of state-rebuilding, obviously. Such arrests occurred with less restraint southward, however, due to the absence in the Confederacy of opposition political parties and other private associations to mediate between power and persons.

Consider the paltry routes open to the Confederate president when, in early 1864, North Carolina's chief judge ruled against the Confederacy's conscription law. By this time many southerners were opposing CSA national policies in states' courts. In Richmond the question rose as to what to do if the North Carolina judge discharged from military service individuals already conscripted. Confederate War Secretary James Seddon knew only one way to cope with a state judge: "I will not hesitate a moment to arrest him." And Seddon's assistant, former United States Supreme Court Justice John A. Campbell, agreed sadly: "That is a point to which it is coming."[57]

That incident slid by. But others did not. Such communications as this by War Secretary Seddon to North Carolina Governor Zebulon Vance reflected the inability of Confederate constitutionalism to sustain war federalism adequately:

The want of a Supreme Court in the Confederate States leaves them [officers of the central government] unprotected against the . . . actions of State Judges by the regular and accustomed course of review by an appellate tribunal. And when the action of the State Judges involves the assumption of powers not conceded to belong to them, . . . this Department cannot discover any course more suitable for making its objection known than to communicate to the Executive of the State those objections in the form of a respectful remonstrance.[58]

We cannot know if a Supreme Court—authorized by the Constitution but never created—would have improved the effectiveness of the Confederate nation in its relationships with states. But the absence of the Supreme Court did not inhibit the Confederacy from

[57]Edward Younger (ed.), *Inside the Confederate Government: The Diary of Robert Garlick Kean* (Oxford, 1957), p. 138.
[58]Seddon to Vance, May 23, 1863, in National Archives, R.G. 109, Confederate Secretary of War, Letters Sent, IX, 81.

exercising war powers. In 1864, Confederate federal judge Alexander Clayton offered views to President Davis on war powers that Lincoln would have welcomed from Taney:

> During a state of war, it is not easy to draw a precise line, between civil and military authority. Something must be yielded to the necessity of the occasion. Precedents heretofore have been of rare occurrence. Resort must therefore be had to principle, and to such interpretation of the Constitution, as will give harmony and consistency to all its parts, and best secure the great ends of its adoption—justice, tranquility, and liberty.[59]

Informed contemporaries concluded that the Confederacy's constitutional arrangements, and, therefore, its political processes, were unworthy of emulation. Instead, it was the United States Constitution and government that became a model for many foreign writers.[60] Its combination of adequate crisis authority to the nation and sensitivity to state needs, plus its capacity to accommodate rising perceptions about individuals' civil rights, by late 1865 won admiring comment here and abroad.

But that favorable estimate of the 1787 Constitution was possible only because the old Constitution survived. In the dark days of secession winter, that survival was anything but assured. Would the Constitution be found adequate to a crisis challenging its very existence, especially when its framers never anticipated that crisis? Could the Constitution of "a more perfect Union" cope with secession and an ensuing Civil War? Could the old federal system tolerate the immense expansion of federal authority, and the curtailment of traditional civil liberties, necessary to meet the threat of war from without and subversion from within?

[59]Clayton to Davis, Nov. 25, 1864, in Pritchard von David Collection, University of Texas–Austin.

[60]Harold M. Hyman (ed.), *Heard Round the World: Impacts Abroad of the Civil War and Reconstruction* (New York, 1968), *passim*.

CHAPTER 8

Reconstruction: The Union Preserved

A LMOST from its first days the Civil War involved the government of the United States, as well as those of the states, in exercises of power. The federal system ceased to be a synonym for weakness and ineffectiveness. The surrender of Fort Sumter came to mean less another proof that the nation was incapable of defending one of its own properties in one of its own harbors than a measure of the depths from which the nation must climb in part through the exercises of the Constitution's latent powers.

Lincoln's vigorous behavior during the first post-Sumter weeks became initial steps in this painful climb, and probably made possible the Union's salvation. Lincoln bought time by his actions; time for his countrymen to replace with greater firmness the peace-at-almost-any-price spirit that, during the secession winter, had sought a "compromise of 1860" on the most abject terms. The time that Lincoln wrested from events permitted northerners to give up plans for seducing seceders and to ponder ways to overcome them.[1]

Displaying unsuspected capacities for forthright political leadership and a profound insight into constitutional relationships, Lincoln resorted to a permissive legal doctrine developed since Mar-

---

[1] Harold M. Hyman, "The Narrow Escape From a 'Compromise of 1860,' " in Harold M. Hyman and Leonard W. Levy (eds.), *Freedom and Reform: Essays in Honor of Henry Steele Commager* (New York, 1967), pp. 149–166.

shall's time, a doctrine, judicially sanctioned, that favored the use of public power as an instrument of social policy ("instrumentalism," as modern scholars call the doctrine). He resorted also to the Constitution's clauses on the Commander in Chief, martial law, and war powers, and exploited constitutional doctrines resulting from the Dorr Rebellion and from European revolutions in the 1830s and 1840s that significantly increased the relevance of martial law to conditions of 1861. These conditions resulted, in short, from a refusal of the population of a vast region to obey the verdicts of elections or the nation's Constitution or laws; a refusal culminating in the use of armed force against national installations; a refusal which had the support of many thousands of persons including public officials, even in unseceded states.

Among Lincoln's most dramatic reactions to the Sumter bombardment and to subsequent events were his proclamations blockading port cities of seceded states, his unauthorized disbursements of funds to antisecessionists, his calls for volunteers to fill the ranks of additional regiments, and his mustering of states' militias into federal service. Most shockingly, Lincoln authorized soldiers to arrest allegedly disloyal civilians under terms of executive proclamations suspending the privilege of the writ of habeas corpus or instituting martial law. Ultimately, approximately 18,000 civilians suffered military arrests. Almost all those arrested quickly regained their freedom, however, usually after swearing to refrain from active pro-secession activities in the future. Although potentialities for excesses were always present in these extraordinary arrests, no one, it appears, was killed or tortured as a result of them. Soldiers in the field who apprehended spies, guerrillas, or saboteurs, and who tried them under provisions of the Articles of War or of martial law, did impose capital punishments.

The desperate resorts to military arrests resulted from the fact that civilian police in numerous communities were failing to enforce criminal laws against arson, assault, and riot against secession activists. In many instances police and other state officials joined the malefactors. Federal criminal laws were few in number and failed to touch on situations in which masses of citizens defied both national and state laws, and state peace officers were incapable of punishing, or unwilling to punish, offenders. The Lincoln administration's harsh actions in search of what today would be described as internal security helped to save critical border areas, including Maryland, Missouri, and portions of Tennessee and western Virginia, from secessionist domination.

Lincoln perceived a deterrent value in the military arrests, that of keeping minor offenders or would-be offenders from actually committing crimes or from hazarding worse ones. Soldiers who carried out arrests did so in the full view of an attentive and often critical population whose information resources included unfettered journalists, opposition politicians, and inventive lawyers. With respect to the politicians, antiwar spokesmen, chiefly Democratic, denounced Lincoln's emergency measures as dictatorial and unconstitutional, especially in view of the First, Fifth, and Sixth Amendments. Antisecessionist legal and constitutional experts, chiefly Republican, though often deeply troubled by Lincoln's expedients, quickly rallied to his support. They developed what Timothy Farrar, an abolitionist war-horse among legal writers, soon after Sumter labeled as an "adequacy-of-the-Constitution" position. Farrar's argument, quickly and effectively supported by other commentators including Horace Binney, James Russell Lowell, Theophilus Parsons, and William Whiting, was that since 1789 the Constitution had been misinterpreted as primarily a network of negatives. Obeisance to southern dictates by Congressmen and jurists until 1861 had obscured the fact that the Constitution also imposed duties upon the national government, to act positively, as an instrument, to realize purposes that had inspired the creation of the nation. These essential purposes included the nation's duty to preserve itself as the base for the more perfect union, to guarantee to every state a republican form of government (Article IV, section 4), and to provide for the general welfare (Article I, section 8). "Adequacy" writers of antislavery convictions echoed Farrar's insistence that the Declaration of Independence was an additional statement of national duties to those in the Constitution; all adequacy writers agreed on the relevance of Marshall-Webster-Story doctrines to which Lincoln was now giving renewed vitality and exciting expression.

Lincoln's daring extensions of executive authority inspired nonabolitionist, genteel Philadelphia lawyer Sidney George Fisher to write *The Trial of the Constitution.* Published in 1862, the book helped provide Republicans with scholarly support for the continuing antidisloyalty policies of the administration. Fisher, who had become transformed from a disgusted critic of Lincoln because of the new President's sluggish performance before the Confederates bombarded Sumter, to a warm though still critical admirer of Lincoln because of his postbombardment vigor, insisted that both the President and the Congress possessed a discretion to react to a condition—not a theory—of war. And because the administration did not, as many seceders had predicted, immediately fall apart, the Union thereby won a preliminary victory—it endured: for how long, troops, and ultimately voters, would decide.[2]

Sanctioned in time implicitly or explicitly by Congress and by voters as well as by the Supreme Court,[3] the Lincoln improvisations of 1861 (and the Congress's subsequent reaffirmations of them) moved the constitutional-legal-political debate away from tired questions. By mid-1861 Americans were arguing less about formal relationships between the nation and the states (although the topic of federalism never remained muted for very long) than about the nature and extent of the war powers, and about connections between the nation and individuals. Arguments necessarily shifted from the question of whether authority existed, to the uses of authority. The newer debate came to center also on liberty, first the liberty of whites as against the national executive and then of all Americans as against any unjust authority.

It was not easy for a generation that perceived constitutions and bills of rights as limitations on public authority to readjust to perceptions about government as a source of power and of liberty.[4] The President's drastic improvisations shocked patriots. For the first time since the Revolution, and, in a minor way, the War of 1812, Americans searched constitutional and legal history for help in ascertaining if democracy could function in crisis. Both abolitionists and Democratic defenders of state rights and slavery had long felt a need to study the frame of government and the derivative

---

[2]Timothy Farrar, "The Adequacy of the Constitution," *New Englander,* XXI (1862), 52ff. See also Harold M. Hyman, "Reconstruction and Political—Constitutional Institutions: The Popular Expression," in Hyman (ed.), *New Frontiers of the American Reconstruction* (Urbana, 1966), pp. 1–39.

[3]Prize cases, 2 Black 635 (1863); Herman Belz, *Emancipation and Equal Rights: Politics and Constitutionalism in the Civil War Era* (New York, 1978), pp. 1–32.

[4]Phillip Paludan, "The American Civil War Considered as a Crisis in Law and Order," *American Historical Review,* LXXVII (1972), 1013–1034.

grants of public power to justify their special positions. Now, in 1861, others began also to study questions such as the government's need for internal security.[5]

Lincoln's supporters might have taken comfort from the history of earlier American crises, had they known about them. During the War for Independence, for example, soldiers on both sides had arrested civilians for such martial law offenses as espionage, guerrilla activity, and sabotage, as well as for a broad category of offenses equated with disloyalty. John Adams, Thomas Jefferson, George Mason, and George Washington created or employed loyalty tests; the states, the Continental and Confederation Congresses, and King George III and Parliament all forced civilians to commit themselves to a side, employing a variety of loyalty tests as prerequisites for civil and military privileges.

Twentieth-century internal security zealots, including A. Mitchell Palmer in the 1920s, Martin Dies in the 1930s and 1940s, and Joseph McCarthy and Richard Nixon in the 1950s, might also have learned from relevant Revolutionary and Civil War experiences. The antics of such persons have left a tenacious suspicion that all efforts by government to protect itself against internal enemies are partisan, unnecessary, and hazardous to a fragile democracy. To be sure, in the Revolution as in the Civil War, loyalty testing sometimes fell into the hands of vicious individuals seeking mean ends. The antidote history suggests is the sort Lincoln provided—sensitive leadership, the assumption of responsibility for the excesses of subordinates, and the nurture of the most open democratic processes possible. Without glorifying loyalty tests, the following description may be drawn from the Civil War experience: loyalty tests were not used casually or cruelly, and they coexisted with democratic processes and institutions which included a largely uncensored press and unrigged elections plus unfettered popular assembling, petitioning, and litigating in civil courts.[6]

---

[5]Horace Binney, *The Privilege of the Writ of Habeas Corpus under the Constitution* (Philadelphia, 1862), *passim;* Farrar, "Adequacy," pp. 51–73; Sidney George Fisher, *The Trial of the Constitution* (Philadelphia, 1862), ch. 3.

[6]In 1972, the Supreme Court (Laird *v.* Tatum, 408 U.S. 1) sustained the right of military intelligence personnel to investigate civilians' loyalty. In crisis situations— and determination of a crisis is not, the Court implied, a judicial prerogative—

Of course, Lincoln's generation, being largely ignorant of relevant precedents and unable to foretell its future, had to deal with its own fiery present. And so antidisloyalty expedients of the 1860s seemed exotic, perhaps constitutionally justifiable but acceptable only because they were essential to survival. No democratic nation had then mapped the permissible limits of opposition and dissent even in noncrisis times, much less in periods of real and present danger. Lincoln's generation faced, not a distant foreign enemy in a traditional war, but an authentic domestic threat to national existence. However drastic, the Lincoln administration's responses to the threat never degenerated into the condition European law accepted, of *état de siège* or *kriegzustand:* literally, state of war, or arbitrary, extraconstitutional, indefinitely prolonged condition of emergency rule.[7] In this context, the Lincoln record is remarkably good. A majority of Americans, having alternatives always open, accepted the administration's apologies. This support is the more remarkable because few governmental constraints on whites had existed in prewar America save as local communities and states imposed occasional police regulations, as against public drunks or Mormons. The major exceptions were in slave states whose communities censored mail and created pervasive checks on "foreign" travelers, and on Negro assembly and mobility, the better to isolate slaves from abolition "infections."

Americans need not have accepted Lincoln's internal security improvisations; many damned them. Republicans knew that their defense of Lincoln's policies would benefit the Democrats, and, indeed, Democrats took every advantage of the political opportunity that antidisloyalty arrests opened. Lincoln's extraordinary executive policies allowed Democrats to depict themselves as the champions of civil liberties. Democrats piously cited the First Amendment, and, while continuing to argue that black slaves en-

---

soldiers could be ordered to police work without impairing First Amendment restraints on national authority and functions. See also Harold M. Hyman, *To Try Men's Souls: Loyalty Tests in American History* (Berkeley, 1959), chs. 3–4; Harold M. Hyman, *A More Perfect Union: The Impact of the Civil War and Reconstruction on the Constitution* (New York, 1973), pp. 63–72, 78, 124–140; James G. Randall, *Constitutional Problems Under Lincoln* (rev. ed., Urbana, 1951), ch. 7.

[7]Belz, *Emancipation,* p. 6.

joyed no civil liberties or rights, insisted also that even civil war conditions could not lessen whites' civil liberties.[8]

In equating national inaction with individual liberty, Democrats were on familiar state-rights doctrinal territory. Digging in there, party spokesmen obscured the Democratic insistence since the 1790s on vigorous national participation in the return of fugitive slaves as the price of Union. With respect to actual, not theoretical disloyalty, Democrats retained their insistence on national inactivity as a precondition for preserving both state's rights and individuals' liberty.[9] Only six weeks after Sumter, before any major military action occurred, Democrats received from Chief Justice Taney the constitutional-legal text they needed—a quotable feast of libertarian constitutional ideas, unconnected with slavery protection or secession doctrine, from the highest jurist of the nation.

In late April and early May of 1861, Baltimore's pro-secession mobs, encouraged by city officials, police, and Maryland lawmakers, forcibly contested Union troops' transit across the strategically essential city, whose rail lines and depots were Washington's sole links to the loyal North and West. Under Lincoln's authorization to suspend habeas corpus, Union soldiers arrested a notorious pro-secessionist, John Merryman, a socially prominent suburbanite who was using his militia connections to recruit and train armed volunteers for the Confederacy. Did Merryman, by the standards of the Constitution's Article III, section 10,[10] deserve a treason prosecution? In the intense confusion of May, 1861, no one was confident that the seceded states, though confederated against the United States, were enemies within the constitutional definition. A workable clarification was not to come from the Supreme Court until the 1863 *Prize* cases.

Even if executive officials had known in 1861 that the Court would

[8]See Stephen Franks Miller, *Ahab Lincoln: A Tragedy of the Potomac* (Milledgeville, Ga., 1861; reprint Chicago, 1958); Sidney Cromwell, *Political Opinion in 1776 and 1863* (New York, 1863); Charles Ingersoll, *An Undelivered Speech on Executive Arrests* (Philadelphia, 1862), as examples of Democratic criticisms and some Republican responses.
[9]Joel Silbey, *A Respectable Minority: The Democratic Party in the Civil War Era, 1860–1868* (New York, 1977), pp. 3–88.
[10]See Appendix.

one day supply some definition of the conflict, their need was immediate. Besides, the terseness and possible irrelevance of the Constitution's treason clause, and the failures of the treason prosecution of Aaron Burr in 1807 and of the treason processes initiated after fugitive slave rescues noted earlier, inspired little confidence of success in such a prosecution for Merryman. Very few American lawyers, law professors, or judges of 1861 knew much about the law of treason. Few crimes other than for customs violations, obstructing fugitive slave returns, and currency or postal counterfeiting were known to federal law. Maryland criminal law was, unfortunately, irrelevant as a check on Merryman. The alternative of leaving him free to recruit for the Confederacy was drearier than arresting him under martial law.

In the absence of a federal prison, the soldiers lodged Merryman in historic Fort McHenry's guardhouse. There, with the consent of his jailers, Merryman enjoyed a globally unique privilege for a civilian in military custody: access to his lawyer—a privilege the Lincoln administration apparently extended to all "political prisoners" who wished it. Unable immediately to get his client freed, the lawyer, Andrew Ridgeley, hurried to Washington and talked with Chief Justice Taney, also a Marylander. Then they returned the same day to Baltimore.

Taney's duties included presiding over the federal court circuit encompassing Maryland. Stipulating that he was acting as Chief Justice of the United States in chambers rather than as circuit judge, Taney, by habeas writ,[11] directed the Fort McHenry commander to produce Merryman. The officer refused, in obedience to Lincoln's telegraphed command. Thereupon, in a performance shrewdly staged before local and national journalists, Taney read an opinion that alleged the death of civil court processes in the face of military intervention, and that criticized the President severely for usurping Congress's alleged primacy in habeas suspensions. Adopting an adversary lawyer's posture, Taney asserted that he ". . . had supposed it to be one of those points of constitutional law upon which there was no difference of opinion, and that it was admitted on all

[11]See Henry Dutton, "Writ of Habeas Corpus," *American Law Register* (1861), 1–13, and above, ch. 5, for U.S. *v.* Hanway, 26 Fed. Cas. 105, #15299 (C.C.E.D. Pa., 1851).

hands that the privilege of the [habeas] writ could not be suspended except by act of Congress." The Constitution, he continued, "expressed [this point] in language too clear to be misunderstood by anyone." Depicting himself as helpless, however, before tyrannical soldiers, Taney, in a closing peroration, noted that he would file the writ in the court's records, with a copy to Lincoln. "It will then remain for that high officer, in fulfillment of his constitutional obligation to 'take care that the laws be faithfully executed' to determine what measure he will take to cause the civil process of the United States to be respected and enforced."[12]

Throughout his statement, Taney implied that the ancient habeas writ had, since 1789, been an ever-ready defense of all individuals' civil liberties, especially against unjust imprisonment by any national or state official. But in reality, federal habeas had been insignificant as a protection for individuals' liberties. In national jurisdictions, the thin roster of federal crimes occasioned few instances of pleas by defendants' counsel for such writs. State habeas was the one that counted, especially in criminal trials. Federal judges, even Supreme Court justices, had no way to deal effectively with defendants' allegations of unjust state criminal or civil procedures, whether before, during, or after trials. Few poor persons, especially Negroes or Indians, had the means or opportunity to seek redress by state habeas against state constraints. Fewer state judges (the majority of whom were popularly elected) were willing to issue habeas writs against state, county, or civic officials.[13] In short, prewar federalism left the habeas writ all but irrelevant everywhere.

Before the war, habeas litigations almost never allowed lawyers to maneuver between national and state jurisdictions on behalf of imprisoned clients. In 1859, Taney and his brethren had considered litigation arising from such uncommon maneuvering. But this rare

[12]Ex parte Merryman, Fed. Cas. #9487 (S.C.U.S., 1861); The Baltimore lawyer Andrew Ridgeley, who had brought Taney to Baltimore from Washington, was so passionate when soldiers did not honor Taney's habeas order that Ridgeley ". . . was willing to form one of a posse comitatus to proceed to the Fort, demand the prisoner and sustain the majesty of the law." But he collected no followers. Bayly E. Marks and Mark N. Schatz (eds.), *The Narrative of William Wilkins Glenn, 1861–1869* (Rutherford, N.J., 1976), p. 33.

[13]Catherine M. Tarrant, "A Writ of Liberty or a Covenant with Hell: Habeas Corpus in the War Congresses, 1861–1867" (Ph.D. diss., Rice University, 1972), ch. 1.

occasion when a state habeas writ actually served as a key of liberty only proved how exceptional the case was, and how great the prewar abyss between federal and state courts.[14]

As to Merryman, Lincoln refused to obey the Chief Justice. In this posture the President enjoyed impressive support from ordinary citizens as well as constitutionalists. Lincoln occasionally imposed martial law and suspended habeas corpus in nonseceded states throughout the war. Habeas suspensions occurred especially in areas exposed to Confederate invaders or where large-scale resistance developed to emancipation, the employment of Negro troops, or conscription. Yet Taney's circuit court remained open, despite the Chief Justice's premature obsequies about the death of legal process, as did federal and state courts outside the Confederacy or removed from battle areas. Congressmen, not anxious to enter the politically dangerous military arrest morass, waited until March, 1863, before enacting a habeas corpus statute. Then they approved Lincoln's internal security initiatives retrospectively to the War's beginnings.

Taney's Supreme Court colleagues resisted his subsequent efforts to bring the Court into confrontations with President or Congress. For his part, Lincoln tried to keep off the Court's docket other litigation involving habeas corpus, treason, martial law, conscription, emancipation, or the novel wartime income tax.[15] Any of these, decided adversely to the national government, might seriously, even fatally affect its capacity to carry on the war.

The President was wise. Secretly, as noted, the Chief Justice, before the facts of a particular appeal were before him or the Court, prepared opinions that declared unconstitutional the arbitrary arrests, conscription, and emancipation. Unable to employ these ready-made opinions, Taney exerted the judicial review power negatively over relatively minor national actions. For example, Taney condemned Treasury Department administrative policies licensing trade south of the Potomac, as destructive of federalism and the separation of powers. He similarly resisted the collection of a 3 percent tax on federal judges' incomes, authorized by Congress in

[14]Ableman v. Booth, 21 Howard 506 (1859).
[15]Carl B. Swisher, *History of the Supreme Court of the United States: The Taney Period, 1836–1864* (New York, 1974), p. 853.

1863. By administrative action, the Secretary of the Treasury with-held the taxable amount due from federal judges' salaries. In a February, 1863, letter to Treasury Secretary Salmon P. Chase, Taney denounced the deduction as unconstitutional, citing the Constitution's prohibition (Article III, section 1) against salary dim-inution for federal judges during their term in office. He inveighed against the domino consequences he perceived of allowing the 3 percent cut in income; all federal officers might suffer the same or worse fates "at the pleasure of the legislature." But since all judges had interests in the matter, no judge could, with propriety, he con-tinued, decide the vexing policy in a litigation. Unwilling to sanction wrong by silence, Taney saw no recourse but to express his discon-tent by means of this letter to Chase.

Chase passed it on to Attorney General Edward Bates, who agreed that no reply should issue. The Chief Justice deposited a copy of his letter in the Court's records. There the matter rested until, in 1872, a successor to Chase in the Treasury decided that this tax was indeed illegally collected from federal judges, but was not, as Taney had argued, unconstitutional: hence, refunds were due. In 1871, the United States Supreme Court, with Chase now in Taney's place, held, in *Collecter* v. *Day,* concerning federally taxed state judges, that reciprocal immunity from taxation was essential as be-tween officers of the nation and the states, else the federal system would become inoperable whenever popular demands imposed pu-nitive rates on "foreign" officials.[16] But, back in 1863, Taney alone among Supreme Court Justices complained against these govern-ment policies.

Beginning in mid-1861, the basic fact of Confederate experience came to be territorial contraction; contrariwise, the Union story was that of expansion. The reoccupation of seceded areas led to unex-pected responsibilities for military officers. These ranged from the disposition of runaway slaves in Union lines to the re-creation of local and state governments. Army officers dealt with their own immediate security needs and then with the distresses, status, and

---

[16]Samuel Tyler, *Memoir of Roger Brooke Taney* (Baltimore, 1872), pp. 523–525; Carl B. Swisher, *Roger B. Taney* (New York, 1935), pp. 567–569; Philip G. Auchampaugh, *Fundamental Principles of the Ward Case Upheld in a Forgotten Opinion of Chief Justice Taney in 1863* (Reno, Nev., 1945), *passim.*

claims of white and black residents. Union officers coped in various ways with unanticipated legal, political, and racial problems. Little or no guidance on military occupation or government reconstructions came before 1863 from the White House, the Capitol, West Point, or military or legal treatises. Policies that Union generals roughed out in occupied areas became political alternatives that were to help civilians win effective control over the generals. These alternatives became variants on the question: What, under the Constitution and laws, should the nation do in the occupied states with its unexpected power? All the responses that both Lincoln and Congress perceived respected the courts, state lines, and the sanctity of title to property except, ultimately, in slaves; all, without exception, sought social stability. No matter how the Civil War shook this society, its leaders aimed to prevent it from becoming a class war. In this sense, "radical" leadership never existed.[17]

The persisting wartime confusions about Reconstruction reflected uncertainties produced by the underinstitutionalized character of the federal government.[18] These confusions were, ironically, magnified because of the completeness of martial law doctrine. Derived especially from British-European practices of the Napoleonic War, and augmented significantly in the 1840s as a result of civil disturbances, an accepted definition of martial law was that it was largely the will of the commanding general, especially in a civil ("municipal") war when the thin constraints that were supposed to govern international combats did not apply.

Americans fought their Civil War as if it were one between nations. Political imperatives and civilian controls proved to be binding. Limitations on the Union generals' conduct derived from the counsel of such European-trained legalists as Francis Lieber—counsel that, as we will suggest, the War Department developed by March, 1863, into basic military government policy for all Union forces.[19]

[17]"The Legal Status of the Rebel States Before and After Their Conquest," *Monthly Law Reporter*, XXVI (1864), 551–554.

[18]So unready were even lawyers to deal with military law questions that the anonymous editor-author of "Martial Law," *American Law Review*, IX (1861), 498, confused military and martial law; Supreme Court justices were as badly informed on this subject as generals.

[19]"Instructions for the Government of Armies in the Field," in Leon Friedman (ed.), *The Law of War: A Documentary History* (New York, 1972), I, 158–164.

Alert, concerned citizens, including professional politicians in uniform, transformed the Army's problems with security and local government into rehearsals for reconstructions. Union soldiers explained military reoccupation difficulties to home communities. The Union's armies remained indelibly civilian, unprecedentedly literate, and politically active. Lincoln called the bluecoats "thinking bayonets." They formed the world's first "harmless army"—harmless, at least, to their civilian superiors. Thousands of Union troops voted in their states' elections in 1862 and 1864, including congressional and presidential contests. Decisions to allow their soldier-citizens to vote were left to the states. The War Department generally afforded state agents access to camps and regiments or, when states failed to appoint agents, allowed mass furloughs home. By most accounts, these open ballotings were remarkably free of corruption or coercion by superior officers.[20]

The activity of uniformed citizens in both election years, and soldiers' unending correspondence to home communities and political leaders, helped to politicize otherwise obscure, unglamorous military government policies. Two-party political apparatuses of the free states operated, however fitfully, in occupied southern areas, inspiring hopes among both Republican "pros" and emancipationists that the party and its antislavery policy might root permanently in and help to democratize the South.

In unplanned, complex ways, military occupations, involving reactions by field commanders to local security and logistical needs, escalated into national policy options that became known as Reconstruction. In newly occupied areas ill-prepared military men undertook, often by default, the resolution of complex civil relationships, including criminal justice and commercial transfers; they even faced the need to provide fire prevention and sewage disposal. Few officers wanted such gloryless assignments. Company and regimental commanders therefore tended to leave in office most local elective and appointed civil officials, including justices of the peace, sheriffs, mayors, and police chiefs. It appears that few jury-selection venires were changed. Save for state and local legislation supporting Confederate national policies such as sequestration (confiscation), con-

[20]Josiah H. Benton, *Voting in the Field: A Forgotten Chapter of the Civil War* (Boston, 1915).

scription, taxation, and, later, slavery, the Union Army also tended to leave on the books the large share of state, county, and municipal laws and ordinances and to honor local legal procedures and customs.[21]

There were exceptions. Many southern state and local civil officials fled on the approach of Union troops. Oppressed white Unionists and Negroes brought blacklists into service against notorious anti-Union officials. Union provost marshals, the traditional Army policemen, assumed the task of screening candidates for vacated local offices. Provosts decided also which civilians should receive privileges such as scarce commodities like shoes or salt, vote in local elections, and, after December, 1863, participate in Lincoln's state-reconstruction procedures.

Through such piecemeal improvisations, some devised in the field and others in Washington, the Union Army in the South came to discriminate among individuals', communities', and states' rights, and to define individuals' legal remedies and responsibilities. Military commanders came to be aided in these tasks by quasi-official agencies such as the Sanitary and the Christian Commissions, plus other missionary, benevolent, and educational associations, many having special concern about Negroes. The Army cooperated also, more or less, with Treasury, Post Office, Justice, and Interior Department functionaries.[22]

What the Army did in the South inevitably involved, often inspired, and sometimes required political choices. For President or Congress to ignore Army needs was to risk alienating the men and the institution upon which all decisions rested; for President or Congress to move too slowly, swiftly, or irrelevantly was to risk factionalizing the Army and antagonizing the soldiers' home constituencies. From mid-1861 through 1863, Congress and the President supplied the Army and other involved federal agencies with legislation and executive orders that, however partially, shaped Reconstruction contours.

The Union Army's involvement with slaves and free Negroes began in the war's first weeks and never stopped. For the first time

[21]Hyman, *A More Perfect Union*, ch. 10.
[22]*Ibid.;* James E. Sefton, *The United States Army and Reconstruction, 1865–1877* (Baton Rouge, 1977), chs. 1–2.

since 1789, national authority capable of adversely affecting slavery operated within slave states. However racist many bluecoats were, a growing number came quickly to believe, and communicated the lesson homeward, that blacks were the only trustworthy southerners. Black guides never led Yankee troopers into ambushes. Accepting known and fearful risks, ever-increasing numbers of Negroes sought sanctuaries in Union Army camps.[23]

Most moderate abolitionists, attracted by "adequacy" constitutionalism as expounded by Timothy Farrar and other writers, moved into Republican party ranks. The result was a quick melding of antislavery goals with nonabolitionists' desires to preserve the Union. This merging involved, generally, support of the Union's armies as instruments of social improvement and national regeneration. For the adequacy writers, victory, more than the quality of what was to be won, was the primary goal; for abolitionists, victory would make emancipation possible. Abolitionists such as Salmon P. Chase, now Lincoln's Secretary of the Treasury, looked to the Constitution's general welfare clause, to the Declaration of Independence, and to the Bill of Rights as criteria of citizens' rights that the nation, after achieving victory and emancipation, should protect in the states.[24] Antislavery constitutionalists such as Farrar and Whiting perceived, however dimly, the existence of a dual citizenship in which the quality of a national citizen's rights was defined at least by his equality with all other state residents before his state's and communities' customs and laws. To some advanced thinkers on these matters, equality embraced also the protections and responsibilities flowing from private and quasi-public relationships as in contracts, access to public facilities, and education.

The temporary merger, early in the war, of the purposeful patriots and the radical reformers greatly helped the government to win acceptance for some of the most vexatious public policies that Americans had ever known. In 1861–62 abolitionist-adequacy writ-

[23]"They [Negroes] were our guides, our spies, our concealers, our nurses," Alpheus Crosby told Dartmouth Phi Beta Kappa Society members in July, 1865; Crosby, *The Present Position of the Seceded States and the Rights and Duties of the General Government in Respect of Them* (Boston, 1865), pp. 10–11.

[24]Louis Gerteis, "Freedom National: Historic Precedent and Constitutional Traditionalism in the Antislavery Thought of Salmon P. Chase" (Organization of American Historians paper, 1976).

ers justified loyalty tests, arrests of pro-Confederate civilians, conscription, the blockade, and confiscation. By 1863 and 1864 abolitionist-adequacy constitutionalists advocated emancipation and the recruitment of blacks in the Union Army by executive war powers, by legislation, and/or by constitutional amendment, and the reconstruction of states' governments under the war power. In 1865 this shared constitutionalism generated a new Thirteenth Amendment and its ratification by the states as the test of Reconstruction. In short, Reconstruction, both as a political process made possible by military successes and as constitutional thought, grew from wartime as well as post-Appomattox developments, from an amalgam of abolitionist and Unionist ideas. At least to Republicans, Reconstruction was a "bricolage"[25] rather than an ideology. Its abolitionist and Unionist elements were themselves dynamic, and were, after 1866, to prove to be rather easily divisible. But in the early sixties what was important was less the permanence of the juncture than the fact of the joining. While the rebellion lasted the connectives held. They were adequate for the nation to reach not only Appomattox but emancipation. However expressed, this adequacy-abolitionist constitutionalism possessed an adaptable quality that contrasted sharply with static constitutional interpretations insisted upon by Democratic party spokesmen and Roger Taney.

Retaining their antipathy to almost any effective national functions, in 1861–62 antiwar Democrats insisted both that the slavery issue must not change from its 1860 form and that the nation vigorously enforce the 1850 Fugitive Slave Law. That statute required all federal officers to return runaways. Even an owner's patent disloyalty was no bar to return. In General George B. McClellan's burgeoning Army of the Potomac, orders were strict, though often disobeyed by subordinates, to enforce the Fugitive Slave Law. Other generals including the Republican party's 1856 presidential candidate, John Charles Frémont, and Benjamin Butler felt impelled, in part because of the smallness of their commands, as well as for humanitarian reasons, not to enforce the increasingly hated fugitive-return law, especially when disloyal masters were involved. Lincoln countermanded their 1861 orders to this effect. He wished

[25]Gerald Garvey, *Constitutional Bricolage* (Princeton, 1971), p. 5.

civilians to decide bedrock policies; he, and the Republican majority in Congress, nibbled at slavery's edges as long as possible before accepting the greater risks of direct confrontation. But, being educable, they eventually took the risk.

By mid-1862, Congress, after intensive, heated, and partisan debates, repealed the Fugitive Slave statute, by then unenforceable anyway, forbade United States officers from returning runaways, abolished slavery itself in the District of Columbia and the federal territories, and made Negroes subject to militia service. National power was exerted now for antislavery purposes and was rolling back the borders of servitude. Abolitionists celebrated forward motion where immobility and intractability had so long dominated.[26]

In order to increase security in occupied areas of the South, to allot privileges and to enforce law and order among civilians, low-rank Union officers in numerous commands improvised loyalty tests for southern whites (never for Negroes: an instance of segregation-as-compliment). These tests commonly took the form of loyalty oaths. In August, 1861, Congress and the President required, by statute, a loyalty oath for all federal civil and military officers. It was a relatively simple attestation of the subscriber's intention to be loyal to the Union in the future. A year later (July 2, 1862), Lincoln signed a tougher loyalty statute for all federal officials, requiring a statement of both a signer's intent to be loyal and an affirmation of unalloyed past loyalty. From 1862 to 1865 Congress extended the coverage of this "ironclad test oath" (or of very similar ones) to federal claimants, contractors, pensioners, passport applicants, jurors and lawyers in federal courts, and to its own members. The Supreme Court required subscriptions to the oath in a rule of the Court binding on all court officers including justices, marshals, and lawyers. The War Department used the ironclad oath when "galvanizing" captured rebels who claimed to have served the Confederacy only under duress and who wished not only to recant their Confederate allegiance but also to take service in the Union armed forces. Field commanders gratefully adapted these statutory oath forms when screening the ever-growing number of whites in occupied

[26]Statutes and abolitionists' views are in Herman Belz, "Protection of Personal Liberty in Republican Emancipation Legislation of 1862," *Journal of Southern History*, XLII (1976), 385–400.

areas who sought privileges including that of appointment or election to revived community and state political offices, or to enter into private litigation in resurrected local courts.

In both congressional and state debates, Democrats postured as defenders of white Americans' civil liberties and damned the oaths as tools for tyrants. Republicans argued that loyalty tests were not constitutionally excessive weapons in a civil war. Republican legalists stressed the fact that the oaths demanded a primary national allegiance of subscribers. By 1863 the implications of this stress on national allegiance were becoming more apparent; until the war, one's state allegiance was of primary importance.

Allegiance affirmed by oath became a requirement for the enjoyment of numerous rights and social relationships. Democrats retained concepts of liberties only in the traditional context of fixed constraints on wrongs that the government must not commit. These constraints on national power operated at all times, Democrats insisted, except for disfavored state-defined groups such as Negroes. Many Republicans were coming to see the Bill of Rights as a grant of positive power to the nation and a duty upon it to seek that elusive "more perfect Union" of free states and free men. Once found, then the Constitution's injunction to the nation to guarantee each state a republican form of government could be obeyed.

More mundane questions had priority for Army officers in the South. They had to fill local offices and determine who could run in elections and vote for candidates. Soldiers' power to require candidates and/or voters to subscribe to the "ironclad" form could result in a rigorous sifting of southern society. Several nonseceded states also created oath tests for voters and officeholders. American political parties traditionally were built up from localities, often on the shoulders of state officials and of federal officeholders such as a village postmaster, a congressional district's federal attorney and revenue officials, and territorial land surveyors. Exclusion of Confederate veterans or supporters from federal and state officialdom and from local and state parties would greatly alter politics' configurations, easing ways for Republican organizations to grow in communities.[27]

[27]Harold M. Hyman, *Era of the Oath: Northern Loyalty Tests During the Civil War and Reconstruction* (Philadelphia, 1954), chs. 1–3.

Republicans in Congress, aware of the political potential the loyalty requirements embraced, might have been expected to bar a large proportion of southern whites from state officeholding or voting in occupied areas. But the Congressmen, though attending in this manner to federal offices by means of test oaths, left the states' offices alone. Admissions to state privileges such as voting or officeholding remained up to states' majorities.

Congress did incorporate punishments for perjurors into the 1861–62 oath statutes. Transgressors were to face individual prosecutions in federal courts. But not a single recorded perjury indictment ensued; the perjury clauses did not place state offices under federal control. Lying under oath was reportedly common and, it developed, unrisky. Some perjurors, apprehended as saboteurs, guerrillas, or spies, faced military rather than civil trials, involving stiffer penalties than those for perjury. Perhaps compassion aborted prosecutions in many instances of detected perjuries. Union soldiers may have preferred not to push peripheral matters such as false swearing so long as civilians kept the peace. Success for a perjury indictment was always in question. In many occupied areas of the Confederacy, federal attorneys were scarce and United States courts reopened only belatedly. Lower federal courts drew juries from local venires and used standards of evidence, procedure, and competence of witnesses prescribed by the state in which a United States court operated. The result of these factors was that southern white officials and voters, unless of high rank or particularly unsavory reputation among local Unionists and blacks, were likely to retain their positions and influence.

As noted, military officers disdained tasks of civil government and tended to keep incumbents in public offices, especially of low-level sorts, rather than to exclude them. All incumbents were whites, naturally. Union soldiers, though appointing only whites to office, simultaneously asserted assumptions about the superior trustworthiness of Negroes. This illogic, or compartmentalization, troubled few commentators except emancipationists. The distrust of whites as security risks and the employment of recent Confederates in public offices and as voters were paradoxes in Army ways and in Lincoln's and Congress's Reconstruction policies as developed by the end of 1863 and mid-1864. As a result, the test oath laws failed, if judged by the absence of perjury indictments and by the presence of numerous probably perjurious subscribers in local offices and as voters. This failure disappointed persons who had hoped that the oaths would themselves democratize the southern power structure and improve race relationships.[28]

At the same time that it enacted the two oath laws, the Thirty-seventh Congress also passed (August 6, 1861; July 17, 1862) confiscation bills. Debates on the oath bills merged into arguments on confiscation; education for Congressmen on one improved understanding about the other. The 1862 loyalty test and confiscation policies were more rigorous than their 1861 predecessors. Both, especially confiscation, aimed to make the federal courts ". . . the nuts and bolts of Reconstruction legislation."[29]

The 1862 confiscation statute was a compromise measure. Unhappy that the Constitution's treason clause was all but unworkable, yet unwilling to violate the constitutional constraint on attainder,[30] Republican legalists specified new federal offenses of degrees less than treason. These included inciting or engaging in rebellion. After jury trials in federal courts, with established Bill of Rights protections, convictions could result in fines, imprisonments, and loss of property, including slaves, at the judge's discretion. But first the federal courts in the South had to open, individual malefactors or their slaves be captured, indictments issue and trials be won. In brief, except for extending federal criminal law, confiscation was traditional and its impact small. Even its slave confiscation clauses, though spectacular in subject, were not capable of reshaping race relationships.[31]

A radical characteristic of the confiscation laws existed in the legal technique their framers employed. Republican Congressmen knowledgeable in constitutional law agreed that the war power was part of the Constitution and that the nation, using the federal courts, should strike at slavery, the root of the war. But most enemy slaveholders were unindictable in person; i.e., they could not be served

---

[28]*Ibid.;* Peyton McCrary, *Abraham Lincoln and Reconstruction: The Louisiana Experiment* (Princeton, 1978), chs. 6–9.

[29]Patricia A. Lucie, "Confiscation: Constitutional Crossroads," *Civil War History*, XXIII, (1977), 304–322 at 307; and see fn. 32 below.

[30]Art. III, sec. 3; see Appendix.

[31]Lucie, "Confiscation," pp. 307–309, esp. n. 33, for discussion of Lincoln's concern on this point, almost causing a veto, but resolved by an explanatory amendment that forfeiture of real estate was for life alone.

writs or arrested. Therefore, no trial and consequent confiscation could occur. The Republicans incorporated in the 1862 law *in rem* judicial proceedings against property, proceedings derived from admiralty and revenue practices, instead of against persons *(in personam)*.[32]

The confiscation laws posed questions beyond the ability of any legal mode to solve. Slaves, if confiscable as property in *in rem* proceedings, reinforced the *Dred Scott* categorization. Further, the 1862 statute said that confiscated slaves were "forever free." Could this square with the Constitution's requirement that forfeitures occur only for the miscreant's lifetime? Two equally valid readings of the Constitution, one backward-looking and static, one forward-looking and potentially revolutionary, clashed head-on with no chance for compromise in the debates on confiscation. Either the "confiscations" of liberated slaves were an unconstitutional attainder or the liberation of slaves was an extraordinary act sanctioned by extraordinary conditions. But the two interpretations could not coexist. One had to control the other. Next, under the 1862 Confiscation Act, anyone claiming a right to a confiscated, perhaps fugitive slave had first to swear in federal court to his past loyalty to the nation. There, by mid-1862, jurors, judge, and all lawyers had to swear similarly. Slaves were far abler so to swear than most masters. But if a white claimant so swore, though a contrary verdict followed, could this provision clash with the "forever free" stipulation concerning his bondsman? In theory, yes. As matters worked out, no. Few confiscation prosecutions occurred. Presidential emancipation soon (September, 1862) supplemented, then far outclassed what the lawmakers did. The confiscation statutes' ambiguities were, it appears, like the perjury clause in the test oath laws, an imprecise effort to ". . . leave responsibility for a more specific construction to the [federal] courts."[33] Congress's reliance upon the federal courts was to be a Reconstruction habit, with fateful consequences.

Emancipation policy required a broader track and a swifter pace than individual confiscation litigations allowed. Lincoln clung as long as he could to variant schemes of state emancipations with or

---

[32]*Ibid.*, p. 312; Miller *v.* U.S., 78 U.S. 268 (1870), sustained the war power base of the second confiscation law. Earlier discussion of *in rem* proceedings is in ch. 2 above.

[33]Lucie, "Confiscation," p. 319.

without colonization of freed slaves abroad. He continued to advocate federal compensation to loyal owners of freed slaves (options that Maryland and Delaware rejected). But by midsummer 1862 he accommodated aspects of abolition constitutionalism developed since 1840. It was increasingly relevant to the Union's changing condition and needs since 1860 and mixed easily with adequacy constitutionalism. Abolitionists and adequacy spokesmen who were unconcerned about race both stressed the nation's victory as the precondition to the existence of all rights. Like the abolitionists, Lincoln had come to join Union and liberty. He employed adequacy constitutionalism to justify the active intervention of the national government in favor of both, and, like millions of mine-run northerners, shifted to favoring emancipation if it would weaken the Confederacy. In effect, the South's basic strengths against the Union—slavery and the war's longevity—fed a decision in the North to free the South's slaves and thus, hopefully, to shorten the war. Moving with this current, Lincoln developed equalitarian tendencies which abolitionists eagerly nourished.

On April 16, 1862, as noted earlier, Lincoln approved a bill abolishing slavery in the District of Columbia (where the 1860 Crittenden "compromise" proposal had said emancipation must never occur), with compensation to owners. A June 19, 1862, statute prohibited slavery in the federal territories, in effect reversing *Dred Scott*. A second Confiscation Act set free the slaves of persons convicted of treason (no one was) or who supported the rebellion—by what test was unspecified. Still it was clear that Congressmen gauged the North's temper to be moving sharply toward a radical bent with respect to southern Negroes. What in prewar years had been glacial immobility on racial matters was melting swiftly in the heat of wartime reverses and frustrations.

Congress held back from braver steps than these. Lincoln sensed, and relished, the swift winds of changed opinion. Feeling also a need to act on behalf of the men in uniform who were in peril of their lives because of his orders, the President came reluctantly but decisively to judgment. Lincoln issued an Emancipation Proclamation on September 22, 1862, in the wake of the Antietam "victory."

The Proclamation had its base in the President's powers as Commander in Chief. In the Proclamation, Lincoln promised that he would recommend to Congress money aid to loyal slave states for initiation there of "immediate or gradual abolishment of slavery" and for colonization abroad of freedmen. Second, he warned that on January 1, 1863, all slaves of persons still in rebellion "shall be then, thenceforward, and forever free." Lincoln added a positive duty to Congress's prohibition of March, 1862, against the Army's returning of runaways; Union officers must now "recognize and maintain the freedom of such persons and . . . do no act or acts to repress such persons . . . in any efforts they make for their actual freedom." In the rebellious states, only individuals of unalloyed past as well as future loyalty to the United States might hope for compensation for property losses including slave runaways. No hope existed for recompense unless abandonment of the rebellion occurred before the ninety-day grace period ended on January 1, 1863.

Whatever dreams Lincoln had of mass surrenders of Confederates as a result of his Proclamation dissipated during those three months. On January 1, 1863, Lincoln proclaimed that emancipation in the specified rebel areas was in effect—which meant that it would go into effect when and if Union troops won those areas. He had not included loyal slaveholding states and portions of seceded states already under Union military occupation in the Proclamation.

A new element entered when the President ordered that Negroes be enlisted in the Union's armies. In brief, the United States intended to redress its manpower problem by recruiting the South's blacks for the North's cause; the only large number of Negroes was in Confederate lines. Now Lincoln offered them a majestic reason to become runaways. Henceforward suitable Negro men would become uniformed and armed *men.* By 1865 almost 200,000 black bluecoats had served.

It was a fateful reversal of history, and everyone knew it. The war was forcing many whites who had no love for Negroes into elevating them to the status of men equal before the law—even if only martial or military law—to whites; so equal as to have arms. In 1857 the *Dred Scott* decision declared that Negroes were less than men, without rights. In 1863 the President committed the nation, so far as he was able, to views common among the abolitionists that slavery had caused secession and nurtured the capacity of the South to continue fighting, and that Negroes were men enough to be soldiers. Lincoln and most Americans had traveled great moral distances in a short time. If the war could be won—in 1863 this was still a hope, not a certainty—the constitutional law of the land was basically transformed from what had obtained in 1860–61. A future opened envisaging a biracial society, still a federal system of diverse states, a political democracy, and an economic capitalism, in which the races lived on legal terms other than that of master-slave.

The Emancipation Proclamation provided the Union with diplomatic assets abroad despite deserved criticism that it was still reversible and left slavery alive in some areas even if the rebellion collapsed. Henceforward the Confederacy's appeal to foreigners diminished; the Union's rose. Bluecoats were no longer invading Dixie merely in order to restore the nation or even to contain slavery where it existed in 1860. Instead the Union was rolling back the slave tide that for fifty years had been expanding in imperial fashion. At least as far as executive policy was concerned, the Proclamation committed the nation to permanent emancipation as a war aim.[34]

As with loyalty tests, confiscation, and emancipation, conscription became tougher and more effective in 1863, both in the Union and in the Confederacy. Prewar recruitment centering on states' volunteer militias could not meet Civil War demands. Congress retained the "federalized" state militias and employed the draft to supplement low enlistments. But in administrative terms, neither Congress nor President was able to make the prewar militia system dependable. In the face of inadequate volunteering, Congress in 1862 conscripted from among draft registrants (including the small number of blacks in the loyal states) a number adequate to meet each state's unfulfilled militia quota. Corruption flourished because Congress, in nineteenth-century manner, allowed individuals to fulfill military obligations without personal service, by money commutations, purchase of substitutes, and bounties by communities that failed to meet quotas. Gross by modern standards, such evasions became unacceptable in the North, though the Confederacy retained them.

On March 4, 1863, Lincoln signed a new draft law. It created a

[34]Stephen B. Oates, " 'The Man of Our Redemption' Abraham Lincoln and the Emancipation of the Slaves," *Presidential Studies*, IX (1979), 15–25.

Provost Marshal General Bureau in the War Department headed by a regular Army officer, James B. Fry. Congress abolished some of the egregious features of the 1862 law, especially those that allowed moneyed individuals to shift to others the burden of personal service. Fry ended other abuses by administrative orders in 1863 and 1864. The PMGB centralized and regularized the draft's administration, although not in time to relieve conditions that resulted in the July, 1863, antidraft riots, and in effect redefined disloyalty as draft evasion and obstruction. The 1864 law did diminish class resentments that fed on earlier obvious unfairness. Every draft-eligible male now had a direct connection to the national government; this involved far more persons that were affected by the oath requirements for federal commissions or positions. As Union armies advanced southward, Fry's provosts imposed the draft in occupied areas, including the recruitment and conscription of Negroes as Lincoln and Congress had specified.

Lincoln and other civilian leaders kept worrying about attacks on the draft from another civilian branch, the courts. Secretly, Chief Justice Taney waited to void conscription, having, as noted, already written an opinion declaring the 1863 act unconstitutional. But no case came to the Supreme Court in time. Democratic judges on Pennsylvania's supreme court, in a highly politicized situation, declared, in *Kneedler* v. *Lane,* the 1863 conscription act unconstitutional, and that court soon reversed itself. Other state courts granted habeas corpus writs to drafted or volunteered individuals, especially minors, but no constitutional test resulted from these instances before war's end.[35]

No manuals existed (or exist) on how to transform the Constitution's stipulations concerning civilian direction of the military into effective controls. Republicans as well as Democrats feared that the Army might be uncontrollable. As example, some unknowable number of Union officers and men shared General George B. McClellan's antipathy to Emancipation and the use of black soldiers. Lincoln and the congressional Republicans were adroit enough to

[35]John Norton Pomeroy, *An Introduction to the Constitutional Law of the United States* (New York, 1870), pp. 300–304; "Commutation of the Draft," *American Law Review,* n.s. II (1863), 622–628; J. L. Bernstein, "Conscription and the Constitution: The Amazing Case of *Kneedler v. Lane,"* American Bar Association *Journal,* LIII (1967), 708–712, 1133–1136.

develop policies that both increased the Army's duties (as in conscription, confiscation, reconstructions, and loyalty testing) and decreased its initiatives.

First steps in extending civilian controls over the military are visible in several War Department policy guidelines. Lincoln and War Secretary Edwin M. Stanton commissioned legal and constitutional experts to prepare the guidelines, bringing some of the writers including Joseph Holt, Francis Lieber, and William Whiting directly into War Department employment. These compendia required much original research by their authors, for earlier military analysts and constitutional lawyers had not anticipated conditions that developed during the Civil War. In print by March, 1863, the War Department guidelines outlined acceptable procedures, especially in civil affairs matters, that Army officers must follow.

Among the most important of the 1863 guidelines, Columbia Professor Lieber's General Order Number 100, circulated throughout the Army, provided officers with detailed procedures for martial law drawn primarily from European history. The War Department also published Judge Advocate General Holt's numerous circulars and opinions as a book in early 1863. The Kentucky Unionist Holt made the military's top law office a rigorous monitor of military conduct. Holt also established a new Bureau of Military Justice within his department. His lawyers provided counsel for officers sued in state courts by civilians for alleged excesses committed when enforcing conscription or internal security assignments, if those officers had conformed to relevant guidelines of instructions.

Stanton prevailed on a prominent Boston lawyer, the abolitionist William Whiting, to become the War Department Solicitor. In this position Whiting represented the government in numerous contract litigations. More important, he brought together and enlarged his scattered writings on the theme of the nation's constitutional adequacy to deal with the crisis secession had produced and placed them in a war setting. Published as a book in March, 1863, Whiting's *War Powers Under the Constitution of the United States*—note his careful use of the word "under"—was a wide-ranging survey of jurisprudence and history on the capacity of a democracy to amass and rule military force. Holt, Lieber, and Whiting contributed also to the composition and later publication of orders issued by Provost Marshal General Fry, and by the Inspector General's Office in the War

Department, a unit almost moribund when, in mid-1862, Stanton revived it. By spring, 1863, few Army officers, field provosts, or draft officials were without copies of these compendia or analyses. Through incessant reports and investigations and prompt rewards or punishments for subordinates, the War Department labored to lessen military excesses.[36]

So did the Congress. Its efforts in this direction, often more spectacular than those of the executive officers, helped to overcome the innate difficulties of a constitutional government formed of separate branches and of divided, often overlapping powers or functions. That these difficulties were substantially overcome by early 1863 is suggested from examination of efforts by President and Congress not only to formulate but also to implement policy on Emancipation and Reconstruction; to transform administrator's guidelines into effective checkreins on the military. Congress's success in implementing resulted from the work of certain of its traditional committees (military affairs; ways and means) on subjects (promotions, appropriations) essential to military well-being and purpose, and also from the novel work of investigating committees.

Soon after the Thirty-seventh Congress assembled in 1861, it created a Joint Committee on the Conduct of the War. Except for temporary, ceremonial purposes, joint committees were all but unknown in Congress's history. The Joint Committee on the Conduct of the War soon exhibited abilities to focus the attention not only of both House and Senate, but also of the public nationwide, on the subjects of inquiry. For good or ill, the Joint Committee was opening the door of modern times in legislative operations. It favored certain journalists, exploited the muscle of Committee members who held places also on other important committees, and shared with the President the responsibility to control upstart generals. The Committee employed subpoenas to compel testimony (including some from Negroes) and documents. Committee investigators helped (or forced) Army officers to operate within policy limits. At times, Committee hearings were savagely partisan, and blighted some military careers. The Congressmen nevertheless helped greatly to make real the Constitution's essential directive about civil-military relationships, that civilians not generals should create

[36]Hyman, *A More Perfect Union,* ch. 12.

policy. Once officers learned this lesson, Committee rancor lessened.[37]

As with loyalty tests, twentieth-century perversions of legislative investigating committee powers hamper fair evaluations of the Civil War legislative investigations. It is possible to view those investigations as wholly partisan, intemperate attacks on the civil liberties of individuals. Such views attach more recent values to past events. An alternative view of the Civil War congressional investigations is that they were part of a modernization process within the Congress, of paltry growth until the Civil War. Without Congress's determined employment of its subpoena powers in investigations, the accord that developed between it and Lincoln would quickly have withered. As a result partly of the close cooperation between the committee and the White House, by mid-1863 the Union Army was under civilians' control. Policy and implementation were closer than ever before.

Army officers' acceptance of the executive and legislative monitors derived also from their fears of lawsuits. A growing number of officers were being sued by civilians for damages in state courts (sometimes in southern civil courts reopened and staffed through Army efforts). Even in northern state courts, some plaintiffs were recent rebels or their known abettors. They claimed damages for alleged false arrests, trespasses, libels, and a variety of other injuries supposedly incurred in security, confiscation, and conscription operations. Some state judges echoed Taney's *Merryman* opinion before local juries. Lieber, becoming conscious of grumblings about the "intolerable nuisance" of the antiwar opportunists' "unceasing harping upon constitutionality," worried that state court intrusions were transforming the Constitution into a "boulder in the road."[38]

Yet the *Merryman* style of confrontation between sword and robe was never repeated in the high courts. Instead, in March, 1863, triple-purpose legislation on habeas corpus, indemnity, and removal partially filled ancient interstices in the dual judicial system. This statute, in Felix Frankfurter's estimate, made the Civil War "a turning point in the history of the federal judiciary." Remarkably,

[37]William Brock, *An American Crisis: Congress and Reconstruction, 1865–1867* (New York, 1963), p. 8.
[38]Francis Lieber, *Civil Liberty and Self-Government* (3rd rev. ed., Philadelphia, 1875), p. 197.

in light of Chief Justice Taney's known views and those of at least a few other federal judges, Congress and Lincoln agreed, in this law, to increase national court jurisdiction. It is remarkable also that this increase occurred in the midst of a great civil war. Students of the subject no longer believe, as Frankfurter suggested fifty years ago, that "the Civil War put out of men's minds such placid concerns as judicial organization."[39] Instead a consensus has grown recently that Lincoln's Republicans gave a high priority to questions of federal court jurisdiction. This estimate is paralleled by the revision of another which earlier depicted both the Republican majority in Congress and Lincoln as hostile to the federal courts in both words and policies. The President and Congress were friendly to the federal judiciary and willing to place themselves, in a sense, in the judges' hands. Congress and President made the federal judges the primary enforcers of the growing confiscation, antidisloyalty, and conscription legislation, established a new lower federal court circuit, expanded further the authority of the young Court of Claims, and, of primary concern here, substantially expanded federal court jurisdiction over state courts, civil or criminal litigations against military defendants.[40]

Since 1789, national courts had only "federal question" review jurisdiction over state court decisions. Under the Constitution's Article III, as implemented in section 25 of the 1789 Judiciary Act, very few plaintiffs qualified for federal jurisdiction. State courts could, and did, exert concurrent jurisdiction over claims arising under the federal Constitution, laws, and treaties. Those cases that federal judges accepted rose primarily because of the litigants' real or contrived diverse state residence, combined with a minimum money value in a claim. Once within a federal court jurisdiction, diversity litigants found the forum state's statutes, procedures, and standards for qualifying witnesses and jurors governing the federal tribunal.

A defendant in a state court proceeding who alleged that a federal constitutional right was infringed had to wait until an adverse verdict issued before he could seek an appeal to the United States

[39]Felix Frankfurter and James M. Landis, *The Business of the Supreme Court: A Study in the Federal Judicial System* (New York, 1928), p. 55.

[40]Stanley I. Kutler, *Judicial Power and Reconstruction Politics* (Chicago, 1968), p. 6 and *passim*.

Supreme Court by writ of error. It was the only federal court allowed but not required by the 1789 Judiciary Act to hear such an appeal. No order, including habeas corpus, to a state court by any federal judge could shift a pretrial state defendant to a federal court. No federal judge could abort a state trial under way. In short, until 1863, justice, even when federal constitutional standards were at issue, was overwhelmingly state justice.

The 1863 Habeas Corpus statute lessened this imbalance, at least for federal officers who were state court defendants.[41] Among other matters, the law legitimized Lincoln's earlier suspensions of the habeas privilege and authorized future suspensions, and indemnified federal officers who had already been declared guilty in state courts of civil wrongs against civilians or paid the plaintiffs the damages awarded by the state court. The law provided also that officers properly enforcing executive orders or legislation, if sued in a state court, should, through counsel (usually provided by the War Department or Attorney General), raise the new federal statute in their defense. If a state proceeding appeared to defendant's counsel to be prejudiced by reason of the defendant's status as a national officer, the 1863 law authorized a shift of jurisdiction from the state court to a federal district or circuit court. There, the case had to proceed upon the basis of forum state procedures, except that by 1863 federal laws stipulated that Negroes could testify even against whites (the question of Negro testimony in fugitive slave renditions had long troubled the federal courts), and that court officers, including judges, lawyers, and jurors, had to be sworn to their past as well as future loyalty to the Union. The 1863 statute did not require a money minimum or state diversity for the federal jurisdiction. It did require that plaintiffs initiate suits against officers within two years of the alleged damage.

More uniform policy in lawsuits permitted also more uniform procedures in implementing the 1863 conscription law. Once the 1863 Habeas Corpus law was effective, federal conscription officials were better able to resist the increasing number of attempts by state judges to wrest apprehended violators, by habeas, from military custody. Affected officers did not themselves have to face irate state

[41]William M. Wiecek, "The Reconstruction of Federal Judicial Power, 1863–1876," *American Journal of Legal History*, XIII (1969), 333–359.

judges, attorneys, sheriffs, and juries. Instead federal justice provided counsel and covered costs. And the lawyer's treasured quality, uniformity, now obtained in greater measure.[42] Congress, in 1866, 1867, and 1871, was to build on 1863 beginnings, extending federal court alternatives to state court defendants, especially Negroes, who were not federal officials. The 1863 Act was, in effect, like confiscation and revenue laws and executive emancipation, a Reconstruction enactment for the entire nation, not only for the South.

Now the military had civilian, national protectors, the federal judiciary. But Congress, in the 1863 statute, exacted a price for this protection. Cabinet Secretaries (especially of War) in charge of internal security and draft operations had to report to federal district and circuit judges all civilian arrests and prisoner dispositions. By far the greatest number of rear-area arrests involved violations of conscription, Emancipation, and trade control policies. The President and Congress, in partnership with the federal judiciary, were imposing a closer watch over the military and were exhibiting also their growing distrust of many states' judges, by no means only of those in the South.

The several laws, executive orders, War Department guidelines, and congressional investigations helped greatly, by mid-1863, to define civilian control over the military in practical situations, and thus to approach its theoretical qualities. But the Chief Justice of the United States refused to credit the improvements and perceived only the costs. Increasingly alienated even from his fellow justices, Taney carried on his lonely crusade to restrict the President, the Congress, and the Army; to maintain the Constitution in its prewar, artificially separate, largely unused categories, however irrelevant these were to existing conditions. Taney saw no reason to celebrate

[42]William Whiting, *War Powers Under the Constitution of the United States* (Boston, 1871), p. 377. Randall, *Constitutional Problems*, p. 214, and Swisher, *Taney*, p. 443, considered this statute to be hasty and ill-advised legislation, suitable merely for wartime use. But contemporary legal specialist Alfred Conkling, *A Treatise on the Organization, Jurisdiction and Practice of the Courts of the United States in Suits at Law, Including Municipal Seizures and Criminal Prosecutions* (5th ed., Albany, 1870), p. 80, thought the 1863 law "a studiously devised and carefully framed act" well constructed "to meet the exigencies of the rebellion then at its height." And Frankfurter and Landis's comment in *Business of the Supreme Court*, p. 107, wants repetition: "Framers of judiciary acts are not required to be seers; and great judiciary acts, unlike great poems, are not written for all time. It is enough if the designers of new judicial machinery meet the chief needs of their generation."

the increases in federal court jurisdiction over the Army and over state courts allowed by the 1863 Habeas Corpus Act. Instead, through 1863 and 1864, aging and ill, Taney clung to life and to his office long after contemporaries thought either was possible. He mustered his energies to try to overcome his colleagues' timidity in two major instances, the *Prize* cases and Clement L. Vallandigham's petition for a Supreme Court order that would free him from the grasp of a military court in Ohio.

In the *Prize* cases the Court determined the nature of the Civil War. The litigation derived from Lincoln's blockade orders on southern ports. A dozen suits involving naval seizures of contraband, lumped together as the *Prize* cases, rose from enforcements of these orders. Summed up by a Washington newspaper, the *Prize* cases raised "two great questions." These were, first, "is our Government engaged in a war in the sense in which that term is understood, so as to bring it within the principles and regulations which affect foreign and commercial nations in their commercial dealings on the seas?" Second, "whether, if so, the blockade declared to exist of the rebel ports has been established in such a manner as to make the vessels captured lawful prizes, subject to condemnation in our Admiralty [i.e., federal district] Courts?"[43] If the Court held that what was going on was a war rather than an insurrection, the blockade was legal but the Confederacy was sovereign. If, however, the Court ruled that it was an insurrection then the Union had no right to blockade its own ports.

The able lawyer James Carlisle argued against the legitimacy of the blockade. Only Congress could declare war, he insisted; Lincoln's blockade proclamations made him a virtual dictator. The Union's consistent opposition to the recognition of the Confederacy by European nations because the war was a civil domestic affair further invalidated the President's orders blockading America's own ports. Necessity—a plea as "old as the reign of Tiberias, its limits should be looked for in Tacitus," Justice Catron wrote privately—created no constitutional powers, Carlisle and his co-counsel pleaded.

Counsel for the United States, Charles Eames and Richard Henry Dana, among others, insisted that the international law of blockade

[43]Washington *Republican,* Feb. 12, 1863, in Swisher, *Taney Period,* p. 885.

was a legitimate weapon against internal enemies. Federalism, "the complex frame of State and Federal power," considered only as a constitutional theory, enabled the Confederates to insist that the impact of blockade orders on neutrals was limited. But, co-counsel William Maxwell Evarts insisted, a war was a fact, independent of declaration, and violators of blockade orders assumed the risk for their ships and cargoes.[44]

In March, 1863, the Supreme Court issued its decision. To the government's dismay, it was divided 5–4; to its relief, the majority accepted its counsel's basic positions. Justice Grier offered the majority opinion. Like Evarts, Grier asserted that a civil war was never proclaimed. Congress's approval was needed for a foreign war. Commander of the armed forces, the President, was obliged to see to the faithful execution of all laws. The Court was no blinder than the President, the Congress, or foreign nations to the fact that a great war was being fought here. It was up to the President and Congress, not the Court, to determine the existence of a civil war and what powers the nation should employ. These were political not justiciable decisions. Grier accepted the concept of seizable "enemies' property" that Dana had advanced, deriving from principles of public policy, not common law. All residents of the Confederate states were technically enemies, subject to the nation's martial grasp. Active supporters of the rebellion had, properly, their property subject to seizure on the seas or confiscation on land. They were not less enemies because they were traitors, Grier stated.[45]

The Court's Democratic members spoke through Nelson. Though a minority statement, the dissent embarrassed the government and delighted antiwar spokesmen. Of course a war existed, Nelson stated. But it was neither a legal nor a constitutional war. Instead it had been and would remain "a personal war" by the President against "those in rebellion . . . until Congress . . . acted upon this state of things." The President had no war powers until the Congress provided him with them. All maritime seizures before July 13, 1861 (the date that Congress by statute approved the blockade), were illicit.[46] Joined by Taney, Catron, and with reservations,

[44]*Ibid.,* pp. 885–889.
[45]Prize cases, 669; Swisher, *Taney Period,* pp. 885–890.
[46]Prize cases, 690; Swisher, *Taney Period,* p. 892.

Clifford, Nelson's dissent skirted both a *Merryman* confrontation and a *Dred Scott* denial of adequate powers.

Dana, whose brief for the government had helped to shape the majority opinion, learned that many commentators misjudged the nature of the *Prize* cases decision. Responding to expressions of concern that the Court's judgment threatened the integrity even of the loyal states if a President chose to be a military dictator, Dana insisted the Court had given the President no undue authority. Secession by a state did not transform its land into enemy territory or its people into enemies; did not end that state's relationships with the nation; did not terminate any individual's responsibilities as a citizen either of the United States or of a state. The Court had confirmed the nation's power to deal with the fact of territorial control of an area by a domestic or foreign foe by seizing property whose owners were domiciled there.[47] Like the 1863 decision, or nondecision, by the Court on the government's power to issue paper money as legal tender,[48] the *Prize* cases decision deeply disappointed persons who, like Taney, wanted the Court to constrain national policy in the war, a disappointment soon reinforced by the Court's avoidance of the issues in Clement Laird Vallandigham's appeal.

Vallandigham was an extreme antiwar, Negrophobe Democratic Congressman. He had knowingly violated orders by the Army commander in Ohio against public expression of pro-Confederate sympathies, especially by persons known to have actively, rather than by mere advocacy, aided the rebellion. As prescribed by the 1863 Habeas Corpus Act, the Army apprised a federal district court judge that it had arrested Vallandigham and was initiating a military trial. The judge refused Vallandigham a habeas release from the military court's jurisdiction on the ground that only the Army commander was competent to decide security needs. Thereupon Lincoln altered the military court's sentence (confinement for the war's duration) against Vallandigham to banishment into Confederate lines. From there, the Ohioan ran the blockade first to Canada, then back to Ohio. He appealed to the United States Supreme Court for a certi-

[47]See Richard Henry Dana and Issac Redfield in Swisher, *Taney Period*, pp. 894–897.
[48]Roosevelt *v.* Meyer, 1 Wall. 512 (1863).

orari order[49] directed to Judge Advocate General Holt, to annul the Army court's sentence and to void its proceedings, on the grounds that he, Vallandigham, had been illegally arrested.

The Supreme Court entertained Vallandigham's petition. Holt, invited by the Court to comment, responded in writing that the Court could with as little propriety enjoin Congress by certiorari as inhibit the President's officers. For the Court, Justice Wayne decided that it could not issue a certiorari even if Vallandigham's arrest, trial, and sentence were illegal (though the Court made no decision on this claim). The Court found no common-law authority to grant relief in the mode requested and no statutory authority on the basis of which it could hear an appeal from a military court. No dissent, even from Taney, is recorded.[50] The President, along with his coadjutors, drew comfort from the fact that the Court's brief but uncontradicted statement agreed with the augmenting body of "adequacy" constitutionalism, that not all legimate authority came from the precise words of Constitution or statutes. Taney drew no comfort at all. He confided to friends that he had lost hope for the Court. Like the Constitution, it could never revive from such blows.[51]

In manner and degree unpredictable in 1860, the President, Congress, and a majority of the Court were cooperating by mid-1863. The nation and the states were also performing with few confrontations. Even the midsummer 1863 antidraft riots in major cities, though allowed to develop far too long by some inept state and community authorities, especially in New York, did not generate the direct clashes between federal and state authorities that pro-Confederates hoped for and patriots had feared. Unflappable de-

[49]A discretionary writ from a superior to an inferior court, requiring the latter to supply the superior court with the record of the relevant case. Unlike habeas corpus or writ of error, certiorari could serve in a pretrial situation or during the course of a trial in a lower court, if the superior court wished so to act.

[50]But see Taney's memorandum on U.S. *v.* Gordon, 25 Fed. Cas. 1364, #15,231 (C.C.S.D., N.Y. 1861), concerning non-Article III lower courts, a memorandum that Chase used in 1865; below, ch. 10.

[51]Swisher, *Taney Period,* pp. 925–930; Ex parte Vallandigham, 1 Wall. 243 (1864). Justice David Davis, on circuit in Indianapolis, discussing Vallandigham with antiadministration Congressman Daniel Voorhees, told him, "Voorhees, you had better look out—they [federal detectives] have got down to the V's." Photostat, Willard King Collection, Chicago Historical Society.

spite the tragic news of racist, murderous rioting in the cities, Lincoln and Stanton in Washington, and Union field commanders, saw the Vicksburg siege and the Gettysburg battle to their conclusions. Then Grant ordered combat units to the riotous cities, and that crisis ended. Suppression of the antidraft rioters fell—or, in the hands of able politicos and lawyers like Lincoln, Stanton, and Whiting, could be made to fall—into the Constitution's Article IV, section 4, provision both for martial law and for federal aid to states when violent individuals overstretched the resources of local police and state militia.[52]

Concerning the South, by 1863 eclectic United States policies were diverging significantly over whether individuals or states there should be the primary object of the nation's attention in a Reconstruction. Some Republican Congressmen, including Thaddeus Stevens and Charles Sumner, talked and wrote a great deal about the southern states' constitutional place in the federal system, about "state suicide," "territorialization," and "conquered provinces." When the time came to act, however, Republicans, including Lincoln, remaining states' rights nationalists, retained the existing states, thus creating Reconstruction processes in which the nation possessed a monitor's role over a state only until that state was readmitted to representation. There was also affection and respect for the localities that made up states, and for the politics of democracy built up from communities, that made Americans incurably state-focused.

One apparent exception existed to this reverence for the states. Unionist western Virginians created the new state of West Virginia in mid-1863. They enjoyed quick formal recognition from Washington and from a puppet Virginia state government propped up by the Union Army. The latter contrivance permitted the Lincoln administration to avoid the Constitution's prohibition against a state being dismembered without its consent.

West Virginia proved a sideshow to the major policy drama developing since 1861, a drama becoming known as Reconstruction. State reconstructions became a political question as Union troops occupied whole states or enough portions of states to make possible the resumption of civil government. But at what pace; with what

[52]See Appendix.

federal role; what status for surrendered rebels, for recent closet-Unionist whites, and for always-loyal Negroes, especially for black Union soldiers? The redevelopments of civil government by Union forces in substantial portions of Arkansas, Louisiana, Tennessee, and Virginia by mid-1863 raised these questions. The controlling context for replies was final military victory. Only victory would permit the preservation of the federal union of states, of civilian control over the military, of political democracy, and of unfettered capitalism. Republicans proceeded from these premises to ask other questions centering on the quality of legal and political life in the states to be reconstructed. Such questions raised again the option for federal policy of concentrating on states or individuals.[53]

In 1861 and 1862, Republicans asked such questions only fitfully; Democrats contented themselves with mocking Republicans' inescapably complex positions and with holding fast to their simpler view of the prewar Constitution's rigid constraints upon any national prescriptions about restored states. But raise them Republicans did. The questions came up in congressional debates on the confiscation and test oath statutes of 1861 and 1862, and on Lincoln's Emancipation order, as example. These aimed in obvious ways at dissident individuals. The laws, by exclusions and prosecutions, could significantly alter the characteristics of southern political and economic leadership if rigorously enforced after Confederate surrenders. Lincoln expressed no substantial opposition to the enforcements of the punitive statutes in the occupied South or in unseceded states. Emancipation came to have the President's firm support, of course. But emancipation, as an executive military order, was worrisomely revocable, Republicans complained.

Prominent Republicans who supported confiscation, test oaths, and Emancipation came to advocate federal policies to affect primarily whole states of the defiant South. All notions of state suicide had fallen flat. In December, 1863, Lincoln, in a war power order, proclaimed a uniform state-remaking procedure. It required 10 percent of 1860's voters (meaning whites only) in affected Confederate states to swear to renounce the Confederacy, to be loyal to the

[53]*Ibid.*, Art. IV, sec. 3; Michael Les Benedict, "Preserving the Constitution: The Conservative Bases of Radical Reconstruction," *Journal of American History*, LXI (1974), 65–90.

Union in the future, and to recognize Emancipation. When that minority had taken the prescribed oath, the President would appoint a military governor over the state and require him to organize a constitutional convention. It, in turn, had to change the state's constitution, renouncing secession and accepting emancipation. A reconstructed state must move, in short, in the direction of that "republican form" guaranteed to every state in the 1787 Constitution, and newly defined by the Civil War's escalations of objectives to mean a state without slaves. Lincoln would then recommend to Congress the readmission of the "galvanized" state. Congress's autonomous parliamentary control of the admission of its members and the Supreme Court's review authority on constitutional issues including Emancipation had to be respected, Lincoln reminded southern whites.[54]

Lincoln was now convinced that northern racism was softening to the extent of approving national interference with slavery in the South as part of state reconstructions, in addition to the military abolition he had proclaimed earlier as a form of punishment on recalcitrant individuals. The President's resort to the Constitution's clause guaranteeing a republican form of government to every state paralleled fairly closely the direction and pace of leading Republican Congressmen. Like them, he found fortuitously in the guarantee clause a civilian alternative and supplement to the war powers, though he rarely hesitated to employ the latter.

Some of his party's leaders on Capitol Hill assigned leadership in state restorations to Congress. The Constitution was silent. Reasonable men could, and did, select alternative forms of the republican form of government argument. By the new year 1864 virtually all Republicans defined republican as slaveless. Beyond this, popularity was growing for federal stipulations that a returning state must exhibit evidence of its republican quality by going further than slavelessness, to equality of individuals before that state's laws. Some Radical Republicans advocated political equality. Such priorities moved Congressmen holding them to concentrate on the status of individuals more than on the formal restructuring of states. Many Republicans took inspiration from Whiggish weak-executive tradi-

[54]James D. Richardson (ed.), *A Compilation of the Messages and Papers of the Presidents, 1789–1897* (New York, 1901), VI, pp. 213–215.

tions and yearned for a formula that would allow national effectiveness for both war and peace purposes, without centralization or the use of the military. Law-trained Republican Congressmen, including Maryland's Henry Winter Davis and Illinois's Lyman Trumbull, though supporting the President in basic matters, sought better ways to contain the military and perhaps to prevent a need for future national interventions within states. Davis, a pioneer of the adequacy-of-the Constitution argument, found another means to his goals in the guarantee clause, a combination advanced also by War Department Solicitor Whiting. Senator Sumner drew attention to the guarantee clause in an 1863 *Atlantic Monthly* article on Congress's power over the rebel states. All this educated Republicans. But as a body Congress stayed out of the overall Reconstruction arena until mid-1864.[55]

By then it had become clear that Lincoln's 10 percent policy was imperfect. Although it possessed, of necessity, elements of concern about individuals within states (i.e., it forbade slavery), Lincoln aimed primarily at restoring states quickly by weakening the will of southern whites to continue warring, rather than antagonizing them further and reinforcing their will to carry on the war. Though Arkansas and Louisiana were largely restructured according to the December, 1863, procedures, and a rump Virginia government sent delegates to Washington, Congress admitted none to representation in both houses. Critics of Reconstruction in those states, especially in Louisiana, complained that prewar laws and customs on race remained in force except for formal slavery. Even slaverylike relationships endured, charged some commentators, including special investigators the War Department and the Congress sent to Louisiana. These hangovers from slavery resulted from Union military commanders' tendency to retain most incumbents in local civil offices, but also from the rapid state-restructuring pace set in Lincoln's proclamation. Lincoln's Reconstruction policy was not restructuring states or communities in a manner to protect individual Unionists and freedmen, to whom the nation owed special debts, in the exercise of their civil rights and preservation of their personal

[55]Charles Sumner, "Our Domestic Relations: Power of Congress over the Rebel States," *Atlantic Monthly*, XII (1863), 507–529; Farrar, "Adequacy," pp. 51–73; Joel Parker, *Constitutional Law: With Special Reference to the Present Condition of the United States* (Cambridge, 1862), pp. 18–19.

safety. Congress was uneasy also because statemaking, that most sacred and original process of American constitutionalism, depended upon a war power executive order. It wanted to base the process more soundly upon a statute.[56]

Whatever the merits or defects of his 1863 Reconstruction order, Lincoln, having moved first, had established the contours of Reconstruction policies to which both critics and supporters had to react. He was "first in the field," noted Eben Greenough Scott's pioneering study of wartime Reconstruction. Lincoln's plan, Scott continued, was ". . . satisfactory to nobody . . . [and] Democrats and Republicans joined in one cry, that it was a creature unknown to the Constitution, and [both] parties, as if inspired with the same motive, fell upon it and stripped it of its raiment, and lashed it in mockery naked through the world."[57]

In June, 1864, Lincoln easily won his party's nomination for a second term. Leading Republicans, barely back in the capital from the nominating convention, on July 2, 1864, passed the Wade-Davis bill through both Houses. It appeared to contradict directly the policy of the man they had just chosen again as presidential candidate. Constituent pressures on Congressmen, and the legislators' own perceptions, were moving sharply to mesh more closely with "radical" definitions of a republican form of government as demanding equal rights, and more rights, for all residents.

The Wade-Davis bill attempted to enlarge civilian control over essentially military elements in state reconstructions. Subject to Senate approval, the President was to appoint a provisional governor for each conquered state in place of the military governors he had appointed without Senate participation. The governor, paid as a brigadier general, was responsible for civil administration until Congress recognized the new state government he was to initiate. Congress specified procedures for creating the new state government. As soon as the Union Army reestablished peace in the state, the provisional governor was to direct United States marshals (the federal "police" in congressional districts) to enroll all white male "citizens of the United States resident in the state." Once a majority

---

[56]McCrary, *Lincoln and Reconstruction*, ch. 9 and *passim*.
[57]Eben Greenough Scott, *Reconstruction During the Civil War in the United States* (Boston, 1895), p. 273.

(not 10 percent of the 1860 voters, as in Lincoln's scheme, but still all-white) of enrollees swore to be loyal to the Union in the future, the governor was to initiate elections to a constitutional convention. The convention was to reestablish the state's ties to the Union and conform state laws to the federal Constitution. Convention delegates faced a stiffer oath requirement than voters. They had to swear to the ironclad oath of past loyalty. Poll-watchers were to exclude possible perjurious voters and convention delegates though they offered to swear the oath; southerners' deceit in swearing oaths had become notorious.[58]

Wade and Davis then defined a republican state in manner to meet the federal Constitution's guarantee responsibility and required the constitutional conventions to incorporate the definition in their product. A republican state was one, first, whose voters and elective officers, from governor or legislator down to pettiest juror, sheriff, or justice of the peace, had held no civil or military office "under the usurping power" of military rank of colonel or above, or civil rank above the clerical (Wade and Davis declared persons of higher civil duties or military rank not to be citizens of the United States). Second, a republican state must forever prohibit involuntary servitude, "and the freedom of all persons is guaranteed in said State." Third, republicanism required the repudiation of Confederate war debts, an issue of such concern to Republicans as to persist until the Fourteenth Amendment forbade any honoring of the rebel war costs.[59] Thereupon, the convention, through the governor, was to submit the proposed new constitution to the enrolled voters. Once approved by a majority of voters, the governor was to send the constitution to the President. After obtaining Congress's assent, the latter was to recognize the state by proclamation. Only then might the provisional governor initiate statewide elections for all civil officers including Congressmen, and, when appropriate, for presidential electors. During the process, the provisional governor was to enforce all state laws "in force when the State government was overthrown by the rebellion" except that

[58]Herman Belz, *Reconstructing the Union: Theory and Policy During the Civil War* (Ithaca, 1969), ch. 8.

[59]Republicans were deeply concerned that, somehow, the Democrats would help regain their political primacy in the South by promising to pay the rebel war debt, pensions to Confederate soldiers, and the like.

. . . no law or usage whereby any person was heretofore held in involuntary servitude shall be recognized or enforced by any court or officer in such State; and the laws for the trial and punishment of white persons shall extend to all persons, and jurors shall have the qualifications of voters under this law for delegates to the convention.

Taking trouble further to spell out their purposes, Wade, Davis, and a majority of Congressmen stipulated that

. . . all persons held to involuntary servitude or labor in the States aforesaid are hereby emancipated and discharged therefrom, and they and their posterity shall be forever free. And if any such person or their posterity shall be restrained of liberty under pretense of any claim to such service or labor, the courts of the United States shall on *habeas corpus,* discharge them.[60]

Differences between Lincoln's and the Wade-Davis reconstruction processes were substantial but not, seemingly, irreconcilable. Emancipation was shared. The obvious greater democratization in the congressional version was, of itself, no bar to accord between President and Congress; the prescription of prominent past rebels from elective positions including constitutionmaking could, it seems, be merged in the two formulas. The enlargement of federal court jurisdiction was a technique that Lincoln supported in other legislation. What remains as a significant difference was Lincoln's search for swift pace as military necessity, and consequent concentration on the status of the states rather than on the conditions of individuals.

The Wade-Davis formulation had wide appeal on its merits. If rigorously enforced, it might have prevented or solved problems that emerged in 1865–67. It gave state reconstructions a statutory base and, therefore, tied the fortunes of supportive Congressmen and the majority party to the success of the policy. The bill removed growing causes of strain between Capitol Hill and the White House. Its relatively democratic stipulation concerning a minimum electorate, its requirement of a past-loyalty oath for constitutional conventioners and jurors, and its exclusion of prominent ex-rebels from state and community offices reflected popular concerns in the North. The Wade-Davis perception of equal civil status for southerners of both races in their states' courts, with appeals by habeas

---

[60]Richardson, *Messages and Papers,* VI, 222–226.

to federal courts, as a right of United States citizens, if on the statute books in early 1865, would have committed Lincoln's successor as President to relatively precise courses of action. But no one can say what such prescriptions would have meant to Andrew Johnson.

And no one has yet made fully clear why Lincoln decided to pocket-veto the Wade-Davis bill. His decision not to sign the bill, which came to him in the last hour of the congressional session, but to let it die by pocket veto, was a resort to a constitutional power rarely used by any President until Richard Nixon, and almost never on important bills. Further to accent the surprising impact of his veto on his fellow Republicans (Democrats were delighted), Lincoln, after Congress dispersed, issued (July 8, 1864) a curious explanation: he asserted that he was unprepared to become "inflexibly committed to any single plan of [state] restoration," Congress's or his own. Under his 1863 order, Arkansas and Louisiana were well advanced toward their reformations. Lincoln did not wish to disturb their progress or to disappoint the Unionists there who were cooperating with the President, often at some risk. Further, Lincoln remained unsure if Congress possessed power, by statute, to emancipate (he had already admitted doubt that the President's war power allowed such action). A constitutional amendment was in order to resolve all doubts. However, Lincoln conceded that he was "fully satisfied" with the Wade-Davis "system of restoration . . . as one very proper plan for the people of any State choosing to adopt it." In short, southern states were free to come back his way or Congress's.[61]

Lincoln's was an odd suggestion, since he had prevented the Wade-Davis bill from becoming law and had based his own "system of restoration" on the uncertain executive war power. Wade and Davis were quick to pounce on Lincoln's stand in a New York *Tribune* "manifesto" (August 4, 1864). Their lengthy statement pointed to the insecurity of southern Negroes with respect to Emancipation, an insecurity unrelieved by the President's Reconstruction plan:

If it [the Emancipation Proclamation] be valid and observed, it [the President's plan] exacts no enactment by the State, either in law or in constitution, to add a State guaranty to the [Emancipation] proclamation title [to freedom]; and the right of a slave to freedom is an open question before the State courts. On the relative authority of the State law and the proclama-

[61]*Ibid.*

tion . . . what the State courts would say of the proclamation, who can doubt? . . . What the [United States] Supreme Court would say, who can tell? When and how is the question to get there? No *habeas corpus* lies for him [i.e., the freed Negro] in a United States Court [in Lincoln's plan]; and the President defeated . . . the extension of that writ to his case.

Though forceful and perceptive in substantial parts, the Wade-Davis criticism of the President did not lead to party schism. In 1864 the Lincoln position was as credible as Wade's and Davis's, unless the heightened race consciousness of 1866–70 is advanced to the earlier year. The telling points Wade and Davis made about defects in Lincoln's procedures concerning habeas appeals from state to federal courts were oversubtle for most nonlawyers. In any event, Lincoln's educability was outstanding. He had, Sumner commented happily to Orestes Brownson, come a very long way on race since 1860.[62]

Lincoln's progress made reasonable an expectation of further, even faster pace to come. If awarded a second term, Lincoln would serve until March, 1869. He was already committed in favor of a federal bureau to aid freedmen and an abolition amendment to the Constitution. No hope existed that the Democrats' platform or candidate, ex-general George B. McClellan, would move toward an emancipation amendment. Odds were high that Lincoln would appoint a Chief Justice of congruent views to his own (Taney died in October, 1864). Pressures favoring Republican unity for the 1864 election were great enough to bring Wade and Davis back into the party fold. The party platform was emphatically emancipationist and accepted adequacy constitutionalism without qualifications. Lincoln's victory at the polls in November, helped by the support he received from voting Union soldiers, inspired widespread commentaries on the implications of approaching military victory both for the reconstructions of states and for the statuses of individuals in those states.

One way or another, the war and Reconstruction joined the once-

---

[62]Sumner wrote that Lincoln's January and December, 1863, war power orders had made the Negroes the "corner-stone of reconstruction" and treated the southern states as "subverted and practically out of the Union." Lincoln's position on the latter point was so close to the territorial status that some Republicans favored for the crumbling Confederate states, as to make differences not worth a quibble, Sumner felt. Dec. 29, 1863, in Henry F. Brownson (ed.), *The Works of Orestes A. Brownson* (New York, 1966), III, 394.

disparate themes of state restorations and of individuals' rights. Until the Civil War, the protection of individuals' civil rights, and the list of what constituted those rights, had rarely been the nation's business. By 1864, to many observers, the nation should no longer remain aloof from such concerns. State secessions and civil war had obliterated all legal stability in the southern states, insisted the Connecticut abolitionist and combat veteran William Mason Grosvenor. "Do the civil rights under our government, once vested in certain States and the citizens of those States, still exist, and, if so, in whom are they vested?" he asked. His answer was that they were now in the nation's hands; hands that grasped not only "the remedial agencies of the courts, but the . . . sword of the conqueror."[63]

Sword and law together was the theme also of Indiana Representative George W. Julian's speech in the House on February 7, 1865. The Hoosier stressed the congruence about slavery that had developed between White House and Congress since 1861. For a long time Congress was in the lead "in ushering in the new dispensation" that recognized slavery "as the enemy of our peace"; by the new year 1865, Lincoln was no longer behind Congress. Now, Julian concluded, it was time for "further and inevitable measures of justice . . . looking to the repeal of all special [state] legislation intended for his [the Negro's] injury, and his absolute restoration to equal rights with the white man as a citizen as well as a soldier."[64]

In February, 1865, the Republican majority in Congress, with Lincoln's hearty endorsement, sent a proposed Thirteenth Amendment out to the states for ratification:

Section 1. Neither slavery nor involuntary servitude, except as a punishment for crime whereof the party shall have been duly convicted, shall exist within the United States, or any place subject to their jurisdiction.
Section 2. Congress shall have power to enforce this article by appropriate legislation.

Chapter 11 will suggest that this brief text reflected elastic, organic, dynamic understandings about individuals' rights under the Constitution, about positive duties on nation and states to secure

[63]William M. Grosvenor, "The Law of Conquest the True Basis of Reconstruction," *New Englander*, XXIX (1865), 111–131. Civil rights are examined more closely below, ch. 9.
[64]*Congressional Globe*, 38th Cong., 2nd sess., app. 65–68 (Feb. 7, 1865).

these rights, and about limitations on states in the federal Union. In Congress, Democratic opponents to the proposed Amendment, unable any longer to defend slavery as a specific state right, resorted to defenses of immutable states' rights in general (i.e., of a federal system unchanged since 1860). Charges of centralization were raised by Ohio's Samuel S. "Sunset" Cox and New York's Fernando Wood, the latter decrying emancipation by amendment, as making the Constitution do what the Constitution forbade. The Amendment, New York's Elijah Ward warned, would make Negroes equal to whites before the law; women equal to men, children to parents, and wards to guardians.

Scare tactics aside, Democrats were correct that many Republicans intended the Amendment to create (i.e., to stipulate) equality before state laws for all state residents. Sumner wanted a section 2 that stated so specifically. He deferred to majority preference for a general enforcement authority. Lacking prescience, Sumner and his colleagues assumed that abolition could lead only to equality before state law, that no halfway houses existed, and that equality was roughly equivalent to the protections the Bill of Rights afforded (or should afford) to whites as well as blacks. A fair consensus existed that suffrage was not one of those protected rights. Abolitionists disagreed whether the Amendment merely declared what should have been the proper condition of the Constitution since 1787, or whether the Constitution, having sanctioned slavery for so long, required an amendment for correction. But once the Thirteenth Amendment was ratified such questions faded. What remained was concurrence that Congress now had power to enforce freedom in the states—if necessary.[65]

Lincoln was moving ahead of many of his Republican colleagues on these points. By the spring of 1865 he had advanced his perceptions about postwar America into radical categories. In part the war itself carried him beyond Jefferson's position that liberty existed so that individuals might, on their own, seek and protect their rights, to one that perceived liberty as equality, as obligations under society actively to support individuals in their efforts to enjoy rights. Lincoln showed that he was both educable and predisposed against

[65]G. Sidney Buchanan, *The Quest for Freedom: A Legal History of the Thirteenth Amendment* (Houston: Reprint from *Houston Law Review*, 1976), pp. 6–13.

servitude. Soon after Taney announced the *Dred Scott* decision, Lincoln, in 1857, had attacked the hopeless place to which the Chief Justice relegated Negroes. By contrast, Lincoln insisted even then that the Declaration of Independence was part of the Constitution, and that the Declaration's message was hope, not despair. The Declaration included "all men" as equal, Lincoln stated. Tragically, not all men enjoyed equality. The nation could not then confer or enforce that boon, but it could, and did, declare its right to state it "so that enforcement of it might follow as fast as circumstances should permit."[66] Lincoln, seven years later, concluded what circumstances at last permitted: that the aspiration of 1776 was both the prize and the price of victory in 1865. Therefore Lincoln enthusiastically supported the Thirteenth Amendment in terms commonly understood then of the dynamic nature of rights and of the nation's responsibility to intervene in their protection.

What rights? On April 11, 1865, Lincoln publicly included in the emancipated status what every Republican and some Democrats agreed was present—civil (i.e., primarily economic) rights. But, Lincoln indicated, he was moving toward the Radicals' positions and enlarging civil rights from the traditional lawyers' view of them as narrowly economic to broader social and even political areas. Lincoln suggested that in the southern states—perhaps in all the states—at least some blacks (he specified ex-Union soldiers and literate Negroes) should also have political rights. He applauded the reformed Louisiana constitutional provision empowering the legislature to give the vote to all blacks (it had not done so), and the one "giving the benefit for public schools equally to black and white [children]." Lincoln promised announcement of a new Reconstruction policy on these tender subjects.[67] Three days later he was assassinated.

[66]Roy P. Basler (ed.), *Collected Works of Abraham Lincoln* (New Brunswick, 1954) II, 390–391, 398–410.
[67]Stephen B. Oates, *With Malice Toward None: The Life of Abraham Lincoln* (New York, 1977), pp. 423–425.

1. George Caleb Bingham, "County Election Day." This genre painting captures the robust spirit of the democratic political system in Jackson's day.

(State Historical Society of Missouri.)

Chief Justice Tanner
U S Court

2. Chief Justice Roger B. Taney. A photograph (the subject's name is misspelled on the mat) taken in the 1850s.

(National Portrait Gallery, Smithsonian Institution.)

3. Justice Joseph Story.

(Courtesy of Curator, U.S. Supreme Court.)

4. John C. Calhoun.

(National Archives.)

Lemuel Shaw, Chief Justice of the Supreme
icial Court of Massachusetts.

tropolitan Museum of Art. Gift of I.N.
lps Stokes, Edward S. Hawes, Alice Mary
wes, Marion A. Hawes, 1938.)

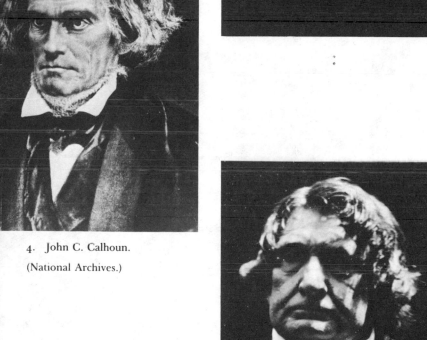

6. The Charles River Bridge. An engraving done shortly after the bridge wa completed in 1786.

(Library of Congress.)

7. The United States Senate during debates on the Compromise of 1850. Henr Clay holds forth right of center. In the lower left, cheek resting on his left hand Daniel Webster stares into space. To the right, just below the presiding officer's lef elbow, John C. Calhoun glares at Clay. Vice-President Millard Fillmore is the presid ing officer.

(Library of Congress.)

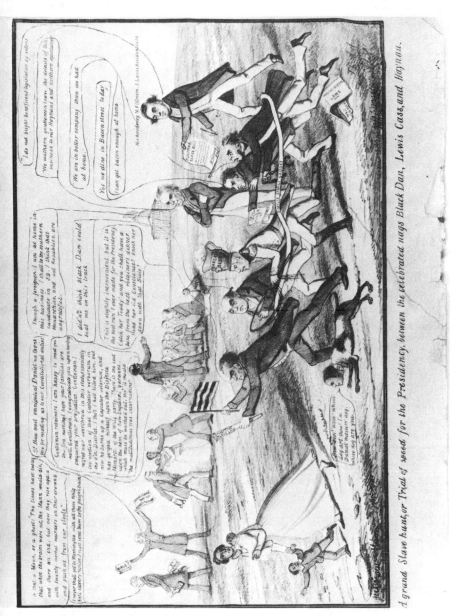

8. "A Grand Slave Hunt," 1852, reflects northern bitterness at Daniel Webster's support for the Fugitive Slave Act of 1850. Webster leads a pack of slave-catchers pursuing runaway slaves. Joining him in the chase are Lewis Cass (Democratic Senator from Michigan), General Julius Haynau (an Austrian General who bloodily suppressed the Hungarian freedom struggle in 1849) and two anonymous Massachusetts attorneys. Henry Clay and Millard Fillmore look on approvingly.

(Louis A. Warren Lincoln Library and Museum, Fort Wayne, Ind.)

9. Stephen A. Douglas.
(National Archives.)

THE ORIGINAL SQUATTER SOVEREIGN.

10. "The Original Squatter Sovereign." An unflattering cartoon portrait of Stephen A. Douglas, lampooning his support for the principle of territorial sovereignty.

(Louis A. Warren Lincoln Library and Museum, Fort Wayne, Ind.)

11. "The Political Quadrille: Music by Dred Scott." This well-executed and even-handed 1860 political caricature suggests that the presidential candidates of that year were forced to dance to the music of Dred Scott; issues raised by slavery overrode other political considerations. In the upper left, the southern Democratic candidate, John C. Breckinridge, dances with "Old Buck," James Buchanan, outgoing pro-slavery president. Lower left, Stephen A. Douglas, northern Democratic candidate, dances with an immigrant Irishman, symbolic of the New York Tammany wing of the party. Upper right, Abraham Lincoln dances with a black belle, suggesting his alleged fondness for miscegenation. Lower right, John Bell, Constitutional Union and ex-Whig, dances with an American Indian, symbolic of Bell's earlier support for the Know-Nothing movement, called the "Native American Party" in some areas.

(Library of Congress.)

12. Justice Benjamin R. Curtis.
(Library of Congress.)

13. Justice John McLean.
(Library of Congress.)

14. Justice Peter V. Daniel.
(Library of Congress.)

15. Justice John Catron.
(Courtesy of Curator, U.S. Supreme Co

1. South Carolina
R. Barnwell Rhett
C. G. Memminger
Wm. Porcher Miles
James Chesnut Jr.
R. W. Barnwell
William W. Boyce
Laurence M. Keitt
T. J. Withers

5. Mississippi
Alex. M. Clayton
James T. Harrison
William S. Barry
W. S. Wilson
Walker Brooke
W. P. Harris
J. A. P. Campbell

2. Georgia
R. Toombs
Francis S. Bartow
Martin J. Crawford
Thos. R. R. Cobb
Benjamin H. Hill
Howell Cobb
E. A. Nisbet
Augustus R. Wright
A. H. Kenan

6. Louisiana
John Perkins Jr.
Alex. de Clouet
Duncan F. Kenner
Henry Marshall
Edward Sparrow

3. Florida
Jackson Morton
Jas. B. Owens
J. Patton Anderson

Texas
John Hemphill
Thomas N. Waul
John H. Reagan
Williamson S. Oldham
Louis T. Wigfall
John Gregg
William Beck Ochiltree

4. Alabama
Richard W. Walker
Robt. H. Smith
Colin J. McRae
William P. Chilton
Stephen F. Hale
David P. Lewis
Tho. Fearn
J. L. M. Curry

16. The signatures to the permanent Constitution of the Confederate States of America. Signatories include the fervent secessionists Robert Barnwell Rhett and Laurence M. Keitt, Confederate Cabinet officials Christopher Memminger and John H. Reagan, and even such pre-1860 opponents of secession as Howell Cobb, Robert Toombs, Benjamin H. Hill, and Alexander H. Stephens.

(Courtesy of the Library of the University of Georgia, which is now the repository of this document.)

17. Abraham Lincoln: the last portrait painted from life, by Matthew Wilson.

(Louis A. Warren Lincoln Library and Museum, Fort Wayne, Ind.)

18.   A popular, fanciful reproduction of the Emancipation Proclamation (1863).

(Louis A. Warren Lincoln Library and Museum, Fort Wayne, Ind.)

19.   William H. Seward's alleged boast of his power to make arbitrary arrests provided ammunition for critics of the Republicans during the war and for years to come. "The Little Bell" was the frontispiece of John A. Marshall's *American Bastile,* a history of the sensational arbitrary arrests of many apparently innocent Democratic politicians.

(Louis A. Warren Lincoln Library and Museum, Fort Wayne, Ind.)

20. Chief Justice Salmon Portland Chase.
(Ohio Historical Society.)

21. Portrait painter David G. Blythe showed President Lincoln hobbled in trying to crush the dragon of rebellion, both by his own sense of the Constitution as a source of authority, and by the overscrupulous constitutionalism of the Democratic party, in this 1862 work.

(Museum of Fine Arts, Boston. M. and M. Karolik Collection.)

22. The Supreme Court in 1865, from left to right: David Davis, Noah H. Swayne, Robert C. Grier, James M. Wayne, Chief Justice Salmon P. Chase, Samuel Nelson, Nathan Clifford, Samuel F. Miller, Stephen J. Field.

(Courtesy of Curator, U.S. Supreme Court.)

THIS LITTLE BOY WOULD PERSIST IN HANDLING BOOKS ABOVE HIS CAPACITY.

AND THIS WAS THE DISASTROUS RESULT.

23. "Andrew Johnson Flattened by the Constitution."

(From *Harper's Weekly*, March 21, 1868, p. 192.)

Thomas McIntyre Cooley.
Scott, *Distinguished American Lawyers.*)

stice Joseph P. Bradley: portrait by
Peter Alexander Healy, 1876.

ersey Historical Society, Newark.)

26. "The Electoral Commission of 1877," painting by Cornelia A. Fassett (1879). Formed to decide the disputed Hayes-Tilden presidential election of 1876, the Commission met in the Supreme Court Chamber (now the Old Senate Chamber in the Capitol). Commission sessions were often attended by crowds of prominent Washingtonians and visitors. Sitting in the gallery are members of the press. On the dais are the Commissioners (left to right): Senators A. G. Thurman, O.; T. F. Bayard, Del.; F. T. Frelinghuysen, N.J.; O. P. Morton, Ind.; G. F. Edmunds, Vt.; Associate Supreme Court Justices W. Strong, Pa.; S. F. Miller, Ia.; N. Clifford, Me. (President of Commission); S. J. Field, Cal.; J. P. Bradley, N.J.; Representatives H. B. Payne, O.; E. Hunton, Va.; J. G. Abbott, Mass.; J. A. Garfield, O.; and G. F. Hoar, Mass. Addressing the Commission is William M. Evarts, a counsel for Hayes.

CHAPTER 9

The Dominion of Well-Administered Law

A RGUMENTS about the status of the states in the former Confederacy after Appomattox intrigued scholars then and since. Yet at the time of Lincoln's murder, and for several months thereafter, the fact that no agreed Reconstruction policy existed appeared to trouble primarily some legal scholars.

There were exceptions. On the right of politics, northern Democrats were eager to repair the party's historic base in the South. They, many southern whites, and Negrophobes generally asserted that the ex-rebel states were, with Appomattox, instantly states in the Union again; that the nation had no continuing rights or duties in the occupied region. On the Republican left, radicals such as Massachusetts' Senator Charles Sumner and Pennsylvania's Representative Thaddeus Stevens suggested that the former Confederate states were reduced to the status of conquered provinces or, at best, territories. Such a position failed to attract mainstream Republicans in 1865, although it did interest those abolitionists who retained concerns about the freedmen and persons who fretted over the fates of black and white Unionists, some of whom wore blue uniforms and who were returning to their southern communities.

Like most Democrats, most Republicans assumed that the ex-Confederate states still existed, and that the immediate question before the nation was to restore them to their proper relationship in the Union. But at what pace? Northern opinion, as expressed by

295

party spokesmen in 1865, split on the question of speed, not of the nation's right to impel state restorations. Republicans generally disagreed with the Democrats' sense of a need for swift pace. Why rush? A few days before his death Lincoln had spoken of the ex-Confederate states as having forfeited their rights though retaining their identities as states; as being in a suspended status under national "grasp of war" supervision for some indefinite time. The seceded states, Lincoln stated, "are out of their practical proper relation with the Union; and . . . the sole object of the government . . . is to again get them into proper practical relation." Restating Lincoln's views in January, 1866, Ohio Congressman Samuel Shellabarger rejected theories of state suicide or territorialization. A consensus appeared to exist in 1865 on Capitol Hill that the nation did have a duty in the South, one defined by the Constitution's command to the nation to "guarantee to every State in this Union a Republican form of government."[1]

Therefore questions of defining the status of the southern states, though capable in 1865 of ruffling theoreticians' feathers, seemed unlikely to strain relationships between the branches of the national government. "Adequacy," "grasp of war," and "forfeited rights" constitutionalism applied to the South after Appomattox as before. Charles Francis Adams saw "the Executive, the Legislature, Judiciary, and Army . . . working together in one harmonious whole like the strands of a cable. It is a pleasant vision."

The new President, Andrew Johnson, appeared at first to share it. In harmony with the pragmatic views on Reconstruction of many Republicans, he kept the Army policing the South, reviving local governments, and reinitiating civil and criminal courts.[2] The government's success in crushing the rebellion "filled the air with the spirit of union," wrote Octavius Brooks Frothingham; it was time that "divisions should cease." James Russell Lowell worried "a little

[1]A variant form of this chapter is in Harold M. Hyman, *Lincoln's Reconstruction: Neither Failure of Vision Nor Vision of Failure* (Third Annual R. Gerald McMurtry Lecture: Fort Wayne, 1980); see also Roy P. Basler (ed.), *Collected Works of Abraham Lincoln* (New Brunswick, 1953), VIII, 399–405 at 403; Samuel Shellabarger in *Congressional Globe*, 39 Cong., 1 sess. (Jan. 8, 1866), pp. 142ff; and see Texas *v.* White, 7 Wall. (74 U.S.) 700 at 725, 727 (1869).

[2]W. C. Ford (ed.), *A Cycle of Adams Letters 1861–1865* (Boston, 1920) II, 206; John Codman Hurd, "Theories of Reconstruction," *American Law Review*, I (1867), 237–264.

about reconstruction, but am inclined to think that matters will very much settle themselves." How? By evidence from the South's states, once they functioned again, that they would behave properly.

The visible sign of decent behavior would be, initially, ratification by those states of the pending Thirteenth Amendment. "My idea," wrote a Radical Republican confidant of West Virginia's governor, "is that once we can insure ratification of the Abolition Amendment . . . we can safely give the South rope and let them arrange and discuss their internal and municipal policies almost without . . . hindrance."[3]

Some Republicans, recalling the 1864 Wade-Davis debates and other criticisms of Lincoln's Reconstruction experiments since 1862, asserted that little safety was likely for the nation's soldiers, white Unionists, or blacks in the southern states if those states enforced presurrender laws and customs. Better guarantees were needed on this point of state laws and customs than the Thirteenth Amendment, if considered only as an abolition amendment, provided. What guarantees? At least those emphasized in the Wade-Davis bill and in Lincoln's April 11, 1865, suggestions, Republican radicals asserted. All the ex-Confederate states, out of their proper relationship with the Union because of their own acts since 1861, should grant political rights (the vote) to Unionists and Negroes. But, if the vote was an unreal aspiration, then an expanded catalog of civil rights (such as Lincoln's idea of the states providing public education to black children) was appropriate. At the same time the southern states should not harass Unionists or soldiers or permit unpunished harassments. Instead, states must protect them against assaults. Let Reconstruction advance slowly until such proofs of state responsibility existed, Republicans counseled, because the states, once again in the Union, would no longer be responsible to the national government.[4]

Charles Sumner, among other advanced Radicals, in addition to

[3]Rev. O. B. Frothingham, *Recollections and Impressions, 1822–1890* (New York, 1890), p. 155; Lowell to C. E. Norton in C. E. Norton (ed.), *The Complete Writings of James Russell Lowell* (Cambridge, 1904) XV, 100; R. Curry (ed.), "A Note on the Motivations of Three Radical Republicans," *Journal of Negro History*, XLVII (1962), 273–277 at 277.
[4]Michael Les Benedict, "Preserving the Constitution: The Conservative Bases of Radical Reconstruction," *Journal of American History*, LXI (1974), 65–70.

propounding the notion of a subordinate status for the ex-rebel states, argued also that the Declaration of Independence and Bill of Rights set minimum standards for defining the rights that the nation should guarantee to all Americans. He saw the Thirteenth Amendment as including such an expanded catalog of rights.[5]

Sumner's perceptions were premature in 1865. Yet by early 1866, a heavy majority of the Congress had accepted some of his radical aspirations. Their support for a positive federal concern with civil rights mounted as evidence accumulated of southern white behavior that contradicted the anticipated effect of ratifications of the Thirteenth Amendment.

Unpunished attacks on the property and persons of freedmen, Unionists, and soldiers in the ex-Confederate states frustrated Adams's vision of harmony among the branches of national government. By early 1866 the Congress was preparing to protect by law the civil rights of national (and therefore of state) citizens in the states, and to improve statutory protections for southern Unionists and federal soldiers in the South. The Republicans' concern for ex-slaves, Unionists, and soldiers, plus the Republicans' instinct to look to recent history for guidance, and their propensity to employ adequacy and grasp-of-war constitutionalism after Lee's surrender, help explain why congressional action for the protection of the slaves received widespread support from a racist society.[6]

Congressional action was never prompted primarily (i.e., near-exclusively) on behalf of Negroes, although, to be sure, the condition of blacks in the laws of southern states became an essential measure of Reconstruction progress. Many northern whites were racist by modern measures. Yet northern states, during and after the war, sharply diminished the harshness of their race laws, thus sensitizing many people to the question of blacks' status before the laws of other states. Along with white equalitarians, northern Negroes were themselves demanding and winning improved civil rights from their states. These factors suggest that an understanding of events after Appomattox requires frequent references to wartime developments, that the Reconstruction problem of civil

[5]Thirteenth Amendment relationships to the Fourteenth are suggested below, ch. 11.

[6]Robert J. Kaczorowski, "Searching for the Intent of the Framers of the Fourteenth Amendment," *Connecticut Law Review*, V (1973), 3.

rights has a historical context out of which the need for national protection arose.[7]

This chapter accepts, therefore, the need to look backward from 1865, if we are to understand the growth of pro–civil rights sentiment among Republican Congressmen and constituents during the early years of Reconstruction. It recognizes the necessity of examining the rising standards of civil rights prevailing in some northern states during and after the war, as well as certain wartime policies including the 1862 ironclad test oath, the 1865 Freedmen's Bureau statute, and the measures concerned with the admissibility of Negroes' testimony in courts. In short, we must view the issue of civil rights as did Lincoln's contemporaries.[8]

In their nineteenth-century sense, civil rights were primarily factors of a person's state and community. After 1865 civil rights were to be increasingly the nation's responses to state conduct—or misconduct, a policy which left civil rights initiatives in the hands of southern whites.

A century ago most Americans separated civil rights from civil liberties. Civil rights pertained to a free individual's legal status; to legal rights, remedies, and responsibilities. Although civil rights were commonly defined, especially by lawyers, as primarily economic, even so the full magnitude of life and labor were encompassed in that term. They included at a minimum the right to contract, as in labor, commerce, or marriage; to sue, be sued, and witness; to travel; to bequeath or inherit; to be licensed in a trade or profession where one's state or community required a license; and to enjoy protection by the state from private violence. State power did not, properly, either impel a free individual to encumber himself with any of these relationships or bar him from them once he met appropriate qualifications. Whether for marriage or for the practice of law, few formal, as distinguished from customary, qualifications existed. Self-reliant freeholders and entrepreneurs were able freely to choose among civil relationships. Free exchanges between individuals who were equal in rights and responsibilities

[7]Robert J. Kaczorowski, *American Historical Review,* LXXXVIII (1978), 811, reviewing Raoul Berger, *Government by Judiciary: The Transformation of the Fourteenth Amendment* (Cambridge, 1977).

[8]Patrick W. Riddleberger, *1866: The Critical Year Revisited* (Edwardsville, 1979), p. vi.

before the law for the commitments they made were the norm. States, counties, and cities facilitated individuals in the exercises of their civil rights, by providing police, courts, and licensing officials.

There were many civil rights. How many, no one knew, although lawyers tended to classify them neatly in terms of primarily economic, contract relationships. Free men entered into relationships they found attractive and ignored others that seemed uninviting. One simply practiced civil rights as a reflection of residence and of free status. Unlistable and dynamic, civil rights differed from one place to another. Communities, by ordinance or custom, forbade certain commodities or activities (liquor, Sabbath commerce), relationships (racially mixed marriages), or legal remedies (gambling debts). Accommodated by the theory of plenary state powers, local initiatives about civil rights were as limitless within states' constitutions, laws, or customs as majorities wished to make them. The local quality of civil rights helped to give the federal system its special flavor of diversity.[9]

In this federal union of dual (i.e., national and state) constitutions and laws, one's "national" civil rights had been relatively minor and few in number compared to the endless quantity and fundamental quality of the civil relationships the states affected. This power of states to limit civil rights began seriously to be a factor in national politics, as distinguished from private lawsuits, as 1865 progressed. Few useful remedies existed in the federal courts for private interests that declared themselves to be adversely affected by state action or nonaction. Popularly elected and locally selected, state judges and juries rarely opposed majority will or community fears.

Up until 1865, there had been little occasion for the courts to protect individuals' civil rights against the federal government, much less against state or private acts. In 1833 the United States Supreme Court had ruled unanimously that the federal Bill of Rights applied only to federal laws; the due process clause of the Fifth Amendment did not protect a Marylander from having his state expropriate his property without compensation. A dozen years later the Court discerned no First Amendment protection against Louisiana's regulation of church services. "Some of the then un-

[9]Belz, *Emancipation and Equal Rights: Politics and Constitutionalism in the Civil War Era* (New York, 1978), p. xiii.

hampered State powers are startling today," wrote Arthur Sutherland, of the decades when only the first twelve Amendments existed.[10]

Of evils deriving from "unhampered State powers," slavery was
preeminent. Slave states relegated all Negroes to varying unfree
statuses, defective in both civil rights and civil liberties. Many northern states, especially those bordering the slaveholding states, had
kept their relatively small number of Negro residents in second-
class status with respect to civil rights. But conditions for all blacks
in the free states were always less onerous than for even free
Negroes in slave states. And by 1865, most northern states had
made, or were making, strides toward greater equality in civil
rights.[11]

But concerns about civil rights, even in their Reconstruction context, were never wholly race-centered: they included wide and growing attention to the condition of white Unionists and bluecoats.
Northerners, especially Republicans, were accustomed to blending
these commitments. "Original" Republicans had focused in their
first national platform, in 1856, on free labor, free soil, and free
men, not on one alone. That trinity involved perceptions about civil
rights for whites as well as blacks (although it is clear that many
Republicans also hoped the "free soil" would be lily-white as to
residents). In 1863 Republican backers of the Habeas Corpus law
attended to soldiers' interests by providing for removals of prosecutions against national officers from state to federal courts when
prejudice existed; in 1865, the Freedmen's Bureau law and the
Thirteenth Amendment enhanced respectively the interests of ex-
slaves and white Unionists.

The right Americans—white Americans, at least—enjoyed the
opportunity to enter into almost limitless civil relationships, and to
gain or lose from these involvements was considered a precious
right. This right underlay what Republicans meant by free labor.

[10]Arthur E. Sutherland, *Constitutionalism in America* (New York, 1965), p. 382; Barron *v.* Baltimore, 7 Pet. 243 (1833); Permoli *v.* First Municipality of New Orleans,
3 How. 589 (1845).

[11]See, *passim*, Leon Litwack, *North of Slavery: The Negro in the Free States, 1790–1860*
(Chicago, 1961); Richard Curry (ed.), *Radicalism, Racism, and Party Realignment: The
Border States During Reconstruction* (Baltimore, 1969); James C. Mohr (ed.), *Radical
Republicans in the North: State Politics During Reconstruction* (Baltimore, 1976).

Slavery diminished that quality, both for affected blacks and for whites. Secession and rebellion were defenses of slavery. An interest by the nation in the quality of free labor in the states as a civil right made sense to increasing numbers of northerners as 1865 progressed.

But the national government had no experience in sustaining civil rights within states. Even the wartime state Reconstructions to which the Civil War drove the nation did not regularly or intensively involve it in civil rights. Veteran abolitionist Elizur Wright, writing in mid-1865, warned that "there is little use and much waste of power in working a State government by Federal machinery." Former slave Frederick Douglass agreed. He envisioned a "let-alone" Reconstruction after Appomattox in which the nation need do nothing about civil rights because, he fondly believed, the states (and the numerous communities) would no longer inhibit blacks from doing whatever was lawful locally. Douglass included among such rights access for Negroes to the ballot, public entertainment, public schools, and franchised transit facilities, plus protection in all private rights, as "simply justice."[12]

Significant numbers of northerners assumed that Appomattox and the Thirteenth Amendment had already roughly won what Douglass and others sketched. Later, E. L. Godkin, editor of *The Nation*, was to argue that bluecoats at Appomattox killed the state sovereignty and slavery cancers that the too-timid Framers of 1787 had left to fester. Legal commentators concluded that the demise of state sovereignty and slavery automatically ushered into the South more equal civil rights such as those that prevailed in northern states. This assumption was in part a product of legal doctrines, evolving since Jackson's time, to the effect that no halfway houses existed between slave and free status. On this, Texas legal writer George W. Paschal noted that with slavery ". . . stricken out of the Constitution, we all, in some sort, stand upon a new era in regard to the protective principles and the guarantee of liberty it affords."[13]

[12]Wright in George L. Stearns (comp.), *The Equality of All Men Before the Law Claimed and Defended* (Boston, 1865), pp. 40–41; Douglass in Philip S. Foner (ed.), *The Life and Writings of Frederick Douglass* (New York, 1950–55), IV, 158–165.

[13]Edwin Lawrence Godkin, "Some Things Overlooked at the Centennial," *The Nation* (Sept. 2, 1887), p. 226; George W. Paschal, *The Constitution of the United States Defined and Carefully Annotated* (Washington, 1868), p. xvi.

The South's misuse of state powers respecting civil rights would delay the "new era" and escalate demands for a national interest in the civil rights of blacks, an interest based on the letter and spirit of the Thirteenth Amendment. This escalation in 1866 raised America's sights beyond the Thirteenth Amendment to laws augmenting the Freedmen's Bureau and creating the world's first civil rights statute. No one in 1865 could reasonably predict the creation of federal guarantees for the practice of civil rights, much less of political rights, in the Fourteenth and Fifteenth Amendments, supportive legislation, a military reconstruction, or the impeachment of a President.

Andrew Johnson failed to understand that American society had advanced and was still advancing on race and civil rights since 1861. Scholars no longer depict him as a premature New Dealer who fought "the interests" on behalf of the common man. Johnson, a growing literature suggests, lacked Lincoln's educability on race. He encouraged the frustration in the South of blacks' aspirations for civil equality. Johnson's constitutionalism stressed states' rights, yet his employments of national executive authority in the ex-Confederate states were extraordinary, perhaps unprecedented. Again and again in the months to follow, he was able to force Congress to consider primarily the restorations of southern states. Republicans had the far harder task of providing for state restorations that, at the same time, at least promised to maintain individuals' rights.[14]

Johnson, a former Democrat, lacked the manifold party connections to Congress and to a nationwide constituency that Lincoln enjoyed. American history offered scant guidance to an accidental President save to avoid party upsets of the sorts John Tyler had created. Johnson expected that the Republican–War Democratic "Union party" coalition he headed would give him its 1868 nomination no matter how he tried to reshape it. He proceeded to alienate himself from the Republican party professionals and from their broad-based constituency that had grown up everywhere except in the slave states.

On May 9, 1865, Johnson, in a proclamation based on the war

[14]Cf. Michael Les Benedict, *A Compromise of Principle: Congressional Republicans and Reconstruction, 1863–1869* (New York, 1974), pp. 126–133; James E. Sefton, *Andrew Johnson and the Uses of Constitutional Power* (Boston, 1980), ch. 7.

power, recognized the Lincoln state governments in Arkansas, Louisiana, Tennessee, and Virginia. Three weeks later (May 29), relying on the Constitution's guarantee clause, he proclaimed, first, amnesty to the great mass of ex-Confederates who would swear future loyalty to the Union, excepting prominent rebels who could petition for executive pardon. By a second May 29 order Johnson established procedures for North Carolina's reconstruction, which became a model for other states. He chose this state because no Union government had been set up there during the war, thus avoiding the dilemma Lincoln faced with the Wade-Davis bill. For each state, Johnson named a provisional governor, of authority and responsibility like Lincoln's wartime military governors, the position Johnson had held in Tennessee from 1862 to 1864. Reasons for the change in the governors' title are still obscure. Whatever the title, the appointed governors had to depend for initial and ongoing support upon the United States Army (no longer the "Union" Army), at least until the processes of state restoration ensured each governor an adequate base of constituents. Johnson ignored any question of Senate approval for these appointees, aiming, it appears, to have the states reconstructed before the Thirty-ninth Congress, elected (except for one-third of the Senate) as he was, in November, 1864, would convene in December, 1865. The governors, in turn, initiated in each state elections for delegates to the constitutional conventions the President's proclamations required, conventions which were to renounce slavery. Then, by terms of the new constitutions, the provisional governors set elections in motion for slates of officials ranging from governors to county, town, and village officers. The President ordered the Army to aid each step in this process, thereby escalating its role from police to policy functions. Every one of the elected and appointed officials and voters was white. A substantial proportion were ex-rebels, and, presumably, Johnson amnestied or pardoned all of them. Pardon-brokering became a new Washington growth industry.[15]

This was the most spectacular exhibition of unilateral national executive authority in American history. The reconstructions of thirteen states transcended any independent action by Lincoln ex-

[15]James D. Richardson (ed.), *A Compilation of the Messages and Papers of the Presidents, 1789–1897* (New York, 1901), VI, 310–314.

cept Emancipation and, perhaps, the blockade. Lincoln, announc-
ing his reconstruction program as a sketch, not a blueprint, at a time
when Union hopes were flagging, was bidding for the best he could
hope for at that moment. With respect to both state restorations and
emancipations, Lincoln had admitted freely the tentative, reversible
nature of unilateral wartime executive action. He anticipated correctly that his December, 1863, proclamation would be a central
issue in the November, 1864, election, then less than a year away.
Johnson, proclaiming his reconstruction policy after the Confederate surrender, though basing the policy on the war power, would
not face voters until November, 1868, more than three years off. In
the meantime he was making the presidency imperial.[16]

A few constitutional experts criticized the fact that the President
required the reconstructing states to ratify the Thirteenth Amendment. Other experts, countering, noted that all states entering the
Union agreed to abide by amendments approved by three-fourths
of the total number. The Johnson provisional states, excepting
Florida and Texas where Reconstruction proceeded slowly, did ratify the Thirteenth Amendment, though reluctantly, with spokesmen
expressing special distaste for the enforcement clause. On Johnson's behalf, Secretary of State Seward both pressured recalcitrant
provisional governors with threats of indefinite military rule if ratification failed and calmed southerners by asserting that the enforcement clause restricted Congress to enforcing only a prohibition on
formal slavery, a dubious interpretation. On December 15, 1865, he
proclaimed the Amendment to be in effect.

Were the southern states truly states for purposes of ratifying not
only the Thirteenth Amendment, but, as events transpired, two
other Amendments as well? James G. Randall concluded that such
questions were "idle speculation." Ratification "was a mandate to
the National Government, not an act of that government." The
southern states ratified in number beyond that needed to reach the
Constitution's requirement that three-fourths of the states approve
an amendment. Additional states ratified subsequently to end all
doubts as to the Amendment's validity.[17] But in 1865, those doubts

[16]Cf. Sefton, *Johnson*, pref., chs. 8–9; Albert Castel, *The Presidency of Andrew Johnson*
(Lawrence, 1979), intro., chs. 1–2.
[17]James G. Randall, *Constitutional Problems Under Lincoln* (rev. ed., Urbana, 1951),
pp. 399, 404.

existed and enhanced concerns about the President's seemingly unlimited authority.

Lincoln had also greatly expanded executive initiatives. But he did so by means of familiar political arts, with great effectiveness. Lincoln determinedly avoided divisive confrontations with his party's congressional or state leadership. The Wade-Davis clash is vivid because it was so exceptional. Lincoln courted Congressmen with commissions and contracts for constituents. He matched executive policies that touched public sensitivities—Emancipation, the use of black soldiers, Reconstruction, conscription—to congressional rhythms. Accepting responsibility for initiating these and for other controversial policies, Lincoln insulated a fair number of his party's Congressmen from the consequences of such policies. Then, if adequate public support of a policy such as Emancipation or the enlistment of black soldiers emerged, Congress safely ratified it, if only by appropriate legislation.

Lincoln's maneuvers with Congress won him substantial discretion in areas of war emergency and foreign affairs that, initially at least, required no statutes. He acknowledged his responsibility to execute laws. Politics, to Lincoln, lubricated separation-of-power and check-and-balance frictions rather than blocked them. He came to wield great power and influence on Capitol Hill because he tied the presidency to party operations both there and in the home districts of favored Congressmen. Lincoln, never ignoring the state bases of the federal system, effectively employed the carrots-and-sticks of patronage. As Lincoln's views escalated on race and Reconstruction, he managed to impose them on the relevant federal bureaucracy, especially the Army.

Andrew Johnson could not distribute war contracts or shift draft quotas. Johnson's primary patronage arena was one region—the South. In superficial terms, Johnson inherited an office little altered from the one Buchanan bequeathed to Lincoln save in its potentialities for the executive to initiate, not implement, large public policies. From building transcontinental railroads to reconstructing states, the governmental habit of the time favored little direct national participation beyond initiation of a policy and having Congress authorize the revenue to start its operation.[18]

    [18]Morton Keller, *Affairs of State: Public Life in Late Nineteenth Century America* (Cambridge, Mass., 1979), ch. 3.

Unlike Congress or the Supreme Court, the presidency remained unmodernized. Once the Union Army was demobilized and the draft ended, the nation's executive apparatuses were little changed from prewar times. The nation casually disbanded its only public administrators, except for the Treasury's specialists, who were experienced in executing national policies within states. Several new federal bureaus such as the Department of Agriculture were modest, small-budget operations. Cabinet officers' duties after Appomattox were, save for those of the War Secretary concerning Reconstruction, and the Treasury Secretary concerning the public debt, substantially what they had been before the Civil War.

Of homestead, tariff, banking, and tax laws, all designed to outlast the outbreak of peace, only the last two required substantially enlarged permanent staffs. These were all but invisible federal presences, performing largely traditional work. The Post Office was most visible, with a branch in each of thousands of communities, and was also wholly traditional in its operations.

The nation's law officers were not experienced administrators; the Attorney General, not a cabinet member,[19] was a part-time public official who retained private practice. Most federal departments and bureaus retained their own legal counsel, so that the Attorney General's influence rarely ran across the legal bureaucracy or even vertically through the Justice Department. Until 1861 the administrative superintendence of inferior national law officers of the Justice Department was not part of the Attorney General's duties, and Edward Bates, who held the office under Lincoln for most of the war, was never a vigorous administrator. The Attorney General had only two assistants in Washington. His office staff of eight clerks in 1865 nominally oversaw seventy-eight judges and ninety-three district attorneys, marshals, bailiffs, and court clerks. Since 1861 the nation's legal work had increased sharply at a time when Attorneys General and district attorneys changed frequently. Consistency in federal justice procedures was often thin or lacking entirely. The 1863 Habeas Corpus Act seemed unlikely to affect the Justice Department's work load after Appomattox.

The decentralized quality of federal justice affected few Americans prior to the war. Federal attorneys prosecuted only a thin catalog of relatively traditional national crimes (counterfeiting, pi-

---

[19]He became a cabinet officer in 1870.

racy, admiralty felonies, obstructions of federal justice, bribery, and perjury). Special federal counsels dealt with civil litigation involving national interests in Spanish or Mexican land claims in California. With the war, federal legal work expanded substantially. Confiscation proceedings, to take one example, necessarily involved the nation's lawyers.[20] But the new President was soon to suspend, then halt, confiscation proceedings permanently.

Johnson, like Lincoln, resorted to the only appropriate federal agency, the Army, to police the South. But as we shall see, the Army, by the terms of the 1865 Freedmen's Bureau law, was also responsible for enforcing civil rights. Army administration, like that of the Justice Department, resisted uniformity. But career officers possessed a corporate identity drawn from their West Point experiences, something that federal attorneys never developed. Now professional officers again ran the Army. Their instinct was to respect each President, but always to look to and to court the Congress, especially the committeemen who determined the Army's composition, assignments, promotions, and budgets. Presidents, all save Lincoln single-termers since Jackson, came and went, a fact underscored by Lincoln's assassination. Congress was eternal. Its invigorated committees, especially on appropriations, military affairs, and the Conduct of the War, had deeply impressed career officers. Civilian control over the military involves the question, which civilian? That question became mixed with others on Reconstruction and civil rights because of laws on these matters and the President's policies in the South.

Johnson had almost free rein from April through November, 1865, with respect to the South. National authority there was complete, although the President later obfuscated that fact. In September, 1863, Johnson was quoted as saying, "The ever-changing condition and wants of the people require ... improvement ... of [i.e., by] the Government."[21] But by midsummer of 1865 it was to be clear that the changed condition and wants of black or Unionist southerners, and of soldiers on duty in that region by his orders, did not inspire the President to align the government in their favor. In

[20]Paul P. Van Riper and Keith A. Sunderland, "The Northern Civil Service, 1861–1865," *Civil War History,* XI (1965), 357.
[21]Boston *Commonwealth,* Sept. 4, 1863.

effect, he refused to advance beyond Lincoln's 1863 Reconstruction position. Johnson did not, as Lincoln had done on April 11, 1865, publicly recommend that Unionists or blacks hold office or vote, although he pleaded secretly with the provisional governors to let a few Unionists and even blacks do both. But he did not insist, and no provisional governors responded affirmatively to the President's confidential, flaccid plea.

An early, easy acquiescence by southern states in more decent formal patterns of biracial coexistence, in accepting returning Unionists, and in cooperating with army personnel could have been a symbolic resolution of the war of the sort that most northerners expected. The visible proof of the resolution would have been roughly equal civil rights. Token black suffrage would have been a bonus. Examples were available in the Wade-Davis bill and in the improvements in civil and criminal laws in the new constitutions and statutes of some northern states. Lincoln had publicly held up Louisiana as a model reconstructed state whose constitution, laws, political practices, and standards of civil rights were democratized. Instead, Johnson set lesser stipulations, with sharply different effects, and then he refused publicly to alter his stand.

Although intense public interest in his policies manifested itself all through 1865, Johnson forbore from calling Congress into special session. Johnson had been a Senator. He knew that once the Thirty-ninth Congress convened in regular session in early December, 1865, its members would attend to southern matters.

Far more than the presidency, the Congress re-formed itself during the war and was unlikely to regress. By 1865, members of the Thirty-eighth and the Thirty-ninth Congresses were self-consciously proud of their representative nature and augmented efficiency. Congress more effectively divided legislative labor, controlled and accelerated the flow of bills, and oversaw the military and civilian executive bureaucracy. An invigorated and improved committee system proved to be Congress's major reform instrument, and its rise presaged a decline in the importance of floor debates. There were to be no more dramatic scenes on the House and Senate floors such as those attending the 1850 "compromise" legislation. Congress moved such business into committee rooms.

Few prewar committees were permanent or powerful. Congressmen avoided committee service, especially as chairmen. Prewar joint committees were primarily ceremonial and always temporary. Congress conducted its business in closed party caucuses and/or open floor operations. Either way, public input was minimal and politicians' responsibility usually diffused. Such conditions served admirably the long-tenured southern delegates.

Wartime Congressmen made committee assignments desirable and chairmanships prizes to be sought. Committees investigated war contractors' frauds, military operations, Confederate atrocities, and emancipation's results; nonwar committees concentrated on appropriations, homesteads, railroads, revenue, and banks.

At the same time, the House speaker, and to a lesser degree, the Senate president, made themselves more effective controllers of legislative traffic than was true before the war. Committees permitted a more effectual division of labor; the speaker or the Senate president was frequently able to move bills from committees onto the floor or to keep them off. These improvements, added to the more amiable relationships enjoyed by Congress as a body with the White House under Lincoln, paid off. An impressive growth occurred in information gathered, in legislation enacted, in confirmations of presidential appointments and commissions, in divisions of patronage, and in a greater sensitivity of the legislative process to public sentiment.[22]

A wartime illustration emerges from attention paid to the office of the House clerk. This seemingly innocuous staff official had the duty of officially listing states' delegates on his roster. In 1863, Democrats plotted with incumbent Clerk Emerson Etheridge to exploit anti-Emancipation Proclamation sentiment. Etheridge was to omit prominent Republicans from the roster. Lincoln sniffed out the plot. He suggested to Indiana Congressman Schuyler Colfax that if Etheridge persisted in the conspiracy, soldiers would carry the clerk out of the House "on a [manure] chip." Learning of Lincoln's awareness, the plotters abandoned the scheme. More sensitive now to the clerk's potential, Republicans placed Edward McPherson, a Pennsylvania disciple of Thaddeus Stevens, in the office.[23] In the summer and autumn of 1865, Republican members

[22]Joseph Cooper, "Strengthening the Congress: An Organizational Analysis," *Harvard Journal on Legislation*, XII (Apr., 1975), 338.

[23]Herman Belz, "The Etheridge Conspiracy of 1863," *Journal of Southern History*, XXXVI (1970), 549–567.

of the Thirty-ninth Congress, through conference and correspondence, determined to conduct a holding action concerning predictable demands for admission by southern delegations. Their entrances would have meant the formal acceptances of their states to full status in the Union, an end of the nation's jurisdiction over their internal affairs, and, as an ironic bonus for rebelling, a substantial increase in House representation now that the three-fifths clause of the Constitution was obsolete and Negroes counted for full persons.

Congress possessed the right, precious in all parliamentary bodies, to control admissions to its membership. Beyond this traditional right, House and Senate had established a rule that every member had to swear to his past loyalty according to the formula in the 1862 ironclad oath law. The southern delegates of December, 1865, included the Confederacy's former vice-president and two C.S.A. generals. They and other southern delegates of lesser Confederate rank had received the President's pardon.[24] Yet, conscious of the Wade-Davis definition of ineligibles for office as including persons of high rank in the Confederacy, Johnson had cautioned state lawmakers and nominating conventioners to choose congressional delegates able to swear to the ironclad test oath. But they disregarded his advice.

Prepared, Republicans in House and Senate avoided a direct confrontation with the President over his pardoning power while refusing to admit the southern delegations. Employing, first, the House clerk's duty to assemble the roster, and then the parliamentary privilege of themselves determining the qualifications of members, both Houses referred the question of the southern state delegations' admissibility to a new joint standing committee on the restoration of the ex-rebel states (soon known as the Joint Committee on Reconstruction).

A fateful pattern was already set. If a national institution possessed traditional constitutional authority over a subject at issue, and was politically alert and ready to take a stand, as with the exclusion of the southern delegates, the South lost a round. But when the nation stepped into novel functional arenas such as civil rights, the white South kept high cards. Yet, despite successive

[24]Richardson, *Messages and Papers*, VI, 358; see also ex parte Garland, 4 Wall. 333 (1867).

disappointments, northern majorities continued to expect that southerners would obey the Thirteenth Amendment and supportive laws. Republicans, as if mesmerized by the dream of law and order, resorted reluctantly to coercion even when evidence of blatant violations and overt defiances accumulated. Southern whites in thousands of communities (not merely in a dozen state capitals) could, by disobedience, test the limits of northerners' patience and willingness to enforce new standards of national justice. A kind of guerrilla warfare was to develop in the interstices of federalism. The United States fought, when it chose to fight, with law, order, and politics. Southern whites responded with evasions and, increasingly, with violence. If patient and fierce, guerrillas, especially those living in a federal system, have great advantages, described by then Attorney General Robert Kennedy a century later. "The hardest problems of all in [national] law enforcement," Kennedy said, "are those involving a conflict of [federal] law and local custom."

Kennedy's concerns speak across the century to "Second Reconstruction" civil rights activists of the 1960s. In both the 1860s and 1960s the nation perceived a need to sustain its officials who were trying to protect individuals' civil rights against adverse state action or inaction. The problem was most acute in the numerous small, isolated, rural communities where federal power never reached effectively. Community resistance to civil equality required, in the 1860s and 1870s, techniques for federal intervention not yet conceived.[25]

As soon as the Thirty-ninth Congress convened on December 6, 1865, its Republican majority established the famous Joint Committee on Reconstruction. Composed of nine Representatives and six Senators, carefully brokered to represent a variety of interests, regions, and approaches to race, its membership was never Radical-dominated. The Committee, as W. R. Brock noted, became a kind of "congressional cabinet." In the absence of effective presidential

[25]Quotation in Arthur M. Schlesinger, *Robert Kennedy and His Times* (Boston, 1978), pp. 294, and see 304–305; Lee Hyman Gudel and Henry J. Escher, "Community Resistance to School Desegregation: Enjoining the Undefinable Class," *University of Chicago Law Review*, LIV (1977), 111–167. Section 2 of the Fourteenth Amendment provided another federal weapon for use against a state: the diminution of its delegation in the House. It has never been employed.

leadership, the Committee helped to bridge the dangerous gap that began in 1865, between executive actions, party programs, and legislation. No Star Chamber, the Committee's Republican members, including the Radicals, still aimed at harmony with the President, if possible. William P. Fessenden of Maine, James W. Grimes of Iowa, Ira Harris of New York, Jacob Howard of Michigan, and George Williams of Oregon were Republican Senators; Reverdy Johnson of Maryland was a Democrat (and perhaps the most learned and effective constitutionalist in Congress). House Republicans of the Committee were Thaddeus Stevens of Pennsylvania, John A. Bingham of Ohio, Henry Blow of Missouri, George Boutwell of Massachusetts, Roscoe Conkling of New York, Justin Morrill of Vermont, and Elihu Washburne of Illinois; Democrats were Henry Grider of Kentucky and Andrew Rogers of New Jersey (the last a constitutional and racial reactionary). Of the Republicans, Boutwell, Conkling, Howard, Morrill, Stevens, Washburne, and Williams were Radicals; the rest, moderates.[26]

High on the list of the Committee's concerns were two federal statutes. On the face of things, this priority should have directed the President toward policies in the southern states different from those he chose to follow. The statutes were the ironclad test oath law (1862) and the Freedmen's Bureau Law (1865). In addition, the Committee concerned itself especially with the southern states' constitutional clauses and statutes known as the Black Codes, as well as with the behavior of public officials and private persons to freedmen, Unionists, and soldiers. Out of the Committee's review came inspiration and justification for a federal statute to protect civil rights.

The President failed to see either the ironclad oath or Bureau laws as limitations on his initiatives with respect to the southern states, or on his pardoning power. Johnson flagrantly violated both laws in order to hasten state restorations. Notwithstanding the 1862 law's requirement of an oath of past as well as future loyalty from every federal civil and military official before salaries were paid, Johnson ordered the Secretary of the Treasury to pay out of surplus

---

[26]William Brock, *An American Crisis: Congress and Reconstruction, 1865–1867* (New York, 1963), pp. 255–256; Benedict, *A Compromise of Principle*, pp. 140–145.

War Department funds the provisional governors and numerous inferior state officials, few of whom could swear to their past loyalty.[27]

These transgressions of the oath law increased dramatically as the result of Johnson's decision to develop his own party organization in the South, not necessarily aligned with the Republican party nationally. He left virtually all determination of state residents' political and civil status in the hands of southern whites, most of whom were recent rebels he had amnestied or pardoned. This was the constituency he had discerned as the one he wished to favor with a monopoly not only of state and local offices but also of federal appointments. Johnson rebuilt the southern Democracy.

Almost every one of the many thousands of federal offices in the South was vacant. Johnson enjoyed the greatest federal patronage opportunity of any President in terms of the numbers of jobs he could fill. Vacant positions connecting Washington to the many layers of state political organizations included federal judges, commissioners, attorneys, marshals, and court clerks; plus the tens of thousands of postmasters and tax collectors. Commonly, such persons served both the local party and the party in power in Washington. If the general Republican aspiration of organizing their party in the South out of Unionists and some blacks was to be realized, adequate sharing of positions, federal contracts, public advertising, and other benefits that flowed from the President's patronage was essential. Because Johnson encouraged pardoned ex-rebels to dominate both federal and state offices in the South, the former in defiance of the oath law, Republican locals generally failed to organize. Where they did come together, they were commonly weak. State and federal officials in the South owed Johnson gratitude, but that gratitude never extended to obedience.

Johnson exercised the distributive function of party head. He exacted far too small a price, however, in terms of imposing upon his new southern constituency a requirement for preventing or punishing hostile actions against blacks, white Unionists, and soldiers. Johnson's confidential appeals to southern governors to prevent

[27]The confiscation laws, though theoretically applicable to all participants in the rebellion, affected relatively few persons. The government had to initiate prosecutions in every instance. In any event, Johnson halted most confiscation proceedings by the end of 1865; see below, fn. 30.

such actions reflected not his opposition to national interventions but a lack of will to intervene on behalf of groups he did not favor. Johnson, six months after becoming President, had let the spoils control the victor.[28] His unilateral actions left him vulnerable to criticism from disappointed Republican "pros," from Negroes, from Freedmen's Bureau officials, and from nonpartisan observers of events.

The second federal statute that should have altered the President's course, the Freedmen's Bureau Act, was especially pertinent to the raised northern standards for civil rights. The Bureau law was shaped by the coalition of private benevolent associations that entered into various auxiliary relationships with the national government, especially the Army, during the war. This coalition celebrated, in March, 1865, the statute creating a Bureau of Freedmen, Refugees, and Abandoned Land in the War Department. Despite its martial, permanent sound, the Freedmen's Bureau was a temporary civil-military hybrid, whose leaders were, on the one hand, believers in racial equality and, on the other, ardent apostles of laissez-faire. The Bureau was to aid white refugees as well as Negroes, a duty insisted on by Republican Congressmen to avoid Democrats' charges that the Bureau would discriminate in favor of blacks.

The law conferred upon the Bureau "control of all subjects relating to refugees and freedmen in the rebel States." Congress provided few other particulars. The President was to appoint a commissioner and ten assistants, with the Senate's consent. The assistant commissioners would supervise Bureau work in the states, appointing agents as needed for community operations. Congress appropriated virtually no funds for agents' salaries or expenses. Contributions were expected, and were received, from church and Negro welfare groups, and the War Department was to supply redundant Army officers to serve as supervisors and agents, as well as surplus military supplies. A Reconstruction involving one-sixth of all Americans was to be won on the basis of almost no government budget, and a lifetime for the Bureau, set in the 1865 law, of one year after hostilities ceased. These were Herculean tasks. They would have weighed heavily upon a President wholeheartedly committed to

[28]Richard L. McCormick, "The Party Period and Public Policy: An Exploratory Hypothesis," *Journal of American History*, XLVI (1979), 279–298.

their successful realization and upon an adequate and trained staff sufficiently funded for the work. Success would have required also the continuing good will of officials down to the lowliest justice of the peace, magistrate, constable, and sheriff.[29]

Lincoln had chosen career General Oliver O. Howard as Bureau commissioner. He assumed office May 12, 1865, one month after Johnson became President. Howard's staff learned almost at once that in the southern states the Bureau's first responsibility was to afford freedmen legal protection not only against discriminatory community customs, but also against the new state constitutions and laws (the Black Codes), and against discriminatory nonenforcements of state criminal laws when whites committed unpunished criminal acts against blacks, Unionists, and soldiers.

Expectations had been raised that the Bureau would have, as a highest priority, the task of redistributing to white and black Unionists the lands taken from rebels under the Confiscation Acts. Quickly puncturing these hopes, President Johnson informed federal attorneys that he wanted few if any new confiscation proceedings begun; as noted, he ordered a halt to prosecutions already under way when he took office, and he pardoned thousands of former rebels. For these reasons, Freedmen's Bureau agents felt impelled to seek, not a basic alteration of southern society by means of democratized land ownership, but relatively limited improvements in the legal relationships of individuals.[30]

Bureau agents tried, largely unsuccessfully, to obtain legal protection in state courts for their charges in disputes about labor contracts between black workers and white employers, and in instances of physical assaults against blacks that local or state peace officers refused to punish. The Bureau felt impelled to afford the sufferers more decent legal remedies and created "bureau courts" —like justice of the peace or magistrate courts—as an alternative to defective community courts.[31] Bureau courts were to set the law in

[29]The most conservative Democrats (New York's John Chanler, as example) suggested that Congress make the Bureau permanent, since Negroes could never be self-sufficient; *Congressional Globe*, 39 Cong., 1 sess., app. (Feb. 3, 1866), 85–86.

[30]LaWanda Cox, "The Promise of Land for the Freedmen," *Mississippi Valley Historical Review*, XLV (1958), 413–440.

[31]Donald G. Nieman, *To Set the Law in Motion: The Freedman's Bureau and the Legal Rights of Blacks, 1865–1868* (New York, 1979), intro.

motion, to create enough familiarity and ease with the experience of equality in law to make southern whites willing to continue the practice after retirement of the federal presence.

What was decent practice? Even Bureau officers with legal training such as General Wager Swayne in Alabama, though insisting that the Negro's legal status in his state required first attention, were uncertain whether Negroes were state citizens, much less national citizens, or if either status brought in a federal presence in the form of some national court, civil or military, when state tribunals were racially inequitable. The adequacy of civilian justice became a new topic for Army officers assigned to the Freedmen's Bureau. That subject grew in interest also for Army regimental officers on "police" assignment in the South. Like many Bureau agents, they would face damage suits and even some felony indictments in state courts for acts done under orders. Unable to obtain fair justice in state courts for uniformed defendants, Army units established "provost" courts for their personnel, akin to the humble Bureau courts in jurisdiction. The Army also created ad hoc military commissions to try civilian violators of martial law and, as always, punished soldiers' violations of military law in court-martial proceedings.

The Bureau and Army courts were reluctant responses to inadequate, prejudiced civilian law and justice. Whether on "police" assignment in the South by executive orders or on Bureau duty as stipulated by statute, federal officers were enlarging the definition of civil rights both for themselves and for Negroes, to include noneconomic relations. Preeminent among these relations were the even-handedness of local police and the fairness of civilian courts.[32]

Like the war power in 1861, the power of local police (not "police power") had been largely ignored by legal writers. Police institutions had grown in diverse ways in the federal system. All local policing existed under explicitly or implicitly delegated state power. State and local judges provided law, order, and justice for most Americans. The most common police presence consisted of county sheriffs and town constables; the supportive judicial structure was the town magistrate or the rural justice of the peace, whose tribunals

[32]Gen. O. O. Howard to Stanton, Dec. 1, 1866, reviewing 1865–86 operations, in Letterpress Copies of Letters Sent, Freedmen's Bureau Commissioner's Office, II RG 106, No. 794, National Archives.

were not courts of record and who dealt primarily with minor offenses and claims.[33]

By mid-1865, Army provost courts and Bureau courts in the South had replaced or paralleled the lowest-level civil courts, but not everywhere or for protracted periods of time. Provost courts quickly faded out of the picture. Bureau courts dealt with minor breaches of the peace where local justice processes broke down or were otherwise unacceptable. Like magistrates or justices of the peace, Bureau judges were rarely law-trained and frequently fell into absurd errors. Thus, circumstances conspired to tie questions about equal civil rights and justice (as required by the Freedmen's Bureau statute) to the law requiring all lawyers in federal courts to swear to the ironclad oath.

Most civilian lawyers in the state courts and in the Army-Bureau tribunals had received the President's pardon for wartime support of the Confederacy. Generally abler than the government's counsel, these lawyers, in addition to becoming rich, as one Tennessean complained to the President, ". . . ingratiate themselves with members of the [military] court and gradually draw them under the influence of the governing class—It seems to me just and politic for the War Department to apply the [oath] law of the last Congress to the Military Courts."[34] But Johnson was disinclined to remedy the situation, leaving the Secretary of War helpless to define the Bureau courts as federal courts where the oath law must apply.

Such unanticipated developments, plus tenacious racism even among some Bureau officers, tended to lead to judgments in Bureau courts favoring whites, especially in labor contract suits and other economic relationships. Perhaps to redress this imbalance, the Bureau headquarters in Washington took on a full-time solicitor. Unsalaried at first and later skimpily paid, the position never had a distinguished, vigorous incumbent. The Bureau did not reach across executive departments to obtain legal professional services from the small corps of federal lawyers.[35]

[33]Samuel Walker, *Popular Justice: A History of American Criminal Justice* (New York, 1980), chs. 1–5.
[34]A. Lovering to Johnson, Apr. 24, 1865, #2951, Johnson Papers, Library of Congress.
[35]Howard C. Westwood, "Getting Justice for the Freedman," *Howard Law Review,* XVI (1971), 492–531; Nieman, *To Set the Law in Motion,* chs. 1–3.

Every new southern state constitution and revised laws accommodated, if grudgingly, in its Black Code to the fact that slavery was
illegal. The Codes accomplished several purposes: (1) to specify the
legal rights basic to the condition of freed blacks; (2) to supply a
special criminal code for Negroes; and (3) to provide both protection and control for freedmen. Beginning with Mississippi's in October, 1865, the Black Codes were published nationwide. Many northerners, including Republican rank-and-file in Congress, saw in the
Codes thinly disguised efforts to reenact the substance of slavery,
including race control and labor discipline, while retaining the
Democratic party's domination that had brought on secession.

Most white southerners insisted that emancipation of itself did
not create a civil status for freedmen equal to that which whites
enjoyed. The Black Codes, therefore, acknowledged the Negroes'
free status but provided blacks only severely truncated forms of
freedom. On the one hand, the southern state constitution-writers
and legislators specified that Negroes should enjoy these incidents
of free status: the right to buy, sell, own, and bequeath real and
personal property; the right to make contracts including valid marriages to other blacks and to enjoy a legally recognized parent-child
relationship; the right to locomotion and personal liberty; the right
to sue and be sued, and to testify in court in cases in which blacks
were a party.

On the other hand, the Black Codes provided detailed lists of civil
disabilities by re-creating the race-control features of the slave
codes. They defined racial status; forbade blacks from pursuing
certain occupations or professions (e.g., skilled artisans, merchants,
physicians, preaching without a license); forebade owning firearms
or other weapons; controlled the movement of blacks by systems of
passes; required proof of residence; prohibited the congregation of
groups of blacks; restricted blacks from residing in certain areas;
and specified an etiquette of deference to whites, as, for example,
by prohibiting blacks from directing insulting words at whites. The
Codes forbade racial intermarriage and provided the death penalty
for blacks raping white women, while omitting special provisions for
whites raping black women. They excluded blacks from jury duty,
public office, and voting. Some Codes required racial segregation
in public transportation. Most Codes authorized whipping and the
pillory as punishment for freedmen's offenses.

Different states' Codes salvaged labor-discipline elements of slave law by various master-and-servant statutes, vagrancy and pauper provisions, apprenticeship regulations, and elaborate labor contract statutes, especially those pertaining to farm labor. Other provisions permitted magistrates to hire out offenders unable to pay fines.[36]

Some northern states enacted attenuated counterparts of the southern Black Codes in the same period, usually by prohibiting the ingress of blacks into the state, imposing Jim Crow in public facilities, or prohibiting blacks from voting. The southern Codes, however, profoundly offended the northern ideal of equality before the law because of their overt, comprehensive racial discriminations extending to almost every area of civil and criminal conduct.

In effect, the Black Codes made all Negroes free but not equal to whites in civil rights; made the ex-slaves roughly equivalent to the free Negroes of slave times without elevating even the Negroes who had not been slaves to a status of equality with whites. The Black Codes created a class of Americans excluded by law because of race and color from the capacity to protect itself in courts equally with whites through testimony, to be fully responsible for marketplace decisions, or to live without fear of prejudiced application of criminal justice. The Codes afforded Negroes status as persons in certain civil relationships such as marriage (to another Negro), litigating and witnessing (again, respecting other Negroes), and labor commitments (but prohibitions existed in the Codes against Negroes testifying against whites, who, of course, were the employer class). The notorious vagrancy and apprentice clauses commonly placed unemployed and minor blacks whose parents lacked funds under white employers' control, and permitted employers to exercise penal authority. Persons, including whites, who "enticed" contracted black labor to change jobs were themselves subject to prosecution by the state. Pass laws, reminiscent of slave days, limited blacks' mobility. The Codes encouraged leasing of prison labor to private contractors, restricted Negro assemblies, harassed them with trespassing violations, and punished speechmaking or preach-

[36]Chief Justice Salmon P. Chase, on circuit, held a typical Maryland apprenticeship statute unconstitutional under the Thirteenth Amendment (in re Turner, 24 Fed. Cas. 337, 14, 247, (C.C.N.D. Md., 1867), but the practical enforcement of labor discipline was taken over by the Freedmen's Bureau.

ing without a license or other permission. Blacks were unrepresented on juries, in peacekeeping agencies, or in militias. All rights
and remedies, in short, were unevenly distributed by law (to say
nothing of the formidable hand of custom) and enforced by pardoned whites.[37]

A good many northerners were fast losing their patience with
southern whites who were trying to make the transition from a slave
society, based on a legal regime of status, to a free, capitalist society
based on will and contract. The southern states' overt subordination of their black residents sparked a move on the part of concerned white Americans toward a search for equality in state justice
as a civil right protected by the nation. By 1866 a majority of northerners were determined to have the Black Codes repealed and to
force the former slave states to create new structures of racial equality.[38] Bureau head Howard, after reviewing the escalation in his own
perceptions about civil rights triggered by the white South's ada-
mant stand on race, concluded that "Efforts have been made [in the
South] to render their [Negroes'] citizenship [i.e., free status] a
mere abstraction recognized technically, but utterly inoperative to
secure them the exercise of the cardinal right of a freeman or citizen." Continuing, Howard noted that the Black Codes defied the
essence of the Thirteenth Amendment, which, to him, was that all
Americans were now both free and equal under their states' laws.
Instead, the southern states treated blacks as aliens and imposed
numerous "civil and legal disabilities." To Howard and to an unknowable but influential number of northern whites, it was outrageous that the Black Codes made not only the black who left his
plantation a criminal, but also criminalized the actions of the white
would-be employer who, seeking a free market in labor, "enticed"
the Negro away.[39]

This sense of outrage helped to feed, and was fed by, a rising

---

[37]William Cohen, "Negro Involuntary Servitude in the South," *Journal of Southern History*, XLII (1976), 31–60.

[38]Later Redeemer and Conservative state legislatures reenacted the Jim Crow provisions and dusted off the labor contract statutes to provide the statutory component of the twilight zone of semifreedom that characterized the legal status of south-
ern blacks through the First World War.

[39]Howard to Stanton, Dec. 1, 1866, Letterpress Copies of Letters Sent, Freedmen's Bureau Commissioner's Office, II, no. 794, RG 105, National Archives.

sensitivity nationwide, especially among lawyers, to revelations about the low quality of criminal justice. By the end of 1865, many northern lawyers were outspoken critics of the Black Codes. This disappointed professional reaction to the Codes reflected the hopes of persons who had expected that the "new" southern states would show the rest of the nation the way toward higher standards of ethical practice in criminal law. Instead those states institutionalized some of the worst aspects of contemporary professional practice by enshrining injustices, unfairnesses, and prejudices in constitutions and laws.[40]

At Johnson's request, Carl Schurz, a former Union general, had toured the South. Schurz reported to the President his conclusion that whites, by keeping blacks on the periphery of the rebuilt civil institutions, were looking toward a permanent race hierarchy with whites on top. The Black Codes' legal disabilities performed this basic service. Under the Codes blacks were no longer the slaves of individuals. Instead, Schurz reported, the ex-slaves, and former "free" Negroes, were now considered to be "the slaves of society, and all independent State legislation will share the tendency to make him [i.e., the black] such." The President found Schurz's observations unwelcome and ignored the report, while Schurz would become a leading Republican politician and exponent of federal civil rights laws.[41]

The war had led to Emancipation; the first nine months of peace were taking northerners somewhere beyond it, toward championship of a federal duty to define and enforce at least nominally equal civil rights for blacks. Probably the ascent would not have occurred so quickly had southern whites refrained from harassing Army and Bureau officers.

In the first post-Appomattox year, many hundreds of white southerners initiated suits in the southern state courts against Army and Freedmen's Bureau personnel. Defendants found to their dismay that state and local judges, police, lawyers, and juries were applying the civil and even the criminal sanctions of the Black Codes against

[40]See, generally, Walker, *Popular Justice*, ch. 5; Blake McKelvey, *American Prisons* (Chicago, 1936), ch. 1.

[41]Frederic Bancroft (ed.), *Speeches, Correspondence, and Political Papers of Carl Schurz* (New York, 1913), I, 303, 348.

them for interfering in Negroes' labor contracts. National officers and Negroes fared no better as plaintiffs when, in local and state courts, they sued whites who reneged on labor contracts, who assaulted blacks, or who harassed or obstructed Bureau personnel. State and local judges and peace officers refused to obey Bureau or provost court decisions. War Secretary Stanton, Generals Grant and Howard, and Bureau of Military Justice head Holt had not anticipated such actions from southern courts. At the same time, in northern state courts, many wartime damage suits against military men were still pending for alleged excesses committed under antidisloyalty, trade control, emancipation, and conscription statutes and executive orders. To defend accused soldiers, Lincoln had assigned the Attorney General, War Department Solicitor Whiting, the Bureau of Military Justice, or federal attorneys. Discretionary War Department funds covered costs and damages in instances of uniformed defendants pronounced guilty in state courts, but whose conduct appeared in the War Department not to merit blame. In preverdict situations the 1863 Habeas Corpus law allowed removals from state courts to federal courts, and Lincoln's forthrightness in authorizing removals comforted defendant officers.[42]

But under Johnson, changes occurred in the nation's officialdom. In part to cut expenditures but also to advance his Reconstruction views, Johnson sharply curtailed the operations of Holt's Bureau of Military Justice. Solicitor Whiting, bitter at the course of events, left government service. Confidence ebbed swiftly in the Army and Freedmen's Bureau about the readiness of federal attorneys to protect uniformed colleagues. Further unsettling matters, the new southern lawsuits rarely involved issues made familiar in wartime litigation. The latter involved a relatively small number of national statutes and executive orders. But the post-Appomattox suits derived instead from numerous, largely unfamiliar state and community laws, ordinances, and customs. Charges against federal officers, alleging enticements and other violations of labor contracts, criminal vagrancy, obstruction of justice, and illicit gatherings, though brought under some state or local law, were often vindictive harassments, defendants complained. They insisted also that persons who cheated and assaulted them commonly went unpunished

[42]Fry to Stanton, Jan. 6, 1866, HR 39A-F 13.7, National Archives.

as a result of race prejudice and antinational sentiment on the part of whole communities, including local and state peace officers, judges, and juries. It was tough enough to fight against injustices resulting from positive acts. But it was far more difficult for federal officers and Negroes to combat acts and nonacts by state and local officials that permitted crimes committed by private persons to flourish.

Both federal officers and Negroes wanted to stand on an equal footing in state and local courts with persons suing them or whom they wished to prosecute. Many harassed Negroes were Union Army veterans and were special targets of unpunished violence. Southern white Unionists returning home after wartime exiles and new white residents from Union states also fell afoul of legal and customary disabilities. They begged for federal intervention to achieve equality in state administration of state laws. President Johnson, however, proved to be unsympathetic. Increasingly bitter because of these unanticipated hazards and frustrations, General Manning Force, on duty in Mississippi as 1865 drew to a close, asked his historian-father, "How far are we bound in honor, to supervise the State laws, upon the subject of Freedmen, is a nice point." Continuing, Force noted that "the public expression here becomes continuously more hostile."[43]

What alternatives existed? Resume mass military operations? Impossible. Abandon all pretensions of a national interest? Equally distasteful. Maintain a façade of national interest, but, like the President, let white southerners carry on in whatever manner they chose? Increasingly difficult. In the summer of 1865, to cite one instance, Stanton learned that a Mississippi court, before whom a Confederate veteran pardoned by the President and since accused of the murder of a Negro was standing trial, refused to admit the testimony of the only witnesses to the assault, who happened to be black. Stanton, who had favored legislation to admit Negro testimony in all federal courts, now learned from Attorney General Edward Bates that no statute governed the admissibility of Negro testimony in military courts. Having failed to restrict legal practice in Army or

[43]Manning Force to Peter Force, Dec. 3, 1865, in Manning Force Private Journal, I, 231–232, University of Washington Library; Holt to Stanton, Policy Book, pp. 148–149, RG 110, National Archives; Holt to Gen. P. Sheridan, Apr. 28, 1866, Sheridan Papers, Box 1, Library of Congress.

Bureau courts to civilian lawyers who could swear to the ironclad oath, Stanton, in July, 1865, ordered a Freedmen's Bureau court in Mississippi to accept the blacks' testimony. Military courts were embraced by Congress's several statutes on the admission of Negro testimony in national tribunals of justice, he ruled. According to Francis Lieber, Stanton's decision earned the War Secretary "every citizen's warmest thanks."[44] At least it earned Stanton the gratitude of Grant and of Freedmen's Bureau officers in the South. Military officers began to look to the War Secretary, to Grant, and to the Congress for support in executing the responsibilities laid out in executive orders and statutes.[45]

The Army leadership determined to conduct a holding operation on the civil rights front until the Congress prepared firmer positions. In this context, with the Thirteenth Amendment just ratified (December, 1865), Grant, on January 12, 1866, issued General Order 3: "To protect loyal persons against improper civil suits and penalties in late rebellion States." General Order 3 fit neatly with the growing civil rights sensitivities of Republican Congressmen. It required commanders in the South who had not already done so to "issue and enforce orders protecting from prosecutions in the State or Municipal Courts of such States" all Army and Bureau officers for lawful acts done under orders. Grant also instructed subordinates to protect white Unionists against unjust state court suits for wartime acts committed against rebel forces or authority. With these categories of whites attended to, Grant further ordered that commanders were to protect "colored persons from prosecutions in any of said States [who are] charged with offenses for which white persons are not prosecuted or punished in the same manner and degree." Widening the relatively narrow coverage of the 1863 Habeas Corpus law's removal provisions in a manner to protect Negro and Unionist civilians as well as government officers, General Order 3, though a mere Army order, represented a substantial step

<hr>

[44]Bates to Hon. Benjamin G. Harris, July 2, 1864, Attorney General's Letterbooks B & C, RG 60, National Archives; Francis Lieber to Edwin Stanton, July 30, 1865, Stanton PP, Library of Congress.

[45]Harold M. Hyman, "Johnson, Stanton, and Grant: A Reconsideration of the Army's Role in the Events Leading to the Impeachment," *American Historical Review*, XLVI (Oct. 1960), 85–100.

forward toward the nationalization of civil rights.[46] Grant's order, reprinted in numerous newspapers, was an open signal from the war hero to the President that the nation was still bound in honor to protect certain Americans in the recent rebel states.

No one, including President Johnson, would openly attack or criticize Grant in early 1866. The President made no public reference to General Order 3. It prevailed, with implicit presidential assent, as policy in all the ex-rebel states.[47] Grant's order rested firmly upon the general Republican constitutional conviction that the southern states, though no longer actively in rebellion, were still in the nation's temporary "grasp of war."[48] That Johnson's orders had created those state governments provided additional support for the validity of federal intervention. Grant's order deserves attention, therefore, as an expression of Republican constitutionalism. Grant intended General Order No. 3 to be, like Congress's exclusion of state delegations from the South, a defensive act, not an assault. He aimed to keep southern matters marking time until Congress clarified the situation created by the President.

The Congress proceeded with hearings on a bill to expand the duration and duties of the Freedmen's Bureau, and on another bill to define and protect civil rights, plus a measure to create a Fourteenth Amendment. Not deterred, the President pushed ahead on an opposite path. On April 2, 1866, he proclaimed that the rebellion was entirely suppressed and the southern states fully restored. That same month, the Supreme Court issued its *Milligan* ruling[49] while withholding its full opinion until the succeeding January. Thereupon Johnson ordered a halt to Army and Freedmen's Bureau trials of civilians in the South (although the Court, in *Milligan,* did not touch the South at all).

In July, a defiant Grant issued General Order 44, authorizing Army and Bureau officers in the South to arrest and hold for trial in military courts persons accused of having violated state civil or

[46]U.S. Army, *General Orders, 1866* (Washington, 1866), No. 3.
[47]Edward McPherson (comp.) *The Political History of the U.S.A. During the Period of Reconstruction* (New York, 1871), pp. 36–38, reprinted Sickles's responsive Jan. 17, 1866, order for South Carolina, q.v.
[48]Richard H. Dana, Jr., in R. H. Dana III (ed.), *Speeches in Stirring Times and Letters to a Son* (New York, 1910), pp. 243–259.
[49]See ch. 10.

criminal laws, against whom state authorities failed to act.[50]

It was unusual for nineteenth-century military leaders to take positions favoring race equality and civil rights, especially against a head of state who held opposing views. Viewing American society of 1865 as a whole, it appears that the Army was more closely tuned to civilian values about civil rights than the President. Supporting this conclusion are the backing constituents gave Republican Congressmen in 1866 for their dynamic positions on civil rights and race equality already embraced by the Army, and the growing enlargement of civil rights in northern states.

By 1865, most northern states had dropped their old Black Code clauses from constitutions and laws, not always enthusiastically. Race equalitarians tried, in several states, also to win the vote for Negroes, with limited success. But the improvements in blacks' civil rights were substantial. The process of winning the improvements educated a generation about the intimate connections that civil rights had to community customs as well as to state laws.

As an example of the workaday character of some of these reform efforts, one might cite the demonstration in 1865 by Philadelphia blacks against the daily injustices they suffered in racially segregated municipally franchised streetcars. When Negroes and sympathetic whites boycotted the cars, Pennsylvania, by statute, forbade racial discrimination. A black pamphleteer, explaining the concern of Philadelphia Negroes about obtaining equal treatment on streetcars, admitted that the question must appear petty after the grandeur of wartime issues. But he admonished readers to realize that equal access to public transportation affected Philadelphia black workers every day. Beyond this practical level, the pamphleteer argued that equal access to public conveyances ". . . is immediately connected with the great policy of equality before the [state and local] law, which is now offering itself [in the Thirteenth Amendment] to the national acceptance." He noted also that Congress, in 1863, had prohibited race discrimination in District of Columbia streetcars, and hoped that all states would follow the nation's example.[51]

[50]Richardson, *Messages and Papers*, VI, 429–432; 440; McPherson, *Reconstruction*, pp. 15–17.

[51][Anonymous], *Why Colored People in Philadelphia Are Excluded From Streetcars* (Philadelphia, 1866), p. 5 and *passim*.

The question of blacks' testimony, already familiar from fugitive-slave controversies, commanded attention as a civil rights issue for whites as well as blacks. Before the war, few states permitted any parties to civil suits to testify as a right, since, either as plaintiff or as defendant, such testimony was naturally self-interested. In criminal trials, prohibitions in federal and state Constitutions against self-incrimination kept defendants from testifying. Maine and Connecticut pioneered in permitting parties in civil suits to testify as a right. In 1864, Maine became the first state to permit defendants in criminal trials to testify in their own defense if they wished to do so.[52]

Maine's chief justice John Appleton, the legal profession's outspoken champion of the cause of extending the right to testify to all parties, raised the issue of admitting Negro testimony in the federal courts. In essays in the late 1850s and early 1860s, addressed to lawyers and legislators, Appleton, along with Senator Sumner and other knowledgeable Congressmen, insisted that in diversity suits, when, as the 1789 Judiciary Act required, the laws of forum states determined federal standards and procedures, the nation must see to it that all residents of the diverse states had opportunities to contribute to the court's knowledge of what went on. Exclusion of testimony by race, gender, or height would make "the attempt to do justice . . . almost hopeless." Color, he insisted, was no better reason for excluding witnesses and testimony. Informed testimony was not a racial matter. Judges and juries would be no less able to weigh a Negro's testimony than a white's, unless it be admitted that Negroes somehow could exert peculiar "seductive influence" upon jurists.[53]

Sumner reminded lawyer-Congressmen already impressed by Appleton that only custom excluded Negro testimony in federal courts. To be sure, in July, 1862, Congress reaffirmed the applicability of forum state laws and rules of decision in federal courts. Thereafter, Congress, Lincoln, and the legal profession became less willing to exclude the testimony of blacks. Respect for states' rights

[52]Privileges against self-incrimination in state constitutions were maintained by stipulations in derivative statutes in Massachusetts (1866), Connecticut (1867), and Iowa (1878) that no presumption existed against defendants who chose not to testify.

[53]Details and quoted phrases in Charles Hamlin, "John Appleton," in William Draper Lewis (ed.), *Great American Lawyers* (Philadelphia, 1980), p. 51; *American Law Register* (Aug. 1865), 577–581, and (Oct. 1866), 705–715.

must no longer be permitted to validate injustice to black Americans in federal trials, reformers insisted, especially in the light of Emancipation. Laws of April and July, 1862, on slavery in the District of Columbia, and of July, 1864, on appropriations, forbade, respectively, the district courts and then all federal courts from excluding any witness on racial grounds in civil cases, or because he was either a party to or had interest in the stakes at issue.[54] By this much, the federal courts, still accepting all other forum state laws in diversity cases, were, in effect, by 1865 reforming state court practices when diversity permitted federal court jurisdiction.

On occasion during the war in resurrected southern states, federal judges lectured juries on the need to follow the model of the free states and of Congress concerning Negro testimony. In one widely reported instance in late 1864, in occupied Virginia, United States district judge John Underwood insisted that the Union came into existence in order that diverse state citizens might, as national citizens, travel and carry on commerce without hazarding their persons or property. These were "privileges so fundamental and important to the security of domestic and personal peace, as to make their denial one of the greatest wrongs, next to slavery itself, which can be inflicted on a human being," Underwood asserted. The Constitution's Article IV stipulated: "The citizens of each State shall be entitled to all the privileges and immunities of citizens in the several States." Hamilton, in *Federalist* 80, had underscored the bedrock significance of Article IV: "It may be esteemed the basis of the Union." And Justice Bushrod Washington's 1823 enumeration of an American's national rights in *Corfield* v. *Coryell* (on which case, more later) had stressed trade and travel. Now Underwood agreed that no state law or court should diminish this superior national privilege and immunity.

However, Underwood concluded, as a federal judge he could only decide negatively the petition before him. It was for an injunction against the legal disability that the Negro petitioner, a black Massachusetts lawyer now a "carpetbagger," suffered in Virginia's courts as a witness because of his race. Underwood felt that no federal

[54]For statutes, see *Statutes at Large,* XII, 377, 539, 588; *ibid.,* XIII 362. Congress did not extend testimony privileges, as a right, to criminal cases, until 1878 (20 *ibid.,* 30–31).

judge had authority to enjoin state court processes, however defective they might be. The Constitution was deplorably incomplete in this matter of a nation-state court interaction involving protection for individuals' civil rights, an incompleteness newly discernible because of the growing interest in civil rights. Underwood prayed, futilely, that the forthcoming Virginia legislature

. . . may do itself and our old Commonwealth the honor of wiping the wicked enactment, excluding the testimony of colored men in any of our Courts, from our code of laws, burying it in the same grave with its barbarous twin brother, slavery, thus obviating the necessity of further action by this court [or by Congress].[55]

Obviously, perfect racial equality did not prevail in the North. But from 1861 through the end of the decade, improvement for northern Negroes struck the dominant note in such matters as the admissibility of blacks' testimony, tax equalization, access to public transportation, redistricting, and the vote. Setbacks and tenacious bigotries notwithstanding, in the free states Negroes and their sympathizers celebrated the "rising race." The weekly *Freedmen's Bulletin* calendared these hopeful state and community auguries. It noted approvingly that the nation, as well as the states, was opening doors long closed to blacks, as in the admission of Negro testimony, the selection of a Negro chaplain to preach in the House of Representatives, and the admission of a black lawyer to practice at the bar of the United States Supreme Court.

Critics mocked contradictions in the northern situation. Neatly summarized recently by J. R. Pole, these contradictions derived from the fact that "Americans wanted a society run on egalitarian principles without wanting a society of equals." Skeptics pointed especially to denials of Negro suffrage in some northern states. Champions of racial equality before state law responded with a reminder that relatively few Negroes lived in northern states; that civil rights were more immediately important, citing the Philadelphia streetcars boycott as an example. What the South's states did,

[55]Virginia blacks printed Underwood's statements along with the facts of the diversity litigation involved, in a pamphlet, addressing copies to Massachusetts newspapers and interested association officers and supplying Freedmen's Bureau headquarters with others. *Address from the Colored Citizens of Norfolk, Virginia, to the People of New Bedford, Massachusetts* (New Bedford, 1866), pp. 17–26.

or failed to do, about the civil rights of black residents affected millions of people representing almost half the southern population, and the free states had not been in rebellion. While conceding that the rejection of black voting in northern states was disappointing, it created no danger to the nation. The northern states' self-reconstructions had at least excised old Black Codes and substantially equalized civil rights practices.[56]

The escalation of demands about Negro rights in northern states, from access to streetcars in Philadelphia to voting, disturbed and wearied persons who had no fixed positions on racial equality. "It seems our fate never to get rid of the Negro question," Philadelphia lawyer-constitutionalist Sidney George Fisher complained. "No sooner have we abolished slavery than a party . . . growing in power, proposes Negro suffrage, so that the problem—What shall we do with the Negro?—seems to be as far from being settled as ever."[57]

Many northerners who, like Fisher, had loyally sustained Lincoln's exploitation of the idea of the "adequate" Constitution during the war and voted Republican then and after, shared his attitude toward the issue of racial equality. The war over; Fisher was swiftly losing interest in Negro questions. He disliked the continuing employment of war powers in the South once the fighting ended, primarily because they were novel and rasping. The war had been waged to preserve the Union of states. However repugnant as diminutions of civil rights, the Black Codes did express state self-determination on internal affairs. State police power was familiar doctrine to every lawyer trained, as Fisher was, before the war; it was a doctrine legitimized by Vermont Chief Justice Isaac Redfield, Lemuel Shaw, and Roger Taney. Unusual circumstances were necessary before Fisher was prepared to sustain national limitations on state power, especially over extended periods of time. The South would derive great advantages during the years ahead from such perceptions and priorities held by Fisher and many other northerners.

With Appomattox, those priorities were shifting sharply away from southern blacks. Even many old abolitionists lost interest in

[56]J. R. Pole, *The Pursuit of Equality in America* (Berkeley, 1978), p. 333; [Chicago], *Freedmen's Bulletin* (Mar., 1865), 89–90.

[57]Nicholas B. Wainwright (ed.), *A Philadelphia Perspective: The Diary of Sidney George Fisher Covering the Years 1834–1871* (Philadelphia, 1967), p. 499.

free labor questions, whether or not connected with racial quality. Others threw their energies and funds into drives for, or against, revised state constitutions, including reapportioned election and school districts, voters' qualifications, licenses for professionals, liquor prohibition or inhibition, required Bible reading in the schools, Sabbath closing for merchants, the reform of the criminal law, state aid to private enterprises such as railroads, and maximum hours of labor for public employees. Still other antislavery veterans concentrated on the Cretan revolt against the Turks, evangelical efforts in China, or their particular professional association's efforts to raise standards of practice.

While most northerners had not been abolitionists until the war linked the causes of Union and antislavery, the war had given that generation a heightened sensitivity to social evils. With Appomattox, veterans of wartime service, both civilian and military, discovered in their cities and states evils that they wished to attack, for, as Emerson had written, the war illuminated "every putrid spot" in American life. Associating in numerous causes, especially in large cities, such reformers as Dorman Eaton and Anthony Comstock obtained delegations of state power to apply against abusers of draft animals and purveyors of pornography, as well as numerous other "evils," according to their definition. Associated physicians in eastern and Gulf coastal cities applied Union Army techniques to fend off a threatened invasion of cholera in 1865–66; again, delegated state power gave effect to epidemiological understandings.[58]

These postwar reform emphases reflected also the success of several northern states in managing large-scale enterprises during the war. Looking to victory, Harvard law professor Emory Washburn's prediction that "the dominion of well administered law"[59] was at hand derived in part from this record. States, counties, and cities had sought to protect soldiers' morals through the issuance of antivice regulations, the inspiration for Anthony Comstock's postwar crusades. Some states (South as well as North) tried to

[58]Edward Waldo Emerson and Waldo Emerson Forbes (eds.), *Journals of Ralph Waldo Emerson with Annotations* (Boston, 1913), IX, 462; Morton Keller, "The Politics of State Constitutional Revision, 1820–1930" (Paper, Project 87 Conference on the Constitutional Convention as an Amending Device, 1979), pp. 10–17.

[59]Emory Washburn, "Reconstruction: The Duty of the Profession to the Times," *Monthly Law Reporter* (July, 1864), 27–28.

shield citizens' purses by price controls. Others ran industries, frequently employing convict labor themselves or leasing it to contractors. Professional associations—law, medical, pharmacological, teaching—lobbied successfully for state license requirements for practice. The common technique of each association was to make itself the state's administrator for licensing, though retaining a private character. State legislators commonly added some form of loyalty test to licensing requirements.

In varying legal relationships with the states, and sometimes also with the nation, remarkably effective associations of mixed public and private character had "organized" the war, in Allan Nevins's apt phrase, in ways unthinkable in 1860. State-based federalism had not prevented the effective conduct of a great war. It hardly seemed likely now to inhibit the conduct of peace. The nation's war power and the states' police powers not merely coexisted but complemented each other admirably. What was it not possible to achieve in this slaveless "new era"?

War-toughened realists apotheosized the Union as the necessary vehicle for all good social purposes while insisting on the essentiality of the states as the basis of that Union. Such persons saw no contradictions in a continued attachment to self-sufficient individualism even while they responded to paternalistic concerns for special classes and groups such as soldiers and freedmen.

By 1865 the war work that dramatized the existence of untapped state and community resources could now be transformed by alert entrepreneurs, social reformers, and, as in the South, racial bigots. Constitutional theory did not inquire into legislators' or constitution writers' motives when applying state power.[60]

All of this had helped to create the generalized optimism of the Appomattox year. State power was an essential element in ordered business growth and social stability. Normally, state power was not the nation's concern. Yet state power had led to secession and war. The sensitivities of many northerners had sharpened during the war to certain evils that state power sanctioned. Those sensitivities proved to be sharp enough to react to the Black Codes and to the attacks on Army and Bureau officers in the South as evils in them-

[60]T. D. Woolsey, "Nature and Sphere of Police Power," *Journal of Social Science,* II (1970), 97–114.

selves and as hazards to the nation. It is difficult to explain the readiness of the Thirty-ninth Congress to deal with civil rights, without acknowledging the enlarged perception of civil rights that had developed during the war.

Joined to this new sensitivity to civil rights was the perception that southern whites were incurring remarkably few penalties from their four-year-long experiment in rebellion and from their behavior during the preceding three decades that had so often unsettled politics. There was no federal policy of mass exilings, executions, or confiscations; no spate of treason trials (even Jefferson Davis was to escape such a prosecution). Instead, state reconstructions involved, at least potentially, enlarged electorates *if* white Unionists and blacks were permitted to participate in politics. But the Black Code states not only effectively disfranchised these potential new electorates but seriously diminished the civil rights of whole classes of their residents.

The Black Codes called back to the colors, as it were, many old abolitionists. They, like a majority of the Republican Congressmen of 1866, were ready-on-the-mark to respond to the Black Code assault because the Thirteenth Amendment, that supreme abolition achievement, possessed an elastic enforcement clause. We will suggest that the framers of the Thirteenth Amendment included the enforcement clause precisely in order to allow posterity to cope with an imprecise future. By 1865 that future had been pressing upon present realities at a much swifter pace than anticipated. At the least, however, an appropriate response by Congress to southern initiatives was possible in early 1866, unlike early 1861.

CHAPTER 10

A Reconstruction of Law and of Judicial Review, 1863-1867

I N July, 1864, Harvard Law School Professor Emory Washburn lectured the legal profession on both its opportunity and its duty in Reconstruction. The opportunity was for personal enrichment out of legal practice; the duty for lawyers was, essentially, to lead the nation in formulating and executing Reconstruction policies. If lawyers and judges failed in their responsibility to define and to contain public programs, then "mad or selfish politicians" would wield government power. The consequence must be continuing social and commercial unsettlement, Washburn warned; the chances for professional gain would disappear; the sacrifices of the war would be wasted.[1]

Profession-proud elitists, lawyers had been voluble about the need for society's most concerned and responsible elements— themselves—to lead their countrymen away from demagogic pitfalls.[2] By 1860, some legal spokesmen had conceived of government run largely by means of apolitical commissions, staffed by appointed experts, as a means of circumventing the excesses of elective democracy.[3] The nation's weakness in the secession winter, and law-

[1]Emory Washburn, "Reconstruction: The Duty of the [Legal] Profession to the Times," *Monthly Law Reporter* (July, 1864), 478.

[2][Anonymous], "The Legal Profession and General Culture," *American Law Record,* I (1872), 366–367.

[3]Emory Washburn, *Lecture Before the Members of the Harvard Law School, January 11, 1861* (Boston, 1861), pp. 17–18; Maxwell Bloomfield, *American Lawyers in a Changing Society, 1776–1876* (Cambridge, 1976), ch. 5.

yers' inability to direct events into pacific channels, had caused a depression of spirit among leading spokesmen of the profession. But although this depressed mood proved to be temporary, when Washburn spoke to the Harvard law students in 1864 his call to judges to lead in Reconstruction was far off the mark. Even the nation's highest law court, the United States Supreme Court, with a new Chief Justice, Salmon P. Chase, since late 1864, carried on work that to outsiders seemed to be of minor importance compared to that of the Congress and the President. The Court lacked commanding authority. Yet, by 1867, it was to shoulder its way into a far more equal share of federal governing than seemed possible only three years earlier. And by 1873, when Chase died, the Court was close to a full partnership among the federal branches and an alert if occasional monitor over certain kinds of state actions. Indeed, it ventured so aggressively in terms of extending its review functions between 1864 and 1873 as to justify G. Edward White's estimation that, under Chase, there was a "potential renaissance of Marshallian judging."[4]

How to account for the rise in the Court's position relative to the other branches of government, and to the states, since the *Dred Scott* decision? In what manner did the Civil War and Reconstruction encourage a reconstruction of law as well as of states and escalate the quality of justice as well as of politics? Why did the legal profession rise, like the Court, in public esteem and influence?

Undoubtedly, in 1857, in *Dred Scott,* the Court had grossly overstepped the limits of discretion in the use of its review power. But it appears that the resulting expressions of distaste about the Court were largely aimed at Taney and his *Dred Scott* majority associates rather than at the institution. The fact that, in *Merryman,* Taney stood alone among the justices in defiance of the President, and that he was in dissent in the *Prize* cases decision, apparently confirmed a widespread opinion that he, not the Court or the legal profession, was the problem.[5]

This renaissance of High Court prestige was particularly important to lawyers in the light of unsettlements and tensions that affected the profession. Secession itself, as noted, in its early phases,

[4]G. Edward White, *The American Judicial Tradition: Profiles of Leading American Judges* (New York, 1976), p. 86.
[5]*Ibid.,* pp. 82, 83; Don E. Fehrenbacher, *The Dred Scott Case: Its Significance in American Law and Politics* (New York, 1978), chs. 8, 20, 21.

had a profound impact upon many lawyers and judges. Whatever their politics, the onset of the Civil War found them in a mood of pessimism and even gloom. They looked backward to what they nostalgically transformed into a Jacksonian golden age when they believed that the profession had come close to eradicating basic obstacles to the smooth conduct of both law and politics.[6]

Then, during the war, lawyers harmonized what John Codman Hurd described as the "chaos of doctrines" concerning the nature of the war and the status of the seceded states. Harvard law professor Joel Parker, albeit a critic of the Lincoln administration, admitted that "the innumerable speeches, in Congress and out of Congress, within the last few years, . . . show with what diligence, if not with success, constitutional law has been recently studied." Parker thought his contemporaries had not "put the authors of the Federalist [Papers] to shame." But, he added with mild sarcasm, the wartime ". . . researches into the mysteries and rules of constitutional construction, . . . have at least shown that there may be expositions of the provisions of the Constitution of which Hamilton, Madison, and Jay never had any conception." Law professor William Duer, late president of Columbia College, one of the few institutions of higher learning in America with a law school, was to express his gratification at the increasing interest exhibited by law alumni in "the origin, structure, and principles of our political institutions." Columbia would no longer send forth its graduates better informed on the constitution of the ancient Roman Republic than on "the fundamental laws in their own country."[7]

The importance of the several legal and constitutional compendia and commentaries prepared by such lawyers-in-Union-service as Joseph Holt, Francis Lieber, and William Whiting, among others, helped to restore the self-esteem of the profession. So did the Lincoln administration's consistent respect for legal and constitutional processes. In Lincoln's as in Tocqueville's time, Americans

---

[6]David Dudley Field, *The Magnitude and Importance of Legal Science: An Address, at the Opening of the Law School of the University of Chicago, September 31, 1859* (New York, c. 1869), pp. 13–14; Grant Gilmore, *The Ages of American Law* (New Haven, 1971), p. 41.

[7]John Codman Hurd, *The Theory of Our National Existence as Shown by the Action of the Government of the United States Since 1861* (Boston, 1881), p. 41 n.; Joel Parker, *Constitutional Law: With Special Reference to the Present Condition of the United States* (Cambridge, 1862), pp. 9–10; William Alexander Duer, *A Course of Lectures on the Constitutional Jurisprudence of the United States: Delivered Annually in Columbia College* (New York, 1868), pp. 19–21.

delighted in trotting out legal authorities on almost any occasion and remained tied to the Constitution as to a civil religion. An English writer in America fell into argument with a Boston lady about Britain's stance toward the Confederacy. " 'But there's Grotius' I said, to an elderly female, who had quoted to me a half-dozen writers on international law, thinking thereby that I could trump her last card. 'I've looked into Grotius, too,' she said, 'and as far as I can see, &c. &c. &c.' So I had to fall back on the convictions to which instinct and common sense had brought me." Boston heard of the seizure of the British ship the *Trent* in 1861, and, reported Anthony Trollope, "Before twenty-four hours were over, every man and every woman in Boston was armed with precedents." Trollope thought it "pretty to hear the charming women of Boston, as they become learned in the law of nations. 'Wheaton is quite clear about it,' " one young woman told him.[8]

Not only did familiarity with legal and constitutional writers grow more widespread during the war; Americans expressed an increasing respect for law, lawyers, and judges. An English visitor in 1865 noted, "Whether it be constitutional, general, state, or only municipal, Law is nobly respected by the native American. The Judge of the Supreme Court is treated in Washington with a degree of respect unknown to lawyers in Europe. . . . The State Judges take the place in society held among us by the bishops. Even the village justice [of the peace] is always styled the Squire." Americans, he marveled, cling to written law "as to a rock in the midst of a storm."[9] Rather smugly, one New York legal commentator of 1865 estimated that there were no giants in the law: "We know at this day of no such names as Kent, Story, [or] Marshall, . . . either upon the Bench or at the Bar." Well enough, he continued; the increasing number of law books and journals would quickly fill the gap, in quantity at least. Meanwhile lawyers must consciously seek to retain the recent affection, or at least respect, the public exhibited toward them.[10]

[8]For Grotius, see review of Anthony Trollope's *North America* (London, 1862), in *Fraser's Magazine for Town and Country*, LXVI (1862), 250; for reference to Henry Wheaton, former U. S. Supreme Court Reporter and expert on international law, see Trollope, *North America*, I, 367–368.

[9]William H. Dixon, *New America* (London, 1867) II, 294–295.

[10]For the quote, see undated New York *Transcript* article, copied in Pittsburgh *Legal Journal* (Aug. 16, 1865), 45–46.

How to do this? By creatively adapting legal training and jurisprudence to the altering characteristics of the business world. The growing number of law schools must bear the lion's share of this work, the argument ran. The 1857 depression had created numerous bankruptcies; the war added confiscations and arbitrary arrests. Peace would usher in new entrepreneurial novelties. The corporation had long challenged lawyers, and the use of this business form was burgeoning. But its characteristics varied greatly from state to state. In agriculture and extractive industries, as in commerce and manufacturing, changes were accumulating. Americans lived under diverse local arrangements that federalism allowed, not only as between states, but between neighboring communities within a state. Traditionally, these local variances in laws were directly associated with agriculture, as in road, milldam, and water rights. As voters, farmers also affected legislation close to their basic concerns, including bankruptcy and usury policies, which also varied greatly from community to community and state to state. The result, Harry Scheiber has noted, was "astonishing variety" in statutes and in judge-made law as well. The Civil War was ending one basic variation: the laws of slavery. But other diversities were increasing.[11] New and improved technology such as the telegraph was altering contract law, wiping out time in negotiations, and introducing unknown participants, the sending and receiving operators. Contract law was in early stages of development, and lawyers and judges were anxious to guide its direction. Since the war started, businessmen were getting into a habit of shortening the duration of contracts out of uncertainty over the nation's stability. Were such changes, if authorized by state law or judicial decisions, in violation of the Constitution's prohibition against violations of contract under state authority? And would constitutional disagreement about contract violations, if that is what the new business mode was, be as disruptive after victory as slavery was before the war? Whole categories of new civil wrongs—torts—had become visible by 1865. They were coming increasingly before judges for settlement, as with many more of the novel issues arising in the 1860s, often without

---

[11]Harry N. Scheiber, "Federalism and Legal Process: Historical and Contemporary Analysis of the American System," *Law and Society Review*, XIV (1980), 663–722; Harold Woodman, "Post-Civil War Agriculture and the Law," *Agricultural History*, LIII (1979), 319–337.

statutes to guide or direct decisions. Law reformers considered mergers of law and equity as a means of freeing state judges to refer to independent legal authorities rather than to statute law.[12]

During the decades running from mid-century past the centennial, the legal profession sought both to order society and yet to serve the interests of an unprecedentedly mobile, creative, and achieving population. Preindustrial America was changing into an industrial, urban, and technology-mad society, noted law professor Washburn. With peace, lawsuits would multiply. Constitutional questions were more likely now than ever before to grow out of private lawsuits. Individuals' consciousness about their rights and remedies had grown mightily since the war started. Much wartime legislation affecting both personal and property rights, and amendments to the constitutions of the United States and of the states, were raising awareness in the profession about rights. Several important new legal treatises were in print, and more were in preparation, on the constitutional implications of legal changes.

In lawyers' self-imagery, they were trained to understand the law but to stand outside it in pleading their clients' causes or, as judges, in deciding the litigation's merits. Legal training was creating "so much of identity in the conclusions to which well-trained minds come upon any given question submitted to them, that there will be scattered all through the land a body of men who not only can and will think for themselves, but will make their own convictions tell upon the convictions of others," Washburn asserted.[13]

Nationwide, Washburn's major suggestions were well received. Optimism dominated the mood of many lawyers. The law could not only supplant politics but supplement the Constitution, and so allow the pacific settlement of even major public policy differences. The fact that during the war, the Supreme Court, as in the *Prize* cases, had taken hold of such differences suggested to Richard Venable, a later president of the American Bar Association, that judges should never permit their capacity to constrain, or even to refine,

---

[12]Henry W. Taft, *A Century and a Half at the New York Bar* (New York, 1938), pp. 144–164.

[13]Washburn, "Reconstruction," pp. 477–484; Joel Parker, *Revolution and Reconstruction: Two Lectures Delivered in the Law School of Harvard College, in January, 1865 and January, 1866* (New York, 1866), *passim.*

public policies, to be diminished.[14] Timothy Farrar perceived that the military victory enhanced the Constitution, because the Constitution was less separated from workaday legal relationships and was no longer venerated in the abstract. The Constitution had been "cautiously and intelligently accepted . . . during the late civil war," wrote Farrar: "The results of our marked experience should be noted and studied."[15]

One way lawyers "noted and studied" the Civil War experience was in the greatly increased number of case reports, legal treatises, and law periodicals issued since 1861. Such publications both eased and complicated the practitioner's life. As assets, the new literature helped to nourish a sense of professionalism. But the growing number of case reports, legal periodicals, and specialized treatises and commentaries were expensive, and they tended to divide the profession into factions, one of which indulged in the use of the latest aids, and another that eschewed them in favor of traditional modes of research and pleading. Codification helped further to widen this breach.

Isaac Arnold, a pioneer Chicago lawyer since 1834, noted of the 1860s that "almost an entirely new system of law has been developed, which has required the exercise of sound judgment, . . . profound study, and extensive research by our legal tribunals." He listed, as the most open, lucrative, and exciting fields for beginning lawyers, those involving municipal corporations, agency, torts, insurance, and eminent domain. "The genius of our institutions requires our courts to break the shackles . . . of the old feudal [common law] system and to apply the principles dictated by a sound common sense . . . and a progressive age," he wrote. This venerable prairie lawyer, like most legal writers of his time, was exhilarated rather than depressed by the law's increasing complexity.[16]

Opportunities for lawyers to profit were growing even as—or

[14]Richard M. Venable, "The Partition of Power Between the Federal and State Governments," American Bar Association Reports, VIII (1885), 1235–1239.

[15]Timothy Farrar, Manual of the Constitution (Boston, 1867), pp. viii–ix; Herman E. Von Holst, Constitutional and Political History of the United States (Chicago, 1876), I, 68, 75.

[16]Isaac Newton Arnold, Recollections of the Early Chicago and Illinois Bar (Chicago, 1882), pp. 38–40.

because—legal complexities multiplied. Clients were launching challenging ventures, as in the railroad and telegraph industries, and linking them to federal or state resources. Now that the southern opposition to internal improvements was removed, further dramatic, innovative relationships between entrepreneurs and government were likely.

So with social reforms. The war experience with mass armies educated physicians and "sanitarians" (public health specialists) about benefits for cities from improved water supplies, prevention of fires, and antiepidemiology. Associated schoolteachers, arguing that illiteracy encouraged secession and disloyalty, demanded more public schools for northern states and the introduction of tax-supported school systems in the South as a basic element of Reconstruction. In addition to litigations about contracts and tort liability, new water supply systems, trolley lines, and school buildings frequently involved communities in legal contests about taxing limits and uses of the state's delegated eminent domain power.[17]

Eminent domain power had become linked in America to the principle of compensation to the despoiled owner. But no agreement existed as to what constituted adequate compensation and whether lawmakers or judges should prescribe it. Furthermore, as of the 1860s, the accepted legal opinion was that only a taking involving formal alienation of title to a property justified compensation. Property not formally taken, though injured or even, in extreme instances, destroyed by eminent domain action, did not rate compensation.

As an example of injury and destruction, Chicago raised the grade level of the entire downtown section seven to fifteen feet, a heroic achievement, in order to decrease flooding. The stability of some buildings diminished; doors and windows were blocked or distorted; neighboring structures were damaged by the collapse of weakened structures. Courts disallowed claims of indirect damage, however. Was this Daniel Webster's 1848 warning in a brief before the Supreme Court come true, that if a state, exercising its eminent domain power, could take a company's franchise, any transient ma-

---

[17]Keller, *Affairs of State,* pp. 390–391; Harry N. Scheiber, "The Road to Munn: Eminent Domain and the Concept of Public Purpose in the State Courts," *Perspectives in American History,* V(1971), 327ff.

jority could be an "unlimited despotism"? The answer was suggested in 1866, when the Supreme Court sustained a state in an uncompensated taking.

But the tide was turning. In 1866, Illinois's supreme court gave hope to lawyers who were worried about the excessive permissiveness, as they saw matters, in existing eminent domain doctrine: ". . . the theory [the Illinois judges stated] that private rights are ever to be sacrificed to public convenience or necessity without full compensation, is fraught with danger, and should find no lodgment in American jurisprudence." Here was a firm stand against a tendency that some legal commentators discerned for legislators to bring about an egalitarian redistribution of wealth by using law politically. The legal profession became more unified in favor of compensation for all takings, including injuries to property. The profession's task was to recruit enough judges to their cause to oversway voting majorities.[18]

Advocates of aggressive Supreme Court interventions against unwise state policies had to be patient. In 1865, Chase joined with the majority of the justices in denying a request for an injunction. The plaintiff asserted that Pennsylvania's charter to a bridge construction company would injure him by diminishing the value of his wharf. Justice Noah Swayne concluded for the majority that the state could charter companies which exercised the state's eminent domain power, and that no injunction was to issue. The prospect of abuse of state power did not allow courts to limit its exercise. State citizens must protect themselves against their state: "they can unmake constitutions and laws; and from that tribunal there is no appeal," Swayne concluded.[19]

This reluctance on the part of judges to forestall prospective injury was also evidenced in litigations over private contracts. Forty years earlier, in *Ogden* v. *Saunders* (1827), the United States Supreme Court had stated a self-limiting rule when considering the Constitution's contract clause: that the clause applied only against past, not prospective, state action. English judges, less constrained, in the latter 1860s began, in small numbers, to issue injunctions in labor

[18]Joseph McCormack, "Legal Concepts in Cases of Eminent Domain," *Yale Law Journal,* XLI (1931), 421–461, esp. app. A.
[19]Gilman *v.* Philadelphia, 3 Wall. 713 at 730–731 (1865).

disputes. Twenty years were to pass before American judges, pressured by lawyers whose clients were worried by unions, dared to emulate British colleagues (who by then had abandoned the injunction remedy). But, as with eminent domain, the potentialities for social control and for aiding business by resort to the injunction and by a less restricted stand by the Supreme Court on remedies intrigued some among the American bench and bar.[20] Reconstruction policies reflected both the repugnance concerning anticipatory remedies and the tendency toward legal change. That change involved a stricter judicial scrutiny of personal rights, both civil and economic, while retaining a traditional deference toward public action.

Lawyers were attempting also to accommodate older professional methods, especially the writ system, to changing relationships. As an example, lawyers, until the 1850s, employed an ancient writ to sue in tort in instances when a client suffered a noncontract civil wrong at the hands of another person. By the 1850s, however, the frequency of such injuries, especially those suffered at the hands of strangers, as in locomotive explosions or in factory accidents, plus the trend among legal leaders to think in broad, conceptual terms associated with formalism, was leading the profession toward a theory and a practice of torts independent of writs. Glossators—i.e., commentators—on torts, usually lawyer-academics, produced the first American treatise on torts in 1859. In 1870, torts became a separate law school subject for the first time, and in 1874 the first torts textbook appeared.

Familiar contract, negligence, and criminal law modes had to be rethought in newer torts categories and procedures. The emergence of torts contributed to the idea of law and society as being in an evolutionary, organic phase of development. G. Edward White has noted that the tendency of the law in the 1850–80 decades was to derive monistic theories while applying them in fluid manner. What was permanent in natural laws was change. Order and unity, as in torts, were to emerge from productive, ordered changes.[21]

This belief in both order and change is one reason why legal

[20]Felix Frankfurter and Nathan Greene, *The Labor Injunction* (New York, 1930), p. 20.

[21]G. Edward White, "The Intellectual Origins of Torts in America," in White, *Patterns of American Legal Thought* (Indianapolis, 1978), pp. 163–191.

writers fretted over oscillations in state court judgments, as in the Pennsylvania draft cases. According to an increasingly popular view among lawyers, these oscillations were caused by the fact that almost all state judges were both poorly educated and dependent on the political parties that elected them.[22] Therefore federal judges, being appointed for life, must exhibit independence, be impartial arbiters of justice, and keep high the standards of the profession.

Lawyer-critics of professional standards justified these estimates by decrying signs of general deterioration. Commentators exploited prewar writings on legal ethics by David Hoffman and, more important, by George Sharswood. In 1865 Sharswood was a member of the Pennsylvania supreme court; in 1867 he was its chief justice. Back in 1854, he had published an *Essay in Legal Ethics*. This slim volume gained in readership during the Civil War, and, revised and enlarged, it was to be a major weapon in the hands of reform-oriented state bar associations.[23]

Law reformers linked the politicization of state judges to the rise in crime that appeared to be in sway. Violence and vigilantism, especially in the South, turned attention to criminal justice, including that revered institution, the jury. Lawyers, most of whom accepted accused felons as clients, knew that juries commonly expressed community prejudices. The Revolutionary heritage was that juries decided both facts and law. In 1835, the Supreme Court denied federal juries in criminal prosecutions a right to judge the law, but state juries still determined both facts and law. The conclusion seemed to be that uniformity and reliability in criminal law were impossible under existing arrangements. Unprofessional and unpredictable, state criminal justice was a source of shame to leaders of the bar.[24]

State attorneys, swamped by rising case loads and, like judges and

[22]Kermit Hall, "The Judiciary on Trial: State Constitutional Reform and the Rise of an Elected Judiciary" Organization of American Historians (paper, 1980), pp. 5–13.

[23]Walter B. Jones, "Canons of Legal Ethics: Their Genesis and History," *Notre Dame Lawyer*, VII (1932), 483.

[24]Lawrence Friedman, "The Development of American Criminal Law," in Joseph Hawes (ed.), *Law and Order in American History* (Port Washington, N.Y., 1979), pp. 8–9; Samuel Walker, *Popular Justice: A History of American Criminal Justice* (New York, 1980), pp. 111–112; Mark A. DeWolfe Howe, "Juries as Judges of Criminal Law," *Harvard Law Review*, LII (1939), 582–616.

juries, enmeshed in local politics, were also targets of the law reformers. Defendants' lawyers and states' attorneys were, increasingly, resorting to unprecedented maneuvers, later to be known as
plea bargains (i.e., exchanging a reduced charge for a guilty plea on
behalf of clients accused of crime). The fact that state judges accepted such deals offended purists.[25] Those lawyers who were also
members of voluntary associations concerned about prisons expressed growing dissatisfaction about scandalous conditions in
penal institutions. In part by reason of interest in soldiers and slaves
who received criminal sentences during the Civil War, long-
moribund prison-reform associations revived. In 1865, the results
of wartime investigations into prison conditions seemed to parallel
those about criminal trials: inconsistency, prejudice, and favoritism
prevailed.[26]

The "rough justice" in lower courts and the regrettable professional behavior of some lawyers inspired efforts toward organizing
practitioners into statewide bar associations to seek higher standards. The associations were intended to improve the bar's public
image and to help members master the avalanche of case reports
and treatises. Beginning in 1865, state after state chartered bar
associations. Each association, linking itself with state power, became the exclusive licensing agency for lawyers in its state. In effect,
the private bar associations became state agents without becoming
public officials. The associations generally opposed the old appren-
ticeships and supported increases in the length of formal legal education. They favored the joining of law schools to colleges and
universities. With respect to curriculum, association makeweights,
especially in the northeastern cities, stressed the newer categories:
corporation, insurance, and municipal law practice; torts, contract,
and criminal law.

Bar association leaders argued the plausibility of both legal and
general social improvements, in part from ideas then spreading
about applied social science. A Social Science Congress met in
Boston in October, 1865, presided over by Governor John Andrew
of Massachusetts, to hear, among other lecturers, Francis Lieber

[25]Albert W. Alschuler, "Plea Bargaining and Its History," *Columbia Law Review*,
LXXIX (1979), 1–43, and see Swang v. The State, 42 Tenn. (2 Cold.), 213–215
(1865).
[26]Walker, *Popular Justice*, pp. 83–84.

and Yale's president and law professor Theodore Woolsey. It established the American Association for the Advancement of Social Science, with sections devoted to education, health, trade, and jurisprudence. In years to come, AAASS locals, including lawyers and judges prominent in bar associations, were at the forefront of reforms in several states. These locals became identified especially with novel uses of delegated state power, as in the pioneering New York Society for the Prevention of Cruelty to Animals (1866) and the same state's Society for the Prevention of Cruelty to Children (1873). Some AAASS affiliates also perceived and institutionalized new uses for federal authority, as in Anthony Comstock's half-century-long role in banning pornography and contraceptives from the mails, and in Dorman B. Eaton's quarantine successes in the 1866 cholera epidemic. Applied social science seemed to have arrived in splendid shape to serve public law and to shape private and criminal law.[27]

In AAASS and bar association meetings, in legal periodicals, in law school classrooms, and in courtrooms, arguments proliferated about alterations that were affecting professional life in America. These discussions reflected, in addition to matters mentioned earlier, a shift that was occurring in ideas about the law and about the law's distrust of democracy and of many elected legal practitioners; the change from instrumentalism to formalism. Antecedents of the change long predated the Civil War; it was to continue long after Appomattox. As with all alterations in intellectual climate, this shift was uneven in pace and coverage. It was affected by the diverse nature of the law in a federal system and by the uncentralized character of legal education. The Civil War, roughly speaking, was an intersection for old and new ideological roads in the law.

Instrumentalism was the older path. Its source was in efforts by legal leaders, including Marshall, Kent, Shaw, and Taney, to replace eighteenth-century anticommercial legal doctrines with others that allowed more marketplace independence. Instrumentalists argued against applications of the law that were overly regulative. Instead, law was an instrument with which government could aid enterprise in nonregulatory ways, as in eminent domain proceedings, in mill-dam acts, and in road condemnation laws. The encouragement of

[27]*Round Table* [Boston] (Oct. 21, 1865), 105.

enterprise through state interventions such as the creation of easier bankruptcy and corporation procedures allowed diminished individual responsibilities for investors while permitting them to risk again. They could "contract out" of a bad situation. Adaptation of law to change, rather than obedience to fixed natural law principles, was the goal.

In public as in private law, instrumental ideology justified sporadic judicial interventions against undesirable marketplace intrusions by legislators, notwithstanding plenary police power doctrine.[28] Flexible, freewheeling, expedient, and adaptive, instrumentalism's advantages were similar to those of wartime "adequacy" constitutionalism. Combined adequacy-instrumental defenses of national and state powers were potent. The state-restoration emphasis in all war aims underscored the validity of police power interventions, for example. Nevertheless, antilegislature (i.e., antidemocratic) attitudes were increasing in the legal community, as in the distrust of state judges.

Long before the war, legal leaders had despaired over the antics of democracy and hoped to depoliticize the law. They had been sounding a retreat from concentration on results, as in instrumentalism, toward concern with the formal procedures that led to a result; thus, "formalism." Essentially, formalism was antilegislative, strongly favored judicial review, and advocated longer, more restrictive state constitutions. Formalists wished to police the processes of representation. Gaining momentum in the 1860s, formalist elements already present in the *Swift* doctrine were, in 1864, to expand greatly in the *Gelpcke* v. *Dubuque* decision, dealt with later in this chapter. Formalism, as an attitude about the law, had, ostensibly, universal truths rather than transitory legislation at its base. Judges of this persuasion tended to magnify their own role from will-less to oracular, to exclude questions of legislators' intent in deciding cases involving public law, and to wrest control from juries in criminal trials when questions of law wanted decision. Formalism enhanced the status of appellate judiciary, deified judge-made law as in equity, and applauded high judges' refusals to consult legislative documents when seeking lawmakers' intentions. A process was under way by 1865, as Edward Dumbauld later described, whereby

[28]Horwitz, *Transformation*, ch. 1.

". . . statutes are ordinarily regarded as isolated or sporadic encrustations upon the rational body of judge-made common law."[29]

Formalism appealed to bar associations–AAASS critics of state attorneys, judiciaries, and juries. The alternative to state courts was the federal, where appointed rather than elected judges reigned. It is a paradox that the growth in popular control of state judges should have helped to justify leaders of the bar in their belief that a great increase in the power of federal judges was essential. Only by accepting this paradox is it reasonable that the least representative courts should have turned their attention to judicial protections for civil liberties and rights. Such matters involved the question whether an official procedure or requirement substantially diminished individuals' rights, no matter what the government insisted were the intentions of the legislators and executives who created and administered the law or procedure in question. Appellate judges were ready, if unevenly, to raise this question by scrutinizing strictly, and substantively, the product of state lawmakers and even of state constitution writers, as well as, occasionally, of Congressmen or Presidents.[30]

By 1865, formalism was one current in the legal stream where permissive instrumentalism still flowed. The ratification of the Thirteenth Amendment lessened the abolitionist-instrumentalist community of interests. Legal leaders were eager to transform the abolitionist stress on the broad ethical values of human dignity into juridical defenses of individuals' (not racial groups') particular rights. The stress on natural laws and moral imperatives, long familiar in abolitionist constitutionalism, remained available both to instrumental spokesmen and to advocates of legal formalism. Formalism became a legal style for defenders of many kinds of rights. Judicial review of national and state laws became the occasional formalist defense against erring majorities.[31]

[29]Edward Dumbauld, "Legal Records in English and American Courts," *American Archivist*, XXXVI (1973), 30.
[30]Gerald Gunther, "In Search of Evolving Doctrine on a Changing Court: A Model for a Newer Equal Protection," *Harvard Law Review*, LXXXVII (1972), 1–48.
[31]William E. Nelson, "The Impact of the Antislavery Movement Upon Styles of Judicial Reasoning in Nineteenth Century America," *Harvard Law Review*, LXXXVII (1974), 513–566; Charles W. McCurdy, "Justice Field and the Jurisprudence of Government-Business Relations: Some Parameters of Laissez-Faire Constitutionalism, 1863–1897," *Journal of American History*, LVI (1975), 970–1005.

Formalist legal ideas did not dominate either federal or state appeal courts in 1865 when Chase assumed the chief justiceship, or in 1873, the year he died. With often-spectacular exceptions, appellate judges still felt impelled to sustain almost all public policies enacted by Congress and state legislators. Concepts of adequate national authority and of plenary state powers proved to be durable. During the same years, however, if only in exceptional court decisions, and, more commonly, in dissents and in legal treatises, the apostles of formalist restraints on majorities' acts disseminated their views.[32]

Their subsequent triumph was to occur in part because a new body of legal writings on states, cities, and individuals took form beginning in 1863 and became very important among lawyers and jurists relatively soon after Appomattox. The new literature differed from that produced by prewar abolitionists and by adequacy writers of 1861–63, who, reacting primarily to what the southern states did about slavery and secession, aimed at relatively broad audiences and at political action. Their essays tended to appear in popular periodicals and, when in book form, were handled by general publishers. By contrast, the authors of the new literature responded to events in northern cities and states as well as to those in the South; aimed to influence legislators and lawyers, especially judges and law teachers, rather than voters; published articles in technical law journals and turned to specialized law publishers to get their books into print.

Events of 1863 inspired men who were to be major legal writers to begin labors. In that year, terrible antidraft, anti-Negro riots occurred in major northern cities. Links appeared to exist between active disloyalty, alien (Roman Catholic) churches, and urban political parties (Democratic). Combined with the fiscal maneuverings of certain cities, maneuverings which spawned litigation about defaulted municipal bonds, the riots confirmed prejudices concerning the subversive effects of cities on traditional values, including those of the Constitution. The lesson of 1863 seemed to be that the law and the federal system were ill-equipped to restrain urban barbari-

---

[32]Harry N. Scheiber, "Instrumentalism and Property Rights: A Reconsideration of American 'Styles of Judicial Reasoning in the 19th Century,' " *Wisconsin Law Review* (1975), 1.

ans. County and state authorities, in too many instances, were either indifferent to their cities' behavior or joined in city excesses. For such reasons, legal spokesmen praised the Lincoln administration's military interventions against the urban rioters of 1863 and the Supreme Court's stern position against Dubuque (to be discussed below).

Because Dubuque and other cities defaulted on bond obligations, legal scholars, independently of each other, began research into the history of "municipal corporations." Like inquiries into the war powers since 1861, those into urban legal history were practical in their purposes. The investigators aimed to control cities' fiscal behavior. Legal scholars had overlooked the city's place in American constitutional arrangements. Instead, nation-state tensions had preoccupied the Jeffersons, Madisons, and Calhouns. "Lawyers in . . . commercial and industrial communities seldom find application for the principles of ethical and philosophical law which arise out of the relations of government," complained the prominent New Orleans attorney Louis Janin, "and their libraries are but scantily supplied with works upon these . . . unpractical branches of the law."[33]

The effect of such sparse attention to "unpractical branches of the law" were dismayingly evident by 1863, stated Yale law professor Theodore Woolsey. Repelled by the "democratic abstractions" so pervasive in the 1860s, Woolsey insisted that

safe liberty existed only within limited government: one which is articulated, one which by institutions of local self-government educates the whole people and moderates the force of [states' political] administrations, one which sets up certain well-defined limits against United States power, one which draws a broad line between the unorganized masses calling themselves the people formed into bodies joined "together and compacted" by constitutions and institutions.[34]

Iowa supreme court jurist John F. Dillon's *Law of Municipal Corporations* (1872), begun in 1863, would have greatly eased the tasks of the lawyers and jurists involved in issues such as those the Dubuque default spawned, issues that were central to the 1864 Supreme

[33]Janin to Francis Lieber, Jan. 16, 1871, Lieber Papers, Huntington Library.
[34]Theodore D. Woolsey, in preface to Francis Lieber, *On Civil Liberty and Self-Government* (Philadelphia, 1853; 3rd rev. ed., 1874), p. 10.

Court decision in *Gelpcke* v. *Dubuque,* had it been available a decade earlier. Dillon, Fairman wrote, "knew *everything* about municipal bonds." Later named a federal judge, Dillon spread the gospel of national judicial constraints on city bond policies when parent states failed adequately to control their urban offspring. Dillon's *Municipal Corporations,* the source of what quickly became known among lawyers as "Dillon's Rule," to the effect that cities were totally subject to their states, became a durable textbook in the growing number of law schools.[35]

So did another volume begun in 1863. In the 1850s New York lawyer John U. Taylor had published a slim treatise on landlord-tenant relationships. With the war, the city's tenant population soared. By 1863, landlords' associations won greater advantages over tenants, especially swifter eviction procedures (from three months to forty-eight hours!) from state and city lawmakers. That year, Taylor began revising his once-modest treatise. Imbued now with ideas about the universality of common law principles in landlord-tenant relationships, Taylor surveyed and contrasted relevant judicial decisions, as well as statutes, in half a dozen of the most urbanized states. Published in 1866, his now-substantial *Treatise on the American Law of Landlord and Tenant* became an essential source for both practicing lawyers and law academics.

Cities, in legal and constitutional theory, were creatures of their states. Researchers into urban legal subjects felt impelled also to inquire about general limits on state power. Except for the southern state secessions, the most blatant claim to limitless state power occurred in Illinois. In 1862, an Illinois constitutional convention declared that its product was immune from any review, including judicial. Chicago municipal judge John A. Jameson was outraged by the claim to "inherent powers amounting almost to absolute sovereignty." The downstate convention was allegedly dominated by wooly-headed farmers, Copperhead disloyalists, and antiproperty radicals. Learning that no useful scholarship existed on state constitutional conventions, Jameson resigned his judgeship and proceeded to create a legal history on the theme. Published in 1867, his *Treatise on Constitutional Conventions, Their History, Powers, and Modes of Proceeding,* according to former Attorney General James Speed,

[35]Fairman, *Reconstruction,* p. 923.

"taught and proved . . . that [state] constitutional conventions are normal to our institutions and that the powers of such conventions can be as well and accurately defined [i.e., restrained] as the powers of any department of any organized [i.e., level of] government—the book will be of great service."[36]

The most important of the postwar commentators to consider limitations on the states was Michigan judge and law professor Thomas McIntyre Cooley. Courts and judges were Cooley's first line of defense against popular majorities. In 1868, Cooley gave lawyers and jurists a potent weapon, his *Constitutional Limitations Which Rest Upon the Legislative Power of the States of the American Union.* It has long been supposed that Cooley was, rather simply, an economic conservative who compressed liberty from its older protean sense to economic activity. But alternative interpretations are supportable. In certain ways Cooley's views paralled those of the new Chief Justice, Salmon P. Chase. Both were products of Jacksonian America; both opposed slavery; both had come to believe that an individual possessed liberty so long as law did not constrain him in ways that it did not constrain others, while protecting him against unlawful injuries by others. The two men assumed that the federal government had no rightful permanent role in states, and that no authority existed for the nation to create coercive, permanent bureaucratic institutions even for purposes specified in the Constitution, except for national defense and maintaining the law. But Chase, tempered by his years of service as governor and administrator, accepted expedients and compromises such as the Freedmen's Bureau in order to make it possible for federal authority to protect individuals in states. Cooley, as abolitionist as Chase, never faced a need to institutionalize freedom. Instead, as judge and law professor, Cooley's concerns about states' wrongs were rarely reactions to events in the South.

Even so, Chase's "freedom national" ideas and Cooley's insistence that personal liberty was more than "grubbing and getting" without discrimination, were not far apart from each other. Later, other lawyers and judges joined Cooley's ideas set down in *Constitutional Limitations* to the Fourteenth Amendment's due process and

[36]Speed to Francis Lieber, Mar. 3, 1867, LI 3218, Lieber Papers, Huntington Library.

equal protection clauses. Cooley's book and the Fourteenth Amendment became defenses primarily of economic liberty (liberty of contact) against state action. But as Chase did, Cooley, in 1865 and later, considered liberty to be a value transcending economic relationships. Both saw liberty as a dynamic condition embracing numerous person-to-person and government-to-person relationships impossible for legislators to pin down in statutes.[37]

Cooley, born in 1824, rose from hardscrabble rural New York origins in a region famous for religious ferment and moral questings. Cooley's family and neighbors taught that individuals made decisions and were responsible for their consequences. Since slaves were forbidden both the right to make decisions and the responsibilities from their moral and contract choices, slavery was immoral. By 1848, the first year in which he could vote, Cooley was a Michigan organizer for the Free-Soil party, and he carried abolition politics into the new Republican organization. Meanwhile, he moved up in his profession. As Michigan chief judge and University of Michigan law professor, Cooley, like other legal writers of antislavery conviction, resorted to laws higher than statutes or constitutions. Ethical and moral convictions infused Cooley's interpretations of the rights and duties of individuals and government to each other.

Cooley espoused abolitionism because he believed in equal rights of all men before all laws, not in racial equality. So considered, *Constitutional Limitations* is a devotion less to abolition won than an alarm about hazards to liberty that Cooley was determined to resist. Cooley's chapter in *Constitutional Limitations* on "The Formation of State Constitutions" suggests why he, like Jameson, hit so precisely some of the major concerns of his generation of lawyers. Equal rights is the chapter's theme, as everywhere in Cooley's book. A state constitution must serve its citizens by providing representative government. But it must be a government that not even the largest majorities can overturn or alter fundamentally. With such a guaran-

[37]Alan Jones, "The Constitutional Conservatism of Thomas McIntyre Cooley" (Ph.D. diss., University of Michigan, 1960), p. 117; Phillip Paludan, "Law and the Failure of Reconstruction: The Case of Thomas Cooley," *Journal of the History of Ideas*, XXXIII (1972), 597–614; Michael Les Benedict, "Laissez-Faire, Class Legislation, and the Origins of Substantive Due Process of Law" (Paper, Woodrow Wilson International Center for Scholars, 1980). Used with permission.

tee, Cooley's general principles of morality would serve all. And he meant all; race minorities were his concern only as their members, as individuals, suffered discriminations under the law. In this part of *Constitutional Limitations,* Cooley based his high-flying aspirations on allegedly accepted principles of constitutional law. In short, he constructed a thesis and presented it as fact; wrote a brief and insisted that it was the only reasonable interpretation.

Cooley indulged in such inventions also as chief judge. In 1870 he heard a case lacking precedent. It involved a local community's power to tax in order to raise money for private railroad construction. In order to deny the community that power, Cooley created a theoretical Michigan which could not favor any township or business over any other. Inflexible, absolute restraints bound the state, and if state officials did not know this, he, the judge, would tell them.

Similarly, a year earlier Cooley condemned racially segregated public schools in Detroit. The Detroit school board, in strikingly modern terms, defended itself by insisting that any diminution in segregation invited violence and white flight. Further, the city's attorneys argued that school policy should be determined by majorities in the community and the state legislature, not judges. Cooley was contemptuous of both the school board's experience and its constitutionalism. All Michigan children must be admitted to public schools; the legislature had decreed admission, he stated. It had a right so to decide. But, having so decided, it could not, either directly or through delegated authority to a city school board, discriminate between students. The students, possessed of a right to admission, bore also the responsibility to meet prevailing standards. Nothing less than equal admission; nothing more than a chance to perform successfully—that was Cooley's measure of liberty and justice. The state must play no favorites. If it did, then judges must deny the state policy.[38]

The new formalism had a prophet. Liberty (as distinguished from democracy), often equated with a distrust both of direct popular decisions and of those deriving from delegated authority, as from police and other administrative officials, was his goal. To reach it

[38]The People *ex rel.* the Detroit and Howell Railroad Co. *v.* The Township Board of Salem, 20 Mich. 487 (1870); People *v.* Board of Education of Detroit, 18 Mich. 400 (1869).

Cooley and other writers of the 1860s and 1870s developed a theory of First Amendment freedoms that ultimately was to put the moral profits supposedly generated by laissez-faire economics and public policies against the moral imperatives to equal rights that Republicans discerned in Reconstruction. Cooley noted that every state Constitution contained some form of free speech guarantee. It was therefore virtually a common-law right, Cooley decided, justifying protection for political speech transcending Blackstone's idea of freedom from prior restraint (Cooley would not, however, protect, under the Amendment or its state analogues, obscenity, blasphemy, or libel).

Cooley's free speech ideas were, except as practiced in a few courtrooms like his own, theoretical.[39] He was nonetheless pleased that the law schools immediately seized upon his, Dillon's, and Jameson's books as texts. Practicing lawyers and judges were to use them as handy digests. The *Swift* doctrine, in 1864 reinforced by the *Gelpcke* v. *Dubuque* decision, of a federal common law in certain diversity situations was at hand to supplement those books as sources of coherent legal doctrines that limited cities and states. Yet earlier doctrines of legislative primacy in defining the public purpose in a law, and of judicial restraint, prevailed. Concerning statutory regulation of gristmills, Tennessee's supreme court held in 1867 that "the grist-mill is a public mill, [and] the miller is a public servant."[40] But the United States Supreme Court, between 1863 and 1880, was ready to impose at least occasional controls over both economic and noneconomic state activities. In addition to the federal Court's reins, in several states delegates to constitutional conventions who shared concerns expressed by law writers and judges themselves constrained state powers.

First, to states' self-limitations achieved in new or revised Constitutions. Constitutional conventions occurred frequently throughout the 1860s and 1870s. The approaches of Cooley, Dillon, and Jameson circulated among delegates. The new or revised Constitutions began sharply to limit the fields that states could enter, curbed state (and city) budgets, fixed debt limits, and prohibited debt repu-

[39]Alexis J. Anderson, "The Formative Period of First Amendment Theory, 1870–1915," *American Journal of Legal History*, XXIV (1980), 56–75.
[40]Memphis Freight Company v. Mayor and Alderman of Memphis, 44 Tenn. (4 Cold.) 419 (1867).

diation. Illinois forbade its legislature from acting at all in twenty areas of former legislative concern; Pennsylvania in forty; and California in thirty-three. Proscribed subjects included social functions, as in name changes to evade responsibilities, divorce, adoption, women's and children's rights, and inheritance. They included economic functions such as interest rates, tax exemptions, special incorporation laws, and local indebtedness; and political functions, such as locations of county seats, town incorporations, the conduct of elections, the power of local officials, the discretion of grand juries, and certain municipal improvements.[41]

Some revised Constitutions abolished city police departments, transferring the responsibility to the state. Others increased the frequency of legislative sessions and decreased the autonomy of city governments by making city charters more specific. Such changes notably enlarged the size and increased the complexity of states' Constitutions. One result was that lawyers, who could better make their ways through the increasingly complex Constitutions and statutes, grew more important in state politics and government. By the 1870s, each American Bar Association president offered the membership his annual summary of changes in states' Constitutions. Every ABA president stressed the growing limitations on state power and the constraints on lower governments, especially cities, in the states' Constitutions, plus the need for state judges to enforce these constraints.[42]

States, curtailing some functions, introduced many others. These included school truancy punishment, saloon licensing, coercive public health policies (especially against social diseases), controls over certain kinds of corporations, and requirements for humane treatment to animals. The states' inventiveness impressed the Western world as a new social science, and foreign observers tagged America as a "great transatlantic workshop" that their nations should copy. Heavy electoral majorities supported most of these

[41]Morton Keller, "The Politics of State Constitutional Revision, 1820–1930" (paper, Project 87 Conference on the Constitutional Convention as an Amending Device, Houston, 1979), pp. 13–17.

[42]Henry Hitchcock, *American State Constitutions: A Study of Their Growth* (New York, 1887), pp. 12–14, 59; W. G. Hastings, "The Development of Law as Illustrated by the Decisions Relating to the Police Power of the State," American Political Science Association *Proceedings*, XXXIX (1900), 360.

innovations. When adversely affected individuals brought suits against administrators of a state enterprise, few state judges chose to limit state powers, though Cooley and other writers touted judiciaries as the proper officials to do so. The prewar educations of incumbent judges had taught them differently. Before the Civil War, judges, obeying the dictates of self-restraint, commonly deferred to the political branches even on ordinary legislation. Federal judges gave the presumption of constitutionality to state laws brought to the bar; state Constitutions, asserted Henry Winter Davis in 1864, "can be questioned in no court." They involved fundamental political relationships that were outside the Supreme Court's or any court's competence.[43] But in 1863, and again in 1866–67, the justices' self-restraint occasionally slipped—spectacularly.

Next, then, to the Supreme Court's own interventions. To Chief Justice Chase, grumbling about the trivial issues involved in almost all the Court's case load when he assumed the office in late 1864, the prospects were dim for vigorous action on the part of his new colleagues. Chase himself had been an activist for a long time. Born in 1808, a Dartmouth College graduate in 1826, Chase studied law under then Attorney General William Wirt. Chase described his legal training as haphazard, a view most of his critics sustain, but almost every lawyer's education then deserved this description. George A. Brown, ex-governor of Georgia, an old enemy to Chase, in 1865 described him as "pregnant" with the law.[44]

Chase learned constitutionalism as well as law from Wirt, then linked abolition ideas to those about "freedom national" flowing from the Declaration of Independence and Bill of Rights as well as from the Constitution. As time passed, Chase became what Peter Walker calls "litigious abolition's stalwart . . . its leading constitutional theorist and one of the founders and chief strategists of abolition's political wing." Though adaptable—or slippery—on many political issues, Chase, whether as governor of Ohio or Lincoln's Secretary of the Treasury, stressed the need for freedom to be national. Free labor was far more than a marketplace relationship; it was also a complex of moral relationships; free labor made

[43]Davis, *Congressional Globe*, 38th Cong., 1st sess. (Mar. 22, 1864), app., 85.
[44]Brown to Simon B. Buckner, Dec. 15, 1865, SP 127, Huntington Library.

the Constitution more than a piece of paper. With free labor, the Union was a precious, indeed a sacred entity that deserved sacrifice and effort to preserve.[45]

In Lincoln's cabinet, Chase was the most consistent abolition spokesman. He clawed out a role for like-minded Treasury officials in the Army's Sea Island experiment for freed blacks. For persons like Chase, possessed of dynamic perceptions about freedom and Union, Reconstruction necessarily involved more than the states' political restorations. The quality of life of state residents was an inescapable national interest. But Chase was always a pragmatist and a states rights nationalist. As a governor and Treasury Secretary, he had learned a great deal about the complexities of government operations. Yet his ideas about federalism were comfortingly simple because they required no administration to achieve. All that was needed was for southern whites not to diminish the equality of all state residents engaged in any lawful activity.

"Freedom national" enhanced rather than diminished states' rights. By 1862 Chase had perceived the position he was to enshrine as Chief Justice:

While I think that the government, in suppression of rebellion in view of the destruction by suicide of the State governments with the actual or strongly implied consent of the majority of the citizens of the several rebel States, have so far forfeited all rights to be regarded as States, might justly treat them as Territories, I have never proposed to make this opinion the basis of political measures. I am willing and indeed much prefer to regard each state as in existence, and to have no change of boundaries, except such as may be freely consented to by them. I want to keep all the stars and all the stripes.[46]

White supremacists feared that Chase would radicalize the Court. As one of his initial acts as Chief Justice, Chase admitted John S. Rock, a Negro, into practice. The first black lawyer so honored,

[45]Peter Walker, *Moral Choices: Memory, Desire and Imagination in Nineteenth-Century American Abolition* (Baton Rouge, 1979), p. 308 and see ch. 13; Louis Gerteis, "Freedom National: Historic Precedents and Constitutional Nationalism in the Antislavery Thought of Salmon P. Chase" (Organization of American Historians paper, 1976).
[46]Chase to William Mellen, Mar. 26, 1862, in Robert B. Warden, *An Account of the Private Life and Public Services of S. P. Chase* (Cincinnati, 1874), pp. 421–422; and see Chase to J. M. McKim, Nov. 20, 1865, in David Hughes, "Salmon P. Chase: Chief Justice" (Ph.D. diss., Princeton University, 1963), p. 223.

Rock preceded by many months the first admission of Negroes into Congress. "Chase on de bench, nigger at de bar / Go away, white man, what you doin' dar?" the reactionary Columbus, Ohio, *Crisis* lampooned Chase (January 15, 1865). Rock's admission was not, tragically, destined to alter racial attitudes or conditions much or soon. Nevertheless the symbolism of a black attorney at work where the *Dred Scott* decision had been pronounced only eight years earlier reflected swift changes in race matters, and conservative Democrats among Court-watchers continued to mourn Taney. An antislavery writer in the Boston *Commonwealth* predicted that "the questions to be presented for the next decade to the tribunal over which he [Chase] is to preside—such as the freedom of millions and the restoration of civil society over one-half the nation—far transcend those which have heretofore been adjudged by it [the Supreme Court]."[47]

Both the race equality advocates and the race conservatives were to be disappointed. Almost all the cases before the Court in 1865 seemed irrelevant to the momentous race-centered concerns that occupied the attention of President and Congress; few of the landmark decisions of the Court beginning in 1866 were explicitly central to the Negro's rights. Perhaps the Chase Court's failure, as twentieth-century writers have estimated the record, to take sides with congressional Republicans contributed to the low estimate in which Chase is held by scholars.[48] Such estimates are less wrong than glancing. For, granting his excesses of personality and ambition, Chase requires measurement in his context, not ours. By its terms, Chase's performance, at least in reasserting the Court's authority to review certain national and state actions, would not have saddened Marshall or Taney.

In Chase's restored Union of States, color was not the only touchstone. Every man, being equal, defended his own rights and interests by voting and litigating. The states had duties both to their residents and to the national government to see that every resident had adequate forums for self-defense.

Chase, in 1865, was not far in advance of most of the Republicans

[47]George Ticknor Curtis, *Life of James Buchanan, Fifteenth President of the United States* (New York, 1883), II, 655; Boston *Commonwealth*, Dec. 10, 1864.
[48]Gerhard Casper in *Columbia Law Review*, LXXIII (1973), 196–221.

in Congress in his views on civil rights. But he was radically distant from the nominal Republican in the White House. Now Chief Justice, he was to serve an institution that enjoyed little authority even among the legal profession, an institution with its own history, values, and pace; an institution whose other servants, the associate justices, were also men of strong views and differing emphases.

James Moore Wayne, a Georgian, born in 1790, was the senior associate justice. He had sat with Marshall on the Court. Jackson's last surviving appointee, Wayne, a former slaveholder, was a confirmed believer in Negro inequality. Above all he was a nationalist in a Jacksonian context that left ample room for state rights.

Tyler had appointed Samuel Nelson to the Court in 1845. Seventy-two years old in 1865, Nelson had rich judicial experience in New York's appeal courts before ascending to the Supreme Court. Far more discreet than Taney, with whom he agreed on many war issues, Nelson, wrote David Hughes, was "out of touch with the prevailing political tides . . . , conservative, predisposed to the Democrats and the Southern interpretation of the Constitution, and self-assertive . . . Nelson was at the same time one of the most influential members within the court."[49]

Almost the same age as Nelson, Robert C. Grier, a Polk appointee, was a Pennsylvanian and a devout Democrat. Grier despised proponents of almost all professional changes. In the secession crisis and throughout the war he was strongly pro-Union, writing the *Prize* cases majority opinion. But though supporting the government, Grier was restless during the war. He was also sometimes indiscreet about Court affairs. It was Grier who slipped advance information to President Buchanan on Dred Scott's fate, and, in 1863, he confided to Richard Henry Dana, the government counsel in the *Prize* cases, how he would vote.[50]

Nathan Clifford, sixty-one years old, was a Buchanan appointee. Clifford rose in Maine politics and was Congressman and Polk's Attorney General. Associated with the southern wing of the Demo-

[49]Hughes, "Chase," p. 65; Harold M. Hollingsworth, "The Confirmation of Judicial Review Under Taney and Chase" (Ph.D. diss., University of Tennessee, 1966), chs. 2, 3; Leon Friedman and Fred L. Israel (eds.), *The Justices of the United States Supreme Court, 1789–1969: Their Lives and Major Opinions* (New York, 1969), II, 817–842, 873–894, 963–1152.
[50]Charles F. Adams, *Richard Henry Dana* (Boston, 1891), II, 270.

cratic party, Clifford was publicly antiabolition and, during the Civil War, he ". . . was critical of the [Lincoln] administration's use of arbitrary power, and he refused to recognize that in wartime it could exercise emergency power." Stubborn, perhaps senile by the early 1860s, Clifford was an often erratic and sometimes immovable conservative on war and Reconstruction questions.[51]

A Virginian transplanted to Ohio, Noah Swayne made his reputation as a private corporation lawyer. This, combined with his strong antislavery views, won him a Supreme Court seat as Lincoln's first appointee, in 1862. Sixty years old in 1865, Swayne, undistinguished as a jurist, though moved privately to complain to Lincoln about arbitrary arrests, was a dependable Republican in his approaches to war and Reconstruction litigation.

Chase would have virtually no contact with John Catron because the seventy-eight-year-old Tennessean was ill throughout the 1864–65 term of the Court. Catron died in May, 1865, and because Congress, in 1866, reduced the size of the Court, his place remained unfilled.

Lincoln's second appointee, the influential and brilliant Samuel Miller, in his late forties, had been a doctor in Kentucky. He tired of both medicine and a slaveholding environment and qualified as a lawyer, quickly becoming a luminary of the young Iowa bar. An Anti-Nebraska Whig, Miller moved easily into the new Republican party, and, in 1862, Lincoln named him to the Supreme Court. Though a successful lawyer, Miller was not known as a learned one. He had held no public office. Yet he rapidly became a dominant justice. A prodigious worker, totally lacking in humility, Miller was nevertheless capable of great tact with his colleagues. Possessed of views on Reconstruction close to the Radical Republican perception, Miller was to be very influential in determining the course of decisions.[52]

Third among the Lincoln appointees was his Illinois friend and 1860 nominating convention manager, David Davis. A former Whig, also almost fifty in 1865, Davis disliked both abolitionists and slaveholders, though he retained his fondness for the southern re-

[51]David M. Silver, *Lincoln's Supreme Court* (Urbana, 1956), p. 23.
[52]Charles M. Fairman, *Mr. Justice Miller and the Supreme Court* (Cambridge, 1939), pp. 43–53.

gion. It was primarily his affection for Lincoln that moved Davis into the Republican party. He advised Lincoln to rescind the Emancipation Proclamation and to end military arrests of civilians. A conservative in the sense of distrusting the capacities of majorities to conduct even large private business wisely, much less public affairs, Davis was also incurably addicted to involvement in behind-the-scenes political maneuvers.[53]

Far more important was Stephen J. Field, born in 1816, whom Lincoln appointed in 1863, from California. Congress created this tenth seat in part because the narrow margin in the *Prize* cases (5–4) dismayed legislators, and another safe justice was wanted. Further, the booming West badly needed a handy federal circuit, if only because chicanery and imprecision in Mexican land grants in California were encouraging numerous claims to great tracts of land in the state. A member of an unusually talented New England family —his brothers were David Dudley Field, the nationally prominent lawyer, and Cyrus Field, the inventor—Field was a War Democrat. Strong-minded and energetic, he was to be the Court's most vigorous exponent of nonrestraint in review. Field held essentially southern views on Reconstruction, and these meshed neatly with his emphatic laissez-faire approaches to the desirable limits of public economic interventions. To Field, judges must make law at least in peculiarly vital matters because the judgment of majorities can rarely be trusted.[54]

The Chase Court was more politically oriented than any that preceded it. Every justice maintained close political connections outside the Court. Chase aspired to the presidency. Several associates yearned to succeed him as Chief. Such ambitions, combined with variant views on race and Reconstruction among the justices, promised lively Court sessions, but not necessarily about Negro rights.

Perhaps champions of racial equality erred so badly in expecting support in the Supreme Court because of the sweeping views of constitutional rights such equalitarians possessed. "My mind is

[53]Silver, *Lincoln's Supreme Court*, pp. 74–78.
[54]Carl Brent Swisher, *Stephen J. Field, Craftsman of the Law* (Washington, 1930), *passim.* In 1869, Grant nominated Stanton to replace Grier, but Stanton died too soon to take the seat. Grant also nominated Joseph Bradley of New Jersey and William Strong of Pennsylvania.

deeply impressed with the importance of establishing the principle of the obligation of the Government to protect the people in their personal rights," wrote a close friend to Senator Sumner in July, 1865. The obligation existed as "one of the fundamental principles of our Constitution to which all other rights are subservient."[55] The hope persisted among equalitarians of aid and comfort from the reconstituted Court. Recalling his expectations for judicial confirmation of eternal moral principles as constitutional law, the prominent New York abolitionist lawyer John Jay II, a descendant of the jurist and diplomat, in early 1867 advised Chase:

The decision which I most wish to see pronounced by your Court is that the adoption of the [Thirteenth] Amendment abolishing slavery destroyed the only exception recognized by the Constitution to the great principle of the Declaration of Independence and that from the date of the adoption of the Amendment all persons black and white stand upon an equal footing, that all State legislation establishing or recognizing distinction of race or color are void.[56]

The Court, as noted, frustrated the hope of such old abolitionists as Jay. It would not escalate civil rights and liberties to the status of positive duties for the nation and states to provide to all Americans, in response to either direct impediments to race equality by states or nonacts by state and local officials allowing private actions that resulted in inequalities. Republican and Democratic justices alike revered the traditional protections Americans—white Americans, at least—enjoyed, by reason of government inaction: "minimum scrutiny," in Gerald Gunther's phrase. Judicial inquiry into the substantive effects of state action or nonaction on civil rights necessarily required the Court to involve itself in more than minimum scrutiny.[57]

Congress, not the Court, was to feel impelled to assume a guardian democracy stance on civil rights. But the aggressive qualities of the Chief Justice and of several of the associates, combined with the fact that major war and Reconstruction issues other than those aimed to raise up the ex-slaves were justiciable, made a volatile mix.

[55]W. J. Demarest to Sumner, July 8, 1865, vol. 10, no. 74, Sumner PP, Houghton Library, Harvard University.
[56]Jay to Chase, Jan. 5, 1867, Chase Paper, vol. 98, no. 14727, Library of Congress.
[57]Gunther, "In Search of Evolving Doctrine on a Changing Court," pp. 1–48.

Those issues involved primarily civil liberties, not civil or political rights. Persons held in military custody or barred from practicing a profession by a federal or state loyalty oath were to find an interested quorum in the Court; debt repudiations by state or city governments intrigued the justices. They all believed devoutly in laissez-faire economics and, one way or another, despised "class legislation" that diminished the substance of legal procedures. Appellants from such situations were white. Blacks, and their champions, were concerned as a first priority to win civil rights for Negroes, although their list of what constituted civil rights was growing.[58] The Chief Justice of the United States was abolition's honored champion. But the Supreme Court of the United States was to remain the white man's last refuge, not the Negro's.

David Hughes concluded that the Chase Court developed very little lasting legal doctrine. But the law transcends the technical, and, as freshman Minnesota Congressman Ignatius Donnelly noted in 1866, anyone who was "fearfully cramped by the old technicalities" was unlikely to understand the law and the Constitution in Appomattox America.[59] The Chase Court contributed to the law in large social senses in part because it respected and exploited continuums from Taney's tenure as well as evolving doctrines of its own —doctrines which increased options for Chase and his brethren.

First, with respect to doctrines Chase inherited from Taney, the 1863 *Prize* cases added to the Court's slim store of popular good will. Then the decision in the Iowa bond litigation, *Gelpcke* v. *Dubuque* (1864), brought the Court the gratitude of major spokesmen for investment, banking, and law interests. Such persons viewed any repudiation of public debt with great apprehension. Overextended state and local governments had defaulted on debt commitments with upsetting frequency since the 1830s. Iowa, as was true elsewhere, competed for railroad building in the 1850s, in part by authorizing the issue of state bonds to develop funds for use by private corporations. But Iowa's Constitution limited the state debt to $100,000 and forbade state investment in private corporations. The Iowa legislature, upon pressure from Dubuque boosters,

[58]Benedict, "Laissez-Faire, Class Legislation, and the Origins of Substantive Due Process of Law."
[59]Hughes, "Chase," p. 4; Donnelly, *Congressional Globe*, 39th Cong., 1st sess. (Feb. 1, 1866), p. 586.

authorized its cities to do what the state could not do. Dubuque issued bonds in excess of $100,000 to encourage railroad building, not only inside the city's limits but throughout the state.

Rail construction faltered. Dubuque and other cities had to increase tax rates because the anticipated railroad income did not materialize to pay interest on the bonds and avoid default. Taxpayers, and speculators who bought risky securities at discounts, sought relief in Iowa courts, asserting that the state Constitution forbade the city's policy. Iowa judges, including those of the supreme court, sustained the state and city actions. Increasing popular indignation brought about the defeat, in elections, of enough of the acquiescent jurists to reverse views in the Iowa supreme court. It declared unconstitutional the state authorization to Dubuque. Dissatisfied bondholders then sued in the federal court in Iowa to recover interest on the bonds. The federal district judge had to choose between the earlier or the later Iowa court decisions concerning the Iowa constitution. He chose the most recent decision. The Dubuque interest coupons became worthless. In effect, a default occurred. Holders of Dubuque bonds appealed to the United States Supreme Court on a writ of error, and it considered the case in 1864.

Relevant forum state law and procedures governed in the Supreme Court. Did this acceptance of state law in federal courts include state court verdicts? What should federal judges do when a state's jurists put forth several self-contradictory judgments, as in the *Gelpcke* litigation? And what if the federal judges disagreed with state court decisions? Should federal judges ". . . immolate truth, justice, and the law, because a state tribunal has erected the altar and decreed the sacrifice[?]" Justice Swayne demanded.[60]

Indeed not, the Supreme Court decided in *Gelpcke*. Contrary to the tradition of a Supreme Court virtually immobilized during the Civil War, both by a supposed fear of the Republican majority in Congress and by the justices' views of the limits of their authority, the Court, in *Gelpcke*, impressively expanded its review power over high state court judgments. The Court created, in effect, a new dimension of general federal common law jurisdiction and jurisprudence. It employed the municipal bond issue for the expansion, an issue so complex as to loom "like a wilderness—tackless even to

[60]Gelpcke *v.* Dubuque, 1 Wall. 175 at 206 (1864).

knowledgeable students of the Supreme Court," in Charles Fairman's analysis. In *Gelpcke,* the Court did more than repudiate a state high court judgment. It required Iowa to honor bonds that the state's supreme court held to be invalid: construed state statutes on the power of municipal officials, on statutory and constitutional debt limits, and on corporations, contrary to state court interpretations.[61]

State supreme courts had been trying for more than a decade to resolve disputes over muncipal bond defaults satisfactorily. The United States Supreme Court, in 1862, speaking through Justice Swayne, had restated a long-honored principle, that "if the highest judicial tribunal of a State adopt new views as to the proper construction of . . . a [state] statute, and reverse its former decisions, this court will follow the latest settled decisions." But in *Gelpcke,* only two years later, Swayne accepted instead Taney's contrary view expressed in 1853. A contract valid by state law when made, and so construed by a state court, could not be invalidated by subsequent legislative action or altered state court judgment, Taney stated.[62]

Dissenting in *Gelpcke,* Justice Miller, an Iowan, decried the federal encroachment upon the right of a state court to speak finally upon the construction of its state Constitution and laws. No infraction of the federal Constitution had occurred in Iowa. It was occurring in Washington, Miller insisted. The Supreme Court was fraying federal-state court relationships. State court prosecutions of federal officers, which Congress addressed in the 1863 Habeas Corpus Act's removal provisions, were no more abrasive than the national Court's *Gelpcke* thrust.

Fairman has recently posed the issue in different terms. "On what rational basis can one justify the Supreme Court's refusal [in *Gelpcke*] to follow the State court's decision on a matter of State law?"[63] Taney's position of 1853, noted above, was hinged to the federal Constitution's-Article I, section 10 contract clause, which forbids a state to pass any law impairing a contract. State court decisions, not state law, were the *Gelpcke* problem. The *Gelpcke* decision rested upon the Constitution's Article III provision that the judicial power

---

[61]Fairman, *Reconstruction,* pp. 918–919.

[62]Swayne in Leffingwell *v.* Warren, 2 Black 599 (1862); Taney in Ohio Life Insurance Trust Co. *v.* Debolt, 16 Howard 416 (1853).

[63]Miller, in Gelpcke *v.* Dubuque, 207–220, and Fairman, *Reconstruction,* p. 937.

of the United States extended to controversies between diverse state citizens. In such instances, federal judges decide which state's laws, procedures, and customs to apply. Are national jurists possessed of the capacity to render conclusions independent of views expressed by the forum states' jurists?

The Supreme Court's *Gelpcke* position was that it enjoyed an independent authority. Its justification was the 1842 decision of *Swift* v. *Tyson,* and the diversity jurisdiction assigned to the federal courts by section 34 of the 1789 Judiciary Act.[64] The latter required federal judges to follow local law in diversity cases. But *Swift* permitted independent federal judicial interpretation, a "general law," in diversity litigations of *Gelpcke*'s sort, where a state court judgment, not a law, was flawed through reversal by the same tribunal, or which, in the justices' opinion, was erroneous. In 1864, the Court, combining in *Gelpcke* aspects of the 1789 statute and the 1842 *Swift* decision, gave itself a discretionary initiative concerning state high court judgments that it had not asserted earlier. Interstate commerce now had a more powerful, elastic, and sensitive guardian than ever before. On the foundation established in *Gelpcke,* the Supreme Court in later years, according to Tony Freyer, "erected a bulwark against the uncertainty and prejudice of local law."[65] *Swift* and *Gelpcke* became a team thereafter, serving the federal courts through the 1930s as a curb on municipal debts, repudiations of contracts, and tort liability, among other matters.

Gelpcke engaged the interest of the legal community even more than the *Prize* cases. Both sustained the nation's authority. But *Gelpcke,* as the Supreme Court Reporter John Wallace pointed out in his introduction to the 1864 volume of the *Reports,* was the initial enforcement by the Court of "high moral duties . . . upon a whole community [i.e., a city] seeking apparently to violate them." The Reporter's evident distrust of urban fiscal morality reflected dominant opinion among the justices and a growing consensus among lawyers. Debt repudiation in Dubuque seemed to be as dangerous

[64]Note that the 1789 Judiciary Act also provided a route for Court judgment on the validity of wartime greenbacks, but in Roosevelt *v.* Meyer, 1 Wall. 512 (1863), the Court avoided the duty.

[65]Tony Freyer, "The Federal Courts, Localism, and the National Economy, 1865–1900," *Business History Review,* LIII (1979), 351; Erie *v.* Tompkins, 304 U.S. 64 (1938), for the repudiation of Swift.

as secession in South Carolina. "Our court," wrote Justice Miller privately, "or a majority of it, are, if not monomaniacs, as much bigots and fanatics on that subject [municipal debt repudiation] as is the most unhesitating Mahemodan in regard to his religion. In four cases out of five the case is decided when it is seen by the pleadings that it is a suit to enforce a contract against a city, or town, or a county. If there is a written instrument its validity is a foregone conclusion."[66]

After the *Gelpcke* decision Iowa state officials denied the validity of the Supreme Court's pronouncement, thereby deeply troubling Timothy Farrar, who had helped to develop adequacy constitutional doctrine. Farrar combined the adequacy argument, so far as the nation was concerned, with a thesis from *Gelpcke* justifying federal judicial restraints on state excesses North and South. He preferred to have state judges hold their own states and localities to acceptable behavior. But if state judges would or could not, national judges must do the work, even at the risk of unsettling the delicate federal balance. All claim to limitless state power, he wrote, was "false doctrine and antagonistic practice, leading, and terminating in, treason, rebellion, and civil war."[67]

Iowa resistance to *Gelpcke* inspired the Supreme Court further to increase its review outreach, thereby linking more solidly Taney's and Chase's tenures as Chief Justice. Back in 1861, for the first time, federal judges granted writs of mandamus (i.e., an order by a superior court directed to a public official, or to one of a private corporation, commanding the performance of a specified act) directed to city and county officers. These writs ordered the state officials, in support of a previous judgment by the federal court, to levy and collect special taxes to pay off bonded indebtedness. After *Gelpcke*, Iowa, like Wisconsin in the *Ableman* case, forbade state and county officers from obeying the federal writs. By this time Chase was Chief Justice. He joined the Court majority that reinforced Taney's 1861 mandamus innovation. The recalcitrant state and local officers went to jail for contempt. In 1868, bondholders' lawyers convinced the Supreme Court that it need not wait for a first federal court judg-

---

[66]John William Wallace, Reporter, in 1 Wall. xiv (1864); Miller in Fairman, *Reconstruction*, p. 920.
[67]Farrar, *Manual of the Constitution*, p. 515.

ment to be defied by a state before seeking a federal mandamus in a separate proceeding. Instead, petitioners could acquire both initial judgment and mandatory writ in a single suit. In 1870, Iowa's supreme court bowed before the *Swift-Gelpcke-*mandamus combination. Iowa restored all bonds to pre-*Gelpcke* validity. In this manner, for a time at least, uniformity in federal and state law was achieved concerning the essential subject of railroad financing.[68]

How far the Court had recovered by 1865 from its near-disaster in *Dred Scott* is apparent also in several actions of Chase and his colleagues in this first months as Chief Justice. Chase quietly sustained Taney's 1863 protest about the tax on the salaries of federal judges. On circuit in Baltimore, where Taney had presided, Chase, in April, 1865, decided an admiralty case in a manner that would have delighted his predecessor. Chase held that the admiralty jurisdiction of United States courts embraced all contracts involving waterborne commerce, even when, as in the case at hand, every act under the contract being litigated occurred in ports within a single state.[69]

The Court's return to prominence is visible also in the manner in which Chase and his fellow Justices confirmed political judgments of President and Congress concerning West Virginia. In 1863, as noted earlier, Lincoln had proclaimed the existence of the state. Considerable uncertainty existed whether Congress would accept West Virginia's representatives, or the Court list it in its order of states on the docket. Either occurring, the status of West Virginia would be in doubt, as was true of the southern states. In January, 1865, Chase's first official act was to direct the clerk to include West Virginia. All justices present (Catron alone being absent) concurred in the propriety of the action, according to journalist Whitelaw Reid: "One question therefore, upon Mr. Thad. Stevens and others have been accustomed to hold high debate in Congress, without ever having been formally raised, may be considered henceforth

---

[68]Knox County *v.* Aspinwall, 25 How. 376 (1861); Von Hoffman *v.* Quincy, 4 Wall. 535 (1867); Riggs *v.* Johnson County, 6 Wall. 166 (1868); Butz *v.* City of Muscatine, 8 Wall. 575 (1869); Stewart *v.* Board of Supervisors, 30 Iowa 9 (1870).

[69]The Mary Washington (1865) in Bradley T. Johnson (comp.), *Reports of Cases Decided by Chief Justice Chase in the Circuit Court of the United States, Fourth Circuit, 1865–1869* (New York, 1876), pp. 125–131 (cited hereafter as *Chase's Circuit Court Decisions*).

practically *res adjudicata* [i.e., already adjudicated]," Reid wrote.[70]

Also in 1865, the Court, less respectful this time of Congress and President, quietly invalidated a section of a federal law, only the fourth time in American history that the Court held a statute, or part of one, to be unconstitutional. The opportunity rose from the law establishing a Federal Court of Claims. The 1855 law substituted court procedures for the vexatious private legislation on each claim against the federal government. Claims swelled in number once the Civil War started. In 1863 Congress decided that the Court of Claims would decide each claim, not merely report on it, and authorized appeals to the Supreme Court. But the Secretary of the Treasury and the Congress had, as it were, more final appeals. The Secretary had discretion on awarding money; Congress, on appropriating it.

Back in the 1790s, in *Hayburn's* case, the Court refused to advise President Washington on pension matters. It was a court of law and decided cases; it did not advise coequal branches of government. In 1864, the Supreme Court accepted jurisdiction in an appeal from the Court of Claims. As was his habit concering much wartime legislation, Taney had prepared a draft opinion denying the government's jurisdiction even before he heard arguments. Taney's opinion held that Congress could not, by statute, "authorize or require this court to express an opinion on a case . . . where its judgment would not be final and conclusive upon the rights of the parties, and process of execution awarded to carry it into effect." Chase, succeeding Taney, found the draft opinion convincing both for the case at hand and for its general endorsement of judicial review. Chase contented himself with a brief opinion, denying Supreme Court jurisdiction because the Treasury Secretary could override a judicial decision by not assigning funds. Congressmen, being apprised of the Court's position, in December, 1866, repealed the objectionable clauses, and the Court thereafter heard Court of Claim appeals.[71]

This adroit maneuvering gave the Court what its members wanted without a confrontation with Congress or President. The

[70]Cincinnati *Gazette*, Jan. 7, 1865, in Reid Papers, vol. 219, Library of Congress.
[71]William Wiecek, "The Origin of the U.S. Court of Claims," *Administrative Law Review*, XX (1968), 387–406.

pacific resolution of the West Virginia and Court of Claims issues, though ignored by the public, may have confirmed some of the justices in a view favoring vigorous review action by the Court in other questions.

The circuit duties all the justices performed in addition to their annual session in Washington offered Chase and his colleagues numerous opportunities to express this spirit favoring invigorated review. Most ordinary litigation reached final resolution in the circuits. In 1865, circuit case loads were growing swiftly in volume. Many technical legal questions hung over from the war. These ranged from insurance claims by soldiers' heirs to demands for compensation for unfulfilled slave contracts (demands that did not become null, plaintiffs' lawyers insisted, upon ratification of the Thirteenth Amendment). In the southern states, great uncertainty existed among lawyers in 1865 whether a multitude of civil relations as in marriage or business contracts since 1861, unconnected with the war, were voided by defeat. Virginia lawyer Bradley Johnson, who was to become Chase's circuit reporter, worried that if, as legal and constitutional theory suggested, every southern white was an enemy of the United States, then all wartime "acknowledgements of deeds, protests of notes, records of courts, judicial proceedings, contracts based on the existing state of things, would, on that theory, all be void, and inextricable confusion would be the consequence."[72]

In 1865 it appeared as though Chase was adding to the confusions. He forbore from assigning circuits in the southern states. Traditionally, his reason was supposed to be an abhorrence of the military presence in the South, especially of the Army and Bureau courts. But, Chase felt, Congress had provided for them by statute; they were as legitimate as the circuit or district courts. In the Reconstruction context, military courts "were competent to the exercise of all jurisdictions, civil and criminal, which belongs, under ordinary circumstances, to civil courts," Chase stated. His concern was with the military presence in the South on the basis only of executive orders. Therefore Chase himself carried on his Fourth Circuit work only in Maryland, though the circuit included Virginia and the Carolinas, until, in March, 1867, Congress substituted the Military

[72]Johnson, *Chase's Circuit Court Decisions,* p. iv.

Reconstruction law for the President's orders. Chase saw to it that the often-forgotten fact was broadcast widely in the southern legal world (by Bradley Johnson) that a federal district judge could carry on a circuit alone, as occurred, without a Supreme Court justice joining him. Federal justice forums were available in adequate number to cope with the litigation load. Peace brought continuums, not disruptions. The major inadequacy was not in traditional legal relationships but in newer ones that the peace was nourishing.[73]

In its 1866–67 term, the Court accepted jurisdiction of three cases that directly involved Reconstruction and, in each, decided against the relevant national and state policies. The first two were known as the *Test Oath* cases. One, *Ex parte Garland,* derived from the Court's own rule made agreeably to Congress's 1862 ironclad oath statute, requiring all court officers including attorneys to swear to their past as well as future loyalty before entering into practice. *Cummings* v. *Missouri,* the second *Test Oath* case, derived from a clause in Missouri's 1865 constitution that required a similar oath from all licensed professionals, voters, and public officers, among other residents. Only once earlier (*Dodge* v. *Woolsey,* 1854) had the Court even accepted jurisdiction of a case involving allegations of a state Constitution's violating the federal Constitution. In *Cummings,* the Court held against the state—a virtually unprecedented enlargement of federal judicial review. The third case of the trio, *Ex parte Milligan,* involved once again the wartime question of the trial of civilians by military courts and touched upon deep concerns about the durability both in the war and in the Reconstruction of Cooley's concern, First Amendment liberty.

In these decisions the justices, in search of doctrine, employed inventively eclectic clauses of the Constitution. These included the Article I, sections 9 and 10, prohibitions against state or nation imposing bills of attainder and ex post facto laws against states violating the obligations of contracts, and the limitations in the Bill of Rights (especially the First and Sixth Amendments) on the nation, rights pertaining particularly to criminal law procedures. Taken together, *Garland, Cummings,* and *Milligan* revealed the unsuspected potentialities of these parts of the Constitution as defenses—now visible as interim defenses—against state and national

[73]*Ibid.* p. 133, and Bradley Johnson's comments, *ibid.*, pp. iii–viii.

actions too obnoxious for the justices to overlook or condone, until in later decades the possibilities in the Fourteenth Amendment's due process clause became apparent.[74] Now to the details of these three decisions.

During the war, unresistible patriotic pressures led legislators and delegates to state constitutional conventions to disfranchise southern activists and sympathizers by means of loyalty oaths, to deprive them of the right to vote, hold state civil or military office, bear arms, practice a licensed profession, hold corporation office, or serve on juries. The most numerous occurrence of proscriptive loyalty oaths was in the Border States and those of the South. Persons favoring the abolition of slavery and race equality commonly supported exclusionary loyalty tests in their state Constitutions, as in Arkansas, Louisiana, Maryland, Missouri, Tennessee (where military governor Andrew Johnson was a notorious hardliner on loyalty oaths), "restored" Virginia, and West Virginia. Louisiana's 1864 Constitution abolished slavery and authorized Negro suffrage, free public education for all, a progressive income tax, a nine-hour workday, a two-dollar-a-day minimum wage on public works, and the disfranchisement of ex-rebels by means of oaths. Missouri's 1865 Constitution, in addition to introducing some reforms analogous to Louisiana's, required its "drakonian" (after its sponsor, the state's senator Charles Drake) oath of past loyalty for all voters, state officers, jurors, officers of corporations, church officials including ministers, and licensed professionals to swear. Oaths were more than a symbol of patriotism. Their enforcement, wrote Schuyler Colfax, meant ". . . giving rebels to understand that they must take back seats, and that reconstruction must be in the hands of the loyal alone."[75]

A tradition existed, and persists, that such oaths are untraditional, even un-American. But they are not strange to American history. In the Civil War period, these oath tests were far milder than the mass

[74]See Dodge v. Woolsey, 18 How. (59 U.S.) 416 (1854), described above, ch. 3; Ex parte Milligan, 4 Wall. 2 (1866); Cummings v. Missouri, 4 Wall. 277 (1866); Ex parte Garland, 4 Wall. 333 (1867). Attainders were legislative acts that defined a crime, named offenders, and set penalties, without trials; ex post facto acts made actions crimes that were not offenses at the time they were allegedly committed.

[75]Colfax to Joseph R. Hawley, Mar. 5, 1866, Hawley PP, vol. 14, Library of Congress.

punishments and individual penalties that losers in other civil wars suffered abroad.[76]

After a decade of violence, little toleration existed in Missouri for resolving political conflicts. In this combustible context, Father John Cummings, a Roman Catholic priest-teacher, refused to swear to the required constitutional oath. He feared state interference by the rural, Protestant majority with the dogma he taught in St. Louis. Cummings persisted in teaching without a license. Missouri arrested and fined him. The priest then appeared in Missouri's appeal courts, represented by one of America's most expensive lawyers, the Marylander Montgomery Blair, Lincoln's Postmaster General. Missouri appeal judges sustained the validity of the oath requirement both as against Cummings and as applicable to lawyers and to nonjuring voters (the last point being raised in a companion suit brought by Montgomery Blair's brother, the Missouri resident Francis P. Blair, Jr., a former Union general).

The Blair brothers sought to put themselves at the center of a conservative national political coalition. They seized upon Cummings's appeal, involving religious and teaching freedom, and contrived Francis Blair's voter case as issues to gain support in courts among all licensed professionals and among the general population. Through the Blairs' efforts, complainants in Missouri and in other states with oaths like Missouri's joined their cases to Cummings's and to Blair's. Montgomery Blair recruited Maryland Senator Reverdy Johnson and David Dudley Field, two of the nation's finest constitutional law experts, as co-counsel. Senator Johnson, who had voted in favor of the federal ironclad oath and repented, became notorious for publicly recommending that ex-Confederate Marylanders should deliberately commit perjury, sign the state's required oath, and vote. He was, in Justice Miller's estimation, an "old political prostitute." This redoubtable trio took Cummings's appeal to the United States Supreme Court, where, joined by Wisconsin Senator Matthew Carpenter, they also represented the Arkansan Augustus Hill Garland in a suit against the federal oath.

Once a lawyer practicing in the federal courts and a United States

---

[76]Willmoore Kendall and George W. Cary, *The Basic Symbols of the American Political Tradition* (Baton Rouge, 1970), pp. 5–6; Peyton McCrary, "After the Revolution: American Reconstruction in Comparative Perspective," (Organization of American Historians paper, 1979).

Senator, thereafter a Confederate general and legislator, Garland had received a pardon from the President. Now he wished again to practice law in the Supreme Court. But he could not swear to the ironclad oath required by the Court as a rule in conformity with the amended 1862 oath statute.[77] A lesser gun of the law, Missouri's attorney general pleaded his state's case. The United States Attorney General argued, or was supposed to argue, against Garland's admissibility to the Court bar.

Cummings's lawyers insisted, in formalistic manner, that the Missouri oath substantively violated the United States Constitution's prohibition of any state law that was ex post facto or a bill of attainder. Persons refusing to sign the oath incurred disfranchisements and exclusions, "all . . . accomplished . . . without any trial or judicial proceeding whatever." Cummings had a property and a contract right to the practice of his profession, and Missouri had violated both. No matter that Missouri's constitution called the oath a police regulation; "In practical operation and essential nature" the oath identified, judged, and sentenced its victims, the substance of a bill of attainder. Despite the Missouri supreme court's judgment that persons suffered from the oath only after refusing to sign it, Cummings's lawyers argued that the refusal to sign was occasioned by events antecedent to the oath's existence. Therefore it was ex post facto. The contrary Missouri court interpretation simply reflected the low quality of the state's judges. Cummings's lawyers concluded that the spirit of the Constitution required the Court to hold against Missouri's Constitution.

Missouri's counsel replied more specifically. The federal government's judicial power extended only to questions rising from the national Constitution, not from a state's Constitution. Federal judges should always review state laws "with great caution." How much more "caution" for state Constitutions? All states had always claimed, often exercised, and retained a right to qualify at their own discretion all voters, and teachers, lawyers, and other licensed groups. Further, the Missouri oath was not a bill of attainder be-

[77]Reverdy Johnson, *Opinion, Oct. 7, 1864* (Baltimore, n.d. [pam. reprint]); Lieber's disgusted reaction is in Lieber to Binney, Nov. 12, 1866, Lieber PP, LI 918, Box 52, Huntington Library. Justice Miller in Fairman, *Reconstruction*, pp. 283.

cause it involved only civil, not criminal, matters.[78] It was not ex post facto, because all consequences followed refusal to sign, not the commission of earlier offenses. If Missouri's Constitution writers wished to catalog refusals to subscribe the oath requirement as crimes they would have done so. Since they did not, the federal judges could not go behind the state Constitution and impute hidden intentions to its writers.[79]

Whereupon the Court heard Garland's petition. Save for the pardon element, arguments repeated those Cummings's counsel made against Missouri. Garland's lawyers admitted that he (unlike Cummings) could not swear to the ironclad oath by reason of his Confederate activities. But Garland had received a pardon from the President. That pardon released him from all penalties of his rebel past, including those imposed by nonsubscription to the oath. The President's pardoning power overcame the consequences of Garland's guilt; "The petitioner's right to practice in this court is property" and deprivation of that property by operation of the oath law was essentially without due process of law and violated the Fifth Amendment. Neither the nation nor the state could enact bills of attainder or ex post facto laws and immunize them against judicial review by calling them by other names. "Would the [oath] law accomplish a result which the Constitution forbids?" asked Senator Carpenter. If so, then "no matter what may be the form of the act, it is unconstitutional."[80]

For the government, Attorney General Henry Stanbery simply noted his opposition to Garland's position, but offered no argument. The government's weak stand contrasted unfavorably with the plaintiffs' impressive briefs in both cases and led to speculation that the President wanted the nation to lose its case.

Justices Field, Clifford, Grier, Nelson, and Wayne held against both Missouri and the nation. In his opinion for the bare majority, Field analyzed the text of the Missouri oath, declaring that it was, "for its severity, without any precedent that we can discover." Field agreed with Missouri that the Supreme Court ". . . cannot decide

---

[78]Calder v. Bull, 3 Dallas 386 (1798), sustained the position that bills of attainder applied only to criminal matters.
[79]Cummings v. Missouri, 327.
[80]Ex parte Garland, 367.

the case upon the justice or hardship of these provisions." But a conflict of constitutions did give jurisdiction to the Supreme Court. Was Missouri's oath a civil qualification or a criminal penalty? Field claimed a right for the Court to go behind the text of the state Constitution, to learn if ". . . under the form of creating a qualification or attaching a condition, the state can, in effect, inflict a punishment for a past act which was not punishable at the time it was committed." Which allowed Field a next step.

He asserted that the Court was not questioning Missouri's Constitution or the adequacy of the state's police power to accomplish what majorities wished. Instead, it was concerned with Missouri's veiled distortion of its legitimate power by impermissible means.[81] "The Constitution," Field continued, "deals with substance, not shadows. Its inhibition [against ex post facto laws and bills of attainder] was levelled at the thing, not the name." However "disguised," laws of this character violated the Constitution because they diminished liberty.

Field defined liberty in formalist, Cooley-like terms. Liberty included the Bill of Rights' protections (against a state, in this instance!), those in the Declaration of Independence (Field intoned "life, liberty, and property"), plus "freedom from outrage on the feelings as well as restraints on the person." A right to practice a profession was a precious property, immune from deprivation by a state through the inadequate procedure the oath provided. Therefore the Court felt impelled to reverse the judgment of Missouri's supreme court. It ordered Cummings freed and restored to his profession.

For the same bare majority of the Court, Field, concerning Garland, held that the federal oath was "a legislative decree of perpetual exclusion" from professional practice. It was in essence a punishment and impermissible. Lawyers practicing in the Supreme Court were not government officials but officers of that court. Qualifications for admission or exclusion, as distinguished from minimum standards for general practice, were up to the justices, not to Congress. A professional practice was too precious a property right to be held by "a mere indulgence." A lawyer should lose it only by a court judgment that he was morally or professionally substandard.

[81]*Ibid.*, 360–361.

Field insisted that Congress could set qualifications for admission to federal practice, but could not make qualifications disguise punishments. Additionally, a President could pardon and remit all punishments for any offense. This power was not subject to legislative limitation. Pardoned, Garland was "a new man" with "a new credit and capacity." The oath law, as a rule of the Court, limited the total effect of Garland's pardon; the oath requirement must give way.[82]

In asserting that both Garland and Cummings had property rights in their professions, Field exploited one of the most urgent concerns of mid-nineteenth-century lawyers and judges: the judicial protection of the right to property against legislators. With roots in jurisprudence extending back to the 1815 Supreme Court decision in *Terrett* v. *Taylor,* against a Virginia law confiscating Anglican Church lands in the state, this concern about property rights had increased through the Ages of Jackson and Lincoln. A visitor to America in 1867, the English lawyer H. R. Droop, reported to his Lincoln's Inn colleagues that "American lawyers regard this constitutional restriction upon legislation as to corporate as well as individual property as something essential to really free government." And, in 1963, Mark A. DeWolfe Howe concluded: "The intense interest of nineteenth century jurists in problems of possession is somewhat mystifying to the lawyers of the twentieth."[83]

Yet, though worries over property rights were compelling to many jurists, contrary strains of jurisprudence existed, strains that held robed believers to practices of restraint in deciding on legislation and constitutions. Therefore, for both *Test Oath* cases, Justice Miller, joined by Davis, Swayne, and the Chief Justice, dissented from the majority. Miller reminded his colleagues of the judges' need for extreme restraint in pronouncing against the legislative enactments of either the nation or of a state, especially against the constitution of a state. Concerning Garland, Miller recalled that Congress possessed a right and duty to establish all federal courts below the Supreme Court. Since the 1789 Judiciary Act, Congress and President had prescribed qualifications for all court officers.

[82]*Ibid.*, 362, 379–381.
[83]Terrett v. Taylor, 9 Cranch 43 (1815); H. R. Droop, *Decisions in the United States as to the Constitutional Limits of the Legislative Power, and American Legislation as to Churches Formerly Established* (London, 1869), p. 5; Mark A. DeWolfe Howe, *Justice Oliver Wendell Holmes: The Proving Years, 1870–1882* (Cambridge, 1963), pp. 201–202.

Clients possessed rights, not lawyers. A lawyer's admission to practice was a privilege that the government and the bar granted him. All governments excluded lawyers for many reasons set down in statutes or expressed in the common law. The oath Congress prescribed faced all government officials, jurors, and claimants in federal courts. Why should not those courts acquiesce in the legislative will and, in a rule of the Court, require the same oath for lawyers practicing there?

Miller insisted that no American court had defined bills of attainder; that the majority relied wholly upon foreign case law; and that attainder applied only to criminal cases. Nor were the oath laws of Missouri or of the nation ex post facto, Miller insisted. The majority's contrary view ". . . can only be found in those elastic rules of construction which cramp the powers of the Federal government when they are to be exercised in certain directions, and enlarges them when they are to be exercised in others." Garland was suffering as a result of his own disloyalty, not by reason of a vindictive criminal law enacted by a majority of Congress and approved by a humane President. Miller agreed that Garland's pardon cloaked the Arkansan from punishments for his disloyalty. But the oath, a qualification, not a punishment, survived the pardon. Turning to Cummings, Miller contrasted the Court majority's defense of the priest against a requirement imposed by a state Constitution, with the Court's 1845 ruling that the federal Constitution did not protect a minister against even municipal regulations of church services.[84]

The justices, keenly aware of their institution's weakness since *Dred Scott,* split so evenly in 1866–67 only as the result of deeply held feelings. In seventy-five years there had been few 5–4 decisions by the Court. The strong tendency among appeal judges was to go with a majority in a divided court, if only for the reason that a majority decides. Chase, in 1870, explained why he chose an extended dissent. "No doubt," Chase wrote, "the Missouri oath is detestable, but that was not the question." It was: Could the state properly regulate the numerous concerns expressed in its Constitution, by the prescribed oath? "There was too much injustice, and needless harshness" in the Missouri oath, Chase continued; ". . . I was natu-

[84]Miller, in *Ex parte* Garland, 374, cited Permoli *v.* First Municipality of New Orleans, 3 How. 489 (1845).

rally inclined to go as far as possible against it; but I thought and think still it safer not to interfere with the right of the State to regulate her own internal concerns."[85]

In the same 1866–67 term of the Court, the justices in *Ex parte Milligan* redefined their authority to include determination of martial emergency in unseceded states—a large step beyond the *Prize* cases position. Lambden P. Milligan was a militant antiwar Indianan. In 1864 an Army court in Indianapolis sentenced him to death for disloyal activities. Lincoln, reviewing his sentence, let Milligan stew in prison. In the first passions after Lincoln's murder, President Johnson approved the death sentence. Milligan's lawyer petitioned the United States Circuit Court in Indiana for his client's release by terms of the 1863 Habeas Corpus Act. Justice Davis, on circuit with the sitting district judge, divided with him on the question of their jurisdiction in an appeal from a military court. Because of the technical question of jurisdiction, the substantive question of the legitimacy of military trials of civilians became a possibility in the Supreme Court—if the justices wished to transform technicality into substance.

For the government, Henry Stanbery attended to the question of jurisdiction. Congressman Benjamin F. Butler assisted with a brief sustaining the plenary power of the nation to impose military justice in critical areas. Their language, Fairman states, was "suited to the royal Stuarts."[86] Milligan's lawyers, including Ohio Congressman James A. Garfield, Jeremiah Sullivan Black (late Attorney General in Buchanan's administration), and David Dudley Field insisted that Milligan, if indictable, was triable by civil courts. The Army court in Indiana had failed to follow procedures of the 1863 Habeas Corpus law requiring it to report on civilian prisoners to the local federal district court. Beyond this defect, Black, insisting upon a fixed, nonorganic view of the Constitution, argued that its barriers against military power were "unchangeable and irreparable." All ancient rights of free men where in force in war as in peace. Field, in an

---

[85]To Alexander Long, Feb. 10, 1870, Letterbook, Chase Papers, ser. 4, vol. 118, p. 11, Library of Congress, Fairman, *Reconstruction,* pp. 766–767, notes that Chase hoped to see Garland reversed; and, *ibid.,* p. 159, that Field originally was determined to hold against Missouri's oath, but not against the federal oath. He then changed his mind. On Miller's private view of oaths, *ibid.,* p. 244.

[86]Fairman, *Reconstruction,* p. 201.

argument he would regret, asserted that Indiana was not the South where Congress had authority under the Constitution to determine the Reconstructions of states and to submit civilians to military justice.

All the justices agreed that the military court in Indiana was derelict in its duty to comply with the reporting provisions of the 1863 Habeas law. For a bare majority of the Court, Justice Davis paid the Bill of Rights such respects as had not sounded in that chamber since Taney's tributes to the Fifth Amendment in *Dred Scott:* "The Constitution . . . is a law for rulers and people, equally in war and peace, and covers with the shield of its protection all classes of men, at all times, and under all circumstances." The President undoubtedly had a right and duty to suspend habeas privileges where civil courts were overthrown. But courts were open in Indiana. Therefore Milligan deserved his freedom.

Differing on the basic point whether the judiciary could decide when a sufficient crisis existed to warrant imposition of military justice, the Chief Justice, Miller, Swayne, and Wayne concluded that only Congress possessed the initiative. "We have confined ourselves to the question of power," Chase stated; "it is for Congress to determine . . . expediency." The Bill of Rights did not apply in areas the Congress determined were crisis zones.[87]

Milligan proved a severe blow to the aspirations of the Republicans concerning Reconstruction for the reason that, along with the *Test Oath* decisions, it sharply diminished ways available for either federal or state governments to prevent ex-rebels from controlling administration, justice, and politics. At least by extrapolation (and the President and Democrats extrapolated), *Milligan* implied that the Army had no rightful role to play in states in the absence of war or invasion. Yet both the President and the Congress had assigned the Army to duties in the South; the Thirteenth Amendment gave authority—indeed, a duty—to the nation to act without defining instruments.

Hailed ever since as a landmark of liberty, the majority's points in *Milligan,* as Fairman noted, ". . . should not be taken as precise tests for all future emergencies. They might allow too little, and they

[87]*Ex parte* Milligan, 141–142.

might invite too much." In 1866, the President and Democrats generally insisted upon "too much." The fact is that *Milligan* did not deal at all with the South. In 1867 Justice Davis, dismayed by both the Democrats' exaggerations about the outreach of the decision and the Republicans' emotional denunciations of the position taken by the Court majority, noted that there was "not a word said in the opinion about reconstruction and the power is conceded in insurrectionary States." Nevertheless, the President and Congress concluded that the decision forbade the imposition of military courts there even if required by statute. Combined with the President's orders on peace, pardon, and amnesty, *Milligan* made Grant's General Orders 3 and 44 suspect, raised serious doubts about the Freedmen's Bureau and Civil Rights laws, and obscured the meaningfulness of the Thirteenth Amendment's enforcement clause.[88] Reviewing a report demanded by Congress, on numerous unpunished violations of that Amendment and those laws, Stanton, in mid-February, 1867, told the President that "In view of . . . Milligan's case . . . this Department is unable to determine what cases, if any, . . . can be acted upon by the military authority." Stanton recommended that the Attorney General should investigate and specify "which [violations of law] . . . are cognizant by the [state and/or federal] civil authorities, and such as are cognizant by military tribunal."[89]

Stanton understood that the President's purposes were now to confuse and hinder rather than to clarify and execute. But this insight was still uncommon. More general among Republicans was the sense of unanticipated frustration; even constitutional expert Lieber decried the Court more than the President. Lieber, in a lecture he was preparing on the Constitution, asked:

Why has not any . . . [critic of the military courts] objected to the [President's] amnesty . . . proclamation? . . . The exclusive ground on which these . . . vast measures [the Freedmen's Bureau and the Thirteenth Amendment] can be explained . . . is that it is . . . not righteous [for states] to cut off the

[88]Stanley I. Kutler, *Judicial Power and Reconstruction Politics* (Chicago, 1968), p. 67, on Davis; Fairman, *Reconstruction,* pp. 214–215, has other data.
[89]Stanton to Johnson, Feb. 15, 1867, Attorney General's Records, Letters Received, Box 8, RG 60, National Archives.

heads of some three or four millions of people . . . whether the Constitution says anything about it or not.[90]

Constitutionalists generally condemned the Court's imperial expansions of review authority in the *Test Oath* and *Milligan* decisions. The thin 5–4 majorities and the Court's unprecedented jurisdictional assertions in those cases left the justices vulnerable, Lieber asserted. Pomeroy held to a position that martial law "is not in any true sense a judicial proceeding, or a means of executing the civil laws, but a method of waging war." The Court had paid too little attention to the fact that neither the bill of attainder nor war power clauses of the Constitution had much history in the form of case law. *Dred Scott* should have cured the Court of reaching beyond the facts because the justices yearned to establish or proscribe policies.[91]

Republican Congressmen repeated the argument they had held since 1857, that majorities of the Congress, not of the Court, created the law of the land. They exhumed for libertarian purposes celebrated Court decisions that had extolled broad national powers, powers exercised in defense of slavery, and endorsed Story's 1842 *Prigg* v. *Pennsylvania* opinion. Now Republicans turned Story's emphasis on national power into support for Congress's efforts to raise the condition of civil rights in the South.[92] Taney, in *Dred Scott,* had applied the Fifth Amendment's due process clause substantively, claiming that a federal law limiting slavery expansion violated property rights. Republicans in 1866 asserted that anti-Negro state discriminations substantively violated Fifth Amendment rights. Referring to *Prigg* and *Dred Scott* in debates of 1866, Iowa's James Wilson insisted:

I am not willing that all these precedents, legislative and judicial, which aided slavery so long shall now be brushed into oblivion when freedom

[90]Francis Lieber, "Notes for Lectures on the Constitution," LI 165, Lieber PP, Huntington Library.
    [91]John Norton Pomeroy, *An Introduction to the Constitutional Law of the United States* (New York, 1870), pp. 321, 345, 477–478; Lieber to Sumner, Apr. 15, 1867, LI 3903, Lieber PP, Huntington Library.
    [92]Of Prigg, Mark DeWolfe Howe was to say: "If constitutional law had terminated with Prigg . . . , scholars and lawyers could confidently assert that there is nothing in the nature of American federalism that disables the Congress from controlling private conduct affecting the civil rights of others," In Archibald Cox et al., *Civil Rights, the Constitution, and the Courts* (Cambridge, 1967), p. 45.

needs their assistance. Let them now work out a proper measure of retributive justice by making freedom as secure as they once made slavery hateful. I cannot yield up the weapons which slavery placed in our hands now that they may be wielded in the holy causes of liberty and just government. We will turn the artillery of slavery upon itself.[93]

Had the Court not taken the plunges of 1863–67, Cooley's future domination of legal thought would have been less likely. Perhaps the body of legal theory justifying federal limitation on state power would have remained largely confined to the commercial law and diversity situations of the 1863 *Gelpcke* case. Situations like the one in Iowa, where successive state supreme court judges contradicted one another, were rare and did not speak to the condition in Missouri, where a constitution required state action and where state judges did not disagree.

The *Milligan* and *Test Oath* decisions seriously undercut the Republicans' assumption that they could use the courts as libertarian artillery. The very volume of negative reaction to the *Milligan* decision suggests the awareness in Congress of the Court's ascent from the depths of *Dred Scott*. Republicans and Democrats both hoped to exploit judicial power in their favor. The Republicans were creating Reconstruction policies. It was inevitable that the Court, given the energies and ambitions of its members, would hear other litigations deriving from those policies.

[93]*Congressional Globe*, 39th Cong. 1st Sess. (Mar. 1, 1866), p. 1118. See also Shellabarger, *ibid.* (Mar. 9, 1866), p. 1204.

The Fourteenth Amendment in Light of the Thirteenth: Not Cramped by the Old Technicalities

THOUGH notable for much else, the Thirty-ninth Congress (December, 1865–March, 1867) created, above all, the Fourteenth Amendment, described in a 1972 Supreme Court opinion as "a basic alteration in our federal system." Passionate arguments persist whether the Congressmen of 1866 intended the basic alteration; whether, whatever the Amendment's framers intended, twentieth-century justices properly transformed it into a catalyst for or against states' policies.[1]

The modern Court's perceptions about the intentions of the Thirty-ninth Congressmen involve the tenderest relationships and most hotly contested policies of our time. These include the incorporation of the Bill of Rights through the Fourteenth Amendment as limitations on states' authority in matters of abortions, school desegregation, civil rights and liberties, private race discrimination in housing, juveniles' rights, and race priorities in higher education or in a corporation's training program.[2] Constitutional scholars

---

[1]Mitchum v. Foster, 407 U.S. 225 at 238 (1972); Raoul Berger, *Government by Judiciary: The Transformation of the Fourteenth Amendment* (Cambridge, 1977).

[2]Adamson v. California, 332 U.S. 46 (1947); Brown v. Board of Education of Topeka, 347 U.S. 483 (1954); Monroe v. Paper, 365 U.S. 167 (1961); In re Gault, 387 U.S. 1 (1966); Jones v. Alfred H. Mayer Co., 392 U.S. 409 (1968); Runyon v. McCrary, 427 U.S. 160 (1975); Regents of the University of California v. Bakke, 438 U.S. 268 (1978); Weber v. Kaiser Aluminum, 443 U.S. 193 (1979).

have both fed the justices' perceptions on these matters and been nourished by them. A love affair between Clio and the Court has been consummated, an affair in which historians, justices, and lawyers periodically reconceive Reconstruction. The legitimacy of the offspring of these unions has been uncertain. No one has yet "proved" that the framers and ratifiers of the Fourteenth Amendment intended, or did not intend, the federal Bill of Rights to limit state authority and for the federal Supreme Court to guard civil rights and liberties against state action or nonaction and private impediments; that only what constituted civil rights and liberties in the "black-letter" constitutional law of 1865–66 properly defines Americans' aspirations in the late twentieth century.[3]

Perhaps inquiries into the Fourteenth Amendment have gone about as far as they presently can; perhaps, as the late Jacobus tenBroek and Mark A. DeWolfe Howe suggested decades ago, we should look more at 1865, when the Thirteenth Amendment was written and ratified, in order to learn what Congressmen and their constituents perceived and intended in 1866–68; perhaps the perceptions of 1865 permitted Congressmen of 1866 to build both explicitly and by implication on the understandings and aspirations of the earlier year. Such a reconsideration of the Thirteenth Amendment helps to relieve at least some of the accumulated and hardening qualities of arguments about the Fourteenth, for, as we will suggest, the men who framed and ratified both also connected them as to purposes and means.

Thirty years ago, Jacobus tenBroek insisted that the Thirteenth Amendment, not the Fourteenth, initiated the "revolution in federalism"; that the Thirteenth went far beyond merely declaring the elimination of "immediate bondage." It not only nationalized freedom in that narrow sense, but also nationalized "the right to freedom" in a far broader, organic contemporary meaning and required Congress to enforce those open-ended rights. The Thirteenth

---

[3]Charles Fairman and Stanley Morrison, *The Fourteenth Amendment and the Bill of Rights: The Incorporation Theory,* ed. Leonard W. Levy (New York, 1970) intro. and *passim;* Alfred H. Kelly, "Clio and the Court: An Illicit Love Affair," *Supreme Court Review* (1965), 119–158; Aviam Soifer, "Protecting Civil Rights: A Critique of Raoul Berger's History," *New York University Law Review,* LIV (1979), 651–706, and Michael K. Curtis, "The Bill of Rights as a Limitation on State Authority: A Reply to Professor Berger," *Wake Forest Law Review,* XVI (1980), 45–101.

Amendment, tenBroek wrote, was the "consummation to abolition-ism in the broad sense in which thirty years of agitation and organi-zation had defined that movement."[4]

If tenBroek is correct, then generations of Supreme Court jus-tices, by concentrating on the Fourteenth Amendment's clauses on due process, privileges and immunities, and equal protection of the laws, aimed at the wrong target. The tenBroek analysis justifies recasting the much-debated judgments of Justice Hugo Black and of Professor W. W. Crosskey, that the creators of the Fourteenth Amendment "incorporated" the Bill of Rights as against the states, into queries: Did the creators of the Thirteenth Amendment so intend? Was Justice Field correct in his 1866–67 *Test Oath* case opinion, in so arguing? Was Civil War veteran Colonel George W. Williams correct in his 1889 judgment that "the thirteenth amend-ment contains the logical, legal results of the war"? Before useful replies are likely to emerge, the 1870 comment by Texas Unionist judge and jurisprudent George W. Paschal deserves attention: "It [the Thirteenth Amendment] not merely swept the name and the fact of the [slavery] system from all our laws, and took from the States the power to restore them, but it also opened new fields of inquiry."[5]

Scholars, like the justices, have lavished thought and energy on the Fourteenth Amendment and all but ignored the Thirteenth. A better balance may result from recognizing the perception of John Roche that ". . . the concept of substantive due process . . . was rattling around both in legal circles and in some state courts" in the 1860s.[6] That concept, or concern, about the actual, as against nomi-nal, protection states afforded to residents emerged out of the de-

---

[4]Jacobus tenBroek, *Equal Under Law* (New York, 1965), p. 196; Mark A. DeWolfe Howe, "Federalism and Civil Rights," Massachusetts Historical Society *Proceedings,* LXXVII (1965), 24–25.

[5]George Williams, *The Constitutional Results of the War of the Rebellion* (Worcester, Mass., 1889), p. 15; tenBroek, *Equal Under Law,* p. 196; Black dissenting, in Adamson *v.* California, 67–124; W. W. Crosskey, "Charles Fairman, 'Legislative History,' and the Constitutional Limits on State Authority," *University of Chicago Law Review,* XXII (1954), 1–21; George Washington Paschal, *Lecture Delivered to the American Union Academy of Literature, Science and Art at Its Second Meeting Called for the Purpose March 7, 1870* (Washington, 1870), p. 24.

[6]John P. Roche, *Courts and Rights: The American Judiciary in Action* (New York, 1961), p. 63.

bates on Emancipation. The conjoining of Emancipation and protection led even constitutional experts of the 1860s to express impatience with technicalities. Their special scorn was reserved for persons who insisted that any fixed constitutional relationships equaled protection, or that formal procedures meant that the substance of protection existed. This impatient spirit infused the rhetoric of supporters of both the Thirteenth and the Fourteenth Amendments. Francis Lieber's comment of 1866 is typical: "There are things higher, holier than constitutions. Such things are nations and men composed of nations."[7] Americans "must not underestimate, neither must we overestimate the Constitution," asserted a July 4, 1867, orator in Pennsylvania. "It is not infallible. It is not something stationary. It moves with the nation. It is always to be adapted to the wants of the nation. . . . The freedom of all the people; the equality of citizens & . . . States—these are the grand principles of the reconstructed Union."[8]

In considering links between the Thirteenth and Fourteenth Amendments, it is desirable also to keep in mind the admonition that persons who enacted the Thirteenth in early 1865 and who ratified it later that year did not know that *a* Fourteenth (much less *the* Fourteenth) was to be needed. In 1865, the Thirteenth Amendment received consideration in its own context. That context does not suggest a tightly limited meaning for the Thirteenth Amendment. If the Amendment aimed only at the termination of formal slavery without leaving a door open for further federal intervention in the states, why the enforcement clause? The *Congressional Globe* provides evidence that the Thirty-eighth Congressmen argued little about the enforcement clause—the Constitution's first. This fact does not, however, justify a conclusion about the Thirteenth Amendment of the sort Andrew Johnson insisted on by early 1866: that the Amendment affected only formal slavery and did not change other nation-state relationships.

Southern provisional governors, legislators, and delegates to constitutional conventions bridled at ratifying the Thirteenth

[7]Francis Lieber, "Notes for Lectures on the Constitution," LI 165, Lieber PP, Huntington Library.
[8]J. J. Creigh, *Address Delivered at Paoli Massacre Grounds, July 4, 1867* (West Chester, 1867), pp. 16–17.

Amendment. Its enforcement clause worried them. It left open the possibility of more changes of unspecifiable nature.[9] Democrats, with few exceptions, argued against further changes. The Thirteenth Amendment simply ended slavery, many Democrats insisted, as their views merged with Andrew Johnson's. No more federal action was necessary or proper, the position the President popularized.

Disagreeing, Republican constitutional experts such as John Jay II, Francis Lieber, John N. Pomeroy, Lyman Trumbull, and Charles Sumner argued that the Constitution's Article IV, section 4, clause requiring the nation to guarantee each state a republican form of government had, in the Thirteenth Amendment, a better, though minimal definition of republican. Now no power, whether national, state, or individual, could make people into property.

Many Republicans were moving beyond even this position.[10] They had written the Thirteenth Amendment in an evolutionary, abolitionist context at a time when instrumentalism dominated legal thought and adequacy constitutional assumptions prevailed. In recent years Charles Fairman has criticized tenBroek's reliance upon the "unschooled jurisprudence" of abolitionists. Yet Fairman accepts a "vocabulary of freedom" as a dominant contextual quality of the time. Abolitionists created that vocabulary: Republicans, often despite their own disinclination to do so, institutionalized it.

That vocabulary, and those institutions, embrace far more than the immediate end of legal slavery. To be sure, the Congressmen of 1865, creating the Thirteenth Amendment, failed fully to specify their immediate intentions. But positive enforcement was part of the Thirteenth Amendment's context. Enforcement of what? Of protection ("against the whole world," wrote Mark DeWolfe Howe) from involuntary servitude and violence, and of all the full and equal rights of freedom, some of which history had identified and a multitude of which remained for the inscrutable future to reveal. The very fact that, as Fairman noted, only in 1866 did "the extent of

[9]TenBroek, *Equal Under Law,* p. 196; Charles Fairman, *Reconstruction and Reunion* (New York, 1971), p. 1135; G. Sidney Buchanan, *The Quest for Freedom: A Legal History of the Thirteenth Amendment* (reprinted from *Houston Law Review,* Houston, 1976), ch. 1.

[10]Herman Belz, *Emancipation and Equal Rights: Politics and Constitutionalism in the Civil War Era* (New York, 1978), intro., chs. 1–2; Fairman, *Reconstruction,* ch. 19.

power generated by the Thirteenth Amendment become a sharply drawn issue"[11] suggests that in 1865 Republicans assumed the existence of that power.

Indeed, "many good lawyers" among Republicans thought the enforcement clause superfluous, stated Louisianan Michael Hahn, a veteran of Lincoln's oldest and most controversial state reconstruction. Hahn, addressing a Washington meeting in November, 1865, which included members of both the Thirty-eighth and the Thirty-ninth Congresses, was applauding what they had accomplished and instructing newcomers about their resources for action. Of the Thirteenth Amendment, Hahn asserted that the abolition clause alone was a wholly adequate source of power to Congress to carry out the nation's duty of enlarging liberty for all Americans. But it was well that the enforcement clause existed. It was the nation's reserved authority to intervene in states to thwart limitations on freedom as the future illuminated freedom's now-unfettered, unpredictable contours; to intervene without again risking the dangerous arguments about immobile limits on national powers so common in prewar decades. It erased questions about Congress's authority to "enforce the principles which it [the Thirteenth Amendment] embodies," Hahn stated.

Though overoptimistic about the enforcement clause ending questions about the nation's authority, Hahn was otherwise correct. In 1866 Republicans were grateful to have the clause available when southerners' intractable behavior made national responses necessary.[12] The need to respond in detail to specific southern situations was to transform the abolitionist-Republican expectations of 1865, that the nation would continue the positive task of enlarging freedom, into a need to reply negatively to southern initiatives. Slavery had delayed and thwarted that enlargement of freedom since 1789. The demise of slavery made freedom the condition not only of constitutions but of law—of all laws. The "vocabulary of freedom," not the defunct vocabulary of slavery, now defined policies.

Freedom was much more than the absence of slavery. It was, like slavery, an evolving, enlarging matrix of both formal and customary

[11]Fairman, *Reconstruction*, pp. 1134–1135; Howe, "Federalism and Civil Rights," p. 24.

[12]Michael Hahn, *Manhood the Basis of Suffrage: Speech Before the National Equal Suffrage Association of Washington, November 17, 1865* (Washington, 1865), pp. 2–4.

relationships rather than a static catalog. Such assumptions helped Republicans and their constituents to accept arguments favoring the nation's capacity and duty to move beyond the Thirteenth Amendment's immediate abolition effect.

Supporters of the Thirteenth Amendment expressed their convictions in organic imagery. "Organic" was a favored adjective among Republicans. They meant by organic their society's triumph over diseased elements and steady growth from sound foundations. Education from the past, forward motion, and adaptability to change were the constitutional qualities Republicans praised. According to Francis Newton Thorpe, a pioneering constitutional analyst, it became popular after Appomattox to depict the Union as an organic relation growing out of "the mutual sympathies, the kindred principles, and the similar interests of the American people."[13] Graying veterans of the antislavery crusade and youthful politicos shared such attitudes. Minnesota Congressman Ignatius Donnelly bridged any generation gap in the early days of the Thirty-ninth Congress:

Shall nothing be born of this mighty convulsion, mightier by far than the old Revolution . . . ? . . . [T]his is a new birth of the nation. The Constitution will hereafter be read by the light of the rebellion; by he light of the emancipation; by the light of that tremendous uprising of the intellect . . . going on everywhere around us. He is indeed fearfully cramped by the old technicalities who can see in the enormous struggles only the suppression of a riot and the dispersion of a mob. This struggle has been as organic in its great meaning as the Constitution itself.[14]

Congressmen who framed the Thirteenth Amendment in 1865 and who enforced it in 1866 perceived themselves to be in a constitutional world characterized by both continuities and changes. They linked freedom to the future as they had opposed slavery in the past. It was challenging to be involved in a process which marked the first instance when the Constitution was being changed in order to establish a nationwide social reform. And it was the more challenging

[13]Francis Newton Thorpe, *The Constitutional History of the United States* (Chicago, 1901), III, 520–521.
[14]*Congressional Globe*, 39 Cong., 1 sess. (Feb. 1, 1866), p. 586; Theodore Nydahl (ed.), "The Ignatius Donnelly Diary, 1859–1885" (Ph.D. diss., University of Minnesota, 1941), I, 248–249, 372–373.

to achieve basic reform at the conclusion of a searching civil war and in a period of fundamental changes, Francis Leiber remarked in 1865. "The heat of a civil war of such magnitude would alone be sufficient to ripen thoughts and characteristics which may have been in a state of incipiency before," he continued.[15]

The Republicans misapprehended the pace with which the future would crowd in on them as result of southern white resistance to freedom as equality. If their timing was off, the instrument they crafted in the Thirteenth Amendment proved to be flexible, responsive, and "organic." Republicans saw the Thirteenth Amendment as a surgery which cut the slavery cancer from the body politic, the Black Codes as persisting remnants of slavery, and the enforcement clause as the tool to sever the loathsome residuals. Unpunished harassments of federal officials in the South renewed painful memories of prewar years when physical violence marred proceedings in the federal Senate and when mobs attacked critics of slavery.[16] By 1866, Republicans generally accepted a view that the nation must respond to the assaults, since the affected states failed to do so, and that the nation possessed the constitutional authority to respond.

That authority derived also from the "grasp of war" power, at least for immediate responses. No one knew when a civil war ended. If the "slave power" endured in the Black Codes despite the amended Constitution, then, Republicans such as Samuel Shellabarger and Richard Henry Dana insisted, that Constitution's war power remained a legitimate authority for the nation's response. The more palatable authority for national action derived, however, from the Thirteenth Amendment, which was, wrote Columbia College's law professor and ex-president William A. Duer, not only "for national protection" of individuals' rights but also for "local imitation and example."[17]

Other Republican constitutional experts added the privileges and immunities clause (Article IV, section 2) to the Thirteenth Amend-

[15]Francis Lieber, *Amendments to the Constitution Abolishing Slavery* (New York, 1865), p. 11.
[16]Colorado Chief Justice B. F. Hall to Sumner, Dec. 13, 1865, Sumner PP, vol. 75, no. 103, Houghton Library, Huntington Library.
[17]William Alexander Duer, *A Course of Lectures on the Constitutional Jurisprudence of the United States: Delivered Annually in Columbia College* (New York, 1868), p. 107; Richard H. Dana III (ed.), *Speeches in Stirring Times and Letters to a Son* (New York, 1910), pp. 243–259.

ment and to the war power as authority for Congress to create remedies when the other branches of the national government, and the states, failed in their duty to do so. An early advocate of the Thirteenth Amendment, Chief Justice Chase extolled it on several grounds. First, it was just, and nationalized freedom in a single, grand, simple, clear action. Second, in his view (as in Justice Field's), it connected the Declaration of Independence and Bill of Rights to the Constitution. Third, it kept open, perhaps included, the question of votes for Negroes. Chase was delighted that Lincoln, on April 11, 1865, publicly took sides with him on the need for the surrendered rebel states to adopt black suffrage. Paired with abolition, suffrage, for Chase, was "the frank recognition of every citizen, white or colored, to protect his and his neighbor's welfare by his vote." Last, the Amendment stymied efforts of conservatives to work a deal with the crumpling Confederacy, to return the rebellious states to the Union with slavery undisturbed.[18]

Michael Hahn summarized many of these elements in his November, 1865, speech. An opportunist of chameleon agility, Hahn shifted his opinion on race to match all changing winds about civil rights and liberty. In his estimate, winds were propelling the nation toward new frontiers of equality and liberty. Equal justice measured both. Hahn argued that the Thirteenth Amendment was an openended national commitment about rights. Under both Lincoln's and Johnson's Reconstructions only whites controlled government and society, from state capitals to tiniest hamlets. Congress should require suffrage for all state residents under the Thirteenth Amendment so that every individual could protect himself against public or private wrongs. But such heavy opinion existed in 1865 against including the vote as a civil right that, a few weeks after Hahn spoke, Congress dropped a suffrage requirement from the 1866 Civil Rights Bill. Congress's action should not, however, be misconstrued as a narrow definition of civil rights. Rather, Republicans dropped suffrage because in the 1860s only "radicals" merged civil and political rights. Suffrage was not a right of an American citizen,

[18]Chase to J. M. McKim, Nov. 20, 1865, in David Hughes, "Salmon P. Chase: Chief Justice" (Ph.D. diss., Princeton University, 1963), p. 223; Alfred B. Hart, *Salmon P. Chase* (New York, 1899), pp. 263–264; Jacob W. Schuckers, *The Life and Public Service of Salmon Portland Chase* (New York, 1874), p. 399.

but a privilege a state should extend to its citizens.[19] The nation owed all its citizens its protection; every state resident was a dual citizen of the nation and of his state. The Thirteenth Amendment both authorized and required protection.

Americans of the Civil War era did not entertain late-twentieth-century conceptions of "civil rights"; the phrase came freighted with a different meaning for them than it does for us. As applied to the freedmen, the phrase "civil rights," as used for example in the title of the Civil Rights Act of 1866, was both hierarchical and developmental. That is, they thought of the rights of a free individual, especially a black one, in terms of strata, some essential and basic, others optional. Moreover, because they were learning intensively from their historical experience in the Civil War and Reconstruction, they were also coming to see, none too clearly, that the rights of black people were expanding and developing over time. What was inconceivable in 1855 was enacted into law a scant twenty years later: equal access to public accommodations.

This nineteenth-century sense of "civil rights" can be conveyed by a pyramidal diagram (see page 396). While slavery prevailed, a free black person in any of the slave states was stripped of all but one or two elemental rights, represented by the two substrata of the diagram. Even in the free states of the time, the concession of any further rights remained optional with white freemen. The transition from slavery to freedom by emancipation and abolition placed the question of blacks' rights in an altogether different light; hence the developmental aspect of "civil rights," admittedly poorly represented by a static and stable pyramid. By the very fact of their transition into free status, the freedmen of necessity automatically acquired certain fundamental rights: by definition, those rights essential to differentiate a slave from a free person. At the end of 1865, the substantive content of these rights was well known, at least in terms of the responses needed to the limitations on freed-

[19]Hahn, *Manhood*, pp. 2–5; John Codman Hurd, *The Law of Freedom and Bondage in the United States* (Boston, 1862), II, 295, 319; Thomas M. Cooley, *A Treatise on the Constitutional Limitations Which Rest Upon the Legislative Powers of the States of the American Union* (Boston, 1868), pp. 131–134. Congressman Wilson, referring to the dropped clause on suffrage, stated, "I do not think it materially changes the bill." *Congressional Globe*, 39 Cong., 1 sess. (Mar. 9, 1866), p. 1296.

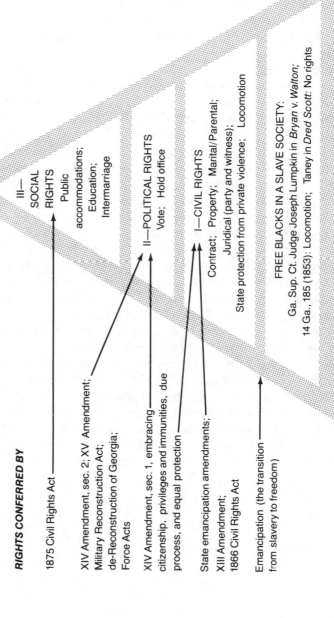

RIGHTS CONFERRED BY

1875 Civil Rights Act

XIV Amendment, sec. 2; XV Amendment;
Military Reconstruction Act;
de-Reconstruction of Georgia;
Force Acts

XIV Amendment, sec. 1, embracing
citizenship, privileges and immunities, due
process, and equal protection

State emancipation amendments;
XIII Amendment;
1866 Civil Rights Act

Emancipation (the transition
from slavery to freedom)

III—
SOCIAL
RIGHTS
Public
accommodations;
Education;
Intermarriage

II—POLITICAL RIGHTS
Vote;   Hold office

I—CIVIL RIGHTS
Contract;   Property;   Marital/Parental;
Juridical (party and witness);
State protection from private violence;   Locomotion

FREE BLACKS IN A SLAVE SOCIETY:
Ga. Sup. Ct. Judge Joseph Lumpkin in *Bryan v. Walton;*
14 Ga., 185 (1853): Locomotion;   Taney in *Dred Scott:* No rights

men the southern states were imposing in the Black Codes. Perhaps, many Republicans asserted, the Thirteenth Amendment (not ratified until December, 1865) conferred these rights of its own force. In any event, their specification in a statute might be useful and, the Republicans of the Thirty-ninth Congress were to prove in the spring of 1866, would not be difficult once the the necessity for a statute was accepted.

Historical experience demonstrated, however, that Republicans could not rely on the good faith of southern whites or on the self-executing provisions of the 1866 Civil Rights law to provide substantive protections to blacks. Both black spokesmen like Frederick Douglass and white friends among Republicans like Charles Sumner perceived a need for American society to ascend to a next level of the pyramid where, they hoped, the whole cluster of rights would finally be self-executing. Section 2 of the Fourteenth Amendment, the various voting provisions of the Military Reconstruction Acts, the Fifteenth Amendment, and the Force Acts were responses to the growing perception of this need for ascent.

That left the highest and most controversial stratum: social equality. Access to public accommodations was, in the nineteenth century, wholly discretionary, at least from the perspective of many whites. The Civil Rights Act of 1875 conveyed these rights, and the very name of that statute, in light of its subject matter, indicated once again how whites' concepts of civil rights were developing.

This transition of the concept of rights took place mostly outside the white South. It was an unplannable growth, occurring largely as reactions to what white southerners did or failed to do (see chart on page 398).

But the evolution of the concept of rights was not wholly a reaction to the initiatives of southern whites. The Thirteenth Amendment itself was a propellant that, for a while at least, pushed people from liberty toward equality. In a technical sense, slaves became free not by action of the Thirteenth Amendment, but by the Emancipation Proclamation as reaffirmed at Appomattox, and by the actions of state statutes or constitutional amendments. By December 6, 1865, when the Thirteenth Amendment was ratified, almost all blacks were already free. This fact contributed, in some subtle and pervasive way, to the Republicans' consensus that the Amendment's force went beyond emancipation-as-liberty, for liberty al-

INITIATIVE	RESPONSE	
Emancipation ⟶ (XIII Amendment)	Black Codes; 1866 Civil Rights Act	CIVIL RIGHTS
XIV Amendment 1. section 1 2. section 2 XV Amendment		CIVIL RIGHTS; POLITICAL RIGHTS
First Military Reconstruction Act; Force Acts	Redemption (1870s) ↓ Mississippi Plan (1890s)	CIVIL RIGHTS; POLITICAL RIGHTS
XV Amendment 1875 Civil Rights Act	*Civil Rights* cases (1883) ↓ *Plessy* v. *Ferguson* (1896)	SOCIAL RIGHTS

ready existed. Emancipation-as-equality was a logical next step, whether or not one favored it.

Those who opposed further climbs on the pyramid of rights tried to hold fast to the idea that adequate rights for freedmen clustered around a core of liberty; an ex-slave was simply someone who had been a slave and was one no longer. Sometime in the mid-1870s, the Republicans, as though frightened by the grandeur of their own thrusts toward equality, lost both their vision and constituent support. They fell back in loose disaggregation, finding comfort and justification in their retreat in a stress on a newer kind of liberty, deriving from prewar constitutional traditions, from postwar legal doctrines, and from innovative notions about science and society. This retreat left southern blacks exposed to discriminations and assaults sanctioned in state laws and customs.

That the Republican members of the Thirty-ninth Congress, assembling for the first postwar session in late 1865, were aware of the dynamic currents that swirled around the questions of emancipation and civil rights is evident from Michael Hahn's speech to them, introduced earlier. Obviously, Hahn stated, the Black Codes must go. "Congress should see to it that no slave codes [i.e., Black Codes] are enacted in any states or districts which, in substance and reality, revive all the features of the [slave] institutions except in name. . . . Under the color of such laws, the most insidious approaches to slavery may be instituted. . . ." Congress must ensure not only that state laws call for fair treatment of citizens but also that state officers execute laws without "difference or partiality." By prejudiced differentiations, "the most execrable tyranny may be practiced on one race, while the other would be partially exempt." Still further, all state institutions including asylums, courts, hospitals, and schools must treat citizens without discrimination. States should equalize taxes and not, by design and administration, burden most those individuals who were least able to defend themselves through protest or litigation. Therefore the nation must protect all citizens' civil liberties as well as civil rights. If Negroes and their white friends could not assemble, petition, or vote without official hindrance and unofficial violence, then civil rights were always in hazard. How to protest if landlords refused to rent offices or residences to Negroes and Unionists without a permit from employers, in situations where only landlords and employers had recourse to a sheriff or constable to support a refusal to give a permit? If by town council order or custom, a community forbade Negroes or white Unionists from establishing residence, both civil rights and liberties were diminished. Hahn cited the instance of a grand jury in Louisiana that indicted a champion of Negro suffrage for sedition "as against the peace and dignity" of the state. Such a fuzzy formula always provided a local majority with a crushing weapon.[20]

Other persons accepted positions analogous to Hahn's upon reading the periodicals of evangelical and teachers' societies associated in the Freedmen's Bureau work, and the popular accounts of touring journalists in the South. Philadelphia lawyer and legal writer Sidney George Fisher, whose 1862 book, *The Trial of the Constitution,* had become a mainstay of adequacy constitutionalists, learned about civil rights in the South during conversations in Philadelphia with a visiting ex-Confederate. Fisher asked him what his neighbor's response would be if a Negro, although enjoying ordinary economic civil rights, when defending himself against assault struck his white attacker. "Most [white] men would kill him [the Negro]," the visitor replied. Would community opinion justify the murder? Fisher asked. "Certainly, . . . more than justify it, almost require it," was the forthright response. Fisher swung toward Hahn-like attitudes (though temporarily, as matters worked out).

Individual insights into the relationship of civil rights and national protection against state and private acts ranged from Hahn's view of suffrage and of access to private accommodations to Fisher's reaction concerning self-defense in criminal assaults. All shared an organic view of the amended Constitution. Senator John Sherman, in mid-December, 1865, expressed this proposition succinctly: the Thirteenth Amendment's enforcement clause gave Congress the express power "to secure all . . . [Americans'] rights of freedom by appropriate legislation."[21]

No one could know that northerners like Fisher would lose their capacity to be shocked at violence and that they would become fatigued instead with "the eternal Sambo," or predict when fatigue would be decisive in politics. Republicans were prisoners of their own tenacious respect for state-based federalism. State sovereignty was dead; state rights were more vigorous than ever. But, in the Republican constitutional view of 1865 and 1866, federalism no longer meant that the nation possessed only disabilities. Federalism meant instead that states, like individuals, bore responsibilities; that the nation, like individuals and states, possessed remedies. State wrongs that threatened the nation's stability by diminishing individuals' rights were unacceptable. States could no longer be "a congeries of despotisms," the abolitionist writer John Cheever asserted in an 1866 petition to Congress favoring Negro suffrage. The nation had a positive duty to prevent a state, or any persons in a state, from withholding rights from any residents.[22]

Abolitionists had referred endlessly to the Declaration of Independence. It was, preached Illinoisan Edwin Larned in a July 4, 1865, oration, the rock upon which the nation was built in 1776, and should now build higher. Compromise with the Declaration's prin-

[21]Nicholas B. Wainwright (ed.), *A Philadelphia Perspective: The Diary of Sidney George Fisher Covering the Years 1834–1871* (Philadelphia, 1967), p. 510; see also pp. 509, 511; Sherman, *Congressional Globe*, 39 Cong., 1 sess. (Dec. 13, 1865), p. 41.

[22]George B. Cheever et al., *Petition and Memorial of Citizen of the U.S. to the Senate and House of Representatives in Congress Assembled, November 30, 1865* (Washington, 1865), pp 4–5.

ciples would undermine the nation's structure. The Bill of Rights, considered only as a list of wrongs like the Ten Commandments that the government must not commit, compromised the Declaration. The proper way to see the Declaration was as a roster of positive duties for the nation, the states, and the people; the nature of those duties was spelled out in the Bill of Rights and the Thirteenth Amendment. Agreeably, an anonymous pamphleteer of 1865, fulminating at Roger B. Taney as "the unjust Judge," concluded that the Declaration and the amended Constitution were now in perfect harmony. "The Constitution is but the Declaration in action," he insisted, and likened the Declaration to a Christian's view of the Gospels, as "the model for imitation . . . [and] the acme of attainment."[23]

As northern reaction to southern events created support for such views, equalitarians hoped that the Thirty-ninth Congress would move the nation beyond reunion. The hope was reasonable because the Thirteenth Amendment was now part of a mobile constitutional platform suitable for continuing ascent. "Lift up your hearts," pleaded former slaveowner Moncure Conway. Remember that America began with the Declaration of Independence but reached *Dred Scott.* Abjure the President's worship at "the tomb of the Old Union." Johnson was re-creating Buchanan's constitutional posture. "There is not a thinking man in America but must see that any permanent 'reconstruction' must imply a reconstruction of the whole organic law of the country," Conway wrote.[24]

By 1866 most Republicans in and out of Congress had caught up with abolitionist, organic, increasingly formalist perceptions about the war's causes and about American society and government, especially about dynamic relationships among liberty, rights, and federalism. Slavery, abolitionists had preached, had made social stability and civil liberties uncertain for whites and blacks, northerners and southerners. The liberties of whites and blacks withered in the face of hostile local majorities, especially when delinquent peace officers failed to protect rights. The war that slavery provoked had resulted in abolition. Now a duty existed to follow through on abolition by eradicating the remaining traces of impaired liberty because they

[23]Edwin Channing Larned, *The Great Conflict* (Aurora, Ill., 1865), pp. 14–15; [Anonymous], *The Unjust Judge: A Memorial of Roger Brooke Taney* (New York, 1865), pp. 18–19.
[24]Moncure Daniel Conway, "Sursum Corda," *The Radical,* I (1866), 291–292.

caused social instability. Therefore the guarantees of the Declaration of Independence and of the Bill of Rights were needed against both mobs and community officials who did not perform their duty to quell mobs. Until such guarantees were obtained everywhere, until the nation, employing the Thirteenth Amendment's enforcement clause, held state and local offices to their duty by appropriate legislation, individuals' rights and liberties could never be secure.[25]

These rights, wrote abolitionist John Weiss, were growing in number and mixing together in ways that defied old technicalities in constitutional law. The rights of American citizens—and such commentators as Cheever, Jay, and Weiss insisted that, by the Thirteenth Amendment, Negroes were "naturalized" citizens of their states as well as of the nation—included civil rights, traditionally defined as economic relationships. But, by the new definition, Americans' civil rights had grown to include also equal civil liberties and social rights such as access to hotels, trolleys, and the like. Republicans, especially those who proudly described themselves as Radicals, had substantially enlarged their definitions of constitutional rights to dimensions that would have pleased both abolitionists of the decades of the 1830s to the 1850s and civil rights frontiersmen of the 1950s and 1960s. The Radicals were an informal, changing, nonideological coalition within the party. They differed sharply with one another and with moderate and conservative Republicans on such matters as tariffs or fiscal policy. But, in 1866, the Radicals proved not to be far ahead of their party colleagues on rights.

The Republican-abolitionist judgment was that the nation must supply security for person, property, and society when states did not, though the states' own Constitutions and laws required them to do so. In a secure society, some authority must insulate individuals against wrongful actions, whether those actions were perpetrated by a private individual, by officials, or by conspiracies or mobs unrestrained by officials. Negroes knew all this from a far longer tuition—knew that not only positive law but officials' acts and nonacts, plus customary private and community relationships, determined the quality of life and labor. Simple justice required that federalism no longer deny individuals some remedy against wrongs

[25]See John Sherman, *Congressional Globe*, 39 Cong., 1 sess. (Dec. 13, 1865), p. 41; Belz, *Emancipation*, pp. 112–117.

when wronged individuals wished to seek remedies.[26]

Foreign antislavery spokesmen, many of whom had supported the United States with their home governments during the war, made similar views known also in America. "So long as the slavery question shall continue," advised the influential Agénor de Gasparin, "the war will not have ended." Emancipation must not be separated from its results. The past clearly imposed on the present a task both to equalize the freedmen's status and to protect him in his transition to equality. The Union's unconditional abolition of slavery necessarily proclaimed equality, he insisted. No Black Code restrictions and reservation were admissible. They separated emancipation from its result, equality. "At the bottom, it is the slavery question that continues under discussion."[27]

Particular concerns about southern states competed for attention with more general apprehensions of misdirected state power everywhere. The Thirteenth Amendment permitted—no, required—further national interventions in opposition to state or private acts that substantively lessened individuals' protections. The measure of adequate protection was the Bill of Rights, including the Declaration of Independence.[28]

As time passed and unanticipated events crowded in, these assumptions and aspirations lost firmness. Old abolitionists sickened, died, or drifted into other crusades. Republicans, including some Radicals, oscillated between a view that they were aiming at obnoxious public and private acts, and one that concerned itself only with positive state acts. The Bill of Rights appeared to be less than adequately "incorporated" into the Thirteenth Amendment. The nationalization of civil rights revealed itself as still incomplete. Greater completeness required more federal interventions. Almost every Republican, however disposed in favor of the broadest view of the Thirteenth Amendment, could not overcome an assumption that the states would obey state and federal law and themselves punish violators of residents' rights; could not diminish the Repub-

[26]Cheever et al., Petition, pp. 4–5; John Jay, The Political Situation in the United States: A Letter to the Union League Club of New York (London, 1866), p. 7; John Weiss, "Is the Negro Naturalized?" The Radical, I (1866), 253–255.

[27]Mary Booth (tr.), Letter from Agénor de Gasparin . . . to the Loyal Publication Society of America (New York, 1866), p. 5.

[28]John N. Pomeroy, An Introduction to the Constitutional Law of the United States (New York, 1870), pp. 149–152; Lieber to Sumner, Apr. 15, 1867, LI 3903, Lieber PP, Huntington Library.

licans' traditional priority to preserving federalism. And it was fair to ask, could, or should, the nation police every southern hamlet? Such oscillations, assumptions, and uncertainties were to frustrate equalitarians' and Negroes' hopes. Those persons, including lawyers and judges, who wished to limit the impacts of the Thirteenth Amendment, of its successor Reconstruction Amendments, and of their enforcement laws were able to capitalize on the equalitarians' uncertainties and sense of limitations.[29] But this foreknowledge of frustration wrenches history from its course, and to that course, so far as opinion and action in Congress on these matters are concerned, this account returns.

Hearings by the Thirty-ninth Congress's Joint Reconstruction Committee and the Senate's Judiciary Committee, chaired, respectively, by Maine's learned, cautious William Pitt Fessenden and Illinois's scholarly, respected Lyman Trumbull, followed by full-scale debates in both Houses, transformed the abolitionists' concept of the Constitution as "ought" into responses primarily, but never exclusively, to what was occurring in the South. Representative James Wilson, chairman of the House Judiciary Committee, had argued in debates on the Thirteenth Amendment that First Amendment rights belonged "to every American citizen, high or low, rich or poor, where ever he may be within the jurisdiction of the United States. With these rights no State may interfere without breach of the bond which holds the Union together." Wilson and other House Republicans such as John Kasson of Iowa and John F. Farnsworth of Illinois had reiterated their conviction that the First Amendment and others of the Bill of Rights defined the "privileges and immunities" of state and national citizens.[30] Upon accepting the speakership of the House, Representative Schuyler Colfax of Indiana, repeating a theme he had stressed in speeches during the preceding autumn, insisted that Congress must both ensure the nation against renascent disloyalty in the South and honor its commitments to

[29]Michael Les Benedict, "Preserving Federalism: Reconstruction and the Waite Court," *Supreme Court Review* (1978), 39–79 at 47; Brotherhood of Liberty, *Justice and Jurisprudence: An Inquiry Concerning the Constitutional Limitations of the Thirteenth, Fourteenth, and Fifteenth Amendments* (Philadelphia, 1889), *passim.* The "Brotherhood" was composed of Negro lawyers who made, inter alia, the points noted above.

[30]Wilson in *Congressional Globe*, 38 Cong., 1 sess., (March 19, 1864), pp. 1202–1203; others in *ibid.* (March 31, 1864), p. 1369, (June 15, 1864), p. 2979; (June 15, 1864), p. 2990; 2 sess. (Jan. 12, 1865), p. 193.

freedom for Negroes. Colfax strove to make clear his dynamic perception that the nation's responsibility was also to protect all persons' rights to property and personal security. The Declaration of Independence, he asserted, defined the inalienable rights of free men as broad principles. Colfax applied those eighteenth-century principles to present needs, stressing the nation's responsibility to individuals who wished to sue, testify, travel, or contract. The Thirteenth Amendment also imposed on the nation the duty to protect in detail freedom's broad categories; the Black Codes made clear the particular evils against which the nation must protect. The popularity of Colfax's speech suggests how widespread the idea was both of envisioning broad categories of freedom and of responding to specific attacks on the practice of freedom.[31]

Other members of the Thirty-ninth Congress frequently repeated such views, especially during the thorough debates on the Fourteenth Amendment and the Civil Rights and second Freedmen's Bureau bills. Alabama's Black Code prohibition against blacks owning firearms violated the Bill of Rights provision on "the right of the people to keep and bear arms," insisted Representative Sidney Clarke of Kansas; a republican form of government, which the nation must guarantee each state, was one in which a state's citizens enjoyed "all privileges and immunities of other citizens," which the Bill of Rights in turn defined.

On the Thirty-ninth Congress's first day (December 6, 1865) Congressman John Bingham of Ohio introduced a resolution for a Fourteenth Amendment that authorized Congress to pass all laws necessary to secure every person in each state equal protection for the rights to life, liberty, and property.[32] Soon after, Trumbull submitted a draft of what later became the second Freedmen's Bureau and the Civil Rights laws. Bingham was unsure how adequately the Thirteenth Amendment's enforcement clause sanctioned such direct federal interventions as Trumbull was proposing. The Presi-

---

[31]O. J. Hollister, *Life of Schuyler Colfax* (New York, 1886), pp. 269–279; *Congressional Globe*, 39 Cong., 1 sess. (Dec. 4, 1865), p. 5; Gideon Welles, *Diary of Gideon Welles* (Boston, 1911), II, 385, 410.

[32]Sec. 1. No State shall make or enforce any law which shall abridge the privileges or immunities of citizens of the United States; nor shall any State deprive any person of life, liberty, or property, without due process of law, nor deny to any person within its jurisdiction the equal protection of the laws. *Congressional Globe*, 39 Cong., 1 sess. (Mar. 24, 1866), p. 1629; for Clarke, *ibid.*, p. 1838.

dent's March 27 veto of the Civil Rights bill determined Bingham to "constitutionalize" civil rights protections, regardless of whether Congress repassed the bill over the veto. The Joint Committee fashioned alternative versions of a Fourteenth Amendment, and by the end of April it issued to both Houses a revised text.[33] Both Houses of Congress further altered the Fourteenth Amendment proposal into its present form (see Appendix) and, in mid-June, sent it out to the states over the President's objection (itself unprecedented concerning a proposed Amendment).

The Congressmen made clear in their warm debates, especially on section 1, that they were not merely voiding *Dred Scott* or creating a shorthand restatement of the Civil Rights bill, simultaneously under consideration. They were also fashioning a long-hand restatement (not a revocation) of the Thirteenth Amendment. Bingham and his colleagues were, demonstrably, not referring in the Fourteenth Amendment only to the Civil Rights bill's catalog of rights. Instead the Congressmen embraced "this immortal bill of rights" in the panoply of organic contemporary meanings. Those meanings encompassed the fundamental rights of free men, an uncatalogable array of rights included in the Constitution's privileges and immunities clause (Article IV, section 2), James Wilson insisted. Had the states observed their obligations under that clause, no Fourteenth Amendment or Civil Rights Bill would now be needed, he continued. The oaths of state officers to sustain the Constitution were insufficient; federal enforcements were needed.[34]

William Brock and others have criticized the authors of the Amendment's first section, and, though less so, of the Civil Rights bill, for their vagueness concerning the meaning of civil rights, a vagueness that seemed to signify a sluggish commitment to Negro freedom. Instead this vagueness may have reflected the difficulties inherent in any attempt to incorporate a natural law concept into a constitution or public law, especially in a federal system. No legal authorities supplied neat definitions of civil rights; none does today,

[33]"The Congress shall have power to make all laws which shall be necessary and proper to secure to the citizens of each state all privileges and immunities of citizens in the several states; and to all persons in the several states equal protection in the rights of life, liberty and property." Benjamin B. Kendrick (ed.), *The Journal of the Joint Committee of Fifteen on Reconstruction, 39th Congress, 1865–1867* (New York, 1914), p. 106; *Congressional Globe*, 39 Cong. 1 sess. (Dec. 20, 1865), p. 97–99.

[34]*Congressional Globe*, 39 Cong., 1 sess. (Mar. 1, 1866), p. 1115; (Mar. 9, 1866), p. 1294; (Apr. 7, 1866), p. 1832.

or can. In 1866 the most widely known and best available legal statement was still that by Justice Bushrod Washington in *Corfield* v. *Coryell* (1823), a case arising from litigation about the rights of Americans from "foreign" states to fish oysters. These rights, Washington had stated, are at least those "which are in their nature fundamental; which belong of right to the citizens of all free Governments; and which have at all times been enjoyed by the citizens of the several States which compose this Union, from the time of their becoming free, independent, and sovereign." But, Washington continued: "What these fundamental principles are it would perhaps be more tedious than difficult to enumerate."[35] He tried to enumerate these fundamental rights, at least in interstate situations. They included

. . . protection by the government; the enjoyment of life and liberty with the right to acquire and possess property of every kind, and to pursue and obtain happiness and safety; subject nevertheless to such restraints as the government may justly prescribe for the general good of the whole. The right of a citizen of one state to pass through, or to reside in any other state, for purposes of trade, agriculture, professional pursuits, or otherwise; to claim the benefit of the writ of *habeas corpus;* to institute and maintain actions of any kind in the courts of the state; to take, hold and dispose of property, either real or personal; and an exemption from higher taxes than are paid by the other citizens of the state.[36]

However encouraging to prewar abolitionists Justice Washington's natural law catalog was, so broad in categories (touching, in one rarely quoted paragraph, even political rights), it failed to speak to the 1865–66 situation in which a state refused its own citizens their due. The framers and supporters of the new federal amendments and laws of 1865–66 aimed to make Justice Washington's fundamental rights of all national citizens independent of state action, not only in comity situations, but as rights of citizens immune from discriminations in their own state. Many Republicans saw Justice Washington's general catalog in 1866 not as theoretical natural rights but as real ones vested by the Thirteenth Amendment.[37]

[35]W. R. Brock, *An American Crisis: Congress and Reconstruction, 1865–1867* (New York, 1963), pp. 44–46; Corfield *v.* Coryell, 6 Fed. Cas. 546 (1823).
[36]Corfield *v.* Coryell.
[37]Cooley, *Treatise,* p. 438; Pomeroy, *Introduction to Constitutional Law,* pp. 151–152, 174.

Section 2 of the proposed Fourteenth Amendment sought, first, to overcome the South's advantage deriving from the demise of the three-fifths clause (Article I, section 2), if blacks did not vote. The Thirteenth Amendment's ratification voided the three-fifths clause. Negroes would be counted as full persons for purposes of state representation in the House, and the South would substantially increase its strength in Congress as a result of its rebellion. A common Republican expectation of 1865, destined for disappointment, was that the South would give Negroes the vote, and the nation would amnesty ex-rebels, thus balancing the South's undeserved advantage.[38] Therefore, in the Fourteenth Amendment, all persons in a state were to be the base for apportioning the number of Representatives. If a state excluded residents from voting in federal or state elections for any reason other than participation in the rebellion or conviction for crime, that state's congressional delegation was reducible in proportion to the numbers of persons disfranchised. This provision which sought to encourage states to provide black suffrage was to remain a dead letter, and, even as it was adopted, received the contumely of George Julian, Frederick Douglass, and Susan B. Anthony, among others. They criticized it for leaving up to the states the suffrage of black men and for ignoring all women. The Radical pamphleteer George Cheever pointed up the contradictions between the Fourteenth Amendment's section 2 and the Thirteenth:

The present proposed amendment . . . , leaving the rebel states at liberty to disfranchise the colored race, is at sword's point with the just amendment [the Thirteenth]. . . . On this ground [i.e., the Thirteenth Amendment's enforcement clause] we have passed the Civil Rights Bill. But if that bill was necessary for security from slavery, if what are called civil rights were necessary to be secured by special law in order that the . . . amendment against slavery be carried out, much more was it necessary, for the same purpose, that the right of suffrage be secured by special law.[39]

[38]Elizur Wright, in George L. Stearns (comp.), *The Equality of All Men Before the Law Claimed and Defended* (Boston, 1865), pp. 40–41.
[39]Rev. George Barrell Cheever, *Impartial Suffrage, A Right: and the Infamy of the Revolution Against It* (New York, 1866), pp. 10–11; George Julian, *Political Recollections* (Chicago, 1884), pp. 272–273; Douglass in *The Radical,* II (1866), 109–110; Susan B. Anthony to Sumner, May 15, 1866, vol. 78, no. 61, pt. 1, Sumner PP, Houghton Library, Harvard University.

Section 3 of the Fourteenth Amendment barred from both federal or state officeholding, whether elective or appointive, persons who had once held office then supported the rebellion. In one sense, this exclusion was more severe than that by the ironclad test oath because it embraced state and federal officeholders. But, in another sense, the Fourteenth Amendment's section 3 formula was softer. It covered only those persons who held office before they supported the Confederacy, thus violating oaths of office. Further, the Fourteenth Amendment provided that Congress, by two-thirds vote in each house, could pardon such persons.

Section 4 reflected concerns about the validity of the United States war debt and the invalidity of the Confederate debt, as well as about claims for emancipated slaves, that had troubled Unionist spokesmen since the days of the Wade-Davis bill. The outrage expressed at the course of the Iowa judges in repudiating Dubuque's bonded indebtedness suggests how deeply Victorians felt about the sanctity of public debts. An assumption of the Confederacy's debt was equally anathema.[40] And section 5 provided that Congress could enforce sections 1–4.

Section 1 engaged most attention. John Norton Pomeroy, dean of New York University's Law School and a "state rights nationalist," wrote that section 1 gave federal officers and courts "complete power" to protect citizens against "local injustice and oppression" even if no diversity jurisdiction existed. "Nor would this Amendment interfere in any way with any of the rights, privileges, and functions which properly belong to the individual states," Pomeroy asserted. The proceedings of any government in America that demeaned the "command" of the Bill of Rights would be void, he concluded. This relationship should have existed since 1789; now it would operate. Therefore Pomeroy applauded what the Republicans of 1866 accomplished in entwining natural with positive law; in making constitutionalism as adaptable and organic as the common law.

The Bill of Rights, defining wrongs the nation might not commit,

---

[40]Irwin Unger, "Money and Morality: The Northern Calvinist Churches and the Reconstruction Financial Question," *Journal of Presbyterian History*, XL (1964), 38–55. Andrew Johnson told Elizabeth Blair Lee that ". . . the [public] debt was his chief solicitude." Lee to Admiral S. P. Lee, Apr. 22, 1865, Box 12, item II-a, Blair-Lee PP, Princeton University.

now defined also inadmissible state wrongs. Congress need pass no enforcing statutes to secure individuals' rights, Pomeroy continued. Injustice was now a violation of the rights Americans possessed against both national and state governments. The old *Barron* v. *Baltimore* rule that Marshall had established, in which the Bill of Rights limited only the nation, was as obsolete as *Dred Scott.* Until 1865–66 the Bill of Rights was of little consequence; the first eight Amendments involved largely concerns about criminal procedure, and few federal crimes existed. "It is not enough [now] that . . . protection should be extended to citizens while abroad; it should be as powerful at home," Pomeroy insisted: "The citizen should be guarded in his enjoyment of his civil rights of life, liberty, limb, and property, against the unequal and oppressive legislation of the states."[41]

"Contemporary history leaves no doubt of what was intended here," the Texas jurist and constitutional commentator George W. Paschal wrote. Congress, by "general terms," aimed in the Fourteenth Amendment to "incorporate those [persons] made free by the thirteenth amendment into the body politic; and to leave no doubts as the [rights of the] naturalized. . . . They are alike entitled to the proud distinction of American citizenship." Congress looked "to past evils" and therefore forbade states from "making or *enforcing*" any law violative of citizens' rights. "For what law can be passed which does not, in some way, affect the privileges and immunities, or the life, liberty, and property of the citizen?" Still, states were wholly free to legislate on any subject so long as the legislation was "in obedience to the paramount law."[42]

Paschal understood precisely the concepts and purposes of the Amendment's major architects such as Bingham. Speaking in this instance in defense of the proposed Civil Rights bill, but in terms appropriate to the Fourteenth Amendment, Bingham stated:

The care of the property, the liberty, and the life of the citizen, under the solemn sanction of an oath imposed by your Federal Constitution, is in the States, and not in the Federal Government. I have sought to effect no

---

[41]Pomeroy, *Introduction*, pp. 150–152. James Wilson noted that Congress's civil rights concern must not aim at creating a criminal code for any state. *Congressional Globe*, 39 Cong., 1 sess. (Mar. 1, 1866), pp. 1118–1120.

[42]George W. Paschal, *Lecture*, p. 26. Italics are Paschal's.

change in that respect in the Constitution of the country. I have advocated here an amendment which would arm Congress with the power to compel obedience to the oath, and punish all violations by State officers of the bill of rights, but leaving those officers to discharge the duties enjoined on them as citizens of the United States by that oath and by that constitution.[43]

The Congress established two levels of protection in section 1 of the Fourteenth Amendment. Citizens were to enjoy all privileges and immunities; other persons, only the fundamentals of due process and equal protection. What were privileges and immunities? To Bingham, they were not only those rights conferred on its citizens by a state. The Bill of Rights was the essential short list. Further, in his view, and in the opinion of many other Congressmen, ex-slaves were citizens. In addition to proofs of these propositions from 1866, Bingham, five years later, reiterated his position of the earlier year, quoting verbatim the Bill of Rights:

Mr. Speaker, that the scope and meaning of the limitations imposed by the first section, fourteenth amendment of the Constitution may be more fully understood, permit me to say that the privileges and immunities of citizens of the United States, as contradistinguished from citizens of a State, are chiefly defined in the first eight amendments to the Constitution of the United States.[44]

One of the problems facing Republicans in coping with federal guarantees for citizens was that no one was sure how to define "citizen." Legal scholar Horace Binney and constitutional expert Francis Lieber, exploring the meaning of "citizen" in 1866 on behalf of Republican Congressmen, agreed that original research was necessary because no "precise and accurate opinions" about national citizenship existed.

A citizen, they concluded, was a resident of a society, comprehending all the people, all free residents, white and black, as well as women, infants, paupers, and vagabonds. "All are entitled to protection by the government and owe allegiance to it," wrote Binney. Citizens were native-born or naturalized. No state in the American Union could make a citizen unless he was born in the state. A

---

[43]*Congressional Globe*, 39 Cong., 1 sess., app. (Mar. 9, 1866), p. 1292.
[44]*Congressional Globe*, 42 Cong., 1 sess., app. (Mar. 31, 1871), p. 84. On Luke Poland's agreement in 1866, see *ibid.*, 39 Cong., 1 sess. (June 5, 1866), p. 2961; on Howard, see Berger, *Government*, pp. 38, 148.

citizen naturalized by action of Congress was automatically a citizen of the state of his residence. Therefore, Binney asserted, every citizen of a state was a United States citizen; every United States citizen was a state citizen either by birth or by naturalization. All citizens deserved the privileges and immunities of other citizens in the states. Ex-slaves were as much free citizens as any other Americans. Emancipation had created equality of citizenship. Had the southern states not limited freedmen's privileges and immunities, no national action would now be needed. "The states are foreign to each other in many particulars; but no state can prevent a citizen of another state from enjoying within its limits all privileges and immunities of its own citizens in like circumstances."[45]

Such views about federalism held by Republican "true believers" both in and out of Congress faced opposition from Democrats. They, and President Johnson, insisted, accurately enough, that, save for expatriates, travelers abroad, importers, and residents of the federal District and territories, national citizens' rights had been irrelevant. Except for abolitionists, legal commentators had long shunted aside questions of national rights with generalities. As recently as 1862, Lincoln's Attorney General Edward Bates, in a widely circulated opinion, could offer only this puzzled nonreply to a request for a definition of the rights adhering to national citizenship:

I have often been pained by the fruitless search in our law books and the records of our courts for a clear and satisfactory definition of the phrase citizen of the United States. . . . Eighty years of practical enjoyment of [the rights of national] citizenship, under the Constitution, have not sufficed to teach us either the exact meaning of the word or the constituent elements of the thing we prize so highly.[46]

Congressmen of 1866 had learned a way around this inescapable difficulty. The states would, in effect, define "the thing we prize so highly," by the public and private actions and nonactions that individuals encountered. It was a brilliant approach to a solution, because it accommodated all the diversity a federal system could contrive while avoiding a need for a permanent, coercive national

[45]Binney to Lieber, Apr. 11, 1866, Lieber PP, Box 51, LI-917, Huntington Library; John Jay, *Address*, p. 9; Hahn, *Manhood*, pp. 2–3.
[46]U.S. Attorney General, *Opinions*, X, 383.

bureaucracy for enforcement. That is, it was brilliant if southerners accepted the new era.[47]

While Congressmen argued about the Fourteenth Amendment, they considered also the Civil Rights and second Freedmen's Bureau bills, the former to flesh out the Thirteenth Amendment, and all to define and enforce one another. Debates on the Civil Rights and Bureau bills, and the Fourteenth Amendment, are all but inseparable, and contemporaries did not separate them. Indeed, attempts to do so too sharply incur the risk of obscuring the essentials which the proponents of these measures sought.

In the Senate, John Sherman stressed the point that the Thirteenth Amendment expressly required Congress "to secure all these rights of national citizenship." To John Jay, the Civil Rights bill was "the proper complement of the Anti-Slavery Amendment, since it relieves all misapprehensions . . . as regards the relationship of our people towards each other." Chief Justice Chase approved of the Civil Rights bill for the same reason, and because it defined national citizenship on this basis: ". . . the people in May 1866 were not the same people as in December 1860, having been then constituted of white freemen only, and now being constituted of white and colored citizens together." Trumbull, a leader in the civil rights cause, noted that the Thirteenth Amendment was not a mere declaration, without effect. He hoped "to secure freedom to all persons within [all of] the United States, and protect every individual in the full enjoyment of the rights of person and property and furnish him with the means of their vindication."

Trumbull saw to it that his aspirations found expression also in the Freedmen's Bureau bill, which prohibited refusal or denial of rights "in consequence of any State or local law, ordinance, police or other regulation, custom, or prejudice." Protection, Trumbull insisted, was "a positive duty" upon the nation that the Thirteenth Amendment imposed. He "never doubted that the Amendment was fully adequate to sustain Congress in carrying out its responsibility "to protect every person in the United States in all the rights of person and property belonging to the free citizen." Congress must act against "any legislation or any public sentiment . . . if the states and local authorities, by legislation or otherwise, deny these

[47]Belz, *Emancipation*, ch. 5.

rights. . . ." The nation, benefiting from the allegiance individuals offered, must protect them in their rights.

Not many years later, Joseph Bradley, one of the most systematic analysts ever to serve as an associate justice, noted in his *Slaughter-house* cases opinion that Congress, enacting the Fourteenth Amendment in 1866, though carefully appending the enforcement clause, did not then pass enforcement legislation. He reasoned that the 1866 Civil Rights bill, then also before Congress, served to enforce the prospective Fourteenth Amendment as well as the Thirteenth.[48]

Trumbull and the other Republicans intended the Civil Rights bill to continue the controlled revolution in the federal system, the system that the Thirteenth Amendment had so greatly advanced. In it, the national government would not likely need to intervene in New York, Illinois, or Massachusetts, Trumbull remarked on one occasion, because those states would probably carry out their duties to protect their citizens. Trumbull overestimated the dedication of northern and western states to legal equality. But his position, that all American governments bore a burden positively to protect rights, was not diminished by the fact that states outside the South were failing in the performance of that duty.[49]

Negroes, as such, were not always central to the framers of the Civil Rights and associated measures; constraints now faced whole classes of persons. Chief Justice Chase noted that ". . . it [the Civil Rights Act] is as important to the prosperity of whites as to the security of blacks." Trumbull emphasized an ancient proposition of which abolitionists were fond: "Allegiance and protection are reciprocal rights."[50]

The Civil Rights bill redefined (section 1) national citizenship so as to void Taney's *Dred Scott* formulation, more narrowly than in the

[48]*Congressional Globe,* 39 Cong., 1 sess. (Dec. 13, 1865), pp. 41, 43; (Jan. 12, 1866), p. 209; (Jan. 19, 1866), p. 323; (Jan. 29, 1866), p. 474; (Feb. 2, 1866), p. 605; (Feb. 20, 1866), p. 937; (Apr. 4, 1866), p. 1757; Bradley, in Slaughterhouse cases, 16 Wall. 34 (1873).

[49]Trumbull in *Congressional Globe,* 39 Cong., 1 sess. (Jan. 26, 1866), p. 460. Similar expressions by, respectively, Hubbard, Shellabarger, Thayer, and Windom are in *ibid.* (Feb. 5, 1866), p. 650; (Mar. 2, 1866), pp. 1151–1152, 1159; (Mar. 9, 1866), pp. 1293–1295.

[50]Robert B. Warden, *An Account of the Private Life and Public Service of Salmon P. Chase* (Cincinnati, 1874), p. 651; Trumbull in *Congressional Globe,* 39 Cong., 1 sess. (Apr. 4, 1866), p. 1757.

Fourteenth Amendment (the latter definition prevailed upon ratification of the Amendment in 1868). Any person born in any state or territory, not an Indian or of foreign allegiance, was a citizen, regardless of color, and would have "full and equal benefit of all [state, local, or territorial] laws and proceedings for the security of persons and property, as is enjoyed by white persons." Equality of state court punishments was also to prevail, "any law, statute, ordinance, regulation, or custom, to the contrary, notwithstanding." Sections 2 and 3 specified that violators were subject to misdemeanor punishment in United States district or circuit courts, whose jurisdiction Congress expanded accordingly. This expanded federal court jurisdiction also embraced appeals from state courts by persons unable to secure section 1 rights, or by United States officer-defendants in state courts whose alleged trespasses or other offenses were made in efforts to protect citizens' section 1 rights, or when carrying out duties imposed in the newly amended and sometimes duplicative Freedmen's Bureau law. The Civil Rights law specified the removal procedures of the 1863 Habeas Corpus statute, and required that in removed litigations, United States laws would apply as suitable. If unsuitable (and federal commercial and criminal law were little developed), the common law of the forum state should apply, but only if consistent with United States statutes including that on Civil Rights. Great discretion rested with the federal judge, and important index to the swift rise of formalism among the lawyer-legislators. The new, post-Appomattox formalism was embracing an enhanced role for judicial initiatives, as contrasted to prewar exponents of the legal doctrine who extolled will-less judges as more likely to regularize economic relationships.

Sections 4 through 9 authorized all federal law officers, including those of the Freedmen's Bureau, to initiate proceedings against violators. Federal judges were to appoint commissioners to achieve enforcement (a use of old Fugitive Slave law arrangements, for opposite purposes). Posses and the military, including federalized states' militias, were backup enforcers, subject to the President's command. Last, Congress expanded the Supreme Court's appellate jurisdiction to include "questions of law" rising from execution of the statute.[51]

---

[51]*Statutes at Large*, XIV, 27 (1866).

The Civil Rights bill, taken together, as it should be, with the Thirteenth and Fourteenth Amendments, especially the former, and with the Freedmen's Bureau and Habeas Corpus laws, suggests that Congress aimed at tying national interventions usually but not exclusively to racially discriminatory actions. The bill created a latent national presence within all the states, a presence triggered into action when a state resident, who was, by the bill's definition, also a national citizen, or a responsible federal officer, became frustrated by inequitable state procedures or by private injustices that states failed to punish, and sought an alternative national forum. These might include Freedmen's Bureau or Army provost courts, though Congress preferred the use of federal circuit and district courts, not all of which were yet functioning.

The Congressmen were accustomed to federal court jurisdiction limited to instances of diverse state citizenship of litigants. As a first step toward federal court protection for Negroes and other beneficiaries of the Civil Rights bill, Congress made them citizens. Congress further widened federal court jurisdiction in instances of alleged discriminations to accommodate situations lacking diversity,[52] and to serve better the Army and Bureau officers who suffered from state or private harassments.

State inequities included those Congress had listed recently in the second Freedmen's Bureau law. These ranged across public and

[52]In an 1866 amendment to the 1863 Habeas Corpus Act, Congress stipulated that if a state judge or prosecuting attorney persisted in a litigation after removal to a federal court had begun under the 1863 statute, the court officer was liable to the litigant requesting removal, for damages and double costs (In Justices v. Murray, 9 Wall. 274 [1867], the Supreme Court held unconstitutional the Habeas Corpus Act's clauses allowing retrial in federal courts of both facts and law, if a state trial had been by jury). In the 1866 Separable Controversies Act, Congress countered state courts' substantive impediments to civil rights litigations not involving race. To avoid federal jurisdiction, alert lawyers got dummy litigants from diverse states to join southern white plaintiffs in damage lawsuits against federal officers, and against southern white defendants in civil rights cases. Such mixtures invoked John Marshall's formula in Strawbridge v. Curtiss, 3 Cranch, 267 (1806), that required every litigant on one side of a suit to have different state citizenship from every litigant on the other side before federal diversity jurisdiction applied. The Separable Controversies law allowed, for the first time, a splitting of federal from state elements in a suit. Now a nonresident party (Army or Freedmen's Bureau officer, usually) could ask a federal court to hear that which that court had statutory jurisdiction to hear, save for the trumped-up diversity complication. William M. Wiecek, "The Reconstruction of Federal Judicial Power, 1863–1876," *American Journal of Legal History*, XIII (1969), 333–359.

private disputes, official actions and failures to act, and civil and criminal justice processes. Congress also extended indefinitely the Bureau's lifetime (the initial statute's year-length expectation was now seen as illusory). In a clause applicable only to the ex-Confederate states, the Bureau bill stipulated that whenever

. . . in consequence of any State or local law, ordinance, police or other regulation, custom or prejudice, any of the civil rights or immunities belonging to white persons, including the right to make or enforce contracts, to sue, be parties, and give evidence, to inherit, purchase, lease, sell, hold and convey real and personal property, and to have full and equal benefits of all laws and proceedings for the security of person and estate, including the constitutional right of bearing arms, are refused or denied to negroes, on account of race, color, or any previous condition of slavery or involuntary servitude, or wherein they . . . are subjected to any other different punishment, pains, or penalties, for the commission of any act . . . than are prescribed for white persons committing like acts . . . it shall be the duty of the President of the United States, through the [Freedmen's Bureau] commissioner, to extend military protection and jurisdiction over all cases affecting such persons so discriminated against.[53]

The second Bureau bill prefigured future Reconstruction laws and policies. Community, state, or private action or nonaction caused the problem and initiated the solutions. A state could cut off the national intervention "whenever the discrimination on account of which it [the case removal] is exercised ceases," Trumbull noted to a confidant, adding "[This] . . . is as far as the country will go at the present time."[54] In national courts (including the Bureau's), existing statutes and habits required the employment of forum state precedents, statutes, and rules of procedure and decision not repugnant to federal laws. Nothing in the Bureau law (or in the Civil Rights bill simultaneously under consideration) altered this state-centered definition of justice.

President Johnson vetoed both the Civil Rights and Freedmen's Bureau bills. Though Congress overrode both (actions that further enhanced legislative authority and widened political differences), the President's vetoes were important. They provided southerners

[53]*Statutes at Large*, XIV, 173 (1866).
[54]Trumbull to T. W. Jayne, Jan. 11, 1866, Jayne PP, Illinois State Historical Society.

with reasons to criticize and blunt the laws. Johnson invoked the *Milligan* decision, stressed familiar notions of plenary state power, predicted that America was becoming a centralized military despotism, and appealed to the lowest racial views of the time. But the President never touched the question of the nation's remedies, or of national citizens' rights, when states failed to carry out their responsibility to treat their own citizens equally. Johnson's view of constitutional history divorced the substance of local justice from the daily lives of Americans. The President insisted that Congress was unconstitutionally creating black state citizens at a time when the southern states, where most Negroes lived, were unrepresented —an irrefutable point to which Congress responded, in effect by admitting his state, Tennessee, to representation upon its ratification of the Fourteenth Amendment. Johnson objected to the Civil Rights and Freedmen's Bureau measures as violations of fixed, unchangeable state-national relationships. Yet Johnson's executive orders kept the Army "policing" the South under "grasp of war" martial authority, while he simultaneously blunted the nation's sword by his interventions against effective Army and Freedmen's Bureau administration. The President insisted that civil rights deriving from birthright citizenship, now coming under national protection, were and should remain wholly the states' to award and protect. His concern was with only one kind of rights—state rights, and Johnson was returning them to the state sovereignty locus from where the war had presumably removed them.[55]

Concepts of fixed natural rights no longer dominated in Congress or among lawyers or judges. Of the Civil Rights bill, Rutherford Hayes noted to an Ohio constituent that he look to the state's evolving practices as the measure of residents' rights:

I know [Hayes wrote] that it [the Civil Rights bill] is grossly misrepresented and greatly misunderstood in Ohio . . . as if it gives increased and unheard of rights as privileges to negroes—as if it would compel the [Ohio] school to receive negro children, the hotels negro guests . . . [etc.]. Now please to note what I say. It undertakes to secure the negro no rights which he has not enjoyed [legally] in Ohio since the repeal of the [state's] Black Laws in 1849.[56]

[55]James D. Richardson (ed.), *A Compilation of the Messages and Papers of the Presidents, 1789–1897* (New York, 1901), IV, 394–413.

[56]Apr. 8, 1866, in Bernard Schwartz, *The Law in America: A History* (New York, 1974), p. 95.

Congress made judges the potential creators and particular guardians of some unknowable catalog of organic rights. The law, still largely instrumentalist in 1866, harmonized easily with the first section of both the Civil Rights law and the Fourteenth Amendment, and with the remedies clauses of the Freedmen's Bureau law. The Thirteenth Amendment made the harmony necessary and proper. No longer, Francis Lieber was to write, was the question, what were an American's rights, as irrelevant as asking newlyweds to define love. The Civil Rights and Freedmen's Bureau laws, General Howard predicted, "will enable us to regulate the judicial features of our work without difficulty."[57]

Howard was oversanguine. Reconstruction was exhibiting intractable qualities of the sort that evoked Claudius' complaint in *Hamlet:* "When sorrows come, they come not single spies, but in battalions." Congress's efforts notwithstanding, the nation was far from ready in 1866 effectively to cope with Reconstruction. At least some Republicans were aware that their structure was fragile. But, perhaps because this structure seemed to be the only relevant one, the assumption prevailed that it would work if everyone acquiesced in the laws. Yet the Republicans' determination was still strong to erase every one of slavery's persisting remnants as they surfaced; "to remove every shackle which . . . constitutes a link in its chain," wrote *Nation* editor E. L. Godkin.[58]

One basic means to "scotch" slavery in any guise was the nurturing of a two-party political organization in every southern state and community. Republicans hoped to encourage such development even without Negro suffrage. Votes for blacks were by no means acceptable to white majorities in several northern states where it was considered 1865–69. But, in the South, President Johnson's patronage and pardon policies, so favorable to Democrats, were frustrating the growth of even a second lily-white party.

Many wartime Unionists in antisecession mountain states had become Republicans because of the party's patriotic appeal. Racial equality efforts by Congress and the Freedmen's Bureau, as depicted by the President and his supporters, eroded support for Republican party locals. All of which encouraged unpunished vio-

[57]Howard to General A. Baird, Apr. 9, 1866, Letterpress Copies of Letters Sent, Commissioner's Office, II, 301, RG 105, National Archives; Francis Lieber, *On Civil Liberty and Self-Government,* (3d rev. ed., Philadelphia, 1874), pp. 35–36.
[58]*The Nation* (Apr. 5, 1866), 422.

lence and vigilantism in numerous communities, culminating in massive race riots such as those in Memphis and New Orleans during 1866. And the President, in messages to Congress and in speeches aimed nationwide, confused people about the constitutional and legal elements in civil rights while at the same time he exploited effectively the tenacious racial attitudes and deep state-centeredness of almost all Americans including Republicans.[59]

Under these conditions Freedmen's Bureau officers tried to cope with a burden of more than 100,000 complaints in 1866. The South was increasingly hostile to Bureau policies; the reception of the enforcement legislation in state courts was at first uncertain and then, as cases reached decision, depressing. The Bureau depended upon the Civil Rights law as its main support and definition of purpose. Bureau officials had anticipated that state judges would, if only from self-interest, see to the standards the statute required. This was not a foolish anticipation; there were hopeful signs.[60]

But the mass of southern opinion was hardening against cooperation; indeed, it was becoming overtly hostile toward the federal presence. This shift was encouraged by the President's ways and by visible changes in racial attitudes among new cadres of Army and Bureau officers. Wartime volunteers were giving way to professionals. West Pointers commonly found southern white society more agreeable than that of blacks. Many Bureau officers and other federal officials were more eager to restore agricultural production than to reinforce civil rights.[61]

A Florida-based field agent of the Bureau, once a prisoner of the Confederacy, complained in December that he and others were "leaving [Florida] in disgust." He had spent "thousands of dollars in feeing lawyers." Remedies of the Civil Rights law were useless, however. They required that injuries occur before efforts toward

[59]Gordon B. McKinney, *Southern Mountain Republicans, 1865–1900; Politics and the Appalachian Community* (Chapel Hill, 1978), chs. 2–4.

[60]The hopeful signs are in *The American Freedman*, II (Philadelphia, 1866), 47.

[61]Donald G. Nieman, *To Set the Law in Motion: The Freedmen's Bureau and the Legal Rights of Blacks, 1865–1868* (New York, 1979), pp. 12–13. Back in 1865, antislavery veterans failed in efforts to have Congress create a commission to do for state restorations, as a process, what the American Freedmen's Bureau Inquiry Commission had done for slaves; i.e., prepare the way for the Freedmen's Bureau. Harold Schwartz, *Samuel Gridley Howe: Social Reformer, 1801–1876* (Cambridge, 1956), p. 267 and n.

redress could begin. The President had the Justice Department in his pocket and was hamstringing the Army. "We have a military but it is so hampered with 'Orders' that it is useless," he mourned; "We have a Civil Rights Bill but no Civil Rights Commission. We have a Freedmen's Bureau but it is divested of vitality." Southern Unionists and Negroes could take care of themselves if only Congress destroyed "these bogus [state] governments. . . . But as it is now we are bound hand and foot."[62]

Congress was unable to unbind such complainants in 1866. Its inability to create effective administration was, in addition to the President's failure to execute the laws, part of the American habit. This society of "self-helpers," wrote Charles Fairman, rested upon law and politics, not administration. "I apprehend great difficulty," Timothy Farrar worried to Sumner, "in rendering a [civil rights] statute efficient, in the present condition of machinery for its administration. Deficiency [in enforcement] is . . . [the nation's] worst fault, and I suppose is incurable."[63]

The new statutes could hardly succeed, considering the broad purposes enshrined in them and in the Thirteenth Amendment, with the existing enforcement mechanisms. The Army, in the South by the President's orders, was by early 1866 depending for authority on Grant's special orders. Enforcement would have been tough enough even if the President had not transformed his vetoes and other messages into public lectures on the evils of the very national policies that Congress had charged him to enforce. The Freedmen's Bureau enjoyed the comfort of a statute as base. But the Bureau had to rely on the Army for support if the courts proved to be inadequate, and the bluecoats were themselves insecure.

On August 20, 1866, Johnson proclaimed that law and order obtained everywhere southward and that the need for all martial authority had ended. Yet, as noted, racial violence exploded at New Orleans and Memphis and was only narrowly averted at Baltimore. Dismayingly, numerous lesser assaults took place on Negroes and on their civilian and uniformed would-be benefactors. Perpetrators included many state and local police and other officials. Almost all

[62]Rev. J. C. Emerson to Col. Liberty Billings, Dec. 21, 1866, in Billings to Sumner, Jan. 7, 1867, vol. 80, no. 18, Sumner PP, Houghton Library, Harvard University.

[63]Farrar to Sumner, May 11, 1866, Sumner PP, Houghton Library, Harvard University; Charles Fairman, *Reconstruction and Reunion,* p. 92.

went unpunished save in Army–Freedmen's Bureau courts, and there spottily. All of which meant that if the Army provost courts and the Freedmen's Bureau courts shut up shop or curtailed operations conformably to the President's peace order, no practical alternative to state courts would be available in the ex-rebel states.

Added to continuing *Milligan* tremors, the President's peace order eroded Army and Bureau self-confidence and capacity to affect conditions. "Does it deprive me of the exercise of command? Of the exercise of martial law in cases of conflict between the authority of the Acts of Congress and orders of my military superiors and the State or municipal authorities?" asked General J. G. Foster, from Florida, of Army superiors. Buoyed by the President's peace proclamation, Tallahassee police were arresting Army and Freedmen's Bureau officers "for trifling causes."[64] The proclamation effectively nullified the Civil Rights law and undercut Grant's efforts to stabilize the situation by means of Army orders based on statutes, thus avoiding a need for the President's formal assent.

Grant, on July 6, as noted earlier, had issued General Order 44, with wide publicity. Therein, he legitimized Army-Bureau interventions especially in police and justice functions by reference to the new Civil Rights and supportive statutes which specified employment of the Army. Grant authorized subordinates down to the company-post level (equivalent to constables, magistrates, and justices of the peace) to arrest and try civilians who committed crimes as defined by state or national laws, against Army or Bureau personnel or against "inhabitants of the United States, irrespective of color, in cases where the civil authorities have failed, neglected, or are unable to arrest and bring such parties to trial." Persons so arrested were to remain in military confinement "until such time as a proper judicial tribunal may be ready and willing to try them." His order was still essential, Grant advised Secretary of War Stanton in November, because "It is evident . . . that the provisions of the Civil Rights Bill cannot be properly enforced without Order No. 44 or a similar one."[65]

[64]Foster to General L. Hartsuff (AAG), Aug. 20, 1866, and endorsements, Box 98, RG 108, National Archives.
[65]Grant to Stanton, Nov. 22, 1866, Letterbook, Letters Sent, 1866–1868, RG 108, National Archives; *General Orders, 1866* (Washington, 1867), No. 44.

Grant's letter to Stanton reflected the deep disappointment and frustration Republicans generally shared. Justice still depended upon military and paramilitary alternatives to the more familiar but untrustworthy state courts.

Violence in the South and the President's policies polarized politics that fall. The 1866 state and congressional contests centered on state ratifications of the Fourteenth Amendment. Ratification by an ex-rebel state would have meant immediate restoration of that state to representation in Congress and an end to military interventions, so anxious were Republican majorities to end the Reconstruction business. Yet, Tennessee excepted, every former seceded state rejected the Fourteenth Amendment. Elsewhere, states ratified (it became effective May, 1868), and Republicans earned nationwide majorities. The Republicans' tragic error of 1866 was to defer to state rights by asking the South to ratify the Fourteenth Amendment instead of compelling ratification, as Congress was to do in the 1867 Military Reconstruction Act and its amendments.[66] But to require the alternatives of 1866 to be those of 1867 is to create historical anachronisms. Thaddeus Stevens may have been correct on these matters in 1866. He could not, however, obtain majority support until the South's disappointing reaction to the Civil Rights law and stunning rejection of the Fourteenth Amendment were in—until it became generally obvious that election triumphs in 1866 did not cure Reconstruction ills.

Soon after the 1866 election, Senator Sumner heard from a Freedmen's Bureau officer in Selma, Alabama, whose report stressed these points: (1) low-level judges and peace officers paid little attention to complaints by Negroes against whites, but acted with "eagerness and severity" in reverse situations; (2) a practice so general as to be systematic existed in rural areas, of employers driving Negroes from jobs near the end of a work contract, so that blacks forfeited pay under the state's law; (3) in towns naked terrorism and extortion kept blacks obedient to analogous extortions; (4) many counties separated families of alleged vagrants or of accused

---

[66]Brock, *An American Crisis*, p. 149; C. Vann Woodward, "Seeds of Failure in Radical Race Policy," in Harold M. Hyman (ed.), *New Frontiers of the American Reconstruction* (Urbana, 1966), pp. 134–135.

labor contract violators, assigning members to different contract-labor projects; (5) the Bureau had become a weak reed because of the President's curtailment of martial law remedies; (6) General Order 44 was invocable except that few Negroes dared "to test the efficacy of the remedy"; (7) recourse to the federal district or circuit courts under the Civil Rights law was ". . . too cumbersome for the effect. It is like using the Great Eastern [the world's largest ship] for a ferry-boat. It is remote and infrequent, and homeless complainants [who] are compelled to get a livelihood where they can, often drift out of reach and knowledge. The same is true of witnesses"; (8) The results? Income losses in the first freedom year crushed many individuals' spirits; labor contracts that Negroes filed with the Bureau proved to be unenforceable.[67]

As General E. O. C. Ord wrote on the last day of 1866 to Howard, concerning Arkansas, the Army and Freedmen's Bureau were able to function relatively well in major towns and cities (but the Memphis and New Orleans experiences suggested that even here severe limitations on effectiveness existed). Even in southern cities it was necessary to have Army and Bureau courts to protect both the blacks and the whites responsible for the execution of national policy. But "in remote and thinly settled areas, a freedman's life is but of little importance; and even white men are in the habit of shooting one another upon small provocation," Ord wrote. Rural citizens seemed to be simply incapable of obeying state laws, much less national. To be sure, Ord added, "we can arrest even under the present laws of Congress—but we cannot hold anyone in the face of the [state] writ of habeas corpus—this should be provided for." Ord reported that he had to free at least half a dozen murderers because of habeas writs from state and local judges. And he added that he had only five hundred infantry and no cavalry to cover all Arkansas.[68]

It became increasingly apparent, as 1866 proceeded, that Congress had not interwoven the protection modes of its Thirteenth Amendment enforcement legislation very well so far as Army and

[67]S. C. Gardner to Sumner, Nov. 19, 1866, vol. 154, no. 2, Sumner PP, Houghton Library, Harvard University.

[68]Ord to Howard, Dec. 31, 1866, copy in Sumner PP, LXXX, no. 17, Houghton Library, Harvard University.

Bureau field officers were concerned. If the officials were not protected their capacity to protect Negroes was severely qualified. To
illustrate, in Texas, state peace officers arrested a Bureau agent for
violating Black Code labor provisions. General Samuel P. Heintzelman, relying on Grant's General Orders and the Civil Rights and
Freedmen's Bureau laws, freed the Bureau officer from county custody. The county clerk ordered the sheriff to arrest Heintzelman.
He refused to accept arrest, alleging to his superior that "I would
not consider my life safe in the hands of the Texas civil authorities."
In Washington, the Heintzelman matter bounced from War Department to Justice Department to White House and back again until
Military Reconstruction overtook the situation.[69]

In 1867's first days, General Howard confirmed to Secretary Stanton every point these officers, and others elsewhere, had made.
Howard reported that states were not merely mal-enforcing their
civil laws, but nonenforcing criminal laws when Negroes were victims and whites the perpetrators. True, by the end of 1866, several
southern states had modified their Black Codes so that, superficially, laws no longer discriminated racially. "Still I am satisfied that
impartial justice is seldom administered," Howard wrote. The Civil
Rights law was failing where it counted most, in local communities
and neighborhoods; failing less due to formal denials of civil rights
by state officers of high visibility than by almost invisible, scattered,
low-rank local officials who administered state laws and community
justice. Denials of civil rights depended, in reality, upon "the temper of the juries and magistrates before whom their cases are tried,"
Howard continued. States were granting some of the forms of protection. But, with obvious community sanction, inferior police and
justice officers were distorting forms into fictions.

What options did responsible United States officers have in this
unhappy situation? Few that overjoyed Howard. "It is difficult to
prove actual [i.e., intentional] 'deprivation' of justice in such a manner as to 'remove the cause' to the U. S. District or Circuit Court,"
he noted. Appeal judges tended to honor positions taken in lower
courts; United States judges felt impelled to wait until all state

[69]Details in Patricia Allen, "Freedom and Federalism: Congress and Courts, 1861–
1866" (Ph.D. diss., University of Glasgow, 1972), pp. 1251–1252.

procedures were exhausted before accepting Civil Rights–Freedmen's Bureau–Habeas Corpus petitions. The result was either that litigants grew discouraged and disappeared or that resort was necessary to the thinly scattered Army–Freedmen's Bureau courts.[70]

Traditional federal legal forums so useful for entrepreneurs were not working well in instances of civil rights violations as alternatives to inequitable state court procedures. Yet the legal amateurishness of the Freedmen's Bureau judges was one "objectionable feature" justifying, to Republicans, the resort in the 1866 Civil Rights law to the legal professionals of the federal courts. Frederick Douglass perceived that the root of difficulty grew from the Republicans' refusal to assume national police authority within the ex-rebel states. Writing in December, 1866, Douglass gloomily advised *Atlantic Monthly* readers:

While there remains such an idea as the right of each State to control its local affairs—an idea, by the way, more deeply rooted in the minds of men of all sections of the country than perhaps any other political idea—no general assertion of human rights can be of any practical value.[71]

For their part, the congressional majority failed to anticipate a President who obstructed the execution of laws. No one predicted the means and the ease with which entrepreneurs and lawyers were metamorphosing slavery into variant forms of economic subordination for blacks in an almost unfettered market situation.[72] Congressmen did anticipate, however, attacks from state supreme courts directed at the historic legislation of 1865 and 1866, an anticipation

[70]Howard to Stanton, Jan. 12, 1867, Letters Sent, vol. III, no. 56, RG 105, National Archives. The question of intent on the part of state officers in policies resulting in segregation is still troublesome. In 1970 a U.S. circuit court, in Dailey *v.* City of Lawton, 425 F. 2d 1037 (10th Cir. 1970) decided that: "If proof of a civil right violation depends upon an open statement by an official of an intent to discriminate, the Fourteenth Amendment offers little solace to those seeking its protection." See, on intent to segregate racially and the Fourteenth Amendment, Mobile *v.* Bolden, 446 U.S. 55 (1980).

[71]Frederick Douglass, "Reconstruction," *Atlantic Monthly,* XVIII (Dec. 1866), 201. In 1964, Thurgood Marshall, then of the NAACP, replied to a suggestion favoring a vast national police intervention in the southern states: "The law is quite clear that the federal government is not the policing authority . . . which rests with the several states." In Arthur M. Schlesinger, Jr., *Robert F. Kennedy and His Times* (New York, 1978), p. 305.

[72]Pete Daniel, "The Metamorphosis of Slavery," *Journal of American History,* LXVI (1979), 88–89.

that was itself a justification for the expanded roles for federal courts in the 1866 laws. But the Congressmen did not foresee the vigor and durability of the state court offensive, or envision interventions by federal judges that would, by the time of the 1873 *Slaughterhouse* decision, greatly diminish the relevancy of the federal laws and courts for blacks seeking protection.

Initial state supreme court decisions on Thirteenth Amendment matters, other than the Civil Rights law, suggest how the views of the equalitarians early became watered down in a period of burgeoning respect for state authority, notably the police power, and for judicial initiatives. Distinguished state supreme court judges including New Hampshire's Charles Doe, Michigan's Thomas Cooley, and Delaware's Edward Woodward Gilpin were in an assertive mood. "Our policy," Yale law professor Theodore Woolsey was soon to write of the police power, "is to get along with the inconveniences which really do grow out of diffused power and local self-government, remedying them in detail as far as the order[ing] of society and the suppression of crime demand, but never giving up the present system for any imagined advantage whatever." Gilpin in 1866 was forthrightly ready to resolve in favor of his state conflicts between Delaware's and the federal constitutions: "But this question will meet us some day when it cannot be avoided, and we do not wish to evade it now."[73]

The very timidity that many elective state jurists exhibited about questioning state laws did not obtain as against the federal. Pennsylvania's supreme court, frequently troublesome during the war about federal policies, continued to condemn them after Appomattox. In mid-1866, speaking through judge William Strong, a future United States Supreme Court justice, the Pennsylvania court declared unconstitutional the March, 1865, federal statute that disfranchised military deserters. It was, Strong asserted, an unacceptable intrusion by the nation into a state's fundamental right to define enfranchised citizens.[74]

[73]T. D. Woolsey, "Nature and Sphere of Police Power," *Journal of Social Science*, II (1870), 111; Gilpin in State *v.* Rash, reported in *American Law Review*, II (1868), 345. On Doe, see *John Reid, Chief Justice: The Judicial World of John Doe* (Cambridge, 1967), esp. chs. 16–20. On Cooley, see this volume, ch. 10.
[74]Huber *v.* Reilly, 53 Pa. 112 (1866); and see Cafferty *v.* Guyer, 59 Pa. 109 (1868); State *v.* Symonds, 57 Maine 148 (1869).

Southern judges, all either newly elected or appointed, were less accountable to constituent reaction than most northern jurists. In the South, wartime litigations hanging over after Appomattox included a clutch of cases concerning the validity of contracts for the sale of slaves entered into before the Thirteenth Amendment was ratified. The post-Appomattox claimants wanted payment, not persons. Several judges, nudged by litigants' lawyers, expressed concerns about the need to reestablish commercial stability and sustained contract performance with respect to payment on slave contracts. Arkansas and Florida judges (plus one in Illinois) in 1866 required that pre-Thirteenth Amendment contracts for slave purchases be honored with respect to the prices pledged. Though balanced by contrary holdings in Louisiana and Georgia, the fact that any judges at all blessed the slave contracts gave credence to arguments that no revolution in federalism had occurred by reason of the Thirteenth Amendment; that the Constitution's contract clause took precedence over the Bill of Rights and the Thirteenth Amendment; and that the Civil Rights and Freedmen's Bureau laws had limited impacts.[75]

Other state decisions concerning the pre-Emancipation status of blacks confused the civil rights picture in 1866 and after. A Kentucky supreme court decision of 1866 held that an 1860 will freeing slaves on the widow's death, and providing each with a $200 legacy on condition of their emigrating abroad, was confirmed by the Thirteenth Amendment. But the slaves no longer needed to emigrate, the Kentucky judge held. Conversely, two years later, the Kentucky court decided that the Amendment ended all obligations of master to slave, and voided a will providing for their burial.[76]

A New York supreme court decision of March, 1866, before the Civil Rights bill became law, enlarged the stream of early restrictive state interpretations of the Thirteenth Amendment. The case rose under a landlord-tenant dispute in rural New York; no Negroes were involved. Was the ejectment of the tenant equivalent to his

[75]Cases surveyed in Allen, "Freedom and Federalism," pp. 177–179, include Hand v. Armstrong, 34 Ga. 232 (1866); Walker v. Gatlin, 12 Fla. 1 (1867); Jacoway v. Denton, 25 Ark. 665 (1869); Roundtree v. Baker, 52 Ill. 241 (1869); Wainwright v. Baker, 52 Ill. 241 (1869); Wainwright v. Bridges, 19 La. Ann. 234 (1867); Austin v. Sandel, 19 La. Ann. 309 (1867); White v. Hart, 39 Ga. 306 (1869); Shorter v. Cobb, 39 Ga. 285 (1869).

[76]Parish v. Hill, 33 Ky. 396 (1866); Farmers Bank of Kentucky v. Johnson, 4 Bush 411 (1868); and see Todd v. Trott, 64 N.C. 280 (1870).

reduction to "involuntary servitude"? No, the New York court decided; the dispute was between private litigants, and the Thirteenth Amendment had no connection with contracts:

[The Thirteenth Amendment] . . . was designed for one specific object, and no other, to wit, the abolition of personal slavery within the United States, the system of personal and involuntary servitude, by which one person owned and could absolutely control the person and services of another. This was the mischief to be remedied—the evil to be abolished—the end to be gained. It was to give personal liberty to the enslaved, emancipation to those who were held in bondage. No other object was ever suggested, in the multitudinous discussions to which the project gave rise. No other would probably have commanded the approval of the country.[77]

Federal quasi-judicial and judicial decisions also diffused the fullness of the Thirteenth Amendment's early impact, before courts had opportunity to comment on the Civil Rights law. Self-described "loyal" Kentuckians claimed payment from the War Department for the services of then-slaves drafted into the Army. Military records suggested that many of the claimants had sustained the Confederacy, although presently they professed unmarred past loyalty. But the claims commission honored the demands.[78]

Though explicitly sustaining the Civil Rights law, some lower federal judges implicitly further minimized the effects of the Thirteenth Amendment and its enforcement legislation. The legal profession, almost instinctively, yearned to stabilize commercial relations as speedily and fully as possible. Chief Justice Chase, on circuit, set the tone. His circuit decisions emphasized the validity of nonwar "business transactions" carried on under the Confederate dispensation. "With a contrary course of decisions we should have been plunged in endless confusion," noted Chase's admiring circuit reporter. "All contracts made during the war and acts done, all judicial proceedings, would have been considered void, and years of turmoil and exasperating controversy would have been before us. He saved us all this."[79]

However, having emphasized commercial stability on circuit, 1865–69, Chase was to find himself a lone dissenter in 1871, when

[77]Tyler v. Heidorn, 46 Barbours Supreme Court Reports (N.Y.) 439 at 458 (1866).
[78]A. G. Hobson to E. M. Stanton, Oct. 19, 1866, Secretary of War Correspondence File, Box 316, RG 107, National Archives.
[79]Bradley T. Johnson (comp.), *Reports of Cases Decided by Chief Justice Chase in the Circuit Court of the United States, Fourth Circuit, 1865–1869* (New York, 1867), p. xiv.

the Court reversed state supreme court decisions that denied the validity of contracts on slave purchases made before the Thirteenth Amendment was ratified. These contracts were valid as to price when made, though the Amendment and statutes subsequent to their execution invalidated their subject matter, the majority decided. The Thirteenth Amendment was not retrospective; states could not, in the Amendment's name, invalidate contracts. Chase argued unavailingly that contracts for slaves had always been adverse to morals and natural justice and that the Court should validate no payment for the sale of a person after the ratification of the Thirteenth Amendment.

The imperative that lawyers and judges felt to look first to the state for stability in contract relations combined early—and perhaps inevitably—with the deep respect that prevailed for state rights. Simply by resorting to lawyers' categories of primarily economic contract relationships when defining civil rights, Republican Congressmen reaffirmed the preeminent role of states in the legal process. In this role, state laws, justice processes, and judges were accepted as the major cast of characters. Little wonder that by 1871 the Thirteenth Amendment and the 1866 Civil Rights law seemed to forbid only the most obvious physical servitudes and compulsion. The implications of the fact that contract law remained state law were not clear in 1865–66. Too late, Chase and others discerned them by the end of the decade.[80]

Compulsions that lawyers and judges felt to stabilize commercial relationships did not, of themselves, define southern reaction to the Civil Rights law in or out of courts. Yet the pressure to stabilize commerce brought with it a common law that, as with the slave sale contracts, undercut (or that could be made by able lawyers to seem to undercut) the full meaning of emancipation, and that seemed also to limit viable Reconstruction goals. Many of these decisions occurred after 1866. But lawyers began in 1866 to weigh legal and constitutional alternatives leading to decisions that favored their clients' interests and perhaps the lawyers' sectional, racial, and/or moral positions and aspirations. This selection among alternatives

[80]White v. Hart, 13 Wall. 646 (1871); Osborn v. Nicholson, 13 Wall. 645 (1871); Boyce v. Taub, 18 Wall. 546 (1873); Aviam Soifer, "Forty Acres, Forty Years: Constitution and Contract Law After Slavery" (Organization of American Historians Paper, 1981).

by lawyers and judges in matters specifically involving the Civil Rights law were to shape Supreme Court arguments in the 1870s on subsequent constitutional amendments and statutes. It is appropriate now to consider specific state and federal court decisions on the Civil Rights law.

State judges generally attacked the Civil Rights law and limited its effects as well as those of the Thirteenth Amendment (and, later, of the Fourteenth). A Freedmen's Bureau agent complained that Florida courts ridiculed the Civil Rights law and that whites ". . . laugh at the idea of its being of any importance." Delaware chief judge Gilpin, though expressing reluctance at the need to decide on a federal statute, felt that he had no alternative as result of a conflict between the Civil Rights law and the state's revised Constitution. The latter admitted a Negro's testimony only if a competent white witness was not available. One party to a damage suit insisted that the adverse party's chief witness, a Negro, should not testify. Responsively, the argument was made that the Civil Rights law required admission of blacks' testimony. Gilpin, for himself and one colleague of the three-man court, held that "the [Civil Rights] Act of Congress, in so far as it attempts to prescribe rules of procedure, pleading, and evidence for State courts, is unconstitutional, null, and void."[81]

Kentucky's supreme court also decided that the Civil Rights law was unconstitutional and that the state law prohibiting Negro testimony against whites remained valid. The Thirteenth Amendment ended slavery, nothing more. The Civil Rights act was not an appropriate enforcement of the Thirteenth Amendment's enforcement clause. Had Senator Sumner's effort succeeded in Congress to incorporate an "equal before the law" phrase into the Thirteenth Amendment, then the Civil Right law might be supportable, stated a concurring Kentucky judge. But, that effort having failed, the Thirteenth Amendment could not authorize Congress to qualify a witness in Kentucky.[82]

[81]On Florida, Rev. J. C. Emerson to Col. Liberty Billings, Dec. 21, 1866, in Billings to Sumner, Jan. 7, 1867, Sumner PP, vol. 80, no. 18, Houghton Library, Harvard University; Gilpin in State v. Rash at 345.

[82]Bowlin v. Kentucky, 2 Bush (Ky.) 5 at 15–29 (1867). Justice Field in Ex parte Virginia, 100 U.S. 339 at 364 (1879), cited Bowlin to suggest doubts about the constitutionality of the 1866 Civil Rights law, and see Hodges v. United States, 203

Contrariwise, in Indiana, a notoriously Negrophobic state, the supreme court reached opposite conclusions. A Negro, a recent immigrant to Indiana despite an 1851 Black Code that forbade Negro incomers and voided private contracts they made, sued a white Hoosier for failure to pay on a promissory note. A lower Indiana court sustained the white defendant. The Negro appealed to the state supreme court. It took cognizance of the new federal Civil Rights law, redefined Indiana citizenship to include Negroes, and reversed the lower court ruling (though it did not invalidate the discriminatory state law).[83]

Some supreme courts of ex-Confederate states, and that of California, sustained the competency of black witnesses as required by the Civil Rights law. In the California decision (subsequently over-ruled), a mulatto enjoyed discharge from custody on the grounds that the only adverse witness was Chinese, and native-born blacks enjoyed the same rights as whites, including one not to be testified against by Asians.[84]

Interracial marriages were sensitive issues, and most state judges concluded that the Civil Rights law disallowed only discriminatory punishments for such unions rather than the state laws forbidding them. Such decisions were not, however, at odds with the views of Republican creators of the Civil Rights law, including Trumbull. But no adequate judgment is yet possible on the sufficiency of state court justice. Records of local courts and police are scanty. The state lower courts were ends-of-roads for most litigants. Few persevered even to state supreme courts, much less to the federal courts. The lower state courts remained sinks of race prejudice, General Howard complained in 1867, despite contrary judgments of superior state or federal judges.[85]

Lower federal courts also took cognizance of the Civil Rights statute and of the Thirteenth Amendment, in ways to please How-

U.S. 1 at 11 (1906). John M. Harlan was the appellee's attorney general in Bowlin.

[83]Smith v. Moody, 26 Indiana 299 (1866); Allen, "Freedom and Federalism," pp. 253–258.

[84]Ex parte Warren, 31 Tex. 143 (1868); Kelly v. Arkansas, 25 Ark. 392 (1869); People v. Washington, 36 Cal. 658 (1869), overruled in People v. Brady, 40 Cal. 198 (1870).

[85]Ellis v. State, 42 Ala. 525 (1868); Burns v. State, 48 Ala. 195 (1872); Green v. State, 58 Ala. 190 (1877); Howard in Allen, "Freedom and Federalism," pp. 253–254.

ard and other race equalitarians (though Fourteenth Amendment litigations were to overshadow these Civil Rights law decisions). In late 1866 *United States* v. *Rhodes* rose from Kentucky, where state law still forbade Negro testimony adverse to white litigants. White vigilantes invaded a black woman's home to rob and assault her and generally to intimidate Negroes. Freedmen's Bureau agents and the unusually energetic federal attorney, Benjamin H. Bristow, brought suit on her behalf. For the United States as plaintiff they insisted that the Thirteenth Amendment and the Civil Rights law both required that Kentucky admit all citizens' testimony. Rhodes's counsel argued that Kentucky's law, forbidding blacks' testimony, must apply. But in a criminal case only the state could prosecute. Only Kentucky and the defendant Rhodes were parties to this suit. Therefore, no Civil Rights law issue of race differentiation existed.

Justice Swayne, on circuit, disagreed. He noted that the Thirteenth Amendment and the Civil Rights law were intimately connected in time and in authorship; many of the framers of the former had helped to construct and had approved the latter. The Amendment and the law revolutionized the federal system, a revolution that was an "act of great national grace." They established everywhere and at all times federal "protection over everyone." Kentucky and all states were now under constraint; all Kentucky's residents were citizens of the nation as well as of the state; the Thirteenth Amendment "trenches directly upon the power of the state and of the people of the state." The state could not limit the rights of free persons by race differentiations.[86]

Chief Justice Chase on his Maryland circuit in early 1867 expressed similar strong views of the Thirteenth Amendment and the Civil Rights law. Chase granted Elizabeth Turner, a former slave, a habeas writ to free her from a nominal apprenticeship agreement she had made with her former master, who was supposed to train her as a house servant. Instead she found herself subject to oppressive conditions of labor sanctioned by her contract. Turner had signed it in ignorance of the limitations she was accepting. Her "employer" failed to appear in court. Chase held for Turner. Negroes were now citizens. Contracts between citizens, though pri-

[86] 27 Fed. Cas. 785 at 788, 794, #16, 151 (C.C.D. Ky., 1866). Swayne's language prevailed in the U.S. Supreme Court until Plessy *v.* Ferguson, 163 U.S. 537 (1896).

vate actions, could not exist without state sanction such as Maryland's apprentice laws, one for whites and one for blacks. The Civil Rights law applied to such private acts as well as to all state actions. The terms Turner faced were not those white workers accepted. Instead they were subterfuges for slavery. Therefore Turner's contract, though "private," violated both the Thirteenth Amendment and the "full and equal benefit" clause (section 1) of the Civil Rights law. Turner was free of the contract.[87]

It was not until 1871 that the Supreme Court considered the Civil Rights law. In the interval, Military Reconstruction had substantially played its role, the Fourteenth and Fifteenth Amendments had become parts of the Constitution, and the "Force Acts" were on the books. By then, we will suggest, Reconstruction was a waning force despite the enforcement laws of Congress, and lawyers and judges were evaluating the Civil Rights law in the context of the Fourteenth Amendment more than of the Thirteenth, which the law had been created to enforce. *Blyew* v. *United States,* the 1871 case, resulted from tragic facts rising out of the murder of a black woman by whites, a murder other Kentucky Negroes witnessed. But the state's witness statutes still disqualified blacks' testimony. Federal attorney Benjamin Bristow argued that Justice Swayne's position in *Rhodes* prevailed. Seemingly in agreement, Justice Strong, for the Court, stated that the Civil Rights act gave:

. . . protection to persons of the colored race by giving the Federal courts jurisdiction of cases, the decisions of which might injuriously affect them either in their personal, relative, or property rights, whenever they are denied in the State courts any of the rights mentioned and assured to them in the first section of the [Civil Rights] Act.

But, Strong held, the black woman was dead and therefore had no rights! No federal jurisdiction existed, since no person, as defined in the Civil Rights law, was suffering inadequate justice. He admitted that Congress had intended the Civil Rights law to eliminate inequalities in state justice, among other goals. But he inter-

[87]In re Turner, 24 Fed. Cas. 339, Abb. U.S. 89, #14, 247 (C.C.C. Md., 1867); Johnson, *Chase's Circuit Court Decisions,* pp. 157–161. Chase's phrases in Turner are like those he employed in the Supreme Court in his License Tax Opinion, 72 U.S. (5 Wall.) 462 at 469 (1866): "There are, undoubtedly, fundamental principles of morality and justice, which no legislature is at liberty to disregard."

preted Congress's intent as one reaching only live persons.[88]
For himself and Swayne, Justice Bradley dissented. Kentucky dis-
favored the whole class of its black citizens by its witness statutes.
Ample federal jurisdiction existed under both the Thirteenth
Amendment and the Civil Rights law, but the Amendment alone was
more than adequate, Bradley insisted.[89]

Another 1871 case in point, *U.S.* v. *Hall,* came from Alabama to
the federal courts and involved a conspiracy to deny citizens freedom of speech and association. These were not privileges and immunities of United States citizens, the defendants insisted. District
Judge William Woods, who was to become in 1880 the first southerner appointed since 1860 to the Supreme Court, decided that the
federal government had both a right and a duty under the Thirteenth and Fourteenth Amendments to reach into states in order to
inhibit the actions of state officials or individuals intended to deprive citizens of First Amendment rights. Woods referred to *Corfield*
v. *Coryell,* that 1823 precedent so favored in 1866 by Republican
champions of the Civil Rights law, as a partial roster of Thirteenth
Amendment rights and of Fourteenth Amendment privileges and
immunities. "Among these," Woods stated, "we are safe in including those which in the constitution are expressly secured to the
people, either as against the action of federal or state governments.
Included in these are the right of freedom of speech, and the right
to peacefully assemble." The privileges and immunities of Americans included those in the Bill of Rights, and Congress rightfully
acted against both "unfriendly or insufficient state legislation."

---

[88]Blyew *v.* United States, 80 U.S. (13 Wall.) 581 at 593, 601 (1873). Yet, on circuit,
Strong was to rule that the "Thirteenth Amendment made the right of personal
liberty a constitutional right," and that the Amendment's "primary object" was to
secure "to persons certain rights which they had not previously possessed." It was
"an exploded heresy that the national government cannot reach all individuals in the
states." United States *v.* Given, 25 Fed. Cas. 1324 at 1325, #15, 210 (C.C.D. Del.,
1873).

[89]"Merely striking off the fetters of the slave, without removing the incidents and
consequences of slavery, would hardly have been a boon to the colored race. Hence,
. . . the amendment abolishing slavery was supplemented by a clause giving Congress
power to enforce it by appropriate legislation. No law was necessary to abolish
slavery; the amendment did that. The power to enforce the amendment by appropriate legislation must be a power to do away with the incidents and consequences of
slavery, and to instate the freedmen in the full enjoyment of that civil liberty and
equality which the abolition of slavery meant." Blyew *v.* United States, 601.

Denial by a state of equal protection of the laws included, Woods concluded, "the omission to protect, as well as the omission to pass laws for protection." An American was entitled to the enforcement of the laws for the protection of his fundamental rights, as well as the enactment of such laws.[90]

Only two years after *Blyew* and *Hall*, in the famous (for Negroes, infamous) *Slaughterhouse* decision (see below, Chapter 13), the Court majority would decide inferentially that the Thirteenth Amendment meant merely formal freedom; that the privileges and immunities of national citizens protected by the Fourteenth Amendment were few and narrow. But in the circuit court decision that was to evoke the *Slaughterhouse* appeal to the Supreme Court, Justice Bradley, referring to the Fourteenth Amendment but also encompassing the Thirteenth, argued concerning the plenitude of federally protectable rights:

It is possible that those who framed the article were not themselves aware of the far reaching character of its terms. They may have had in mind but one particular phase of social and political wrong which they desired to redress. Yet, if the amendment as framed and expressed, does in fact bear a broader meaning and does extend its protecting shield over those who were never thought of when it was conceived and put in form, and does reach social evils which were never before prohibited by constitutional enactment, it is to be presumed that the American people, in giving it their *imprimatur,* understood what they were doing and meant to decree what has in fact been decreed.[91]

In the Supreme Court, Justice Samuel Miller, for the bare *Slaughterhouse* majority, would advert to history ". . . fresh within the memory of us all" in which the Thirteenth as well as the Fourteenth Amendments were "the occasion and the necessity for recurring again to the great source of power in this country, the people of the States, for additional guarantees of human rights; [for] additional

[90]United States v. Hall, 26 Fed. Cas. 79 at 81–82, #15, 282 (C.C.S.D. Ala., 1871). See also United States v. Mall, 26 Fed. Cas. 1147, #15, 712 (C.C.S.D. Ala., 1871). Justice Bradley agreed with Woods; Bradley to Woods, Mar. 12, 1871, Bradley PP, New Jersey Historical Society. O'Neil v. Vermont, 144 U.S. 323 at 361–363 (1892), for Field's, Harlan's, and Brewer's belated agreement with Woods, in dissent.

[91]Live Stock Dealers and Butchers Association v. Crescent City Livestock Landing and Slaughterhouse Co., 1 Woods 21, 15 Fed. Cas. 649 at 652, #8408 (C.C.D. La., 1870).

powers to the Federal government; [for] additional restraints upon those of the States."[92]

Just so. For the federal judges expressed a coherent principle in all the Thirteenth Amendment–Civil Rights act decisions, a principle the majority of the Court (including Bradley) was to undercut when it came to treating the Fourteenth Amendment, beginning with *Slaughterhouse.* This principle was that the Thirteenth Amendment, absolute in its prohibition of servitudes, not only set new state norms but could affect and control the conduct of individuals as well. In their Thirteenth Amendment–Civil Rights act opinions the federal judges agreed that when the nation had a duty to protect rights guaranteed in or depending on the Constitution, state power must defer or even exit (a principle hallowed in *Prigg* v. *Pennsylvania*).

Agreement among the federal judges in Thirteenth Amendment– Civil Rights act cases about authority, did not, however, extend to the question of *means* the Congress might employ to reach the postwar Amendments' new heights of liberty. And *Slaughterhouse,* decided only two years after *Blyew,* helped to create a fateful divergence between ends and means in civil rights.

To say that *Slaughterhouse* was decided "only" two years after *Blyew,* or "only" seven or eight years, respectively, after the writing of the Thirteenth and Fourteenth Amendments, is to slight dramatic alterations in the American mood, as well as tenacious continuums, that formed the context of the *Slaughterhouse* decision. Scholars have made the *Slaughterhouse* decision its own starting point in history as they searched for definitions of both the Thirteenth and the Fourteenth Amendments. No adequate comprehension of the Fourteenth Amendment is possible without reverting to the Thirteenth and even back to *Dred Scott.*

So with *Slaughterhouse.* Countermarching is in order from 1873, the year the Court decided *Slaughterhouse,* back to 1867. Attention is required to the further development of Reconstruction constitutionalism and politics that helped to shape *Slaughterhouse;* to the decision for Military Reconstruction, to the impeachment, and to the Fifteenth Amendment and the Force Acts. Such a review may justify doubts about the accuracy of Justice Miller's *Slaughterhouse*

[92] 16 Wall. 36 at 67 (1873).

comment that in 1872–73 the history of the Thirteenth and Fourteenth Amendments was "fresh within the memory of us all." Instead it appears that Miller's memory and those of the majority of
the robed brethren were dimming when the Supreme Court considered *Slaughterhouse.*

CHAPTER 12

Anxious Passages: Fitting Ends
to All Controversies?

B Y the spring of 1867, accelerated state restorations usurped
equal rights in the priorities of the Republican majority. Now
Republicans became Reconstructors-in-a-hurry as Andrew Johnson
had been in 1865. Their sense of the necessary pace in Reconstruction quickened because they felt it essential to end unforeseen
strains in administration, politics, and society that had appeared
since Appomattox; a period when "the nation . . . survived one
anxious passage only to confront another," as Charles Fairman
observed. E. L. Godkin, *The Nation*'s editor, was to recall in a centennial tribute to the Constitution that in the spring of 1867 congressional Republicans "took hold resolutely of all the seriously obscure
or ambiguous passages in the instrument, and of all compromises
which had proved difficult or incapable of execution, and eliminated
them."[1]

Centennial sentimentalism had obscured Godkin's usually more
perceptive vision. In early 1867, the Fourteenth Amendment, still
out to the states for ratification, was itself filled with "seriously
obscure" and "ambiguous passages" which could by no means
eliminate Reconstruction difficulties. Yet, though mere expediency
would have inspired Republican leaders totally to cut free of Negro

---

[1] Edward Lawrence Godkin, "Some Things Overlooked at the Centennial," *The
Nation* (Sept. 22, 1887), p. 226; Fairman, *Reconstruction and Reunion*, pp. 138–139.

rights, racial equality remained on their agendas through the early seventies. Each expression of national concern about Negroes cost the party support. Alternative preoccupations were taking hold as wartime fervor faded. Southern whites were expressing a preference to live for decades under simple military rule rather than to accept black co-citizenship. Time was on the unregenerates' side; time, running out, now required the Republicans to hurry southern Reconstruction along.

An increasing body of opinion was coming to favor more direct federal intervention in the South and still another constitutional amendment to add political rights—the ballot—to the civil rights and liberties already protected under the Thirteenth and Fourteenth Amendments and relevant statutes. The abolitionist legacy the Radical Republicans inherited in 1865 perceived the Thirteenth Amendment as including the vote. The year-long experience with the Civil Rights and Freedmen's Bureau laws suggested strongly that something more was wanted than faith in southern whites' willingness to obey their own state laws: something that reached to localities, to constables and sheriffs as well as to state capitals and governors. The biracial, if not universal, ballot was widely discerned as the moderate, indeed, conservative, solution to the Reconstruction dilemma, in part because it promised to be the fastest way to get the federal government out of Reconstruction.[2]

As an example, Texas governor Andrew J. Hamilton in 1865 had thanked God that he lived where whites controlled government and society; in early 1867 he advocated black suffrage because true freedom required more than the absence of formal slavery. Freedom required that actual protection be real for every person. Any less left citizens in "the old condition" subject to the tender mercies of the state. Negro suffrage must be an integral part of another Reconstruction effort, Hamilton urged. Frederick Douglass wrote that every "loyal citizen" should have both the litigation remedies of the Civil Rights law and the controls the ballot provided as the minimums for adequate self-protection. General Rufus Saxton offered the Joint Reconstruction Committee his belief that with the

[2]Michael Les Benedict, "Preserving the Constitution: The Conservative Bases of Radical Reconstruction," *Journal of American History*, LXI (1974), 83–85; James M. McPherson, *The Abolitionist Legacy: From Reconstruction to the NAACP* (Princeton, 1975), p. 113.

ballot ". . . in his [the Negro's] hand, there would be little need for any special Freedmen's Bureau. Without it, and left to the oppressive legislation of his late owner, the result would be fearful to contemplate."[3]

To achieve black suffrage even in advance of a Fifteenth Amendment, to substitute a civilian counterpart for Grant's Special Orders, and to replace Johnson's executive orders that had created a "military reconstruction" for two years, Congress now prepared Military Reconstruction legislation. The Republicans' 1867 advance was to a vision of a state-based Union in which black citizens participated in local and state politics. Blacks were now to have access, even if racially segregated, to state and local institutions such as balloting booths, jails, asylums, and schools that whites entered, in addition to self-help remedies for unperformed or malperformed private contracts. Root-and-branch race equalitarians advocated wholly integrated enjoyment of all rights. Most Republicans, including Negroes, however, allowed—indeed, assumed—that racially segregated access (to public facilities, as example) was admissible. Even limited participations were sweet to blacks who, whether once-slave or ever-free, had known only exclusions until a very short time before.[4]

Alexander Bickel and others have suggested that the Republicans' shift to black suffrage was a partisan convenience. So supplemented in constituent strength, Republicans might issue not only new civil rights laws but also new economic proposals, easily overcoming opposition votes in Congress or vetoes.[5]

Alternative judgments are supportable. They are, first, that obstructions and nonenforcements of laws supporting the Thirteenth Amendment had seriously weakened confidence in enforcing legislation; enforcement by voters was surer, it seemed. Second, the pending Fourteenth Amendment was unlikely to perform better than its predecessor unless accommodation by southern whites was

---

[3]Hamilton in Carl H. Moneyhon, *Republicanism in Reconstruction Texas* (Austin, 1980), pp. 56–57; Frederick Douglass, "Reconstruction," *Atlantic Monthly*, XVIII (Dec., 1866), 761–765; Joint Committee on Reconstruction, *Report* (1867), II, 222.

[4]H. H. Rabinowitz, "From Exclusion to Segregation: Southern Race Relations, 1865–1890," *Journal of American History*, LXIII (1976), 325–350.

[5]Alexander Bickel, "The Original Understanding and the Desegregation Decision," *Harvard Law Review*, XLIX (1955), 1 at 62, n. 1; William Gillette, *The Right to Vote: Politics and the Passage of the Fifteenth Amendment* (Baltimore, 1965), ch. 1.

ensured by means of a biracial southern electorate. Third, the continuing need for military forces in the South because whites were not obeying the amended federal Constitution and laws, or their own state criminal laws, was forbidding. A civilian alternative was essential. Fourth, since the prospect of obedience by white southerners was unrealistic, recourse was necessary to Negro suffrage. Blacks, employing both the ballot and the Civil Rights law for self-protection, and whites wishing to avoid the Fourteenth Amendment's diminutions of representation, would coexist in decent manner. Save for the courts a national presence would no longer be needed. Weeks of intensive debate culminated two years after Appomattox, one year after enactment of the Civil Rights law, in the passage (March 2, 1867), over the President's predictable veto, of the Military Reconstruction law. It was an unambiguous statute, ". . . a fitting end to all controversy," Grant wrote mistakenly to E. B. Washburn.[6]

Sponsored by two conservative Republicans, Senator George Williams (Oregon) and Representative Roscoe Conkling (New York), favored by radical Thaddeus Stevens and by moderate John Bingham, the Military Reconstruction law retained the southern states in the "grasp of war" status that had obtained since Appomattox, disavowed the existing "provisional" state governments (though Congress carefully retained state lines), and placed them under federal military authority. The President retained responsibility to oversee the work of the Army officers he was to name to duty in the South. They could use existing state officers and courts or substitute martial equivalents, and, as will be indicated, they chose to retain many incumbents. Each provisional state was to convene a new constitutional convention. Delegates were to be elected by all otherwise qualified male citizens "of whatever race, color, or previous conditions," except for those disfranchised as past rebels or as convicted criminals. The resulting constitution must open the elective franchise to all state residents with the qualifications noted above, be ratified by state voters, and then be approved by Congress. After the new state legislature ratified the Fourteenth Amendment and it became added to the Constitution, the Congress would declare the state entitled to representation.

[6]Grant to Washburn, Mar. 4, 1867, Grant Papers, Illinois State Historical Library.

While all this was proceeding, each Army commander was

... to protect all persons in their rights of person and property, to suppress insurrection, disorder, and violence, and to punish, or cause to be punished, all disturbers of the public peace and criminals, and to this end he may allow local civil tribunals to take jurisdiction of and to try offenders, or, when in his judgment it may be necessary for the trial of offenders, he shall have power to organize military commissions or tribunals for that purpose. . . .[7]

Seemingly, as Grant had commented, Congress at last gave the Army clear goals and adequate authority. But several factors mitigated against success for Military Reconstruction. First, it was too late. Success for such a program might have been probable in 1865 when southern whites would likely have accepted what they could not then prevent. But by 1867, they, and the President, had learned techniques of obstructions and delays precisely applicable to the new statute. For example, the white South dragged its feet about participating in elections, making majorities impossible. Congress had to amend the basic statute aiming at overcoming impediments. Whereupon southerners initiated new impediments, some procedural and others violent; whereupon Congress further amended the Military Reconstruction statute. Each amendment (the last was in June 1868) involved debate, party strains, the President's veto, and public confusion. Increasing numbers of white militants, resorting to violence, mocked the Republicans' law-and-order aspirations.

Second, Military Reconstruction kept local functionaries in their offices during the provisional phases of Reconstruction, with few exceptions. The upshot was that for weeks, then months, into late 1867 and early 1868, the old white "Johnson state government" leadership retained control, even to the point of recommending "qualified" persons as vote registrars. They trained few or no Unionist-Negro apprentices in state-local administration. Inevitably, the successor "black-and-tan" governments were staffed with amateurs.

Next, the Military Reconstruction law did not propose "to blot out State authority, or to station a federal officer at every crossroad," as Frederick Douglass wrote.[8] No politically realistic sugges-

[7] *Statutes at Large,* XIV, 429.
[8] Douglass, "Reconstruction," pp. 762–763.

tion issued from Congress to expand the Army or Freedmen's Bureau to a number remotely up to the task of a real military occupation of the South, or of functioning as a civil rights police. Republicans' antimilitarism and distaste for coercive policies had, considering the span of American history, ancient and tenacious roots. Yet the optimistic aim was to solve problems spawned by centuries of racial prejudice and nurtured in heretofore ignored recesses of the federal system. Congress still wanted Reconstruction-on-the-cheap. The 15,000 soldiers on southern duty and the 900 Freedmen's Bureau field agents were hopelessly inadequate. As result, in 1867 and later, as in 1866, the Army could maintain a presence primarily in state capitals and the more important county seats and cities. Only special circumstances impelled troopers even to visit, much less police, the small communities where most southerners lived. Classic semiguerrilla situations resulted. Southern whites, discouragingly often, evaded justice whether of their states or of the nation. The Freedmen's Bureau was able to add little strength where it was most wanted, in localities. Bureau officers, deeply discouraged by two years of presidential interferences, tended to stay close to Army posts, seeking protection.[9] Army officers, in turn, were increasingly timid by reason of the damage suits filed against them in increasing number in unfriendly state courts for alleged offenses in carrying out the Reconstruction Acts. With the President so set against what the Army was doing, would he assign federal lawyers to protect defendant officers?

Fourth, Military Reconstruction was democratic in goals while military in means. Reconstruction's processes bred counter-Reconstruction. Congress, aiming to increase the number of voters and to democratize officeholding and jury service, specifically disfranchised notably few whites, a policy that tended to fray Republican party unity. Some party weights insisted on disfranchisements by rigorous enforcements of test oaths; others stressed increases in the electorate and jury venires. Commanding generals felt both goads and checkreins on these scores. "There is [sic] . . . statutes in all the states punishing cruelty to animals," mused Senator Matthew Carpenter. "Is there none against cruelty to commanding Generals?"[10] Disharmonies increased between Reconstruction districts as a result

[9]William Miller, "Reconstruction as a Police Problem, 1865–1867" (Organization of American Historians Paper, 1978).

[10]Carpenter to B. F. Butler, Sept. 2, 1867, Butler PP, Library of Congress.

of commanders' differing views on disfranchisements, commonly enough to warrant the comment of General Daniel Sickles, commanding in the Carolinas, that "the truth is we now have two systems of Reconstruction. . . ."[11]

On this matter of disfranchisements and exclusions from voting, officeholding, and jury service, the roles of President Johnson and his adroit Attorney General, Henry Stanbery, proved to be central. Congress, respectful of the check-and-balance system, left Johnson in the Reconstruction law as executive. Johnson publicly denounced Military Reconstruction in his vetoes of the bill and of every amendment as unconstitutional, centralizing, and despotic. Stanbery circularized southern federal attorneys, Treasury and Post Office workers, and Army and Freedmen's Bureau officers with official opinions (which lacked the force of law but not everyone knew this) against disfranchisements. President and Attorney General published their views in "pet" newspapers, even in some that counseled obstruction or violence against Reconstruction.

As an example, the Reconstruction Act excluded certain classes of ex-rebel officeholders from voting. The *Test Oath* decision magnified the effect of the President's pardons. Thousands of pardoned persons held themselves to be immune from both the oath qualification or other disfranchisement under the Military Reconstruction law, a position the Attorney General officially both broadcast and sanctioned. Were minor Confederate officers (notaries, justices of the peace) disfranchised? Stanbery ruled that minor rebel officers were not included, and that the voter registration boards had no power to look behind a voter-applicant's statement on rebel offices held. If he swore that he was not disqualified, he was not, and a perjury prosecution was very remote indeed. Congress thereupon enacted another supplement (July 19, 1867) authorizing Reconstruction commanders to suspend and remove officeholders, and registration boards to look behind an applicant's loyalty qualification. But initiatives came from the southern whites and Stanbery. Congress, if it wished to persist, had to descend ever deeper into local situations, from constitutions to constables. The descent was unwelcome; the path of duty, unclear. For district commanders, it was, William Sherman wrote to Grant, ". . . about as hard to manage

[11]Sickles to Lyman Trumbull, July 1, 1867, Andrew Johnson PP, nos. 16013–16014, vol. 116, Library of Congress.

as two round floating logs drifting down the Mississippi."[12]

Shrewd Stanbery understood perfectly the Republicans' self-imposed Reconstruction constitutionalism. This able lawyer, serving his client the President, played the role of an adversary advocate for political purposes, but he employed the deceptively objective language and logic that the language of the law provided. For example, Stanbery issued an official "opinion" that a Reconstruction commander had only a power "to sustain the existing frame of social order and civil rule, and not a power to introduce military rule in its place. In effect, it is a police power to be used only when the state failed to perform." And the President, not the on-scene commander, would decide if state nonperformance existed.[13]

Another example. A "provisional" state judge, upon complaint of a Negro citizen, refused to give effect to the Civil Rights law in his court, alleging its unconstitutionality. The district Army commander wished to remove the judge. But, upon an appeal to the President by the judge and by prominent Democrats, Stanbery ruled that neither removal nor suspension was in order, that individuals' civil rights, despite the clear contrary language of the Civil Rights and Reconstruction laws, came "within the exclusive cognizance of the state civil courts. . . ."[14]

Such stands by the Attorney General, like the President's several vetoes, impressed Army and Freedmen's Bureau officers, especially when war hero General Daniel Sickles tried to be independent and fell victim to the Attorney General and President. In April, 1867, Sickles, responding to widespread destitution in the Carolinas, suspended the collection of private debts or imprisonment for debt save for fraud. He decreed that wartime judgments of state courts not be executed, that those courts accept no new suits for recovery of such debts, and forbade tax foreclosures for twelve months. Unpaid farm laborers' wages were to be liens on their employers' crops. Homestead exemptions were to keep debtors' homes and tools out of creditors' hands even if courts ordered seizures. Sickles prohibited all personal firearms and subjected all offenders to military trials; prohibited certain criminal punishments including whip-

[12]Sherman to Grant, Mar. 13, 1867, HQA, Box 104, Letters Received, RG 108, National Archives.
[13]*Opinions of the Attorney General,* XII, 182.
[14]Fairman, *Reconstruction,* pp. 340–341.

ping, branding, and maiming; and abolished the death penalty for aggravated larceny and burglary, offenses almost always attributed to Negroes. He stressed that a new federal bankruptcy law and state inheritances, trusteeships, and wardships were unaffected by his order.

One of the most vigorous and Negrophile Reconstruction commanders, Sickles was already anathema at the White House. In addition to southern white outrage at Sickles's order, business spokesmen in the North condemned this military interference with marketplace operations. Johnson opportunistically replaced him, as well as equally energetic Phil Sheridan, in command in Louisiana, whose removals of ex-rebels from local offices were among the most numerous of any district.[15]

The President's and Attorney General's courses drove Army officers, obeying laws, into overt disagreements, either with the Commander in Chief or with Congress. The President was supposed to obey—to execute—statutes, even those passed over vetoes. Now, in effect, he and Stanbery forced Army officers into positions vis-à-vis obedience to statutes that few wished to take. "The Attorney General's opinions have of course not been regarded [in the Army]," wrote Francis Lieber's epauletted son, on Sheridan's staff in New Orleans, "but that such opinions were given and are not followed has a very serious effect."[16]

How serious is suggested by the fact that War Secretary Stanton felt it necessary openly to intervene in the Cabinet in efforts to protect officers and to see to the substantive execution of the laws:

The President has, as Commander in Chief [Stanton stated] a supervision over Military Commanders to see that there is no wilful neglect or wanton abuse of authority by the Generals commanding, but in my opinion the duties assigned to the Military Commanders in the [Reconstruction] Act . . . are specially entrusted to them, and they are not bound to perform their

[15]Benjamin P. Thomas and Harold M. Hyman, *Stanton: The Life and Times of Lincoln's Secretary of War* (New York, 1962), p. 490; Grant to Sheridan, May 26, 1867, in Adam Badeau, *Grant in Peace: From Appomattox to Mount McGregor, A Personal Memoir* (Hartford, 1887), pp. 61–62, 102.

[16]Norman Lieber to Joseph Holt, July 11, 1867, Holt PP, #7783, Library of Congress. See also J. R. Morrill III, "North Carolina and the Administration of Brevet Major General Sickles," *North Carolina Historical Review* (1965), 291–305; J. G. Dawson III, "General Phil Sheridan and Military Reconstruction in Louisiana," *Civil War History*, XXIV (1978), 133–151.

duties in conformity to his [or the Attorney General's] instructions unless they are in conformity to the Acts of Congress.[17]

In July, 1867, Congress, its leadership desperate, over a veto passed an amendment to the Military Reconstruction law to counteract Stanbery's restrictive interpretations. It made all provisional state authorities "subject in all respects to the military commanders," and stipulated that no commander or voter registrar "shall be bound . . . by any opinion of any civil officer of the United States." Congress gave Grant overall authority over Reconstruction commanders and, within each ex-rebel state, specific authority to suspend, remove, or appoint civil officials.

The July statute troubled Chief Justice Chase and many other Republicans. "I shall be sorry," Chase wrote privately, "if . . . [Congress] attempt[s] to supercede the President as Commander of the Army, or to make the District Generals superior to all civil authority as well as all military." But, though Chase was irritated with the Republican majority in Congress, it was a momentary vexation; in his opinion the July statute was less evil than unproductive of ". . . the greater [good] for which the country looks to Con[gress] . . . as the basis of justice and equal rights, firmly secured by the Constitution and laws."[18] Had President Johnson shared Chase's perception about Congress's hold on the respect of the majority of Americans, the presidency might have escaped crisis.

Back in October, 1866, Stanbery, then the newly appointed Attorney General, confided to Stanton that he would neither buy nor rent a house in Washington for his family "while things are so ticklish and uncertain." Stanbery believed "that Johnson will be impeached, and I think [Stanbery] dreads it, as bringing on fresh troubles," Stanton advised his wife. Stanton foresaw no impeachment.[19] But on January 7, 1867, Republican Representatives James M. Ashley (Ohio) and Benjamin Loan (Missouri) introduced resolutions calling for the Judiciary Committee to investigate Johnson's conduct,

[17]June 20, 1867, Stanton PP, #56610, Library of Congress.
[18]Chase to Theodore Tilton, July 9, 1867, Chase ms., Letterbook 1, Library of Congress; *Statutes at Large*, XV, 28.
[19]Stanton to Mrs. Stanton, Oct. 6, 1866, owned by Gideon Townsend Stanton.

looking toward his impeachment. His alleged offenses: obstructing the execution of Reconstruction legislation, in sum. The committee dug for ten months. During the off-year election campaigns, popular media, pulpits, and law journals became forums for sharply variant opinions and much misinformation on the constitutional law and history of impeachments in general and on the consequences of an impeachment of Andrew Johnson in particular.

As with the debate in 1861–65 about Lincoln's war powers, arguments in 1867 (and 1868) about Johnson's impeachability were overprecise. Politicans and professors described the allegedly exact meanings in English and American constitutional history concerning impeachments. But no President had ever been impeached. Earlier American impeachments, excluding a handful of forgotten ones in the colonial period, involved one against Tennessee Senator William Blount in 1799, against federal district judge John Pickering in 1803, against United States Supreme Court Justice Samuel Chase in 1805, and against federal district judge James H. Peck in 1830. None ever defined "high crimes and misdemeanors," one of the Constitution's scattered clauses about impeachments.[20] Johnson and his supporters exploited the imprecisions.

A major area of disagreement concerned the need for a President to have committed an indictable crime before an impeachment should occur, the position Johnson adopted in 1867 (and 1868), as opposed to those who argued that unindictable offenses such as interferences with the administration of statutes were also adequate for an impeachment. Constitutional history and law as understood in 1867 fell on the side of those who argued against the need for an indictable offense. Writing in 1866–68, at the height of the interest on impeachment, John Norton Pomeroy summarized the judgments of Joseph Story, William A. Duer, Timothy Farrar, James Kent, William Rawle, and the authors of *Federalist Papers* 65, 66, and 81:

The importance [Pomeroy wrote] of the impeaching power consists, not in its effects upon subordinate ministerial officers, but in the check which it places upon the President and the judges. They must be clothed with an

[20]Art. I, sec. 2, cl. 5; Art. II, sec. 2, cl. 1; Art. II, sec. 4; Art. III, sec. 2, cl. 3. See Appendix.

ample discretion; the danger to be apprehended is from an abuse of this discretion. But at this very point where the danger exists, and where the protection should be certain, the President and the judiciary are beyond the reach of Congressional legislation. Congress cannot, by any laws penal or otherwise, interfere with the exercise of a discretion conferred by the Constitution. . . . If the offense for which the proceeding may be instituted must be made indictable by statute, impeachment thus becomes absolutely nugatory against those officers in those cases where it is most needed as a restraint upon violations of public duty.[21]

In November, 1867, the committee reported 5–4 in favor of an impeachment resolution. But on December 7, the House, after intense debate centering on the need for proof of an indictable criminal offense for an impeachment, rejected the committee's recommendation, 75–108. Despite the comfort constitutional lawyers offered, Republicans drew back from impeachment in December, 1867, because the Constitution was nevertheless imprecise. Matters were strained enough already without adding a whole new dimension of argument. As a result of the 1866 elections Republicans could override vetoes. But, because they so respected check-and-balance relationships and the presidency, Republicans risked dangerous factionalism each time they did so. Yet the fact that Republicans retained the President as executive of the very bills he vetoed virtually ensured further discord, especially in light of Johnson's personality and purposes. Thus Johnson, nominally executing these laws while substantively distorting them, confused those who worried about his obstructions of the Reconstruction statutes.[22]

Republicans divided also on such questions as whether an impeached President was to continue functioning during his trial. If Johnson was convicted and removed, his successor until March, 1869, was to be Senator Ben Wade, whose fiscal ideas dismayed even Radical Republicans. In any event, by the end of 1867 most Republicans believed that they had tied Johnson up in legislation.

[21]Pomeroy, *Introduction,* pp. 491–492.

[22]The Nixon impeachment effort of 1973 produced a scholarly consensus largely based on the 1868 Johnson impeachment, that impeachable offenses need not be indictable felonies; that impeachment became part of the Constitution in order to make a President accountable to majority will at times between elections if he willfully failed to execute laws and to carry out other constitutional responsibilities; Benedict, *Impeachment,* pp. 192–202.

This legislation, almost all passed over vetoes, included the 1866 law reducing the number of Supreme Court justices to eight (though this was not wholly an anti-Johnson ploy to deny him an opportunity to appoint a justice, as long depicted). In January, 1867, Republicans had resolved that the Fortieth Congress commence its sessions immediately after the demise of the Thirty-ninth, so that Johnson would not, as in 1865, have a period of sole control over administration. The Military Reconstruction law itself was, as amended, the most dramatic effort by Congress to diminish the President's ability to determine policy. Anxious to limit his patronage and to protect incumbents in appointive offices, especially Grant and the Secretary of War, Congress, in a rider to the 1867 military appropriations bill, required the general of the Army (Grant) to be located in Washington, and all orders from the President to the Army were to pass through him. This bill also provided for the dissolution of the southern states' militias. Further, Congress repealed an earlier law that had given the President statutory authority to issue pardons by proclamation. To be sure, the President possessed an independent, constitutional pardoning power. But the repeal reflected Congress's mood.[23]

The Tenure of Office law was to have the profoundest consequences. It required a President not to discharge executive officers whose appointments the Senate had approved without the Senate's consent. If Congress was recessed the President could suspend an officer, then report the suspension to the Senate soon after its reconvening, requesting its consent to the suspension. Did the law cover the cabinet officers including the Lincoln holdovers, especially the War Secretary upon whose department Reconstruction depended? Opinions differed on this point, as on many others.[24]

Johnson's increasing militancy in the last third of 1867 failed to convince majority Congressmen to impeach because he nevertheless appeared to have accepted the constraints these laws imposed. In August, Johnson, carefully conforming to the Tenure law's procedure, suspended Stanton from the War Secretaryship. There-

[23]*Ibid.*, pp. 45 ff.; Stanley I. Kutler, *Judicial Power and Reconstruction Politics* (Chicago, 1968), esp. chs. 4–5.
[24]Benedict, *Impeachment*, pp. 48ff.; Statutes at Large, XIV, 154.

after, he removed from their commands the tough Reconstruction generals Pope, Sheridan, and Sickles and key subordinates of like opinions. Johnson replaced them with generals whose views were known to be like his, more lenient toward the white South: Winfield Scott Hancock, George Meade, and John M. Schofield. Great excitement attended news of these changes. But Johnson cleverly defused the most explosive possible reaction. He appointed Grant to Stanton's place *ad interim,* with simultaneous service as commanding general. While Grant had no option but to transmit the President's orders shifting the southern commanders, his presence both in the cabinet and at the War Department was a token protection for basic Reconstruction commitments. Republicans, though painfully aware of the distress the President was causing to southern Negroes and to Freedmen's Bureau officials by his removals of generals, argued that patience was in order. Grant was holding the central place; the President was obeying the Tenure law; it was time to soft-pedal impeachment. When Congress reconvened, he must report the suspension of Stanton to the Senate as the Tenure law required. If the Senate withheld consent from the suspension, Johnson must accept Stanton back into the cabinet. The administration would then have only a year remaining in office (unless Johnson won a presidential nomination and election in 1868). Surely Congress's peacekeeping efforts would prevail for that brief time.

Little wonder that by the end of 1867 impeachment appeared to be dead. The Republicans had balanced the President's interventions against southern Reconstruction while leaving him unfettered concerning banking, homesteading, railroads, taxation, and foreign affairs. Impeachment, as a *New York Times* correspondent predicted in February, was unlikely to revive. But "there is one qualification to be made," the newsman wrote:

. . . If the President persistently stands in the way . . . , if he fails to execute the laws in their spirit as well as in their letter, if he will forget nothing, if he will learn nothing; if, holding the South in his hand, either by direct advice or personal example he shall encourage them to such resistance to progress as may tend to defeat the public will—in such event . . . the President may, after all, come to be regarded as an 'obstacle' which must be 'deposed.'[25]

[25]*Times,* Feb. 13, 1867, p. 2, in Benedict, *Impeachment,* p. 25 and ch. 4.

Renewed defiance, not accommodation, characterized Johnson's annual message in December, 1867. After descending again to low racial levels, Johnson condemned the Reconstruction law anew as despotism and revealed that he had considered disobeying it in 1867 even to the point of forceful resistance.[26] On December 12, still complying with the Tenure law, Johnson reported to the Senate his reasons for suspending Stanton. He did not question the constitutionality of that law, argue that Stanton was not covered by its protections, or suggest that the Senate had no right to restore Stanton to the cabinet if it failed to consent to the suspension. Later, Johnson was to insist that he always intended a Supreme Court test of the constitutionality of the Tenure law if the Senate failed to concur in Stanton's suspension. But this self-serving argument does not convince. When the occasion arose, Johnson failed to seek a Court hearing. Further, the Supreme Court of 1868 was not that of 1973; Salmon Chase and his brethren were not Warren Burger and his associates who accepted jurisdiction of impeachment questions.[27]

Johnson may have hoped for implicit corroboration from the Court on other pending Reconstruction questions. For, as Yale law professor Henry Dutton, an ex-governor of Connecticut, wrote in early April, 1868, two inextricably entwined constitutional questions, impeachment and military government, simultaneously involved the Court: the former because the Constitution spelled out a role for the Chief Justice in an impeachment; the latter with respect to justiciability. Anti-Reconstruction interests tried in 1867 and 1868 to have the Supreme Court take sides with the President against Military Reconstruction. Mississippi's and Georgia's provisional governments requested injunctions from the Court against the enforcement of the allegedly unconstitutional Reconstruction

[26]Richardson, *Messages and Papers*, VI, 588–581. Reacting confusedly to the President's renewed offensive, Republicans, under the conservative Bingham's sponsorship, passed through the House, but lost in the Senate, an amendment to the Reconstruction Act that would have prohibited the President from removing commanders. Further, the bill declared any interference with its provisions to be a "high misdemeanor" and therefore impeachable. Benedict attributes the failure to pass the bill to Republicans' unwillingness further to disturb separation-of-powers relationships: Benedict, *Impeachment*, pp. 92–94, esp. n. 11–12.

[27]Paul Murphy, "Misgovernment by Judiciary?" *Harvard Civil Rights–Civil Liberties Law Review*, XIX (Fall, 1979), 783–785; Benedict, *Impeachment*, pp. 93–96.

law. Even Johnson and Stanbery felt required to respond on behalf of the United States that the Court should deny Mississippi and Georgia the relief; the requests were historically and constitutionally unsound. The Court agreed.[28]

Then William McCardle, a Negrophobe publisher of Vicksburg, Mississippi, editorialized in favor of violent resistance to Reconstruction. Soldiers arrested him for violating military orders under the Reconstruction law about keeping the public peace. McCardle's lawyer sought his release from military custody by appealing to a federal circuit court for a habeas corpus writ. Denied a writ, McCardle's counsel, now including Jeremiah Black and David Dudley Field, appealed to the Supreme Court, justifying the appeal on the basis of the Habeas Corpus law, as amended in 1867, in order to avoid the jurisdiction limits the Court had set in the *Vallandigham* and *Milligan* decisions. Stanbery, exhibiting curious behavior for an Attorney General, refused to represent the government. Grant obtained the services of Senators Lyman Trumbull and Matthew Carpenter as special counsel for the Army. Only a week after denying itself jurisdiction in the Georgia appeal, the Court accepted McCardle's.

By now it was February, 1868; as we shall see, impeachment was again in train. Congress, its Republican members' patience worn thin, overcame weak Democratic resistance and a tepid veto and repealed provisions of the 1867 law that gave the Court jurisdiction in McCardle's appeal. The Court acquiesced in the limitation. Deeply disappointed by the Court's restraint in *McCardle,* anti-Reconstruction conservatives, who wanted the Court in politics, insisted that federalism, democracy, and private property were everywhere in danger. Stung by accusations of judicial cowardice, Chase stipulated that Congress had the constitutional right to define by statute the Court's jurisdiction in all save matters provided for originally in the Constitution. The legislators had, however, Chase reiterated, only limited the Court's habeas jurisdiction relevant to petitions such as McCardle's; the Court, as it soon proved

[28]Henry Dutton, "Impeachment and Military Government," *New Englander,* XXVII (April, 1868), 360–368; Mississippi v. Johnson, 4 Wall. 476 (1867); Georgia v. Stanton, 6 Wall. 50 (1867).

in *Ex parte Yerger* in 1869, retained all other habeas prerogatives.[29]

On January 10, 1868, the Senate's Military Affairs Committee had recommended against consent in Stanton's suspension. Grant, who like most career Army officers was deeply respectful of the military affairs committees, relinquished the War Department to Stanton despite earlier promises to the President not to do so. Johnson thenceforward insisted, contrary to his earlier conformity to the Tenure law, that Stanton's suspension had occurred legitimately under the President's independent constitutional authority. More dangerously, Johnson tried secretly to inveigle General Sherman into accepting command of a completely unauthorized new Army department near Washington. These troops would be his to control outside the Army–War Department hierarchy. He recommended to the Senate that it give Sherman rank like Grant's. Sherman refused to be used to beget violence or to Balkanize the Army into presidential and congressional factions, and left Washington for the less dangerous Indian frontier.

Nevertheless, on February 21, Johnson, without consulting his cabinet, ordered Stanton's removal and named a new Secretary of War *ad interim*, Adjutant General Lorenzo Thomas, a career officer of little stature in the Army. Stanton remained self-immolated on the War Department. Greatly agitated, Congressmen recalled that only on the tenth, they had smothered impeachment; now, in the twenty-first, the President had revived it.[30]

Johnson had decided that he, as President, possessed the executive privilege to decide unilaterally on the legitimacy of the Tenure Act and, with it, of major Reconstruction alternatives. So deciding, Johnson was assuming an unprecedented constitutional posture, one not revived until Nixon's misadventures of the 1970s. Not only did Johnson assert an imperial view of executive privilege; by this view he was, as President, perilously close to a claim that he embodied the national will. Therefore, he had, he felt, a right to enforce or nonenforce laws he favored or did not favor. Johnson's (and Nixon's) presidencies suggest that our check-and-balance structure

[29]Ex parte Yerger, 8 Wall. (74 U.S.) 506 (1869); Kutler, *Judicial Power*, pp. 101–104 and chs. 5–6.
[30]Benedict, *Impeachment*, pp. 98–101; Thomas and Hyman, *Stanton*, pp. 583–586.

skews precipitously when a President applies such principles.[31]

By February 24 the House, in a party vote (128–74; 15 not voting), resolved for impeachment. A special House committee (Bingham, Boutwell, Julian, Logan, Stevens, James Wilson, and Hamilton Ward) hurriedly drafted articles. Not well composed, they were heavily legalistic. Perhaps this reflected the fact that the committee was strongly Radical in membership, yet Bingham and Wilson had opposed the 1867 impeachment effort. It all meant that for impeachment to proceed, much less to achieve a conviction, both Republican moderates and conservatives had to support if not run the show.

The committee reflected also the prevailing uncertainty whether indictability was an essential test for impeachability. The committee's Articles 1–10 were largely of indictable offenses. Articles 1–8 concentrated on Johnson's violations of the Tenure law; Article 9 charged that Johnson violated the 1867 Appropriations Act by not issuing orders through Grant; Article 10 attended to Johnson's allegedly "intemperate, inflammatory, and scandalous" harangues against Congress in the 1866 campaign; Article 11, added on the House floor at Radical insistence, was a catchall aimed at holding the votes of those who believed that nonindictable offenses were adequate for impeachment and conviction.

The House then chose its managers: moderates Bingham and James Wilson; Radicals Butler, Boutwell, Logan, Stevens, and Thomas Williams. On March 4 the managers appeared before the Senate which organized itself into a "court," two-thirds of whose members had to vote to convict in order for the removal of the President to occur, perhaps to be followed by indictment and trial in courts. Chase appeared on the fifth to "preside." The Constitution's impeachment machinery for a President was in operation for the first time.[32]

Of Nixon's aborted impeachment procedure, Paul Murphy asked: "Was the constitutional impeachment machinery useable in a modern setting?"[33] The "moderns" of 1868 were to learn that the ma-

[31]Murphy, "Misgovernment," pp. 783–786; cf. James E. Sefton, *Andrew Johnson and the Uses of Constitutional Power* (Boston, 1980), pp. 155–160.

[32]This treatment follows Fairman, *Reconstruction*, pp. 521–527; Benedict, *Impeachment*, ch. 4.

[33]Murphy, "Misgovernment," p. 786.

chinery was useable. But, though Johnson's trial was to run into May, its participants never made the machinery whose use they were pioneering run smoothly. The mixed political-constitutional-legal qualities of an impeachment in a check-and-balance system of government, that was itself the center of a complex federal system, remained obscure.

Consider defects in the Articles of Impeachment. Their concentration on indictable offenses gave the President's able defense counsel, including Stanbery, who resigned the attorney generalship in order to serve Johnson, and Benjamin R. Curtis, William Evarts, T. A. R. Nelson, and William S. Groesbeck, opportunity to cast very wide defensive nets. Even admitting that Johnson had committed them, were actions such as those the Articles enumerated truly indictable? Further, the Tenure law failed to protect Stanton, a Lincoln holdover, Johnson's counsel insisted. Next, the President had as much right as Congress to decide if a law was unconstitutional and undeserving of enforcement. Last, the President aimed always at a Court test.

These are lawyerlike arguments-in-the-alternative. They fit the legal procedures of the impeachment "trial" as well as the "prosecution" Articles, yet served also to tug at interests and principles of uncommitted Senators. The major problem with the defenses is that they are unfactual and leave government unworkable. Granting that a President might refuse to enforce a law because he thinks it unconstitutional. What if courts, Congress, or the electorate disagreed?[34] Could he continue nonenforcements and obstructions? When would they stop?

Johnson's impeachment suggests that in 1787, as in 1868, it is better not to expect precise answers for which Constitution, history, or law cannot formulate exact questions. As example, the impeachment managers wisely chose to let slide the question of Johnson's status during the impeachment. The President kept on with his work, carefully refraining from further interferences with Reconstruction; the Senate and House carried on regular business in nonimpeachment hours; the Chief Justice returned to the Supreme Court at those times. As the French observer Adolphe de Chambrun noted:

[34]Benedict, *Impeachment*, pp. 108–112.

The United States then presented an unexampled spectacle in the history of the world: that of a President continuing the administration of affairs, whilst a high court of justice deliberated on his fate. Those who ordered his impeachment, did not dare to suspend him from the exercise of his functions during the trial.[35]

Another question that rose in the proceeding's first days concerned the role of the Chief Justice. Chase had studied carefully the available literature on his status and duties in the impeachment. He decided that though he did not have a vote he did have more than a parliamentarian's power; could, in short, pass on points of admissibility of testimony and other evidence. When Democrats protested that Senator Wade, who would succeed Johnson if the latter was convicted and ousted from office, should not sit because of self-interest, Chase ruled in favor of Wade. In an impeachment the Senate was a court; Wade's status as president of the Senate was irrelevant, Chase decided. "Chase could not lose," Michael Les Benedict concluded.[36]

All this involved lengthy, tedious debate, to the President's and the Democrats' ultimate advantage. The President's counsel dragged their feet. Sumner had hoped for a trial of ten days. Instead, five weeks were consumed in procedural arguments before the Senate accepted any testimony. But the Republicans could not push too hard, though every day accentuated their political problems. They could not both insist on a speedy trial and convince themselves and their constituents that it was a fair one.[37]

Through March and April the nation observed the increasingly ludicrous antics of some of the House managers. Their bombast and harassments of witnesses contrasted sharply with the calm demeanor of the President's counsel. They, unlike the managers, had a single clear position, that impeachability required an indictable offense and that Johnson had committed no felonies. The fact that this position was historically and legally unsound did not detract

[35]Madeliane V. Dalhgren (tr.), Adolphe de Chambrun, *The Executive Power in the United States: A Study of Constitutional Law* (Lancaster, Pa., 1874), p. 266.
[36]Benedict, *Impeachment*, pp. 118–124.
[37]As Stanbery argued: "A case like this, Mr. Chief Justice, in which the President of the United States is arraigned upon an impeachment presented by the House of Representatives, a case of the greatest magnitude we have ever had, is, as to time, to be treated as if it were a case before a police court, to be put through with railroad speed on the first day the criminal appears." Quoted in Benedict, *Impeachment*, p. 122.

from its political utility or appeal. Johnson's restrained behavior seemed to be an implicit promise no longer to obstruct Reconstruction. He thereby helped finally to detach from the pro-conviction ranks enough Republican Senators to escape conviction—by a single vote—when, in May, the balloting took place.

Johnson's implicit sacrifices on the altar of nonconviction included his naming during the trial, as Secretary of War, General Schofield, who, though hardly a Reconstruction enthusiast like Sickles, as commander in Virginia at least had administered the Reconstruction laws. The President stayed quiet in the White House while biracial voting in six states created new Constitutions. As April ended, only Mississippi, Texas, and Virginia might still be arenas for presidential obstructions. Tensions diminished in Washington. Impeachment's primary goal, the safeguarding of Reconstruction, was won before the senators voted.[38]

Despite the anxieties of the pro-conviction Republicans that Johnson would impede Reconstruction once the trial ended in his nonconviction, the President honored his implicit commitment to equilibrium during the ten months left of his administration. Johnson had, however, lost his chance to get the Democratic party's presidential nomination in 1868. But in a larger sense Johnson won. As in 1865, so in 1868: his buccaneering had reinvigorated the will of southern whites to resist race equality and tired many northern whites concerning Reconstruction. Johnson's danger in 1868, though self-created, raised fears of dangers to the presidential office that many persons grew determined to avoid. For many contemporaries the impeachment was an added proof that Reconstruction itself was too risky to pursue.[39]

Along with Congress, the Supreme Court greatly increased its prestige and significance in 1868 and 1869. Partly this increase was a factor of the growth of the work load of all federal courts under way in the sixties, a growth that by decade's end was to double the docket compared to that of the preceding ten years; then to double it still again by 1880. The increases in the jurisdiction of the federal courts voted by Congress, plus the jurists' awakening willingness to

[38]*Ibid.*, pp. 137–139.
[39]*Ibid.*, p. 180.

hear cases of uncertain justiciability, were also factors in the swelling docket of the Supreme Court. After the furor aroused by the *Test Oath* and *Milligan* decisions and the impeachment, the possibility that the Court might intervene against Reconstruction seemed to recede, especially when the justices declined to challenge Republican policy in the Georgia and Mississippi petitions and in McCardle's case. In none of those cases did the Court pass on the substantive issued of Reconstruction itself; each was a "jurisdictional" case. Hence the possibility persisted, as Reconstruction went on, that the Court might intrude on Reconstruction policymaking in some drastic way. Many Republicans feared that military Reconstruction was constitutionally vulnerable, especially if lawyers and judges should abandon discretion to seek out Republican dragons to slay in the South. A case already on the Supreme Court docket when Congress passed the first Military Reconstruction Act might provide the occasion; the Court issued its decision early in 1869.

Texas v. *White* was a suit in the original jurisdiction of the Supreme Court because one of the parties was a state—at least in the opinion of its attorneys, the Texas Unionist George Washington Paschal and Richard T. Merrick. The state sought to recover bonds originally given to it in partial fulfillment of the Compromise of 1850, in which Texas got ten million dollars in exchange for surrender of her claims to lands incorporated in New Mexico Territory. After secession, the Confederate state government sold the bonds to pay for supplies to support its war effort.[40]

Attorneys for the respondents, Albert Pike, a flowery Confederate general, and the learned Alabaman Philip Phillips, denied that Texas was a "state" within the meaning of the Constitution. But a year earlier, Paschal had anticipated this argument in his treatise, *The Constitution of the United States,*[41] in which he argued that the Union was indestructible but that the seceding states' relation to it might become so abnormal that Congress, acting under its power to guarantee republican forms of government, would have power to rehabilitate them. Paschal's argument fell on receptive ears before the United States Supreme Court: Chase had previously twice de-

[40]7 Wall. (74 U.S.) 700 (1869). On the original, as opposed to the appellate, jurisdiction of the United States Supreme Court see Art. III, sec. 2, cl. 2, in Appendix
[41]George W. Paschal, *The Constitution of the United States Defined and Carefully Annotated* (Washington, 1868), pp. v–xvi.

nied that states could sever their relations with the Union.[42]

Chase wrote the majority opinion in *Texas* v. *White* for a divided court. He began by pointing out that the term "state," as it is used in various places in the Constitution, is ambiguous, meaning variously the geographic entity, the people residing there, or the political entity comprised of people, territory, and government. Given this ambiguity, it would be possible for a state to remain in the Union, yet have its political relationship with its sister states deranged. But in any event, in Chase's sonorous phrase, "the Constitution, in all its provisions, looks to an indestructible Union, composed of indestructible States." For that reason, the attempted secession was void.

But, Chase went on, the status of Texas as a state at the time the suit was filed (February 14, 1867, before Military Reconstruction) might nonetheless be abnormal. "During this condition of civil war, the rights of the State as a member, and of her people as citizens of the Union, were suspended."[43] In this crucial sentence, Chase validated the "forfeited-rights" theory of the status of states that had earlier been put forward by Lincoln and by Republican stalwarts such as Ohio Congressman Samuel Shellabarger. The forfeited-rights theory reassured Republican moderates about the majority report of the Joint Committee on Reconstruction and the Military Reconstruction Acts; even about the temporary de-Reconstruction of Georgia in 1868, a state which Congress had admitted to representation, then excluded again.

Chase declared that, as a result of secession, there was "then no government in Texas in constitutional relations with the Union," and it was the duty of the federal government, acting in wartime under the President's powers as Commander in Chief, and in peacetime under the guarantee clause, to restore the proper relationship between states and union. Though he was careful to point out that nothing in his opinion spoke one way or the other to the constitutionality of the Military Reconstruction Acts, the effect of his opin-

[42]Draft Memorandum of Chase, dated "1865," quoted in Fairman, *Reconstruction*, pp. 629–630; Shortridge *v.* Macon, 22 Fed. Cas. 20, #12,813 (C.C.D. N.C., 1867).
[43]Texas *v.* White, at 725, 727. Grier, writing for himself, Swayne, and Miller on the jurisdictional point, maintained that Texas was, realistically speaking, effectively out of the Union between 1861 and 1868, whatever its theoretical status might have been.

ion was to validate at least the theoretical bases of Republican Reconstruction. But Chase went further: Congress enjoyed a "discretion in choice of means" in working out Reconstruction policy. So long as its measures are, in the phrase of Article I, section 8, "necessary and proper" and not "unsanctioned" by the Constitution, the Court would decline to upset congressional policy.[44]

If Roger B. Taney was looking on from some judicial Valhalla, he must have been aghast at the irony of Chase's reliance on the guarantee clause. In *Luther* v. *Borden* (1849), which Chase cited, Taney had laid the foundations for Chase's reading of the powers of Congress under the guarantee clause, never dreaming that his political-question doctrine would justify a later Court's refusal to interfere with restoration of the Union on the ruins of the Confederacy. Chase's position was not, as Taney doubtless would have considered it had he survived, an abdication of judicial responsibility. Rather, it was a recognition that, in Eric McKitrick's words, "there are occasionally problems of such magnitude that the Court itself must simply look to the principle of majority rule as the key to their ultimate settlement."[45]

The Court, with Chase dissenting on other grounds, reaffirmed doctrines of *Texas* v. *White* three years later, in *White* v. *Hart,* where the Court held that the status of Georgia during war and Reconstruction was a political question, to be determined by Congress. The rights of the states were suspended by the war, not destroyed. With some irony, the result in the later case upheld the enforceability of contracts for the sale of slaves.

Perhaps with greater irony, the Court's obeisances to Congress in *Texas* v. *White* and *White* v. *Hart* spotlighted the basic Republican dilemma—how, given Republican commitment to state rights and federalism, to guarantee adequate state conduct after Congress readmitted the state? One way was for Congress to encourage or, indeed, to require would-be states to write national supremacy into state Constitutions; another way was to require Negro suffrage as a "fundamental condition" to statehood, as with Colorado and Nevada in 1867. In June, 1868, with Johnson squelched and Grant nominated, Congress amended the Military Reconstruction law yet

[44]Texas *v.* White, at 729.
[45]Eric McKitrick, *Andrew Johnson and Reconstruction* (Chicago, 1960), p. 118.

again. This time it required Alabama, the Carolinas, Georgia, Florida, and Louisiana to accept, before readmission, in addition to the Fourteenth Amendment ". . . the following fundamental conditions: that the constitutions of . . . said States shall never be amended or changed as to deprive any citizen of the United States of the right to vote in said State, who are entitled to vote by the constitution thereof. . . ."[46]

Only the Republicans' intent, to cement equality into the states' Constitutions, excused the method, editorialized *The Right Way:* "We hope, . . . from the act, . . . the beneficial result contemplated by Congress in its enactment." Still, the editorialist worried, the fundamental condition method suffered from "a looseness." For no matter what a would-be state promised to win admission, once admitted, what could Congress do if that state, once restored, broke its commitments on equality?[47]

Such questions diminished Republicans' pleasures in their 1868 triumphs. Party leaders put the best face they could on things. The 1868 platform, like the *Texas* v. *White* decision, suggested that all basic constitutional questions were settled in favor of the party's definitions and beneficiaries. Preparing notes for a political speech in early 1870, Ignatius Donnelly wrote: "Not a single issue of the many which agitated us in the past remains alive today—slavery—reconstruction—rebellion—impartial suffrage—have all perished as issues. Let us bury them and . . . reconstruct from the bottom upward."[48]

How? The Fifteenth Amendment, ratified in February, 1870, appeared to be the appropriate, politically realistic response. Like the Thirteenth it was brief and, seemingly, uncomplicated; like the

[46]White v. Hart, 13 Wall. (80 U.S.) 646 (1872); Statutes at *Large,* XV, 73–74; M. J. Brodhead, "Accepting the Verdict: National Supremacy as Expressed in State Constitutions, 1861–1912," *Nevada Historical Society Quarterly,* XIII (1969), 3–16. One part of Georgia's Constitution that worried Lieber and others was the stipulation, perhaps for the first time in a state Constitution, that state judges should declare unconstitutional laws void: Ethel K. Ware, *A Constitutional History of Georgia* (New York, 1947), p. 123. Lieber wrote: "The very bill of rights of Georgia . . . declares that the [state] law courts shall decide upon questions of constitutionality. This is nothing less than destroying the constitutional fabric that has been reared." Memo on the Supreme Court, LI, 463, Lieber PP, Huntington Library.
[47]*The Right Way* (Jan. 22, 1867).
[48]Theodore Nydahl (ed.), "The Ignatius Donnelly Diary, 1869–1885" (Ph.D. diss., University of Minnesota, 1941), I, 372–373.

Thirteenth and Fourteenth, the Fifteenth had an enforcement clause (see Appendix).

Was the new Amendment primarily a Republican device to overcome northern states' refusals to allow Negroes to vote, and so win blacks' ballots for the party? A proponent of this view, William Gillette, suggested that such a goal did not exclude sincere moral concerns. As in the Bill of Rights, amendments to the federal Constitution that set standards higher than many states afforded their citizens were familiar in American history. The Fifteenth Amendment can be seen also as a lurch backward in a retreat from Reconstruction.[49] But it was also a great leap forward toward a "reconstructed" American polity—or, it could have been had the Fifteenth Amendment, like the Fourteenth, not helped to turn the attention of President, Congress, and Court primarily to state action and to ignore state nonaction or private behavior.

The Thirteenth Amendment, in imperial manner, forbade every American individual as well as every American government from holding persons in bondage; the Fourteenth restrained only states, a growing consensus insisted. The Fifteenth added strength to that consensus. While the Fifteenth inhibited both national and state actions, it did not constrain individuals' behavior—*if* the Thirteenth was assumed to have been superseded or was otherwise ignored.

And that is what happened. Between 1870 and the mid-1880s, administrators, judges, lawyers, and legislators all but lost sight of the Thirteenth Amendment as the standard by which to measure the nation's duty to every individual as against every other person or unit of government, concerning defenses of national rights. Perhaps this spreading myopia helps to explain the retreat from adequate enforcement of the Reconstruction laws by both Presidents Grant and Rutherford Hayes.[50] Congress's growing fuzziness on which Reconstruction Amendment sanctioned enforcements both added to the Presidents' uncertainties and fed the Supreme Court's tendency to shift away from the Thirteenth to the narrower Fourteenth and Fifteenth. Reciprocally, the jurists' shifts encouraged legislators to narrow their concentration.

[49]William Gillette, *Retreat from Reconstruction, 1869–1879* (Baton Rouge, 1979), chs. 1–2.
[50]Gillette, *Retreat,* p. 43, offers statistics on criminal prosecutions under the Enforcement Acts, 1870–77, by section and by year.

As result, the nation's sense of responsibility for rights become confined to official state action rather than to both private and state action. The Thirteenth Amendment not only faded. It lost its dynamic meanings of 1865. By 1880 it was almost a relic. Its potential, as expressed in the 1866 Civil Rights Act, to protect Americans against any offender was sadly diminished.

No one in 1866, or 1870, anticipated that lawyers and judges would reverse the stream of history and begin to interpret the 1866 Civil Rights act in light of the Fourteenth and Fifteenth Amendments rather than the Thirteenth Amendment. The result was that the Fourteenth, as reinterpreted by the Court, in a period of skyrocketing respect for state rights and for judicial review, was seen to safeguard "an almost unlimited number of rights primarily against a very few persons—those who represented the State," Mark DeWolfe Howe noted.[51]

Perhaps a diminished concentration on the Thirteenth was inevitable. The Fourteenth and Fifteenth Amendments simply loomed larger in men's minds by the fact of recency of composition; they perhaps seemed to be more appropriate for more recent conditions. Further, the Thirteenth's "force act," the 1866 Civil Rights law, had received favorable judicial treatment. That Amendment and enforcement law were safe, it appeared. The newer Amendments and their enforcement laws had now to be safeguarded. One way was to subsume the Thirteenth and the 1866 Civil Rights law into the successor enactments as a reinforcement.

Reinforcements were needed. Violence grew in the South. Democrats, who had denounced the 1866 Civil Rights law as dangerously radical in that federal power reached individuals, continued to condemn that novel linkage as a cause of violence. By 1870 some leading Republicans including Lyman Trumbull were coming to agree that federal authority must never reach private conduct, else fatal upsets to federalism might occur.

Still further, the impeachment had frightened Republicans. The Fifteenth Amendment, so clear in its command, promised to stabilize the revered check-and-balance structure. And it was stability and

[51]Mark A. DeWolfe Howe, "Federalism and Civil Rights," Massachusetts Historical Society *Proceedings*, LXX (1965), 24–25; G. Sidney Buchanan, *The Quest for Freedom: A Legal History of the Thirteenth Amendment* (reprinted from *Houston Law Review*, Houston, 1976), p. 34.

order for which Republicans had been searching for a decade. The shift of attention in the Fourteenth and Fifteenth Amendments to official action, while not formally retracting the Thirteenth Amendment's boundless commitment against servility, reflected limitations that white America wished to set on the search for justice-as-equality.[52]

These elements mixed together unsystematically beginning in 1870. Enforcement legislation enacted very soon after the ratifications of the Fifteenth Amendment included clauses punishing private diminutions of rights. Contemporaries were doubtless confused about what they had wrought. The three amendments were hardly a neat, systematic package. Much of what occurred 1866–1870 and later was, as noted, planless responses to Andrew Johnson's policies, southern white violence, and party needs. But this fact does not lessen the validity of another fact, that Negroes' inability to vote had been a concomitant of servility. In 1870, political rights became, or could have become, defendable against both private and state interferences almost in the dynamic, twentieth-century Warren Court sense. Taken together, as they should be, the Fourteenth and Fifteenth Amendments can be seen, as some contemporaries saw them, to have advanced the goals of the Thirteenth Amendment and the 1866 Civil Rights law.[53]

What became the Republicans' civil rights program after the Fifteenth Amendment was ratified employed three enforcement mechanisms. The first was the most dearly wanted, but least obtained: it was that the states themselves enforce equal rights by the standards of their own Constitutions and laws. Federal troops were the second enforcement machinery. They were little used. State restorations successively excluded the national military from the list of available options. The federal courts and the new Justice Department, together, were the last of the enforcement machineries, and would outlast state restorations. But case-by-case litigations were unlikely to create systematic replies to questions about the legacy of the war and Reconstruction.

Which is to say that in 1870, an advance from civil to political

[52]Buchanan, *Quest,* pp. 36–37.
[53]John Bascom, "The Three Amendments," *Annals of the American Academy of Political and Social Science,* XXVII (1906), 135–147.

rights, seen then as separable, had become mandatory. This advance resulted from a progression, with much slippage, toward goals that unforeseeable events disclosed. The May 31, 1870, Civil Rights–Enforcement Act spearheaded the new advance; its champions did not know that they were retreating.

As soon as possible after ratification of the Fifteenth Amendment, Congress, with President Grant's hearty assent, enacted the May 31, 1870, "Civil Rights" or "Enforcement" statute. In twenty-three sections, the 1870 law "reenacted" the guarantees of the 1866 Civil Rights law, this time under the Fourteenth and Fifteenth Amendments. Further, the 1870 statute forbade every state election official from enforcing discriminatory state laws or from using violence, intimidation, bribery, or force to interfere with voting because of race, and prohibited (section 16) disguised groups intending to oppress voters. The latter section aimed at felonious private acts, it will be noted. Congress assigned enforcement to the brand-new Department of Justice, expanded the jurisdiction of federal courts to hear prosecutions brought under the statute, appointed federal election supervisors, authorized federal judges and marshals to call for troops to maintain peace at elections, and embraced aliens under national protections.[54]

Then, in 1874, a long-awaited compilation of the United States laws, known as the *Revised Statutes*, came into existence. It rearranged the nation's laws into allegedly relevant, logical groups. This rearrangement reflected growing notions in the profession that the law was a science and harmonized well with the new library arrangements of the Harvard Law School. But, inexplicably, the *Revised Statutes* failed to list the 1866 Civil Rights law either in the published text or in the "historical" documentation. The parts of the 1866 law were scattered in the *Revised Statutes* under different chapter (i.e., subject) headings. Civil rights as an independent subject worthy of the attention of lawyers, judges, law professors, and an entire new generation of future professionals then studying in the schools was neither easily researched nor, seemingly, important.

Further, in 1874, the codifiers, through inadvertence or design, dropped the word "custom" from the scattered sections of the *Revised Statutes* devoted to the 1866 Civil Rights law, though custom

54*Statutes at Large*, XVI, 140, sec. 16.

was a prominent element in that law's first section. This omission left only officials' actions made in conformity to formal statutes as prohibited by the "reenacted" 1866 Civil Rights law, *if* one could find the parts of that law in the *Revised Statutes.*

Almost simultaneously with the *Revised Statutes,* in the *Slaughterhouse* decision, as well as in two subsequent decisions (*Ex parte Virginia* and *Virginia* v. *Rives,* 1879–80), Justice Field was to argue that the 1870 "reenactment" of the 1866 law under the Fourteenth and/or Fifteenth Amendments, plus the dropping of any prohibition against discriminatory customs, helped to prove that the federal interest in rights under any of the Reconstruction Amendments was restricted to official acts, not private or customary ones; that the Act did not protect against "popular prejudices and passions"; that protectable federal rights were still, as before the war, relatively traditional in nature and few in number. And his position was eventually to triumph. The Field deemphasis in *Slaughterhouse* of the Thirteenth Amendment, echoed heavily, if implicitly, in the simultaneous work of the revisers of the federal laws, was, as Patricia Allen described it: ". . . to separate the pieces of Republican policy, and to isolate them from their historical connections." Her judgment merges with that of Mark DeWolfe Howe's that, because of the ahistoricism of the Court and of the legal profession, the Fourteenth Amendment, an effort to ensure Negroes what the Thirteenth Amendment and the Civil Rights law promised, became "the source of their undoing."[55]

Congressmen favorable to the anticonspiracy section 16 of the 1870 bill found ample authority in both the Thirteenth and the Fifteenth Amendments; implied that the Fifteenth in effect ex-

[55]Allen, "Freedom and Federalism," p. 263; Howe, "Federalism," pp. 24–25; Buchanan, *Quest,* pp. 69–70; Field in Virginia *v.* Rives, 100 U.S. 313 at 333 (1879); Ex parte Virginia, 100 U.S. 339 at 349–370 (1879). Francis Biddle noted that the 1874 revision "effectively concealed the whole scheme for the protection of rights established by the three amendments and five [enforcement] acts." "Civil Rights and the Federal Law," in Robert Carr (ed.), *Safeguarding Civil Liberty Today* (Ithaca, 1945), p. 131. Harold M. Hyman, *Era of the Oath,* pp. 146–147, noted how the 1862 law requiring a test oath of jurors in federal courts, having been repealed in the April, 1871, Enforcement Act, 3d section, reappeared in the 1874 *Revised Statutes,* and was reaffirmed as good law by the Supreme Court, in Atwood *v.* Weems, 9 Otto 183 (1876). See also Justice Field's opinion, Burt *v.* Panjoud, 9 Otto 188 (1876).

panded the Thirteenth. But extended statements on the Thirteenth Amendment were rare. Perhaps there was little need for them. A Republican consensus still obtained in 1870 that the Fifteenth Amendment, like the Fourteenth, supplemented, not repealed or superseded, its precedent Amendments. Yet, as noted, the Congress contributed to this distorted time sense about the Thirteenth and Fourteenth Amendments when, in section 18 of the 1870 law, it specifically "reenacted" the 1866 Civil Rights law, but this time under the Fourteenth and Fifteenth, not the Thirteenth.[56] So doing, Mark DeWolfe Howe wrote, Congress encouraged lawyers and judges ". . . to forget the [1866] statute's Thirteenth Amendment paternity and to see it as the fruit of powers conferred on Congress by the Fourteenth Amendment." In this manner the consensus grew that only official discriminations counted. But, Howe reminded us, in 1866 when writing the Fourteenth Amendment, Congress retracted no authorities the Thirteenth Amendment granted;[57] a position relevant also in 1870 when Congressmen wrote the Fifteenth Amendment and the Enforcement law.

To be sure, section 18, the "reenactment" part of the 1870 law, seemed to bear out Field's positions. Yet, Senator William Stewart, chief drafter of the 1870 Enforcement bill, wanted to apply (not to reenact) the administrative apparatus of the 1866 law in defense of aliens, a class not covered in 1866. A section of Stewart's early drafts of what became the 1870 bill "reenacted" the 1866 law, specifically deleting from the restatement its sections that excluded aliens. No one seemed to think this "loss" of the offending sections important. "Reenactment" of the 1866 law simply gave the 1870 Republicans the machinery of 1866 to use.[58]

No one repealed the Thirteenth Amendment. It made sense to support the 1870 law under the newer Amendments as well. Perhaps proponents of the 1870 law wished to diminish all doubts as to their creation's constitutionality in this multi-Amendment ap-

---

[56]For Thirteenth Amendment statements, see *Congressional Globe*, 41 Cong., 2 sess., app. (May 20, 1870), p. 473; and Senator William Hamilton, *ibid.*, p. 354; Buchanan, *Quest*, pp. 38–39; *Statutes at Large*, XVI, 140; sec. 18.

[57]Howe, "Federalism," pp. 24–25.

[58]Buchanan, *Quest*, pp. 38–39; W. T. Hamilton (Maryland) in *Congressional Globe*, 41 Cong., 2 sess., app. (May 18–19, 1870), pp. 354–361.

proach, thus to make future Congresses hesitate before repealing the rights laws. They may have been trying to protect the 1866 law, criticized since its passage as an unwarranted extension by Congress of authority granted in the Thirteenth Amendment, by reinforcing it by the Fourteenth. No doubt the 1870 law was sloppily drafted; unquestionably its legislative history is murky and inconclusive. But these very factors suggest that courts, judges, and historians erred grievously by insisting unqualifiedly that the 1870 "reenactment" diminished the outreach of the 1866 law only to state action.[59]

Unpunished racist violence increased in the South. Congress responded on April 20, 1871, with the "Ku Klux Klan" Act, enforcing now the Fourteenth Amendment. This law aimed to create remedies for persons deprived of federal rights under color of state law; the Fourteenth Amendment was clearly appropriate. But major portions of the KKK law extended to private conspiracies that intentionally deprived persons of the equal protection of state law, while establishing litigation remedies for the victims of these conspiracies. Representative Bingham, the Congressman best acquainted with the 1866 Civil Rights law, responded incredulously to Democrats' assertion that the KKK bill could not also find Thirteenth Amendment authority to inhibit criminal conspiracies:

The . . . [Thirteenth Amendment, Bingham stated] provides that involuntary servitude, or slavery, shall not exist in the United States. That is negative. Then we have the further provision that Congress shall have power to enforce, by appropriate legislation, this amendment. That is affirmative. Do gentlemen undertake to say today that this does not impose a new limitation upon the power of the States, and grant a new power to Congress? . . . Let any State try the experiment of again enslaving men, and we will see whether it is not competent for the Congress of the United States to make it a felony. . . . In such case the nation would inflict the penalty for this crime upon individuals, not upon States. Will gentlemen undertake to tell the country that we cannot enforce by positive enactment that negative provision, the thirteenth article of amendment?[60]

[59]Buchanan v. Warley, 245 U.S. 60 (1917); Corrigan v. Buckley, 271 U.S. 323 (1926); Young v. International Telephone & Telegraph Co., 438 F. 2d 757 (3 Cir., 1971); Shelley v. Kramer, 443 U.S. 1 (1948); United States v. Morris, 125 Fed. 322 (D.C.F.D. Ark., 1903), is an important exception to the trend toward a state-action-only formula.
[60]Congressional Globe, 42 Cong. 1 sess., app. (Mar. 31, 1871), p. 85.

Representative James Garfield asserted that all the Reconstruction Amendments had beneficently altered federal relationships so that clear authority existed for direct connections between the nation and individuals. George Edmunds insisted that the Thirteenth Amendment imposed a duty on the nation to crush Klan conspiracies. Democrats inveighed against such views, insisting wearyingly that the abolition Amendment ended only formal slavery. Samuel Shellabarger, the House manager of the 1871 anti-Klan bill, moving rightward, was himself ambivalent, not about the nation's constitutional adequacy to act but about the effects of action on federalism. He wrote to an intimate that "the full idea of the Fourteenth Amendment . . . interpreted by the old rules of construction [i.e., those obtaining in 1866 when Congress wrote the Amendment?] and pushed to their full logical consequences, would so invade what has been the exclusive domain of the States, that I do not, now at any rate, wish to go any further in that direction than the exigency of the country require [sic]." The Klan bill reserved the nation's right to act. But it did not, Shellabarger insisted, "push the federal authority into doubtful latitudes." He would ". . . lean, for more mature deliberation on the Courts and on Congress to decide, in the future, where the line between the two authorities is; or where they are concurrent." Confusions spread by Shellabarger's daintiness grew greater when Trumbull argued that the anti-Klan bill was superfluous. All the Reconstruction Amendments were self-enforcing, he insisted—a view best described as unrealistic.[61]

The KKK bill passed, as did laws of July 14, 1870, and February 28, 1871, in which Congress increased the numbers and duties of

[61]Shellabarger to J. Comly, Apr. 10, 1871, Comly MSS, Ohio Historical Society. Trumbull stated that "the civil rights act [of 1866] did not undertake to protect those who had been slaves, nor whites, in particular rights; but it declared that the rights of the colored people should be the same as those conceded to the white people in certain respects, which were named in the act. The necessity for that legislation grew out of the laws in several of the then late slave-holding States which denied to persons of color the ordinary and fundamental rights which were conceded to white citizens. . . . We both agreed [speaking of Senator Reverdy Johnson] that after the abolition of slavery everybody born in and subject to the jurisdiction of the United States was a citizen of the United States; but we both thought that in consequence of the declaration which had been enunciated in the Dred Scott case, and also in order that there might be no cavil about it, it was better to declare it by law." *Congressional Globe*, 42 Cong., 1 sess., app. (Apr. 4, 1871), p. 150; app. (Apr. 11, 1871), p. 208; (Apr. 11, 1871), pp. 575–580; (Apr. 14, 1871), p. 695; (Apr. 18, 1871), p. 758.

federal election monitors to oversee state ballotings for national officials. In cities of 20,000 population or more, federal district judges were to appoint the special commissioners. The *Gelpcke* heritage of distrust of Democratic-dominated cities endured.[62]

What William Gillette calls a "double liability" was developing for race equalitarians. The presidential election of 1872, involving the misnamed "liberal" Republican schism, made clear that increasing numbers of Republicans saw the Negro as a party liability. Congress let the Freedmen's Bureau fade out of existence. Supporters of civil rights were falling into confusions concerning the limits of national authority to secure those rights. Henceforward the earlier Republican stress on extending protections diminished at an accelerated pace as attention concentrated on limits. Not until 1875 would the question of the nation's power to regulate private actions again command adequate votes in Congress to achieve legislation.[63] And before then, in 1873, the Court's *Slaughterhouse* decision would further distort vision on Capitol Hill.

[62]*Statutes at Large*, XVI, 140–146 (1870).
[63]Gillette, *Retreat*, ch. 3; McPherson, *Abolitionist Legacy*, chs. 1–4, 9–11.

CHAPTER 13

The 1870s and 1880s: Eras, Not Decades, Removed from the 1860s

S UPREME Court justices attended closely to the confusions in Congress over the Reconstruction Amendments and enforcement statutes, to the Republicans' ambiguities, and to the Democrats' impressive, if ignoble, consistencies. The numerous new legal and constitutional commentaries both extolled the Union's survival and stressed the state-based nature of the federal system. By 1870, Republican legal writers, reflecting on the "Force" Acts, though sustaining them, recognized the strain the laws placed on prevailing doctrines of federalism and private rights.

Like these authors, several justices had become ambivalent on Reconstruction. State-centered nationalism suffused the Supreme Court as well as the legal profession. The justices were sensitive to the growth in jurisdiction that Congress had lavished on the Court since 1863 and to other expansions in its authority the Court itself had created in the *Gelpcke, Test Oath,* and *Milligan* decisions, among others. Some justices, like Stephen J. Field, were frightened by socialist elements of the 1871 Paris Commune and worried that continued federal interventions in favor of blacks' rights might spread dangerous ideas to white laborers. A devotion to laissez-faire economic principles was spreading swiftly in the still-small, but growing, higher-education world of Morrill Act America. Devotees diffused these principles, though unevenly and against resistance, in the legal profession among others. In the process laissez-faire thought became entwined with many matters of public policy, including race relations.[1]

Among Supreme Court justices, Justice Field was prominent in the diffusion effort as well as being the judicial architect of the deemphasis of the Thirteenth Amendment and the constraining of the Fourteenth. Though in his 1873 *Slaughterhouse* dissent Field was to stress the Thirteenth Amendment's organic and universal outreach, by 1879, in his *Ex parte Virginia* dissent, he imprecisely, though probably not thoughtlessly argued that both Amendments were "merely prohibitory on the states."[2] Later in the 1879–80 term of the Court he asserted that Congress, having "reenacted" the 1866 Civil Rights law in the 1870 Enforcement Act, in effect transferred the 1866 statute from an enforcement of the Thirteenth Amendment, able to reach both state and private acts, to an enforcement of the Fourteenth, able to reach only state action. According to Field, the 1866 law, though enacted before ratification of the Fourteenth Amendment—indeed, before its composition was fully complete—now enforced it. He accomplished this judicial sleight-of-hand by adverting to the fact that some judges in the late 1860s doubted the constitutionality of the 1866 law. But Field was unable to cite any federal judge to this effect. He had to rest this argument on the plaint of one obscure state judge. At the same time, Field in his 1879 opinion sustained the 1866 Act by reason of its alleged reenactment in 1870 under the Fourteenth Amendment.

A poor historian, Field nevertheless was advancing his purpose of constraining the 1866 Civil Rights law within a state-action context.[3] In the *Slaughterhouse* cases, he ". . . brought into focus the Fourteenth Amendment's potential for revolutionary change in American federalism in a way the black-oriented legislation of Congress

[1]Michael Les Benedict, "Preserving Federalism: Reconstruction and the Waite Court," *Supreme Court Review* (1978), 39–53; Michael Les Benedict, "Laissez-Faire, Class Legislation, and the Origins of Substantive Due Process of Law" (paper, Woodrow Wilson International Center for Scholars, 1980), pp. 5–13.

[2]100 U.S. 339 at 361 (1879).

[3]Virginia *v.* Rives, 100 U.S. 313 at 324–338, esp. 333 (1880), citing Bowlin *v.* Kentucky, 2 Bush (Ky.) 15 (1867). Justice Strong's majority opinion in Virginia *v.* Rives, though agreeing that the 1870 Civil Rights law enforced the Fourteenth Amendment, accurately identified sections 1977–1978 (now 1981–1982) as provisions of the 1870 law rather than of the 1866 law.

simply had not," concluded Michael Les Benedict.[4]

This decision of 1873 is a major step toward Field's end-of-decade triumph. *Slaughterhouse,* occurring seven years after Congress wrote the Fourteenth Amendment, and five years after Seward declared it to be ratified, has become the major source of definitions for both the Thirteenth and the Fourteenth Amendments. The men seeking federal protection in *Slaughterhouse* were not beleaguered freedmen or Unionists, but rather white butchers being victimized by what they alleged was monopolistic legislation greased through the Louisiana legislature by bribery. The 5–4 decision in *Slaughterhouse* gave a permanently narrow reading to the new privileges and immunities clause; it began blighting the constitutional hopes of the freedmen, leading to the nadir of legally enforced segregation and discrimination. Its dissenters, Field and Bradley, disclosed embryonic doctrines—liberty of contract and substantive due process—that were, after Chase's death, to dominate American jurisprudence for two generations. Any one of these points would have earned the case a prominent place in casebooks; together they made it epochal.

In 1869, the Louisiana legislature incorporated the Crescent City Stock Landing and Slaughterhouse Company, prohibiting landing and butchering livestock anywhere in New Orleans except at its premises, and setting fees for all animals butchered in its "Grand Slaughterhouse." The statute, creating a lucrative monopoly, was nevertheless a routine police measure of a sort that was common throughout the Union in the postwar years. It localized slaughtering for health reasons (control of rats, restricting the stench of abattoirs, policing the butchering trade).

A group of New Orleans butchers not admitted into the monopoly decided to sue. Their counsel challenged the monopoly's constitutionality, alleging that it violated the Thirteenth Amendment, the 1866 Civil Rights law, and section 1 of the Fourteenth.[5] The plaintiff's chief lawyer was former United States Supreme Court Justice John Archibald Campbell, who, though an opponent of secession, had resigned his seat and served the Confederacy as an assistant secretary of war. Campbell was opposed by Jeremiah S. Black and the influential Republican Senator Matthew Carpenter of Wiscon-

[4]Benedict, "Preserving Federalism," p. 57.
[5]Charles Fairman, *Reconstruction and Reunion, 1864–1868* (New York, 1971), ch. 21.

sin. For the excluded butchers, Campbell claimed that their right to work was protected by the Thirteenth Amendment's ban on servitude, by the 1866 Civil Rights Act's broad enforcements of that ban, and by the Fourteenth Amendment's clauses on guaranteed privileges and immunities, equal protection of the laws, and due process. Campbell's appeal to the 1866 Civil Rights act had, in an earlier stage of the litigation, prompted the editorialist of the New Orleans *Picayune* to marvel (June 7, 1870):

> Few of our people would have dreamed that it would have been found necessary to appeal to the civil rights bill to protect the rights of the [white] people in this or any other southern city from invasion. . . . What reasonable man could have thought, ten years ago that any of our citizens, whose rights were threatened under any pretense, could have gone before a federal court and solemnly sworn that he could not obtain justice in the state courts?

A majority of the Court, speaking through Justice Miller, was unprepared to accept Campbell's novel extension of federal authority, especially the judicial, over the states.[6] Instead, Miller stressed the police power aspect of the statute to show that regulation of abattoirs was within the regulatory power of the states, drawing on Kent's *Commentaries, Gibbons* v. *Ogden,* and *Commonwealth* v. *Alger* for authority. That brought him to what he called the most important question to "have been before this court during the official life of any of its present members": whether Louisiana's monopoly legislation deprived the appellants of freedom, privileges and immunities, equal protection, or due process.

Miller held that "the one pervading purpose found in [the Thirteenth through Fifteenth Amendments], lying at the foundation of each," their "unity of purpose," was the liberation of black slaves, not the enlargement of whites' rights.[7] In light of that purpose, he dismissed Campbell's arguments based on the word "servitude" in the Thirteenth Amendment, holding that the word did not pertain to common-law servitudes on property, but rather only to enslavement or cryptoenslavement. As authority, he cited the recent *Turner* circuit decision of Chief Justice Chase that had struck down a Mary-

---

[6]John V. Orth, "The Fair Fame and Name of Louisiana: The Eleventh Amendment and the End of Reconstruction," *Tulane Lawyer* (1980), 3–15; The Slaughterhouse Cases, 16 Wall. (83 U.S.) 34 at 36 (1873), and fn. 39, below.

[7]Slaughterhouse cases, 67, 71, 69.

land Black Code apprenticeship provision as being a subterfuge for slavery.[8]

Turning to the Fourteenth Amendment, Miller analyzed its section 1 clause by clause. He declared that there were two sorts of privileges and immunities, federal and state, and that "the latter must rest for their security and protection where they had heretofore rested [that is, in the states, not the federal government]; for they are not embraced by this paragraph of the amendment."[9] The privileges and immunities of state citizenship included the most significant substantive rights of citizens, black and white, in the day-to-day conduct of their lives.

Herein lay a terrible irony for blacks. After having construed the "pervading purpose" of the Civil War amendments to be the freedom of black people, Miller relegated freedmen, for the effective protection of their new freedom, to precisely those governments—the southern states—least likely to respect either their rights or their freedom should the Republican regimes fall from power. The federal government could protect only the privileges and immunities of federal citizenship. As enumerated by Miller, these included the right of access to Washington, D.C., and the coastal seaports; the right to protection on the high seas and abroad; the right to use navigable waters of the United States; the right of assembly and petition; the privilege of habeas corpus. Of these, only the last two would be significant for most blacks.

Miller's orthodoxy made it impossible for him to imagine that the postwar Amendments made any significant change in the federal system. The consequences of adopting Campbell's argument would be "so serious, so far-reaching and pervading, so great a departure from the structure and spirit of our institutions"; they would "fetter and degrade the State governments by subjecting them to the control of Congress" and radically change the whole theory of the relations of the State and Federal governments"; they "would constitute this court a perpetual censor upon all legislation of the States."[10] Miller could not share the vision of the framers of the Thirteenth and Fourteenth Amendments—a vision of federal privi-

[8]In re Turner, 24 Fed. Cas. 337, #14,247 (C.C.D. Md. 1867),
[9]Slaughterhouse cases, at 75.
[10]Ibid., at 78.

leges and immunities defined not by the nation but by the states, and so involving no centralization or loss of state initiatives. He concluded: "we do not see in those amendments any purpose to destroy the main features of the general system."

Miller then summarily dispensed with the arguments of due process and equal protection. Pointing out that the due process clause had existed in the Fifth Amendment since 1791, he argued that more than two generations' experience with it furnished "no construction of that provision that we have ever seen, or any that we deem admissible," that would support the position of the butchers.[11] To make such a statement, Miller had to shut his eyes to Taney's dictum in *Dred Scott,* and to the entire rich history of the due process or law-of-the-land clauses in the state Constitutions before the war. Yet as late as 1878, Miller would respond to due process arguments by harrumphing impatiently that "there exists some strange misconception of the scope of this provision as found in the Fourteenth Amendment."[12]

Miller shrugged off the equal-protection argument as abruptly: "we doubt very much whether any action of a State not directed by way of discrimination against the negroes as a class, or on account of their race, will ever be held to come within the purview of this provision."[13] Thus, though seeming to protect blacks, Miller consigned them to the ingenuities, subterfuges, and legal chicane of white Democrats already returning to power in the South. The process of "Redemption" had begun, and it would be consolidated within a decade. *Slaughterhouse* was the first great judicial setback suffered by blacks in their quest for effective constitutional protection of their liberties.

Miller's *Slaughterhouse* opinion did not weather well, except in his privileges and immunities reasoning. Forty years after it was handed down, Justice William H. Moody observed that "criticism of this case has never entirely ceased, nor has it ever received universal assent by members of this Court."[14] But Miller's narrow reading of

---

[11]*Ibid.,* at 81–82.

[12]Davidson *v.* New Orleans, 96 U.S. 97 at 104 (1878).

[13]Slaughterhouse cases, 81.

[14]Moody in Twining *v.* New Jersey, 211 U.S. 78 at 96 (1908). Miller's limited view of the Thirteenth Amendment received employment in federal district judge Halmor Emmons's 1875 charge to a Tennessee grand jury: 30 Fed. Cas. 1005 #18,260

privileges and immunities has indeed stood the test of time. Only once, in 1935, has this clause ever been used to overturn state legislation, and even that decision was itself overruled five years later.[15] The remaining parts of the majority opinion proved to be short-lived. The future belonged to the dissenters, Field and Bradley.[16]

Differing between themselves chiefly in emphasis, these two exemplars of judicial conservatism produced dissents that became a pivot point in American constitutionalism of the later nineteenth century. Field and Bradley reached back to the natural-rights philosophy of Justice Samuel Chase's 1798 opinion in *Calder* v. *Bull* and to Justice Bushrod Washington's often-cited circuit court opinion in *Corfield* v. *Coryell* (1823). They built also on the enlarged scope for judicial discretion in the *Swift–Gelpcke–Prize* cases–*Test Oath* line of decisions, to establish the reality of innate rights of free citizens in a federal republic.[17]

Though Field argued in *Slaughterhouse* that the butchering monopoly constituted a "servitude" within the ban of the Thirteenth Amendment, he placed his principal reliance on the privileges and immunities clause of the Fourteenth, perceiving it as establishing equality among all "citizens of the United States" as its ancestor, the Constitution's Article IV, section 2, had established equality in privileges and immunities among the "Citizens in the several States." As Justice Bushrod Washington had argued in 1823, Field saw in the clause a guarantee of "the fundamental rights, privileges and immunities which belong to him as a free man and a free citizen," rights that did "not derive their existence from [state] legislation, and cannot be destroyed by its power." On this basis, Field insisted on an "equality of right, with exemption from all disparaging and partial enactments, in the lawful pursuits of life, throughout the whole country." Though the state might regulate occupations under the police power, "when once prescribed, the

---

(1875) and see United States *v.* Harris, 106 U.S. 629 (1882).

[15]Colgate *v.* Harvey, 296 U.S. 404 (1935), overruled by Madden *v.* Kentucky, 309 U.S. 83 (1940).

[16]Justice Swayne dissented in a brief opinion that added nothing to the substance of the Field and Bradley efforts. Chief Justice Chase joined in Field's dissent.

[17]Calder *v.* Bull, 3 Dall. (3 U.S.) 386 at 387–388 (1798); Corfield *v.* Coryell, 6 Fed. Cas. 546, #323C (C.C.E.D. Pa., 1823).

pursuit or calling must be free to be followed by every citizen who is within the conditions designated, and will conform to the regulations."[18]

Field's dissent, in which Chase concurred, was essentially a condemnation of monopolies and discrimination among citizens; of class legislation in short. But his words had a retrograde potential that was to be realized in the hands of jurists less respectful of the states' regulatory power than he. Gaining the ascendency in Justice Rufus Peckham's opinion in *Allgeyer* v. *Louisiana* (1897),[19] while being cut free of its moorings to the privileges and immunities clause, Field's (and Bradley's) concepts of the "lawful pursuits of life" and of vested rights became transformed after their deaths (1899 and 1892, respectively) into the doctrine of liberty of contract and substantive due process. As such, they stalked through the pages of the *United States Reports* for the next generation, disemboweling federal and state efforts to protect workers from predatory employers in such constitutional monstrosities as *Lochner* v. *New York* (1905), *Adkins* v. *Children's Hospital* (1923), and *Morehead* v. *Tipaldo* (1936).[20] Not until Chief Justice Charles Evans Hughes rudely slew the doctrine in 1937—"the Constitution does not speak of freedom of contract"[21]—was Field's concept returned to its original, tolerable scope.

Bradley, by now retreating from his position in the *Blyew* decision, joined in Field's dissent, while shifting the emphasis away from Field's almost exclusive reliance on the privileges and immunities clause to the due process clause. He too adopted the Chase-Washington-Field notion of "valuable rights . . . which the legislature of a State cannot invade." But in a passage that advanced far beyond the salient established before the war in Taney's *Dred Scott* dictum and *Wynehamer* v. *New York*, Bradley called "substantive due process" into being:

these . . . fundamental rights . . . can only be taken away by due process of law, and . . . can only be interfered with, or the enjoyment of which can

[18]Slaughterhouse cases, at 110.
[19]165 U.S. 578 (1897). For Field's respect for the police power, see his concurrence in Bartemeyer v. Iowa, 18 Wall. (85 U.S.) 129 at 138 (1873).
[20]Respectively, 198 U.S. 45 (1905); 261 U.S. 525 (1923); 298 U.S. 587 (1936).
[21]West Coast Hotel Co. v. Parrish, 300 U.S. 379 at 391 (1937).

only be modified, by lawful regulations necessary or proper for the mutual good of all. . . . This right to choose one's calling, when chosen, is a man's property and right. Liberty and property are not protected where these rights are arbitrarily assailed.[22]

Substantive due process is an elusive concept, difficult to pin down. Procedural due process, deriving its ancestry from Magna Charta and legislation of the time of Edward III, is the pursuit of fair and impartially applied procedural steps, usually in criminal cases. It is the basis of Justice Felix Frankfurter's famous assertion that "the history of liberty has largely been the history of observance of procedural safeguards."[23] Substantive due process, on the other hand, assumes that all persons possess rights to life, liberty, and property, rights anterior to the Constitution, which the legislature may not transgress. Procedural due process regulates the action of courts; substantive due process scrutinizes the acts of legislatures. Procedural due process demands that the game be played by fair rules fairly applied; substantive due process *is* the game itself. Substantive due process is a judicial doctrine empowering courts to hold statutes unconstitutional because the policy they embody deprives certain persons of property or freedom.

This notion was, of course, nothing new among the judges of the United States Supreme Court in 1873. But except for Samuel Chase's *Calder* v. *Bull* opinion, some ambiguous language of Marshall in *Fletcher* v. *Peck* (1810) and of Story in several cases both on the Supreme Court and on circuit, and Taney's evanescent *Dred Scott* dictum in 1857, substantive due process had always been linked with a specific clause of the Constitution—chiefly, in the prewar years, the contracts clause. After Bradley's bold dissent, however, substantive due process took on a life of its own, not moored to any textual dock but to the due process clauses of the Fifth and Fourteenth Amendments.

Remaining on the road which would lead to *Munn* v. *Illinois* (the "Granger Cases") in 1876–77, the justices continued to sustain exercises of state police power. Nevertheless, successive warnings that the states' police powers were not unlimited appeared in deci-

[22]Slaughterhouse cases, at 114.
[23]McNabb *v.* United States, 318 U.S. 332 at 347 (1943).

sions between 1873 and 1890.[24] The concept of substantive due process achieved its first triumph in 1890, when the Supreme Court held that a state legislature could not permit a state regulatory commission to set binding railroad rates, holding that the issue of "reasonableness . . . is eminently a question for judicial investigation, requiring due process of law for its determination." If courts did not supervise administrative ratemaking, a railroad might be "deprived of the lawful use of its property, and thus, in substance and effect, of the property itself, without due process of law."[25] From thence, in protean form, substantive due process inhibited state and federal economic regulation until 1937. After its repudiation in the economic realm, it burgeoned in the area of civil liberties, protecting intangible freedoms, especially those enumerated in the First Amendment: religion, speech, press, assembly, and petition. Yet in their economic guise as well as in their civil liberty context, the Field and Bradley notions in *Slaughterhouse* remain remarkably tenacious.[26]

Allan Nevins concluded that on Chase's death, May 7, 1873, "Men . . . realized that during the past seventy-five years the Supreme Court had been ruled over by three jurists of consummate ability. Could Grant find a leader worthy to stand beside John Marshall, Roger B. Taney, and Salmon P. Chase?"[27]

On January 19, 1874, Grant named Morrison R. Waite to be Chief Justice. Known outside of Ohio chiefly for his service as American counsel in international arbitrations rising from the Civil War, Waite possessed what Chase did not: a capacity to get on with his colleagues. Born in Connecticut in 1816, a Yale graduate of 1837, Waite read law with his father, then moved to northwest Ohio and

[24]See, e.g., Field's dissent in Munn v. Illinois, 94 U.S. 113 (1877); Davidson v. New Orleans, 96 U.S. 97 (1878); Stone v. Farmers Loan and Trust Co., 116 U.S. 307 (1886).

[25]Chicago, Milwaukee, and St. Paul Railway Co. v. Minnesota, 134 U.S. 418 at 458 (1890).

[26]Even after Jones v. Alfred H. Mayer Co., 392 U.S. 409 (1968), some judges assumed that the 1866 Civil Rights law had lost its Thirteenth Amendment roots and been transplanted into the Fourteenth; see Cook v. Advertiser Co., 323 F. Supp. 1212 (N.D., Ala., 1971 [affirmed Civil Case #71-1748, 5th Cir. Mar. 21, 1972]).

[27]Allan Nevins, *Hamilton Fish: The Inner History of the Grant Administration* (New York, 1957), pp. 659–660.

quickly established himself as a leading practitioner. As years passed, Waite served increasingly important corporate clients, then the government as well. This latter service resulted in his nomination to be Chief Justice of the United States. He was to serve until 1888, a term almost twice the length of Chase's yet only half the periods of time that Marshall and Taney held the Court's reins. Of Waite's associate justices, the roster as of 1874 included the Chase Court survivors, among whom the most influential were Bradley, Field, and Miller, with Field becoming the would-be prophet of enhanced judicial review. Clifford, Davis, and Swayne formed a second rank of influence and reputation. Grant had appointed the Pennsylvanian William Strong in 1870 and the New Yorker Ward Hunt in 1872. In 1880 the President would name William B. Woods to the Court.[28]

Waite took the helm of an institution that was rising swiftly in its influence and reputation vis-à-vis the other branches of national government and the states. Since 1862 the Congress and Presidents had favored the Court by substantially increasing its jurisdiction; in 1875 the Congress was to complete the process, as it were, by extending jurisdiction to the fullest extent of the Constitution's Article III, section 2, categories. During this same period, the Court on its own had added jurisdiction over both national and state policies through inventive, opportunistic doctrinal sorties, as in the *Gelpcke, Test Oath,* and *Slaughterhouse* cases.

By 1873, the justices were able to employ the increased jurisdictions the Congress provided, and the flexible legal doctrines that they themselves contrived, almost at will. Thus, in *Crandall* v. *Nevada,* in 1868, the Court dealt with that brand-new state's exit tax of one dollar each on departing travelers. President Johnson had criticized this allegedly unjustified bar to interstate commerce in his 1865 annual message. Earlier, in the 1849 *Passenger Cases,* the Court had held unconstitutional certain state taxes on immigrants though the states involved insisted that the taxes supported essential public health "police" policies. But a state tax on emigrants? Both the commerce clause and Congress were silent. Any Supreme Court verdict had to be by implication. Yet the Court was unanimous that

[28]C. Peter Magrath, *Morrison R. Waite: the Triumph of Character* (New York, 1963), pp. 91, 99–103, and chs. 1–4, *passim.*

the state's tax was unconstitutional; that the federal constitutional right of a citizen to travel interstate was independent of congressional acts or those of any state through which he must travel. As Fairman wrote, "the basic principle [of *Crandall*] was old, although the language rang with the assurance derived from the recent triumph of the Union."[29]

In 1873, Myra Bradwell appealed to the Court under the Fourteenth Amendment to compel Illinois to admit her to legal practice. No question existed about her professional qualifications. The state admittedly denied her admission by reason of her sex. Bradwell depended on one aspect of the Court's position in the Missouri *Test Oath* decision *(Cummings* v. *Missouri):* on its holding that even in pre-Fourteenth Amendment days a professional practice was a property right and that the Court might question the reasons for the limits a state placed on access to practice. But not for Bradwell. Playing now a self-restrained role, the Court held that Illinois controlled admission to the practice of law there and that no federal rights were involved in her exclusion. "As a demonstration of man's superior fitness for the law this opinion was not a shining example," wrote Charles Fairman.[30]

Chase bequeathed to Waite the largest tally of federal laws or policies held to be in violation of the Constitution, since the nation's start. This tally included *Gordon* v. *United States* (on the finality of Supreme Court judgments in appeals from the court of claims); *Ex parte Garland* (on the federal test oath for lawyers); *Hepburn* v. *Griswold* (on legal tender); *United States* v. *Klein* (on excluding judges from considering a claimant's pardon or amnesty under the Abandoned and Captured Property Act); and *United States* v. *Dewitt* (on Congress's attempt to prohibit interstate traffic, by means of a tax, of an adulterated, explosive kerosene-naphtha mixture). Each involved the Court's holding that Congress could not hide a substantive intent that, in the justices' view, was contrary to expressed or implied values in the Constitution even behind a clear grant of constitutional authority. Thus, in *Garland,* for example, the oath requirement could not stand, though the Constitution authorized

[29]Fairman, *Reconstruction,* p. 1125 for the quoted phrase, and see pp. 1302–1306; Crandall *v.* Nevada, 6 Wall. 35 (1868).

[30]Fairman, *Reconstruction,* pp. 1308, 1364–1368; Bradwell *v.* Illinois, 16 Wall. 130 (1873).

Congress to organize the federal courts. In *Dewitt,* the Congress could not disguise as a revenue measure a clearly "police" purpose that was a state matter. Congress, if beyond its authority, had, like the states, a potential monitor in the Court.[31]

In 1865, Chase's first term, the state of the law gave the Court only occasional control over state actions; an "incomplete federalism" still prevailed despite the Appomattox victory. By 1873, federalism was far more complete in the sense of acknowledged causes for federal judicial intervention against both federal and state policies. Skirting both extreme interpretations of plenary federal authority and equally extreme positions against federal involvements developed by Jeremiah Sullivan Black and David Dudley Field, the Chase Court ". . . sustained its authority by exercising and refusing to exercise its power with a delicate sense of the possible, never allowing anyone to mistake its essentially conservative stance," concluded David Hughes. Chase and his brethren were able to pass on to the successor Chief Justice an institution that was secure in its authorities, was sustained by its professional constituents, and was becoming almost revered by the general population.[32]

Chase helped the Court to invigorate and to expand judicial review, a process that Waite would carry on. To be sure, review under both Chase and Waite failed the modern justification for its existence—that of affording protections for persons and groups who are underfavored by the political process.[33] Employing this test—and only Chase among his brethren came close to accepting anything like the modern view—the Chase Court obviously did not leave a distinguished record. Congress rather than the Court concerned itself with blacks, the major underfavored group of Americans. Yet the Court's success in advancing its own authority and in

[31]Gordon *v.* United States, 2 Wall. 561 (1865); Ex parte Garland, 4 Wall. 333 (1867); Hepburn *v.* Griswold, 8 Wall. 603 (1870); United States *v.* Klein, 13 Wall. 128 (1872); United States *v.* Dewitt 9 Wall. 41 (1870). Minor "instances of invalidity" include: Reichar *v.* Phelps, 6 Wall. 160 (1868); The Alicia, 7 Wall. 571 (1869); and Justices *v.* Murray, 9 Wall. 274 (1870). Differences exist between invalidity and inapplicability, as in Collector *v.* Day, 11 Wall. 113 (1871) and United States *v.* B. & O. Railroad Co., 17 Wall. 322 (1873), both of which held that the statute did not apply to plaintiffs, as the government claimed; *ibid.,* pp. 1435–1436.

[32]David Hughes, "Salmon P. Chase: Chief Justice" (Ph.D. diss., Princeton University, 1963), pp. 359–360; Fairman, *Reconstruction,* pp. 1124–1127.

[33]Alexis J. Anderson, "The Formative Period of First Amendment Theory, 1870–1915," *American Journal of Legal History,* XXIV (1980), 56–75.

harmonizing at least some dangerous elements in federal-state and check-and-balance relationships deeply impressed that generation. Its Reconstruction decisions—and nondecisions—placed it in the center of national politics.

In the 1870s, the Court's reputation was such that a French bar association, anxious to reconstruct post-Commune France, sent an observer to study the Court and its work; in the 1890s, Brazil's Emperor encouraged his minister to the United States to "Study with special care the organization of the Supreme Court of Justice at Washington. I believe that in the function of the Supreme Court is the [secret of the] successful operation of the American Constitution."[34]

Yet, however highly some of Chase's (and Waite's) contemporaries valued the Supreme Court's work and status, scholars have created a differing consensus. "History has not been kind to Chase —and rightly," Gerhard Casper wrote in 1973, in a shorthand for prevailing opinion. Indeed, Chase's chief justiceship became, for some contemporaries, one proof that American institutions had eroded from a golden to a gilded age. Depressed because the Chase Court would not lead a crusade against Civil War and Reconstruction policies, fearful that the then newly appointed Chief Justice intended instead to muster a quorum on the high bench in favor of race equality, former President Buchanan fretted in 1867: "What is to become of the Supreme Court of the United States—the conservative part of the Government?" Buchanan recalled the ". . . pure, able, and venerable men who have filled the office of Chief Justice, from John Jay to Roger B. Taney." Now, ". . . witness[ing] the efforts of the present Chief Justice to drag the judicial ermine through the dirt to propitiate radicalism, I cannot help thinking we have fallen upon evil times. But now I am an old fogey."[35]

Buchanan had many "old fogeys" for company: mourners after the good old days before the Civil War. And persons of views

[34]In Percy A. Martin, "Causes of the Collapse of the Brazilian Empire," *Hispanic American Historical Review,* IV (1921), 23. The French survey is in Horace Heilbronner, *Le pouvoir judiciare aux États-unis; son organization et ses attributions: Discourse prononcé le 23 Decembre 1871 à la conference des advocats* (Paris, 1872).

[35]George Ticknor Curtis, *Life of James Buchanan, Fifteenth President of the United States* (New York, 1883), II, 655; Gerhard Casper, in *Columbia Law Review,* LXXIII (1973), 916.

opposite to Buchanan's by the mid-1870s were commonly swinging around to the former President's stance. As an example, back in 1865, the year after Chase became Chief Justice, Edwin L. Godkin, editor of the new periodical *The Nation,* a weekly of impeccable Republican constitutional views, had been optimistic about the nation's capacity to cope with all post-Appomattox responsibilities; James Russell Lowell's "Commemoration Ode" of that year rejoiced at the Union's total victory and was confident about its destiny as a biracial, slaveless society. But in 1876, three years after Chase died, the year of both the Revolution's centennial and of the disputed presidential election, Lowell's "Ode to the Fourth of 1876" expressed disillusionments and fears: "Is this the country that we dreamed of in youth / Where wisdom and not numbers have weights / Seed-field of simpler manners, braver truth / Where shame should cease to dominate / In household, church and State? / Is this Atlantis?" Godkin by then was morosely skeptical about government interventions for almost any purposes, including those to help blacks. To both men Reconstruction had already become, veritably, a fool's errand. All American society had deteriorated sharply in a materialistic, technology-mad age; tradesmen had displaced statesmen; majority judgments were untrustworthy.[36]

The centennial came shortly after Chase's death. A retreat from Reconstruction was under way before he died, to be sure, and the Chase Court, especially its *Slaughterhouse* decision, was a significant element in that retreat. *Slaughterhouse* is not, however, a proof that the Negro was by then an expandable pawn in the Republicans' cynical maneuverings both for votes and for a sectional reconciliation on southern whites' terms, as some scholars argued. The major retreat from Reconstruction awaited Waite's years as Chief Justice and those that followed him. Yet the judgment has persisted well into the twentieth century that the Chase Court has as its central value the protection of business interests against government, and had already begun to reinterpret the Fourteenth Amendment's due process and equal protection clauses to that end.[37]

Continuums were strong between doctrines created, or advanced,

[36]Richard Clark Sterne, "Political, Social, and Literary Criticism in the New York *Nation,* 1865–1881; A Study in a Change of Mood" (Ph.D. diss., Harvard University, 1957), I, 29–75; James Russell Lowell, *Poems* (Cambridge, 1848), IV, 96.

[37]See, e.g., Robert McCloskey, *The American Supreme Court* (Chicago, 1960), p. 105.

during Chase's chief justiceship and that of Waite. But, as noted, leadership in the judicial retreat from Reconstruction should be assigned to Waite's term. For during his years on the Court (1874–88) the justices accelerated the relegation of the Thirteenth Amendment almost to invisibility and the Fourteenth to state-action-only futility. Congressmen also played a role in this relegation, as in the 1870 "reenactment" of the 1866 Civil Rights law under the Fourteenth Amendment rather than the Thirteenth, and in accepting the 1874 *Revised Statutes* with its curious and still-unexplained scatterings of parts of the 1866 Civil Rights act to obscure parts of the volumes. In effect, during Waite's chief justiceship, the pieces of Republican race and Reconstruction policies, like the text of the 1866 Civil Rights law, were becoming separated from each other.

Federal circuit and Supreme Court decisions widened this separation. These decisions emphasized the growing opinion in the legal community (a growth that Cooley nourished in his later editions of *Constitutional Limitations*) that the Reconstruction Amendments protected only a finite roster of federal rights against states only.

To cite an example, on circuit in Texas, Judge Woods held in 1874 that a black beaten by whites for daring to testify in a prosecution against them had no federal rights infringed. The Negro had claimed redress under the 1871 Enforcement law. Woods stated that ". . . where an act of Congress is directed exclusively against the action of individuals, and not of the states, the law is broader than the amendment by what is attempted to be justified, and is without constitutional warrant."[38]

In "redemptionist" Louisiana, whites attacked a predominantly black posse under carpetbag authority, killing over one hundred Negroes. The Justice Department indicted an almost equal number of whites under the 1870 Enforcement Act, but managed to arrest only nine. A federal circuit court jury brought in guilty verdicts. But Judge Woods and Justice Bradley (the latter on circuit) disagreed on the validity of the indictments. Woods took a position akin to that of his Texas opinion. Bradley, though agreeing that "ordinary crimes" would always fall to the state to punish, held that the Thirteenth Amendment embraced crimes inspired by the "war of race"

[38]Texas *v.* Gaines, Fed. Cas. #13,837 (1874). On Cooley, see Fairman, *Reconstruction*, pp. 1368–1370.

and that the indictments were proper. As result of the division the case, *United States* v. *Cruikshank,* went to the Supreme Court. There, in 1876, the unanimous Court (Bradley included) held that the indictments were indeed defective and that Cruikshank and the other defendants were unpunishable by terms of the Thirteenth or Fourteenth Amendments or the 1870 Enforcement law. Murder, even a mass murder, though racially motivated enough to convince a local jury, was not a deprivation of a federal right.[39]

Refusals by Kentucky election officials to accept blacks' ballots in a local election led to indictments in federal circuit court for violations of the 1871 Enforcement law. The Kentuckians claimed that, as in *Cruikshank,* the indictments were faulty. In the Supreme Court, the Kentuckians' counsel, David Dudley Field, also exploited *Slaughterhouse.* Field insisted that the nation had no duty to punish local breaches of the peace or to police local elections. The rights assertedly infringed were not merely anterior to the Reconstruction amendments; they preexisted the Constitution. Therefore these rights were exclusively the states' to defend. With only Justice Hunt dissenting on the basis that Congress intended in 1871 precisely to reach situations like that in Kentucky, the Supreme Court declared sections 3 and 4 of the 1871 Act to be void.[40] Thus, before 1876, the Court was well on a state-action-only path of interpretation; before, not after the dramatic events culminating in passage of the 1875 Civil Rights law and in the installation of Rutherford B. Hayes as President in 1877.

Charles Sumner's death in 1873, like Chase's that same year, was widely perceived as the passing of a generation. In substantial part as a tribute to Sumner, Republicans in Congress created in 1875 another—and, as we know, the last—Civil Rights Act of Reconstruction. Within seven years after its enactment, the Supreme Court of the United States would decimate the 1875 law.

Back in 1870, the most visible signs of legal inferiority most blacks suffered were exclusions from privately owned public facilities such as hotels, theaters, mass transit, and other public accommodations. Sumner had raised the exclusion question intermittently since 1870.

[39]United States *v.* Cruikshank, Fed. Cas. #14,897 (1874); United States *v.* Cruikshank, 92 U.S. 542 (1876); Magrath, *Waite,* pp. 120–121.
[40]United States *v.* Reese, 92 U.S. 214 (1876); Magrath, *Waite,* pp. 122–129.

He tried in 1871 and 1872 to expand federally protected rights to include access to public accommodations (as well as to schools and juries) as a "supplement" to the 1866 Civil Rights law—a matter especially urgent to Sumner in 1871 because an amnesty measure for ex-Confederates was sliding through the Senate then. Sumner's strong arguments on the Thirteenth Amendment inspired resistance both from Democrats and from self-styled "Liberal" Republicans in 1872—Republicans like Lyman Trumbull and Carl Schurz, who were entering an antigovernment, anticorruption "mugwump" phase in their careers even before the label was invented. Republican Senator Lot Morrill of Maine offered the Democratic-sounding response to Sumner that the Thirteenth Amendment ended formal slavery only. Sumner replied that slaves could not enter public accommodations; therefore the formal ending of slavery required that freed blacks should be able to enter as a minimum definition of freedom. Trumbull asserted that the 1866 Civil Rights law had already reached the outer edge of allowable federal interventions under the Thirteenth Amendment. Not so, replied Vermont's Edmunds. Congress might have included public accommodations in the 1866 Civil Rights act had ordinary legislative procedure been involved. But a need to override Johnson's veto existed, and so Congress did not include public accommodations.[41]

Debate moved from the Thirteenth Amendment to the Fourteenth's privileges and immunities clause. After complex parliamentary maneuvers, Sumner's bill died at the end of session. He reintroduced it in 1873, after the Supreme Court issued its *Slaughterhouse* decision. The Court's *Slaughterhouse* emphasis on state action and the Fourteenth Amendment in that decision shaped Congress's discussions of Sumner's perennially resurfacing Civil Rights bill. *Slaughterhouse* raised the question whether equal protection could coexist with state police powers—i.e., whether state-based federalism was viable if Congress enacted the proposed civil rights legislation.

Self-consciously seeking to speak for Sumner, now dead, was Robert Brown Elliott, a Massachusetts-born Negro who became a

[41]Hans Trefousse, "Carl Schurz, the South, and the Politics of Virtue," in Abraham L. Eisenstadt et al. (eds.), *Before Watergate: Problems of Corruption in American Society* (New York, 1978), pp. 99–116; Wilbert H. Ahern, "Laissez Faire vs. Equal Rights: Liberal Republicans and Limits to Reconstruction," *Phylon* (1979), 520–565.

carpetbagging South Carolina Representative. In the 1874 debates on a civil rights bill, Elliott asked the House if *Slaughterhouse*'s support for state powers denied the efficacy of the Fourteenth Amendment's equal protection clause. Answering his own question negatively, Brown insisted that the Thirteenth *and* Fourteenth Amendments, by the Court's own insistence in *Slaughterhouse*, had as their primary purposes not only the nominal freedom of blacks "but their complete protection from those who had formerly exercised unlimited dominion over them." The Amendments' essential common purpose was "to secure the perfect equality before the law of all citizens of the United States." Therefore no conflict could exist between equal protection and state power. A state could create exclusive privileges, as in *Slaughterhouse*, only on behalf of the common good. Racial inequality—the assignment of privileges to one color of citizens over another—could never advance the common good; the dilemma between equal protection and federalism was contrived, Elliott concluded.[42]

In 1875, enough Republican Congressmen temporarily accepted Elliott's views and those of Mississippi Senator James Alcorn, that *Slaughterhouse* was irrelevant, to overcome strengthening Democratic and conservative Republican resistance to the proposed legislation. Indeed, the gains of Democrats in voter appeal, both in the North and in the "redeemed" South, helped to convince some Republicans to favor Sumner's Civil Rights bill. Republicans lost heavily in congressional and state elections in 1874. In the early 1875 lame-duck congressional session, the holdover Republican majority, in part to reinvigorate the Republicans' losing grip on the House majority, in part as bait for black votes, patched together the Civil Rights act of 1875.[43] But even surviving "original Republicans" were deeply confused on the issue of the Thirteenth Amendment's relevance to civil rights. Democrats were united on the most constrained interpretations, especially that the Reconstruction Amendments and laws attended only to state action. Debates on the 1875 Civil Rights bill meandered haphazardly in a Fourteenth Amendment jungle partially of the Congressmen's own creation.

[42]David Donald, *Charles Sumner and the Rights of Man* (New York, 1970), ch. 13.
[43]Alfred Avins, "The Civil Rights Act of 1875: Some Reflected Light on the Fourteenth Amendment and Public Accommodations," *Columbia Law Review*, LVI (1966), 873.

The Thirteenth Amendment as a source of independent authority, and as a referrent to both the Declaration of Independence and the Bill of Rights for federal defenses of civil rights and liberties, was suffering a virtual demise.[44] Of debaters in the Congress few still had Sumner's confidence in the incorporative quality of the Thirteenth and Fourteenth Amendments with respect to both the Declaration and the Bill of Rights. Instead, in 1875, debaters on the Civil Rights bill such as Morrill, Trumbull (who had helped to write the 1866 Act), and Massachusetts' Ebenezer Hoar, a former Attorney General, acknowledged no absolute guide to the scope of federal authority.

Like the justices, the Congressmen, including Republicans who finally passed the Civil Rights bill in 1875, were unwilling to acknowledge that a revolution in federalism had occurred and that the nation now had a duty to see to the equality of federal citizens before state law and customs. Reference in the 1874–75 debates by enemies to the bill, not only to the *Slaughterhouse* decision but to that in the *Bradwell* case, were common currency among many Republicans as well as virtually all Democrats. To be sure, Ben Butler's comment, that interpretations such as those in *Slaughterhouse* and *Bradwell* allowed the nation to protect American citizens anywhere in the world except in the states,[45] evoked laughter. But the majority views of the Republicans had changed toward limiting what the nation had to do to formal state action, and Butler's caustic wit could not reverse the heavy drift. In 1875, the Republicans were barely able to muster votes in Congress to enact a Civil Rights law that made racial discriminations in public accommodations illegal. Their effort was to be one of Reconstruction's last hurrahs.

As enacted, the 1875 Civil Rights law recognized the government's duty "to enact great fundamental principles into law." Section 1 stipulated that all Americans must have equal access to all public accommodations and places of amusement. Section 2 created causes of action for violations, and set fines and lengths of imprisonments; in 1883 the Supreme Court declared both sections 1 and 2 to be unconstitutional. Section 3 afforded the federal lower courts

---

[44]G. Sidney Buchanan, *The Quest for Freedom: A Legal History of the Thirteenth Amendment* (reprinted from *Houston Law Review*, Houston, 1976), pp. 48–49.
[45]*Congressional Record*, 43 Cong., 1 sess. (Dec. 19, 1873), p. 341.

exclusive jurisdiction in Civil Rights law litigations and instructed peace officers to institute relevant proceedings. Section 4, still in force today, forbade race discriminations in federal or state juries and set misdemeanor penalties for violators. Section 5 extended Supreme Court review jurisdiction to derivative cases without a money minimum.[46]

But in the presidential election in 1876, neither presidential candidate, Republican Rutherford B. Hayes nor Democrat Samuel J. Tilden, received the necessary 185 electoral votes. Disputed counts of all the electoral votes in three still-Reconstructing states, plus one from Oregon, created a stand-off. The Constitution allows no delay in an inauguration. As threats and fears of crisis grew in the first weeks of 1877 a compromise procedure was patched up by terms of which an Electoral Commission, including five Supreme Court justices among its members, accepted the Hayes electoral count. The price of southern acquiescence included the Republicans' commitment to end Reconstruction; to withdraw the remaining troops from the South (the Freedmen's Bureau's life had ended in 1872); and to cease enforcing civil rights laws including the brand-new one of 1875.

Some scholars argue that many Americans, including Supreme Court justices, were profoundly troubled by fears of a breakdown in the nation's political and constitutional processes in 1876–77. According to some accounts, including those by leading legal specialists, the justices, especially those who participated in the Electoral Commission, became embittered by aspersions cast upon their integrity both as individuals and as jurists, a bitterness that hastened the whole Court on its retreat from Reconstruction.[47] More recently, alternative responses hold that sectional reconciliation did involve the Court and the nation, but hardly in such gross terms as long perceived.[48]

[46]*Statutes at Large*, XVIII, 335–337 (1875); Civil Rights cases, 109 U.S. 26 (1883).
[47]Buchanan, *Quest*, pp. 70–71; Arthur Kinoy, "The Constitutional Rights of Negro Freedom," *Rutgers Law Review*, XXVI (1967), 396.
[48]Michael J. Horan, "Political Economy and Sociological Theory as Influences Upon Judicial Policy-Making: *The Civil Rights Cases* of 1883," *American Journal of Legal History*, XVI (1972), 7186; Orth, "The Fair Fame and Name of Louisiana," p. 14, notes how from 1877 to 1890, the Court, retreating from prewar precedents such as Osborne *v.* Bank of the United States, 22 U.S. (9 Wheat.) 738 (1824), permitted the Eleventh Amendment to become an impediment to the exercise of federal juris-

We will return to the question of changes occurring in the intellectual condition and the constitutional and legal climate of the country that helped to bring on the abandonment of a national concern with blacks' rights. For the present, it is clear that the 1877 "deal" manifested itself almost at once in the form of contradictory imperatives the justices felt toward the nation's, and their, duty under the Reconstruction Amendments and laws.

What were these contradictory imperatives that created a legal anomaly for the justices? Before them were cases involving the Reconstruction Amendments and enforcement laws. By statute or self-assumption of authority, the Court was a major implementer of federally protectable civil rights. But, after the 1877 Compromise, what rights should the justices define as within the nation's ambit? Which should they seek to protect? And how to proceed obediently to the Amendments and laws in light of the Compromise's commitment against further federal interventions? In brief, the Court could help in the sectional reconciliation so obviously desired by the great majority of white Americans; could follow the election returns, as it were. But blacks would have to pay the price.

Individualists all, Supreme Court justices could not have been expected to accept all the implications of the 1877 Compromise at one time, or at all in certain instances. Consider that to the justices, as lawyers, the jury system was peculiarly precious; the justices, as citizens and national officials, resented intensely any tamperings with ballots in federal elections. Both outrages occurred in the closing years of the decade in situations involving race. In 1879–80, despite the 1877 Compromise, the Court perceived valid, enduring federal interests in individuals' rights not to be barred from either jury service or from voting in congressional elections. The Court invalidated a West Virginia statute that excluded blacks from jury service and a Virginia law that authorized state selection officials to exclude blacks from jury lists. Dissenting, Justices Clifford and Field predicted the imminent destruction of federalism—predictions

---

diction in litigations involving repudiated state bonds issued by Republican administrations during Reconstruction. "The key figure in this switch . . . was . . . Bradley," who became central in the Court's confirmation of the fact that federal interventions were at an end, Orth concluded. As in civil rights matters, Bradley, before 1873, had expressed strong views about the need for federal judicial interventions in instances of state repudiations of debts, then reversed his earlier views.

echoed by constitutional expert George Ticknor Curtis.

But, later the same year, the Court also decided *Virginia* v. *Rives.* Two blacks charged with murder in a county where no Negroes had ever sat on a jury claimed that their indictments and trial—the process due to them as citizens—were unconstitutional; the protections afforded them, unequal. The Supreme Court, however, expressed faith that the Virginia courts would sustain all Virginians' rights, and denied that the monochromatic character of juries reflected partiality. No one had a right to be on a jury. As a consequence of this decision, according to C. Peter McGrath, ". . . the Negro's right to freedom in the selection of juries became meaningless. All that was necessary to keep Negroes off juries was the avoidance of open, public discrimination."[49]

Next, to voting in federal elections. Also in 1880, the Court upheld the conviction of state election officers who had stuffed ballot boxes in order to overcome blacks' votes, and, second, upheld the conviction of nine whites for beating a Negro who had voted in a congressional election. In these decisions, the Court sustained one federal right—that of voting in an election for national officials—against both public and private infringements. But discriminations in voting, though involving federal elections, were not the key to Court judgments supporting a general right to vote for all disfavored persons. In an earlier case, a Missouri woman, Virginia Minor, claimed a Fourteenth Amendment right to vote as one of her "privileges and immunities" despite Missouri's men-only laws. Missouri was so certain, because of the *Bradwell* decision, of favorable Court treatment that it did not contest Minor's appeal in Washington. For a unanimous Court, Waite denied her appeal. The Fourteenth Amendment did not add to the citizen's privileges and immunities; it only guaranteed those that existed. The Chief Justice stated that suffrage was not a right. Mrs. Minor could not vote.[50]

Contrariwise, in considering nonfederal elections (and balloting

[49]Magrath, *Waite,* pp. 146–147, which also has information on Curtis. Cases are Strauder *v.* West Virginia, 100 U.S. 303 (1880) and Ex parte Virginia, 100 U.S. 339 (1880); and see Virginia *v.* Rives, 100 U.S. 313 (1880). During the same period exclusions from juries of past disloyalists, by means of oath tests, all but ended; Drew L. Kershen, "The Jury Selection Act of 1879, Theory and Practice of Citizen Participation in the Judicial System," *University of Illinois Law Forum,* III (1980), 707–715.

[50]Magrath, *Waite,* pp. 147–149; Ex parte Siebold, 100 U.S. 371 (1880) Ex parte Yarbrough, 110 U.S. 651 (1884); Minor *v.* Happersett, 21 Wall, 162 at 171 (1875).

for federal officials took place almost always as part of simultaneous state elections), the Court also implied an end to federal protection for participation by blacks. These elections would select the local and state officials who counted most in individuals' daily lives. By 1880, federal attorneys had stopped or sharply diminished efforts to apply the federal enforcement laws in state contests, and also in federal elections, the number of prosecutions dropping from two hundred in 1875 to twenty-five in 1878. "In practical terms . . . the Court, in facing the Southern question, marched in step with the national mood," wrote McGrath; sectional reconciliation was in the air; federal interferences were no longer acceptable; justice and rights were to rest in states' hands as before the war. Justices Miller and Bradley and Chief Justice Waite, the "principal architects" of the Thirteenth–Fifteenth Amendment decisions, responded also to specific imperatives, McGrath continued. To Miller, Justice Field's desire to convert the Fourteenth Amendment into "a roving license for judicial supervision of the economy" required resistance. Bradley was engaged in a philosopher's quest after some remote truth. And Waite, "consistently devoted to the concept of broad state powers in all areas," could come to no other conclusions.[51]

The decisions in the jury service and federal elections cases through 1880 were only preludes to the judicial avalanche that buried adherents of race equality later that decade. In 1882, the Court, in *United States* v. *Harris,* declared unconstitutional section 2 of the 1871 Enforcement Act, which made it a federal offense for two or more persons to conspire in order to deprive anyone of the equal protection of the laws or of equal privileges and immunities. An armed mob of Tennessee whites had wrested several Negroes from the custody of a sheriff, killing one and beating the others. An indictment against the whites rested upon the 1871 law's section 2. After examining all the Reconstruction Amendments, the Court determined that section 2 was broader even than the Thirteenth Amendment, as Justice Woods stated for the majority, for it covered instances even where whites assaulted whites. That is, Woods, for the first time, read into constitutional law a necessity for color as a quality of the servitude the Thirteenth Amendment forbade. The

[51]Magrath, *Waite,* pp. 132–134.

Thirteenth Amendment, he blandly reasoned, "simply prohibits slavery and involuntary servitude," completely ignoring the fact that in *Harris* whites did conspire against blacks in order to prevent enjoyment of equal legal protection. Further, Woods propounded that individuals who harmed others transgressed no constitutional rights criminally; that the Amendment gave Congress no warrant to punish ancient crimes such as murder or assault. Section 2 of the 1871 Act must fall or else the nation would be involved massively in every local crime. It was the same argument Bradley had refuted in *Cruikshank*, on circuit. Now it became Supreme Court doctrine.[52]

The *Harris* decision dismayed proponents of race equality and of the 1875 law. But the *Harris* circumstances seemed to be special if dramatic. By contrast, the 1875 Civil Rights law had vastly extended the potential range of federal interests under the Thirteenth and Fourteenth Amendments into more prosaic quasi-public and even private accommodations that served the public. Soon challenges rose to the constitutionality of the 1875 statute; the *Civil Rights* cases joined five litigations. Four were criminal prosecutions against persons who excluded Negroes from hotels or theaters; the fifth was a civil action by a black woman excluded from a ladies' railroad car. All raised the question of the constitutionality of sections 1 and 2 of the 1875 law.[53]

For all the justices save for the Kentucky Unionist John Marshall Harlan (appointed 1887), Bradley denied the validity of sections 1 and 2 under either the Thirteenth or the Fourteenth Amendment. Adverting first to the latter, he escalated a "state action" doctrine to a supraconstitutional level. By this doctrine the Amendment prohibits only states, not individuals, from infringing upon the equal protections and due process that citizens enjoy by right. Individuals, whether in mobs or other conspiracies, were susceptible only to state punishments. Innkeepers, theater managers, and railroad conductors were individuals, though deriving their rights to operate from state authority in form of licenses, safety and health permits, or corporate franchises. Exclusions of blacks from such facilities

---

[52]United States *v.* Harris, 641; cf. Stewart in Griffin *v.* Breckenridge, 403 U.S. 88 at 100–102 (1971).
[53]109 U.S. 3 (1883).

were private acts by nature. Congress, seeking to enforce the Fourteenth Amendment, had violated the Tenth. *Slaughterhouse* reigned.[54]

Moving to the Thirteenth Amendment, Bradley denied that exclusions from public amusements and other accommodations were badges of servitude; such a conclusion ran the slavery argument into the ground, he said. The Thirteenth Amendment, Bradley continued, had no state-action limitation. It was an absolute declaration against positive laws sanctioning slavery. The Amendment also proscribed servitudes of any involuntary sort. It was both self-executing, in the sense that its existence nullified all state laws on slavery, and possessed of what he called "a reflex character in the enforcement clause."[55]

Did Congress's undoubtable enforcement authority extend to inns, taverns, theaters, and ferries? Were exclusions from such places badges of servitude? Lumping access to these accommodations as social rights, Bradley returned civil rights to those primarily economic ones familiar to lawyers since the 1823 *Corfield* v. *Coryell* opinion, discussed earlier (although Bradley ignored the sweeping natural rights elements in that opinion). Referring to the 1866 Civil Rights law that enforced the Thirteenth Amendment, Bradley suggested erroneously that it dealt all but totally with fundamental and legal economic relationships from which slaves had been excluded. By Bradley's analysis, the Thirteenth Amendment forbade only racial exclusions from exercises of these fundamental rights to sue, contract, and give evidence.[56]

Harlan's lonely dissent has, deservedly, become a much-anthologized classic. Congress, not the Court, he insisted, had the right and duty to enforce the Thirteenth Amendment; Congressmen, not justices, were responsible to define any carryover traces of slavery; private or quasi-private race discriminations could not exist without support in state law and/or local customs. The nation was responsible to see that freedom existed everywhere within its boundaries. Slavery had never been a static condition, Harlan concluded after a keen analysis of servility in America; neither was freedom static.

[54]Civil Rights cases, 14–15.
[55]*Ibid.* at 20.
[56]*Ibid.* at 20–24.

Exclusions of blacks from public accommodations might have been acceptable in 1865. But in 1866 it was clearly less so (as in the Civil Rights law of that year and in the boycott of segregated streetcars in Philadelphia). And in 1883? Thinking of the heartbreak that the Court had caused by *Dred Scott,* Harlan was moved to say:

I hold that since slavery, as the court has repeatedly declared, . . . was the moving or principal cause of the adoption of . . . [the Thirteenth] Amendment, and since that institution rested wholly upon the inferiority, as a race, of those held in bondage, their freedom necessarily involved immunity from, and protection against, all discrimination against them, because of their race, in respect of such civil rights as belong to freemen of other races.

Therefore, Harlan continued, Congress had the express power to do what it had done in 1875. That law was valid. It looked backward, as he had done while composing his dissent, to *Dred Scott;* it looked also to the present and future by punishing individuals who discriminated against race minorities. But the majority view that individuals' offenses could not be reached by federal punishment locked the nation to the sad past more than to the potentially brighter future. And so Harlan came to the matter's heart. Responding to Bradley's insistence that only the states rightly defined and protected social relationships, Harlan asked:

Was it the purpose of the Nation simply to destroy the institution [of slavery], and then remit the race, theretofore held in bondage, to the several States for such protection, in their civil rights, necessarily growing out of freedom, as those States, in their discretion, might choose to provide?

An affirmative response to this question rendered the Thirteenth Amendment a "phantom of delusion," Harlan concluded, and Congress never so intended.[57]

The decision in the *Civil Rights* cases was a crushing additional disappointment to black Americans, especially to those few who were versed in the law. A group of Negro lawyers in Philadelphia, writing as "The Brotherhood of Liberty," felt impelled to review the history of the Reconstruction Amendments and of the intentions of their creators and supporters. The result of their research was a large book, published in 1889, entitled, rather touchingly, *Justice and*

[57] *Ibid.* at 34.

Jurisprudence. In it, the authors lamented the gap that had grown up in two decades between legislators' purposes and jurisprudents' applications. A view of federalism that kept enough of the prewar dual citizenship so that much of what was important in rights remained for the states to enforce was tragedy for blacks. The political parties were partly to blame. It was bad enough, but hardly surprising, that Democrats opposed equality in law. But that Republicans should have chosen to water down the positions the party had reached in the years 1865–70, in favor of clean-government "Liberal Republican" reformers or mercenary standpatters! That decision made politics and the Constitution all but irrelevant for most Negroes, the Brotherhood stated. And what of the federal courts, the special Reconstruction institution of the Republicans since 1863? By 1883 federal judges had chosen, in effect, to reamend the Reconstruction Amendments; to walk around the purposes of the framers of the Amendments and to pervert their effects. Justice and jurisprudence could not coexist for blacks so long as jurisprudents chose to favor states over citizens.[58]

The Brotherhood of Liberty, Benjamin F. Butler, Louis A. Post, and a few other still-Radical Republicans, if self-serving, were correct in their essential judgments on the federal judiciary. The gap grew ever wider between justice and jurisprudence in the eighties and nineties, and well into the next century. That liberty in law, rather than equality, was the true condition of constitutional doctrine and legal relationships, at least for whites, was the message the Supreme Court offered in its *Plessy* v. *Ferguson* decision of 1896. Plessy protested a Louisiana Jim Crow statute, enacted since the *Civil Rights* cases, requiring blacks to use segregated but allegedly equal railroad cars. He had refused to obey that law and sat in the whites-only coach, and railroad employees had forcibly removed him. Faced with a criminal prosecution by Louisiana under the statute, Plessy sought a writ of prohibition and certiorari against the state proceedings on the grounds of his rights under the Thirteenth and Fourteenth Amendments. The state court refused him relief. On appeal to the United States Supreme Court, the justices, with

---

[58][Brotherhood of Liberty], *Justice and Jurisprudence; An Inquiry Concerning the Constitutional Limitations of the Thirteenth, Fourteenth and Fifteenth Amendments* (Philadelphia, 1880) pp. 110–111.

only one dissenter, again Harlan, sustained Louisiana.

The Court's blessings upon state "separate but equal" public accommodations all but completed the quarter-century-long process of standing the Reconstruction Amendments and laws on their heads. The Court majority, including Justice Brewer, Field's relative and intellectual twin, stated in *Plessy* that slavery was only formal bondage. Civil rights were those traditionally associated with economic relationships and did not include social or political relationships. Racial segregation did not create servitude. Louisiana gave black citizens equal protection under state law because the cars for blacks were substantially equal to those whites rode—the state had said so. The majority opinion narrowed the meaning of rights protectable by the Thirteenth Amendment even more than was true of the decision in the *Civil Rights* cases of 1883.[59]

Harlan's vigorous dissent in *Plessy* echoed his *Civil Rights* cases statement. The Thirteenth Amendment meant what it said; it "not only struck down the institution of slavery . . . but it prevents the imposition of any . . . badges of slavery or servitude. It decreed universal civil freedom in this country." Any railroad exists by reason of public law—state law in this instance. Racial segregation on a public road was inadmissible because it was "a badge of servitude wholly inconsistent with . . . the Constitution," Harlan insisted.[60]

Plessy was outdistanced in 1906 by the even more constraining Supreme Court decision in *Hodges* v. *United States*. Hodges derived from a conspiracy among three whites to prevent, by violence, black laborers in a lumber mill from fulfilling the work the Negroes had contracted to perform. The race prejudice of the defendants was clear. Their violations of the Civil Rights acts of 1866 and of May 31, 1870, resulted in indictments and convictions in federal district court. The defendants, on writ of error, appealed to the Supreme Court. There, Brewer all but completed the federal judiciary's dilution of Reconstruction, holding that the federal courts did not have jurisdiction over conspiracies to deprive citizens of contract rights —the most traditional civil right—and reversed the lower court's judgment.

Brewer insisted that only the Thirteenth Amendment could sus-

---

[59]Plessy *v.* Ferguson, 163 U.S. 537 (1896), esp. 542–552.
[60]*Ibid.*, 553, 555, 562.

tain the indictment. If it did not, then plaintiffs must seek relief in the state courts, not the federal. That Amendment did not favor or disfavor a race. It ended slavery for everyone, reaching every individual in a universal prohibition of one specific condition, but did not touch crimes or torts. And the Fourteenth Amendment did not help the excluded Negroes either. It required state action, and none existed in this offense. No crime existed against the United States in the *Hodges* situation despite the clear language of the 1866 and 1870 laws. Jobs were not the nation's business, Brewer asserted; private wrongs did not create federal rights.[61]

Joined in dissent by Justice William Day, Harlan echoed himself, rather cruelly noting the majority opinion in the 1883 *Civil Rights* cases which had recognized the fundamental civil right involved in making contracts. Being free from slavery's "incidents or badges" was a universal right, not a sign of class advantage. Freedom's rights were, to Harlan, distinct, established in the amended Constitution, and specified in the enforcement laws.[62]

Brewer was not denying that the Thirteenth Amendment removed from the states their once exclusive authority to allow some residents to enslave other residents. But the power, assigned in the Thirteenth Amendment to the nation, to prohibit slavery throughout the land did not otherwise enlarge the nation's functions and duties to the giving of preferential status to blacks or any other class. Brewer perceived the Fourteenth Amendment to be a proof for his position on the Thirteenth. The Fourteenth Amendment limited state action adverse to federal citizens' rights; it did not enlarge those rights. Therefore the Fourteenth Amendment was Brewer's touchstone. It protected both civil rights, in the narrow sense he allowed, and state rights, the latter the keystone of the federal system, while eschewing what he perceived as preferential class legislation. Laissez-faire had found still another formula.

As in the *Civil Rights* cases, the Justices in *Plessy* and *Hodges* were unanimous about the federal plenitude concerning slavery. What caused dissent was the amount of slavery or servitude that admitted the exercise of national power. Both Harlan and Brewer agreed in

[61]Hodges v. United States, 203 U.S. 1 at 17–18, and see 1–8, 14–20 (1906); cf. Clyatt v. United States, 197 U.S. 207 (1905).
[62]Hodges v. United States, 27.

Hodges that the Thirteenth Amendment prohibited both state and private actions. The question was: at what point in a line of actions did conditions of slavery, or enough like it to be involuntary servitude (peonage, involuntary apprenticeship), exist? Harlan is now honored as a prophet of our own consensus in favor of looking far down the line—to public schools and to private businesses' in-service training programs, as examples. He perceived the Thirteenth Amendment to be a broad grant of responsibility and power to the nation to police the actions of persons who, because of race, interfere with individuals' enjoyment of the full measure of freedom, as defined at any one time and place. Brewer, hailed in his own time as a spokesman for the most respected professional values and social ethics, insisted upon a far narrower vision of the Amendment's coverage. It existed to prevent anyone from imposing involuntary servitude on anyone else, not to anticipate the imposition in situations when individuals wronged other persons of a different race.

It is possible to read the relevant case law since 1866 several ways on these essential points. Harlan resorted, among many other references, to *Ex parte Yarbrough,* in which conspirators intimidated by violence a Negro who was trying to vote in a federal election. In *Yarbrough,* Justice Miller, sustaining the nation's right to punish these felons, admitted that the Constitution did not specifically authorize such punitive statutes. But "what is implied is as much a part of the instrument as what is expressed." Clearly, Miller's language allowed Congress to punish intimidations because of race.[63]

But Brewer, in *Hodges,* though considering the same statute and kind of situation, decided that a citizen's right to perform a labor contract, if interfered with, did not reduce him to a condition close enough to involuntary servitude to warrant resort to federal justice. Disagreeing, Harlan had raised up also an 1884 opinion, also by Miller, this time not on a race discrimination issue. The defendant in the 1884 case had prevented a would-be homesteader from making good his entry, by intimidation. Miller found in Article IV, section 3, of the Constitution, on the territories, adequate authority to punish the personal violence the defendant committed. If a right an American wished to exercise, based on the Constitution or laws,

[63]Ex parte Yarbrough, 655–656.

faced unlawful impediments, the nation possessed a duty to remove the blockage, even if by criminal indictments, Miller had concluded.[64]

Harlan seized also upon *In re Neagle,* an 1890 habeas corpus proceeding involving the killing by a federal marshal of a would-be murderer of Justice Field while the latter was on circuit in California. The marshal was immune from state justice, the Court ruled. No federal statute assigned the marshal to guard the justice; none defined an intention to assault and kill a federal judge as murder. The Court in *Neagle* reached out for implications. The Constitution authorized such inferior federal courts as Congress allowed. Courts required judges. Judges therefore required protection by federal peace officers. The "peace of the United States," Miller stated, created constitutional rights that the nation must protect.[65]

Another precedent of seemingly unrelated nature to Hodges that Harlan resorted to in his *Hodges* dissent was *Logan* v. *United States,* an 1892 decision involving a conspiracy to murder the prisoner of a federal marshal. Justice Horace Gray found in the general nature of the Constitution, and of the nation it created, adequate and paramount authority to maintain law and order in its jurisdictions. Any government must punish crime. Therefore the United States government possessed the duty to protect prisoners in its custody, and their custodians, from violence.[66] Harlan did not refer in Hodges to the 1903 *United States* v. *Morris* lower federal court decision, which sustained a Negro's right to lease land without private interference because of race, under the 1866 Civil Rights law. A citation to *Morris* would probably have made no difference in *Hodges;* the dissenters were too few.

Harlan's position in *Hodges* was like that of Chase in *In re Turner* and Swayne in *United States* v. *Rhodes,* in 1866–67. Swayne, we have noted, on circuit in Kentucky, stated precisely and accurately that the Thirteenth Amendment "trenches directly upon the power of the states and of the people of the states." He nullified a Kentucky law that forbade blacks from offering testimony adverse to whites. Reviewing the history of slavery and that of free Negroes in the

[64]Miller in United States *v.* Wadell, 112 U.S. 76 (1884).
[65]203 U.S. 16 (1890).
[66]144 U.S. 263 (1894).

South for definitions of what Congress intended in the just-enacted
Thirteenth Amendment and Civil Rights law, Swayne asserted mov-
ingly that:

Slaves were imperfectly, if at all, protected from the grossest outrages by
the whites. Justice was not for them. The charities and rights of the domestic relations had no legal existence among them. The shadow of the evil fell
upon the free blacks. They had but few civil and no political rights in the
slave states. Many of the badges of the bondman's degradation were fas-
tened upon them. Their condition, like his, though not so bad, was helpless
and hopeless.

Congress, Swayne continued, had specific authorization and command in the Amendment's enforcement clause to select appropriate
means to abolish slavery in every manifestation of its existence.
Emancipation meant more than individual manumissions. It encompassed a people, a nation, a society, and a duty.[67] At least it did in
1866.

But not in 1906. In *Hodges* that year, Harlan, like Chase and
Swayne before him, had kept for the nation a tiny but essential
doctrinal toehold that, a century after *Rhodes* and sixty years after
Hodges, their robed successors would appropriately enlarge.[68] But
during those decades the Court kept on the *Hodges* road concerning
tight limits both on the persisting vestiges of slavery for Thirteenth
Amendment action and on state involvement as a prerequisite for
federal intervention under the Fourteenth Amendment. In 1926, in
Corrigan v. *Buckley*, the Court refused to consider a real estate covenant restricting purchase from blacks as a violation of the Thirteenth Amendment. The Court cited *Hodges*. The *Hodges-Corrigan*
perception stripped the Thirteenth Amendment of its potential as
a civil rights weapon, just when, in the early twentieth century,
small, weak civil rights associations, with litigation as their primary
weapon, were forming. But their lawyers, looking on *Hodges*, resorted only sporadically to the Thirteenth Amendment, by then
such a weak reed.[69]

[67]United States v. Rhodes, 27 Fed. Cas. 20 at 788, 793, #16,151 (C.C.D. Ky.
1886).
[68]Robert L. Kohl, "The Civil Rights Act of 1866: Its Hour Come Round at Last,"
Virginia Law Review, LV (1969), 272–300.
[69]Buchanan, *Quest,* pp. 85–86; Corrigan v. Buckley, 271 U.S. 323 (1926).

For almost fifty years after *Hodges,* the Thirteenth Amendment, all but forgotten by almost everyone, received almost no further interpretation in the Supreme Court. Attacks on peonage (i.e., servitude from debt not race) proved the exceptions. Legislation against peonage in New Mexico and elsewhere dated from the same date (March 2, 1867) as the Reconstruction law. The 1905 *Clyatt* v. *United States* decision, though it reversed a lower court judgment against an alleged violator of the statute, sustained the 1867 law, holding that "It is not open to doubt that Congress may enforce the Thirteenth Amendment by direct legislation, punishing the holding of a person in slavery or involuntary servitude. . . ."[70]

Further, the Court evidenced willingness to look behind what Sidney Buchanan called "disguised forms of peonage." An Alabama statute regulating criminal fraud embraced persons who entered into labor contracts intending not to complete them, and making failure to complete an evidence of such intent. One Alabaman received $15 in advance payment of a labor contract, then quit the job before the termination of the contract period without returning the advance. Alabama courts found him guilty of fraud and fined him, but the Supreme Court, in 1911, reversed because the state fraud statute contravened the Thirteenth Amendment and the antipeonage law and was therefore void.[71]

But the Court also found that the Thirteenth Amendment did not apply to sailors' contracts that required the forcible return to personal service of unfulfilled portions of the contracts of deserting seamen; to a Florida law that imposed on residents a duty to work on roads a set number of days per year; or to the draft law in World War I.[72] In 1964, in the famed *Heart of Atlanta Motel* case, the Court rejected arguments that a federal requirement for racially blind access to motel accommodations, under the 1964 Civil Rights act, exceeded the boundaries of involuntary servitude under the Thirteenth Amendment.[73] But that peers too far toward our day.

During the writing of the Thirteenth Amendment, Congress lost an unrecoverable opportunity to specify, as Sumner desired, that all

[70]197 U.S. 207 (1905); *Statutes at Large,* XIV, 546.
[71]Buchanan, *Quest,* p. 87, and see 86–90; Bailey *v.* Alabama, 219 U.S. 219 (1911).
[72]Respectively, Robertson *v.* Baldwin, 165 U.S. 275 (1897); Butler *v.* Perry, 240 U.S. 328 (1916); Selective Draft Law Cases, 245 U.S. 366 (1918).
[73]Heart of Atlanta Motel, Inc., *v.* United States, 379 U.S. 241 (1964).

Americans were equal before all laws; that emancipation required positive duties upon government to secure all free men's rights against any offenders, governmental or private, in any guise.[74]

Subsequent congresses through 1875 failed to connect the 1870 Enforcement Act and the 1875 Civil Rights law to the Thirteenth Amendment and thus helped to confirm notions that the Amendment was superseded by the Fourteenth. Congress thereby lent credence to arguments that the Thirteenth Amendment prohibited only formal slavery or peonage and was thus largely irrelevant to less formidable inferiorities.

As matters worked out, the 1875 law was the last civil rights statute of Reconstruction. To be sure, all the civil rights laws 1866–75 were enacted before the Supreme Court fixed a state-action-only definition onto the Fourteenth Amendment. All through the decade 1865–75 many Republicans persisted in the belief that any or all of the Reconstruction Amendments were equally good sources of authority for the nation to act against either private or state acts; that the passage of one Amendment did not revoke any of its predecessors.

Indeed, to the Republicans through the 1870s and 1880s who kept the race-equality faith, the accumulation of Reconstruction Amendments and laws represented great and inspiring progress: ever increasing commitments to sustain the best cause Americans had ever perceived. This sense of advance further defined their perceptions and purposes in the Thirteenth and Fourteenth Amendments. They wanted to harmonize the broad (perhaps, in a dynamic, questing, aspiring society, the indefinable) catalog of free men's rights with the state-based federal system. That catalog was and is not neatly discoverable in any printed record, including congressional debates. The debaters, especially those with law training, knew how uncertain the legal literature was on rights. They could only leave the catalog of rights for posterity, for the politics of democracy, to make specific in nondiscriminatory terms. There was

[74]In the 1867 Bowlin decision in Kentucky, that state's supreme court derided Sumner's view that "the power to make the freedman a competent witness [in state courts, against whites]," as "simply an absurdity, a broad and unmitigated perversion of language and the well-defined meaning of the term [i.e., slavery]." Bowlin v. Kentucky, 27, 29. Field cited Bowlin in Ex parte Virginia, 364; and plaintiff cited Bowlin in Hodges v. United States, 11.

no consensus that courts would have the final word. A view of the Reconstruction Amendments that comes to tighter conclusions may repeat Taney's *Dred Scott* error that the Constitution "must be construed now as it was understood at the time of its adoption."[75]

The abolitionists had expressed their grand design in the simple, brief Thirteenth Amendment. It was of a moral nation in which slavelessness equaled equal freedom for all. What resulted after 1866 was a complex, confused kaleidoscope. Every Reconstruction and Enforcement statute was longer, more detailed, and less comfortable to live with than its predecessor. The Fourteenth Amendment was both more complex than the Thirteenth, superficially at least, and less effective. Endless (it seemed) national interventions were to be necessary because southern whites were willing to resort to obstructions, harassments, and raw violence. Events proved that Lincoln's generation was ill-prepared to cope in a sustained, patient way with problems of voter registration in South Carolina, rabble-rousing newspaper editors in Mississippi, monopolistic butchers in Louisiana, or brutal vigilantes almost anywhere in the "redeemed" South or elsewhere.

The Chase and Waite Courts both contributed to and responded to these cross-cutting influences. As example, according to Charles Fairman, Chase and his associates felt "relief . . . when the strain of Reconstruction was at an end."[76] This sense of relief at a job completed was easier for those holding it to accept because Reconstruction policy since 1861 had delegated so much of the job of protecting individuals' rights to courts and to legal procedures. Then as now, the lawyer's truism existed, that justice must be visible to be believed. The Reconstruction experience suggests that a "flip" side exists to the truism: that the mere existence of legal procedures can convince a populace predisposed to believe in their effectiveness to accept them as sufficient remedies, thus ending a duty to do more. The modern view is that more than legal procedures are wanted; that civil rights are dynamic not static; and that knowledge of their number and nature at any one time demands close scrutiny of the substance of a situation affecting rights.

[75]Robert Kaczorowski, "The Congressional Approach to Citizenship and Civil Rights During Reconstruction" (Southern Historical Association paper, 1973), 1–9; Arthur Selwyn Miller, "Notes on the Concept of the 'Living' Constitution," in Miller (ed.), *Social Change and the Fundamental Law* (Westport, 1979), pp. 345–382.
[76]Fairman, *Reconstruction*, p. 1481

In the late 1860s the Court, like all branches of the national government, had virtually no experience with a federal duty to protect individuals' civil rights. Fifteen years after passage of the 1866 Civil Rights act, in the 1883 *Civil Rights* cases, the Court, no matter how precisely the Justices spoke, was in fact dealing with a host of imprecisions concerning civil rights, so far as legal knowledge existed.[77]

The Civil Rights act of 1866 derived from the abolition Thirteenth Amendment. The fact that the death of slavery was indeed a product of wartime expediency clouded the history of emancipation in the 1860s and obscures its characteristics even now. Clearly, by the 1880s, white America lost the sense of moral anger and escalating common national purpose that brought it to emancipation and then to the protection of civil rights as they understood them, then of political rights, and of civil liberties with both. That sense lost, the Negro, its initial and primary beneficiary, became all but invisible.

In this relegation of blacks and other race minorities to obscure corners of our constitutional closet, the growth of formalist legal thought played a part, impossible to weigh precisely, but significant at least in contextual terms. Instrumentalism retained popularity among lawyers and legislators. Judicial self-restraint, a concomitant of instrumentalism, continued to characterize at least the rhetoric of jurisprudents through the first three post-Appomattox decades. And, indeed, instrumentalism synchronized satisfyingly with the busy, inventive, eclectic characteristics of America in matters of public law and administration. On every level of the federal system, American governments and private associations, or quasi-public ones, were the globe's pioneers in efforts to institutionalize the public good. This record is the more remarkable in light of the dismal descriptions common about the quality of government and the alleged domination of laissez-faire principles in the Gilded Age. The vigor of state-based federalism here contrasts strikingly with the centralizations occurring abroad.

Lincoln's generation was excited and proud of the post-Appomattox novelties in public law and administration, including the Freedmen's Bureau. Jurists sanctioned New York's Metropolitan Health

---

[77]Jones *v.* Alfred H. Mayer, 413, 445, 449–50. Fairman, *Reconstruction,* pp. 1207–1216, offers opinions contrary to ours on these points.

Board, the Society for the Prevention of Cruelty to Animals, and the Society for the Prevention of Cruelty to Children. One may point also to Louisiana's assignment of a butchering monopoly as a public health measure, and to Illinois's Granger commissions, being armed with coercive authority from the state to enforce maximum railroad and associated rates, as additional examples. It must have seemed that the dream of leading spokesmen among lawyers, of government run apolitically by commissions of experts, was becoming a reality. It all added to the optimism that Appomattox had engendered; a "can-do" optimism that lent itself, ironically, to the very kind of moralistic politicking that the lawyers wished to avoid.

The political history of the 1870s and 1880s suggests how disappointed both voting and nonfranchised groups were by the inadequacies they perceived in these and other proud "inventions" of the 1860s; inventions that, in a fundamental sense, included immediate and unqualified emancipation. After initial successes, the Freedmen's Bureau failed to set southern law into motion toward color-blindness; the New York SPCA and Metropolitan Health Board failed to end abuses of beasts or to prevent epidemics; the favored Louisiana butchering monopoly failed to improve public health or stop the overpricing of meats; and the Illinois Granger commission failed to hold down railroad and warehousing rates. These and other administrative contrivances could not of themselves overcome the effects of race prejudice, industrialism, urbanization, or finance capitalism. The men who created these institutions probably did not comprehend the vast forces to which they reacted.

The do-gooders of the SPCA and the Freedmen's Bureau proved to be Davids with weak slings. But in terms of constitutional and legal theory these responses to change tapped deep American wellsprings. The nation's war powers and the states' police powers, respectively, were appropriate for the tasks of that time, by the test of ascertainable evidence. But by the 1880s even major participants in the chief events of the years since 1860 began to separate the prewar past from the Civil War, the war from Reconstruction, and both from post-Appomattox events such as the Granger response to being gouged by the Illinois Central Railroad.[78]

[78]Morton Keller, *Affairs of State: Public Life in Late Nineteenth Century America* (Cambridge, 1979), *passim;* Hyman, *A More Perfect Union,* chs. 18–22.

In terms of constitutional and legal history, these decades are less easily severable from one another. The same generation in the 1870s and 1880s accounted Reconstruction a fool's errand, registered its frustrations with politicians in the southern states and in cities, and worried about the decline in American public ethics from the allegedly austere virtues of prewar times. Nostalgia for a lost golden age, exposures of corruption among public officials, fatigue with the "eternal Sambo," the Democrats' relentless opposition to race equality, all combined with unlikely elements of contemporary thought. In the growing university population, both on private campuses and in the new tax-supported state institutions, Charles Darwin's, Herbert Spencer's, and William Graham Sumner's teachings were coming to dominate relevant curricula. The ideas of these men, and others, were to result in both a pessimistic, reactionary Social Darwinism and a progressive, optimistic Reform Darwinism that favored enlightened government interventions. Social and Reform Darwinism infused the teaching of law and the practice of jurisprudence in the 1870s and 1880s. Law schools, increasingly associated with colleges and universities, made Cooley and Dillon required texts. Law as a science found the social implications of other sciences, chiefly the biological, respectable and relevant. The new social sciences, accepting both Social and Reform Darwinian notions about the need for unfettered competition to advance progress by permitting the most deserving to survive proved very incomplete as ideologies. In seeming inconsistency the new science of society and law also sanctioned the regulation of businesses "affected with a public interest," as in the *Slaughterhouse* and *Granger* decisions, while leaders of the new science inveighed against worse; against the "fantastic" schemes of Single Taxers, Greenbackers, Knights of Labor, trade unionists—and who knew what might come up next?[79]

Laissez-faire champions rarely fell into a trap of ideological overconsistency. The revised editions of Cooley and Dillon, and the first major writings of other glossators such as Christopher Tiedeman that the law schools snapped up as texts, reserved for judges a duty to intervene in Reconstruction or non-Reconstruction matters when

[79]Cf. Richard Hofstadter, *Social Darwinism in American Thought* (rev. ed., New York, 1955), pp. 35–60; Robert C. Bannister, *Social Darwinism: Science and Myth in Anglo-American Social Thought* (Philadelphia, 1979), *passim.*

government went too far. In the oncoming body of formalist legal doctrine, activist judicial review was not merely an acceptable exception from laissez-faire. It was an obligation upon jurists, who rose steeply and quickly in importance both in Washington and in the several states. In this rise, as John W. Johnson noted,

. . . the leading judicial opinions that announced substantive due process principles—Justice Field's dissents in the Slaughter-House Cases and Munn v. Illinois, Judge Earl's majority opinion in the New York case of Matter of Jacobs and, of course, Justice Peckham's opinion for the Supreme Court in Lochner v. New York—were largely predicated on the objections to melioristic state legislation posited in such influential treatises as Thomas Cooley's *Constitutional Limitations* and Christopher Tiedeman's *Treatise on the Limitations of Police Power in the United States.* [80]

Ideas about liberty and the rise of individuals to elite positions were the major concern of the intellectual leadership in the postwar decades. Concerns about equality and the protections of individuals sharply diminished. This fateful shifting of concern occurred despite the fact that the Reconstruction legislation of the decade 1866–75, especially the bedrock Civil Rights law of 1866, had paired equality under law as a value with liberty. But in 1873, when Chase died, liberty had assumed a clear if not yet overwhelming priority for the justices. The lead that liberty enjoyed grew at a time when the Congresses from 1866 and Presidents Grant and Rutherford B. Hayes, as well as the Supreme Court, continued to speak of liberty under law, and of equality, as roughly equal priorities for the national government. These ostensibly paired values had come to be seen, however, in the evolving context of Republican constitutional thought about federalism, the separation of powers, and individuals' rights of both economic and noneconomic sorts.

The growing lead that liberty came to enjoy over equality both reflected and helped to shape dominant trends in American society as a whole, including law and jurisprudence. Within these swiftly changing configurations of life, labor, and thought, American's

[80]John W. Johnson, "Creativity and Adaptation: A Reassessment of American Jurisprudence, 1801–1857 and 1908–1940," *Rutgers-Camden Law Journal,* VII (1976), 635; Clyde Jacobs, *Law Writers and the Courts: The Influence of Thomas M. Cooley, Christopher G. Tiedeman, and John F. Dillon Upon American Constitutional Law* (Berkeley, 1954), *passim;* Arnold Paul, *Conservative Crisis and the Rule of Law: Attitudes of Bar and Bench, 1887–1895* (New York, 1960), *passim.*

decisionmakers (including those in the political parties, the legal profession, and the Court) were, as noted earlier, dedicated to preserving liberty and the federal system more than individuals' rights by means of governments' interventions. Chase's Court wrestled to reshape the Constitution's Reconstruction Amendments and enforcement legislation into elements useful in that preservation. Conciliation with the South's states was to prove to be not too high a price to pay for stable federal relationships; stability permitted safer play for the newer economic forces, production technologies, and legal contrivances. Race equality was a sacrifice that relatively few whites objected to making by the centennial year 1876, in part because the disputed presidential election that year frightened many whites; in part because the new science appeared to validate ancient race prejudices; in part because the Court, in *Slaughterhouse* and other decisions, had already glossed over the sacrificial nature of what was occurring.

Liberty required government to do virtually nothing save to encourage entrepreneurs as in transcontinental railroad construction. A view requiring government (except for judges) to keep hands off both race relations and the marketplace was increasingly sweet to persons of anti-Granger or antiunion attitudes—a view that gained avalanching support from late-nineteenth-century considerations by "classical" economists. But equality—it required vexing, often frustrating, unsettling interventions on behalf of disfavored and largely unloved groups (or classes, and the concept of class legislation was itself repugnant to the majority of Americans): southern blacks, southwestern Mexicans and Indians, and the Far West's Asians. It proved to be difficult—indeed, all but impossible—for champions of equality to maintain in the seventies the fervor of the sixties, a phenomenon that civil rights veterans of the 1960s will recognize as a characteristic of the 1970s and, perhaps, of the 1980 decade.

All of which is to suggest that formalism in the law reflected complex and numerous approaches to social problems; indeed, to the very perception of improvable problems. No "conspiracy theory," such as the tenacious one concerning the alleged adoption of the Fourteenth Amendment's due process clause to favor businessmen, need rise concerning formalism. The exaltation of the federal judiciary resulted from a distrust of elected state jurists plus a sense of deep antipathy to legislation overfavoring classes.[81]

None of which mitigates the tragedy involved in the nation's abandonment of equality as a national goal (or, if "abandonment" is hyperbolic, then C. Vann Woodward's phrase, "the deferred commitment to equality," serves admirably). The Chase Court did not lead in the abandonment. Indeed, Chase himself, and Swayne, on circuit, bequeathed enduringly important doctrines about the broad outreach and strength of the Thirteenth Amendment and 1866 Civil Rights law that their heirs picked up again in the 1968 *Jones* decision. The Chase Court did not rule on the Freedmen's Bureau (although its *Milligan* and *Test Oath* decisions affected Bureau operations negatively), or the New York Health Board or SPCA. Its *Slaughterhouse* decision sustained the state, albeit the insight that hindsight affords allows us to see *Slaughterhouse* as a step toward the Court's apogee of substantive due process interpretations, decades ahead.

In *Slaughterhouse* and in the *Granger* cases, however, even the majority opinions reserved for the jurists a right to inquire into both the legislators' intentions and the substantive effects of the respective legislation. By the *Slaughterhouse* year, political parties, immigrant groups, and the freedmen appeared to be cancers in the American polity. The distrust of popular decisionmaking led to an exaltation of the judiciary, especially the federal judiciary, as an essential brake on popular passions.

In the new graduate schools of the 1880s, budding Ph.D.s in history and political science justified, by "scientific" principles, the ascent of judicial review. "The Courts the Conscience of the People" was the heading for the concluding chapter of Horace Davis's 1885 dissertation at the new Johns Hopkins University, a dissertation that stressed the Supreme Court's function ". . . so often to bring back the people from a state of excitement and fury to a calm sense of right." Davis asserted: "The Court can go no further towards absolute right than it is sustained by popular opinion, and its decisions must represent the average public sentiment; not the froth and fury of a political campaign, but the calm, settled conviction of thinking men." To Davis, as to Cooley, Dillon, Jameson, Tiedeman, and other major writers whose views were tending to dominate legal education and practice and the new graduate education in the social sciences and history, judicial review, was, to borrow Davis's panegyric phrases, "the ripened fruit of our experience . . . this modern idea of government, which lifts up the Judiciary to an exalted and independent position, and places law, impersonal, impassive, and serene, in the innermost shrine of the temple, jealously guarded from profane intrusion."[82]

The nation had survived all the monumental hazards deriving from slavery, secession, Civil War, and Reconstruction, hazards jeopardizing its survival from the time of its semicentennial to the centennials of the Revolution and of the Constitution. Courts and laws had contributed mightily to that survival and to the social stability most Americans desired, though not to the racial quality that many Americans still aspired to realize. Slavery, so long protected, by the time of the centennials was dead; political mechanisms had become greatly democratized. In most ways the capacity of the states to create internal policies that defined, or redefined, the relationships of individuals to authority, thereby modifying the equation between liberty and equality, remained virtually undiminished. State power remained the principal challenge to the new constitutional order after the Civil War. High judges, along with the leaders of the legal profession, were ready to meet that challenge as the nation started on its second century.

[82]Horace Davis, *American Constitutions: The Relations of the Three Departments as Adjusted by a Century* (Baltimore, 1885), pp. 62–63.

Appendix

The Constitution of the United States

We the People of the United States, in Order to form a more perfect Union, establish Justice, insure domestic Tranquility, provide for the common defence, promote the general Welfare, and secure the Blessings of Liberty to ourselves and our Posterity, do ordain and establish this Constitution for the United States of America.

ARTICLE I

SECTION 1. All legislative Powers herein granted shall be vested in a Congress of the United States, which shall consist of a Senate and House of Representatives.

SECTION 2. The House of Representatives shall be composed of Members chosen every second Year by the People of the several States, and the Electors in each State shall have the Qualifications requisite for Electors of the most numerous Branch of the State Legislature.

No Person shall be a Representative who shall not have attained to the Age of twenty-five Years, and been seven Years a Citizen of the United States, and who shall not, when elected, be an Inhabitant of that State in which he shall be chosen.

Representatives and direct Taxes shall be apportioned among the several States which may be included within this Union, according to their respective Numbers, which shall be determined by adding to the whole Number of free Persons, including those bound to Service for a Term of Years, and excluding Indians not taxed, three fifths of all other Persons. The actual Enumeration shall be made within three Years after the first Meeting of the

Congress of the United States, and within every subsequent Term of ten Years, in such Manner as they shall by Law direct. The Number of Representatives shall not exceed one for every thirty Thousand, but each State shall have at Least one Representative; and until such enumeration shall be made, the State of New Hampshire shall be entitled to chuse three, Massachusetts eight, Rhode-Island and Providence Plantations one, Connecticut five, New-York six, New Jersey four, Pennsylvania eight, Delaware one, Maryland six, Virginia ten, North Carolina five, South Carolina five, and Georgia three.

When vacancies happen in the Representation from any State, the Executive Authority thereof shall issue Writs of Election to fill such Vacancies.

The House of Representatives shall chuse their Speaker and other Officers; and shall have the sole Power of Impeachment.

SECTION 3. The Senate of the United States shall be composed of two Senators from each State, chosen by the Legislature thereof, for six Years; and each Senator shall have one Vote.

Immediately after they shall be assembled in Consequence of the first Election, they shall be divided as equally as may be into three Classes. The Seats of the Senators of the first Class shall be vacated at the Expiration of the Second Year, of the second Class at the Expiration of the Fourth Year, and of the third Class at the Expiration of the sixth Year, so that one third may be chosen every second Year; and if Vacancies happen by Resignation, or otherwise, during the Recess of the Legislature of any State, the Executive thereof may make temporary Appointments until the next Meeting of the Legislature, which shall then fill such Vacancies.

No Person shall be a Senator who shall not have attained to the Age of thirty Years, and been nine Years a Citizen of the United States, and who shall not, when elected, be an Inhabitant of that State for which he shall be chosen.

The Vice President of the United States shall be President of the Senate, but shall have no Vote, unless they be equally divided.

The Senate shall chuse their other Officers, and also a President pro tempore, in the absence of the Vice President, or when he shall exercise the Office of President of the United States.

The Senate shall have the sole Power to try all Impeachments. When sitting for that Purpose, they shall be on Oath or Affirmation. When the President of the United States is tried, the Chief Justice shall preside: And no Person shall be convicted without the Concurrence of two thirds of the Members present.

Judgment in Cases of Impeachment shall not extend further than to removal from Office, and disqualification to hold and enjoy any Office of honor, Trust, or Profit under the United States: but the Party convicted shall nevertheless be liable and subject to Indictment, Trial, Judgment, and Punishment, according to Law.

SECTION 4. The Times, Places and Manner of holding Elections for Senators and Representatives, shall be prescribed in each State by the Legislature thereof; but the Congress may at any time by Law make or alter such Regulations, except as to the Places of chusing Senators.

The Congress shall assemble at least once in every Year, and such Meeting shall be on the first Monday in December unless they shall by Law appoint a different Day.

SECTION 5. Each House shall be the Judge of the Elections, Returns, and Qualifications of its own Members, and a Majority of each shall constitute a Quorum to do Business; but a smaller Number may adjourn from day to day, and may be authorized to compel the Attendance of absent Members, in such Manner, and under such Penalties as each House may provide.

Each House may determine the Rules of its Proceedings, punish its Members for disorderly Behavior, and, with the Concurrence of two thirds, expel a Member.

Each House shall keep a Journal of its Proceedings, and from time to time publish the same, excepting such Parts as may in their Judgment require Secrecy; and the Yeas and Nays of the Members of either House on any question shall, at the Desire of one fifth of those Present, be entered on the Journal.

Neither House, during the Session of Congress, shall, without the Consent of the other, adjourn for more than three days, nor to any other Place than that in which the two Houses shall be sitting.

SECTION 6. The Senators and Representatives shall receive a Compensation for their Services, to be ascertained by Law, and paid out of the Treasury of the United States. They shall in all Cases, except Treason, Felony and Breach of the Peace, be privileged from Arrest during their Attendance at the Session of their respective Houses, and in going to and returning from the same; and for any Speech or Debate in either House, they shall not be questioned in any other Place.

No Senator or Representative shall, during the Time for which he was elected, be appointed to any civil Office under the Authority of the United States, which shall have been created, or the Emoluments whereof shall have been encreased during such time; and no Person holding any Office under the United States, shall be a Member of either House during his Continuance in Office.

SECTION 7. All Bills for raising Revenue shall originate in the House of Representatives; but the Senate may propose to concur with Amendments as on other Bills.

Every Bill which shall have passed the House of Representatives and the

Senate, shall, before it become a Law, be presented to the President of the United States; if he approve he shall sign it, but if not he shall return it, with his Objections to that House in which it shall have originated, who shall enter the Objections at large on their Journal, and proceed to reconsider it. If after such Reconsideration two thirds of that House shall agree to pass the Bill, it shall be sent, together with the Objections, to the other House, by which it shall likewise be reconsidered, and if approved by two thirds of that House, it shall become a Law. But in all such Cases the Votes of both Houses shall be determined by Yeas and Nays, and the Names of the Persons voting for and against the Bill shall be entered on the Journal of each House respectively. If any Bill shall not be returned by the President within ten Days (Sundays excepted) after it shall have been presented to him, the Same shall be a Law, in like Manner as if he had signed it, unless the Congress by their Adjournment prevent its Return, in which Case it shall not be a Law.

Every Order, Resolution, or Vote to which the Concurrence of the Senate and House of Representatives may be necessary (except on a question of Adjournment) shall be presented to the President of the United States; and before the Same shall take Effect, shall be approved by him, or being disapproved by him, shall be repassed by two thirds of the Senate and House of Representatives, according to the Rules and Limitations prescribed in the Case of a Bill.

SECTION 8. The Congress shall have Power To lay and collect Taxes, Duties, Imposts and Excises, to pay the Debts and provide for the common Defence and general Welfare of the United States; but all Duties, Imposts and Excises shall be uniform throughout the United States;

To borrow money on the credit of the United States;

To regulate Commerce with foreign Nations, and among the several States, and with the Indian Tribes;

To establish an uniform Rule of Naturalization, and uniform Laws on the subject of Bankruptcy throughout the United States;

To coin Money, regulate the Value thereof, and of foreign Coin, and fix the Standard of Weights and Measures;

To provide for the Punishment of counterfeiting the Securities and current Coin of the United States;

To Establish Post Offices and post Roads;

To promote the Progress of Science and useful Arts, by securing for limited Times to Authors and Inventors the exclusive Right to their respective Writings and Discoveries;

To constitute Tribunals inferior to the supreme Court;

To define and punish Piracies and Felonies committed on the high Seas, and Offenses against the Law of Nations;

To declare War, grant Letters of Marque and Reprisal, and make Rules concerning Captures on Land and Water;

To raise and support Armies, but no Appropriation of Money to that Use shall be for a longer Term than two Years;

To provide and maintain a Navy;

To make Rules for the Government and Regulation of the land and naval Forces;

To provide for calling forth the Militia to execute the Laws of the Union, suppress Insurrections and repel Invasions;

To provide for organizing, arming, and disciplining the Militia, and for governing such Part of them as may be employed in the Service of the United States, reserving to the States respectively, the Appointment of the Officers, and the Authority of training the Militia according to the discipline prescribed by Congress;

To exercise exclusive Legislation in all Cases whatsoever, over such District (not exceeding ten Miles square) as may, by Cession of particular States, and the acceptance of Congress, become the Seat of the Government of the United States, and to exercise like Authority over all Places purchased by the Consent of the Legislature of the State in which the Same shall be, for the Erection of Forts, Magazines, Arsenals, dock-Yards, and other needful Buildings;—And

To make all Laws which shall be necessary and proper for carrying into Execution the foregoing Powers, and all other Powers vested by this Constitution in the Government of the United States, or in any Department or Officer thereof.

SECTION 9. The Migration or Importation of Such Persons as any of the States now existing shall think proper to admit, shall not be prohibited by the Congress prior to the Year one thousand eight hundred and eight, but a tax or duty may be imposed on such Importation, not exceeding ten dollars for each Person.

The privilege of the Writ of Habeas Corpus shall not be suspended, unless when in Cases of Rebellion or Invasion the public Safety may require it.

No Bill of Attainder or ex post facto Law shall be passed.

No capitation, or other direct, Tax shall be laid, unless in Proportion to the Census or Enumeration herein before directed to be taken.

No Tax or Duty shall be laid on Articles exported from any State.

No preference shall be given by any Regulation of Commerce or Revenue to the Ports of one State over those of another: nor shall Vessels bound to, or from, one State be obliged to enter, clear, or pay Duties in another.

No money shall be drawn from the Treasury, but in Consequence of Appropriations made by Law; and a regular Statement and Account of the

Receipts and Expenditures of all public Money shall be published from time to time.

No Title of Nobility shall be granted by the United States: And no Person holding any Office of Profit or Trust under them, shall, without the Consent of the Congress, accept of any present, Emolument, Office, or Title, of any kind whatever, from any King, Prince, or foreign State.

SECTION 10. No State shall enter into any Treaty, Alliance, or Confederation; grant Letters of Marque and Reprisal; coin Money; emit Bills of Credit; make any Thing but gold and silver Coin a Tender in Payment of Debts; pass any Bill of Attainder, ex post facto Law, or Law impairing the Obligation of Contracts, or grant any Title of Nobility.

No State shall, without the Consent of the Congress, lay any Imposts or Duties on Imports or Exports, except what may be absolutely necessary for executing its inspection Laws: and the net Produce of all Duties and Imposts, laid by any State on Imports or Exports, shall be for the Use of the Treasury of the United States; and all such Laws shall be subject to the Revision and Control of the Congress.

No State shall, without the Consent of Congress, lay any duty of Tonnage, keep Troops, or Ships of War in time of Peace, enter into any Agreement or Compact with another State, or with a foreign Power, or engage in War, unless actually invaded, or in such imminent Danger as will not admit of delay.

ARTICLE II

SECTION 1. The executive Power shall be vested in a President of the United States of America. He shall hold his Office during the Term of four Years, and, together with the Vice-President, chosen for the same Term, be elected, as follows:

Each State shall appoint, in such Manner as the Legislature thereof may direct, a Number of Electors, equal to the whole Number of Senators and Representatives to which the State may be entitled in the Congress: but no Senator or Representative, or Person holding an Office of Trust or Profit under the United States, shall be appointed an Elector.

The Electors shall meet in their respective States, and vote by Ballot for two persons, of whom one at least shall not be an Inhabitant of the same State with themselves. And they shall make a List of all the Persons voted for, and of the Number of Votes for each; which List they shall sign and certify, and transmit sealed to the Seat of the Government of the United States, directed to the President of the Senate. The President of the Senate shall, in the Presence of the Senate and House of Representatives, open all the Certificates, and the Votes shall then be counted. The Person having the greatest Number of Votes shall be the President, if such Number be a Majority of the whole Number of Electors appointed; and if there be more than one who have such Majority, and have an equal Number of Votes, then the House of Representatives shall immediately chuse by Ballot one of them for President; and if no Person have a Majority, then from the five highest on the List the said House shall in like Manner chuse the President. But in chusing the President, the Votes shall be taken by States, the Representation from each State having one Vote; A quorum for this Purpose shall consist of a Member or Members from two thirds of the States, and a Majority of all the States shall be necessary to a Choice. In every Case, after the Choice of the President, the Person having the greatest Number of Votes of the Electors shall be the Vice President. But if there should remain two or more who have equal Votes, the Senate shall chuse from them by Ballot the Vice President.

The Congress may determine the Time of chusing the Electors, and the Day on which they shall give their Votes; which Day shall be the same throughout the United States.

No person except a natural born Citizen, or a Citizen of the United States, at the time of the Adoption of this Constitution, shall be eligible to the Office of President; neither shall any Person be eligible to that Office who shall not have attained to the Age of thirty-five Years, and been fourteen Years a Resident within the United States.

In case of the removal of the President from Office, or of his Death, Resignation, or Inability to discharge the Powers and Duties of the said Office, the same shall devolve on the Vice President, and the Congress may by Law provide for the Case of Removal, Death, Resignation or Inability, both of the President and Vice President, declaring what Officer shall then act as President, and such Officer shall act accordingly, until the Disability be removed, or a President shall be elected.

The President shall, at stated Times, receive for his Services, a Compensation, which shall neither be increased nor diminished during the Period for which he shall have been elected, and he shall not receive within that Period any other Emolument from the United States, or any of them.

Before he enter on the Execution of his Office, he shall take the following Oath or Affirmation:—"I do solemnly swear (or affirm) that I will faithfully execute the Office of President of the United States, and will to the best of my Ability, preserve, protect and defend the Constitution of the United States."

Section 2. The President shall be Commander in Chief of the Army and Navy of the United States, and of the Militia of the several States, when called into the actual Service of the United States; he may require the Opinion, in writing, of the principal Officer in each of the executive Departments, upon any subject relating to the Duties of their respective Offices, and he shall have Power to grant Reprieves and Pardons for Offenses against the United States, except in Cases of Impeachment.

He shall have Power, by and with the Advice and Consent of the Senate, to make Treaties, provided two thirds of the Senators present concur; and he shall nominate, and by and with the Advice and Consent of the Senate, shall appoint Ambassadors, other public Ministers and Consuls, Judges of the supreme Court, and all other Officers of the United States, whose Appointments are not herein otherwise provided for, and which shall be established by Law; but the Congress may by Law vest the Appointment of such inferior Officers, as they think proper, in the President alone, in the Courts of Law, or in the Heads of Departments.

The President shall have Power to fill up all Vacancies that may happen during the Recess of the Senate, by granting Commissions which shall expire at the End of their next Session.

SECTION 3. He shall from time to time give to the Congress Information of the State of the Union, and recommend to their Consideration such Measures as he shall judge necessary and expedient; he may, on extraordinary Occasions, convene both Houses, or either of them, and in Case of Disagreement between them, with Respect to the Time of Adjournment, he may adjourn them to such Time as he shall think proper; he shall receive Ambassadors and other public Ministers; he shall take Care that the Laws be faithfully executed, and shall Commission all the Officers of the United States.

SECTION 4. The President; Vice President and all civil Officers of the United States, shall be removed from Office on Impeachment for, and Conviction of, Treason, Bribery, or other high Crimes and Misdemeanors.

ARTICLE III

SECTION 1. The judicial Power of the United States, shall be vested in one Supreme Court, and in such inferior Courts as the Congress may from time to time ordain and establish. The Judges, both of the supreme and inferior Courts, shall hold their Offices during good Behaviour, and shall, at stated Times, receive for their Services a Compensation which shall not be diminished during their Continuance in Office.

SECTION 2. The judicial Power shall extend to all Cases, in Law and Equity, arising under this Constitution, the Laws of the United States, and Treaties made, or which shall be made, under their Authority;—to all Cases affecting Ambassadors, other public Ministers and Consuls;—to all Cases of admiralty and maritime Jurisdiction;—to Controversies to which the

United States shall be a Party;—to Controversies between two or more States;—between a State and Citizens of another State;—between Citizens of different States;—between Citizens of the same State claiming Lands under Grants of different States, and between a State, or the Citizens thereof, and foreign States, Citizens or Subjects.

In all Cases affecting Ambassadors, other public Ministers and Consuls, and those in which a State shall be Party, the supreme Court shall have original Jurisdiction. In all the other Cases before mentioned, the supreme Court shall have appellate Jurisdiction, both as to Law and Fact, with such Exceptions, and under such Regulations as the Congress shall make.

The Trial of all Crimes, except in Cases of Impeachment, shall be by Jury; and such Trial shall be held in the State where the said Crimes shall have been committed; but when not committed within any State, the Trial shall be at such Place or Places as the Congress may by Law have directed.

SECTION 3. Treason against the United States, shall consist only in levying War against them, or, in adhering to their Enemies, giving them Aid and Comfort. No Person shall be convicted of Treason unless on the Testimony of two Witnesses to the same overt Act, or on Confession in open Court.

The Congress shall have power to declare the Punishment of Treason, but no Attainder of Treason shall work Corruption of Blood, or Forfeiture except during the Life of the Person attainted.

ARTICLE IV

SECTION 1. Full Faith and Credit shall be given in each State to the public Acts, Records, and judicial Proceedings of every other State. And the Congress may by general Laws prescribe the Manner in which such Acts, Records and Proceedings shall be proved, and the Effect thereof.

SECTION 2. The Citizens of each State shall be entitled to all Privileges and Immunities of Citizens in the several States.

A Person charged in any State with Treason, Felony, or other Crime, who shall flee from Justice, and be found in another State, shall on demand of the executive Authority of the State from which he fled, be delivered up, to be removed to the State having Jurisdiction of the Crime.

No Person held to Service or Labour in one State, under the Laws thereof, escaping into another, shall, in Consequence of any Law or Regulation therein, be discharged from such Service or Labour, but shall be delivered up on Claim of the Party to whom such Service or Labour may be due.

SECTION 3. New States may be admitted by the Congress into this Union; but no new State shall be formed or erected within the Jurisdiction of any other State; nor any State be formed by the Junction of two or more States, or parts of States, without the Consent of the Legislatures of the States concerned as well as of the Congress.

The Congress shall have Power to dispose of and make all needful Rules and Regulations respecting the Territory or other Property belonging to the United States; and nothing in this Constitution shall be so construed as to Prejudice any Claims of the United States, or of any particular State.

SECTION 4. The United States shall guarantee to every State in this Union a Republican Form of Government, and shall protect each of them against Invasion; and on Application of the Legislature, or of the Executive (when the Legislature cannot be convened) against domestic Violence.

ARTICLE V

The Congress, whenever two thirds of both Houses shall deem it necessary, shall propose Amendments to this Constitution, or, on the Application of the Legislatures of two thirds of the several States, shall call a Convention for proposing Amendments, which, in either Case, shall be valid to all Intents and Purposes, as part of this Constitution, when ratified by the Legislatures of three fourths of the several States, or by Conventions in three fourths thereof, as the one or the other Mode of Ratification may be proposed by the Congress; Provided that no Amendment which may be made prior to the Year One thousand eight hundred and eight shall in any Manner affect the first and fourth Clauses in the Ninth Section of the first Article; and that no State, without its Consent, shall be deprived of its equal Suffrage in the Senate.

ARTICLE VI

All Debts contracted and Engagements entered into, before the Adoption of this Constitution shall be as valid against the United States under this Constitution, as under the Confederation.

This Constitution, and the Laws of the United States which shall be made in Pursuance thereof; and all Treaties made, or which shall be made, under the Authority of the United States, shall be the supreme Law of the Land; and the Judges in every State shall be bound thereby, any Thing in the Constitution or Laws of any State to the Contrary notwithstanding.

The Senators and Representatives before mentioned, and the Members of the several State Legislatures, and all executive and judicial Officers, both of the United States and of the several States, shall be bound by Oath or Affirmation, to support this Constitution; but no religious Test shall ever be required as a Qualification to any Office or public Trust under the United States.

ARTICLE VII

The Ratification of the Conventions of nine States shall be sufficient for the Establishment of this Constitution between the States so ratifying the Same.

ARTICLES IN ADDITION TO, AND AMENDMENT OF, THE CONSTITUTION OF THE UNITED STATES OF AMERICA, PROPOSED BY CONGRESS AND RATIFIED BY THE SEVERAL STATES, PURSUANT TO THE FIFTH ARTICLE OF THE ORIGINAL CONSTITUTION

AMENDMENT I

Congress shall make no law respecting an establishment of religion, or prohibiting the free exercise thereof; or abridging the freedom of speech, or of the press; or the right of the people peaceably to assemble, and to petition the Government for a redress of grievances.

AMENDMENT II

A well regulated Militia, being necessary to the security of a free State, the right of the people to keep and bear Arms, shall not be infringed.

AMENDMENT III

No Soldier shall, in time of peace be quartered in any house, without the consent of the Owner, nor in time of war, but in a manner to be prescribed by law.

AMENDMENT IV

The right of the people to be secure in their persons, houses, papers, and effects, against unreasonable searches and seizures, shall not be violated, and no Warrants shall issue, but upon probable cause, supported by Oath or affirmation, and particularly describing the place to be searched, and the persons or things to be seized.

AMENDMENT V

No person shall be held to answer for a capital, or otherwise infamous crime, unless on a presentment or indictment of a Grand Jury, except in cases arising in the land or naval forces, or in the Militia, when in actual service in time of War or public danger; nor shall any person be subject for the same offence to be twice put in jeopardy of life or limb; nor shall be compelled in any criminal case to be a witness against himself, nor be deprived of life, liberty, or property, without due process of law; nor shall private property be taken for public use, without just compensation.

AMENDMENT VI

In all criminal prosecutions, the accused shall enjoy the right to a speedy and public trial, by an impartial jury of the State and district wherein the crime shall have been committed, which district shall have been previously ascertained by law, and to be informed of the nature and cause of the accusation; to be confronted with the witnesses against him; to have compulsory process for obtaining witnesses in his favor, and to have the Assistance of Counsel for his defence.

AMENDMENT VII

In suits at common law, where the value in controversy shall exceed twenty dollars, the right of trial by jury shall be preserved, and no fact tried by jury, shall be otherwise re-examined in any Court of the United States, than according to the rules of the common law.

AMENDMENT VIII

Excessive bail shall not be required, nor excessive fines imposed, nor cruel and unusual punishments inflicted.

AMENDMENT IX

The enumeration in the Constitution, of certain rights, shall not be construed to deny or disparage others retained by the people.

AMENDMENT X

The powers not delegated to the United States by the Constitution, nor prohibited by it to the States, are reserved to the States respectively, or to the people.

AMENDMENT XI [1798]

The Judicial power of the United States shall not be construed to extend to any suit in law or equity, commenced or prosecuted against one of the United States by Citizens of another State, or by Citizens or Subjects of any Foreign State.

AMENDMENT XII [1804]

The electors shall meet in their respective states and vote by ballot for President and Vice-President, one of whom, at least, shall not be an inhabitant of the same state with themselves; they shall name in their ballots the person voted for as President, and in distinct ballots the person voted for as Vice-President, and they shall make distinct lists of all persons voted for as President, and of all persons voted for as Vice-President, and of the number of votes for each, which lists they shall sign and certify, and transmit sealed to the seat of the government of the United States, directed to the President of the Senate;—The President of the Senate shall, in presence of the Senate and House of Representatives, open all the certificates and the votes shall then be counted;—The person having the greatest number of votes for President, shall be the President, if such number be a majority of the whole number of Electors appointed; and if no person have such majority, then from the persons having the highest numbers not exceeding three on the list of those voted for as President, the House of Representatives shall choose immediately, by ballot, the President. But in choosing the President, the votes shall be taken by states, the representation from each state having one vote; a quorum for this purpose shall consist of a member or members from two-thirds of the states, and a majority of all the states shall be necessary to a choice. And if the House of Representatives shall not choose a President whenever the right of choice shall devolve upon them, before the fourth day of March next following, then the Vice-President shall act as President, as in the case of the death or other constitutional disability of the President.—The person having the greatest number of votes as Vice-President, shall be the Vice-President, if such number be a majority of the whole number of Electors appointed, and if no person have a majority, then from the two highest numbers on the list, the Senate shall choose the Vice-President; a quorum for the purpose shall consist of two-thirds of the whole number of Senators, and a majority of the whole number shall be necessary to a choice. But no person constitutionally ineligible to the office of President shall be eligible to that of Vice-President of the United States.

AMENDMENT XIII [1865]

SECTION 1. Neither slavery nor involuntary servitude, except as a punishment for crime whereof the party shall have been duly convicted, shall exist within the United States, or any place subject to their jurisdiction.

SECTION 2. Congress shall have power to enforce this article by appropriate legislation.

AMENDMENT XIV [1868]

SECTION 1. All persons born or naturalized in the United States, and subject to the jurisdiction thereof, are citizens of the United States and of the State wherein they reside. No State shall make or enforce any law which shall abridge the privileges or immunities of citizens of the United States; nor shall any State deprive any person of life, liberty, or property, without due process of law; nor deny to any person within its jurisdiction the equal protection of the laws.

SECTION 2. Representatives shall be apportioned among the several States according to their respective numbers, counting the whole number of persons in each State, excluding Indians not taxed. But when the right to vote at any election for the choice of electors for President and Vice President of the United States, Representatives in Congress, the Executive and Judicial officers of a State, or the members of the Legislature thereof, is denied to any of the male inhabitants of such State, being twenty-one years of age, and citizens of the United States, or in any way abridged, except for participation in rebellion, or other crime, the basis of representation therein shall be reduced in the proportion which the number of such male citizens shall bear to the whole number of male citizens twenty-one years of age in such State.

SECTION 3. No person shall be a Senator or Representative in Congress, or elector of President and Vice President, or hold any office, civil or military, under the United States, or under any State, who, having previously taken an oath, as a member of Congress, or as an officer of the United States, or as a member of any State legislature, or as an executive or judicial officer of any State, to support the Constitution of the United States, shall have engaged in insurrection or rebellion against the same, or given aid or comfort to the enemies thereof. But Congress may by a vote of two-thirds of each House, remove such disability.

SECTION 4. The validity of the public debt of the United States, authorized by law, including debts incurred for payment of pensions and bounties for services in suppressing insurrection or rebellion, shall not be questioned. But neither the United States nor any State shall assume or pay any debt or obligation incurred in aid of insurrection or rebellion against the United States, or any claim for the loss or emancipation of any slave; but all such debts, obligations and claims shall be held illegal and void.

SECTION 5. The Congress shall have power to enforce, by appropriate legislation, the provisions of this article.

AMENDMENT XV [1870]

Section 1. The right of citizens of the United States to vote shall not be denied or abridged by the United States or by any State on account of race, color, or previous condition of servitude.

Section 2. The Congress shall have power to enforce this article by appropriate legislation.

Bibliographical Essay

General

The primary sources of constitutional history are mostly public documents. Archival materials are ancillary and do not occupy the central place that they do in the best political history.

The Constitutions themselves of nation and states have been reprinted with painstaking care and completeness by Francis N. Thorpe: *The Federal and State Constitutions* (Washington, 1909) in seven volumes paginated consecutively from first volume to last.

Legislative material consists of statutes and codes; records; and working and documentary papers of the federal Congress and the state legislatures. Federal statutes from the period of this book are published in a compilation known as *Statutes at Large*. The conventional form of legal citation is to: date of enactment or popular name, followed by chapter (which is simply the numerical designation of the act in the biennium's series), followed by references to sections, if appropriate, and concluding with the volume and page in *Statutes at Large* where the statute begins. For example, the Kansas-Nebraska Act of 1854 can be cited either by that popular title or as Act of May 30, 1854, ch. 59, 10 Stat. 277. Toward the end of the period of this study, Congress authorized the compilation and codification of all federal laws enacted before 1873; this was published as the *Revised Statutes*.

The collections of state statutes are more various. Each biennium of a state legislature publishes its statutory work-product, both public and private laws, in a biennial publication that is known as the Session Laws. These are customarily simply cited, e.g.: Laws of Maine 1846, ch. 34; usually any more bibliographic data would be superfluous and pedantic. States too authorized codifications and compilations, usually called the Revised Statutes.

Records of legislative bodies consist of the *Journals* of the houses, recording motions and votes. We have not had occasion to make use of these here.

Legislative documents at the federal level are an invaluable primary source, and are commonly referred to as the "Serials Set" by librarians. They consist of Reports, Executive Documents, and Miscellaneous papers that both houses of Congress have ordered published. These contain a wealth of constitutional material. They are customarily cited by the category of document (e.g., House Executive Documents), Congress and session, date of document if any, and two numbers, the series number and document number, that enable the user to find the document in the Serials Set.

Congressional debates were taken down by shorthand reporters and reported verbatim by private publishers before 1873. We have used two reports herein: *Congressional Globe,* published between 1833 and 1873, when it was superseded by the official report that continues to this day, *Congressional Record.* The *Globe* and *Record* often contain useful documentary material besides debates: copies of bills, inserted newspaper articles, etc. They are organized by Congress and session; and within each volume by day, and within day by Senate and House. Thus the debates on the Kansas-Nebraska Act are found in the relevant volumes (including the Appendix volume) of *Congressional Globe,* 33 Cong., 1 sess., for January–May 1854. A particular quotation is cited to the page and date. Unfortunately, no comparable reporting service exists for the state legislatures of the period, though important debates would often be covered in newspapers. The *National Intelligencer,* though published mostly at Baltimore, offered selective nationwide coverage; among the states, Thomas Ritchie's Richmond *Inquirer* covered the Virginia legislature nicely.

Primary sources from the executive branch include messages of the chief executives and reports of executive departments. We have used both at the federal level in this study. The Presidents' official messages were collected by James D. Richardson: *A Compilation of the Messages and Papers of the Presidents* (New York, 1897–1917). Some correspondence and other unofficial papers of the presidents are available in the Presidential Papers microfilm series available from the Library of Congress. Some Presidents' papers have been published; the most important for us in this study was Roy P. Basler (ed.), *The Collected Works of Abraham Lincoln* (New Brunswick, N.J., 1953–55). Of the executive departments, the most frequently used by constitutional historians are the *Official Opinions of the [United States] Attorneys-General,* published by the federal government and cited by volume and page, thus: 9 Op. A.G. 64.

The primary sources of the judicial branch consist almost entirely of the published reports of appellate decisions. Occasionally, however, the private papers of the justices contain revealing material; the Roger B. Taney Papers at the Library of Congress are rewarding, as are the Salmon P. Chase Papers at the Library of Congress and the Historical Society of Pennsylvania. But for the most part, the documentary sources are the case reports. In the post–Civil War period, cases are cited to the official reports, by case name. Thus, for the United States Supreme Court, e.g.: Plessy v. Ferguson, 163 U.S. 537 (1896), meaning that the report of the case, decided in 1896, may be found at volume 163, page 537 of the *United States Reports*. The report includes the majority, concurring, and dissenting opinions, together with headnotes, which were usually prepared by the court reporter, which are occasionally erroneous or misleading, and which are never an adequate substitute for reading the opinions themselves. State reports in the modern period are cited similarly; thus: Lemmon v. The People, 20 N.Y. 562 (1860).

But a problem arises with the citation of reports of both national and state supreme courts before the war, which requires a word of explanation here for the lay reader. These reports are cited by the name of the individual reporter, with the official volume number, if any, added parenthetically. In the period covered by this study, the reporters of the United States Supreme Court (with the customary abbreviation of their names) were: Richard Peters (Pet.); Benjamin Howard (How.); and John William Wallace (Wall.). Thus a citation to their reports would be: Luther v. Borden, 7 How. (48 U.S.) 1 (1849). The state supreme courts were similarly reported and cited; a listing of all the states' reporters (plus Commonwealth and federal) is in an appendix to *Black's Law Dictionary*, fifth edition.

In addition to the official reports of the United States Supreme Court, two privately published sets of reports duplicate the official ones: *Supreme Court* and *Lawyers' Edition*. The latter, L.Ed., contains much useful data not found in the official reports, such as the exact date of decision and more extensive summaries (in some cases, verbatim reports) of attorneys' arguments. We have occasionally used it here; it is cited by its own set of volume and page numbers, thus: 10 L.Ed. 567.

The decisions of the lower federal courts (United States district courts and United States circuit courts) were not contemporaneously published before 1880. But you will find lower court opinions before that date published in a collection called *Federal Cases* (cited Fed. Cas.), where they are reprinted alphabetically without distinction of court. Such cases are cited by name, volume and page of Fed. Cas., the identifying number assigned by the publisher, and the court and date. Thus: U.S. ex rel. Garland v. Morris, 26 Fed. Cas. 1318 (No. 15811) (D.C.D. Wis., 1854), meaning that

536 BIBLIOGRAPHICAL ESSAY

it can be found at volume 26 of Fed. Cas. at page 1318, and is a published opinion of the United States District Court for the District of Wisconsin handed down in 1854.

Several compilations of primary sources are available for this era. The most generally useful is Henry Steele Commager's judicious, copious *Documents of American History,* 9th ed. (Englewood Cliffs, 1973), which, though it includes documentary material from all areas of American history, is particularly rich in constitutional history. Three documentary collections are limited to constitutional history: James M. Smith and Paul L. Murphy (eds.), *Liberty and Justice* (New York, 1965), a two-volume selection that is regrettably now out of print; Donald O. Dewey (ed.), *Union and Liberty: A Documentary History of American Constitutionalism* (New York, 1969); and Stanley I. Kutler (ed.), *The Supreme Court and the Constitution: Readings in American Constitutional History* (New York, 1977), which, as its title indicates, consists of excerpts of opinions of the High Court. Three constitutional casebooks are useful: Gerald Gunther, *Cases and Materials on Constitutional Law* (Mineola, 1975); Paul A. Freund et al., *Constitutional Law: Cases and Other Problems,* 4th ed. (Boston, 1977); and William B. Lockhart et al., *Constitutional Law: Cases, Comments, Questions* (St. Paul, 1975). Stephen B. Presser and Jamil S. Zainaldin's recently published *Law and American History: Cases and Materials* (St. Paul, 1980) contains constitutional materials.

Two valuable collections of legal-constitutional materials are limited to the antebellum era: Perry Miller (ed.), *The Legal Mind in America, From Independence to the Civil War* (Ithaca, 1962); and Charles M. Haar, *The Golden Age of American Law* (New York, 1965). The period is dominated by two giants: Joseph Story, *Commentaries on the Constitution of the United States,* 1st ed. (Boston, 1833) and James Kent, *Commentaries on American Law,* 1st ed. (New York, 1826–30). For the latter part of the period of this study, Thomas M. Cooley's *A Treatise on the Constitutional Limitations Which Rest Upon the Legislative Power of the States* (New York, 1868) is equally valuable.

Constitutional history is one of the classical fields of American historical scholarship. Its long and honorable tradition began after the Civil War with the publication of Herman E. von Holst's magisterial, dogmatic *Constitutional and Political History of the United States* in seven volumes (Chicago, 1877–92). This tradition produced giants whose work has never been entirely superseded. It includes John W. Burgess, Edward S. Corwin, Howard J. Graham, Homer C. Hockett, Leonard Levy, Andrew C. McLaughlin, Alpheus T. Mason, Allan Nevins, Herman Pritchett, James G. Randall, James Schouler, Carl B. Swisher, James N. Thorpe, William W. Willoughby, and Benjamin F. Wright. The body of Corwin's long lifetime of constitutional scholarship is itself a small library of indispensable studies. His *The Constitution and What It Means Today,* 13th ed. (Princeton, 1973) is an especially useful commentary on the documentary Constitution, though the only grist for its mill consists of cases of the United States Supreme Court. The last in this line of magisterial scholarship is Alfred H. Kelly and Winfred A. Harbison's *The American Constitution: Its Origins and Development*, 5th ed. (New York, 1976), currently being updated (since its senior author's untimely death) by Herman Belz. Lawrence Friedman, *A History of American Law* (New York, 1973), contains much constitutional material. Harry Scheiber, "American Constitutional History and the New Legal History," *Journal of American History*, LXVII (1981), 337, discusses the conjunction of both approaches.

Four scholarly aids will prove useful to the student of nineteenth-century constitutional history: Morris L. Cohen, *How to Find the Law*, 7th ed. (St. Paul, 1976); *Black's Law Dictionary*, 5th ed. (St. Paul, 1979); Stephen M. Millett (comp.), *A Selected Bibliography of American Constitutional History* (Santa Barbara, 1975); and Alpheus T. Mason and D. Grier Stephenson (comps.), *American Constitutional Development* (Arlington Heights, Ill., 1977), one of the most valuable of the Goldentree Bibliographies in American history.

Chapter 1: The Democratic Constitution

Alexis de Tocqueville's *Democracy in America,* in the elegant Henry Reeve translation (1835, reprinted New York, 1945), remains the classic introduction to American democracy, but it should not be read uncritically. Democracy emerged from the popular sovereignty foundations of republican ideology. The best survey of the origins of that ideology is Gordon Wood's *The Creation of the American Republic* (Chapel Hill, 1969), especially full and sensitive on questions of popular sovereignty. The meaning and direction of popular sovereignty after a generation under the federal Constitution were worked out in three epochal constitutional conventions of the 1820s in New York, Massachusetts, and Virginia. Merrill Peterson supplies generous excerpts of these concon debates in his *Democracy, Liberty, and Property: The State Constitutional Conventions of the 1820s* (Indianapolis, 1966), together with a graceful interpretation. Fletcher M. Green, *Constitutional Development in the South Atlantic States, 1776–1860* (1930, reprinted New York, 1966), surveys constitutional trends from Maryland through Georgia, but does not give sufficient attention to slavery as a constitutional issue.

One of the great crises of popular sovereignty occurred in the Dorr Rebellion of 1842 in Rhode Island, an event that one scholar, George Dennison, sees as a climacteric in republican theory. For three differing interpretations of the Rebellion and its constitutional dynamic, see: Marvin E. Gettleman, *The Dorr Rebellion: A Study in American Radicalism, 1833–1849* (New York, 1973); George M. Dennison, *The Dorr War: Republicanism on*

Trial, 1831–1861 (Lexington, Ky., 1976); and two articles by William M. Wiecek that view the Rebellion from the perspective of the conservatives: " 'A Peculiar Conservatism' and the Dorr Rebellion: Constitutional Clash in Jacksonian America," *American Journal of Legal History,* XXII (1978), 237–253; and "Popular Sovereignty in the Dorr War: Conservative Counterblast," *Rhode Island History,* XXXII (1973), 35–51.

The meaning of popular sovereignty was also explored and extended in the vigilante movements of the era. Tracing their origins back to the Regulator movements in the Carolinas of the Revolutionary era, antebellum vigilante movements represented not a cancer of democracy but rather its expectable manifestation in an era of minimal government. For introductions, see Richard M. Brown, "Legal and Behavioral Perspectives on American Vigilantism," in Donald Fleming and Bernard Bailyn (eds.), *Law In American History* (vol. 5 of *Perspectives in American History*) (Cambridge, Mass., 1971), and the same author's "The American Vigilante Tradition," in Hugh D. Graham and Ted R. Gurr (eds.), *The History of Violence in America: Historical and Comparative Perspectives* (New York, 1969). See also the more specialized study by Leonard L. Richards, *"Gentlemen of Property and Standing": Anti-Abolition Mobs in Jacksonian America* (New York, 1970).

The nature of Jacksonian Democracy has long been sharply debated by scholars and others. The issues and party divisions of the era display a curious ability to stir passions as strongly today as they did in their own times. Only one of those issues is directly relevant to this study: the attitude of Jacksonian Democrats toward slavery, black people, and abolitionists, a pervasive concern that colored their views toward everything else. A neo-Jacksonian defense of the Democracy's position on these three interrelated subjects is John M. McFaul, "Expediency vs. Morality: Jacksonian Politics and Slavery," *Journal of American History,* LXII (1975), 24–39, who argues that the Jacksonians' foremost value was the Union; that they saw slavery and abolition as threatening the Union and therefore tried to suppress the issues; and that they were not so much opposed to freedom for black people as determined to preserve the fundamental guarantor for freedom of whites, the constitutional, democratic order. Other scholars reject this view and see most Jacksonians, with only a handful of exceptions, as spontaneously, enthusiastically racist, antiabolitionist, and militantly proslavery. The most emphatic statement of this view is in Edward Pessen's survey/interpretation, *Jacksonian America: Society, Personality, and Politics,* rev. ed. (Homewood, Ill., 1978). See also Leonard L. Richards, "The Jacksonians and Slavery," in Lewis Perry and Michael Fellman (eds.), *Antislavery Reconsidered: New Perspectives on the Abolitionists* (Baton Rouge, 1979), pp. 99–118. The proslavery reorientation of the Democracy in the second party system was first suggested by Richard H. Brown, "The Missouri Crisis, Slavery, and the

Politics of Jacksonianism," *South Atlantic Quarterly,* LXV (1966), 55–72.

On the Union and challenges to it, consult Paul C. Nagel, *One Nation Indivisible: The Union in American Thought, 1776–1861* (New York, 1964). Nullification is admirably surveyed by William W. Freehling, *Prelude to Civil War: The Nullification Controversy in South Carolina, 1816–1836* (New York, 1966). Calhoun's constitutional thought is surveyed with admirable brevity in Richard N. Current's little intellectual sketch, *John C. Calhoun* (New York, 1963).

On the impact of slavery itself on constitutional development, two older studies made solid beginnings at explicating a topic that still awaits full development: William S. Jenkins, *Pro-Slavery Thought in the Old South* (Chapel Hill, 1935), and Jesse T. Carpenter, *The South as a Conscious Minority* (New York, 1930). The controversies stirred by the abolitionists have, on the other hand, gotten a fuller airing lately. For all its tendentiousness, Dwight L. Dumond's massive neo-abolitionist *Antislavery: The Crusade for Freedom in America* (Ann Arbor, 1961) set a standard for thoroughness and passion that will keep it the starting point for all subsequent investigations of the anti-slavery movement, particularly in its constitutional aspects. The Jenkins, Carpenter, and Dumond books have that quality rare in historical studies of not becoming dated, of always speaking freshly to each generation, of not being buried and forgotten by later revisionism. One example of a study that used Dumond as its starting point, truly a book that stands on the shoulders of a giant, is William M. Wiecek, *The Sources of Antislavery Constitutionalism in America, 1760–1848* (Ithaca, 1977), a synoptic survey of the early period of abolitionist constitutional argumentation. For the later period of the slavery controversy, two superb studies fill the landscape of constitutional history with light: Arthur Bestor, "State Sovereignty and Slavery: A Reinterpretation of Proslavery Constitutional Doctrine, 1846–1860," *Journal of the Illinois State Historical Society,* LIV (1961), 117–180, and the body of Howard Jay Graham's work collected in his *Everyman's Constitution: Historical Essays on the Fourteenth Amendment, the "Conspiracy Theory," and American Constitutionalism* (Madison, 1968).

Chapter 2: The Public Law

All histories of the law in America contain extensive material on public law. General histories include: Lawrence M. Friedman, *A History of American Law* (New York, 1973); Bernard Schwartz, *The Law in America: A History* (New York, 1974); Frederick G. Kempin, *Historical Introduction to Anglo-American Law,* 2nd ed. (St. Paul, 1973); Grant Gilmore, *The Ages of American Law* (New Haven, 1977); J. Willard Hurst, *The Growth of American Law: The Law-Makers* (Boston, 1950); Spencer L. Kimball, *Historical Introduction to the*

Legal System (St. Paul, 1966), a casebook; Presser and Zainaldin, *Law and American History* (mentioned above); two studies by Charles Warren, *A History of the American Bar* (Boston, 1913) and *A History of the Harvard Law School* (Boston, 1908). Two collections of essays are especially rich in historical materials: American Association of Law Schools, *Selected Essays on Constitutional Law* (4 vols., Chicago, 1938), and the more recent Lawrence M. Friedman and Harry N. Scheiber (eds.), *American Law and the Constitutional Order: Historical Perspectives* (Cambridge, Mass., 1978).

Legal histories limited to the nineteenth century include: J. Willard Hurst, *Law and the Conditions of Freedom in the Nineteenth-Century United States* (Madison, 1956); Perry Miller, *The Life of the Mind in America: From Independence to the Civil War* (New York, 1965) (its second part deals with the legal profession); Morton J. Horwitz, *The Transformation of American Law, 1780–1860* (Cambridge, Mass., 1977), winner of the Bancroft Prize; Jamil S. Zainaldin, *Law in Antebellum Society,* and Jonathan Lurie, *Law and the Nation: 1865–1910,* both published under the auspices of the American Bar Association's Commission on Undergraduate Education in Law and the Humanities in 1980; William E. Nelson, *Americanization of the Common Law: The Impact of Legal Change on Massachusetts Society, 1760–1830* (Cambridge, Mass., 1975); Wythe Holt (ed.), *Essays in Nineteenth-Century American Legal History* (Westport, Conn., 1976), a collection of essays; Maxwell Bloomfield, *American Lawyers in a Changing Society, 1776–1876* (Cambridge, Mass., 1976); Charles M. Haar (ed.), *The Golden Age of American Law* (New York, 1965), a collection of primary sources; Roscoe Pound, *The Formative Era of American Law* (Boston, 1938); and Leonard W. Levy, *The Law of the Commonwealth and Chief Justice Shaw* (Cambridge, Mass., 1957).

On higher law, see Edward S. Corwin's seminal works: *Liberty Against Government: The Rise, Flowering and Decline of a Famous Juridical Concept* (Baton Rouge, 1948), ch. 3, "Liberty into Property Before the Civil War," and "The Basic Doctrine of American Constitutional Law," *Michigan Law Review,* XII (1914), 247–276. See also William B. Scott, *In Pursuit of Happiness: American Conceptions of Property from the Seventeenth to the Twentieth Century* (Bloomington, Ind., 1977), and Harry N. Scheiber, "The Road to Munn: Eminent Domain and the Concept of Public Purpose in the State Courts," in Fleming and Bailyn, *Law in American History,* pp. 329–402.

The emergence of the private, profitmaking business corporation is treated in Edwin M. Dodd, *American Business Corporations Until 1860* (Cambridge, Mass., 1954). For the experience of two states with the new entity, see John W. Cadman, *The Corporation in New Jersey: Business and Politics, 1791–1875* (Cambridge, Mass., 1949), and George J. Kuehnl, *The Wisconsin Business Corporation* (Madison, 1959).

G. Edward White provides an admirable view of the historical evolution of torts in *Tort Law in America: An Intellectual History* (New York, 1980). Charles O. Gregory's article "Trespass to Negligence to Absolute Liability," *Virginia Law Review*, XXXVII (1951), 359–397, remains valuable. Grant Gilmore sketches the history of contract law in America in his provocative and much-attacked *The Death of Contract* (Columbus, 1974). For brief sketches of contract's evolution, see Friedrich Kessler and Grant Gilmore, *Contracts: Cases and Materials*, 2nd ed. (Boston, 1970), pp. 25–35, and Kempin, *Historical Introduction to Anglo-American Law*, pp. 190–209. See also Lawrence M. Friedman, *Contract Law in America* (Madison, 1965).

Many scholars have traced the profound effect of the Transportation Revolution on the law, including: Robert S. Hunt, *Law and Locomotives: The Impact of the Railroad on Wisconsin Law in the Nineteenth Century* (Madison, 1958); Harry N. Scheiber, *Ohio Canal Era: A Case Study of Government and the Economy, 1820–1861* (Athens, Ohio, 1969); Lee Benson, *Merchants, Farmers, and Railroads: Railroad Regulation and New York Politics, 1850–1887* (Cambridge, Mass., 1955); Edward C. Kirkland, *Men, Cities and Transportation: A Study in New England History, 1820–1900* (Cambridge, Mass., 1948); Carter Goodrich, *Government Promotion of American Canals and Railroads, 1800–1890* (New York, 1960); Louis Hartz, *Economic Policy and Democratic Thought: Pennsylvania, 1776–1860* (Cambridge, Mass., 1948).

For the evolution of American criminal law, see Samuel Walker, *Popular Justice: A History of American Criminal Justice* (New York, 1980). On the death penalty: David Brion Davis, "The Movement to Abolish Capital Punishment in America, 1787–1861," *American Historical Review*, LXIII (1957), 23–46. Eleanor Flexner includes law-related material in her *Century of Struggle: The Woman's Rights Movement in the United States* (Cambridge, Mass., 1975).

Chapter 3: The Taney Court

The achievements of the Taney Court are evaluated in all surveys of the entire history of the United States Supreme Court. For lists of these, consult the Millett and Mason/Stephenson bibliographies cited at the beginning of this bibliographic note. Studies of the Taney Court in particular are: Carl B. Swisher, *The Taney Period: 1836–64* (vol. 5 of the Holmes Devise *History of the Supreme Court of the United States*) (New York, 1974); Charles G. Haines and Foster H. Sherwood, *The Role of the Supreme Court in American Government and Politics, 1835–1864* (Berkeley, 1957); Charles Warren, *The Supreme Court in United States History* (Boston, 1922); and Kent Newmyer, *The Supreme Court Under Marshall and Taney* (New York, 1968).

Biographical studies provide some insight into the workings of the Court. Chief Justice Taney: Carl B. Swisher, *Roger B. Taney* (New York, 1936);

Swisher, "Mr. Chief Justice Taney," in Allison Dunham and Philip B. Kurland (eds.), *Mr. Justice* (Chicago, 1964); Walker Lewis, *Without Fear or Favor: Chief Justice Roger Brooke Taney* (Boston, 1965); Robert J. Harris, "Chief Justice Taney: Prophet of Reform and Reaction," *Vanderbilt Law Review,* X (1957), 227–257; Samuel Tyler, *Memoir of Roger Brooke Taney, LL.D.* (Baltimore, 1872). Justice Story: James McClellan, *Joseph Story and the American Constitution: A Study in Political and Legal Thought* (Norman, 1971), which sees Story as an archetypal conservative; Gerald T. Dunne, *Justice Joseph Story and the Rise of the Supreme Court* (New York, 1970); William W. Story, *Life and Letters of Joseph Story* (Boston, 1851); and William W. Story (ed.), *The Miscellaneous Writings of Joseph Story* (New York, 1852), which includes a brief autobiographical sketch. The others: Francis P. Weisenburger, *The Life of John McLean: A Politician on the United States Supreme Court* (Columbus, 1937); John P. Frank, *Justice Daniel Dissenting: A Biography of Peter V. Daniel, 1784–1860* (Cambridge, Mass., 1964), an exceptionally fine and sensitive study of a mind utterly alien to the modern era; Alexander A. Lawrence, *James Moore Wayne: Southern Unionist* (Chapel Hill, 1943); Benjamin R. Curtis, Jr., *A Memoir of Benjamin Robbins Curtis* (Boston, 1879).

For biographical sketches and brief evaluations of their judicial contributions, see the relevant entries in vols. I and II of Leon Friedman and Fred L. Israel (eds.), *The Justices of the United States Supreme Court, 1789–1969: Their Lives and Major Opinions* (New York, 1969). Gerald T. Dunne contributed the articles on Story and Thompson; Frank Otto Gatell those on Taney, McLean, Baldwin, Barbour, Daniel, Wayne, McKinley, Catron, Nelson, Grier, and Woodbury; William Gillette those on Curtis, Clifford, and Campbell. All entries have good bibliographic references.

On particular topics see: Stanley I. Kutler, *Privilege and Creative Destruction: The Charles River Bridge Case* (Philadelphia, 1971), and Kent Newmyer, "Justice Joseph Story, the Charles River Bridge Case, and the Crisis of Republicanism," *American Journal of Legal History,* XVII (1973), 232–245; Felix Frankfurter, *The Commerce Clause under Marshall, Taney, and Waite* (Chapel Hill, 1937); Gerard G. Henderson, *The Position of Foreign Corporations in American Constitutional Law* (Cambridge, Mass., 1918), on Bank of Augusta *v.* Earle; Maurice G. Baxter, *Daniel Webster and the Supreme Court* (Amherst, 1966); William M. Wiecek, *The Guarantee Clause of the U.S. Constitution* (Ithaca, 1972), for the Dorr Rebellion, Luther *v.* Borden, political questions, and slavery.

Swift *v.* Tyson has provoked more controversy among scholars than any other decision of the Taney Court except *Dred Scott,* and there is no indication that the debate over its significance is likely to abate. See the following: Tony A. Freyer, *Forums of Order: The Federal Courts and Business in American History* (Greenwich, Conn., 1979); Charles A. Heckman, "The Relationship of Swift v. Tyson to the Status of Commercial Law in the Nineteenth Century and the Federal System," *American Journal of Legal History*, XVII (1973), 246–255; [Mark Tushnet], "Swift v. Tyson Exhumed," *Yale Law Journal*, LXXIX (1969), 284–310; Joseph McClellan, *Joseph Story and the American Constitution: A Study in Political and Legal Thought* (Norman, Okla., 1971), pp. 180–189; Horwitz, *Transformation of American Law*, pp. 245–252; Randall Bridwell, "Theme v. Reality in American Legal History," *Indiana Law Journal*, LIII (1978), 450–496 (critical of the Horwitz interpretation).

Chapter 4: The Nemesis of the Constitution

The literature on slavery's impact on the Constitution is extensive and of high quality. Two excellent surveys of the whole field are Dumond, *Antislavery*, discussed at the beginning of this bibliographic note, and Paul Finkelman's *An Imperfect Union: Slavery, Federalism, and Comity* (Chapel Hill, 1981), a valuable addition to the "Studies in Legal History" series. William M. Wiecek surveys slavery-related cases in the High Court in "Slavery and Abolition Before the United States Supreme Court, 1820–1860," *Journal of American History*, LXV (1978), 34–59.

For slavery's early constitutional impact, see William M. Wiecek, "The Statutory Law of Slavery and Race in the Thirteen Mainland Colonies of British America," *William and Mary Quarterly*, XXXIV (1977), 258–280; A. Leon Higginbotham, *In the Matter of Color: Race and the American Legal Process: The Colonial Period* (New York, 1978); David Brion Davis, *The Problem of Slavery in the Age of Revolution, 1770–1823* (Ithaca, 1975); Donald L. Robinson, *Slavery in the Structure of American Politics, 1765–1820* (New York, 1971); Howard A. Ohline, "Politics and Slavery: The Issue of Slavery in National Politics, 1787–1815" (Ph.D. diss., University of Missouri–Columbia, 1969); Ohline, "Republicanism and Slavery: Origins of the Three-Fifths Clause in the United States Constitution," *William and Mary Quarterly*, XXVIII (1971), 563–584; Wiecek, *Sources of Antislavery Constitutionalism*, mentioned above; Arthur Zilversmit, *The First Emancipation: The Abolition of Slavery in the North* (Chicago, 1967). Two studies provide indispensable intellectual background: Winthrop D. Jordan, *White Over Black: American Attitudes Toward the Negro, 1550–1812* (Chapel Hill, 1968), and George M. Frederickson, *The Black Image in the White Mind: The Debate on Afro-American Character and Destiny, 1817–1914* (New York, 1971).

Two collections of primary sources are especially valuable: Helen T. Catterall, *Judicial Cases Concerning American Slavery and the Negro* (Washington, 1926–36), and Richard Bardolph, *The Civil Rights Record: Black Americans and the Law, 1849–1970* (New York, 1970).

Abolitionists are beginning to receive their due. See Jacobus ten Broek,

Equal Under Law (New York, 1965); Howard Jay Graham, *Everyman's Constitution: Historical Essays on the Fourteenth Amendment, the "Conspiracy Theory," and American Constitutionalism* (Madison, 1968), and William E. Nelson, "The Impact of the Antislavery Movement Upon Styles of Judicial Reasoning in Nineteenth Century America," *Harvard Law Review*, LXXXVII (1974), 513–566. On moderates: Eric Foner, *Free Soil, Free Labor, Free Men: The Ideology of the Republican Party Before the Civil War* (New York, 1970), and Richard H. Sewell, *Ballots for Freedom: Antislavery Politics in the United States, 1837–1860* (New York, 1976). On Garrisonians: James B. Stewart, "The Aims and Impact of Garrisonian Abolitionism, 1840–1860," *Civil War History*, XV (1969), 197–209; Staughton Lynd, "The Abolitionist Critique of the United States Constitution," in Martin Duberman (ed.), *The Antislavery Vanguard: New Essays on the Abolitionists* (Princeton, 1965).

On highlights of the constitutional confrontations over slavery: Thomas D. Morris, *Free Men All: The Personal Liberty Laws of the North, 1780–1861* (Baltimore, 1974); Edmund Fuller, *Prudence Crandall: An Incident of Racism in Nineteenth-Century Connecticut* (Middletown, Conn., 1971); Robert Cover, *Justice Accused: Antislavery and the Judicial Process* (New Haven, 1975); Levy, *Law of the Commonwealth and Chief Justice Shaw*, chs. 5–7; John T. Noonan, Jr., *The Antelope: The Ordeal of the Recaptured Africans in the Administrations of James Monroe and John Quincy Adams* (Berkeley, 1977); Bertram Wyatt-Brown, *Lewis Tappan and the Evangelical War Against Slavery* (Cleveland, 1969), on the Amistad incident; Joseph C. Burke, "What Did the Prigg Decision Really Decide," *Pennsylvania Magazine of History and Biography*, XCIII (1896), 73–85; William M. Wiecek, "Latimer: Lawyers, Abolitionists, and the Problem of Unjust Laws," in Perry and Fellman, *Antislavery Reconsidered.*

Finally see two studies on the public and private law of slavery in the states: A. E. Kier Nash, "Reason of Slavery: Understanding the Judicial Role in the Peculiar Institution," *Vanderbilt Law Review*, XXXII (1979), 7–218 (the footnotes and to a great extent this book-length article itself are a survey of the literature), and Mark Tushnet, "The American Law of Slavery, 1810–1860: A Study in the Persistence of Legal Autonomy," *Law and Society Review*, X (1975), 119–184.

Chapter 5: Free Soil

Perhaps the most agreeable introduction to the issues of this period can be found in a spate of excellent biographies of principals of the era, particularly those opposed to slavery's expansion. Among the best are: Richard H. Sewell, *John P. Hale and the Politics of Abolition* (Cambridge, Mass., 1965); David H. Donald, *Charles Sumner and the Coming of the Civil War* (New York, 1960); Samuel F. Bemis, *John Quincy Adams and the Union* (New York, 1965),

BIBLIOGRAPHICAL ESSAY 545

and Adams's priceless diary, Charles Francis Adams (ed.), *Memoirs of John Quincy Adams, Comprising Portions of His Diary from 1795 to 1848* (Philadelphia, 1874–77); James B. Stewart, *Joshua R. Giddings and the Tactics of Radical Politics* (Cleveland, 1970); Frank Otto Gatell, *John Gorham Palfrey and the New England Conscience* (Cambridge, Mass., 1963); Henry Steele Commager, *Theodore Parker* (Boston, 1936); Irving H. Bartlett, *Wendell Phillips: Brahmin Radical* (Boston, 1961); and Charles G. Sellers's splendid political biography, *James K. Polk* (Princeton, 1957–66). The towering figure of Salmon P. Chase has yet to find his modern biographer, a strange omission considering the wealth of personal papers left by him and his associates.

Frederick Merk's study of *Slavery and the Annexation of Texas* (New York, 1972) is definitive and full of documents. The constitutional problems posed by the maneuverings preceding the war with Mexico are surveyed in their modern form in Anon., "Congress, the President, and the Power to Commit Forces to Combat," *Harvard Law Review*, LXXXI (1968), 1771–1805, and Francis D. Wormuth, "The Vietnam War: The President versus the Constitution," in Richard A. Falk (ed.), *The Vietnam War and International Law* (Princeton, 1969). The most recent interpretation of the Wilmot Proviso's political background is Eric Foner, "The Wilmot Proviso Revisited," *Journal of American History*, LVI (1969), 262–279. On the debated question of Negrophobia among Free-Soilers, see Eric Foner, "Politics and Prejudice: The Free Soil Party and the Negro, 1849–1852," *Journal of Negro History*, L (1965), 239–256; Frederick J. Blue, *The Free Soilers: Third Party Politics, 1848–54* (Urbana, 1973), and Eric Foner, "Racial Attitudes of New York Free Soilers," *New York History*, XLVI (1965), 311–329. See also Eugene H. Berwanger, *The Frontier Against Slavery: Western Anti-Negro Prejudice* (Urbana, 1967). Richard H. Sewell's excellent *Ballots for Freedom: Antislavery Politics in the United States, 1837–1860* (New York, 1976) is a definitive recent interpretation. But Joseph G. Rayback, *Free Soil: The Election of 1848* (Lexington, Ky., 1971), and Chaplain W. Morrison, *Democratic Politics and Sectionalism: The Wilmot Proviso Controversy* (Chapel Hill, 1967), also remain useful. Theodore Smith's *The Liberty and Free Soil Parties in the Northwest* (New York, 1897) continues to be surprisingly fresh, another of those rare studies that wears well over time.

So too with Milo M. Quaife, *The Doctrine of Non-Intervention with Slavery in the Territories* (Chicago, 1910), though Quaife's sense of the meaning of the term "nonintervention" differs from that herein. Robert R. Russel provides an updated survey of the controversy in "Constitutional Doctrines with Regard to Slavery in the Territories," *Journal of Southern History*, XXXII (1966), 466–468. For Congress's invitation to the Supreme Court to try its hand at the problem, see Wallace Mendelson, "Dred Scott's Case—Reconsidered," *Minnesota Law Review*, XXXVIII (1953), 16–28.

There are numerous accounts of the Crisis and Compromise of 1850. Four of the best are David M. Potter, *The Impending Crisis, 1848–1860* (New York, 1976), ch. 5, "The Armistice of 1850"; Michael F. Holt, *The Political Crisis of the 1850s* (New York, 1978), ch. 4, "Dynamics of the Party System and the Compromise of 1850"; Holman Hamilton, *Prologue to Conflict: The Crisis and Compromise of 1850* (Lexington, Ky., 1964); Allan Nevins, *Ordeal of the Union* (New York, 1947), I, 219–404.

On the constitutional aspects of the Fugitive Slave Acts and their enforcement see Stanley W. Campbell, *The Slave Catchers: Enforcement of the Fugitive Slave Law 1850–1860* (Chapel Hill, 1970), ch. 2, "The Constitutionality of the Fugitive Slave Law of 1850"; Dumond, *Antislavery: The Crusade for Freedom in America*, ch. 38, "Fugitive Slaves and the Law," and *passim;* Allen Johnson, "The Constitutionality of the Fugitive Slave Acts," *Yale Law Journal*, XXXI (1921), 161–182 (of little persuasive force today, and dubious even in its own time).

Chapter 6: The Crisis of the Union

Surveys of the period handle constitutional questions well. Three of the best are: Potter, *Impending Crisis*, chs. 7–15; Roy E. Nichols, *The Disruption of American Democracy* (New York, 1948); and Allan Nevins, *Ordeal of the Union: A House Dividing, 1852–1857* (New York, 1947).

On Kansas-Nebraska, in addition to the works above, see also Robert R. Russel, "The Issues in the Congressional Struggle over the Kansas-Nebraska Bill, 1854," *Journal of Southern History*, XXIX (1963), 187–210; Robert W. Johannsen, *Stephen A. Douglas* (New York, 1973), chs. 16–18; and Harry V. Jaffa, *Crisis of the House Divided: An Interpretation of the Issues of the Lincoln-Douglas Debates* (1959; reprint Seattle, 1973). The formation of the Republican party, the most significant consequence of Kansas-Nebraska, is surveyed in Eric Foner, *Free Soil, Free Labor, Free Men: The Ideology of the Republican Party before the Civil War* (New York, 1970), and Sewell, *Ballots for Freedom.*

Because of the case's importance, and the confusion of the issues, the scholarly literature on *Dred Scott* threatened to proliferate endlessly. Two excellent guides to the earlier writings are Thomas B. Alexander, "Historical Treatments of the Dred Scott Case," *Proceedings of the South Carolina Historical Association*, XXIII (1953), 37–59, and Frederick S. Allis, "The Dred Scott Labyrinth," in H. Stuart Hughes (ed.), *Teachers of History: Essays in Honor of Laurence Bradford Packard* (Ithaca, 1954). Stanley I. Kutler provides a judicious selection of documents in *The Dred Scott Decision: Law or Politics* (Boston, 1967), as well as a good bibliographic survey. Probably the only treatment of the case sympathetic to Taney that the modern reader will find persuasive is Carl Brent Swisher, *Roger B. Taney* (New York, 1936); Swisher, *Taney Period*, chs. 24 and 25, is less apologetic. But at last, two complementary studies provide what should prove to be, respectively, a definitive evaluation of Taney's performance and that of his colleagues, and a compendium of every detail of the case that could ever be relevant. They are: Don E. Fehrenbacher, *The Dred Scott Case: Its Significance in American Law and Politics* (New York, 1978), and Walter Ehrlich, *They Have No Rights: Dred Scott's Struggle for Freedom* (Westport, Conn., 1979). Finkelman, *An Imperfect Union*, is indispensable on the implications of the case. Bestor, "State Sovereignty and Slavery," places the case in the trajectory of the development of proslavery constitutional thought.

Chapter 7: Secession: The Union Destroyed

Emory Thomas surveys the movement toward secession and the experience of the Confederacy in *The Confederate Nation, 1861–1865* (New York, 1979). Ralph A. Wooster traces the process of secession state by state in *The Secession Conventions of the South* (Princeton, 1962). Studies of particular states include Steven A. Channing's *Crisis of Fear: Secession in South Carolina* (New York, 1970); William L. Barney, *The Secessionist Impulse: Alabama and Mississippi in 1860* (Princeton, 1974); and Michael B. Johnson, *Toward a Patriarchal Republic: The Secession of Georgia* (Baton Rouge, 1977). Dwight L. Dumond's older study, *The Secession Movement, 1860–61* (New York, 1931), remains useful.

Four books successfully capture the drama of secession winter: Allan Nevins, *The Emergence of Lincoln* (New York, 1950); David M. Potter, *Lincoln and His Party in the Secession Crisis* (1942; reprint New Haven, 1962); Kenneth M. Stampp, *And the War Came: The North and the Secession Crisis, 1860–61* (1950; reprint Chicago, 1964); and Bruce Catton, *The Coming Fury* (Garden City, 1961).

For the Old Gentlemen's Convention, see Robert G. Gunderson, *Old Gentlemen's Convention: The Washington Peace Conference of 1861* (Madison, 1961), and Jesse L. Keene, *The Peace Convention of 1861* (Tuscaloosa, 1961). Charles R. Lee surveys the Confederate provisional and permanent Constitutions in *The Confederate Constitutions* (Chapel Hill, 1963). On the Confederate judiciary, see J. G. de Roulhac Hamilton, "The State Courts and the Confederate Constitution," *Journal of Southern History*, IV (1938), 425–448.

Chapter 8: Reconstruction: The Union Preserved

Don E. Fehrenbacher's *The Changing Image of Lincoln in American Historiography* (Oxford, Eng., 1968), and Mark E. Neely, Jr., "The Lincoln Theme since Randall's Call: The Promises and Perils of Professionalism," Abraham Lincoln Association *Papers,* I (1979), 10–70, grapple with the mountain of "Lincoln and . . ." publications. Tensions between government survival and liberty are treated in James G. Randall's enduring *Constitutional Problems Under Lincoln* (rev. ed., Urbana, 1951); see also Harold M. Hyman, *A More Perfect Union: The Impact of the Civil War and Reconstruction* (New York, 1973), chs. 5, 8. On their subjects, see George F. Dennison, "Martial Law: The Development of a Theory of Emergency Powers, 1776–1861," *American Journal of Legal History,* XVIII (1974), 52–72; Morgan D. Dowd, "Lincoln, the Rule of Law and Crisis Goverment: A Study of His Constitutional Law Theories," *University of Detroit Law Journal,* XXXIX (1962), 633–649; Don E. Fehrenbacher, "Lincoln and the Constitution," in Cullom Davis (ed.), *The Public and Private Lincoln: Contemporary Perspectives* (Carbondale, 1979), pp. 121–166; James A. Rawley, "The Nationalism of Abraham Lincoln," *Civil War History,* IX (1963), 283–298.

Instrumentalism receives attention in Morton J. Horwitz, *The Transformation of American Law, 1780–1860* (Cambridge, 1977), ch. 1, and Harry N. Scheiber, "Instrumentalism and Property Rights: A Reconsideration of American Styles of Judicial Reasoning in the 19th Century," *Wisconsin Law Review* (1975), 1.

Phillip S. Paludan, "The American Civil War Considered as a Crisis in Law and Order," *American Historical Review,* LXXVII (1972), 1013–1034; Paludan, *A Covenant With Death: The Constitution, Law, and Equality in the Civil War Era* (Urbana, 1975); and Wilbert H. Ahern, "Laissez-faire vs. Equal Rights," *Phylon* (1979), 52–65, analyze tensions between liberty and order, and the Republicans' commitment to both federalism and civil rights, as expressed chiefly by legal writers. These themes are developed also by Herman Belz, *A New Birth of Freedom: The Republican Party and Freedmen's Rights, 1861–1866* (Westport, 1976); Arthur Bestor, "The American Civil War Considered as a Constitutional Crisis," *American Historical Review,* LXIX (1964), 327–352; Harry N. Scheiber, "American Federalism and the Diffusion of Power," *University of Toledo Law Review,* IX (1978), 619–680; Scheiber, "Federalism and Legal Process: Historical and Contemporary Analysis of the American System," *Law & Society Review,* XIV (1980), 663–722; Daniel Elazar, "The Civil War and the Preservation of Federalism," *Publius,* I (1970), 39–58. On political institutions, see Willmoore Kendall and George W. Carey, *The Basic Symbols of the American Political Tradition* (Baton Rouge, 1970); Eric L. McKitrick, "Party Politics and the Union and Confederate War Efforts," in W. D. Burnham and W. N. Chambers (eds.), *The American Party Systems: Stages of Political Development* (New York, 1967). Democrats' exploitations are detailed in Joel H. Silbey, *A Respectable Minority: The Democratic Party in the Civil War Era, 1860–1868* (New York, 1977), chs. 2–3. Habeas corpus history was enriched by William F. Duker's *A Constitutional History of Habeas Corpus* (Westport, 1980). Herman Belz, *Reconstructing the Union: Theory and Practice During the Civil War Era* (Ithaca, 1969), treats wartime Reconstruction efforts by both President and Congress. Patricia Allen Lucie, "Confiscation—Constitutional Crossroads," *Civil War History*, XXIII (1977), 304–322, is essential; see also John Syrett, "The Confiscation Acts: Efforts of Reconstruction during the Civil War" (Ph.D. diss., University of Wisconsin, 1971);

On their subjects, see Robert M. Spector, "Lincoln and Taney: A Study in Constitutional Polarization," *American Journal of Legal History*, XV (1971), 199–214; Eugene C. Murdock, *One Million Men: The Civil War Draft in the North* (Madison, 1971); Frank L. Klement, *The Limits of Dissent: Clement L. Vallandigham and the Civil War* (Lexington, 1970). Adrian Cook, *The Armies of the Streets: The New York City Draft Riots of 1863* (Lexington 1980), provides needed coverage. On Congress, see Donald G. Morgan, *Congress and the Constitution: A Study of Responsibility* (Cambridge, 1966). A full-fledged history of *a* Congress, if not of *the* Congress, is badly wanted.

William F. Messner's *Freedmen and the Ideology of Free Labor, 1862–1865* (Lafayette, 1978) complements William M. Wiecek, *The Guarantee Clause of the U.S. Constitution* (Ithaca, 1972). Military emancipation and related questions receive evaluation in Richard Hofstadter's essay on Lincoln in *The American Political Tradition* (New York, 1948); Jacques Voegeli, *Free But Not Equal: The Midwest and the Negro During the Civil War* (Chicago, 1967); Louis S. Gerteis, *From Contraband to Freedman, 1861–1865* (Westport, 1973); Mary Berry, *Military Necessity and Civil Rights Policy: Black Citizenship and the Constitution, 1861–1868* (Port Washington, 1977); Stephen Oates, " 'The Man of Our Redemption': Abraham Lincoln and the Emancipation of the Slaves," *Presidential Studies Quarterly*, IX (1979), 23.

Chapter 9: The Dominion of Well-Administered Law

Scholars including Benedict, Castel, Paludan, and Trefousse continue to differ on Andrew Johnson with respect to his purposes, policies, and constitutional perceptions, as is evident in titles cited in this and in the preceding chapter, as well as in several that follow. See also Eric L. McKitrick, *Andrew Johnson and Reconstruction* (Chicago, 1960); William R. Brock, *An American Crisis: Congress and Reconstruction, 1865–1867* (New York, 1963); James Sefton, *Andrew Johnson and the Uses of Constitutional Power* (Boston, 1980); LaWanda Cox and John H. Cox, *Politics, Principle, and Prejudice, 1865–1866: Dilemma of Reconstruction America* (New York, 1963); Michael Perman, *Reunion Without Compromise: The South and Reconstruction, 1865–1868* (Cambridge, Eng., 1973).

On the federal judiciary and Reconstruction, the several titles by Fairman, and by Patricia Allen, "Freedom and Federalism: Congress and Courts, 1861–1866" (Ph.D. diss., University of Glasgow, 1972); Stanley I. Kutler, *Judicial Power and Reconstruction Politics* (Chicago, 1968); William M. Wiecek, "The Reconstruction of Federal Judicial Power, 1863–1875," *American Journal of Legal History,* XIII (1969), 333–359; J. David Hoeveler, "Reconstruction and the Federal Courts: The Civil Rights Act of 1875," *The Historian,* XXXI (1969), 604–617, are essential.

For indicated themes, insight is afforded by William Miller, "Reconstruction as a Police Problem, 1865–1877" (Organization of American Historians paper, 1978); Michael Les Benedict, "Preserving the Constitution: The Conservative Basis of Radical Reconstruction," *Journal of American History,* LXI (1974), 65–90; James Oakes, "Failure of Vision: The Collapse of the Freedmen's Bureau Courts," *Civil War History,* XXV (1979), 66–76; Robert Horowitz, "Land to the Freedmen: A Vision of Reconstruction," *Ohio History,* LXXXVI (1977), 187–199. Mitchell Wendell, *Relations Between the Federal and State Courts* (New York, 1949), remains useful.

Some legal questions in this chapter are examined by Henry P. Weihofen, "Supreme Court Review of State Criminal Procedure," *American Journal of Legal History,* X (1966), 189–200; and W. G. Carleton, "Cultural Roots of American Law Enforcement," *Current History,* LIII (1967), 1–49. Legal-constitutional interactions are discussed further in the bibliographical sources for ch. 10.

Chapter 10: A Reconstruction of Law and of Judicial Review, 1863–1867

Fairman's, Keller's, Kutler's, and White's works, among others cited in footnotes, are basic for questions in this chapter. See also the relevant biographical essays in Friedman and Israel, *The Justices of the United States Supreme Court,* II; Maxwell Bloomfield, *American Lawyers in a Changing Society, 1776–1876* (Cambridge, 1976); Harold Hollingsworth, "The Confirmation of Judicial Review Under Taney and Chase" (Ph.D. diss., University of Tennessee, 1966); Robert V. Bruce, "Universities and the Rise of the Professions: Nineteenth Century Americanists" (Organization of Ameican Historians paper, 1970); Morton Horwitz, *The Transformation of American Law, 1780–1860* (Cambridge, 1977); James Willard Hurst, *Law and the Conditions of Freedom in the Nineteenth Century United States* (Madison, 1956), and Hurst, *The Growth of American Law: The Law Makers* (Boston, 1950); Sanford Levinson, "The Constitution in American Civil Religion," *Supreme Court Review* (1979), 123–151; Benjamin Schwarz, "Old Wine in New Bottles? The Renaissance of the Contract Clause," *Supreme Court Review* (1979),

95–121; Harry N. Scheiber, "Property Law, Expropriation, and Resource Allocation by Government: The United States, 1789–1910," *Journal of Economic History,* III (1973), 232–251 (recently reevaluated in M. H. Cersonsky, "Setting the Record Straight: Eminent Domain and the Concept of Public Use in Late Nineteenth Century America" [M.A. thesis, Rice University, 1980]). John W. Johnson, "Retreat from the Common Law? The Grudging Reception of Legislative History by American Appellate Courts in the Early Twentieth Century," *Detroit College of Law Review* (1978), 413–431, is perceptive for the nineteenth century as well. James E. Herget's "The Missing Power of Local Governments: A Divergence Between Text and Practice in Our Early State Constitutions," *Virginia Law Review,* LXIII (1976), 999–1015, and his "The Impact of the Fourteenth Amendment on the Structure of Metropolitan and Regional Governments," *Hastings Law Journal,* XXIII (1972), 763–790, are thoughtful on an ignored theme. More generally, see Clyde E. Jacobs, *Law Writers and the Courts: The Influence of Thomas M. Cooley, Christopher G. Tiedeman, and John F. Dillon Upon Ameican Constitutional Law* (Berkeley, 1954); Alan Jones, "Thomas M. Cooley and 'Laissez-Faire Constitutionalism': A Reconsideration," *Journal of American History,* LIII (1967), 751–771.

West Virginia's role is noted in V. A. Lewis, "How West Virginia Became a Member of the Federal Union," *West Virginia History,* XXX (1969), 598–606. Erwin Surrency, "The Legal Effects of the Civil War," *American Journal of Legal History,* V (1961), 146–165, pioneered this topic. On loyalty tests, judicial review, and rights, see Harold M. Hyman, *Era of the Oath: Northern Loyalty Tests during the Civil War and Reconstruction* (Philadelphia, 1954) and George Fletcher, "The Concept of Punitive Legislation and the Sixth Amendment," *University of Chicago Law Review,* XXXII (1965), 303ff.; P. J. Avillo, "Ballots for the Faithful: The Oath and the Emergence of Slave State Republican Congressmen, 1861–1867," *Civil War History,* XXII (1976), 164–174; David D. March, "The Campaign for the Ratification of the Constitution of 1865," *Missouri Historical Review,* XLVII (1953), 223–232; L. D. Asper, "The Long and Unhappy History of Loyalty Testing in Maryland," *American Journal of Legal History,* XIII (1969), 97–109. A useful supplement to Kutler's and other treatments of the rise of High Court review is J. G. Gambone, "Ex Parte Milligan: The Restoration of Judicial Prestige?" *Civil War History,* XVI (1970), 246–259. The scope of the Thirteenth Amendment and 1866 Civil Rights Act is usefully analyzed in Robert L. Kohl, "The Civil Rights Act of 1866; Its Hour Came Round at Last: *Jones* v. *Alfred H. Mayer Co.,*" *Virginia Law Review,* LV (1969), 294–300.

Chapter 11: The Fourteenth Amendment in the Light of the Thirteenth

Like the literature on Lincoln and on Reconstruction, that on the Fourteenth Amendment continues to attract constitutional, legal, political, and social history specialists, lawyers, and jurists. Footnoting in ch. 10 and earlier bibliography entries suggest specific items in this rich, growing literature. The most useful titles for the present study were Howard D. Hamilton, "The Legislative and Judicial History of the Thirteenth Amendment" (Ph.D. diss., University of Illinois, 1950); Herman Belz's, Jacobus tenBroek's, Sidney Buchanan's, Michael Curtis's, Mark A. DeWolfe Howe's, and Aviam Soifer's books and articles. Howard Jay Graham's 1938 and 1950 articles, respectively, on the Fourteenth Amendment's "conspiracy theory" and abolitionist background are reprinted in his *Everyman's Constitution: Historical Essays on the Fourteenth Amendment, the "Conspiracy Theory," and American Constitutionalism* (Madison, 1968). Equally convenient, Charles Fairman and Stanley Morrison, *The Fourteenth Amendment and the Bill of Rights: The Incorporation Theory,* ed. Leonard W. Levy (New York, 1970), is also essential. Horace Flack's *The Adoption of the Fourteenth Amendment* (Baltimore, 1908), is still useful, with significant enrichment by Alfred H. Kelly, "The Fourteenth Amendment Reconsidered: The Segregation Question," *Michigan Law Review,* LIV (1956), 1049–1086; Kelly, "Clio and the Court: An Illicit Love Affair," *Supreme Court Review* (1965), 119–158; Robert J. Kaczorowski, "Searching for the Intent of the Framers of the Fourteenth Amendment," *Connecticut Law Review,* V (1973), 368–398; and Arthur Kinoy, "The Constitutional Right of Negro Freedom," *Rutgers Law Review,* XXI (1967), 387–441. Michael Les Benedict's "Laissez Faire, Class Legislation, and the Origins of Substantive Due Process of Law" (Woodrow Wilson International Center for Scholars paper, 1980) illuminates aspects of incorporation and due process too long obscured, and Arthur Bestor, "The American Revolution as World Experiment," *Archiv für Rechts und Sozialphilosophie, Bieheft Neue Folge,* Nr. 10 (Weisbaden, 1977), suggests approaches to Civil War and Reconstruction constitutionalism, centering on the need, perceived by Republicans in the 1860s and 1870s, for an adaptable, "organic" Constitution.

In all this literature, two views of the Constitution, two canons of interpretation, are opposed. The first was articulated by Taney in *Dred Scott:* the Constitution today means exactly what it meant at the time the Framers drafted it, no more; if you want to have it grow, you must amend it. Contrast that view, which was buried at Gettysburg and Appomattox, with two canons of Holmes. The first is in Gompers *v.* U.S., 233 U.S. 604 at 610 (1914): "the provisions of the Constitution are not mathematical formulas having their essence in their form; they are organic, living institutions transplanted from English soil. The significance is vital, not formal; it is to be gathered not simply by taking the words and a dictionary, but by considering their origin and the time of their growth." The second canon is in Missouri *v.* Holland, 252 U.S. 416 at 433 (1920): "When we are dealing with words that are also a constituent act, like the Constitution of the United States, we must realize that they have called into life a being the development of which could not have been foreseen completely by the most gifted of its begetters. It was enough for them to realize or to hope that they had created an organism; it has taken a century and has cost their successors much sweat and blood to prove that they created a nation. The case before us must be considered in the light of our whole experience and not merely in that of what was said a hundred years ago."

Scholars who emphasize the constraints on national protections for civil rights deriving from state-action assumptions include, in addition to Michael Les Benedict, Herman Belz, and Charles Fairman, Alfred Avins, "The Ku Klux Klan Act of 1871: Some Reflected Light on State Action and the Fourteenth Amendment," *St. Louis University Law Journal,* XI (1967), 331–381; Alexander Bickel, "The Original Understanding and the Segregation Decision," *Harvard Law Review,* LXIX (1955), 1–65; and Laurent B. Frantz, "Congressional Power to Enforce the Fourteenth Amendment Against Private Acts," *Yale Law Journal,* LXXIII (1964), 1352–1384. James Kettner, *The Development of American Citizenship, 1608–1870* (Williamsburg, 1978), though very able and useful, does not, unfortunately, come fully to grips with the Civil War's impact.

William McFeely, *Grant: A Biography* (New York, 1981), and *Yankee Stepfather: General O. O. Howard and the Freedmen* (New Haven, 1968), and, in particular, Donald Nieman's *To Set the Law in Motion* enrich George E. Bentley, *A History of the Freedmen's Bureau* (Philadelphia, 1955), especially with respect to Bureau courts. Leon Litwack, *North of Slavery: The Negro in the Free States, 1790–1860* (Chicago, 1961), and Theodore Wilson, *The Black Codes of the South* (University, Ala., 1965), complement each other.

Chapter 12: Anxious Passages

The Johnson impeachment is best surveyed in Michael Les Benedict's *Impeachment and Trial of Andrew Johnson* (New York, 1973); and supplemented in Hans Trefousse, *Impeachment of a President: Andrew Johnson, The Blacks, and Reconstruction* (Knoxville, 1975); John R. Labovitz, *Presidential Impeachment* (New Haven, 1978); Philip Kurland, *Watergate and the Constitution* (Chicago, 1978); and Raoul Berger, *Impeachment: Constitutional Problems* (Cambridge, 1973). David Herbert Donald, "Why They Impeached Andrew Johson," *American Heritage,* VIII (1956), 21–25, and Eric McKitrick, *Andrew Johnson and*

Reconstruction, retain value. David Y. Thomas, "The Law of Impeachment in the United States," *American Political Science Review,* II (1908), 378–395, brought up to date in Paul S. Fenton, "The Scope of the Impeachment Power," *Northwestern University Law Review,* LXV (1970), 719–747, though useful, have inadequate historical dimensions.

Chapter 13: The 1870s and 1880s

On Military Reconstruction, see David Herbert Donald, *The Politics of Reconstruction, 1863–1867* (Baton Rouge, 1967), Brock, *An American Crisis,* and Benedict, *A Compromise of Principle.* W. W. Van Alstyne, "The Fourteenth Amendment, The 'Right' to Vote, and the Understanding of the Thirty-Ninth Congress," *Supreme Court Review* (1965), 33; William Gillette's *Right to Vote;* Alfred Avins's "The Ku Klux Klan Act of 1871," and Everette Swinney, "Enforcing the Fifteenth Amendment, 1870–1877," *Journal of Southern History,* XXVIII (1962), 202–218, center attention on suffrage as a right. See, on its subject, Bertram Wyatt-Brown, "The Civil Rights Act of 1875," *Western Political Quarterly,* XVIII (1965), 763–775; John Hope Franklin, "Enforcement of the Civil Rights Act of 1875," *Prologue,* VI (1974), 225–235; and Alfred H. Kelly, "The Congressional Controversy Over School Segregation, 1867–1875," *American Historical Review,* LXIV (1959), 537–563. Robert J. Harris, *The Quest for Equality: The Constitution, Congress, and the Supreme Court* (Baton Rouge, 1960), plus works by Buchanan, McGrath, Horan, and Scott, are most helpful on the judicial responses to rights legislation. Ruth Whiteside's "Justice Joseph Bradley and the Fifth Federal Judicial Circuit" (Ph.D. diss., Rice University, 1981) illuminates Bradley's jurisprudence on the rights theme, while Ira Nerken, "A New Deal for the Protection of Fourteenth Amendment Rights: Challenging the Doctrinal Bases of the *Civil Rights Cases* and State Action Theory," *Harvard Civil Rights/Civil Liberties Review,* XII (1977), 552–570, offers alternative analyses.

Index